The
NEBI
YEARBOOK
2001/2002

Springer
Berlin
Heidelberg
New York
Barcelona
Hongkong
London
Mailand
Paris
Tokio

The
NEBI
YEARBOOK
2001/2002

North European and Baltic Sea Integration

General Editors:
Lars Hedegaard
and
Bjarne Lindström

Co-editors:
Pertti Joenniemi
Anders Östhol
Karin Peschel
Carl-Einar Stålvant

 Springer

Nordic Centre for
Spatial Development

Lars Hedegaard
Department of History and Social Theory
Roskilde University
DK-4000 Roskilde
Denmark

Bjarne Lindström
Department of Statistics
and Economic Research in Åland
Box 60
FIN-22101 Mariehamn
Åland Islands

ISBN 3-540-43004-0 Springer-Verlag Berlin Heidelberg New York

Library of Congress Cataloging-in-Publication Data applied for
Die Deutsche Bibliothek – CIP-Einheitsaufnahme
The NEBI Yearbook: North European and Baltic Sea Integration / Nordregio, Nordic
Centre for Spatial Development. – 1998 –. – Berlin; Heidelberg; New York; Barcelona;
Hong Kong; London; Milan; Paris; Tokyo: Springer, 1998
Erscheint jährllich. – Bibliographische Deskription nach 2002

Springer-Verlag Berlin Heidelberg New York
a member of BertelsmannSpringer Science+Business Media GmbH

http://www.springer.de

© Springer-Verlag Berlin · Heidelberg 2002
Printed in Germany

SPIN 10859922   43/2202-5 4 3 2 1 0 – Printed on acid-free paper

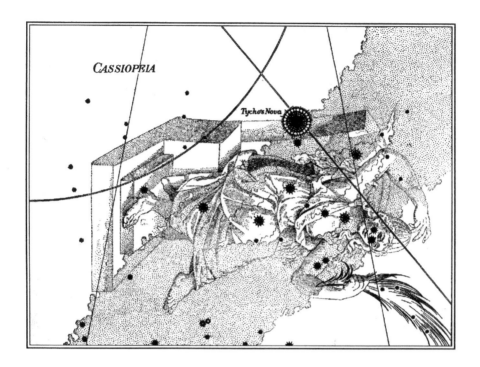

The computer-enhanced photo on the cover shows six bright stars in Cassiopeia and – in the top left-hand corner – the Polar Star. With its characteristic W-shape, Cassiopeia is among the most easily identifiable constellations in the NEBI area's night sky. Its name comes from *Quassio-peaer*, meaning Rose-Coloured Face in Phoenician and being the name of a queen who reigned over a world far from Greece. Ptolemy attributed to Cassiopeia the qualities of Saturn and Venus, meaning power, respect and command. When the combination was negative, however, it generated exaggerated pride and great presumption. Among countless depictions throughout the centuries is the above from Bayer's *Cassiopeia* (1603). *Tycho's Nova* is the famous exploding star discovered by the Danish astronomer Tycho Brahe on 11 November 1572 and described in his book *De nova stella* (1573). The new star quickly dimmed, and in March 1574 it could no longer be seen.

The Editors wish to acknowledge the kind assistance provided by the Tycho Brahe Planetarium, Copenhagen.

Cover design: Rita Baving, Copenhagen

List of Partners

The publication of The NEBI Yearbook 2001/2002 has been made possible by generous grants from the following Partners:

Danish Institute of International Affairs (DUPI), Copenhagen
The Ministry of Foreign Affairs, Finland
The Ministry of Foreign Affairs, Norway
The Ministry of Foreign Affairs, Sweden
The Government of Åland, Mariehamn
Centre for Regional Science (CERUM), Umeå
Copenhagen Peace Research Institute (COPRI)
Council for the Stockholm-Mälar Region, Stockholm
Federation of County Councils, Stockholm
Nordic Centre for Spatial Development (Nordregio), Stockholm
Pan-European Institute, Turku
Schleswig-Holstein Institute for Peace Research (SHIP), Kiel
The Skärgård Co-operation, Mariehamn
Swedish Institute for Growth Policy Studies, Stockholm, Sweden
University of Joensuu

Editorial Advisory Board

Foreword

Thorvald Stoltenberg

President of the Norwegian Red Cross
Chairman of the Editorial Advisory Board

Despite the very optimistic language on the imminence of new accessions to the European Union that came out of the June 2001 European Council in Gothenburg, it will serve no good purpose to neglect the fact that EU membership for the Central and Eastern European applicants remains a difficult process. Painful experience makes it prudent to exercise caution in predicting developments within the European Union. Negotiations may drag out, snags may appear and something may happen on the way to ratification. So perhaps it is wise to take a broader view of European integration – and therefore integration within the North European, Barents and Baltic Sea region that is the focus of this Yearbook.

EU membership for those countries that are able to satisfy the Copenhagen requirements – and the chapters of the *acquis communautaire* that have subsequently been specified – is certainly a prize worth fighting for. But all is not lost if some of the applicants end up not joining the Union as a result of the current enlargement round. Even more important than formal membership is the process of growing together that has taken place simultaneously with the membership negotiations. We are dealing here with integration in the real world of trade, investments, division of labour, politics, environment, hard and soft security, people-to-people relations etc. Many of the contributions to this volume of the Yearbook deal with precisely this real integration between the old East and the old West, which is profound and hard to reverse regardless of the immediate institutional outcome of membership negotiations. The NEBI Yearbook 2001/2002 makes it plain that irrespective of its immediate institutional outcome, the enlargement process has mattered a great deal for the actual integration that has taken place in Europe and thus in the NEBI area.

European integration may be characterised as a process that is larger and more comprehensive than mere EU integration. On the other hand, in the real world it is difficult to imagine how a balanced European integration could have developed and might continue without the existence of the European Union as a prime mover and common point of reference.

Concerning developments in the eastern parts of the NEBI area, the message in this volume is a positive one despite some setbacks and continuous difficulties. Due to a development that has taken no more than ten years – which is astonishing in the light of historical experience – all four EU candidate countries in the NEBI area, i.e. Poland and the three Baltic Republics of Estonia, Latvia and Lithuania, must now be considered functioning democracies endowed with the basic prerequisites for liberty and the rule of law. At the same time determined steps have been taken to develop the judicial competence needed to ensure the rule of law.

The main difficulty lies in the area of economic development. Though economic growth in the most of the eastern NEBI area must be considered rather satisfactory, the candidates for EU membership have accumulated considerable deficits in their trade with the EU. It has also given cause for some concern that with the exception of Estonia, the NEBI applicants have been slow in transforming their economies away from reliance on outmoded industrial production and primary industries and towards internationally competitive, advanced industry and services.

On the whole, however, the European Commission has remained confident that the applicants remain on course towards compliance with the Copenhagen criterion of a functioning market economy. This appears to be a fair assessment. Much has already been achieved in countries that threw off the communist yoke only a decade ago and there is little reason to doubt the capacity of the same countries to eventually catch up in the remaining areas.

Contents

The NEBI YEARBOOK
2001/2002

1 EU Enlargement and Integration in the NEBI Area

Lars Hedegaard and Bjarne Lindström

Accession and Societal Change

In its November 2000 Enlargement Strategy Paper (Commission 8 November 2000), the EU Commission expressed its belief that enlargement of the European Union with several new member states mainly from Central and Eastern Europe was imminent – with the end of 2002 being set as the date of the first entries into the Union.[1] Later developments have dampened this optimism somewhat. Nevertheless it is still the official belief that enlargement is close at hand. At its meeting in Gothenburg, Sweden, 15-16 June 2001 the European Council spoke of breakthroughs in the negotiations for membership and predicted a successful conclusion of the enlargement. Despite the Irish referendum rejecting the Nice Treaty of December 2000 intended to get the EU institutions ready for enlargement, the EU heads of government remained confident that the enlargement process would prove 'irreversible.' As pointed out in the Presidency Conclusions from the Gothenburg Summit, a number of the applicants were far ahead of others in terms of meeting the specific requirements of the EU *acquis*, nevertheless even the laggards among the candidates might count on assistance to reach their objectives. Overall the EU was to apply a 'principle of differentiation' in its dealings with the Central and Eastern European countries, allowing the best-prepared countries to move more quickly (EU Commission 2001b).

The general conclusion of the Gothenburg Summit had a firm ring to it: 'Provided that progress towards meeting the accession criteria continues at an unabated pace, the road map should make it possible to complete negotiations by the end of 2002 for those candidate countries that are ready. The objective is that they should participate in the European Parliament elections of 2004 as members' (EU Commission 2001b).

EU President and Swedish Prime Minister Göran Persson clearly took great pride in the ebullient language, which he saw as a real achievement by Sweden. Many of the applicant countries also appeared genuinely pleased with the outcome of the summit. More sober voices, however, pointed out that little of any substance had been accomplished (e.g. *The Economist*, 23 June 2001). Nothing in the Gothenburg declaration was really new and the key promises were riddled with escape clauses. As the German chancellor Gerhard Schröder made clear, the Gothenburg Conclusions expressed an objective, not a commitment. A modicum of reflection would in fact show that the EU leaders were in no position to guarantee accession by any of the applicants, and if negotiations with some of them could be completed on schedule, that would not guarantee eventual membership. The accession treaties would still have to be ratified by every EU member state and would be subject to referendum in many applicant countries.

As the Irish Nice referendum showed, one should not take the outcome for granted. But even more formidable obstacles to accession loomed in the shape of the unsolved problems of EU farming subsidies[2] and aid to poor regions – very difficult issues unlikely to be addressed by the EU before the first half of 2002 (*The Economist*, ibid.).

It would thus appear prudent to treat the prospects of enlargement with caution. A great number of obstacles – political, institutional, economic and having to do with the national interests of old and new members – would have to be overcome for enlargement to become a reality. However, from the point of view of integration in the NEBI area and elsewhere across the old East-West divide, the concrete steps that may or may not lead to eventual EU membership for certain countries are as important as membership itself. Or, differently expressed, real integration may take place regardless of a country's formal affiliation with the European Union.[3]

From the point of view of integration, what matters most is that a number of societal transformations in primarily the candidate countries are so deep-going that an economic and ideological bonding between the Union and entrance seekers has already taken place.[4] It is also hard to see how this de facto integration can be undone even in countries that may have to – or may decide to – postpone or give up membership.

In the case of a macro-region such as the NEBI area – which comprises EU members, non-members, countries that have applied for membership and countries without any immediate desire to join in addition to various other dividing lines – it is these underlying societal transformations that will, in the final analysis, determine what happens at the political and institutional level. Regardless of the formal status of various countries vis-à-vis the EU enlargement process, once a country's patterns of trade, production, employment, labour force training, foreign investments, ownership structure and other characteristics of an economic nature have been allowed to adapt to the social market norms upheld in the European Union, one can hardly imagine circumstances under which the process could be reversed. This means that the Copenhagen Criteria of 1993,[5] to which were subsequently added a long list of specific 'chapters' with which applicant states would have to comply,[6] have a dual nature. These requirements are of course conditions intended to pave the way for membership in the Union but should membership fail to materialise, the very attempt to fulfil these requirements will in itself lead to fundamental 'western' transformations in the applicant countries. To a large extent this de facto 'westernisation' – and in the case of Estonia 'Nordification' – was already well under way in the majority of the candidate countries by the time the EU heads of state met in Gothenburg.

So irrespective of the timing and the end results, the enlargement process does matter and has mattered a great deal to the actual integration in the NEBI area. Following their applications for EU membership, fundamental changes have occurred in Poland, Estonia, Lithuania and Latvia.[7] Of particular importance are major changes in areas that are usually deemed decisive as determinants of the degree of cross-border integration, i.e. patterns of external trade, foreign investment, fundamental transformations of the productive system and the allocation of manpower.[8]

Accession as Process and Method

It is probably no exaggeration to state that the fundamental demands (Copenhagen Criteria plus the Chapters of the *acquis communautaire*) and the methodology imposed on the applicants amount to a top-down-initiated and controlled revolution in the applicant countries – particularly when the current situation in most applicant countries is compared to conditions under communism.

In the early 1990s the EU Commission started signing so-called Europe Agreements with applicants or prospective applicants as a practical step towards eventual membership. As basic legal instruments of the relationship between the EU and the ten candidate countries in Central and Eastern Europe, the Europe Agreements cover trade-related issues, political dialogue, legal approximation in addition to various other areas of co-operation (European Commission n.d.). The agreement with Poland was signed as early as December 1991 and went into effect in February 1994; the agreements with Estonia, Latvia and Lithuania were all signed in June 1995, i.e. prior to these countries' application dates for membership, and came into force in February 1998 (ibid.). The EU has similar Europe Agreements or Association AgreementsSee Europe Agreements with the other eight applicant countries whose membership negotiations are under way, in addition to Turkey.

The aim of the Europe Agreements is to establish free trade between the EU and the candidate countries. However, countries are accorded differing transition periods. Poland was granted a transition period of ten years before establishing completely free trade with the Union. The corresponding periods for Lithuania were six years and for Latvia four years. In the case of Estonia, free trade was established as early as 1 January 1995, i.e. even before the signing of the Europe Agreement. The Agreements also provide for the progressive adaptation to EU rules in such areas as capital movement, rules of competition, intellectual and industrial property rights and public procurement (ibid.).

In July 1997, the Commission initiated the principle of publishing regular reports on each applicant country's progress towards accession. So far regular reports have been issued in December 1998 and October 1999. The latest set of reports was published on 8 November 2000 (European Commission 2000c-f).

Also in 1997, the Commission effectively split the group of applicants by determining that the Czech Republic, Estonia, Hungary, Poland, Slovenia and Cyprus were better positioned to become eligible for membership and recommended that negotiations with this lead group commence immediately. The laggards according to this classification (among those Latvia and Lithuania) had to wait until the October 1999 Regular Reports before the Commission finally proposed negotiations.

As part of its so-called Pre-accession Strategy, the Commission has created a number of highly specific and rather innovative instruments for the establishment of territorial integration and control. Among them are the PHARE Programme, the ISPA Programme (environment and transport investment support), the SAPARD Programme (agriculture and rural development support), and co-financing with international financial institutions (IFIs) (European Commission n.d.; see also Hallin and Svensson in this volume).

Following the conclusions of the Berlin European Council (24-25 March 1999), pre-accession aid to Central and Eastern Europe was more than doubled from the year 2000 onwards. Through the already existing PHARE Programme and the two new pre-accession instruments, i.e. ISPA and SAPARD, the Commission committed itself to annual payments to the Central and Eastern European Countries of approximately 3.1 billion euro between 2000 and 2006 (ibid.). Of this yearly amount, approximately 1.6 billion euro will be spent under the PHARE Programme, which finances general institution-building measures in addition to investments in areas not covered by the other two instruments, including regional development programmes. ISPA, which finances major environmental and transport infrastructure, has an annual budget of about 1 billion euro. SAPARD, which is entrusted with aid for agricultural and rural development, will have annual expenditures of a little more than 500 million euro (ibid.).

From the point of view of NEBI-wide integration, the SAPAD Programme is of particular importance due to the problems of the huge agricultural sector and the large rural population in Poland, which remains one of the most intractable stumbling blocs for Poland's integration with Europe (Rabinowicz 1998; Neubauer's

Table 1.1: Share of agriculture in GDP and total employment, 1998 or 1999 (percentages)

	Share in GDP	Share in total employment
Estonia	3.3	7.6
Latvia	7.6	16.6
Lithuania	3.8	21.4
Poland	4.9	28

Source: Commission Online (14 September 2000); Commission Online (25 October 2000)

Introduction to the Statistical Section in this volume; Hallin and Svensson in this volume). Poland's and to a lesser degree Lithuania's heavy dependency on agricultural employment becomes evident from Table 1.1, which also indicates the relatively developed state of Estonia compared to the other applicant countries in the NEBI area.

By far the biggest beneficiary of SAPAD aid is Poland with almost 169 million euro per year. Estonia, Latvia and Lithuania are to receive approximately 12 million, 22 million and 30 million euro respectively per year. In all the recipients of SAPAD aid in the NEBI area will receive a yearly amount of close to 232 million euro corresponding to approximately 45 per cent of the entire agricultural pre-accession aid (Commission Online 29 November 2000).

As part of its SAPAD initiative, the European Commission has entered into agreements on Rural Development Programmes with all four countries in the NEBI area. The agreements with Latvia and Poland were signed on 14 September 2000 (Commission Online 14 September 2000) and the agreements with Estonia and Lithuania were signed on 25 October 2000 (Commission Online 25 October 2000). The SAPAD agreements were to be followed by Multi-annual Financing Agreements for each country before SAPAD money would actually start flowing (Commission Online 25 January 2001; Commission Online 5 March 2001).

The specific measures undertaken under each SAPAD Programme vary from country to country. In the case of Poland, three main areas are emphasised in an attempt to diminish the country's excessive dependency on low-yielding agricultural labour: 1) Improvement of the market efficiency of the agri-food sector; 2) improve conditions for economic activities and job creation in rural areas; 3) Human capital enhancement (Commission Online 14 September 2000).

In addition to their general integration into the EU system and *acquis communautaire*, Estonia, Latvia and Lithuania may be said to be undergoing yet another type of integration, namely the one initiated by and carried out under the auspices of the Nordic Council/the Nordic Council of Ministers and by individual Nordic countries, with Finland, Denmark and Sweden being the most active in delivering economic, administrative and political aid. The number of initiatives is far too great to be accounted for here. Suffice it to mention that there are several indications of very strong economic links having developed between the Nordic countries and the Baltic Republics in terms of investments, directly owned companies and trading patterns. This emerges very clearly from a comprehensive survey of the regions of the Baltic States published by Nordregio (Nordregio 2000; see also the Statistical Section in this volume). The new patterns of Nordic-Baltic economic integration are even more impressive for having developed over the course of just one decade.

The Reality of Integrative Change

Real integration of the four applicant countries in the NEBI area, i.e. Estonia, Latvia, Lithuania and Poland, into the EU co-operative structures (including the remaining EEA countries) necessitates comprehensive economic, institutional and social adaptation within these states. To gain access to the European family, applicants must comply with a number of political and economic demands laid down at the 1993 Copenhagen Council, as already mentioned.

The main demand is that 'membership requires that the candidate country has achieved stability of institutions guaranteeing democracy, the rule of law, human rights, and the protection of minorities.' This may be compared with Article 6 of the Amsterdam Treaty, which states that the Union is based on the principles of 'liberty, democracy, respect of human rights and fundamental freedoms and the rule of law.' The corresponding economic requirements for membership are 'the existence of a functioning market economy and the capacity to withstand competitive pressure and market forces within the Union' (European Commission 1999b: 14, 21).

In a general sense, Poland and the three Baltic Republics are in compliance with the Union's political requirements for membership. All candidate countries in the NEBI area must be considered democracies endowed with the basic prerequisites for liberty and the rule of law. The candidate countries of the NEBI area have utilised the pre-accession period to build up their legal systems as much as possible and develop the judicial competence required to safeguard the rule of law (European Commission 2000c-f).

Quite a few problems remain unsolved, however. Two areas in particular stand out, namely the treatment of national minorities and the fight against corruption and crime. Shortcomings in the handling of national minorities are particularly prevalent in Estonia and Latvia. Despite great advances compared with the situation by the middle of the 1990s, it remains the opinion of the European Commission that Estonia's minority policy still does not fully comply with the international standards required for EU membership. To be sure the right kind of citizenship and language legislation is now in place but the implementation still leaves much to be desired in many respects. The same applies to Latvia, where the economic resources to implement current programmes to support the large Russian minority's linguistic and social integration into the Latvian society are still too small (European Commission 2000c; 2000d).

The hardest of the remaining problems for the candidate countries in the NEBI area, however, are related to economic development and the development of the institutions required for a well functioning and stable market economy.

Firstly, the Europe or Association AgreementsSee Europe Agreements concluded between the EU and the Eastern and Central European candidates do not at all appear to have entailed the sort of balanced development of trade that was originally envisaged (Rabinowicz 1998). Even though economic growth has been rather satisfactory, the applicants have accumulated fast-growing deficits in their trade with the EU. For the year 1998 the EU's trade surplus vis-à-vis all candidate countries came to a staggering 33 billion euro of which more than a third was due to Poland's deficit (European Commission 1999b). That same year, the Polish trade deficit equalled 10 per cent of GDP. The situation in the other three applicant countries of the NEBI area was even worse. In 1999 the three Baltic Republics had trade deficits amounting to more than 20 per cent of their combined economies. In the case of Lithuania, the deficit grew from approximately 10 per cent of GDP in 1995 to almost 26 per cent in 1999 (Pautola 1999).

Secondly, with the exception of Estonia, the candidates in the NEBI area have been slow to restructure their economies away from outmoded industrial production and inefficient – and consequently over-sized – primary industries and towards advanced industry and services. Quite the opposite has happened. In both relative and absolute terms, employment in agriculture has continued to grow whereas growth in the advanced industries and services has been rather more modest (Nordregio 2000). In Poland the lack of structural changes and a widening trade deficit have led to inflationary pressures (European Commission 2000f).

Despite such shortcomings, the European Commission remains confident that the candidates are starting to comply with the Copenhagen criterion of a functioning market economy (*Enlargement Weekly*, various issues).

In addition to macro-economic, structural change, a number of adaptations are needed in a number of areas and primarily in the institutional and judicial infrastructure. Other important shortcomings are evident within the formulation and application of regional policies. With the exception of Poland, the NEBI applicants have failed to develop a functional and EU-compatible regional policy. The same may be said of the legislative basis and the administration of environmental policies, whose standards leave much to be desired, compared to EU norms. There are similar problems in the area of transport infrastructure, which is outdated, creating further difficulties for the integration of candidates into the EU. The European Commission has also pointed to regrettable bottlenecks at border crossings resulting from administrative and other impediments to the free flow of the production factors (European Commission 2000c-f; Nordregio 2000).

Integration in Depth

Viewed over a longer term, the candidates' adaptation to the EU's *acquis* may not be the most important determining factor for real integration around the Baltic Sea and in the Barents area. Of much greater importance will be changes to the fundamental social and economic basis of integration.

The first prerequisite for integration in depth in the NEBI area is a much more advanced internal division of labour between the new transitional economies and the more developed market economies to the west. The most reliable indication of real and mutual economic integration is a wide-ranging and comprehensive division of labour among enterprises within the same product area. This will result in widespread intra-industry trade among collaborating enterprises, regions and national economies. The opposite of this type of economic integration is the kind of interaction that may arise among economies that have specialised in certain products, e.g. raw materials that may be traded as inputs to a more advanced industrial mode of production. This type of volume-conscious specialisation in a narrow selection of products or sectors is indicative of trade among economies that are not of the same type and are often at quite different stages of economic development.

At present the economy of the NEBI area is characterised by a wide gap between countries and regions dominated by advanced intra-industry – and consequently strongly integrative – trade and, on the other side, countries and regions whose trade is dominated by exports of high-volume and rather simple-to-produce goods or commodities. Today intra-industry trade in the NEBI area as a whole accounts for upwards of 60 per cent of total trade – due to the heavy impact of such advanced countries as Germany and Scandinavia. The intra-industrial trade of the four candidate countries accounts for approximately one-third of their total foreign trade (Cornett 2000c).

Despite current difficulties, certain facts speak in favour of long-term economic integration in the NEBI area. Fundamental in this respect is the fact that a great part of the area's population and labour resources is found in the transformation economies to the east whereas most of the region's economic activities take place in the old, often sparsely populated economies to the north and·west. This situation cannot fail to create pressures towards more economic interaction in the shape of labour division, cross-border direct investments, labour migration etc. This development is probably enhanced by the fact that the labour force of the transitional economies enjoys a relatively high level of education combined with the existence of the much noted 'technology gap' between the NEBI area's western and eastern halves (Cornett 2000a).

A model analysis of the trading potential in the NEBI area plus Russia shows that until 2011, the greatest trading potential will be found along the west-east axis and within 'intra-eastern' trade. Whereas the long-term growth potential in the trade between the NEBI area's mature market economies is limited to 6-7 per cent, the potential inherent in trade between transformation economies and advanced market economies will be double that figure. This would imply that the share of 'intra-western' trade in the NEBI area's total economic exchange would decline from its current 55 per cent to approximately 35 per cent, whereas the trade between west and east together with the 'intra-eastern' trade would increase from 45 per cent at present to about 65 per cent of the area's total trade volume (Cornett and Iversen 2000).

In this connection it is also interesting to note that since the end of the 1980s – 1988 to be precise – the four candidate countries' share of intra-industrial deliveries has grown from approximately 25 to almost 34 per cent (1997) of their total trade, which clearly indicates a development towards a more specialised economy that is more compatible with the well-integrated economies of the neighbouring world (Cornett 2000c). These figures also include the four countries' agricultural and raw materials-producing sectors. If the latter are left out, the trend towards a more advanced division of labour between the NEBI area's eastern and western parts becomes even more pronounced. Within parts of the textile and electronic industries the development towards a more advanced transnational production system including fast-growing foreign direct investments and intra-industrial trade is already noticeable (Cornett 2000a).

One indication of a growing and above all more high-classed exchange between the transformation countries and the developed market economies within the NEBI area is that by the end of the 1990s, the three Baltic Republics received more than half of their foreign direct investments from other parts of the NEBI area (Cornett 2000b). The investment volumes are far from marginal or economically insignificant. Over the period 1990 through 1999 foreign investors directly placed more than 30 billion euro in the three Baltic Republics and Poland (Nordregio 2000).

Regardless of current problems of adaptation to macroeconomic structures and institutional set-ups, the NEBI region's candidate countries thus seem to possess sufficient prerequisites to participate in a more integrated NEBI economy. And equally clearly, compliance with the political and institutional demands of the EU family will help pave the way for a broader socio-economic integration within the NEBI area.

The Russian Problem

A much larger source of uncertainty concerning the political and economic integration game around the Baltic Sea is Russia. Sooner or later the expansion of the European Union towards Central and Eastern Europe is bound to peter out.[9] This will necessitate the establishment of a stable border zone supplemented by a cross-border structure of co-operation. Most likely this line of demarcation will coincide with the borders around Russia.

Just a few years ago Russia was considered a country destined for economic and political dissolution. Recently, however, the Soviet successor state has regained much of its former role as a regional power (see also Zimine in this volume). Under President Vladimir Putin the Russian centre has re-established part of its former power over the regions that had been lost during the 1990s (*The Economist* 11 November 2000). Also important is the fact that the Russian economy has proved capable of a surprisingly quick recovery following the collapse of August 1998 (Hedegaard and Lindström 1999). For the year 2000 economic growth has been estimated at a healthy 7 per cent, which far surpasses the average in the surrounding world. Industrial production grows even faster and inflation has been reduced to a more manageable level (ÅSUB 2001). To complete this picture, one should consider the enormous Russian reserves of strategic minerals, gas and petroleum, whose importance to Europe and to the NEBI area in particular was underlined in the Finnish EU-initiative on the 'Northern Dimension' (Hedegaard and Lindström 1999; Zimine in this volume).

The issue of Russia's relations to Europe and to the NEBI neighbours is further accentuated by the two Russian outposts lying deep inside or in close proximity to the NEBI area, i.e. the enclave region of Kaliningrad[10] and the city of St Petersburg. St Petersburg's weight as a population centre and as a potential economic powerhouse is undeniable. Even though population has declined precipitously in recent years as a result of exmigration and a growing imbalance between the number of deaths and births, the fact remains that with 5-6 million inhabitants, the St Petersburg region is still the largest concentration of people in the NEBI area (see the Statistical Section in this volume). The region is also the most powerful economic centre for all of north-western Russia. St Petersburg accounts for over 40 per cent of northwestern Russia's GDP, almost 40 per cent of the region's total economic activity, more than 50 per cent of total investments and more than 60 per cent of foreign direct investments in northwestern Russia (Oding 2000). It is thus amply clear that regardless of what direction developments take, St Petersburg's demographic and economic dynamics will continue to have important direct as well as indirect consequences for future integration in the NEBI area and thus for the European Union's entire northern flank (Zimine in this volume).

With its 900,000 inhabitants and an economy which is in a miserable condition even compared to Russian realities, Kaliningrad presents challenges to integration that are of a different kind. One of the European Commission's strategy papers on eastern enlargement (European Commission 2000b) notes that following a successful enlargement, Kaliningrad will be changed into a Russian enclave within Union territory. As the Commission is also aware, this means that the Union must develop a strategy to manage that situation and that this strategy must be developed in collaboration with Russia, Poland and Lithuania. However, the European Commission is very brief not to say vague when it comes to determining what such a strategy might look like. All that is said is that active cross-border regional co-operation 'will be an important element of that strategy.' This seemingly scant attention the Kaliningrad problem is not surprising. The potential political problems inherent in the Union's relations to the Russian enclave are so sensitive that they call for the utmost delicacy if one is to avoid offending the central government in Moscow (Fairlie 1999; Lindström 2000).

Russia thus remains a real problem not only for the chances of integration in the NEBI area but also for EU enlargement. It is equally obvious that the future orientation of Kaliningrad and St Petersburg must be settled within a future, integrated NEBI area. Without a sustainable solution to Kaliningrad's enclave problem and the incorporation of the Baltic Sea region's largest population concentration into the wider European economy, genuine integration and political stability in the NEBI region cannot be achieved.

The Logic of Expansion

EU enlargement will not be a simple process. In addition to the institutional and political problems of adaptation in the candidate countries, their economic starting position is such that even with the growth rates obtained in recent years, it would take several generations before they could catch up with average living standards in the old EU countries.

In its recent Cohesion Report the European Commission has considered a future European Union consisting of 27 members. In this future EU the four applicants in the NEBI area would be among the poorest members with just 40 per cent of the EU-27 average GDP per capita. The same report also notes that it would require investments of a magnitude of not less than 50 billion euro and perhaps as much as 100 billion just to upgrade the candidate countries' physical transport infrastructure to EU standards (European Commission 2001a). A previous study commissioned by the PHARE Multi-Country Transport Programme aimed at estimating the costs to candidate countries of adopting EU transport regulations and directives came to these estimates: 15 billion euro for Poland and approximately 1 billion euro for each of the Baltic States (European Commission 1999a).

It follows that no matter how smoothly enlargement is carried out, it cannot fail to dramatically increase the economic and social gaps within the Union. Of course one may settle for a wider perspective. If Europe is considered as a whole, it would rather appear that enlargement will gradually lead to smaller discrepancies between the countries and regions of Europe – an assumption that applies eminently to the countries and regions in the NEBI area.

Compared to previous EU enlargements, the one that is now being prepared is unprecedented both terms of the number of countries involved and in terms of the severity of the problems that have to be overcome by successful candidates. The closest approximation to the present situation is the Union's second round of enlargement encompassing Greece, Spain and Portugal in 1981 and 1986. Despite these countries' recent experience with repressive, authoritarian regimes, they did not have to undergo the kind of almost total reconstruction in all areas of society demanded from the current applicants from Central and Eastern Europe. Besides, when Greece was accepted as a member, the Union's Single Market was still being prepared. New members did not have to accept the several thousand pages of legislation subsequently passed to make this market function. The same may be said of many other key areas of current EU policy: the elaborate structural policies that were introduced by the late 1980s, Economic and Monetary Union, the common foreign policy, co-operation on legal and internal affairs and others (Friis 2001).

The sheer difficulty of incorporating increasingly weaker countries into an ever-closer Union that demands more and more from those hoping to join begs the question: why do it at all? Why risk the rather fragile political and especially popular consensus behind the current EU-15 construction in order to further complicate matters by letting in countries that might need generations of development to catch up with the EU core? Why indeed, proceed along the enlargement course following the Irish voters' solid rejection of the Nice Treaty intended to pave the way for enlargement – as Europe's heads of state have indicated they will?

The answer has to do with the European Union's very legitimacy and self-perception. Ever since its inception in the 1950s the architects behind the European construction have maintained that the real purpose of their 'ever closer union' was not economic gain but the preservation of peace. Economic integration across the European borders – however desirable for its own sake – was a means towards creating peace. That is the ultimate legitimacy of the EU and for that reason, the Union cannot lightly dismiss requests from other European countries to join if these countries can demonstrate sincere efforts to qualify for membership. The EU cannot close its doors to such applicants without having to re-examine its most cherished beliefs about itself. If the purpose of the European Union is no longer to secure peace on the European continent, what then is the purpose? Surely the idea of a 'rich man's club' would be a hard sell in the current political atmosphere.

To quote the German Foreign Minister Joschka Fischer: 'The decision to expand the EU is irreversible. To reject expansion would entail enormous risks. Enormous. Besides, it would destroy the European idea for that is not reserved for Western Europe' (quoted in Friis 2001: 220).

Regardless of the almost constant disagreements, the EU leaders, governments and national bureaucracies have come to experience the EU as an order of peace. This experience gathered over more than 40 years has increasingly convinced the EU national governments that the best remedy against war and violent turmoil is to offer the trouble areas membership in the EU. And if outright membership is not possible, then one should strive for some accommodation with the actual or potential 'rogue' states or regions.

Developments since outbreak of the Kosovo Crisis in 1999 have been instructive. Not being able to offer the kind of military security along its borders that the United States can provide even across the Atlantic Ocean, The EU leaders have resorted to their best instrument, which is to extend the olive branch of membership to reforming offenders. This strategy has been amply demonstrated in the case of post-Milosevic Serbia.

Though under less dramatic circumstances, the same basic strategy has been followed in the Baltic Sea and Barents co-operations – and with remarkable success.

The benevolent 'empire building' in the NEBI area is due to the shared ideological values shared by the Nordic countries and the European Commission and bureaucracy alike. The EU was never intended to become an instrument of unrestrained, rapacious capitalism. Its socio-economic ideal has remained the social market model demanding a vast amount of collaboration among the social partners. This means that the Union cannot behave as an unrestrained imperialist towards its neighbours. Nor can it tolerate abject poverty and political turmoil right outside its borders.

That explains the array of institutions, programmes and financial instruments created by the European Union – and of course by the Nordic Council and the Nordic states – to ameliorate and calm the situation of neighbours. But to get the aid, the beneficiaries have so submit to the influence and partial control of the EU and Nordic institutions. To receive PHARE, SAPAD or other kinds of pre-accession support, countries must accept more and more of the mighty *acquis communautaire*.

The European Union has no option but to assume an increasingly active role outside its borders. The integrationist logic of this manifest destiny remains whether or not individual countries join the EU.

Notes

[1] The candidate countries in Central and Eastern Europe are Bulgaria, the Czech Republic, Estonia, Hungary, Latvia, Lithuania, Poland, Romania, Slovakia and Slovenia. Four of these countries belong to the NEBI area: Estonia, Latvia, Lithuania and Poland.

[2] This problem is discussed in Rabinowicz 1998.

[3] An oft-mentioned case in point is Norway, whose voters have twice rejected membership of the EU. This has not prevented the Norwegian government and indeed other official and private actors from pursuing a policy of de facto integration with the Union, leading to talk of a Norwegian 'secret membership.'

[4] An instructive case in point is the very close relationship that has developed between Finland and Estonia based on comprehensive economic integration as well as shared political perspectives and cultural proximity. This has led *The Economist* (23 June 2001) to characterise Estonia as an 'honorary Nordic' – a situation that is unlikely to be reversed regardless of Estonia's formal arrangement with the EU.

[5] In addition to the 1993 Copenhagen Criteria, further specifications were introduced by the 1995 Madrid Council, the December 1997 Luxembourg Council and the December 1999 Helsinki Council (European Commission n.d.).

[6] The Copenhagen Criteria are as follows. Membership requires that the candidate country has achieved: stability of institutions guaranteeing democracy, the rule of law, human rights and respect for and protection of minorities; the existence of a functioning market economy as well as the capacity to cope with competitive pressures and market forces within the Union; the ability to take on the obligations of membership including adherence to the aims of political, economic and monetary union. The candidate country must further have created the conditions for its integration through the adjustment of its administrative structures, so that the European Community legislation transposed into national legislation is implemented effectively through appropriate administrative and judicial structures (European Commission 2000a).

As a tool for the overall assessment of the progress of individual applicant countries, the Commission has set up 31 chapters of the *acquis* that must be complied with prior to membership. These chapters are highly specific and cover practically every major area of the economy, legislation and public policy and their implementation is continuously monitored by the Commission (European Commission 2000c-f).

[7] The dates of application for EU membership are as follows: Poland: 05.04.1994, Latvia: 13.10.1995, Estonia: 24.11.1995 and Lithuania: 08.12.1995.

8   There is comprehensive monitoring of several data and criteria relating to all candidate coun-
     tries. Of particular importance are: European Commission (2000c-f)). Up-to date reports
     and assessments are published in *Enlargement Weekly*.

9   This does not necessarily mean that the EU will not continue to exert a strong economic,
     political, institutional and cultural influence in areas beyond its borders.

10   The very special problems of Kaliningrad have been discussed in a number of previous con-
     tributions to the NEBI Yearbook, in particular Pacuk and Palmowski (1998) and Fairlie
     (1999).

References

ÅSUB (2001). *Konjunkturläget våren 2001.* Rapport 2001:1. Mariehamn.

Commission Online (25 January 2000). 'Commissioner Fischler signs pre-accession financing
     agreements with Estonia, Latvia and Poland.' IP/01/113. Brussels.

Commission Online (14 September 2000). 'Rural development programmes for Poland, Hun-
     gary, Bulgaria, the Czech Republic, Latvia and Slovenia endorsed.' IP/00/1009. Brussels.

Commission Online (25 October 2000). 'Rural development programmes for Estonia, Lithuania
     and Slovakia endorsed.' IP/00/1211. Brussels.

Commission Online (29 November 2000). 'Farm aid: Go-ahead for 520 million agreements with
     candidate countries.' IP/00/1370. Brussels.

Commission Online (5 March 2001). 'Agriculture: Commissioner Fischler signs Multi-Annual
     and Annual Financing Agreement with Slovenia and Lithuania.' IP/01/309. Brussels.

Cornett, A.P. (2000a). 'The Baltic Rim Region as an Integrated Part of the European Economic
     System.' Paper prepared at the 6th Nordic-Baltic Conference in Regional Science, Riga, 4-7
     October, 2000.

Cornett, A.P. (2000b). 'Regional development and competitiveness in a regional perspective: The
     case of the Baltic Rim,' pages 43-61 in Bojar, E. (ed.). *Competition and Coexistence in the
     Process of European Integration.* Warsaw, Polish Scientific Publishers.

Cornett, A.P. (2000c). 'Regional Integration through Trade in the Baltic Rim Region: Urban Sys-
     tem and Urban Networkoing in the Baltic Sea Region & Vision and Strategies 2010 around
     the Baltic.' Hørsholm, Denmark.

Cornett A.P. and Iversen, S.P. (2000). 'Regional Integration and Economic Links in the Baltic Sea
     Region: Urban Systems and Urban Networking in the Baltic Sea Region/Economic Trends.'
     Vilnius.

The Economist, various issues.

Enlargement Weekly, various issues.

European Commission: DG Enlargement

(http://europa.eu.int/comm/enlargement/index.htm)

European Commission (1999a). *Multi-Country Transport Programme: Costs and Benefits of
     Enlargement:* 98-0422. Final Report, December 1999. Halcrow Fox.

European Commission (1999b). Composite Paper.

European Commission (2000a). *Enlargement: Overview Progress Report.* November 2000.

European Commission (2000b). Enlargement Strategy Paper (with Annexes), 8 November 2000.

European Commission (2000c). *Regular Report – From the Commission on Estonia's Progress
     Towards Accession*, 8 November, 2000.

European Commission (2000d). *Regular Report – From the Commission on Latvia's Progress
     Towards Accession*, 8 November, 2000.

European Commission (2000e). *Regular Report – From the Commission on Lithuainia's Progress
     Towards Accession*, 8 November, 2000.

European Commission (2000f). Regular Report – From the Commission on Poland's Progress
     Towards Accession, 8 November, 2000.

European Commission (n.d.). European Union Enlargement: A Historic Opportunity

European Commission (2001a). *Second Report on Economic and Social Cohesion.* Brussels, 31.1.2001. COM(2001) 24 final.

EU Commission (2001b). Presidency Conclusions, Göteborg European Council, 15 and 16 June 2001.

Fairlie, L.D. (1999). 'Kaliningrad: Recent Changes in Russia's Exclave on the Baltic Sea,' pages 293-312 in Hedegaard, L. and Lindström, B. (eds). *The NEBI Yearbook 1999: North European and Baltic Sea Integration.* Berlin, Heidelberg, Springer.

Friis, L. (2001). *Den europæiske byggeplads: Fra fælles mønt til europæisk forfatning.* Haslev, Centrum.

Hedegaard, L. and Lindström, B. (1999). 'The Northern Dimension, Russia and the Prospects for NEBI Integration,' ' pages 3-31 in Hedegaard, L. and Lindström, B. (eds). *The NEBI Yearbook 1999: North European and Baltic Sea Integration.* Berlin, Heidelberg, Springer.

Lindström, B. (2000). 'The Northern Dimension: Nordic Regional Policy in a Brave New European World' in *Built Environment* 26:1, pages 21-30.

Nordregio (2000). *Regions of the Baltic States.* Report 2000:2.

Oding, N. (2000). 'The Russian Urban System in the Baltic Sea Region: Urban System and Urban Networking in the Baltic Sea Region & Vision and Strategies 2010 around the Baltic.' Hørsholm, Denmark.

Pacuk, M. and Palmowski, T (1998). 'The Development of Kaliningrad in the Light of Baltic Co-operation,' pages 267-82 in Hedegaard, L. and Lindström, B. (eds). *The NEBI Yearbook 1998: North European and Baltic Sea Integration.* Berlin, Heidelberg, Springer.

Pautola, N. (1999). 'The Baltic States' Integration into the European Union: Institutional Approach,' *Helsingin kauppakorkeakoulu.* Helsinki.

Rabinowicz, E. (1998). 'The CAP: An Obstacle to EU Enlargement?' pages 131-44 in Hedegaard, L. and Lindström, B. (eds). *The NEBI Yearbook 1998: North European and Baltic Sea Integration.* Berlin, Heidelberg, Springer.

Part I

Economic Integration

2 Who Changes Who? Territorial Integration, Enlargement and EU Structural Policy

Göran Hallin and Bo Svensson

While there is broad agreement that the coming eastward enlargement of the European Union will bring change to both new and present member states, as well as to the Union itself, there is also great uncertainty about the nature of change and how it will affect the involved parties. One of the crucial issues is that of economic and social cohesion of the new EU territory. According to the European Commission, the challenges of cohesion can be expressed in different ways. Enlargement will increase the number of people living in regions with a GDP per head less than 75 per cent of the present EU average from 71 million to 174 million. While GDP per head in lagging regions averaged 66 per cent of the EU average, GDP per head was only around 37 per cent in the lagging regions of applicant states. The Commission concludes that the challenge to cohesion will be twice as widespread and twice as large as today and that at current growth rates, it may take two generations bring new members reasonably on par with the present members (European Commission 2001).

The general understanding of European integration is that membership will bring advantages to new members but also expose their economies to stronger competition as they become part of the Single Market. As regional disparities are considered a problem or even a threat to the process of integration itself, almost 90 per cent of the EU budget is devoted to its structural policies, i.e. the Common Agricultural Policy (CAP), the Structural Funds and the Cohesion Fund. Without a doubt, eastward enlargement will pose the greatest challenge ever to EU Structural Policy and will, according to many observers, necessitate substantial reforms. These reforms will also have consequences for existing member states, which may affect their generosity towards applicant states.

This chapter focuses on the link between the cohesion challenge of enlargement and the need for policy reform within the structural policies of the EU. It raises two main questions: Firstly, what is the role of European Union structural policy in relation to the coming enlargement and its cohesion challenges? Secondly, to what extent and how is eastward enlargement likely to affect the structural policies of the EU? As the questions indicate, change is expected to be a two-way process where actual, or expected, changes at one end may have a strong impact at the other, making enlargement a sensitive matter for all parties involved.

The first section analyses the overall objectives of EU structural policies and examines them in relation to a more general debate on territorial integration and social and economic cohesion. In the second section the relations between enlargement and structural policy are examined by referring to previous challenges of integration (enlargement or enhancement) of the European Union. The third section looks at the performance of applicant states in the negotiations over Chapter 21 of the *acquis communautaire* and at the contents of the pre-accession strategies of the EU.[1] The final section discusses possible scenarios pertaining to the relations between structural policy and enlargement.

Why European Structural Policies?

In geographic and economic literature cohesion and territory are intertwined concepts. The general view seems to be that undisputed territories are able to accept larger economic disparities than disputed ones (see e.g. Hallin and Lindström 2000). The problem in relation to this hypothesis is of course one of cause and effect: do disparities generate disputed territories or do disputed territories lead to higher tolerance of economic disparities?

Looking across European territories we find the highest levels of regional disparities, i.e. disparities within the nation states at levels of NUTS2 (Nomenclature commune des unités territoriales statistiques), in the United Kingdom, France, Austria, Italy, and Belgium.[2] Low levels of economic disparities prevail in Greece, Portugal, Ireland, the Netherlands and Sweden (European Commission 2001). It is of course extremely difficult to assess the reasons for this variation. But the main issue here is whether some territories accept greater disparities than others do. Among those with large disparities are states with relatively far-reaching regional self-governance, including the federations of Austria, Belgium and Germany, and the instances of self-governance within the UK. Unitary nation states often have smaller disparities.

Among the motives behind national regional policy, which is the most studied form of territorial cohesion policy, the diminishing of regional disparities, either in social or in economic terms, often stands out as the overruling objective. In the regional policy literature it has been debated whether there is an inherent conflict between economic development in general and diminishing disparities. This debate of course draws on the classic literature about economic development and progress, the liberal argument being that by definition economic development will lead to diminishing disparities – although perhaps with a time lag. During the 1950s Perroux, Myrdal and other economists introduced the view that economic development may in fact underpin territorial polarisation (Perroux 1950; Myrdal 1957).

More recent debates on economic development policy have suggested that putting diminishing disparities at the forefront may lead to flaws in policy formulation, e.g. by focusing on measures which may only serve to support inferior economic structures, such as uncompetitive firms or industries. In line with these studies are others that favour measures tackling structural imperfections and long-term restructuring of the regional economies.

The cohesion of the national territory is only implicitly at focus in the theories of regional policy, or in the political debate. However several analyses of regional policy, in e.g. the UK, Belgium, Italy and even in the Nordic countries, indicate that this motive is not unimportant for the development of regional policy (Hallin 1995; Artobolevskiy 1997).

At the level of the European Union the official aim of regional and structural policy is of course to reduce disparities between regions and countries. Theoretically we can assume that integration may lead to structural change, primarily affecting regional performance, on the one hand. On the other hand, we may assume that integration may also have institutional effects, primarily on national performance.

Already in the early 1990s observers noted that economic disparities were developing in new ways in the integrating Europe (Armstrong and Wickerman 1995; Cheshire 1990; Dunford 1993; 1994). Above all there was a tendency towards diminishing disparities at the national level but with increasing disparities at regional and local levels. These trends are further manifested in the Commission's second report on economic and social cohesion published early 2001 (European Commission 2001).

The so-called Cohesion countries (Greece, Ireland, Portugal and Spain) experienced higher average growth rates than did the EU-12 or the EU-15 during the period 1988-2000. Ireland was in fact the fastest growing economy of the EU-15, with an annual average growth of 6.4 per cent. But also Spain and Portugal grew faster than both the EU-12 and the EU-15, with 2.6 and 3 per cent respectively. Even Greece managed to match the EU-12 but fell slightly behind the EU-15. From the national perspective, therefore, it looks as though the higher pace in European integration has been paralleled by a rapid decrease in economic disparities.

If we look at the development within the member states, we find a somewhat different picture. The cohesion report gives data for the period of 1988 to 1998 and shows an overall increase in disparities at the regional level, measured at NUTS2. While there is still a small decrease in general disparity between regions, from a standard deviation by NUTS2 regions of 29.4 in 1991 to 28.3 in 1998, there are marked increases within a majority of countries. Large increases in regional disparities are noted for the UK, Sweden and Greece. More moderate increases are seen in Finland and in other member states. Decreasing disparities occur in France and in Portugal (European Commission 2001).

We may interpret the above figures as national denominators having become less important for the production of disparities. At the same time, integration or

other developments have opened up for a structurally more volatile situation producing greater disparities at the regional level within individual nation states. All
in all, we have seen a general but moderate decrease in regional disparities over
the last decade, but the main driving forces are not structural changes leading to
more equal regional performance, but national performance strengthened by
institutional change leading to decreasing disparities also at the regional level.

In the second report on cohesion the harmonisation of institutions and the
removal of judicial discrepancies are for the first time clearly defined as tools that
may be used to reduce disparities. In previous communications, e.g. Europe 2000
(European Commission 1991) or the first report on social and economic cohesion
(European Commission 1996), integration in this sense is treated as an unknown
outcome, and the possibility that integration might lead to greater disparities was
always raised. In the second cohesion report the divergence at regional level is discussed in similar terms, but at the national level integration is treated with much
more clarity than previously and is now explained as a driving force leading to
diminishing disparities. In our view the Commission's marked shift in focus –
from that of great concern and uncertainty over the effects of integration as late
as in 1996 to a clear-cut positive view – cannot be explained solely by referring to
empirical evidence.

The History of Structural Policy and Integration

At the heart of the Union's attempts to eliminate economic and social disparities
are the structural policies. This section deals with the empirical relation between
territorial integration and structural policy.

We also need to assess the different steps in European integration. There is an
absolute and a relative dimension to integration. In absolute terms integration is
about changing the physical boundaries of the territory, e.g. manifested in the
enlargement of the territory. In relative terms integration is about changing the
nature of relations within the territory, by reducing barriers in terms of judicial,
economic, political, cultural and social institutions that obstruct or reduce connectivity.

The Difficulties of CAP Reform

The Common Agricultural Policy (CAP) is still by far the largest single item in
the EU budget, corresponding to 54 per cent of the total budget. It is necessary
to include CAP in any discussion on integration and structural policy, because of
its size and because of it entails large transfers. The largest net contributor to CAP
is Germany, followed by Italy, while the largest net beneficiary is Spain, followed
by France. In relative terms the net cost of CAP in Belgium and Luxembourg is
more than 100 EUR per head, while the net gain is highest in Greece (approximately 50 EUR per head). The Irish and Danish farmers are, however, those gain-
ing most per full-time worker in the sector.

The size of the net transfers is quite substantial, Germany contributing over 4 billion EUR in 1998, and Greece and France both receiving over 1 billion EUR. The so-called Cohesion countries are net beneficiaries of CAP with the exception of Portugal.

The reforms of CAP have been relatively modest since its introduction. CAP remains an instrument involving price control and subsidies to production. Since it had been noted that the structure of CAP was in favour of the northern member states, being concentrated on cattle and diary production, strong demands were raised in favour of a reform of CAP. However, reforming CAP proved extremely difficult, mainly due to its strong sectoral connotation. Instead compensation was sought outside of CAP, mainly by two means: firstly by the reinforcement of the structural funds focusing their resources on the Objective 1 regions in the Mediterranean areas; secondly by the introduction of the Cohesion Fund in 1992.[3]

Some reform was, however, undertaken. In 1992 small adjustments in the CAP structure shifted its resource allocation away from price support to performance-related indicators. More area-based support focusing on the rural areas as income generators was also introduced. The significance of these reforms was, however, very limited.

Analysing the development of CAP in relation to the integration challenges facing the EU, the overall impression is one of stability. The legal foundation of CAP has been relatively stable over the years, with CAP surviving the accession of new members and the development of the pace of integration relatively intact. The reforms in 1992 were related to the progress towards the Single Market and may perhaps be seen as attempts to reduce the apparent contradiction between CAP and the principles of the Single Market laid down by the Single European Act.

Our conclusion is that CAP was not an adequate tool to facilitate the entry of new member states. Instead the Structural Funds were expanded, and together with the new instrument – the Cohesion Fund, seen as the main structural policy instrument in this respect. Thus the reform of the Structural Funds in 1988, the introduction of the Cohesion Fund in 1993 and the reform, or rather lack of reform, of CAP in 1992 need to be viewed together. They tell us that there is a degree of communication and interdependency between the various measures adopted within the structural policy instruments in relation to the challenges posed by integration.

The Structural Funds Are Flexible Instruments
Together with the Cohesion Fund the four Structural Funds are the prime policy instrument for achieving economic and social cohesion available to the Commission. Michie and Fitzgerald (1997) identify three phases in the historical development of the Structural Funds. However, before the 1970s regional interventions were relatively small, with the exception of the Mezzogiorno – southern Italy. Regional policy was the responsibility of the member states. In fact Article

92 of the Rome Treaty stated that the member states were allowed exemptions from the general regulations of state aids in certain instances.

The Social Fund and the European Agriculture Guidance and Guarantee Fund were initiated in 1958. At the Paris Summit in 1972 it was decided to create a third fund – the European Regional Development Fund (ERDF). This was introduced in 1975, two years after the enlargement of the EU by the UK, Ireland and Denmark. The main role of the ERDF was to add industrial restructuring outside the agricultural sector to the community agenda. It has been noted by many observers that ERDF was largely called for by the UK, as a mechanism for a financial refund.

In implementation terms regional policy was still very much a mechanism for redistribution, and the Commission's ambitions in relation to targeting or earmarking resources from the ERDF were seen as modest.

The major reform of regional policy came in 1988 when the social fund, ERDF, the fisheries fund as well as a part of the agricultural fund were co-ordinated with national and community initiative multi-annual programmes. It is only from this time that we can begin to talk of an EU regional policy. The co-ordination of resources was also accompanied by large increases of resources. For example, the ERDF was increased tenfold between 1985 and 1995. The total resources of the Structural Funds were doubled between 1987 and 1992.

It is possible to discuss the expansion of the structural resources in terms of adjustments to the integration challenge of new members in 1981/1986. The enlargement of 1981 (Greece) and 1986 (Spain and Portugal) posed more significant disparity challenges than had previous enlargements. It would even be fair to say that the enlargement of 1981/1986 triggered a whole new European concern for economic disparities.

A further tendency is that the co-ordination of resources calls for a much more active role by the European Commission. This has mainly been done through the use of guidelines, through Commission representation on monitoring committees and through evaluations. The Commission has partly used its authoritative role in order to diminish the influence of member states further, by calling for a principle of partnership in the programming and implementation of the funds, involving regions as well as the social partners.

Two further enlargements have challenged the structural policy system. The more significant challenge is of course the accession of six new German *länder* in 1990/91. This is more significant because of the large disparities between the new *länder* and the EU in relation to a series of economic development indicators. However, the integration of the new länder should not primarily been seen as an enlargement of the EU but as the integration of two German territories. The national commitment to integration of course eased the pressure on the EU.

Of less significance was the enlargement in 1995, when Finland, Sweden and Austria became members. Politically the accession of these members was delicate because of the relatively weak support for membership shown in the national referenda. Reform of the Structural Funds in relation to the new members may perhaps to a large degree be understood as a tool for political integration. The introduction of Objective 6 enabled the new member states to raise support for membership from the parts of the countries least in favour.[4] Objective 6 was accepted by the EU-12 partly because of its low costs. The new members were net contributors and the sums flowing into the Objective 6 regions were small because of the small number of people living there.

The Cohesion Fund was introduced in 1993, as a late response to the accession of new members in 1981 and 1986. It has also been linked to the introduction of the Single Market. With the Cohesion Fund the EU shows its concern over economic disparities as a result of absolute or relative integration. The Edinburgh European Council allocated over 15 billion EUR for the period 1993-99, and a further 18 billion was allocated in Berlin for the following period, 2000-2006.

The fund focuses on environment and transport in the so-called Cohesion countries – the idea being that these countries would have major difficulties meeting the demands of investments in the sectors mentioned and at the same time fulfilling the demands raised by the EMU convergence programme. The Cohesion countries are defined as countries with a GDP less than 90 per cent of the EU average. For 1993-98 these countries were Greece, Portugal, Spain and Ireland. In the new period Ireland is no longer a Cohesion country.

Lessons from Previous Enlargements

Based on the experience of earlier enlargements, a few observations concerning the link between integration and policy development may be identified. How integration is achieved is important, since it affects the negotiation powers of the involved parties. In cases of relative integration, negotiation powers are balanced within the Union, thus they are likely to favour the already favoured or serve to preserve existing conditions. Absolute integration, however, represents a unique moment in the negotiations between the parties since the power structures will be resolved as soon as integration is a fact.

The strength of various parties is likely to be determined by factors that determine any negotiation. New member states' strength stems either from their being net contributors to the Union's present policy structure, thus giving them powers to reform policy systems, like in the case of the UK entry in 1973. To a certain degree this was true also for the accession of Austria, Finland and Sweden in 1995. In other situations the strength of new members is politically derived. This seems to have been important in the case of the accession of Greece, Portugal and Spain. For the first time it actually became possible to speak of a European Union while integrating three young democracies in what can be perceived of as an overarching democratic structure.

It is important to notice that pressure for change may not only come from those entering the Union, but also from those already within the structure. The general impression from analysing the interplay between historical integration and reform of the structural policies is one of internal stability and amendments. Whenever integration challenges arise, they are primarily met by amendments to the policy instruments. This works well in cases when new member states are expected to be net contributors to the policy structure. The only previous instance when this was not the case was the accession of the southern European countries in the late 1980s, which led to a budgetary expansion without reductions elsewhere.

Comparing previous enlargements with the coming ones calls for caution. Firstly, economic disparities are much greater. Secondly, the dominance of agriculture in the new member states will prove a significant challenge to the CAP's present structure. Thirdly, the political pressure is fundamentally different from that of previous rounds. The peace and security dimensions of the eastward enlargement cannot be underestimated. The possible outcomes of these conclusions are developed in a number of scenarios in the final section of this chapter. Before that we shall look at the status of the present enlargement.

Before Membership:
Pre-accession Strategies and Negotiations

Preparations for eastward enlargement have been more or less under way since the beginning of the 1990s, although Accession Partnerships came into affect as late as 1998 and confirmed that the ten states were now on the path to membership. Accession Partnerships signify a shift from a multilateral structured dialogue to a mainly bilateral procedure between the EU and applicants. It urges aspiring members to develop national programmes, or timetables, for adoption of the *acquis communautaire*. Apart from being an instrument for measuring progress in the applicant states, the continued flow of EU assistance is now tied to timetables. The function of Accession Partnerships is thus to design individual plans for each of the countries (based on their needs as understood by the Commission and as expressed in membership applications) and to better co-ordinate support to accomplish this (European Commission – Enlargement).

Part of the EU structural policy has been devoted to preparing new members for accession. The PHARE Programme, which has been the main instrument in EU's financial and technical co-operation with Central and Eastern Europe, has been refocused and reoriented for such purposes. In partner countries, PHARE is now concentrated on capacity building for bringing public administrations, industry and infrastructure closer to EU standards. PHARE has an annual budget of 1.5 billion EUR in the current period. Two further accession instruments – ISPA (Instrument for Structural Policies for Pre-Accession programme) and SAPARD (the Special Accession Programme for Agriculture and Rural Development) – have also been introduced from 2000 in order to prepare the new member states for membership. ISPA is designed to facilitate preparations for Structural Funds management. Apart from making applicant countries familiar with the policies and procedures of the EU, support was made available for catching up with environmental standards. ISPA has a budget of 1 billion EUR per year.

With a budget of 520 million EUR per year, SAPARD deals with the structural problems in agricultural and rural area and the adoption of the CAP *acquis* and related regulations (European Commission: Enlargement Directorate-General). These instruments clearly play an important role in the accession process and give the EU a chance to monitor progress or setbacks in applicant states' road to membership. Through these instruments it is possible to observe actual improvements in institutional performance, which is usually much more difficult than the formal change of legislation and regulations. What is not revealed in the formal screening of the *acquis*, might show during the implementation of programmes. While CAP reform and practice in the new member states and the free movement of people stand out as extremely sensitive issues for both parties during the negotiation process, the institutional situation is crucial for judging whether it is at all possible to allow a state to become a member.

The importance of structural assistance as part of the pre-accession strategy is underlined by tendencies in the overall expenditure of the EU. Since 1988 there has been a steady increase in the annual structural expenditures, but after the peak in 1999 overall structural expenditures will decrease each year during the present planning period (2000-2006). Despite this, a steadily growing part of the shrinking resources is spent in applicant states and will make up nearly half this type of expenditure by the end of the period (European Commission 2001). What the picture will be after applicant states have become members and after the present planning period for the Structural Funds, is uncertain and hinges both on reforms and negotiations. The logical guessing seems to be that an even larger share of the resources will be directed to the new territories. There are, however, at least two obvious complications in such a development – enlargement costs need to be kept at a manageable level and opposition by the larger recipients of structural support among the present member states might pose a threat to the timetable for enlargement.

Attempts at measuring budgetary consequences of eastward enlargement are naturally circumscribed by great uncertainty. A recent effort made at measuring Structural Funds spending after enlargement arrived at the conclusion that between five and ten times as much as during the present period would have to be spent on the new members if all were accepted. At the same time, expenditure in the existing member states would need to be more than halved in the period 2007-13 in comparison with 2000-2006. The span in outcome is explained in two alternative scenarios. In the first scenario the present upper limitation to anybody's Structural Fund assistance at 4 per cent of GDP per capita will remain and the SF budget will be maintained at the current level. In the second scenario a more generous approach is taken. In both alternatives a substantial continuation of the redirection of Structural Fund activity will take place (Tarschys 2000). Although these are only two alternative ways of guessing budget effects, it is easy to conclude that Structural Fund policies contain sensitive issues with a bearing both on the reform discussion and on the accession negotiations.

Closely related to the budget issue and different levels of support is the question of future policy instruments. With the existing arsenal of instruments, only Objective 1 would be relevant in the new member states. If existing criteria for Structural Fund support remain, Objective 1 financing will be zeroed or very limited in the Mediterranean states and Ireland. It has been observed, however, that existing instruments are designed to fit EU-15 conditions and not the new potential members. As a consequence, a long period of transition from old to new instruments might be necessary (Karlsson 2001). Such changes seem to fit the needs in new member states and to meet the expectations of existing members of continued assistance. So far Spain has expressed the strongest reaction against a total re-orientation of the funds by threatening to bring the enlargement process to a halt if EU assistance to the country's poorer regions were too much affected. Few would question that other states have similar opinions. The European Commission does its best to bring expectations down to reasonable levels. It points out that the challenge of cohesion will be twice as widespread and twice as large as today, and that it may take two generations bring new members reasonably well into level with the present members (European Commission 2001). While the more generous variant may be based on cohesion arguments, it seems unrealistic and politically difficult from the negotiation perspective.

As this goes to press, negotiations over Chapter 21 of the *acquis communautaire* – regional policy and co-ordination of structural instruments – are still in the early stages and the applicant states on the shores of the Baltic Sea (Poland, Estonia, Latvia and Lithuania) differ in performance. By the end of year 2000 Poland and Estonia had opened this chapter, while Latvia and Lithuania had not reached that stage. In the progress reports of the European Commission (November 2000), steps forward are noted among all four but performance varies. Poland in particular is considered to have made significant progress while the three Baltic States have made only limited progress (see Table 2.1).

Chapter 21 illustrates the institutional shortcomings in applicant states as one of the key problems of the accession process. Insufficient administrative capacities and corruption are general problems among the applicant countries. Financial and budgetary management is another problem area alongside with monitoring and evaluation, where they all have very limited experiences. The legislative framework for regional policy has only begun to emerge and needs to be given priority in the near future, according to the Commission. Concerning statistics, regional data is another issue that remains to be resolved.

The reading of Table 2.1 might give the impression that applicant states still have a long road to go and raise the question of whether problems with the adoption of the *acquis* pose a threat accession. The answer is that failure to adopt the *acquis* certainly is a legitimate reason for refusing membership. We are thus not speaking of negotiations in the ordinary sense since negotiation partners are highly unequal at the table, leaving little room for offers and requests, or even compromise. Applicant states basically have to adopt the *acquis*, which is the result of decades of compromise and negotiations between member states. Real negotiations take place towards the very end of the accession process and usually result

Table 2.1: Status of preparation for Structural Funds

	Poland	Estonia	Latvia	Lithuania
General assessment of progress (since previous year)	Significant progress	Limited progress – but legal and administrative framework not complete	Limited progress, serious difficulties remain with legal and administrative framework	Some progress – but serious difficulties with administrative capacity and co-ordination mechanisms
Territorial organisation	Provincial and county reforms Provisional NUTS classification	State Statistic Act legal basis NUTS classification unsettled	Planning regions corresponding to NUTS III suggested Voluntary amalgamation of municipalities has begun	Some modifications at municipal level Law (below) gives central government right to create new regions
Legislative framework	Law on Regional Development Regional contracts – implementation and SF relevance unclear	State Budget Act allows co-financing and three-year programming Multi-annual local budget plans	None Needs to be given priority	Law on regional development – but relevance for SF partly questioned
Programming	Preliminary National Development Plan Rural development plan in process	Preliminary National Development Plan – improvements needed Responsibilities and administrative capacity unclear	National Development Plan in process	Preliminary National Development Plan approved Regional Development Plans to come Improvements needed
Administrative co-ordination	Ministry of Regional Development created Principles in Law (see above) Co-ordination and division of responsibilities need improvement	Responsibility with National Regional Policy Council – passive so far, role needs consideration Responsibilities and competencies of other bodies only partly settled	Regional Policy working group established Structures for SF still missing at central level	Responsibility given to Ministry of Interior National Regional Development Agency – limited resources Capacity of system poor
Monitoring and evaluation	Responsibility with Ministry, but considerable efforts required	Limited experience – improvements necessary	Structures missing	System missing – should be priority
Financial and budgetary management	Preparatory work under way – but a lot remains	Improvements made concerning selection and assessment of projects Control powers with Ministry of Finance	New principles in the making Structures still missing	No improvement Legislation and structures missing
Statistics	Data partly available	National data partly available No regional data	Most data available at national level Few regional data	Most national data available No regional data

Source: Regular Reports – From the Commission on Progress towards Accession, November 2000

in a package deal that removes the last obstacles. As the previous section illustrated, structural assistance is usually part of that package and is likely to be so also this time. (Nicolaides and Den Teuling 2001). One should, however, not rule out that the accession of certain members might necessitate alterations of the *acquis*, which makes the priorities of candidate states during negotiations a delicate strategic choice.

Conclusion

Finally, what are the future prospects for enlargement and reform of EU structural policy? Enlargement will dramatically exacerbate economic disparities of the EU territory. Only in one instance did previous enlargements lead to increasing disparities, namely the accession of Greece (1981) and Spain and Portugal (1986). The levels of disparity created by those enlargements, however, were much less dramatic.

Historically challenges of enlargement have been met by a) budgetary expansion; b) policy structure reform; and c) policy structure amendment. The way that these challenges have been met is through policy structure amendments, both in relation to the integration of net beneficiaries – the introduction of the Cohesion Fund – and in relation to net contributors – the Regional Development Fund and Objective 6.

CAP has proved more stable than the Structural Funds, possibly because of its more complicated structure and because of its stronger sector-related interests. Hence policy structure reform has primarily taken place within the system of the Structural Funds. Budgetary expansion was chiefly motivated not by the absolute integration of new members, who were net beneficiaries rather than net payers, but instead by referring to relative integration. Introducing the Single Market and the preparations for EMU called for a budgetary expansion, which made it possible to maintain status quo in the CAP structure while the Structural Funds underwent reform and new policy elements were targeted at new members.

We are now facing absolute integration, but with much deeper disparity gaps than in the previous rounds of enlargement. On the basis of the development of the structural policies it is hard to avoid wondering if the time is not ripe for CAP reform, and if eastern enlargement does not call for CAP reform more than anything else (Rabinowicz 1998). Possibly the SAPARD programme is an indication of direction, with its focus on structural change in the agricultural sector and rural development in a broader sense. Whether enlargement will push the CAP out of its reform inertia is of crucial importance to the enlargement process, given the size of the agricultural sector in the applicant states and the threat it poses to the EU budget. Before the future of CAP is settled, little can be known about the costs of enlargement.

Countries likely to lose out on substantial CAP reform are of course its greatest net beneficiaries, in particular Spain and France. But strong sectoral interests may also be voiced in Ireland and Denmark. In particular in the case of Ireland the total net effect of reform and general loss of funds due to rapid economic development may be significant. Spain, which is not only a net beneficiary from CAP but also from the Structural Funds and the Cohesion fund, also perceives a significant threat from the total effects of reform.

One possible scenario may be reduction in and reorientation of CAP, including getting rid of price-control instruments, abolishing production subsidies and increasing the use of area-based development programmes, perhaps coupled with much closer integration with the Structural Funds. In such a scenario we may foresee either a more generous approach allowing for the Structural Funds to maintain a significant level of support for the present Cohesion states, or a less generous approach reducing the interventions in the present member states to a minimum, redirecting funds to the new members. In the latter case successive accession of new members will also allow for a phasing out of the present structural support to the present members. The generous approach in this scenario will of course need to be funded from a budgetary expansion. A third alternative in this scenario is a reform of the Structural Funds favouring the present member states, which may reduce the need for budgetary expansion but allow for more limited structural interventions in the new member states.

A second scenario would perhaps draw on the historically observed difficulties of changing CAP. Instead reform may concentrate on reshaping the Structural Funds. Despite continuous and sometimes radical reforms, the Structural Funds in their current form cannot tackle the expected budgetary consequences of enlargement. In comparison with CAP, the pressure for reform from within is much weaker, which may be another indication of where the defence of existing policies might be strongest. An important question is whether existing members accept budget expansion as a consequence of enlargement, given that they may lose out on resources anyway. Another question is whether pre-accession instruments will survive after accession, as new instruments in the Structural Fund inventory exclusively reserved for new members; or whether a common set of instruments for reasons of justice and simplification will make up the Funds. Again earlier enlargements give a hint that new instruments may be invented exclusively for new members as long as there is a reasonably logical argument for doing so. Possibly the latter variant is the easier way forward, and possibly pre-accession instruments give a clue. If so, institutional improvements may remain a high priority, assuming that institutional change takes much longer than hoped for, which was something the analysis of contemporary developments indicated. A third alternative is perhaps also possible. In this alternative, changes to the present structural policy will be minimal, meaning that most of the resources would automatically go to the new member states. This needs to be compensated for in the present EU area. This compensation may call for a budgetary expansion depending on whether and how substantial reform may be undertaken in the present structural policy systems. The composition of such a compensatory reform may take the form of a policy structure amendment, i.e. a new programme. One way forward may be to strengthen the role of the European Commission in launching a new instrument drawing on the present Community Initiative model. Such a scenario would not beforehand identify the sums that will 'flow back' to the individual member states, it would give a higher profile to the EU and allow for more experimental projects within a wide range of policy fields.

As part of the reform package, EU ambitions in dealing with the cohesion challenge are important for the impact of enlargement on the structural policy field and accession negotiations. The imaginable span is between a position where structural policy as a pawn, among many others, in the negotiation game, to a position where structural policy is treated as a key feature of the integration process and the cohesion problem. From the former perspective, structural policy is used to save the faces of worried negotiators in the eyes of their public opinion back home. Focus is shifted from the needs of new members to the wishes of existing members. Such a position by the EU could perhaps be defensible if applicant states fail to adjust to substantial parts of the *acquis* and if there are extensive demands for temporary derogations. In such a case, the EU could open for a trade-off between derogations and structural policy resources, assuming that the urge for membership among applicants is so strong they will not jeopardise the opportunity by fighting over financial assistance. Existing pre-accession instruments put great emphasis on institutional conditions in the applicant states and may find arguments for letting this focus remain also for some period after new members' accession, meaning that different instruments are used in the old and new parts of the EU territory. If that is the case, structural policy budgets could be kept at present levels also during the 2007-13 period. Such a development emphasises the strong position of the EU at the negotiating table and raises questions as to whether it really believes structural policy is going to even out the differences in economic performance between present and future members.

Notes

[1] The *acquis communautaire* covers the whole range of principles, policies, laws, practices, obligations and objectives that have been agreed upon, or been developed, within the European Union. New members are legally obliged to accept all agreements when joining the EU.

[2] If we include the new *länder*, Germany also appears on the list of states with high levels of economic disparity.

[3] Objective 1is targeted at development and structural adjustment of regions with GDP per capita of 75 per cent or less of EU average.

[4] Objective 6 is targeted at regions with extremely sparse population.

References

Armstrong, H.W. and Wickerman, R.W. (eds) (1995). *Convergence and Divergence among European Regions*. London, Pion.

Artobolevskiy, S.S. (1997). *Regional Policy in Europe*. Regional Policy and Development Series 11. London, Regional Studies Association and Jessica Kingsley.

Cheshire, P. (1990). 'Explaining the recent performance of the European Community's major urban regions,' *Urban Studies* 27:3, pages 311-33.

Dunford, M. (1993). 'Regional Disparities in the European Community: Evidence from the REGIO databank,' *Regional Studies* 27:8, pages 727-43.

Dunford, M. (1994). ' Winners and Losers: The new map of economic inequality in the European Union,' *European Urban and Regional Studies* 1:2, pages 95-114.

European Commission (1991). *Europe 2000: Outlook for the Development of the Community's Territory.* Luxembourg, Office for Official Publications of the European Communities.

European Commission (1996). *First Report on Economic and Social Cohesion.*

European Commission (2001). *Second Report on Economic and Social Cohesion.*

European Commission (2000). Regular Report – From the Commission on Estonia's Progress Towards Accession, 8 November 2000.

European Commission (2000). Regular Report – From the Commission on Latvia's Progress Towards Accession, 8 November, 2000.

European Commission (2000). Regular Report – From the Commission on Lithuania's Progress Towards Accession, 8 November 2000.

European Commission (2000). Regular Report – From the Commission on Poland's Progress Towards Accession, 8 November, 2000.

European Commisson, DG Enlargement (http://europa.eu.int/comm/enlargement/index.htm).

Hallin, G. (1995). *Struggle over Strategy. States, Localities and Economic Restructuring in Sunderland and Uddevalla.* Geografiska Regionstudier 28. Uppsala, Uppsala University, Department of Social and Economic Geography.

Hallin, G. and Lindström, B. (2000). *Det ouppklarade partnerskapet: Om svensk regionalpolitik, strukturfonderna och den territoriella utmaningen.* Stockholm, Institutet för regionalforskning, Rapport 108. Stockholm, Fritzes.

Karlsson, B.O. (2001). *Priset för ett större EU: en ESO-rapport om EU:s utvidgning.* Stockholm, Ds 2001:2. Fritzes.

Moehler, R., Ferrer, J.N. and Fernández, J. (1999). 'The Challenges of Enlargement to EU Agriculture.' Working paper 25, Center for European Policy Studies.

Myrdal, G. (1957). *Economic Theory and the Underdeveloped Regions.* London, Duckworth.

Nicolaides, P. and Den Teuling, A. (2001). *The Enlargement of the European Union: Prerequisites for Successful Conclusion of the Accession Negotiations.* Summary of Conference Proceedings, Maastricht, 19-20 February. EIPA.

Perroux, F. (1950). 'Economic space, theory and applications,' *Quarterly Journal of Economics* LXIV, pages 89-104.

Rabinowicz, E. (1998). 'The CAP: An Obstacle to Enlargement?' in Hedegaard, L. and Lindström, B. (eds). The NEBI Yearbook 1998: North European and Baltic Sea Integration: Berlin, Heidelberg, Springer.

Tarschys, D. (2000), *Bra träffbild, fast utanför tavlan: en ESA-rapport om EU:s strukturpolitik*, Ds 2000:60. Stockholm, Fritzes.

3 Regional Development in Poland

Grzegorz Gorzelak

New Economic Paradigm

For about two decades, three phenomena have shaped contemporary social and economic processes: globalisation, innovation and competition. They are closely interrelated and influencing each other. One may present it in a form of a triad that represents the contemporary paradigm of economic development.

Globalisation is not just more intensive international trade. Globalisation is manifested in the following ways (Amin and Thrift 1999):
- Transnational corporations (TNCs) became the strongest actors on the united global economic scene. They are the greatest producers on innovations and new technologies.
- The strength of the TNCs is supported by the growing magnitude of global flows of 'electronic money' that are very difficult to control (if at all), which leads to greater than ever dependence by public economic agents (international organisations, national governments, city and regional governments).
- Globalisation was made possible by the emergence of global information networks, through which decisions and their economic effects are spread with no physical constrains all around the worlds in almost negligible real time.

Competition, which is an intrinsic feature of a market economy, has acquired new features:
- It has become more acute (*throat cutting,* Kanter 1995).
- It has become global, since several new countries have entered the economic scene.
- It affects all economic agents – also the big TNCs (Christiansen 1997).
- The territorial units have had to become competitive in their efforts to attract capital, especially capital active in innovative businesses.
- It is responsible for economic, social and technological polarisation (Braunerhjelm et al. 2000).

Innovation also is not a new phenomenon. However, in the contemporary world it too has acquired new features:
- Innovation 'produces' innovation, resulting in a synergetic process of constant, accelerating technological change (Castells 1997).
- Global competition is being won only by those who can produce innovation (i.e. belong to the 'high' segment of the global economy) – others compete by production costs, which keeps them in the 'low' segment (Sachs 2000).
- Innovation – through rapid development of telecommunication information networks – enhances globalisation.

The interference of these three phenomena produces a new economic reality with several names: 'third wave' (Toffler 1980), 'knowledge economy,' 'post-fordist' economy' (Malecki 1991: 229-230), sometimes referred to as the 'new economy.' This new economy also produces new location criteria which change the locational attractiveness of the territorial systems. The quantitative categories have been were replaced by qualitative ones that create a favourable business climate for the knowledge-based economy.

Contemporary innovations in the information economy are 'light': they do not weigh much but cost a great deal. The location of innovative activity does not depend on the existence of minerals, sea harbours or abundant labour resources. What matters are the quality, efficiency and reliability of production factors. Cities and regions actively shape conditions for economic activity. They are also becoming entrepreneurial entities competing globally for capital and must provide structures supporting innovation, a superbly qualified workforce as well as the best living conditions.

These processes have an important bearing on spatial processes. The following are of the greatest importance:

- The *metropolises* become the most important and powerful types of spatial unit. Their socio-economic features (high qualifications; rich technical and institutional infrastructure; good accessibility; differentiated business environment; abundance of academic and research institutes; good living conditions) are well adjusted to the modern location criteria (Soja 2000).
- The links of a metropolis with its *hinterland* are weakening, since the region cannot provide its metropolis with high quality inputs, and its main offer is residential land and recreational facilities.
- The metropolises create a *global metropolitan network* in which capital, decisions, innovations and the members of *the world class* (Kanter 1995) circulate.
- *Polarisation* between regions and cities based on quantitative differences in production factors is replaced by a process of segmentation in which spatial differences become more rigid and persistent, since the qualitative differences in innovation potential are more difficult to overcome (Higgins and Savoie 1995).

The Historical Heritage of Polish Regions

Spatial processes take a long time in the making. The physical features of space, its topography, climate, water conditions etc. are changing in cycles lasting hundreds of years. Interference of man may change those features quickly only on a small spatial scale (e.g. dams on a river, urban structures, new agricultural plantations). The distribution of socio-economic processes in space is also subject to long cycles (for instance, the settlement network of Europe had already been shaped in the Middle Ages, even though the flexibility of socio-economic processes is considerably higher than that of physical and natural phenomena.

Most regional studies conducted in Poland reveal a strong impact of historical factors on the current socio-economic spatial patterns of the country. The contemporary shape of the Polish socio-economic space dates back many hundred years. Since the very beginning of Poland's history, division along the western-eastern axis determined different development paths for individual parts of the country. Starting from the very first wave of urbanisation in the 13th-15th centuries, towns were significantly more frequent in the western than in the eastern part of Poland. For many centuries, transport routes in the western part were more dense, and the level of farming culture higher. The period of partitions (1795-1918)[1] reinforced those disparities even more. The differences established earlier were increased not only by the fact of uneven industrialisation (much more intense in the areas situated west of the Vistula river), but also by the fact that individual Polish regions belonged to different political entities, which was reflected in the institutional structures, organisational capabilities, culture of work, self-government traditions etc. Those disparities were not abolished during the so-called Second Republic (1918-39) and efforts at modernisation were interrupted by the outbreak of World War II.

The differentiated developmental conditions of the territories, which in 1918 joined to form the independent Polish State, left behind deep traces in the level of economic development, the infrastructure (roads, railways), the level of urbanisation, the legal system, the education and attitudes of the population and the cultural landscape. After World War II Poland's borders were shifted westward at the expense of eastern – less developed – territories taken over by the former USSR by force of the Treaty of Yalta. During the time of the post-war communist Poland (the People's Republic of Poland) investment efforts mainly targeted areas which had already received some investment, and the newly established centres for natural resource extraction. These processes seldom reached the areas of eastern Poland, which continued to be referred to as 'Poland B.'

To sum up, the historical differentiation of the former and present Polish territories can be presented as follows (Gorzelak 1998):

- Territories situated west of the Vistula (basically west of the Gdansk-Kraków line), long under the influence of the West, undoubtedly constitute a part of Western Europe;

- territories situated east of the line (the so-called Huntington line, see Huntington 1996) across the Vilnius and Lviv regions[2], dividing Slavic Christendom into two parts: western (Roman-Catholic) and eastern (Orthodox), under the influence of the East;
- 'transitory' territories between these two historical borders, in which the influences of Western and Eastern Europe have intertwined and jointly shaped their social, economic and spatial structures.

The Transformation

General Patterns

During the 1960s and 1970s highly developed countries started the process of restructuring, which led them to replace the industrial economy with the contemporary 'information' or 'third wave' economy, briefly described above. The countries of 'real socialism' were well insulated from these changes. Till the end of the socialist system they pursued the path of an industrial (or Fordist) economy, which brought insoluble economic difficulties and resulted in the collapse of the economic system.

There are many analyses of the post-socialist transformation (see, for example, De Melo et al. 1997; Woo et al. 1998; World Bank 1996). These analyses seem, however, to overlook that the post-socialist transformation initiated in 1989 in

Figure 3.1: Transformation trajectories (J-curve patterns)

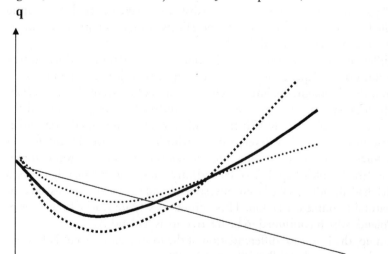

Note: q = quantity, e.g. GDP; t: = time.
Source: Gross domestic Products by *Voivodship*, 1995-97, Katowice, Central Statistical Office, 1999

countries of Eastern and Central Europe resembles the beginning of the structural change which took place in the more developed economies some 20 years ago. This is both a delayed and accelerated restructuring, and one occurring under different conditions. The post-socialist transformation should be demythologised from its ideological underpinnings (though this dimension should not be entirely overlooked) and should be regarded as a normal process of technological and organisational change, performed later than it would have happened if Central Europe (and also other socialist countries) had been incorporated into an open global economy earlier (Gorzelak 1996). As a result of this process, within the economic systems of some post-socialist countries (mostly the Central European ones), some manifestations of a new development model of knowledge-intensive development can be noticed, replacing the traditional patterns of resource-intensive production.

The decline in economic output which occurred in the post-socialist countries after 1990 was the price for restructuring similar to that which the West paid for its change of socio-economic structures after 1973. The restructuring process is often referred to as the J-curve trajectory (Bradshaw and Stenning 1999), see Figure 3.1. The curve indicates that the restructuring process has to be started with a phase of scrapping or deconstructing old, obsolete production stock which cannot be effective under new economic and technological conditions, and only after having done that may the economy system enter the path of growth. This pattern follows the idea of Schumpeterian 'creative destruction,' which refers to the role of innovator in economic development. The systems (firms, cities, regions, countries) which are braver and bolder in the 'destruction phase' may be then better rewarded in the 'creation' or 'growth' phase, since the burden of obsolete structures is much smaller and the freedom for creation is greater. Table 3.1 indicates the differentiated patterns of post-socialist transformation in particular in Eastern and Central European countries.

As Table 3.1 reveals, among the Central European countries Poland has no doubt followed the 'sharpest' J-curve. It entered the 'destruction phase' as early as 1990, which may be regarded as one of the main reasons why the restructuring of the Polish economy has been among the most successful in this part of Europe. It begun to grow already in 1992 and reached the 1989 level of GDP in 1996, to climb in 2000 to 127 per cent of the 1989 GDP value. Ukraine shows the opposite pattern as it – like several other countries – tried to delay the restructuring, and has not been able to return to the path of growth.

The Regional Patterns of Transformation

The transformation from the socialist industry-driven economy to an open market system with elements of the knowledge-driven economy has influenced most of the territorial systems of the post-socialist countries. It has manifested itself in different ways in particular in regions. The following four cases of regional reaction to the post-socialist transformation should be noticed (see also Gorzelak 1998):

(a) *Leaders* – the regions that can be considered as (relatively) well prepared for the new paradigm of the information economy. These are the metropolitan regions, with diversified socio-economic structures, well equipped with technical and institutional infrastructure, with a highly educated population, hosting several academic and scientific establishments. The capitals of the Central European countries, like Prague, Budapest, Warsaw, Moscow, Kiev in the first place, but also St Petersburg, Poznan, Kraków and Wroclaw, Bratislava and Ljubljana fall into this group.

(b) *Winners* – the regions that took advantage of the macro-spatial change that occurred outside of these regions. These are mostly western regions that took advantage of the proximity of Austria and Germany, but also Finland and Sweden (Estonia and Latvia) with their consumer and investment capital. Some tourist regions have also taken advantage of the opening to the outside world.

(c) *Losers* – the regions that have to pay large economic and social costs of restructuring and adaptation to the new conditions. In Central Europe these are the regions with traditional heavy and mining industries. In Poland and in the Czech Republic one must mention Upper Silesia with the main cities of Polish Katowice and Czech Ostrava, in Hungary the north-eastern part of the country with Miskolc and several localities in Slovakia. Hard hit is also the textile industry as in Poland's second biggest city Łódź.

(d) *Laggards* – regions that are to some extent 'sentenced' to backwardness as they have little to restructure and no impulses may come to them form outside. The eastern belt of the Central European countries falls into this category

Table 3.1: Dynamics of GDP in post-socialist countries, 1989-99

Countries	1990	1991	1992	1993	1994	1995	1996	1997	1998	1999	
											1990
	previous year=100										=100
Belarus	98	99	90	89	84	90	103	111	108	-	78
Bulgaria	91	88	93	99	102	102	89	93	104	102	68
Czech Rep.	99	86	94	99	103	106	104	100	98	100	85
Lithuania	93	87	61	70	101	103	104	106	104	97	60
Latvia	103	89	65	85	101	98	102	-	-	-	51[a]
former GDR	84	81	108	106	109	109	-	-	-	-	110[b]
Poland	**88**	**93**	**100**	**104**	**105**	**107**	**107**	**107**	**105**	**104**	**121**
Russia	97	95	86	81	87	96	97	101	95	102	57
Romania	94	87	91	102	104	107	104	93	93	98	74
Slovakia	98	85	94	96	105	107	107	107	104	102	103
Slovenia	92	92	95	102	105	104	104	105	104	105	107
Ukraine	96	88	86	86	77	88	90	97	98	100	36
Hungary	97	88	97	99	103	102	101	105	105	105	101

[a]1996; [b]1995; [c]1998.

Source: Polish Statistical Yearbooks, 1990-2000

since it is mostly agricultural, poorly endowed with infrastructure, with poor-ly qualified inhabitants and bordering the regions of Ukraine and Belarus that do not present promising chances for transborder co-operation.

Two major patterns of regional differentiation are thus characteristic of several post-socialist states: big urban centres, and especially the capital cities, are in a better position than are the non-metropolitan parts of these countries; so are the western regions that flourish due to co-operation with Germany and Austria, while the eastern ones are still peripheral and stagnating.

The following sections will highlight some selected processes of regional restructuring in Poland in more detail.

Regional Differentiation during Transformation

Poland entered the phase of transformation with relatively small inter-regional disparities – only the Warsaw region displayed a much higher level of GDP per inhabitant than the national average.

The transformation period generated an interesting process of regional diver-sification, though formally, in statistical terms, the regional disparities in Poland have not grown considerably during the 1990s (although the distance between the most and the least developed regions increased). Generally speaking, the dynam-ics may be summarised as follows:

1. In the years of the so-called transformation shock (1989-90), the less devel-oped *voivodships* improved their situation. Their smaller economic decline compared to the better developed regions resulted from a higher share of (individual) farming in the structure of the economy, which cushioned them from the recession of the initial years of Polish transformation, brought about mainly by the restructuring of industry. The urbanised and industrialised regions experienced massive breakdowns of their economic input, which was caused by market re-orientation and the necessity of adaptation to new con-ditions.

2. In the years 1991-92, the tendencies of the first stage of transformation were reinforced:
   - *voivodships* with a large share of individual farming saw relatively high GDP increases;
   - *voivodships* with a large share of state-owned agriculture (north-western regions) experienced a decline in GDP, similarly to some underdeveloped *voivodships* (e.g. those with a significant amount of tourism). In some of those regions, acute social problems (mass unemployment) appeared;
   - the majority of regions with huge agglomerations experienced a further decline in GDP caused by recession in industry.

In the period of overcoming recession (from 1992-93 until now), the less devel-oped *voivodships* proved to be relatively less capable of accelerating their develop-ment. *Voivodships* with large agglomerations, which required restructuring of traditional industries, noted a relatively lower rate of GDP increase. The regions with diversified economies were in a more favourable position (large agglomerations, efficient farming), as well as those which underwent successful economic restructuring (e.g. post-state farm regions). The differences in the volume of GDP per capita in 'old' Polish 49 regions are shown in Figure 3.2.

These regional trajectories may be easily interpreted within the cognitive framework presented in the fist section of this chapter. The backward, rural regions proceeded along the shallower J-curve, while the more industrialised ones proceeded along the steeper one. The former regions did not have much to restructure – their agriculture was not (and still is not) oriented towards the market (it is mostly a self-sufficient subsistence agriculture), and therefore market changes did not affect their economies. The 'restructuring price' was not paid – but the 'development price' will be paid, since the ability of these regions to sustain a decent rate of growth is rather limited. The steeper J-curve, which was the trajectory of the industrialised Polish regions, involved higher restructuring costs (bankruptcies, unemployment, temporary poverty), but these costs enabled these regions to enjoy a 'development premium' after the restructuring had passed its critical point.

International Relations as a Factor in Regional Development

To some extent the patterns of regional differentiation that occurred in the 90s can be explained by Poland's international contacts, which changed after the collapse of the centrally planned economy. The systemic transformation of 1989,

Figure 3.2: Regional GDP per capita, 1997

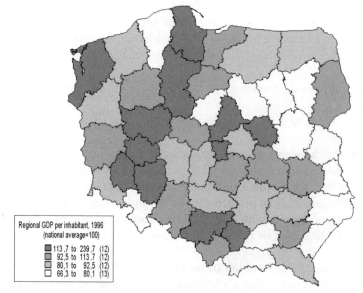

Source: Voivodship Statistical Yearbook 1999, Warsaw, Central Statistical Office

The two following local cases from the same western region of the country (Lubuskie *voivodship*) may be instructive for this line of reasoning:

Żary (40 thousand inhabitants) used to be a concentration of textile and wood industries. In 1990 the main local employers went bankrupt. Unemployment soared to over 20 per cent, and the local budget was run on deficit. The local authorities decided not to assist the bankrupt firms. Instead they chose to create opportunities for new start-ups or for fundamental restructuring (with privatisation) of the old enterprises. It was in Żary that the first big public industrial enterprise went through the bankruptcy procedure, and the local leaders are now proud of it! Since 1992 several new local business-supporting institutions have created in Żary: a loan fund, a foundation for entrepreneurship, a centre for small-firm assistance, a business incubator. The town hosts a genuinely local electric company that has issued shares on the Warsaw stock market, has a daughter company in Mexico and now moves some of its production to Lithuania (lower labour costs). Unemployment has been held below 8-10 per cent; several small and medium-sized firms prosper; and development perspectives are optimistic.

Nowa Sól, located some 20 kilometres from Żary, is inhabited by 42,000 people. Two big plants used to dominate its local labour market: a metallurgical company (with a great share of military production), which employed 4000 people, and a textile factory with 8000 employees. The first stage of Polish transformation took its toll on both companies, which lost their traditional Soviet markets. The managers of both these huge plants and the city authorities tried to postpone the necessary restructuring. Both firms became heavily indebted, and the local budget allocated big sums to assist the enterprises and to guarantee their loans (spent mostly on wages for too many employees). Both firms have now closed down; the local unemployment rate jumped to 30 per cent; social pathologies became widespread; and prospects for the future are darker than 10 years ago.

by destroying the COMECON system, opened Poland to the world. In terms of the country at large, this process was manifested by a radical change of the geographical structure of Polish foreign trade. Regionally, it was displayed in the form of transborder co-operation and a spatially uneven distribution of the activity of foreign capital. Transborder co-operation assumed varied forms. Initially, it was restricted to trade, primarily unofficial trade, which was an obvious response of people's enterprise to the differences in prices on both sides of the border. Owing to the fact that the purchases made by the Germans were approximately two times higher than the aggregate purchases of all the remaining neighbours of Poland, the influence of border trade was much stronger along the western border than along the eastern or southern ones. Border trade became an important development factor for some towns lying on the border. On the one hand, it generated incomes for companies and persons engaged in this activity, and on the other it provided significant support to the local budgets, thanks to proceeds from the marketplaces and taxes.

Recently we have been witnessing a gradual reduction of the role of border trade, which is due to the appreciation of the Polish currency (zloty) and the levelling out of price levels, in addition to the disturbances in the economy of Poland's eastern neighbours and administrative restrictions. New, lasting economic ties such as exports, influx of foreign capital and Polish investments abroad, are being established to a markedly greater extent along the western border than the eastern or southern ones.

For a few years the Polish western regions enjoyed an economic boom stemming from the benefits of the transborder trade. Some 5 billion DM were brought there yearly to pay for products much cheaper than in Germany – mostly basic commodities like food, gas, cigarettes, simple services (also erotic), cheap textiles, leather, carpets, crystal, plastic etc. The merchants came from all regions of Poland, as did the commodities, so a large share of profits was exported to other Polish regions. Even so, the local economy benefited, since jobs were created, local taxes were paid, some income was left on the spot.

However, the golden era seems to be coming to an end. Price differences between Poland and Germany slowly vanish – but profits made in previous years were mostly consumed or located in new houses and not invested in businesses. Recently unemployment has been growing and local transborder trade has been reduced mostly to gasoline, cigarettes and sex. The chances to use the profits made on trade for creating enterprises that might be competitive on the German markets, have not fully materialised.

By opening the borders the Polish western regions have been offered a great chance. The efforts to turn this temporary advantage into a durable competitive advantage have been too weak. Polish western territories have failed to take the 'high road' of economic transborder co-operation and may end up on the 'low road' of dependency on stronger and more technologically advanced German partners and competitors (Krätke 1997).

The most important form of new international economic ties is the influx of capital (Figure 3.3), which came to 50 billion

American dollars by the end of 2000. This influx is distinctly higher in the western part of the country than in the eastern one. German capital, representing about 12 per cent of the aggregate foreign capital invested in Poland, more frequently than capital from other countries is invested in small companies located near the border. The capital from other countries displays different location preferences and is concentrated in large cities, predominantly in Warsaw (approximately 30 per cent of the total foreign capital inflow).

The opening of the Polish space to international co-operation is not complete, partly because of the stagnation in the construction and modernisation of transport infrastructure. Poland has only about 200 kilometres of motorways, whereas over 95 per cent of Polish roads are two-way and one-lane in each direction. There is a shortage of city bypass roads, two-level crossings, and the surface quality is poor. The major east-west transit route, from Świecko on the border with Germany to Terespol on the border with Belarus, crosses several towns and cities, Poland and Warsaw included, which has put a heavy strain on these agglomera-

Figure 3.3: Companies with foreign capital in Poland, 1997

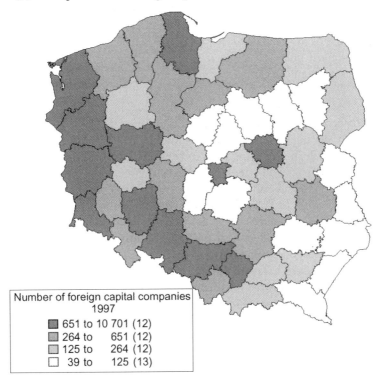

Number of foreign capital companies
1997

■ 651 to 10 701 (12)
▨ 264 to   651 (12)
▨ 125 to   264 (12)
□   39 to   125 (13)

tions and has slowed down the traffic. The condition of Polish railways constitutes a smaller barrier since the railway network density is one of the highest in the world, but the quality and efficiency is low. The transformation period has not alleviated the situation in any way – on the contrary, the tragic and constantly deteriorating state of Polish roads with respect to the rapidly growing needs is one of the most serious barriers to the further opening of Polish space and its integration with the European space (Petrakos 2000).

The Future of Polish Regions

Regional Trajectories
It may be assumed that the Polish space and economy will remain open to the world and to the principles of a global competitive economy. It is also very probable that the country will join the European Union by the middle of the decade 2001-10. It can be also assumed that the Polish economy will grow at the rate 5 per cent yearly and will continue its structural change. Based on these assumptions we may deduce the following perspective for the regional development of Poland at the beginning the twenty-first century:

1. For the period 2001-15, the metropolitan region of *Warsaw* (i.e. an area small-
    er than the former capital *voivodship*) will be the fastest developing region of
    the country. An annual 7-10 per cent growth rate is quite feasible owing to the
    steady influx of investment to this most technologically advanced and at the
    same time most polarised regional economy in Poland. Simultaneously, the
    disparities between the capital metropolis and its vicinity will grow, while the
    range of positive impact of Warsaw will gradually increase. The agglomera-
    tions of *Poznań, Kraków* and *Wroclaw* – cities that, in addition to Warsaw, can
    aspire to become metropolises on the European scale (Jałowiecki 1999) will
    most likely develop at a rate similar to the national average or even higher,
    which will result in increasing the gap between them and the less developed
    regions. These areas will strengthen their current role as centres of techno-
    logical, economic and cultural development and will attract – together with
    Warsaw – the bulk of Poland's contacts with the world. The agglomerations
    of Gdansk (Tri-City) and Szczecin are likely to follow suit, provided they are
    able to develop financial services and other sectors of the modern economy
    related to sea harbours. One may say that the restructuring process in these
    metropolitan regions has gone through a 'sharp' J-curve, and the costs paid at
    the initial stage of industrial restructuring have then led to accelerated growth
    in the second phase of transformation.

    However, fast development of Polish agglomerations may come up against
    an infrastructural barrier, which may be particularly deeply felt in the Warsaw
    agglomeration, whose backwardness, particularly with regard to the transport
    sector, is the most severe. Warsaw makes only slight use of its potential result-
    ing from the fact that it is the capital of a quickly developing country and this
    impairs the opportunities not only of Warsaw itself but of the entire country.
    Lack of a congress centre, architectural chaos, snail pace in the construction
    of the underground, paralysis of municipal authorities are only some of the
    unfavourable phenomena occurring in all Poland's major cities.

2. *Lódz* experienced a very dramatic decline at the beginning of the 1990s. How-
    ever, it was able to revitalise its economy, though mostly in the 'low' sector, i.e.
    textiles directed to less demanding market of the post-Soviet republics. This is
    not too promising as shown by the recent decline in demand due to the
    Russian economic crisis of 1998. If the restructuring of the economy is directed
    towards the expansion of advanced technologies and specialised services, such
    as medical services or design and manufacturing of quality clothing, the
    agglomeration may eventually join the leading cities, and the average annual
    rate of growth in the region will be only fractionally smaller than the national
    average.

3. *Upper Silesia* is still facing serious restructuring. So far, the forecast dramatic
    increase in unemployment has not come true. The region may be said to have
    gone against the general pattern of the J-curve since its trajectory has been

'flat' even with some growth without earlier decline. However, this has been due to subsidies (direct and indirect) transferred to this region: for example the cumulated debts of the coal mining sector are equal to half of the regional product. It can be expected that the current pattern of certain internal and external 'parasitism' cultivated by the region will be exhausted. Two development scenarios for the region are possible, depending on the volume of funds earmarked for the region and the manner they are utilised. The positive scenario envisages a fast reduction of coal mining and parallel intensive restructuring of the region's economy and space[3], which can lead to the redefining of the central area of the mining industrial basin, and not only its boundaries. The unfavourable scenario will involve slow restructuring of the economy and relinquishing the redevelopment of obsolete industrial structures, which will result in the destruction of the social fabric of the region. It is to be hoped that structural funds, launched after 2006, will make it possible to realise the first scenario.

4. The *Central-western regions* (Wielkopolska and adjoining northern and southern areas) will exhibit dynamics comparable to the national average, since the fast development that will occur in non-agricultural sectors will be decelerated as a result of a relatively high share of agriculture in the regional economy. These regions have not gone through a 'deep' curve, since their economies were sufficiently developed and diversified not to have to pay high costs of restructuring.

5. The *eastern* and non-metropolitan *central* parts of Poland have not been touched too severely during the first phase of restructuring as they have experienced much less decline than the more industrialised ones, and some parts of the regions even experienced growth between 1990 and 1992. However, after 1993 they began to be overtaken by the more developed parts of the country – which exactly corresponds to a 'shallow' J-curve. It is therefore almost certain that their development will be slower than the country's average. In other words, these are areas which despite their positive rate of growth will lose out to the most developed regions. In the long-term perspective, the development of the eastern regions will depend on the situation in Russia, Ukraine, Belarus and Lithuania. It is not very likely that favourable stimuli will be generated there in the near future. The development of this part of the country will be concentrated to local entities capable of maximal use of indigenous factors. Such centres should receive support funds from both domestic and foreign sources. Sealing the eastern border following Poland's entry to the EU will not have any negative effects if structures capable of starting cross-border co-operation are established on the other side of the border. This may require Poland's assistance, similar to the support extended to Poland's western regions by Germany.

6. Particularly acute problems may arise in the *south-eastern* part of Poland threatened by stagnation of the highly dispersed, backward and overpopulated agriculture. The revival of industry with traditions dating back to the inter-war period (COP – the Central Industrial District) will be difficult owing to its profile and a considerable share of military industry that is rather redundant in the face of progressing disarmament. The EU funds are not likely to have any significant bearing on this situation. The region may experience increased pressure on the labour market both in rural and urban areas since widespread urban unemployment will coincide with high rural unemployment caused by overpopulated agriculture and currently estimated at 750 – 900 thousand. Even though EU resources earmarked for this region after 2006 will help improve the level of education and infrastructure, this will not be a sufficient stimulus for generating speedier growth of the region. Paradoxically, it may lead to an increased outflow of the most active and best educated individuals. Similarly to eastern and central Poland, development of this region will be concentrated in a relatively small number of dynamic local systems.

7. The *northern* regions, which in the initial phase of the Polish transformation found themselves in a particularly difficult situation owing to the collapse of the unprofitable state farms, seem to be coming out of recession though recovery has been difficult and painful. Reduction of the persisting high unemployment in the area is not very likely since it is largely due to the widespread poor adaptation of those who are currently out of work (mainly former employees of state farms) to the requirements of the contemporary labour market. Part of this region (the coastal strip and lake districts) can hope for the development of tourism, which is expected to become the leading sector of the regional economy. The remaining areas will be subject to depopulation, a phenomenon aided by the increased scope of one of the most effective measures of combating unemployment – education of the young outside their place of residence.

8. For the *western border belt*, the proximity of Germany, and transborder co-operation in particular, has been an essential factor of economic development. However, as the price levels on both sides of the border have become more equal, the profits from this exchange have dwindled. Regretfully, no economic structures have been created that would permit more equal co-operation with stronger German partners. Nonetheless, this region still enjoys the greatest development opportunities but embracing them requires huge effort, mainly related to the development of technical and institutional infrastructure, including educational and research establishments. After 2006, this region will experience a boost in development since the barrier in the form of the state border will be eliminated.

9. In addition to the large regions discussed above, the are many areas in Poland in an exceptional situation. Some of them are dependent on the global demand for the raw materials that are extracted there. For instance, currently the copper-mining basin of Głogów-Legnica in Western Poland benefits from a boom in the copper market, whereas the Tarnobrzeg sulphur basin (south-eastern part of the country) is in a difficult situation, and the future of brown coal mines and associated power plants depends on the mineral resources and demand for energy. In other cases, the development of a given territorial micro-system hinges on the standing of one large state enterprise. In a market economy, many such entities will probably not regain the prosperity they enjoyed under the socialist economy of shortages. The situation of such areas will be only slightly affected by Poland's relations with the European Union, since their performance is determined by the structural changes in the dominant sectors on which the Polish government or the European Union can hardly have any bearing.

In the decentralised system that is now being built in Poland (we now have 16 self-governing regions, 308 districts and approximately 2500 municipalities) it will be the regions' own responsibilities to take advantage of their potentials. The central government should only intervene in the regions when it appears beneficial for the whole country. Examples of nationally beneficial intervention might be construction and modernisation of major transportation corridors, enhancing trans-border co-operation, assisting the regions in developing their educational and R&D potential. Such undertakings might increase the international competitiveness of the Polish regions – and, as result, of the whole country.

Notes

1   In 1795 the last partition took place, and Poland was divided among three states: Russia took the eastern part, Prussia the western and Austria the south-eastern part. In what is now Poland (i.e. after the two World Wars had moved its borders westwards) there is also a fourth historical part, the northern and most western one, which used to belong to German states.
2   After 1945 in Lithuania and Ukraine, respectively. Poland is now entirely located west of the line separating eastern and western Christianity.
3   The experience of Western Europe proves that reclamation of one hectare of post-industrial area for a lawn, square etc. costs around USD 15 thousand. Reclamation for housing purposes requires expenditures of approximately USD 150 thousand (Fothergill 2000: 200).

References

Amin, A. and Thrift, N. (1999). *Globalization, institutions and Regional Development in Europe.* Oxford University Press.
Bradshaw, M. and Stenning, A. (2000). 'The Progress of Transition in East Central Europe,' in Bachtler, J., Downes, R. and Gorzelak, G. (eds). *Transition, Cohesion and Regional Policy in Central and Eastern Europe.* Aldershot, Ashgate.

Braunerhjelm, P., Faini, R., Norman, V., Ruane, F. and Seabright, P. (2000). *Integration and the Regions of Europe: How the Right Policies Can Prevent Polarization*. London, CEPR.

Castells, M. (1997). *The Rise of the Network Society*. Cambridge, Massachusetts, Blackwell.

De Melo M., Denizer, C. and Gelb, A. (eds) (1997). 'Patterns of Transition from Plan to Market,' *The World Bank Economic Review* 19:3.

Gorzelak, G. (1996). *The Regional Dimension of Transformation in Central Europe*. London, Jessica Kingsley.

Gorzelak, G. (1998). *The Regional and Local Potential for Transformation in Poland*. Warsaw, EUROREG.

Higgins, B. and Savoie, D.J. (1995). *Regional Development Theories and Their Application*. New Brunswick and London, Transaction.

Huntington, S.P. (1996). *The Clash of Civilisations and the Remaking of World Order*.

Jałowiecki, B., (1999). *Metropolie*. Białystok, WSFiZ.

Krätke S. (1997). 'Regional Integration or Fragmentation? The German-Polish Border Region in a New Europe.' Paper presented at the Regional Studies Association Conference, Frankfurt (Oder).

Malecki, E.J. (1991). *Technology and Economic Development: The Dynamics of Local and Regional Change*. Longman.

Petrakos G. (2000). 'The spatial impact of East-West integration in Europe' in Petrakos, G., Maier, G. and Gorzelak, G. (eds.). *Integration and Transition in Europe. The economic geography of Integration*. London and New York, Routledge.

Sachs, J. (2000). 'A new map of the world,' *The Economist*, June 24-30.

Soja, E.W. (2000). *Postmetropolis: Critical Studies of Cities and Regions*. Oxford, Blackwell.

Woo, T.W., Parker, S. and Sachs, J. (eds) (1998). *Economies in Transition: Comparing Asia and Europe*. Cambridge, London, MIT.

World Bank (1996). *From Plan to Market: World Development Report*. Oxford, Oxford University Press.

4 Norway and EU Enlargement: Prospects for Further Integration

Ole Gunnar Austvik and Noralv Veggeland

As a participant in the European Economic Area (EEA), a participant in the Baltic Sea region, the North Sea region and the Barents region co-operations and a signature country of the Schengen and the Veterinary Agreements, Norway is part of the flexible integration processes in Europe. However, as a non-member of the EU, she is not a part of the official structure of the EU. The Norwegian EU referendum of 1994 made it clear that the majority of Norwegians were opposed to membership and were afraid of giving up sovereignty to remote supra-national political authorities. In particular, there was profound opposition to losing national control over agriculture and fishery policies, regional policies and the petroleum resources in the North Sea, and against becoming an economic and political periphery in a greater, unitary Europe – The United States of Western Europe. The deficit of democracy was also looked upon as a reason to reject full membership.

Left-wing politicians in particular argued that if Norway joined the Union, it would become a member of a superpower that would leave poor Eastern Europe behind economically and politically. The result would be increased tension and insecurity in the region. They favoured pan-European integration and a 'Europe of Nations.' Concerning national trade and industrial development, the European Economic Area agreement had already given Norway access to the Single Market. Hence the economic argument had little impact on the decision.

Following the rejection of EU membership, the government declared that there would be no new initiative to join the EU for at least ten years. However, since the summer of 1999 the question has received renewed attention in the Norwegian press. This has been accentuated by the fact that more and more policy areas are being drawn into the competence of the Union in addition to economics, especially in the area of security and defence policy. There are signs that Norwegians are becoming aware of the anomalous position in which they have placed themselves, being obliged to take over rules that affect their lives and businesses very deeply (perhaps more than they had ever anticipated), with no say in their formulation.

The enlargement processes and the Nice Summit negotiations on institutional adjustments have reinforcing this feeling of being an outsider in vital European affairs. An extension of the Union to the south and east may contribute to build up pressure for a new membership bid.

Flexible Integration

Flexible integration is a new approach and might be a political option for Norway. The concept was developed in 1995 by a multinational team of academics of the London-based Centre for Economic Policy Research. Flexible integration was introduced as a contribution to the discussion on deepening and widening of the EU before the 1996 Intergovernmental Conference. It made 'predefined flexibility' feasible (Deubner 2000: 8). The dual structure principle made it possible to open up for an expansion and to let the countries in economic and political transition become members. As this is being written, 12 countries are negotiating membership and many of them are likely to become part of the European Union in the years to come. The perspective seems to be a European Community of member states integrating at different speeds.

The main characteristic of flexible integration is its dual structure. The approach consists of *a common base*, a set of policies that has to be accepted by every member state, and *open partnerships*, policies outside the common base. In fact, already in the implementation process of the Maastricht Treaty this dual structure was in use as certain exceptions from the basic principles were granted to Denmark and Great Britain. At the time this approach was called 'case by case flexibility' (Deubner 2000: 8). The No in the Danish referendum on membership in the Economic and Monetary Union in September 2000 confirms the duality.

This perspective raises many challenges to Norwegian EU policies. One question is simply what the enlargement and the existence of a multi-speed Europe will mean to public opinion. Will the principle of flexible integration and the dual structure of the EU make membership and supra-nationality more acceptable? If so, national control over vital petroleum and fishery resources should be secured. Another question is how the new economic structures and an extended market and Euro-zone will influence the Norwegian economy and business interests (Johansson and Person 2000; Straubhaar 2000). A third dimension is how the enlargement coupled with Baltic Sea co-operation influences Norwegian structural policies and developments. A fourth question is what impacts the enlargement and the new Common Foreign and Security Policy (CFSP) will have on Norway as a member state of NATO.

The Single Market and the EMU

The EEA encompasses Norway, Iceland and Liechtenstein. The three countries participate fully in the Single Market with free trade for goods, services, labour and capital, with the exception of agriculture and fishery. Thus, most EU Single Market laws and regulations have become Norwegian policy as well. More than 3000 directives and regulations have been adopted by the Norwegian parliament since 1994. The EEA agreement and intensified competition between Norwegian and EU firms contribute to the harmonisation of Norwegian policies with those of EU countries in a number of areas.

With the enlargement of the Single Market, competition will be further intensified for many industries. The most important sector for Norway in this respect, as it is for many EU countries, will be agriculture. Lower food prices outside Norway will put pressure on Norwegian food prices as well as on farmers' incomes. Together with the negotiations in the World Trade Organisation (WTO) to liberalise international markets for agricultural products, the enlargement of the EU and its agricultural reform (Agenda 2000) may force Norway to change its agricultural policy in the direction of EU agricultural policy. This is what has had to do in many other sectors, irrespective of the fact that Norway is not a member.

Another important area is migration from the new democracies towards the richer west. Free trade and labour markets tend to make wages converge over time. Migration and trade will lower relative wages in the west and make them rise in the east. Even though everyone may benefit in the long run from integrating east and west, workers in the west may lose out in the first phase, and some will lose permanently. The differences in income between business owners and employees in the west will be greater. As a participant in the free labour market, Norway will be confronted with this challenge in line with the EU countries.

Already, the establishment of a common European currency has put tight limits on Norwegian macroeconomic policy. The expansion of the EMU area will increase the competition faced by Norwegian firms. Imported goods may be expected to become cheaper, and Norwegian exports will fetch lower prices and face higher demands for specialisation. Norwegian firms will gain from reduced costs of currency trade and reduced uncertainty in exchange rate fluctuations. At the same time, Norwegian kroner may still fluctuate against the euro and the gains for Norwegian businesses will be less than for businesses in EMU countries. Thus, the emergence of the Euro-zone may lead to a deterioration of *relative* cost advantages for Norwegian firms.

A further enlargement of the Euro-zone will underline the fact that Norway is a small currency area, inter-inked in trade and finance with a very large one. This will lead to pressure for even more harmonisation of Norway's monetary policy with that of the European Central Bank (ECB). In turn, this will reinforce the pressure for a greater degree of fiscal policy harmonisation.

Norway as a Large Energy Exporter

The role of Norway as a major petroleum and gas exporter puts special requirement on Norwegian economic policy in these new and rapidly changing circumstances. Norway is one of the world largest petroleum exporters and the second
largest gas exporter to the European market. The size of Norwegian petroleum
and gas exports makes Norway a strategic actor in markets vital for European
energy supplies. At the same time as Norway has developed as a petroleum economy, the importing countries have become intensively dependent on safe energy
supplies at reasonable prices.

The large and fluctuating petroleum revenues put Norway in a very special
macroeconomic situation compared to the EU countries. The decoupling of
petroleum revenues and the use of petroleum money through the establishment
of the Norwegian petroleum fund is moving some of the wealth from the North
Sea into international financial markets. This contributes to reducing the Norwegian economy's vulnerability in relation to fluctuations in petroleum revenues,
for example when petroleum prices change as much as they have done over the
year 2000. The fund is becoming very large, and is expected to pass the level of
the entire Norwegian annual GDP within 3-4 years.

On the other hand, plans for how this money can be used in the long run to
make the Norwegian economy more competitive are almost not discussed. Traditionally there has been tension between fiscal discipline and the need to spend
on infrastructural development and social expenses. Norway has been more concerned with avoiding the problems connected with the large revenues than with
the benefits that may be derived from them.

The large petroleum revenues in a small economy present Norway with special challenges in relation to developments in the rest of Europe. To a large extent,
the Norwegian economy is counter-cyclical to the other European economies
with respect to changes in petroleum prices. When petroleum prices go up, Norway gains while the others lose, and vice versa. Hence it is argued that Norway
needs a different monetary policy from the EU countries. As freedom in the area
of monetary policy is already reduced, the question arises whether or not Norway
might be better off introducing the Euro in order to keep interest rates down and
abolish the problem of changing exchange rates due to fluctuations in the petroleum revenues. Introducing the euro may also reduce the problem of using more
of the petroleum and gas revenues for structural change in industry without overheating the economy through high interested rates and exchange rate fluctuations.

The widening and deepening of the Union also has specific energy policy
implications for Norway. More economic growth in the EU, in general, and in
the new member states, in particular, will be followed by demands for more energy. This will be to the benefit of Norway as a petroleum and especially gas
exporter. On the other hand, the EU's geographical extension and economic
growth will better enable it to develop energy market policies that may not be

favourable to Norway as a petroleum exporter. Such policies may include energy taxation and the liberalisation of the gas market and may lead to controversy between Norway and the EU.

Norway and the EU countries are interdependent in the field of energy, but may, within certain limits, have asymmetric interests concerning energy price levels. The EU wants to optimise the benefits for its member countries, while Norway wants to optimise the benefits for Norway. The better EU institutions and political instruments are developed, and the more representative the EU becomes of European economic development, the greater the potential to formulate polices detrimental to Norway's interests as major petroleum exporter.

Short and long-term interests must be assessed here. In the short and medium term, which for fossil energy may be 2-8 years, the EU would like Norway to increase petroleum and gases supplies and lower prices in order to meet the increased demand. However, the exhaustion of the non-renewable resources and lack of long-term investments that such a policy might entail, could reduce and possibly endanger energy supplies in the long run.

Security of energy supplies was at the top of the political agenda after the petroleum crises of the 1970s and 1980s. In the 1990s shortages have been almost absent. Over the last year the issue has got a renewed attention both by the EU and the International Energy Agency (IEA), after the petroleum prices in real terms climbed back to the level of the 1970s (Austvik 2000a). Thus, the importance of energy in general economic and political development gives the EU an interest in influencing energy markets as well as Norwegian petroleum decisions, beyond the economic dimension. Norway and the EU should have joint interests in maximising long-run welfare as opposed to short-run welfare. Nevertheless, it is crucial for Norway to be able to influence energy-related decisions in the EU whether or not Norway formally becomes a member (Austvik 2000b).

Structural and Spatial Policy

Despite the strong bonds that bind the Nordic countries together, these states have widely differing economic and geopolitical interests in the globalisation process. Consequently, in recent decades the countries have chosen different paths of international co-operation. Actually, European regional integration projects have the potential of providing a new starting point for common Nordic policies. Particularly important in this respect are the policies advocated by the European Spatial Development Perspective (ESDP 1999).

Norway has been informally involved in the ESDP construction process during the 1990s and has shown great interest in modifying its regional and structural policy. There are several reasons for this. The ESDP is an all-European planning programme for spatially balanced competitiveness that must also interest Norway. Besides, the ESDP focuses on transnational co-operation in macro-regions that involve Norway.

Hence, the ESDP constitutes a challenge to Norwegian structural policies, not least with respect to the Baltic Sea region. The accession of the Baltic States and Poland enlargement to the EU makes the emergence of a new, integrated European core region around the Baltic Sea very likely. This might make traditional territorial models of regional development in Norway inadequate despite the country's fringe position.

According to the ESDP, development policy decisions should be reached on the basis of a multilevel system of governance and the establishment of partnerships. This recommendation is made because spatial power and spatial development are closely connected with a competitive and sustainable urban and regional economy (Porter 1990; Veggeland 2000). In the Baltic Sea region this means that cross-border co-operation should be based on strong subnational units, politically as well as economically.

The effect has been that the small and weak Norwegian counties (*fylker*) have been put on the political agenda. One option has been to eliminate this administrative level and make Norway as such a region in Europe. The other (more serious) option is to reduce the number of regional units, as has been done by the ongoing structural reforms in Sweden, in order to create greater and stronger regional entities (NOU XX:2000; SOU 169: 96). Such a reform may strengthen democracy and revitalise regional economies. It would also make Norwegian regions equal partners in cross-border co-operations. The nine counties of eastern Norway including the municipality of Oslo have already joined to establish a regional partnership called the Eastern Norway Co-operation (*Østlandssamarbeidet*).

The Eastern Norway Co-operation is among other projects involved in city-to-city co-operation in order to realise the ESDP guideline on development of a balanced and polycentric urban system and a new urban-rural relationship, as part of the Baltic Sea region development projects. This project involves the capital of Oslo but not the smaller cities of the region. This indicates that integration into the Baltic Sea region is not without complications. One challenge is that the Norwegian regions on the periphery of this transnational region have indisputably sparse populations. Where scattered cities exist, they are extremely small (less than 50,000 inhabitants). The ESDP does not take such factors into consideration. Rather it equates such peripheral regions with densely populated urban and rural areas to be found on the Continent.

It may be assumed that the ESDP is dominated by Dutch, French and German planners and their perception of their own needs. At any rate, the Norwegian planning solution might be the development of a few greater regional urban centres as 'gateway cities' (regional capitals). As political and economic motors these cities should be able to integrate smaller cities and rural towns into co-operative networks with access to effective infrastructure. By using new information and communication technology they should provide services and counterbalance the urban concentration that will follow the EU enlargement, seen in a Baltic Sea region perspective.

Concerning transportation infrastructure, sea traffic and coastal cities are very important to Norway. On land, the Nordic Link represents one motorway connection from the continent to Norway, from Germany through Denmark, with a ferry connection over Skagerrak to the coastal cities of southern Norway. This is connected to the West Link corridor, which gives access to the west-coast Norwegian cities. The Scandic Link represents the second motorway and railway connection from the capital city of Oslo along the West Coast of Sweden to Gothenburg and Malmø, and then over the new Øresund Bridge to Copenhagen and the Continent. The next large plan yet to be realised is the bridge over Femer Belt to Germany. The Nordic triangle is a planning initiative to improve road and railway communication between the capitals Oslo, Stockholm and Copenhagen. In a Baltic Sea region context, the triangle will be expanded to Helsinki, St Petersburg, the capital cities of the Baltic States (Via Baltica) and back to Copenhagen via Poland and Germany. The planning and development of effective ferries over the Baltic Sea and Skagerrak are both important according to the ESDP's fourth guideline (Nordvision 1999). It is also important to develop air and land-based lines of communication between the smaller cities in the Nordic area, in accordance with the principle of 'pearls and strings.'

The development of these connections will involve a different type of Norwegian spatial planning than today. Traditionally, the national capital Oslo has been the dominant gateway in Norway, upon which all the large traffic ways and lines of communication converge. The Baltic Sea region concept has changed this structural perspective. The regionalisation of the nation state entails an increased density and convergence of communication in a new spatial pattern. The regional capital cities might become networking gateway cities and constitute the basic element in the development of a new urban-rural relationship.

This will represent an attempt to improve the spatial balance, the competitiveness of the regions and a way of relieving the pressure for growth on the national capitals in favour of a change in the distribution of high functions in the networking urban system.

Foreign and Security Policy

The EU Common Foreign and Security Policy (CFSP) was established by the Maastricht Treaty and came into force on 1 November 1993. The provisions of the CFSP were revised by the 1997 Amsterdam Treaty. This revision should make it possible to improve the effectiveness and the profile of this policy. An important decision in this respect was the appointment, as provided for in the new Treaty, of a High Representative for the CFSP in June 1999. Furthermore, the Western European Union (WEU), with Norway as an associated member, is to be integrated into the Union.

The architects of the Amsterdam Treaty assigned an important position to the Petersberg tasks, so named after the place where the WEU Ministerial Council that formulated them was held in 1992. These are humanitarian and rescue tasks, peacekeeping tasks and combat-force tasks in crisis management, including peacemaking. As a result of the Kosovo conflict, the Petersberg tasks were placed at the core of the process of strengthening the European common security and defence policy. And the declaration from the 15 heads of state or government meeting on 3 and 4 June 1999 underlined the following: 'The Union must have the capacity for autonomous action, backed up by credible military forces, the means to decide to use them, and a readiness to do so, in order to respond to international crises without prejudice to actions by NATO.'

The aim of exercising political control and strategic guidance in the Petersberg operations conducted by the European Union is to do that with or without the resources and capabilities of NATO. On the other hand the operations should claim participation of both members of the European Union and the European members of NATO like Norway. Consequently, Norway as a non-member of the EU would be responsible to the High Representative/the Council of Ministers according to the Common European Security and Defence Policy but would have no say in the formulation of this policy or in the actual decision-making process in case of international crises.

Probably the European Security and Defence Policy foresees Norway as an associated member of the alliance. Even so most political observers describe the new situation as threatening, not so much because of loss of sovereignty due to the missing of a chair at the decision-making centre in Brussels but for security reasons. The perspective is one of Norway becoming a *'Randstaat'* in a prospective European security system. *'Randstaat'* is a term well known from the 1920s and 1930s with the small countries in Europe bordering on the great powers and blocs of states. The Baltic Republics of Estonia, Latvia and Lithuania were such states with bad security prospects. The European security and defence integration and the enlargement of EU will literally make Norway a *'Randstaat'* in Europe in relation to the former superpower Russia (unstable but still powerful) and the coming superpower of the EU.

This perspective is further underlined by the withdrawal of US military forces from Europe and especially from its Northern flank as a result of the end of the cold war. Obviously Norway is on the verge of becoming peripheral in both the US and NATO global security and defence context. The CESDP dimension intends to construct new networks for balance, stability and security in Europe, but Norway does not yet know how to become a formal node in these networks because of her non-membership in the EU. At the same time, Norway's huge energy exports and consequent close links with the EU, have wide security implications. Some of these can only be solved in co-operation with such purchasing countries as Germany, France, Great Britain or the EU (Kibsgaard et al. 2000).

In this context the EU Northern Dimension regional action programme, initiated by the Finnish Presidency in 1999, might be promising to Norway. This scheme, like the Baltic Sea co-operation, is sure to be an increasing part of the external relations of the European Union as enlargement brings in new members in the region. The basic aim is to promote security, political stability and sustainable development through enhanced cross-border co-operation between the countries in Northern Europe. To avoid new dividing lines in Europe, the EU is aware of the necessity to involve all external neighbours. Norway is also active in the co-operation in the strategically important Barents Euro-Arctic Region – an area rich in petroleum and gas deposits, fisheries, hot spots of nuclear waste pollution etc. As Commissioner Chris Patten noted in 1999: 'The Commission is convinced that the Northern Dimension can contribute to improved relations and mutual dependence between Russia, *all* countries of the Baltic Sea Region and the European Union' (Patten 1999).

Conclusions

At present, the EEA agreement gives the EU a lot of influence in Norway, while Norway has practically no influence in the EU except through the participation in particular sub-committees (Veggeland, F. 1999). The enlargement connected with the deepening of EU policies will increase the Union's influence on Norway irrespective of her formal relations to the EU. Due to the developments of the Baltic Sea region and the Northern Dimension scheme, Norway is expected to become even more closely integrated from both a spatial and a functional perspective. The free movement of labour will lead to pressure on wages, particularly when the EU includes the Baltic States. Lower prices on agricultural products (Agenda 2000) will increase pressure for lower food prices also in Norway and may entail a large degree of Norwegian agricultural harmonisation with the EU.

The energy sector in particular sets Norway apart from the rest of Europe. Norway's huge energy revenues force it to adopt different economic policies from those of its neighbours. At same time there may be conflicting interests between Norway and the EU as to the speed of energy production, the organisation of European energy markets and energy taxation. Short and long-term considerations may clash as concerns over the security of energy supplies are on the way back on the political agenda.

A common EU foreign and security policy, new command structures within NATO and the establishment of the CESDP dimension, may force Norway to rely more on the EU than on the US for its security. The large energy exports and the close links that they create between Norway and the EU, especially through the natural gas infrastructure, reinforce this challenge and call for a more active Norwegian European policy and participation.

The eventual inclusion of most European countries in the Union may reduce the importance of the centralisation argument and the argument that the EU is only for the rich. Being on the periphery both in Europe as well as in an enlarged Nordic region, and with a raw material-based economy different from that of the EU economies, Norway may need a flexible approach from the EU. A multi-speed Europe and flexible integration of participating countries should make it

easier for Norway to have more active relations with the EU as opposed to rely-
ing exclusively on the EEA agreement. That should be more practical for the EU
as well.

References

Andersen, S. and Austvik, O.G. (2000). 'Nasjonal handlefrihet – nye internasjonale ramme-
    betingelser: Petroleum, makt og demokrati,' Forprosjekt til Makt- og demokratiutredningen
    1998-2003 *(National autonomy – a new international framework: Petroleum, Power and Demo-
    cracy. Report to the National Study on Power and Democracy in Norway 1998-2003)*. Unipub
    Forlag.
Austvik, O.G. (2000a): 'Drivkreftene i oljemarkedet' *(The Driving Forces in the Petroleum
    Market)*, Research Report, Lillehammer College No. 50 /2000. www.kaldor.no/oga.
Austvik, O.G. (2000b): 'Norge som storeksportør av gass' *(Norway as a Large Gas Exporter)*,
    Norge i energiens geopolitikk. Europaprogrammet.
Deubner, C. (2000). *Harnessing Differentiation in the EU – flexibility after Amsterdam*. Brussels,
    Commission of the European Community.
ESDP (1999). *European Spatial Development Perspective: Towards Balanced and Sustainable
    Development of the Territory of the European Union*. Brussels, Commission of the European
    Community.
Johansson, M. and Persson, L.O. (2000). 'Approaching a Single Labour Market: Emerging
    Migration Patterns in the Baltic Sea Area,' pages 77-98 in Hedegaard, L. and Lindström, B.
    (eds). *The NEBI Yearbook 2000: North European and Baltic Sea Integration*. Berlin, Heidelberg,
    Springer.
Kibsgaard (ed.), Aakvaag, Austvik, Johannessen and Nyhamar (2000). 'Norge i energiens
    geopolitikk' *(Norway and the Geopolitics of Energy)*. Europaprogrammet.
Nordvision (1999). *A Spatial Perspectice for the North Sea Region*. (Final draft). European
    Commission/ PLANCO Consulting GmbH Essen.
NOU (2000:XX). *Om oppgavefordelingen mellom stat, region og kommune (On the division of func-
    tions between the state, region and municipality)*. Oslo.
Patten, C. (1999). 'A Northern Dimension for the policies of the Union: Current and future
    activities.' Speech/99/161. Brussels, Commission of the European Community.
Pelkmans, J. (1997). *European Integration: Methods and Economic Analysis*. Open University of the
    Netherlands
Porter, M. (1990). *The Comparative Advantages of Nations*. London, Macmillian.
SOU (1996:169). *Förnyelse av kommuner och landsting (Renewal of Municipalities and Regions)*.
    Stockholm.
Straubhaar, T. (2000). 'Immigration to Scandinavia: Good or Bad for the Nordic Economies?'
    pages 63-76 in Hedegaard, L. and Lindström, B. (eds). *The NEBI Yearbook 2000: North
    European and Baltic Sea Integration*. Berlin, Heidelberg, Springer.
Veggeland, F. (1999). 'Institusjonelle tilpasninger til europeisk integrasjon' *(Institutional adjust-
    ments to European integration)*, Norsk Statsvitenskapelig Tidsskrift 3:99.
Veggeland, N. (2000). Den nye regionalismen. Europeisk integrasjon og flernivåstyring *(Neo-
    regionalism: European integration and multilevel governance)*. Bergen, Fagbokforlaget.

5 Limits of Integration: The Case of North-western Russia

Dmitri Zimine

At the turn of the 21st century Russia continues to look for new forms of social and economic existence and co-existence with the outside World. Now this country faces an enormous spectrum of opportunities ranging from the revival of her traditional forms of statehood and spiritual life to accepting foreign economic and political models and values. This situation is further complicated by the fact that the process of societal transformation in Russia coincides with a worldwide trend of global economic integration and the emergence of new global institutions and norms. Consequently, for Russia the main task is not only to find the optimal internal self-organisation (i.e. to redefine the role of the state within society) but also to find the optimal mode of interaction with the emerging world-scale phenomena.

This chapter focuses on one particular aspect of such interaction, namely, on international economic links between two Northwestern Russian provinces (the Leningrad province[1] and the Republic of Karelia[2]) and their Western neighbours in the Baltic Sea area, primarily Finland. The chapter seeks to establish whether any form of cross-border and regional economic integration takes place in this area. In this context the term 'cross-border' denotes economic links taking place between territories that have a common land border. In our case such territories are (1) the Republic of Karelia and Eastern Finland and (2) the Leningrad province, Eastern Finland and Estonia. Likewise, the term 'regional' means economic links between territories belonging to the same international region, but lacking a common land border, for example, the Leningrad province and Sweden. Three measurements of international economic integration are used here: (1) international trade, (2) foreign investment and (3) the creation of integrative institutions (e.g. international political, co-ordinating and consultative bodies). Thus, an increase in international trade and investment is regarded as a move towards greater economic integration and *vice versa*.[3]

This chapter is a result of a research project which has been financed by a grant from the Finnish Ministry of Foreign Affairs. This project is entitled 'Economic monitoring of Northwest Russia.' At its initial stage it involved four joint groups of Finnish and Russian scholars studying economic performance of the city of St Petersburg, the Leningrad and Murmansk provinces and the Republic of Karelia in the 1990s. For each of these territories the research groups identified the main patterns of economic change, particularly in such fields as industry, agriculture, transportation, construction, investment, trade, natural resources, financial services, environment, public-sector policies and human capital development. The results of the initial stage show that the role of international economic co-operation in Northwest Russia dramatically increased in the 1990s. However, after the economic crisis of August 1998, the character of international contacts has changed: after a decade of industrial decline the provinces have experienced substantial growth, especially due to import-substituting industries.[4]

Macroeconomic Factors Influencing Integration

After the collapse of the USSR, a deep economic crisis rapidly spread across Russia. The Northwestern provinces were no exception. It has been established that the depth of decline at the provincial level was largely predetermined by the particular economic structure that a given province had inherited from the Soviet period. As a rule, provincial economies based upon extraction of exportable raw materials scored much better than those based upon processing industries, because the rate of decline of the latter was much faster than that of the former (Hanson and Bradshaw 2000). In the early 1990s in Karelia and in the Leningrad province, the share of processing industries was relatively low. As a result, the provinces experienced a smaller decline in industrial output than Russia as a whole. For instance, over the period 1990-99 Russian industrial output in physical terms declined by 50.1 per cent, while in Karelia it declined by 44.4 per cent, and in the Leningrad province by 43.3 per cent.[5] Such industrial sectors as fuel, power, timber and metals have grown in significance, while machine-building, metal-working, wood-processing, food and light industries have dramatically declined. Likewise, all other economic sectors depending upon the situation in such industries as transportation, communications, trade, construction and public-sector services have also declined. Personal incomes have dropped, and domestic consumer demand has declined correspondingly. For instance, between 1991 and 1999 real personal monetary incomes declined by 64.2 per cent in Karelia and by 46.2 per cent in the Leningrad province. The most dramatic decline occurred in both provinces in 1998-99 as a result of the financial crisis of 1998, which led to the 70 per cent devaluation of the national currency. Between 1991 and 1999 retail trade turnover declined by 52.7 per cent in Karelia and by 54.5 per cent in the Leningrad province.

In addition, during the 1990s transportation tariffs have risen substantially, thus making problematic economic co-operation between distant Russian regions. Foreign companies have quickly won the competition with local producers in many market niches, thus squeezing out Russian producers. Moreover, economic and regional policies of the Russian federal government have resulted in further destabilisation and deterioration of regional economies. Disinvestment and capital flight have become endemic in the country. Thus, over the 1990s investment in fixed capital declined by 90 per cent in Karelia.[6]

Under these circumstances, only competitive export-oriented enterprises and state-supported natural monopolies have managed to survive the crisis. Weakness and instability of domestic markets, as well as the unfavourable national macro-economic situation, have forced Russian producers to turn towards foreign markets. However, it has appeared that only Russian raw materials could be competitive abroad. This has resulted in a radical shift in the structure of exports: the share of manufactured goods has declined, while that of raw materials has increased. The production equipment and technologies of Russian companies have been so outdated that in many cases the processing of raw materials has been a value-deducting activity.[7] Furthermore, high taxation of industrial operations has served as an additional incentive for exporting raw materials. Likewise, the opportunity to hide profits from taxation through export transactions has also been an export-promotion incentive.

Despite the general liberalisation of economic life in Russia in the early 1990s and the opening up of new border-crossing points, it has not become easier to transport goods across a Russian border. Russian customs regulations and practices and insufficient border infrastructure have turned out to be the main bottlenecks hampering international trade. Transporting goods across the border has remained a complicated matter often connected with corruption and extortion. As a result, the border has remained a dividing line effectively preventing close economic and social integration of bordering regions. In addition, the Russian federal government has pursued a policy of high taxes on imports (which include customs duties, VAT and excises plus numerous fees and penalties to the Customs Office). Such heavy taxation of foreign trade has made many types of cross-border transactions economically impossible.

Another relevant aspect of Russian international economic relations has been her non-participation in international trade agreements and economic associations. Thus Russia remains outside the World Trade Organisation (WTO). At present the country holds talks about joining the WTO, but this lengthy process cannot be completed soon. This non-participation considerably damages Russia's exports (particularly metals) because foreign countries use anti-dumping procedures against Russian producers. Russia's accession to the WTO, as well as an expansion of bi- and multilateral trade agreements, can become powerful incentives for Russia's closer economic integration with the global economy.

In sum, the dynamics of Russia's international economic links have been predetermined by a number of factors, namely the national economic crisis of the 1990s, unfavourable taxation and customs policies and practices and non-participation in the WTO. All these factors taken together have negatively affected

Russia's international trade and foreign investment. Export of raw materials was the only sector that managed to adapt to the economic situation in Russia in the 1990s.

International Trade in Goods

For both the Leningrad province and for the Republic of Karelia foreign trade has become the main pillar of the regional economies. For instance, in 1999 the ratio of total exports to total industrial output reached 1.22 in the Leningrad province, which illustrates the importance of this region as an export hub of Northwestern Russia.[8] In Karelia this ratio was much lower. However, it also had a strongly positive dynamic: 0.15 in 1991, 0.45 in 1995 and 0.65 in 1999.[9] These figures mean that an increasing share of Karelia's and Leningrad's industrial output is exported. In other words, Karelian and Leningrad industries become increasingly oriented towards foreign markets and thus more actively participate in the international division of labour.

After the collapse of the USSR, foreign trade of the Leningrad province dramatically declined due to the loss of markets in countries of the socialist block and in former republics of the Soviet Union. However, since the foreign trade liberalisation in the early 1990s, both exports and imports of the province have begun to grow rapidly. Thus, foreign trade turnover (i.e. the sum of total exports and imports) increased approximately five times between 1993 and 1999. This spectacular growth was achieved mostly on account of the growth of exports to Sweden, which increased from $10.9 million in 1993 to $891.3 million in 1999.[10] Now Sweden is the main trading partner of the Leningrad province. This country accounts for 58.6 per cent of exports and 6.2 per cent of imports of the province. The growth of trade with other countries has also been positive, yet much less significant than that with Sweden. Finland has been the second largest trading partner of the province, responsible for 11.8 per cent of its exports and for 22.5 per cent of its imports in 1999. In 1993-99 Finland strengthened its position as the main supplier of imports to the Leningrad province. Trade turnover with Finland grew 2.3 times during this period. Germany, the USA, the Netherlands and Estonia[11] occupied the third, fourth, fifth and sixth places in terms of trade turnover with the province respectively. Trade with Estonia developed especially quickly: for instance, trade turnover with Estonia grew 14.8 times over the period 1993-99. This was clearly a period of re-establishing trade links that were broken after the collapse of the USSR.

The structure of Leningrad's exports is dominated by fuel, petroleum products and chemicals (75.6 per cent in 1999) and wood and timber products (12.8 per cent). Imports include machinery (48.1 per cent), chemicals (15.2 per cent) and foodstuffs (13.3 per cent). In sum, it can be noted that, firstly, the foreign trade of the Leningrad province is concentrated in the Baltic Sea area. Secondly, in the 1990s the province integrated more closely with this region, particularly with Sweden and Estonia. Thirdly, the rate of growth of trade turnover with Finland was below the average. Nonetheless, Finland has remained the largest importer to the province.

Table 5.1: Foreign trade of the Leningrad province, million US dollars

	1993	1994	1995	1996	1997	1998	1999
Total exports	329.3	379.9	541.2	n/a	1482.6	1444.3	1520.2
Exports to Finland	101.4	284.5	70.9	n/a	195.7	176.2	179.3
Exports to Estonia	4.3	5.3	17.9	n/a	75.6	46.2	66.2
Total imports	56.9	87.4	n/a	n/a	365.8	307.1	357.4
Imports from Finland	12.5	21.1	n/a	n/a	60.4	70.6	80.4
Imports from Estonia	0.4	0.6	n/a	n/a	6.6	9.5	3.4

Sources: Köll (2000: 450-51) and Petersburgkomstat (2000: 64)

The development of foreign trade was less successful in Karelia than in the Leningrad province in the 1990s. For instance, from 1993 to 1999 Karelian foreign trade turnover increased by merely 18.4 per cent. After a peak in 1995, Karelian exports declined noticeably. Likewise, since 1996 imports to Karelia have declined. Over the period 1990-99 the fastest growth was observed in the export of cellulose (16.0 times), iron ore pellets (5.2 times), round-wood (3.9 times) and thin paper (2.9 times). During the same period Karelian exports of sawn timber declined by 70 per cent, fish by 30 per cent, while exports of tractors and machinery ceased completely. As a result, in 1999 Karelian exports consisted mainly of wood, cellulose and paper (60.8 per cent) and metals and ores (25.8 per cent). It should be noted that in Karelia the main industrial goods are produced primarily for export. For instance, in 1999 Karelia exported 98.4 per cent of locally produced aluminium, 63.9 per cent of round-wood, 67.3 per cent of thin paper, 64.0 per cent of cellulose, 76.5 per cent of sawn timber, 40 per cent of fish and 39.4 per cent of iron ore pellets. The structure of Karelian imports was dominated by machinery (32.1 per cent), petrochemical products (20.1 per cent) and cellulose (17.6 per cent).

Despite the negative overall dynamics of Karelian exports from 1996 to 1999, Karelian exports to the neighbouring Finland grew (by 44.1 per cent 1994-99). This growth occurred mostly on account of iron ore, timber, cellulose and paper.[12] However, imports from Finland to the Republic stagnated between 1993 and 1996 and then declined. Only imports of Finnish cellulose increased over the period 1996-99 (by 41.7 per cent).

Finland is the main trading partner of Karelia. In 1999 this country was responsible for 32.5 per cent of Karelian exports and 30.5 per cent of its imports. The next places were occupied by the United Kingdom (9.6 per cent and 2.5 per cent respectively), Turkey (6.5 per cent and 0.9 per cent), Norway (5.2 per cent and 11.1per cent) and Sweden (6.3 per cent and 2.5 per cent).

Table 5.2: Foreign trade of the Republic of Karelia, million US dollars

	1993	1994	1995	1996	1997	1998	1999
Total exports	341.0	380.8	633.0	560.3	520.3	527.5	497.7
Exports to Finland	n/a	112.3	138.0	152.4	162.9	171.4	161.8
Total imports	185.5	167.0	176.6	209.7	158.7	110.4	125.5
Imports from Finland	n/a	40.7	55.5	46.3	33.8	25.8	38.3

Sources: Köll (2000: 444-45), Karelkomstat (2000: 14) and Druzhinin (2000)

In the second half of the 1990s Karelian foreign trade was increasingly concentrated in Northern Europe. For instance, in 1995 Karelian trade turnover with 15 countries of Northern Europe[13] accounted for 50.5 per cent of the total turnover, while in 1999 this figure reached 69.2 per cent. However, this was not a result of growth of trade with these countries.[14] This was rather a consequence of a deep decline in trade with countries outside Northern Europe. In conclusion, it should be noted that the diversity of Karelian foreign trade has substantially decreased, and it has become more concentrated on and integrated with Northern European countries, particularly with Finland. Karelia represents a good example of cross-border trade integration.

International Trade in Services

International trade in services represents one of the fastest-growing business sectors at the global level. However, in the 1990s the situation was quite the opposite in both Karelia and the Leningrad province: trade in services substantially declined there. Thus, Karelian exports of services declined from $114 million in 1994 to $14.8 million in 1999,[15] mainly because most of Karelian commercial sea ships were re-registered in low-tax offshore zones (Druzhinin 2000). Nonetheless, exports of sea transportation services still constitute the bulk (80.1 per cent or $11.8 million in 1999) of the total Karelian exports of services.[16] The second place in terms of exports of services (9.0 per cent or $1.3 million in 1999) is occupied by sewing of clothes from materials provided by Finnish firms.[17] Karelian imports of services were also in decline. For instance, in 1999, by comparison with 1998, it declined by 72.5 per cent to $14.4 million. In previous years it had also declined, though less sharply. Finland is the main exporter of services to Karelia. In 1999 Finnish exports to the Republic included forest logging services (52.0 per cent of the total or $7.5 million), construction services (14.4 per cent or $2.1 million), rent of equipment (4.8 per cent or $693 thousand) and repair and instalment services (4.6 per cent or $666 thousand).

In the Leningrad province the export picture was similar to that in Karelia. By 1999 Leningrad's exports of services declined to $6.9 million of which 46.4 per cent ($3.2 million) was made up of transportation services and 14.5 per cent ($1.0 million) consisted of sewing services. Imports of services were also at a comparatively insignificant level, but it grew by 56.5 per cent in 1999. This growth was caused by Finland: her exports to the province (particularly of legal and marketing services) grew 4.1 times. As a result, the Finnish share in the total import of services to the Leningrad province reached 87.1per cent in 1999.

It may be noted that in both Karelia and the Leningrad province such modern business practices as international outsourcing and subcontracting are not developed. The Russian business climate does not stimulate foreign companies to subcontract certain operations and functions to Russian firms because the latter cannot be fully reliable under given circumstances. The only known form of such co-operation is sewing services, but it has developed very slowly.[18] Another important observation is that the Republic and the province differ substantially in terms of the structure of import of services. Imports to the Leningrad province consisted mostly of legal and marketing services, which was certainly a result of the growing interest of Leningrad's companies in accessing foreign markets. At the same time, imports to Karelia have included mainly logging, construction and repair services. This is a sign of weakness in Karelian companies which have been unable to compete with Finnish companies even in the market for these relatively simple services.

Foreign Investment

Since the early 1990s it has been very popular amongst public officials to declare that they welcome and support foreign investment. In practice, however, the investment climate in Russia worsened considerably in 1992 after Gorbachev's tax breaks for foreign investors were abolished. At that period of hyperinflation and of general turmoil in state affairs, investment in Russia was all but impossible. As the situation gradually stabilised, some Russian regions have begun to play a more active role in attracting foreign investment. For example, the Novgorod province (situated to the South of the Leningrad province) has emerged as a successful leader in this field. In December 1994 the province adopted regional laws granting generous tax concessions to inward investors. The result has been a skyrocketing growth in domestic and foreign investment (Zimine 1998). The Leningrad province, governed then by the publicly elected Governor Gustov, decided to follow the example of Novgorod in 1997. It adopted regional laws similar to those of Novgorod. The result has also been a growth in foreign investment. By contrast, the Republic of Karelia has not pursued such policies, and foreign investment has remained insignificant there.

It should be noted that the bulk of investments in the Leningrad province and the Republic of Karelia has come not from neighbouring Finland but from far more distant countries, such as the USA, Germany and the Netherlands. This fact can be regarded as evidence that there has been no investment-driven economic integration between Finland and the Russian Northwest. In 1999 the share of FDI in total investment in fixed capital was 48.6 per cent in the Leningrad province and just 2.2 per cent in the Republic of Karelia. These data lead to the conclusion that geographical proximity does not play a significant role as a factor predetermining patterns of economic integration. Thus, the Leningrad province is integrating not with Finland, but directly with other global development poles such as the USA and Western Europe, represented by the Netherlands and Germany.

Table 5.3: Foreign direct investment, in million US dollars

	1993	1994	1995	1996	1997	1998	1999
Leningrad province	n/a	0.2	20.1	43.2	16.3	81.3	236.0
Republic of Karelia	3.1	13.7	16.0	2.5	3.7	1.9	4.5

Sources: Köll (2000: 446, 452), Petersburgkomstat (2000: 62) and Druzhinin (2000)

The geographical proximity of Finland does not serve as an incentive for Leningrad-Finland economic integration. Perhaps, this is also a result of a low population density in the territories along the Finnish-Russian border leading to a low density of cross-border business contacts. Another possible explanation is the proximity of St Petersburg. Foreign companies investing in the city benefit from direct access to a large pool of labour and from other scale economies that are not available elsewhere in Northwestern Russia. This five million metropolis, the largest city in the Baltic Sea area, serves as a powerful magnet attracting international economic activities while other territories, such as the Leningrad province and Karelia, remain comparatively neglected. At the time when foreign investment in St Petersburg approaches one billion dollars, in the peripheral Karelia the investment-driven integration process has not even started.

Table 5.4: Main countries of origin of FDI accumulated, 1994-99, percentage of total FDI

	Finland	Germany	Netherlands	USA
Leningrad province	2.0	16.6	44.0	24.7
Republic of Karelia	14.1	19.2	-	33.9

Sources: Köll (2000: 446, 452), Petersburgkomstat (2000: 62) and Druzhinin (2000)

An important aspect of FDI inflows is the nature of output of enterprises with FDI. In Karelia about 70 per cent of FDI was invested in the timber and pulp-and-paper industries, thus increasing Karelia's capacity to export timber, cellulose, cardboard and paper. The character of FDI in the Leningrad province has been different. A substantial share of FDI has been invested in machine-building ventures, such as two Caterpillar plants producing excavators and road machines and a car plant of Ford Motors. Amongst other projects are the renovation of a paper and printing combine by Knauf AG (Germany), a new cardboard factory constructed by AssiDoman (Sweden), an industrial glue factory Era-Henkel (Germany), modernisation of the Svetogorsk pulp-and-paper mill by International Paper (USA), a coffee packaging factory built by Kraft Jacobs Suchard and two new tobacco factories of Philip Morris and Kress-Neva (Krom 2000). It may be noted that enterprises with FDI in the Leningrad province are mostly oriented towards the Russian domestic market, unlike those in Karelia. This fact testifies that, firstly, FDI has a diversifying effect upon the Leningrad economy. Secondly, the character of investment-driven integration creates a domestically oriented economy in the province. Perhaps, this is just the first stage of Leningrad's integration into the global economy. The second stage might involve the creation of export-oriented enterprises with FDI in the Leningrad province.

Public-sector Cross-border Initiatives

Given that international economic contacts play an increasingly important role in the economic life of the Leningrad province and Karelia, public authorities of these regions have become more active in developing international co-operation, particularly in the late 1990s. Of course, the nature of international contacts has been predetermined by the difficult economic situation in Russia. The Republic and province have been recipients of foreign financial and humanitarian assistance, particularly from the European Union, the USA, and from individual West European countries, organisations and private persons. The assistance from foreign public institutions has focused on environment protection, efficient use of energy, agriculture and small business promotion. Apparently, investments from foreign public institutions have been mainly motivated by 'soft security' considerations. These investment projects have reached their principal aims but they have failed to trigger an inflow of private investment (Interfax 1999).

In the late 1990s regional governments began to develop new forms of co-operation. For instance, the Republic of Karelia together with three Finnish regions set up Euroregio Karelia. This is a cross-border alliance of the Russian and Finnish regions aimed at lobbying jointly for EU funding from the TACIS and Interreg programmes (Motylkov 2000a). Another major project of the Karelian Government is the creation of the Kostamuksha Free Economic Zone (Motylkov 2000b). The idea of this Zone has existed since 1995 and it remains unclear why the project was not carried out earlier.[19] In its international economic relations the Karelian Government has acted not only as a public authority but also as an entrepreneur. Thus, after long negotiations, the Government intends to set up a joint venture with the Finnish Stora-Enso company. This venture will produce sawn timber for export in accordance with international quality standards.[20]

The situation has been quite similar in the Leningrad province. As of mid-1999 about 70 EU projects with the total value of $25 million were being implemented on its territory (Motylkov 1999). Several foreign institutions[21] have set up their representative offices in St Petersburg, thus stimulating the province's international contacts. At present the main international project being realised by Leningrad's public authorities is the creation of the 130-hectare Svetogorsk

Industrial Zone on the border with Finland near the Finnish town of Imatra. The Leningrad Provincial Government and the municipalities of Svetogorsk and Imatra have been the main promoters of the project (Andreev 2000). The Provincial Government and Svetogorsk municipality have promised to exempt industrial companies operating in this Zone from local taxes, while the Russian federal government has granted some customs privileges to the zone (Motylkov 2000). A number of Finnish companies[22] have decided to invest in the zone and establish their production outlets there.[23] Amongst planned activities are production of foodstuffs for the Russian market and export of sawn timber and timber products to Finland and Western Europe (Rosbusinessconsulting 2000).

Major Development Projects:
Integration versus Confrontation

The character of international economic co-operation in Northwestern Russia is determined not only by the above-mentioned domestic macro-economic and regulatory factors. National geopolitical considerations play an increasingly important role in this field. Since the mid-1990s the prevailing view amongst Russian public officials and the population at large has been that Russia should restore her economic independence from foreign countries. In practice this means, firstly, the desire to increase domestic output of high-added-value goods and, secondly, to decrease dependence of Russian exporters on foreign transportation facilities (e.g. Ukrainian gas and petroleum pipeline and seaports in the Baltic States, Ukraine and Finland). This point of view is shared not only by federal-level officials but also by regional leaders including those in the Republic of Karelia and the Leningrad province. For instance, at present both these regions stimulate international co-operation in processing of local raw materials while discouraging export of raw materials (e.g. timber). The reason for this attitude has been the desire to create new jobs and to raise more revenues for public budgets.

For instance, in 1999 the Karelian government announced its new industrial strategy, which introduced new forms of control over local exporters of timber. The aims of the policy are (1) to make timber exports more transparent for the government, (2) to decrease the total number of exporting companies and (3) to set up an institutional mechanism which would guarantee optimal prices on exported timber and provide enough revenues to the Karelian budget from the timber industry (Evseenkov 2000). Later, the Government announced that it intends to create "holding companies" which would unite large timber-processing plants and pulp-and-paper mills with timber logging companies. The aims are the same – to stimulate timber-processing activities and to make exporters more accountable (Makarov 2000b). The Leningrad province has pursued a similar policy. Leningrad's government intends to create a network of "forest terminals" or "forest customs warehouses." These terminals will be the only institutions through which Leningrad's companies will be able to export timber.[24]

Another major issue affecting international economic relations of the regions has been the construction of new Russian ports on the Baltic Sea. The Leningrad province is now actively involved in the construction of two new ports in Primorsk and Ust-Luga. It has been planned that the cargo (oil, metals, chemicals and other) which is now shipped through ports of the Baltic States will be shipped mainly through these two new ports in the nearest future. The Russian federal government has been the principal supporter and financier of the construction of these ports. The government also finances the construction of an extension of petroleum pipeline from Kirishi (a town in the Leningrad province) to the Primorsk Seaport.[25] At the initial stage of this project, it was planned to get funding from the European Bank of Reconstruction and Development. However, the bank demanded that the pipeline should be extended to the Finnish port of Porvoo, thus making a port in Primorsk unnecessary (Ershov 2000). This idea was regarded as unacceptable for the Russian side, and now the project is funded by Russian petroleum companies and the government without foreign involvement (Romanyuk 2000b). According to estimations, the cost of petroleum transportation through the Primorsk Port will be $3-$4 per tonne lower than that through the Ventspils Port (Latvia) and the Odessa Port (Ukraine). Another large project in the same vein has been organised together by RAO Gazprom and the Finnish petroleum company Fortum. They intend to build an underwater pipeline in the Baltic Sea to transport natural gas from Siberia to Northern Europe. It has been planned for completion by 2010. At present Russian natural gas can be delivered to Western Europe only through Ukraine (Romanyuk 2000a). If these infrastructure projects are indeed realised, the main losers should be Finland, Ukraine and the Baltic States, while Russia would see the creation of a large number of jobs and an increase in corporate incomes and public revenues.[26]

The current political and economic agenda in Central Europe is focused on the forthcoming EU enlargement. The general attitude of Russian business people towards this issue can be termed 'negatively cautious.' It is expected that Russian exports to the forthcoming members of the EU can be negatively affected because after their accession the new members will introduce protectionist measures against Russian manufactured goods. In addition, capital flows between Russia and these countries might be restricted because of EU anti-money-laundering regulations. This is particularly relevant for Estonia and Cyprus, which are deeply involved in financial business with Russia. Another major issue is the change in border-crossing rules. All forthcoming East European EU members now require visas from Russian visitors, while earlier such travels were visa-free. However, the issue of EU enlargement as such does not occupy a major place in local debates in Northwest Russia. After all, Poland, Hungary, the Czech Republic and Estonia are not amongst the main economic partners of the northwestern provinces.

In sum, the dynamics of international economic relationships in Northwestern Russia involve both co-operative and confrontational trends. Co-operative trends stem from the need to achieve higher economic efficiency through international trade and foreign investment. These trends lead to a greater economic integration. At the same time, confrontational trends stem from an alternative understanding of the Russian national economic and political interests. These interests proclaim the primacy of Russian transportation independence and the priority of domestic manufacturing over exports of raw materials. The combination of co-operative and confrontational trends creates an uneasy environment for a fuller economic integration of Northwestern Russia into the Baltic Sea area.

Conclusions: A Look into the Future

During the 1990s the character of economic relations between the North-western Russian regions and foreign countries was predetermined by (1) the difficult economic situation in Russia, (2) Russian federal and regional economic policies worsening the domestic business climate, (3) increased international competition and (4) a reassessment of Russia's interests as part of the global economy. Under these circumstances, the relationships between Karelia and the Leningrad province, on the Russian side, and their Western neighbours were dominated by exports of raw materials from Russia and imports of machinery and consumer goods to the country. International investment flows remained insignificant. Cross-border subcontracting and outsourcing practices also remained undeveloped. Consequently, it can be said that economic integration between the East and the West was rather weak, though it gradually strengthened in the late 1990s. The Leningrad province developed relatively close links not with her immediate neighbours (Finland and Estonia), but with rather distant countries in or beyond the Baltic Sea area such as the Netherlands, Germany and Sweden. By contrast, Karelia achieved a significant degree of cross-border integration with the neighbouring Finland though only in the field of exports of raw materials. Nonetheless, in both these cases the provinces have failed to create integrated economic structures benefiting from the synergy of international co-operation. There is still no common cross-border business community which would promote international integration of Northwest Russia into the Baltic Sea area and into the global economy as a whole. Cross-border initiatives of public authorities do not change the situation much.

As the economic situation in Russia is gradually normalising, it is possible to hypothesise that the new decade can become the period of a radical qualitative change in the East-West economic relations. If Russia manages to establish a more favourable business climate and to join the WTO, this country has the potential to become a prime site for locating industrial enterprises producing goods for the global market. Of course, Russian internal investment sources are not sufficient to accomplish this ambitious task. It can be achieved mainly as a result of foreign investment, particularly, from global transnational companies. Another feasible source of foreign investment can be money of Russian origin hidden abroad during the period of economic crisis.

Russia has almost all components are required for a rapid economic development (skilled and cheap labour, abundant natural resources, cheap energy and reasonable transportation infrastructure). Utilisation of these advantages through setting up of production operations in Russia can become a powerful cost-reducing strategy for global producers. In addition, the Leningrad province possesses an advantageous geographic position, which favourably distinguishes it from other Russian regions. The access to the Baltic Sea in combination with a good regional investment climate has already allowed the Leningrad province to succeed in its competition for foreign investment with other Russian regions. It can therefore be expected that this province will be among the first to see the emergence of really integrated international economic structures using Russian plants, as well as subcontracting and outsourcing practices, in order to achieve higher global competitiveness. The Republic of Karelia will, due to a number of objective reasons (such as geographical location), remain less integrated with the West, unless the Russian federal government would introduce some special measures to promote Karelia's economic development, which is unlikely. Perhaps the path of Karelia's future development lies in her deeper economic integration with the Leningrad province. The latter will possibly become a conduit of Karelia's interaction with the global economy.

Now there is a growing understanding in Northwestern Russia that this territory is a regional competitor within the global economy. Its immediate neighbours (Finland and the Baltic States) are both partners and competitors. That is why it is natural to expect that cross-border co-operation with them will develop further in some particular fields, while in other fields the co-operation will be suppressed by stiff competition (e.g. in transportation and processing of Russian raw materials). The same is true in respect of the more distant neighbours of Northwestern Russia within the Baltic Sea area. However, at the regional level the fields of competition will be somewhat different. This will be competition for international investment and for a better place in the global division of labour. Therefore, it is necessary to understand that there are limits to a possible economic integration, which are set, on the one hand, by the logic of global competition and, on the other hand, by benefits stemming from economic synergy of neighbouring territories. Which trend will prevail, integration of disintegration, is one of the key research questions for this decade.

Notes

[1] The Leningrad province is one of 89 constituent subjects of the Russian Federation. The province has a government and is administratively independent from the city of St Petersburg. Although the city and the province are closely economically linked, the case of St Petersburg is not included in this chapter. The city represents a unique case of international economic co-operation, which cannot be compared neither with the Leningrad province nor with the Republic of Karelia.

² In terms of legal status there is no difference between the Republic and the province. Both are 'equal constituent parts of the Russian Federation' (Russian Constitution of 1993).

³ The author, nonetheless, recognises that this approach simplifies reality. In practice, it is entirely possible that an increase in, for example, foreign trade does not necessarily mean greater economic integration of the trading partners. A separate study would be needed in order to determine the exact nature and consequences of such an increase.

⁴ Full reports have been published on the Internet, see www.hkkk.fi/~vbi.

⁵ Author's calculations on the basis of Goskomstat Rossii (1999: 360) and Karavaeva (2000).

⁶ Fixed capital (or 'basic capital' in Russian) includes buildings, machinery, technologies and the like, i.e. capital with a period of amortisation longer than one year (according to Russian accounting principles). An opposite notion is 'operating capital,' which includes salaries, materials, parts, etc.

⁷ A value-deducting activity is a process through which an initial value of a product diminishes. In Russia many industrial enterprises have outdated technologies and equipment. As a result, when they process raw materials, the value of the output becomes smaller than the value of the unprocessed materials. Of course, in this case it would be more economically efficient to sell the raw materials than to process them and sell processed goods. However, some enterprises still continue such value-reducing activities because of non-economic considerations (e.g. job preservation, pressure from local public authorities, etc.). Now, however, this situation is much less common than it was in the late 1980s and in the early 1990s.

⁸ Industrial output is calculated in domestic prices of industrial producers, while exports are measured in export prices denominated in US dollars. In the Russian case, domestic prices are always lower than export prices. That is why total exports can be larger than total industrial output. This, however, does not necessarily mean that in such a case all industrial production is exported. Alas, it is impossible to determine exactly what share of industrial output is exported from a given region: such data are simply not available. So, the ratio of exports to total industrial output is used here as an approximate measurement. The hypothesis here is that the higher this ratio the higher the share of exported industrial output. In the Leningrad province this ratio had the following dynamics: in 1993 - 0.21, in 1994 - 0.21, in 1995 - 0.23, in 1997 - 0.59, in 1998 - 0.82 and in 1999 - 1.22. Only the figure for 1996 is missing. The growth of this ratio clearly demonstrates the increasing internationalisation of the Leningrad economy.

⁹ Ibid. and author's calculations on the basis of 'Vneshnetorgovaya deyatelnost Assotsiatsii Severo-Zapad v 1999 godu,' *Ekonomika i vremya*, 17 July 2000, page 4.

¹⁰ Statistical data for this section are taken from Koll (2000: 444-445, 450-451), Karelkomstat (2000: 11-27) and Petersburgkomstat (2000: 64-65).

¹¹ Besides Finland, the Leningrad province has a land border with Estonia.

¹² This exports of raw materials to Finland existed already in the 1920s and 1930s. During the 1990s Karelia not only turned itself into a major exporter of Karelian round-wood but also became the main transit channel for exporters from other Russia's regions, sometimes delivering round-wood from as far as the Urals. It should be noted that the bulk of exported Russian round-wood is represented by small-diameter birch that is processed by paper mills in Eastern Finland.

¹³ The following countries were accounted for here: Belgium, the UK, Germany, Denmark, Ireland, Iceland, Latvia, Lithuania, the Netherlands, Norway, Poland, Finland, France, Sweden and Estonia.

¹⁴ Karelian trade turnover with these countries grew by just 5.5 per cent 1995-99 (calculated on the basis of Karelkomstat, 2000: 11-14).

¹⁵ Statistical data for this section were taken from Karelkomstat (2000: 10, 35-38) and Petersburgkomstat (2000: 66-7).

¹⁶ It is surprising that these services were ordered mainly by companies from such distant countries as Liechtenstein ($7.6 mio.), Malta ($2.3 mio.) and the USA ($1.4 mio.). It is likely that these offshore companies have Karelian owners who use these offshore jurisdictions for hiding profits from commercial exploitation of the Karelian sea-going fleet.

[17] The most famous of these firms is Skila Oy, which concludes contracts with Russian sewing companies in Sortavala (Karelia) and in the Leningrad and Novgorod provinces (Generozova 2000).

[18] In 1999 Karelian exports of sewing services grew by 6.5 per cent, and in the Leningrad province by 11.0 per cent.

[19] In many Russia's regions (e.g. Novgorod, Smolensk, Altay and other) such zones have been created by regional administrations. Nonetheless, the Karelian Government believes that at present the creation of the zone is impossible because of a negative attitude by the Federal Government toward such zones.

[20] However, these plans have not been officially confirmed by Stora-Enso (Makarov 2000a).

[21] City of Stockholm, Helsinki Development Corporation, Representative Office of the German Economy and others.

[22] For example, Marli, IDO Ruokatalo, Nerpish, HK Kylplahuone, VP-Kuljetus and Lemminkainen (Nevskaya, Anna (1999), "Pod Svetogorskom vyrastet finskaya derevnya," *Delovoi Petersburg*, 14 April: 5).

[23] However, these plans are still tentative.

[24] Motylkov, Dmitri (2000). "Lenoblast vozvodit zaslon deshevomu exportu lesa,' *Delovoi Petersburg*, 16 February, page 4.

[25] This project is called the Baltic Pipeline System.

[26] However, as a result of these plans Russia may lose the Finnish market for energy products once Finland has completed its planned pipeline delivering natural gas from the South, thus bypassing Russia.

References

Andreev, B. (2000). 'Finlyandiya – osnovnoi partner Lenoblasti,' *Ekonomika i vremya*, 17 January, page 6.

Druzhinin, P. (2000). *Razvitie Respubliki Karelia v 1990-1999 gg*, mimeo.

Ershov, A. (2000). 'Primorsk stal razmennoi monetoi,' *Delovoi Petersburg*, 24 April, page 5.

Evseenkov, O. (2000). 'Les rubyat,' *Expert Severo-Zapad*, 7 February, pages 10-12.

Generozova, Y. (2000). 'Novgorodtsy skroili novui zakaz,' *Delovoi Petersburg*, 19 December.

Goskomstat Rossii (1999). *Regiony Rossii*, Volume 2. Moscow, Goskomstat.

Hanson, P. and Bradshaw, M. (eds) (2000). *Regional economic change in Russia*. Cheltenham, UK, Edward Elgar.

Interfax (1999). 'Karelia sotrudnichaet s Suomi,' *Delovoi Petersburg*, 19 April, page 11.

Karavaeva, G. (2000). 'Sostoyanie i osnovnye tendentsii razvitiya promyshlennosti,' *Ekonomika i vremya*, 17 July: 4.

Karelkomstat (2000). *Vneshnyaya torgovlya v Respublike Karelia*. Petrozavodsk, Karelkomstat.

Köll, J.(2000). 'North European and Baltic Statistics,' pages 329-466 in Hedegaard, L. and Lindstrom, B. (eds). The NEBI Yearbook 2000: *North European and Baltic Sea Integration*. Berlin; Heidelberg, Springer.

Krom, E. (2000). 'Sinergiya vmesto sorevnovaniya,' *Expert Severo-Zapad*, 24 January, pages 4-8.

Makarov, A. (2000a). 'Karelia postroit lesopilku za $25 mln,' *Delovoi Petersburg*, 21 November, page 8.

Makarov, A. (2000b). 'Karelia sozdaet holdingi,' *Delovoi Petersburg*, 19 December, page 8.

Motylkov, D. (1999). 'Lenoblast rabotaet s evropeiskimi dengami,' *Delovoi Petersburg*, 16 June, page 3.

Motylkov, D. (2000). ' priznala zonu,' *Delovoi Petersburg*, 10 March, page 8.

Motylkov, D. (2000a). 'Sozdayut evroregion,' *Delovoi Petersburg*, 17 March, page 8.

Motylkov, D. (2000b). 'V Kostamukshe sozdaetsya svobodnaya zona,' *Delovoi Petersburg*, 2 February, page 6.

Petersburgkomstat (1999). *Sankt-Petersburg i Leningradskaya oblast v 1998 godu.* St Petersburg, Petersburgkomstat.

Petersburgkomstat (2000). *Leningradskaya oblast '99.* St Petersburg, Petersburgkomstat.

Romanyuk, R. (2000a). 'Fortum ishchet svoe mesto v proekte BTS,' *Delovoi Petersburg,* 7 August, page 3.

Romanyuk, R. (2000b). 'Pravitelstvo Rossii nashlo dengi na trubu,' *Delovoi Petersburg,* 19 July, page 3.

Rosbusinessconsulting (2000). 'Oblast druzhit s Suomi,' *Delovoi Petersburg,* 27 March, page 4.

Zimine, D. (1998). *Economic development in the city of Novgorod and in Novgorod oblast,* Working Paper 14, Russian Regional Research Group. Birmingham, University of Birmingham.

Part II

Spatial Planning and the Environment

6 Cleaning up Hot Spots in the Baltic Sea Drainage Basin: An Appraisal of the Joint Comprehensive Environmental Action Programme

Matthew R. Auer and Eve Nilenders[1]

The Joint Comprehensive Environmental Action Programme (JCP) – a multilateral effort to remediate and 'restore the ecological balance of the Baltic Sea' – celebrates its tenth anniversary in 2002-2003. Programme participants audited the JCP in 1997 at the close of the first five-year phase. The main body overseeing the JCP, the Helsinki Commission (HELCOM) declares the programme a success as do a variety of observers. Indeed, pollution emissions from various JCP 'hot spots' have been reduced, among other accomplishments. However, the JCP is not without shortcomings including problems stemming from the earliest days of its formulation. Detracting from the performance of the first phase were overly ambitious goals for pollution abatement and dubious accounting measures for programme success.

Introduction

In the late 1980s and early 1990s, deteriorating environmental conditions in the Baltic Sea worried political elites, environmentalists and ordinary citizens, alike. These concerns were warranted, as scientists were documenting, among other trends, increasing concentrations of heavy metals in marine sediments and plants and the presence of various persistent organic compounds in fish (SNV 1990: 19-52, 90-118; Andersson and Förlin 1988: 233-36). Perhaps most unsettling were the ill effects from nutrient enrichment of the sea from urban age, agricultural runoff and other sources of nitrogen and phosphorus. By the end of the 1980s, toxic blooms of cyanobacteria – a nitrogen-fixing species of blue green algae – were increasingly common in the Baltic Proper, Danish Sound and Kattegat. Fauna in deep bottom waters were greatly reduced over a 100,000 km² area, and dramatic changes in plant species composition were observed in coastal waters in Latvia, Poland and Sweden – all due to eutrophication, subsequent die-off of algae and oxygen deprivation (Rosenberg et al. 1990: 105; Cederwall and Elmgren 1990: 111). The sea's declining environmental health made headlines from London to Leningrad (Taylor 1990; Rachko 1989).

Worsening environmental problems in the sea were evident despite more than 10 years of environmental co-operation by the region's coastal states. The 1974 Convention on the Protection of the Marine Environment of the Baltic Sea Area (Helsinki Convention), which came into force in 1980, bound Baltic Sea coastal countries to 'take all appropriate legislative, administrative or other relevant measures…to prevent and abate pollution and to protect and enhance the marine environment of the Baltic Sea Area' (International Legal Materials 1974: art. 3). But, in practice, the treaty area extended only to the open waters of the sea and Cold War tensions precluded meaningful application of the agreement in and along inland waters leading to the sea. Contracting parties sent emissaries each year to participate in the convention's governing body – the Helsinki Commission or HELCOM. Over the course of the 1980s, member states from Western Europe were relatively responsive to soft law recommendations issued annually by HELCOM (Auer 1998: 84-85). The same could not be said of the former eastern bloc nations whose governments mostly ignored the environmental problems generated by state-owned industry and underinvested in public environmental infrastructure. But worsening conditions in the sea were not due solely to Communist governments' negligence. Contaminated runoff and direct discharges to the sea from Denmark, Sweden, Finland and Germany contributed to the sea's decline. Significant sources of environmental pressure on the sea included, inter alia, nutrient inputs from farms and feedlots in Denmark and toxins from Swedish and Finnish pulp and paper mills.

Confronted with mounting evidence of the sea's beleaguered health, the region's environmental ministers took action in 1988. A Ministerial Declaration of that year called for a reduction in emissions of heavy metals, toxic and persistent organic substances and nutrients by 50 per cent from their 1987 levels (HELCOM 1988). Several months later, in Ronneby, Sweden, ministers signed the Baltic Sea Declaration which called for a Joint Comprehensive Environmental Action Programme to 'assure the ecological restoration of the Baltic Sea' (HELCOM 1998d: 10; HELCOM 1990: para 1). The latter called for the cleanup of 132 hot spots of pollution in the Baltic Sea drainage basin at an estimated cost of 18 billion ecu, to be implemented over 20 years.

The JCP was innovative in that its participants sought to de-nationalise the basis for co-operation. As specified at the Ronneby Conference, the JCP had a 'joint and comprehensive nature' whereby 'priorities for implementing the integrated programme elements were set for the catchment area as a whole and not just within a national context' (HELCOM 1998d: 10). The JCP partners' integrated, basin-wide strategy exemplifies what some scholars call a 'community of interests' approach to regional environmental co-operation (Dellapenna 1992).

A second unusual feature of the JCP was the makeup of the partners – a collection including not only governmental actors, but also intergovernmental organisations and perhaps most importantly, international financial institutions who promised, in principle, to help finance JCP investment activities. A list of the original partners is shown in Table 6.1. Belarus and Ukraine joined the list of JCP co-operating governments in 1993, and in later years, a variety of non-governmental organisations joined the programme.

Table 6.1: Joint Comprehensive Environmental Action Partners in 1992

Contracting Parties and Co-operating Governments*	Other Parties
Czech and Slovak Federal Republic	*Regional Intergovernmental Organisations*
Denmark	Baltic Marine Environment Protection Commission
Estonia	Commission for the European Communities
Finland	International Baltic Sea Fishery Commission
Germany	(IBSFC) (Observer status)
Latvia	
Lithuania	*International Financial Institutions*
Norway	European Bank for Reconstruction and
Poland	Development (EBRD)
Sweden	European Investment Bank (EIB)
Russian Federation	Nordic Investment Bank (NIB)
	Nordic Environment Finance Corporation (NEFCO)
	World Bank
* Contracting Parties to the Convention on the Protection of the Marine Environment of the Baltic Sea Area (Helsinki Convention) are in bold text.	

Source: HELCOM (1992: Annex I)

The contracting parties and co-operating governments agreed to harmonise national environmental norms with JCP policies and regulatory measures. All partners offered to develop human, financial and technical capacities within JCP countries to implement the programme; participate in or support applied research activities; and promote public awareness and environmental education related to the JCP (HELCOM 1992: Chapter 5). But the centrepiece of the programme was the prospective cleanup of hot spots. Of the 132 sites on the hot spot list, 127 were point and non-point emission sources and five were special management areas in the form of large coastal lagoons and wetlands.

JCP participants audited the programme in 1997 at the close of the first, five-year phase. Based on this audit, HELCOM declared the programme a success (HELCOM 1998a: 6). However, available data indicate that by the end of phase I, the programme fell far short of many of the pollution reduction goals specified by the participants in 1992.

The JCP missed its pollution reduction targets for a variety of reasons. Most importantly, the goals themselves were unrealistic. Targets for pollution abatement relied on uncertain indicators of ex ante emissions from the hot spots and crude projections for emissions reduction. Problems with missing data, low quality baseline data used for target-setting and arbitrary pollution reduction goals undermined (and continue to undermine) HELCOM's ability to measure and report on the programme's achievements. Other problems affecting the performance of the JCP in its first phase included capital constraints in the transitional economies; transitional economies' problems adapting Western-style environmental management practices; and, in some cases, flagging political will to implement projects.

The Joint Comprehensive Environmental Action Programme

Depending on the contaminant, data is available from HELCOM to compare pollution reduction achievements against prescribed goals for as few as 60 JCP hot spots (in the case of nitrogen and phosphorus) and as many as 65 sites (in the case of BOD_5) between 1991 and 1997. Over the course of phase I, HELCOM ceased reporting data on pollution emissions from an additional 15 hot spots that were deleted from the original hot spot list. We obtained emission trend data for more than half of these sites from non-HELCOM sources.

In 1992, HELCOM published expected annual pollution abatement goals for more than 50 per cent of the 132 hot spots. Most but not all hot spots emit oxygen-demanding organic contaminants (BOD_5), nitrogen (tot-N) and phosphorus (tot-P).[2] Annual BOD_5, tot-N and tot-P abatement goals were established for most of the hot spots in 1992. JCP parties submitted hot spot environmental data to HELCOM in 1991, 1994, 1995 and 1997. In each of these years, data were missing for approximately two dozen hot spots. HELCOM, like other environmental programme secretariats, deals with contracting parties whose commitment to data collection and reporting vary and whose environmental monitoring institutions diverge in quality and aptitude. However, missing data is neither the only nor the most significant problem interfering with HELCOM's evaluation of programme successes and shortcomings.

Perhaps the most confounding problem is establishing a baseline against which to compare pollution emission trends. Out of 132 hot spots, HELCOM estimated the annual pollution reduction performance for over half of all hot spots emitting either/or BOD_5, tot-N, or tot-P. Specifically, annual BOD_5, tot-N and tot-P abatement goals were established for 72, 71 and 69 hot spots, respectively. Pollution abatement goals were not specified for several hot spots because of participants' low confidence in indicators of ex ante emissions from these sites. Goal-setting for hot spots in the former centrally planned economies was especially difficult due to absent or otherwise unreliable historical data and problems estimating current emissions (Interview with Peter Marksoo, Tallinn, Estonia, June 19, 2000).

Another problem hampering programme monitoring were differences in both biophysical and economic facets of different hot spots, making intercomparability among hot spots difficult. For example, HELCOM strongly suspects that emissions reduction from agricultural hot spots significantly lagged emissions reduction from industrial and especially municipal hot spots during phase I. But its assessment is tentative because some of its data are estimates rather than direct measurements of discharges and more fundamentally, because participants *are unsatisfied with the criteria used to define agricultural hot spots*. In 1998, HELCOM declared (1998d: 26):

'Experience has shown that there appears to be a problem with the definition of what constitutes an agricultural/livestock hot spot. Present listed sites include both 'point' and 'non-point' sources, but agriculture presents such particular problems that there is a need for more precision in this sector.'

Adding to the ambiguity, some of the JCP's hot spots are collection points for pollution from other point and non-point source hot spots. To illustrate, the Gulf of Riga Management hot spot subsumes polluting activities from a large area, including from other agricultural, municipal and industrial hot spots (HELCOM 1999a: 15). Were HELCOM to measure emissions reduction from the Gulf of Riga Management site, it risks double-counting pollution reduction occurring at other sites. Partly because of the double-counting problem, HELCOM does not report emissions data from coastal lagoon/wetland hot spots. Meanwhile, emissions data are missing for many agricultural/livestock hot spots (HELCOM 1998c: 51-66). Data are also missing for some large point source emitters including all of the St Petersburg sewerage projects and a combined municipal and industrial wastewater treatment project in the eastern region of Katowice. The omission of these sites constitutes a significant setback for HELCOM's verification efforts, since these hot spots are responsible for relatively large, subregional loadings to the Baltic Sea. To illustrate, by HELCOM's own ex ante estimates, the St Petersburg hot spots were responsible for approximately 40 percent of BOD loadings to the Gulf of Finland and around 50 percent of all phosphorus point source loadings to the gulf in 1991 (HELCOM, 1992: 3.4-3.5).

For sites whose pollution emissions *were* reported to HELCOM in 1991 and 1997 and for whom annual pollution reduction goals were specified in 1992, we were able to approximate actual achievements in emissions reduction versus the pollution abatement goals. This type of analysis has not been reported by HELCOM[3] nor, to the best of our knowledge, attempted by other researchers.

Evaluating JCP Phase I Pollution Abatement Achievements

In 1998, HELCOM evaluated the first, five-year phase of the JCP. Using 1991 as a baseline to measure emissions of different contaminants covered by the programme, HELCOM reported impressive indicators of pollution reduction from the hot spots. According to the Commission, hot spot emissions of biochemical oxygen demand (BOD_5), chemical oxygen demand (COD) and total phosphorus (tot-P) declined by around 35 percent while total nitrogen (tot-N) had been reduced by 30 percent. Emissions of chlorinated organic compounds, measured as absorbable organic halide (AOX) fell 67 percent (HELCOM 1998c: 15). Twenty-three hot spots with especially impressive pollution reduction performance were profiled in a separate appraisal (HELCOM 1998d: 24). Stand-outs for emissions reduction included pulp and paper mills in Finland, Germany, Sweden, Estonia, Latvia and Russia and wastewater treatment plants in Poland and the Baltic States. Many of these hot spots reported reduced emissions of BOD by 90 percent or more between 1991 and 1995 (HELCOM 1998d: 24).

An important set of indicators missing in this and other HELCOM appraisals (e.g., HELCOM 1998a; HELCOM 1998b; HELCOM 1998c) deals with programme performance vis-à-vis *goals for emissions reduction* specified at the JCP's outset. When programme achievements are measured against the original pollution reduction goals, results for the first phase of the JCP are less impressive than the selected indicators highlighted by HELCOM in the Commission's various annual reports and program review documents from 1998.

In 1992, JCP parties estimated the annual pollution reduction load for BOD_5 and/or nutrients to be achieved for as many as 72 hot spots on an annual basis between 1991 and 1997. During this six-year period, the parties assumed that pollution emissions from each site would decline by an equal amount, each year. By any reasonable measure, the parties' assumption of a constant, linear trend for pollution abatement was boldly optimistic, because typically, the marginal cost of pollution abatement increases with each additional unit of pollution abated (Teitenberg 2000: 344; Kahn 1998: 57-58). Hence, as marginal abatement costs increase, one can expect the amount of abated pollution to diminish over time. Yet, the parties effectively ignored this principle by projecting unvaryingly large levels of pollution abated, each year.

In estimating actual pollution abatement results from hot spots that reported data, we do not depart from the JCP parties' assumption of static rates of pollution reduction. For each hot spot, pollution loads from 1997 were subtracted from pollution loads in 1991 with the remainder divided by six (to account for the six, two-year periods of pollution abatement separating 1991 from 1997). For any given hot spot with available data, progress toward attainment of the hot spot's pollution reduction goal was measured by dividing average annual pollution abatement from 1991 to 1997 by the pollution reduction goal specified in 1992. Pollution abatement performance for the 60 to 65 hot spots for which there were available data (the number of hot spots examined varies depending on the contaminant in question) are presented in Table 6.2. By the end of the JCP's first phase, the vast majority of the 60 to 65 hot spots missed the average annual pollution reduction goals specified by the JCP parties in 1992. Most hot spots achieved less than 25 per cent of the specified annual pollution reduction goal for BOD_5, tot-N and tot-P.

Table 6.2: Results of pollution abatement efforts at JCP hot spots with available data, 1991-97

Hot spot number	Hot spot name	Hot spot type	Percentage of average annual BOD$_5$ goal achieved	Percentage of average annual tot-N goal achieved	Percentage of average annual tot-P goal achieved
2	Metsä-Botnia Oy Kemi	Industrial	9.3	-68.1	16.7
11	YPT Joutseno	Industrial	13.4	13.3	10.3
12	Kaukas Lappeenranta	Industrial	6.5	16.7	16.9
13	E-G Kaukopää	Industrial	9.6	10.1	34.4
14	Syasstroi	Industrial	38.8	50.0	35.5
15	Volkhov	Industrial	45.2	103.3	11.8
16	Sunila Oy-Kotka	Industrial	15.8	ID	ID
17	Helsinki Region	Municipal	19.2	-5.3	6.1
26	Kohtla Järve	Municipal & Industrial	6.1	1.3	ID
28	Tallinn	Municipal & Industrial	16.0	29.3	18.1
31	Haapsalu	Municipal & Industrial	2.2	-2.1	-1.0
32	Matsalu Bay	Management Program	ID	0.9	19.4
33	Pärnu	Municipal & Industrial	0.7	1.7	3.0
34	Paide	Municipal & Industrial	5.0	0.5	7.1
35	Vohma Meat Combine	Industrial	4.6	2.3	15.0
41	Siauliai	Municipal & Industrial	12.6	23.3	16.9
42	Riga (WWTP Phase II)	Municipal & Industrial	36.5	74.7	-14.3
46	Daugavpils	Municipal & Industrial	11.3	-10.7	-3.9
49	Sovetsk	Industrial	15.8	17.5	121.7
50	Neman	Industrial	15.5	17.0	32.9
51	Kaunas	Municipal & Industrial	9.6	2.2	-0.9
52	Amalg Azotaz	Industrial	ID	0.4	ID
53	Kedainiai	Municipal & Industrial	38.5	ID	3.3
54	Kedainiai	Industrial	ID	1.2	ID
55	Panevezys	Municipal & Industrial	10.7	ID	25.3
58	Alytus	Municipal & Industrial	21.5	18.9	7.7
59	Vilnius/Grigiskes	Municipal & Industrial	19.0	1.3	10.9
61	Grodno	Municipal & Industrial	23.3	ID	ID
63	Klaipeda	Municipal & Industrial	5.0	-15.3	2.3
64	Cardboard Factory	Industrial	16.7	13.3	ID
66	Kursiu Lagoon	Management Program	ID	-166.7	ID
67	Kaliningrad	Municipal & Industrial	121.7	-353.5	-4.9
68	Pulp & Paper No 1	Industrial	9.3	ID	-0.6
69	Pulp & Paper No 2	Industrial	5.3	ID	-43.3
74	Kozalin	Municipal & Industrial	26.1	-12.1	0.0
75	Gdynia-Debogorze	Municipal & Industrial	14.4	-0.3	4.8
76	Gdansk-Wschod	Municipal & Industrial	4.5	-0.6	16.2
77	Swiecie	Industrial	10.5	ID	ID
78	Bydgoszcz-Fordon	Municipal & Industrial	10.6	ID	ID
79	Bydgoszcz-Kapusciska	Industrial	0.0	0.0	0.0
80	Torun	Municipal & Industrial	0.0	ID	ID

Table continued next page

Table 6.2: Continued

Hot spot number	Hot spot name	Hot spot type	Percentage of average annual BOD$_5$ goal achieved	Percentage of average annual tot-N goal achieved	Percentage of average annual tot-P goal achieved
81	Wloclawek	Municipal & Industrial	5.6	3.3	-0.6
82	Warsaw-Czajka	Municipal & Industrial	-20.4	-7.0	-0.5
83	Warsaw-Siekierki	Municipal & Industrial	3.0	-10.4	-8.4
84	Warsaw-Pancerz	Municipal & Industrial	9.1	-79.8	5.7
85	Lublin-Hajdow	Municipal & Industrial	12.0	ID	-3.9
86	Krakow-Plaszow	Municipal & Industrial	-1.9	1.4	6.3
87	Krakow-Kujawy	Municipal & Industrial	3.2	-0.8	8.3
88	Katowice-East	Municipal & Industrial	-5.0	ID	ID
93	Brest	Municipal & Industrial	0.6	ID	ID
94	Lvov	Municipal & Industrial	14.4	ID	ID
97	Szczecin	Municipal & Industrial	57.1	32.7	33.2
98	Szczecin	Industrial	-2.0	-20.6	-2.0
99	Poznan	Municipal & Industrial	-3.0	1.9	-0.3
100	Lodz	Municipal & Industrial	0.3	2.2	-2.9
101	Zielona Gora	Municipal & Industrial	1.2	84.0	3.9
102	Legnica-Glogow	Industrial	-5.1	78.4	887.5
103	Wroclaw	Municipal & Industrial	5.0	-0.1	0.0
104	Wroclaw	Industrial	111.1	ID	ID
105	Ubocz-Luban	Industrial	ID	ID	0.0
107	Katowice-West	Municipal & Industrial	22.5	22.5	25.8
108	Katowice-West	Industrial	ID	513.5	ID
109	Ostrava	Municipal & Industrial	9.1	10.4	12.0
110	Ostrava Area	Industrial	28.1	1.6	ID
114	Greifswald	Municipal & Industrial	23.4	23.5	68.3
115	Neubrandenburg	Municipal & Industrial	38.9	7.4	1.6
116	Stralsund	Municipal & Industrial	41.9	20.1	397.9
117	Stavenhagen-Malchin	Municipal & Industrial	ID	1.9	6.2
119	Lübeck	Municipal & Industrial	0.9	0.4	3.6
120	Wismar	Municipal & Industrial	29.2	-17.3	772.9
121	Rostock	Municipal & Industrial	15.7	-4.3	36.6
123	Copenhagen	Municipal	14.4	19.8	12.5
125	Sweden-Agriculture	Agricultural Runoff Program	ID	0.0	0.0
127	Göteborg	Municipal	ID	ID	-0.3
128	Sweden-Agriculture	Agricultural Runoff Program	ID	0.0	ID
131	Nymölla	Industrial	ID	ID	6.1
132	Sweden-Agriculture	Agricultural Runoff Program	ID	0.0	0.0

ID = insufficient data

Data for the 15 hot spots delisted during Phase I are not shown.

Sources: adapted from HELCOM (1992b; 1998c)

Figure 6.1 exhibits actual annual BOD_5 emissions reduction performance of hot spots versus annual BOD_5 emissions reduction goals specified by the parties at the programme's outset. ArcView images of hot spots' tot-N and tot-P emissions reduction performance are found in a separate publication (Auer and Nilenders forthcoming). Hot spots that achieved at least 50 per cent or more of the phase I goal for BOD_5 are denoted by lightly shaded symbols with darker shades indicating less goal attainment. The darkest symbols are hot spots whose 1997 emissions exceeded 1991 emissions, illustrating negative goal attainment. Square symbols are hot spots delisted by HELCOM over the course of the first phase as JCP participants concurred that these sites achieved the pollution abatement goals specified in 1992. However, and as discussed below, some delisted hot spots may have achieved steep emissions reductions for some contaminants while emissions of other contaminants fell less sharply, did not fall, or actually increased over the course of phase I.

A disproportionately high number of deleted hot spots are located in relatively wealthy countries in the Baltic Sea catchment area. During phase I of the JCP, 13 out of 15 deleted hot spots resided in Sweden, Finland and Germany. These 13 sites were remediated; in contrast, the two delisted hot spots in Estonia were shut down. The predominance of delisted hot spots among wealthy countries is not

Figure 6.1: Average abatement compared to abatement goal, 1991-97

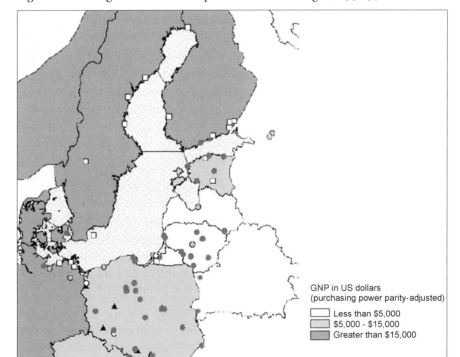

surprising since these countries possess relatively vast financial resources and strong institutional capacities to remediate hot spots. Nevertheless, according to the annual pollution reduction goals specified by JCP partners in 1992, substantial pollution abatement was expected at several hot spots in the transitional economies. To illustrate, 47 'priority' hot spots – sites that were to receive special attention in the programme – all reside in the transitional economies, though none of these hot spots were actually delisted during the first phase.

Among the three contaminants (BOD_5, tot-N and tot-P), the participants were most successful in abating emissions of BOD_5 (Table 6.3) with 12 sites reporting partial goal attainment of at least 25 per cent and 6 sites reporting negative goal attainment.

Table 6.3: Pollution abatement performance of JCP hot spots with available data, by contaminant

Contaminant	Hot spots achieving greater than 50% of abatement goal	Hot spots achieving between 25% and 50% of abatement goal	Hot spots achieving between 0% and 25% of abatement goal	Negative goal achievement	Total hot spots
BOD	3	9	47	6	65
tot-N	5	3	34	18	60
tot-P	5	7	33	15	60

These results are indicative of the pollution control devices installed at many JCP hot spots, namely, activated sludge systems. HELCOM has not systematically collected data on specific environmental technologies installed at hot spots. However, it is evident that site managers installed secondary sewage treatment devices with varying degrees of enhanced biological nutrient removal because hot spots achieved relatively high BOD_5 abatement versus tot-P and tot-N abatement. Conventional activated sludge treatment plants without biological phosphate or nitrate removal tend to remove 10 to 30 per cent of phosphorus loads (Stensel 1991: 141) and only eight to 20 per cent of nitrogen loads from a typical municipal wastewater influent (Eckenfelder and Argaman 1991: 7).

By the mid-1990s, HELCOM realised that JCP parties were struggling to satisfy nitrogen reduction goals, in particular. This realisation inspired contracting parties to the Helsinki Convention to pass HELCOM Recommendation 16-9 (HELCOM 1995) which established nitrogen abatement targets for all municipal sewage treatment plants in the drainage basin and encouraged JCP partners to redouble their nitrogen abatement efforts.

Determinants of the JCP's Phase I Performance

Determinants of the JCP's underperformance in its first phase include JCP partners' financial problems; institutional problems in the transitional economies; and JCP partners' delisting of hot spots that continued to emit relatively large loads of pollution. However, the most important determinants of programme underperformance were the parties' reliance on low quality data for goal-setting and on an overly simplistic algorithm for estimating progress toward pollution abatement goals.

Financial Constraints

Based on survey responses returned to HELCOM by JCP partners in 1998, estimated total cleanup costs at hot spots were revised downward from the original sum of 18 billion ECU to 10 billion ECU (HELCOM 1998c: 7, 14). Nevertheless, HELCOM admitted that investments in industrial hot spots were sluggish in the first phase (HELCOM 1998b: 7) and that cleanup of non-point source pollution hot spots demanded 'increased emphasis' in future phases of the programme (HELCOM 1998b: 15). Only 13 per cent of the 20-year funding target for industrial hot spots was satisfied during phase I (HELCOM 1998c: 14). Through 1999, 0 per cent of the total funding target was achieved for the agricultural sector (HELCOM 1999a: 14). Regarding the latter indicator, HELCOM claims that cleanup occurred at agricultural hot spots though within the context of national rural sector environmental programmes and not the JCP (interview with Ulrich Kremser, Helsinki, Finland, 12 June, 2000; see also, HELCOM 1999a: 14). Furthermore, data submitted by partners on investments in agricultural and other non-point source hot spots tend to be less comprehensive than data on point source hot spots (interview with Ulrich Kremser, Helsinki, Finland, 12 June, 2000).

Lower than expected funding for phase I is also partly explained by the closure of certain factories and their subsequent removal from the hot spot list or their 'inactive' status on that list. A pulp and paper mill and a meat combine in Estonia were removed from the list during JCP phase I because these factories ceased production; three additional sites, a pulp and paper mill in Latvia, a cardboard factory in Lithuania and a pulp and paper mill in Kaliningrad shut down or drastically reduced production and hence were inactive hot spots. HELCOM did not calculate how the temporary or permanent closure of these factories affected the cost-savings to the overall JCP programme. However, over the 20-year life of the programme (1992-2012), estimated cleanup costs (not including operating costs) for these five closed-down or inactive hot spots were approximately 110 million ecu (HELCOM 1992: Table 3).

Other factors contributing to the slow pace of investment were deep economic recessions in Sweden and Finland in the early 1990s and international financial institutions' (IFIs') cautious approach to lending for hot spot cleanup (Auer and Nilenders, forthcoming). From 1991 to 1993, the Swedish and Finnish economies contracted. Disbursement of Swedish and Finnish grants for some JCP projects was delayed in 1993, in particular. Meanwhile, IFI lending for the JCP did not begin in earnest until 1994.

Institutional Problems in the Recipient Countries

The grants and loans for JCP projects that *did* flow to the transitional economies were not always programmed smoothly by recipient governments. Authority fragmentation and flagging political will slowed-down programme implementation in some regions. In capital and secondary cities in the Baltic States and especially in Russia, participants quarrelled with the JCP's rules and procedures and protested when programme advocates demanded short-term financial pain in exchange for long-term environmental gain. To illustrate, IFIs like the World Bank demanded that loan recipients institute user-fee systems to pay for newly installed sewage treatment works. While responsible ministries in recipient countries readily agreed to this condition, local officials were more reticent. Some newly elected mayors were reluctant to transform heretofore free or heavily subsidised public services into fee-for-services. Also, elected officials at the local level challenged the prerogatives of local project managers and their foreign advisers. For example, the Kaunas JCP wastewater project stumbled for lack of support from the mayor's office. Frequent mayoral changes in Kaunas (i.e., five different mayors between 1995 and 1999) caused significant delays in the signing of key loan and related documents (Lariola and Danielsson 1998). Though the first feasibility studies on the Kaunas wastewater project were performed in 1993, actual installation of sewerage infrastructure did not begin until 1999.

Authority fragmentation proved even more debilitating for JCP projects in St Petersburg. Russian representatives who attended JCP meetings were far more enthusiastic about the programme than were ministerial counterparts in Moscow and local officials in St Petersburg. Remarks by a senior official at the Finnish Ministry of Environment epitomise the donors' frustration: 'Personally, I doubt whether the Russian government even knows what HELCOM's aim is. It is possible that none of St Petersburg's municipal offices knows what HELCOM is' (Henttonen quoted by Iloniemi 1999: 35).[4] The Government of Finland was a major bilateral donor to the St Petersburg projects. But Finnish Ministry of Environment officials inferred that counterparts in Moscow were indifferent toward Finnish-sponsored projects in Russia because these projects were located in 'peripheral areas' such as Karelia, Petrozavodsk and Murmansk (sites that are upwind of Finland), or in the case of St Petersburg, in a city that Moscow deems a competitor (Interview, Kristiina Isokallio, Helsinki, Finland, 9 June, 2000). Several other JCP projects in 'non-peripheral' parts of Russia produced anaemic results in phase I. For example, sewerage equipment installed in the Kaliningrad oblast during the mid-1990s may never perform optimally because it depends on shoddy infrastructure installed before the JCP (Roginko 1998: 600-601).

Delisting of Hot Spots with Stubborn Emissions Problems

Problems with pollution abatement efforts were not the exclusive domain of the transitional economies. In the Nordic countries, participants failed to anticipate increases in factory production that worked against pollution load reduction objectives. For example, Swedish sulphate pulp production increased in the mid-1990s which hampered efforts to decrease emissions of nutrients from at least three of four sulphate pulp mill hot spots (Figure 6.2).

Figure 6.2: Annual nitrogen emissions from four Swedish pulp mill hot spots, 1991-97

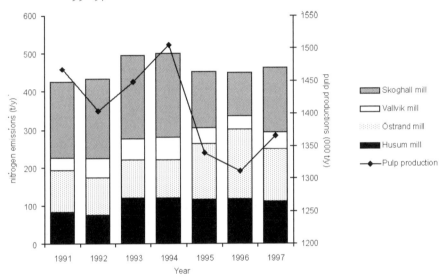

Sources: SNV (1992; 1993; 1994; 1995; 1996; 1998a; 1998b); HELCOM (1998c)

These four pulp mills were entries on the JCP hot spot list primarily because of their discharges of persistent and toxic organochlorine wastes and not because of their emissions of BOD or nutrients. These mills were removed from the hot spot list in 1994 after their organochlorine emissions declined sharply during the early 1990s. However, their aggregate nitrogen emissions did not decrease between 1991 and 1997 and indeed, peaked the same year (1994) that these hot spots were delisted. The aggregate tot-N peak in the mid-1990s corresponds to a peak in pulp production from the mills during this period. From 1995 through 1997, annual pulp production declined versus the previous four-year period, but tot-N emissions did not fall as precipitously. In 1995, Coalition Clean Baltic, a regional NGO and a co-operating party in the JCP, complained that the delisting of Swedish and Finnish pulp mills was premature since some of these hot spots continued to emit large, and in some instances, increasingly large quantities of nitrogen (Coalition Clean Baltic 1995: 2). JCP partners did not relent – the delisted sites were not 'relisted.' However, the partners did address a second, more generic concern aired by Coalition Clean Baltic, namely that the JCP lacked formal criteria for delisting hot spots. In 1999, HELCOM formalised a system for delisting hot spots (HELCOM 1999b) effectively conceding that such a system had not existed during the programme's first phase.

Programme Accomplishments Resulting from Non-programme Activities

The previous section evidences negative goal attainment in the reduction of nitrogen emissions from pulp mill hot spots in Sweden and Finland. However, and as correctly reported by HELCOM, emissions of chlorinated organic substances – measured as AOX[5] – fell sharply from these mills during phase I (see, e.g., HELCOM 1998a: 7, 14). That AOX emissions declined steeply from Swedish and Finnish pulp mill hot spots during the early- to mid-1990s is not disputed. However, one may dispute that the JCP was instrumental to this outcome.

Powerful inducements to Swedish and Finnish mills to cut their AOX emissions predated the JCP by several years. In the mid-1980s, Swedish environmental organisations began promoting 'environmentally friendly paper' (*miljövänligt papper*) and condemning Swedish mills that produced paper bleached with chlorine (Bryntse 1990). In 1987, at a pollution permit hearing of the Swedish Värö pulp mill – a meeting well-attended by the Swedish branch of Greenpeace – Swedish regulators ordered mill managers to reduce Värö's total organically-bound chlorine (TOCl) emissions to 1.5 kg per metric tonne pulp. This was among the earliest in a series of Swedish pulp mill permit hearings dealing primarily with organochlorines in wastewater. Between 1987 and 1990, Swedish regulators ordered 10 of Sweden's 15 sulphate pulp mills producing bleached pulp to sharply reduce their organochlorine emissions (Auer 1998: 77 *passim*). In Finland, comparable permit rules were issued beginning in 1989. By the time the JCP was approved in 1992, all Swedish and Finnish sulphate pulp mills that produced bleached pulp, including the mills on the hot spot list, were busy instituting AOX-reduction plans in response to regulators' demands.

Markets played a role in the AOX story, too, and again, the pulp and paper industry responded to incentives well before the emergence of the JCP. Demand for low- and no-chlorine pulp and paper products blossomed in continental Europe more than three years before the JCP as evidenced in the annual reports of Swedish and Finnish pulp and paper companies and their major customers (see, e.g., MoDo, 1988; ICA, 1988). In 1993, the first year of the JCP, 'totally chlorine free' or 'TCF' pulp – bleached without chlorine compounds – captured 60 per cent of the chemical pulp market in Germany where Swedish and Finnish pulp producers exported more of their product than anywhere else in Europe (Weintraub et al. 1995; OECD 1989: 46). Hence, JCP partners' assumption of credit for that programme's single most impressive environmental result in the first phase – a 67 per cent reduction in AOX emissions (HELCOM 1998c: 15) – must be understood against a background of intensive environmental campaigning, domestic regulatory pressure and profit-oriented inducements to industry to clamp-down on AOX – all predating the JCP.

The case of the pulp and paper industry illustrates broader lessons about the listing of candidate hot spots by JCP members and about HELCOM's claims concerning programme success. The industrialised countries had a strategic interest to carefully designate candidate hot spots from their own countries *that they intended to remediate with or without the JCP*. This strategy was rational because the relatively wealthy JCP countries understood that they, alone, would be responsible for remediating hot spots on their own territories. Little or no help would be rendered from the IFIs not to mention the former eastern bloc countries in the JCP. In contrast, in order to cleanup hot spots in the eastern and southern portions of the drainage basin, the transitional economies could expect foreign aid and loans from the IFIs and from the industrialised partners. Poland, for example, could be relatively cavalier in designating candidate Polish hot spots. It could issue a 'wish list' of prospective sites to cleanup knowing it would not be held as strictly accountable to repair these sites as, say, Denmark would in cleaning-up Danish sites. Hence, it is not surprising that relatively wealthy partners like Sweden and Finland nominated Swedish and Finnish hot spots that were already the subject of long-standing domestic regulatory actions. And since environmental cleanup programs were occurring at these hot spots even before the JCP commenced, it is not surprising that many of these sites were first to be deleted from the hot spot list. Reflecting on these national concerns, one surmises that lurking just below the high-minded 'community of interests' rhetoric of the Ronneby Declaration were self-interested, cost-conscious deliberations within the wealthy countries about which sites to list.

Low-quality Data and Crude Forecasting Method Contribute to Exaggerated Expectations

More than any other factor invoked to explain the JCP's missed targets, low quality baseline data and a rudimentary method for forecasting pollution abatement explain the programme's underperformance. In 1992, JCP participants established goals and targets using, in some instances, rough indicators of current emissions from different hot spots as well as crude estimates of expected investment costs and investment in-flows to the different sites. HELCOM stated from the outset of the programme that load reduction indicators and cleanup cost estimates would be revised periodically (see, e.g., HELCOM 1992: 5.40 *passim* and 5.46 *passim*). In hindsight, it is evident that the original targets for pollution abatement, cleanup costs and expected investments were overestimated both for the programme as a whole and for priority hot spots in particular. Regarding the latter, the severity of environmental problems at these sites as well as the sites' relatively poor commercial prospects may have discouraged investments. As HELCOM observed in the late 1990s, investment in non-JCP pollution hot spots (i.e., sites not listed in the programme) often outpaced investments in JCP hot spots during phase I. HELCOM attributes this trend to the comparatively large and complex problems at JCP industrial hot spots, in particular (HELCOM 1998c: 27).

In addition to poor data on ex ante emissions from several hot spots – a problem largely beyond JCP participants' control – participants relied on a crude method for forecasting annual pollution abatement. Pollution reduction was expected to be constant from year to year at each site. This projection is unrealistic since typically, marginal abatement costs will increase with each additional unit of pollution abated. This fundamental principle of environmental economics (see, e.g., Teitenberg 2000: 344; Kahn 1998: 57-58) has been borne-out empirically for a large range of U.S. and British industries and publicly owned treatment works (Hartman et al. 1994; United Kingdom's Department of the Environment, Transport and the Regions 1999). JCP parties should have been especially cautious in projecting pollution abatement at hot spots with uncertain ex ante emissions. If the latter were underestimated, than expected costs for remediation would likely be underestimated, too. As partners confronted higher-than-expected cleanup costs, the rate of real abatement would probably lag the projected rate of abatement.

At a minimum, JCP partners should renounce expectations for zero emissions from any except various already-delisted hot spots. Partners could adjust the current model by projecting only 80 or 90 percent pollution reduction for any given contaminant during the 20 year life of the programme (1992-2012), and by assuming diminishing rates of pollution reduction in later years as marginal abatement costs increase. It is worthwhile for HELCOM to re-state its forecasts using this straightforward correction (or its equivalent), because when real results are compared against more plausible reformulated goals, genuine programme accomplishments are revealed.

The JCP as a Qualified Success

HELCOM's exaggerated expectations for the JCP obscure that programme's real accomplishments during phase I. The JCP's successes are most apparent when examined at sub-regional levels.

Subregional Results
Hot spot remediation progressed far in the Nordic countries and in Germany, including indications of *post*-phase I progress to correct emissions from pulp mill hot spots that were delisted too hastily. Sweden's four sulphate pulp mills that were delisted during JCP phase I emitted a combined 388 tonnes of tot-N in 1998 versus 463 tonnes in 1997 (SNV 1999). The mills' aggregate 1998 nitrogen emissions were substantially lower than at any time during phase I.

Among the former planned economies, Estonia stood out for its ability to attract investment and actually abate pollution. Through phase I, virtually all Estonian hot spots received at least some foreign investment toward cleanup, including substantial private resources to rehabilitate a pulp and paper mill (Kehra) and nearly 30 million ecu in loans to upgrade the Tallinn wastewater treatment plant. The Tallinn wastewater project may be the most successful JCP activity in the transitional economies measured by pollution abatement, with BOD_5 emissions declining by more than 95 percent during phase I and tot-N emissions falling by almost 50 per cent over this same period (Auer and Raukas 2000). BOD_5 loadings from the Haapsalu hot spot in Estonia fell by almost 65 per cent in phase I though the site's tot-N and tot-P emissions remained stubbornly high. The Pärnu municipal wastewater and Matsalu Bay hot spots in Estonia and the Riga municipal wastewater hot spots in Latvia also achieved steep BOD_5 reductions. Many other sites, especially industrial hot spots in the Baltic countries and in Poland reduced their emissions of BOD_5 and/or nutrients during the first phase though these results were due more to economic recession than to environmental management efforts (Liiv and Marksoo 1998: 416-417).

HELCOM recognises that care should be exercised in linking programme activities with changing environmental conditions in the Baltic Sea, for as HELCOM reasons '…the sea itself reflects any reduction in the pollution load only very slowly' (HELCOM 1998d: 35). Indeed, the most dramatic improvements to environmental quality in the sea during phase I were due not to the JCP but to a large inflow of salt water from the North Sea in 1993 that flushed-out hydrogen sulfide in various bottom waters while replenishing these waters with dissolved oxygen. Unfortunately, the pulse of rejuvenating waters from the North Sea only provided temporary relief: water quality in many parts of the sea degenerated in the mid-1990s as eutrophication problems returned.

JCP partners and HELCOM justifiably take credit for improved conditions in waters near successfully installed wastewater treatment plants. For example, water quality improved in Tallinn Bay, Estonia and along the Journal coast of Latvia after sewage treatment plants were installed or were modernised (HELCOM 1998d: 36).

It may be worthwhile for JCP partners to expend more resources on relating changing environmental conditions to levels and types of JCP investments. A finding, for example, that relatively modest investments yield large positive impacts on the environment would please cost-conscious politicians, concerned environmentalists and ordinary citizens alike. Moreover, these 'success stories' could serve as prototypes for future phases of the JCP and provide models for other regional environmental programmes.

Confidence-building and Co-operation among Partners

Beyond measures of actual pollution abatement, the JCP can claim success in the realms of knowledge- and capacity-building and multi-stakeholder co-operation.

A key success was the programme's ability to instil confidence among prospective investors. Donor countries' and IFIs' willingness to invest was enhanced by the results of JCP-sponsored prefeasibility studies and environmental assessments in eastern and southern parts of the drainage basin. The Nordic countries and multilateral banks were reluctant to issue loans and grants in lieu of these pre-investment studies. Donors mistrusted environmental assessments conducted in the planned economies during the Soviet era (Interview with Peter Marksoo, Tallinn, Estonia, 19 June, 2000).

In addition to facilitating investment, the JCP encouraged regular and systematic project monitoring by JCP partners (Greene 1998). In some instances, monitoring duties required close co-operation and co-ordination between environmental authorities in neighbouring nations (e.g., for appraising environmental activities at hot spots that straddled political boundaries).

Finally, for some governments, the JCP provided a unique forum for working directly with environmental NGOs in project formulation and implementation. JCP working groups summoned NGOs and governmental representatives to work side-by-side on project goal-setting, implementation and appraisal activities and in some instances, demanded that government officials defer to the leadership of the NGOs. Some NGOs were 'lead parties' in working groups to implement core elements of the JCP. For example, the World Wildlife Fund directed a working group overseeing management plans for coastal lagoons and wetlands (HELCOM 1998c: 29-30).

Reconsidering the Expected Accomplishments of Regional Environmental Regimes

In its first phase, the JCP played an important role in jump-starting investment flows to cleanup major pollution hot spots in the Baltic Sea drainage basin and in co-ordinating members states' and other co-operating parties' environmental protection activities in the region. However, JCP partners fell far short of many of their self-prescribed targets for pollution abatement and investments in cleanup. In large part, the gaps separating the programme's goals and its actual achievements reflected the partners' reliance on low quality data for goal-setting and a deficient forecasting method. Programme performance also suffered from a regional recession in the early 1990s, sluggish investment flows to the hot spots, institutional capacity problems in the transitional economies and premature delisting of hot spots with chronic emissions problems. Nevertheless, poor results were not uniform across hot spots; some sites, especially municipal hot spots in the Baltic States and Poland and most hot spots in Germany and the Nordic countries achieved steep pollution load reductions during phase I.

Because the JCP partners were preoccupied with the programme's pollution abatement and investment results, promotion of the programme's real accomplishments was short-changed. Those accomplishments included the nurturance of political and technical co-operation among partners and fruitful intelligence-gathering activities that catalysed investments in site cleanup.

Partly because the JCP's strengths do not include the direct assurance of environmental quality, the programme's importance to overall regional environmental protection efforts will most likely diminish in the future. The JCP accomplished the tasks it was best designed to tackle: namely increasing donors' confidence in the programme; enhancing the sharing of information among participants; and strengthening environmental and project monitoring activities in the eastern and southern portions of the drainage basin. Other European regional environmental programmes are performing functions that the JCP can not easily execute, namely the direct financing of environmental protection activities. Among the most important programmes is the EU's Instrument for Structural Policies for Pre-Accession – a 1 billion euro fund to prepare the transitional economies for EU membership with emphasis on 'economic and social cohesion concerning environment and transport policies...' (European Council, 1999, §1). The instrument is centrally funded by EU member states and the European Commission reviews and alternatively awards or denies pre-accession countries' applications for funding (European Council 1999: §7-9 and §14). In contrast, the JCP has no independent funding of its own and decision-making about project selection and project financing is decentralised. For one, the Finnish Ministry of Environment expects its participation in any future JCP projects to be organised under the auspices of existing or new EU funding instruments (Interview, Kristiina Isokallio, Helsinki, Finland, 9 June, 2000).

Apart from external funding and the lure of regional integration, local public and private financing of project cleanup will become increasingly important as the transitional economies mature. Augmented local investment in pollution abatement will bolster environmental protection efforts in the transitional economies, generally, while advancing the specialised goals of the JCP. As local-, national- and EU-sponsored cleanup activities yield positive environmental outcomes, the real accomplishments of the JCP will be better understood. The JCP's most significant achievements do not include the direct assurance of environmental cleanup. Rather the JCP advances other steps in the policy process that abet cleanup.

Notes

[1] Research for this article was supported by a grant from the United States National Research Council's Office for Central Europe and Eurasia. GIS base maps were adapted from the United Nations Environment Programme's GRID-Arendal map atlas.

[2] HELCOM Recommendation 16-9 ('Nitrogen removal at municipal sewage treatment plants') defines tot-N as all organic nitrogen, ammonium (NH_4^+), nitrate (NO_3^-)-nitrogen, and nitrite (NO_2^-)-nitrogen (HELCOM, 1995). Generally, tot-P includes all forms of organic and inorganic phosphorus, though neither HELCOM Recommendation 16-9 nor other HELCOM Recommendations define it as such.

[3] HELCOM has reported aggregate pollution reduction loads for hot spots that submitted data to the Secretariat between 1991 and 1995 (HELCOM 1998b: 29; HELCOM 1998c: 15; HELCOM 1999a, pages: 15-16). However, HELCOM has not reported, on a site-by-site basis or in aggregate, actual pollution abatement performance of the various hot spots versus the goals specified in 1992.

[4] Elsewhere, Henttonen complained, 'In Russia, it really still seems as if they couldn't care less

about environmental issues, which indeed results in poor funding' (quoted by Lindfors 2000: 41).

5   AOX is a bulk parameter that measures the quantity of halogenated material bound to organic material in a given sample. In pulp mill wastewater, AOX is composed almost entirely of chlorinated organic substances – the waste products from bleaching pulp with chlorine, chlorine dioxide, or other chlorinated chemicals.

References

Andersson, T. and Förlin, L. (1988). 'Biochemical and physiological disturbances in fish inhabiting coastal waters polluted with bleached kraft mill effluents,' *Marine Environmental Research* 24, pages 233-36.

Auer, M. (1997). 'Risk perception and international environmental affairs: The organochlorine debate between Sweden and Finland,' *Ambio* 26, pages 359-62.

Auer, M. (1998). 'Geography, Domestic Politics, and Environmental Diplomacy: A Case from the Baltic Sea Region,' *Georgetown International Environmental Law Review* 11, pages 77-100.

Auer M. and Raukas, A. (2000). 'Determinants of environmental cleanup in Estonia.' Paper presented at the 41st Annual Convention of the International Studies Association, 7-11 March 2000, Los Angeles.

Auer, M. and Nilenders, E. (forthcoming). 'Verifying Environmental Cleanup: Lessons from the Baltic Sea Joint Comprehensive Environmental Action Programme,' *Environment and Planning C: Government and Policy* 19.

Bryntse, G. (1990). 'Environmentally friendly paper: The Swedish Situation,' *Journal of Pesticide Reform* 10, pages 16-17.

Cederwall, H. and Elmgren, R. (1990). 'Biological effects of eutrophication in the Baltic Sea, particularly the coastal zone,' *Ambio* 19, pages 109-12.

Coalition Clean Baltic (newsletter), 1995 (1).

Dellapenna, J. (1992). 'Surface Water in the Iberian Peninsula: An Opportunity for Cooperation or a Source of Conflict?' *Tennessee Law Review* 803, pages 816-17.

Eckenfelder, W. and Argaman, Y. (1991). 'Principles of biological and physical/chemical nitrogen removal,' pages 3-42 in Sedlak, R. (ed.). *Phosphorus and Nitrogen Removal from Municipal Wastewater: Principles and Practice.* Second Edition. Boca Raton, FL, Lewis Publishers.

European Council (1999). 'Council Regulation (EC) No. 1267/1999 of 21 June 1999 establishing an Instrument for Structural Policies for Pre-accession,' *Official Journal of the European Communities* L 161/73 (26 June 1999).

Gerin, R. (1999). 'Building a cleaner future for the Baltic,' *Nordicum* 7, pages 36-38.

Greene, O. (1998). 'Implementation review and the Baltic Sea regime,' pages 177-220 in Victor, D., Raustiala, K. and Skolnikoff, E. (eds). *The Implementation and Effectiveness of International Environmental Commitments: Theory and Practice.* Cambridge, MA and London, MIT Press.

Hartman, R., Wheeler, D. and Singh, M. (1994). 'The cost of air pollution abatement,' *Policy Research Working Paper* 1398. Washington, D.C., World Bank.

HELCOM (1988). *Declaration on the Protection of the Marine Environment of the Baltic Sea Area,* Helsinki, Finland, 15 February 1988.

HELCOM (1990). *Baltic Sea Declaration,* Ronneby, Sweden 2-3 September 1990.

HELCOM (1992). *The Baltic Sea Joint Comprehensive Environmental Action Programme (Preliminary Version).* Conference document no. 5/3, agenda Item 5 of the Diplomatic Conference on the Protection of the Marine Environment of the Baltic Sea Area, Helsinki, Finland. Helsinki, HELCOM.

HELCOM (1995). 'HELCOM Recommendation 16/9: Nitrogen Removal at Municipal Sewage Water Treatment Plants,' adopted 15 March 1995, *Baltic Sea environment proceedings No. 60: Report on the activities of the Baltic Marine Environment Protection Commission during 1994 including the 16th meeting of the Commission held in Helsinki 14-17 March 1995*. Helsinki, HELCOM.

HELCOM (1998a). *Baltic Sea environment proceedings No. 72: Recommendations for updating and strengthening*. Helsinki, HELCOM.

HELCOM (1998b). *The Baltic Sea Joint Comprehensive Environmental Action Programme Ministers Session: Recommendations for updating and strengthening*. Working paper. Helsinki, HELCOM.

HELCOM (1998c). *HELCOM Programme Implementation Task Force (HELCOM PITF) / The Baltic Sea Joint Comprehensive Environmental Action Programme Annual Report 1998*. Helsinki, HELCOM.

HELCOM (1998d). *Baltic Sea environment proceedings No. 71: Final report on the implementation of the 1988 Ministerial Declaration*. Helsinki, HELCOM.

HELCOM (1999a). *HELCOM Programme Implementation Task Force (HELCOM PITF) / The Baltic Sea Joint Comprehensive Environmental Action Programme (JCP) Annual Report 1999*. Helsinki, HELCOM.

HELCOM (1999b). *HELCOM Programme implementation task force (HELCOM PITF) Criteria for inclusion and deletion of hot spots: Procedures and guidelines for inclusion and deletion of hot spots, 21 May 1999*. Helsinki, HELCOM.

ICA (1988). *Aktuellt om miljövänligt* (Guide for Environmentally Friendly Products). Stockholm, ICA förbundet.

Iloniemi, E. (1999). 'Nordic dimension,' *Nordicum* 7:35.

International Legal Materials (1974). *Convention on the Protection of the Marine Environment of the Baltic Sea Area*. 22 March, 17, art. 3.

Kahn, J. (1998). *The Economic Approach to Environmental and Natural Resources*. New York, Dryden Pres.

Lariola, M. and Danielsson, B. (1998). 'Twinning cooperation between Kaunas Water Company, Lithuania and Stockholm Water Company.' Report to Swedish International Development Cooperation Agency, Department for Central and Eastern Europe; copy available from Infocenter, S-105 25 Stockholm.

Liiv, H. and Marksoo, P. (1998). 'The Helsinki Conventions 1974 and 1992: Implementation in the Baltic States,' *International Journal of Marine and Coastal Law* 13, pages 413-20.

Lindfors, L. (2000). 'The Baltic Sea—A common concern,' *Nordicum* 8, page 41.

List, M. (1990). 'Cleaning up the Baltic: A case study in East-West environmental cooperation,' pages 90-116 in Rittberger, V. (ed.). *International Regimes in East-West Politics*. London and New York, Pinter Publishers.

Ministry of Environment of Finland (1991). 'Pre-feasibility study no. 13: Reduction of the environmental effects of the power plants in Narva,' *Environmental Priority Action Programme for Leningrad, Leningrad Region, Karelia and Estonia*. Helsinki, Ministry of the Environment of Finland.

MoDo (1988). *MoDo Annual Report*. Stockholm.

OECD (1989). *The Pulp and Paper Industry in the OECD Member Countries*. Paris, Organization for Economic Co-operation.

Rachko, A. (1989). 'Measures to Prevent Baltic Sea Pollution,' *Tass* (Leningrad), 3 August.

Roginko, A. (1998). 'Domestic implementation of Baltic Sea pollution commitments in Russia and the Baltic states,' pages 575-637 in Victor, D., Raustiala, K. and Skolnikoff (eds). *The Implementation and Effectiveness of International Environmental Commitments: Theory and Practice*. Cambridge, MA and London, MIT Press.

Rosenberg, R., Elmgren, R., Fleischer, S., Jonsson, P., Persson, G. and Dahlin, H. (1990). 'Marine Eutrophication Case Studies in Sweden,' *Ambio* 19, pages 102-108.

SNV (1992). *Forest industry emissions to water and air 1991: Rapport 4086* [in Swedish]. Stockholm, SNV.

SNV (1992). *Marine Pollution '90: Action Programme for Marine Pollution*. Solna, SNV.

SNV (1993). *Forest industry emissions to water and air 1992: Rapport 4233* [in Swedish]. Stockholm, SNV.

SNV (1994). *Forest industry emissions to water and air as well as solid waste and energy consumption 1993: Rapport 4348* [in Swedish]. Stockholm, SNV.

SNV (1996). *Forest industry emissions to water and air as well as solid waste and energy consumption 1995: Rapport 4657* [in Swedish]. Stockholm, SNV.

SNV (1998a). *Forest industry emissions to water and air as well as solid waste and energy consumption 1996: Rapport 4869* [in Swedish]. Stockholm, SNV.

SNV (1998b). *Forest industry emissions to water and air as well as solid waste and energy consumption 1997: Rapport 4924* [in Swedish]. Stockholm, SNV.

SNV (1999). *Forest industry emissions to water and air as well as solid waste and energy consumption 1998: Rapport 4987* [in Swedish]. Stockholm, SNV.

Stensel, H. D. (1991). 'Principles of biological phosphorus removal,' pages 141-66 in Sedlak, R. (ed.). *Phosphorus and Nitrogen Removal from Municipal Wastewater: Principles and Practice.* Second Edition. Boca Raton, FL, Lewis Publishers.

Susiluoto, K. (1998). 'Defusing the ecological time bomb: An interview with Jaakko Henttonen,' *Nordicum* 6, pages 46-47.

SWECO, COWIconsult, VKI (1992). 'Pre-feasibility study of the Vistula River basin and Baltic coast of Poland part I: Synthesis report [draft].' Report produced in association with Hydroprojekt and Stolica (Copenhagen, Stockholm and Warsaw).

Taylor, R. (1990). 'Summit Calls for Baltic Clean-up,' *Financial Times* 5 September, page 13.

Teitenberg, T. (2000). *Environmental and Natural Resource Economics*. Reading, MA, Addison-Wesley.

United Kingdom Department of the Environment, Transport and the Regions (1999). *Economic Instruments for Water Pollution Discharges*. London, United Kingdom Department of the Environment, Transport and the Regions.

VanDeveer, S. (1999). 'Capacity building efforts and international environmental cooperation in the Baltic and Mediterranean regions,' pages 13-37 in VanDeveer, S. and Dabelko, G. (eds). *Protecting Regional Seas: Developing Capacity and Fostering Environmental Cooperation in Europe.* Washington, D.C., The Woodrow Wilson Center Environmental Change Security Project.

Victor, D., Raustiala, K. and Skolnikoff, E. (1998). 'Introduction and overview,' pages 1-46 in Victor, D., Raustiala, K. and Skolnikoff, E. (eds). *The Implementation and Effectiveness of International Environmental Commitments: Theory and Practice* Cambridge, MA and London, MIT Press.

Vistula Joint Venture (SWECO, COWIconsult, Water Quality Institute) (1992). *Pre-Feasibility Study of the Vistula River Basin and Baltic Coast of Poland: Part I Synthesis Report and Part IIB Technical Report Appendices.* Copenhagen, Stockholm and Warsaw, Vistula Joint Venture.

Weintraub, M., Grünfeld, H. and Winsemius, P. (1995). 'Strategic planning cuts green costs,' *Pulp and Paper International* 37, page 45.

Westing, A. (1989). 'Regional security in a wider context,' pages 113-21 in Westing, A. (ed.). *Comprehensive Security for the Baltic: An Environmental Approach*. London, Sage.

Young, O. (ed.) (1997). 'Rights, rules, and resources in world affairs,' pages 1-21 in *Global Governance: Drawing Insights from the Environmental Experience*.

7 National Ecological Networks in the Baltic Countries

Kalev Sepp, Jüri Jagomägi, Are Kaasik,
Zenonas Gulbinas, Oļģerts Nikodemus

Political and economical changes in the Baltic countries during the last decade have caused considerable changes in human interaction with nature. Intensive utilisation of forest resources is now a fact, since almost half of forest areas are becoming privately owned and many private forest owners regard it as a source of rapid income. Due to land reform and development of recreational activities, pressure is also increasing in coastal areas. Valuable agro-habitats are being lost: most of semi-natural grasslands and former pastures are overgrowing with brush, as farmers quite often have no capacity to continue grazing and grass cutting and traditional agriculture practices do not pay themselves off. The slow and incomplete privatisation process and inadequate rural policy have been the main reasons causing arable land abandonment. Currently around 20 per cent of the arable land is abandoned. This creates several environmental problems – decrease in biodiversity and esthetical value of the landscape, distribution of the weed seeds and danger of the fire.

Environmental deterioration, biodiversity decline and disappearance of traditional landscapes in the Baltic countries are some of the costs of increased pressure on natural ecosystems and changed land use, which in turn have called for new remedies such as new approaches and methodologies in spatial planning. The establishment of ecological networks has become one of the most widespread and promising applications through which ecological principles and biodiversity conservation requirements are integrated into spatial planning procedures and land use practices. During the 1990s the ecological network concept was implemented in environmental protection practice, especially in spatial planning in the Baltic countries.

The proposal to establish a Pan-European Ecological Network – PEEN – by 2005 has been endorsed by ministers from 54 countries in the UNECE region in 1995. The network will be one of the principal means through which the Pan-European Biodiversity and Landscape Strategy (PEBLDS) is to maintain and enhance natural diversity on the continent. The PEEN is a coherent assemblage of areas representing the natural and semi-natural landscape elements that need to be conserved, managed or, where appropriate, enriched or restored in order to ensure the favourable conservation status of the ecosystems, habitats, species and landscapes of European importance across their traditional range (Bennett 1998).

This chapter analyses the natural, social and economic preconditions for development as well as theoretical concepts and practical applications of ecological networks in the Baltic States (Estonia, Latvia and Lithuania) in the framework of the Pan-European Ecological Network. In this context the experience in classical nature conservation as well as the controversial impacts of social and economical re-structuring are also discussed.

Theoretical Concept and Practical Applications of Ecological Networks

Since the 1970s the concept of ecological networks has been developed by several authorities and by several scientific institutions throughout the world. This development has been simultaneous and often independent and therefore the concept is known by different names including *nature frame* in Lithuania, *network of compensatory areas* in Estonia, *territorial system of landscape territorial stability* in the Czech Republic and Slovakia, *green belts* and *protected nature areas systems* in Russia, *greenways* in the USA, Australia and Portugal.

The concept of ecological networks developed as a response to the fragmentation, restructuring and intensification of land use. It has gained a lot of support, probably because of an intuitive feeling for its beneficial functions and effectiveness. Unlike other approaches dealing with environmental problems by separate media (water, air, soil), different types and sources of pollution, or nature conservation issues by protection of single species and habitat types, the concept of ecological networks provides a more complex approach to nature conservation and environmental protection issues. It is an attempt to harmonise economical land use practices with environmental protection and nature conservation goals by maintenance or establishment of an interlinked territorial structure of natural and semi-natural ecosystems/areas.

According to the main presumption of the concept, it is particularly important to maintain or re-establish a sufficient network of natural areas throughout agricultural, industrial and urban areas. This network is proposed to have several functions. By providing habitats to local species driven away from neighbouring areas, this network of predominately native vegetation is a strong support to their survival. On the banks of lakes and rivers natural vegetation stabilises banks, filters sediments and nutrient run-off and prevents pollution and eutrofication of water bodies at least during the vegetation period. On roadsides and around urban and industrial areas it filters noise and the spread of pollutants and provides a cleaner and healthier environment for people. It also prevents erosion on slopes and deflation in sandy areas, and offers recreational activities in close to human settlements, etc.

Some authors (e.g. Kavaliauskas 1995) have found the origins of the concept from as early as the eighteenth century, when the idea of an 'ideal city' and the general aspirations of Romanticism radically changed the principles of urban planning. The models of integrated 'green belts' became a necessary part of urban structures in metropolitan areas, both in the USA (Little 1990) and in Europe, e.g. in Berlin, Prague, London, Budapest and Copenhagen in the first part of the twentieth century.

Common environmental challenges but different scientific and planning traditions have led to a situation where many similar issues have emerged. Reviewing recent developments concerning ecological networks, Arts et al. (1995) concluded that 'during the last decade, the nature conservation policies in many European countries have been based on landscape-ecological research, especially concerning the role of land use and landscape structure in the survival of species and in the protection of nature reserves. Plan proposals were made to establish ecological networks on local, regional and national scales.' At the moment, the planning of these networks may be considered to be one of the most important fields in which the results from landscape ecological research find application in territorial planning and nature conservation policies (Arts et al. 1995).

As a result of specific geographical, natural, economical, political and social conditions, and due to different scientific and planning traditions, the concept has developed differently in various countries and regions. Ecological networks have been designed mainly for abiotic purposes: regulating fluxes of water, energy and materials (Bridgewater 1988; Mander et al. 1988, 1995; Kavaliauskas 1994, 1995, 1996) or mainly for biotic purposes, i.e., maintenance of biodiversity (Brandt 1995; Van Zadelhoff and Lammers 1995; De Blust et al. 1995; Burkhardt et al. 1995). According to Jongman (1995) and Jongman and Kristiansen (1998), it is possible to distinguish two main approaches to ecological networks: ecostabilisation and bio-ecological. Landscape ecology from both its ecological and its geographical background has provided the necessary theoretical basis for both of these. Land use is considered to influence the functioning of ecosystems as a whole, its self-purification capacity and the carrying capacity of the landscape (Mander et al. 1988; Kavaliauskas 1995). It also affects habitat quality for wild species and the potential for dispersal and migration that are vital for the survival of populations especially in fragmented landscapes (Jongman and Kristiansen 1998).

Ecostabilisation approaches are based on an extensive analysis of the geographical and abiotic structures of the landscape. Theoretically the approach is based on the idea of a 'polarised landscape' that was suggested by the Russian geographer, Rodoman (1974). This concept means a functional zoning of the landscape elements into natural zones that antagonises the poles of intensive land use. The planning principles derived from this concept require a strict delimitation of natural zones, zones for nature restoration, and zones for recreation united into one coherent zone, which is proposed to polarise the zones selected for agriculture, industry and urban development. The fact that the idea of 'polarised landscapes' and planning concepts derived from it found response and support in Eastern Europe was not a coincidence but a logical consequence of the developed landscape pattern, in which a mosaic of pristine areas and heavily endangered areas/spots lay side by side. Hence it was/is not only a planning concept, but also a descriptive term of reality, and a convincing argument against extensive and monofunctional land use and orientation towards short-term economic profits.

According to Kavaliauskas (1995) the concept of the polarised landscape 'represents a territorial elaboration of the idea of sustainable development.' Rodoman's concept was a dialectical and holistic one developed within a deductive scientific tradition. Later, his formal and geometrical principles were developed to principles for practical ecological planning in the Central and Eastern European countries (in Estonia, Lithuania and Czechoslovakia) in the late 1970s and the beginning of the 1980s. This was done in co-operation between ecologists and territorial planners (Kavaliauskas 1995; Mander et al. 1995) and resulted in concepts like 'nature frame,' 'ecological compensatory areas' and 'ecostabilising functions.' Essential in these concepts are: 1) the determination of some territories to function as an ecological compensation for the territories that are heavily exploited; and 2) to connect these compensatory territories into one united and coherent land-management zone (Jongman and Kristiansen 1998). Designation of ecological networks for ecostabilisation purposes was related with interdisciplinary studies focusing on matter cycling in catchment areas based on computer modelling, and thus based on an analysis of a large amount of data from geology, geomorphology, geography, hydrology, soil physics, etc.

Bio-ecological approaches emphasise first of all the role of ecological networks in maintaining biodiversity. According to these approaches the principal aim of an ecological network is to unite nature reserves into one integrated territorial system in order to give better conditions for the dispersal, migration and survival of species. In general the bio-ecological approaches are more widespread in Western countries. In Northwestern Europe ecological networks have been applied on national and regional levels as a response to fragmentation and isolation in agricultural and urbanised landscapes. Similar approaches in the USA vary from case studies for conserving biodiversity in forests managed for timber production (Harris 1984) to large-scale plans attempting to link all the larger nature reserves and national parks in North America by ecological corridors that would stretch from Alaska to Mexico (Foreman et al. 1992).

The bio-ecological approach is based on the principles of McArthur and Wilson's (1967) 'island theory' that is stated as a 'global conservation strategy' by the World Conservation Union (IUCN), World Wide Fund for Nature (WWF) and United Nations Environment Programme (UNEP); and the concept of metapopulations as a spatially interpretable concept (Jongman and Kristiansen 1998). Several studies have demonstrated the positive effects of ecological linkages in fragmented landscapes for survival of viable populations (Diamond 1975; Opdam 1990; Limpens and Kapteijn 1991; Hanski 1994, 1998; Hanski et al. 1995).

The bio-ecological approach to ecological networks has led to some scepticism, criticism and debate (Hobbs 1992; for an overview, see Bennett 1999). According to Foppen et al. (2000), the criticism has focused mainly on the following aspects:

- Whether sufficient evidence is available to demonstrate the potential conservation benefits of ecological corridors (Simberloff 1988; Dawson 1994).
- Whether the potential negative effects of corridors outweigh the conservation value.
- Whether corridors are a cost-effective option in comparison to other ways of using scarce resources for nature conservation.
- Whether the understanding of ecological systems and the available data are sufficient for real designation of corridors in landscape.

To counterbalance criticism towards ecological networks, Jongman (1995) concluded that 'it is impossible to know ecological systems completely, although we might strive towards a better understanding,' and that 'planning for the future is always planning for uncertainty, also in planning of ecological networks.'

Natural and Social Preconditions for Ecological Network

The Baltic States are situated at the western edge of the East European Plain. The development of the landscape was strongly influenced by glaciers, which formed a typical landscape of lowlands and uplands. The coastal areas are transformed by fluctuations of the level in the Baltic Sea. There are several unique landscape formations especially in the coastal area of the Baltic region. The long Estonian coastline is characterised by the Baltic Glint, following the northern coast, and about 1,500 islands and islets. In Latvia the coastal areas are characterised by freshwater lagoons (Lake Engure, Lake Pape, etc.) important as nesting sites for birds. The most significant formations in Lithuania are the Curonian Lagoon and the Curonian Spit.

Thanks to variable natural conditions the Baltic States are rich in species and habitats and the biodiversity is remarkably well preserved. This is probably due to a relatively low population density and to a lack of economic development during the Soviet period and to long-term nature conservation traditions starting from the beginning of the twentieth century. The preservation of bogs, wooded meadows, wetlands, forests and several other landscape types, mostly destroyed in the rest of Europe, and the establishment of an extensive system of protected areas (Figure 7.1) have been possible thanks to the joint efforts of nature conservation activists, dedicated scientists and general public support.

As concluded in national biodiversity reports, when compared to other regions with similar areas situated between 56th and 59th northern parallels, the diversity of flora and fauna in the Baltic states is one of the richest in the world (EME and UNEP 1999; EPMRL 1998; LMEPRD and UNEP 1998). The main reasons for it are quite similar:

Figure 7.1: Protected areas according to national law, percentage of the national territory (BEF 2000)

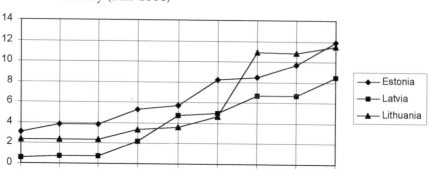

- diversity of climatic conditions;
- the existence of both islands (Estonia) and continent;
- the influence of the Baltic Sea;
- long coastline and large number of inland waters;
- diversity of soils (simultaneous occurrence of limestone and sandstone as a base for the formation of soils, and the resulting incidence of neutral, lime-rich and lime-poor soils);
- varying surface forms and water regimes determined by young and developing post-glacial relief;

Figure 7.2: Land cover types in Baltic countries according to CORINE land cover

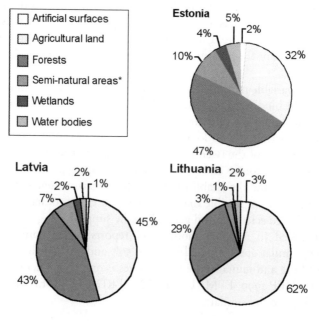

- extension of a large number of species distribution range borders to the territory of the Baltic States;
- large proportion of natural landscapes (Figure 7.2);
- retention of traditional land use methods until the middle (and in many cases until the end) of the twentieth century, and the respective relatively extensive maintenance of semi-natural habitats and the relatively unimportant role of alien tree species in forestry (EME and UNEP 1999).

Despite to drainage activities (Figure 7.3), wide areas of valuable wetlands have remained. Undisturbed coastal areas (wetlands, lagoons and lagoon lakes) are providing important resting and feeding sites for migratory birds. Several species, threatened on a European scale, are abundant in the Baltic States (e.g. beaver, wolf, otter, black and white stork, corncrake, lesser spotted eagle, cranes, etc.).

Figure 7.3: Area drained per year in agricultural land (BEF 2000)

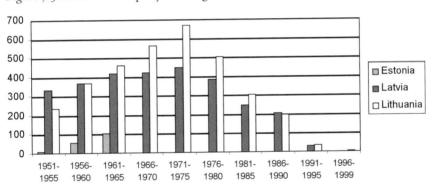

During the Soviet period the patchy mosaic type of landscape, characterised by small fields, grasslands and woodlots, was re-organised and replaced by extensive fields and extensive forests. Cultivated lands were transformed from small to large units especially because of wider use of industrial methods in agriculture. It has brought about contrary tendencies in land use and loss of valuable habitats. Meadows, marshes and fens have been drained for cultivation, and have some decades later been abandoned. Meadows rich in species have been cultivated into grasslands, while others have been afforested or overgrown with scrub. Water bodies have been eutrophicated caused by increasing use of fertilisers. By 1998 the percentage of arable lands (incl. sown lands) in Estonia and Latvia was the same as the European average, whereas Lithuania still has one of largest portion of arable lands (BEF 2000). See Figure 7.4.

However, recent political and economical changes have caused considerable changes in human interaction with nature. Intensive utilisation of forest resources has started as a result of the fact that almost half of the forest areas are becoming privately owned and many private forest owners regard them as a source of fast income. Due to land reform and the development of recreational activities,

Figure 7.4: Sown area, 1969-99, percentage of national territory

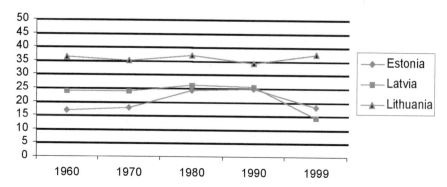

pressure is also increasing in coastal areas. On other hand, agricultural development is experiencing significant decline, which reduces the pressure from agriculture activities on landscapes (e.g. decrease of fertiliser and pesticide use), but also results in the loss of valuable agro-habitats. Most semi-natural grasslands and former pastures are overgrowing with brush, as farmers quite often have no capacity to continue grazing and grass cutting and traditional agriculture practices are unprofitable.

Development of National Ecological Networks

By adopting the PEBLDS in 1995 the Baltic States have pledged themselves to develop PEEN based on the common criteria of naturalness and biodiversity in a pan-European context (Van Opstal 1999). The PEEN is developed 'to ensure that a full range of ecosystems, habitats, species and their genetic diversity and landscapes of European importance are conserved: habitats are large enough to place species in a favourable conservation status; there are sufficient opportunities for the dispersal and migration of species; damaged elements of key systems are restored and the system are buffered from potential threats' (Council of Europe et al. 1996).

Co-operation between the Baltic States in developing ecological networks is justified and could be fruitful for several reasons:

– The natural conditions and general biodiversity characteristics are similar and consequently similar conservation strategies could be used.
– Political and social transition poses similar problems: controversial impacts of privatisation, changes in land use, increased pressure on coastal and forested ecosystems, need for new legislation, etc.
– Similar problems related to accession to the EU and the required approximation of national legislation with European nature conservation standards. Therefore, development of common position for negotiations with the EU is

needed for several purposes. The status of some species listed in the annexes of EU directives is relatively good in the Baltic States and in such cases it is not possible to apply the protection measures established in the directives. Also, there may be species and habitats in the Baltic that might need to be added to the annexes of the directives.

– All three Baltic States have ratified similar nature conservation conventions and are involved in similar international programmes. Complying with these obligations may require common actions.
– All three Baltic States have a remarkable experience in nature conservation and landscape planning.
– All three Baltic States have assumed the obligation to develop the PEEN.

The network will be built up from the following elements:

– *core areas* to conserve ecosystems, habitats, species and landscapes of European importance;
– *corridors or stepping stones,* where these will improve the coherence of natural systems;
– *restoration areas,* where damaged elements of ecosystems, habitats and landscapes of European importance need to be repaired or certain areas completely restored;
– *buffer zones,* which support and protect the network from adverse external influence (Council of Europe et al. 1996).

According to all methodologies the development of ecological networks is a process in which several sequential stages can be distinguished, e.g.:

– analysis of the initial nature conservation problems;
– identification of well-defined objectives of the network;
– defining the methodological approach for designation of ecological network and criteria for identification of its structural elements;
– analysis of existing databases, identifying the location of relevant data and possible gaps;
– identification of potential core areas, ecological corridors, and finally buffer zones and restoration areas if needed;
– designation of implementation strategy.

The Purpose of Ecological Networks

The *Estonian* approach tries to integrate bio-ecological, environmental and landscape aspects in the designation of ecological networks at all of its hierarchic levels. According to this approach the network should fulfil several functions: 1) to maintain natural self-regulation of the environment on acceptable (for human existence) level; 2) to protect valuable landscapes, ecosystems and species; 3) to provide opportunities for sustainable economic activities, life style and recreation;

4) to ensure spatial accessibility of natural areas for public use/enjoyment; 5) to preserve ecological, historical and aesthetic values of traditional cultural landscapes (Jagomägi and Sepp 1999). The network should preserve biodiversity in a wider sense than just at species level by facilitating the spread and migration of certain species. Moreover, it should preserve the diversity of natural and cultural landscapes.

The *Latvian* concept of ecological network is similar to the Estonian one: to conserve and improve important landscape structures, to ensure biological and landscape diversity of territories. Particular attention is paid to forest and meadow ecosystems, which protect surface water from pollutants, act as accumulators and compensators in urban environments, and are important for education and recreation (Nikodemus et al. 2000).

The aim of developing *Lithuanian* ecological network is to form a territorial system supporting landscape stability and preserving biodiversity, integrating it into the complex of a pan-European ecological network. The concept of the ecological network is based on conservation of rare and endangered species and valuable habitats by forming necessary structure of landscape elements. Lithuania's ecological network, on the one hand, has to comply with European requirements, on the other hand it has to fit Lithuanian conditions. The ecological network will be co-ordinated with the existing location of the nature frame as much as possible, and the pan-European requirements for biodiversity conservation will be achieved by adapting and expanding the existing system of protected areas. A very important short-term objective in Lithuania is to incorporate ecological network schemes into the national system of territorial planning as a way to ensure sustainable development and sustainable use of natural resources (Mierauskas et al. 2000).

Criteria for Designation of Ecological Networks

There are two criteria for the designation of structural elements of ecological networks: qualitative (indicating ecological values) and quantitative (e.g. size of core areas, width of ecological corridors and other morphometrical parameters). Various international conventions and agreements use different criteria on the basis of which international areas are designated. Often the criteria are rather broad: e.g., naturalness, biodiversity, threat, representativeness, uniqueness, etc. that cannot be directly measured without further specification.

All three Baltic States have decided to use the same criteria (naturalness and biodiversity) as suggested by Van Opstal (1999) for designation of ecological networks, but due to different natural conditions and experience in ecological networks (Estonian network of ecologically compensating areas and Lithuanian nature frame) additional criteria could be used.

National Approaches and Experience in Ecological Networks

Estonia and Lithuania were among the first countries in Europe where basic principles of ecological networks were developed. The Estonian 'network of ecologically compensating areas,' developed by Jagomägi (1983) and Mander et al. (1988, 1995) as well as the Lithuanian 'nature frame,' established by Kavaliauskas (1995, 1996), were accepted among the first analogous concepts in Europe (Baldock et al. 1993; Jongman 1995). Developed from Rodoman's (1974) purely theoretical concept of polarised landscapes, the Baltic approaches have been applied for functional zoning of landscapes for several purposes (including environmental, economic and social). Built up on the networks of protected areas (as core areas of the ecological networks) and interlinked by natural and semi-natural landscapes, they both support the maintenance of valuable habitats as well as migration and dispersal of species. Although the PEEN has a continental scope, its implementation depends to a great extent on national and regional initiatives, and it should be based on national nature conservation legislation and policies. Therefore, although the Baltic approaches are wider and not totally compatible with the ecological network in a Pan-European sense (designed mainly for European biodiversity conservation purposes), the theoretical and methodological experience, as well as supporting legal systems and planning traditions, provides a strong base for further actions.

The Ecological Network in Estonia

In Estonia a concept of ecological networks has been developed at local, regional and a national level since the 1960s. Elements of the now widely used concept can be found in several applications for functional zoning and landscape planning at regional level. In early 1980s a concept of the Estonian network was developed (Jagomägi 1983). This network was defined as an ecological infrastructure of cultivated landscape that is able to compensate and buffer human impacts, or in other words, influence the flow of matter, energy and information through the landscape as obstacle, accumulator, filter and buffer (Jagomägi et al. 1988). The network of ecologically compensating areas was designed on a scale of 1:200,000. In 1983-88 more detailed maps of ecological networks (1:100,000) were compiled for northeastern Estonia, the surroundings of Tallinn and the western Estonian islands (Saaremaa and Hiiumaa). These maps were intended to be used as spatial reference information for development programmes until 2005.

Despite a wide range of research and implementation capabilities in the country, the ecological network concept was not implemented in environmental protection practice after the country regained independence. Only in the mid-nineties the Act on the Protection of Coastal Areas (1994) and the Water Act (1994), prohibiting all building activities within 200 m of the coast line and lake shores, provided the first pieces of legal background for designing an ecological network as a part of county spatial planning processes. However, at present the ecological network concept is already better reflected in strategic and spatial planning

documents. The need for the formation and improvement of the network of protected areas can be found in the Estonian Environmental Strategy approved by
the *Riigikogu* (Parliament) (EME 1997). It aims 'to establish /by the year 2010/ a
network of nature reserves corresponding to EU recommendations where zones
of strict protection have to cover up to 5 per cent of the terrestrial area of Estonia.' The Estonian Environmental Action Plan (EME 1998) for the period 1998-
2000 provides for such actions as: a) setting principles for ecological network
design, b) defining elements of the ecological network and for the period of 2001-
2006 to update and develop the ecological network concept at the national and
regional level. As described by Sepp and Mikk (1998) the designation of ecological networks should be a part of landscape planning, which is the preparatory step
to spatial planning. The implementation tools may be different at different levels: at state and county level the main instrument is spatial planning.

In 1999 the governmental decree for the second phase of county planning
(1999-2002) on 'Defining environmental conditions for the development of land-
use and settlement structure' was issued. The county spatial plan is considered to
be a general development plan determining the legal framework for land use and
other activities. The main tasks of the second phase of county planning include:

–   design of green network at county level (planners are using a term 'green net-
    work' instead of 'ecological network');
–   defining valuable cultural/historical landscapes.

By 2002 each of the 15 counties must prepare a map of ecological networks as one
of the layers of spatial planning. For that reason at least two methodologies will
need to be elaborated; one for designing green networks and the other one for
defining valuable cultural landscapes.

The long-term strategy, 'Estonia – vision 2010,' approved by the government
in 2000, contains a chapter on 'green networks' and a schematic map on Estonian
green network. It defines an ecological network as a coherent system of extensively used areas in a comparatively good natural state that helps to maintain
biodiversity and stability of the environment. It consists of bigger core areas and
narrower corridors connecting them.

In the first round the present plan stipulates that the natural zones with the
area of more than 100 km² will be included in the category of core areas of national importance. The biggest of them are related to Alutaguse, Emajõe Wetlands,
Kõrvemaa-Lahemaa, Nigula Wetlands-Soomaa, Lower-Pedja region and West-
Estonian shoal and the western part of Saaremaa and Hiiumaa. The aim of the
strategy at the lower level is to guarantee the core areas of national importance
their present area and grant animals sufficient passage through the corridors.

The concept of ecological network in spatial planning has been discussed by
several authors (Mander et al. 1995; Külvik and Sepp 1998; Sepp et al. 1999;
Remm et al. 2001).

Ecological Networks in Latvia

In contrast to other Baltic countries, no national approach to ecological networks has been elaborated in Latvia. However, this does not mean that Latvia is lacking in ecological planning traditions and experience at all. In 1990 the scientific and planning institute Pilsetprojects worked out a 'Complex territorial scheme of nature protection in Latvia' as a first attempt to carry out a comprehensive summary and analysis of factors influencing natural resources (Priednieks and Kreilis 1999). More than 20 thematic overview maps, including a map on the system of particularly protected nature areas in the Latvian SSR, were prepared in the framework of the project. This was also the first time the concept of an ecological network was introduced. Based on an analysis of thematic maps an 'axis of ecological activities' in contrast to 'priority areas for urban development' was designated (Priednieks and Kreilis 1999).

After independence, the planning of ecological networks started at local level. Natural compensating territories (parks, forest parks, forests, rivers and lakes) were identified in the physical plans of Rīga, Jūrmala and Babīte and Pagast, which form a united structure.

A development plan for Kuldiga district in 1998 was the first attempt to introduce the concept of ecological network at a local level and by territorial planning procedures (Priednieks and Kreilis 1999).

Structures of the ecological network (biological centres, corridors, etc.) in the District are grouped by level of importance (national, regional and local) based on their habitat and landscape importance (area, biological and landscape diversity), representativity and uniqueness, presence of threatened and rare species, cultural-historical importance and as landscape elements or for landscape ecology.

The development of ecological networks is associated with laws regarding spatial planning (On spatial development planning (30.10.1998)) and Cabinet of Ministers regulations (Regulations on spatial planning; 05.12.2000) for specific planning levels. As a result, planning of ecological networks is not separated from general spatial planning conducted at various administrative levels, in which specific goals/use of territories are defined. This identification of territories makes it possible to structure requirements and actions needed to ensure participation in the ecological network and the respective land-use. Development of networks and various levels is consistent with the structure of the Latvian landscape or nature system.

National-level biocentres in Kuldiga District are formed by landscapes with high biological diversity which cover 18 per cent of the area, of which 5 per cent is in the prime zone. In Latvia, corridors include linear structures and also mosaic-type landscapes with 'green islands' which ensure seasonal movement and migration of species, population dispersal and connections within distribution areas, as well as appropriate feeding conditions to sustain the populations. The following aspects were analysed in the development of corridors:

- migration paths of salmon-type fish;
- bird migration paths and feeding areas;
- migration paths of land animals;
- elements of mosaic structures within agricultural landscapes;
- drainage divides with bogs between waterbodies;
- water outflow zones, spring areas;
- specific landscape structures; wind barrier zones on lowlands;
- suburban forests; gardens and parks in cities;
- tree hedges in rural areas.

Buffer zones were formed as barriers (land use, geochemical landscape barriers) to prevent negative impact; as areas for research, and for conservation of traditional land-use. Buffer zones included: animal feeding areas and landscapes functionally, visually and geochemically associated with biocentres. Based on the example of Kuldiga District, a national-level ecological network is being developed in Latvia.

Ecological Networks in Lithuania
The idea of Lithuania's nature frame was first raised in the national Integrated Nature Protection Scheme of 1983. Since then the concept of nature frame has become universal in the conservation and protection of Lithuania's natural landscapes (EPMRL 1998). In 1989, nature frame schemes were prepared at a national level and in 1993 at regional level for all 44 administrative districts (Kavaliauskas 1995). At the regional level the basic concern was the evaluation of compensatory ecological potential of the areas. This was done by considering 1) the degree of landscape cultivation and 2) the difference in geochemical activity of the soils that emphasised the need to develop differentiation in land management regimes and a new system of land management zones. These projects are considered as the basis for the detailed planning of agricultural areas on a local level in the scale 1:10,000 (LFN 1999).

The concept model for Lithuanian nature frame, as an integral system of geo-ecological compensation, based on ensuring exchange of substances, energy and information between landscape elements, was prepared by P. Kavaliauskas (1995, 1996). According to the concept, the main functions of the nature frame are:

1) To ensure that links between separate protected areas are protected.
2) To protect natural landscapes and natural recreation resources.
3) To neutralise the impact of economic activities in territories with intensive use.
4) To optimise structure of anthropogenic landscapes by creating conditions for the restoration of forests, and by regulating trends and intensity of agricultural activities and urban development.

The nature frame links all protected areas with other ecologically valuable areas or relatively natural areas that altogether form a system of geo-ecological compensation zones. In this zone land management is focused on forestry, recreation and nature conservation. The nature frame, as a land management system, is composed of three metafunctional subsystems:

1) Geo-ecological divides (geo-ecological watersheds), which are the territorial belts between different geosystems and fulfilling functions of ecological compensation on an intersystem level.
2) Areas of inner stabilisation (areas of conservation and biodiversity significance), which are fulfilling functions of ecological compensation inside the separate geosystems.
3) Migration corridors (linear territories like riverbeds, valleys, pit-grooves, etc.), which are fulfilling the functions of geodynamic exchange and biological information flow.

Among other policy instruments there are two documents which are the most important for biodiversity protection: the *National Environmental Strategy of Lithuania* adopted by the Ministry of Environment in 1996 and the *Lithuanian Biodiversity Strategy and Action Plan* adopted by the Ministries of Environment and Agriculture in 1998 (EPMRL 1998). These two legal instruments are considered to provide a framework for forthcoming environmental and biodiversity protection programmes in Lithuania (LFN 1999).

From a methodological point of view, ecological network and nature frame have different specialisation levels but from an organisational point of view they are analogous functional territorial formations that are understood as continuous hierarchical combinations of concentration centres of certain functions and connecting axes. Both are based of buffering compensation and biodiversity conservation areas from economic activities. According to their main purpose, ecological network and nature frame are in principle compatible.

From the point of view of structure and development, identification of nature frame and ecological network is actually possible, because the most important functional units are identical. At the highest level, structures are based on the same large forest areas, lake and wetland complexes, and river valleys. Both networks cover main protected territories (Lithuanian Fund for Nature (LFN) 1999). Designation of ecological network at the national level in Lithuania would be very important instrument in the development of the general master plan for the country with the particular importance for the conservation of landscape and biological diversity.

Conclusion

Compared with the preconditions in Western Europe, the natural preconditions for a well-functioning ecological network in the Baltic States are fairly good. Because of diverse natural conditions the national biodiversity indicators are high in all Baltic States; and mainly due to low population density and inhibited economic growth during the Soviet period, the biodiversity is remarkably well preserved. In Estonia and Latvia vast natural areas (forests and wetlands) still exist, and in all Baltic States anthropogenic impacts have not yet affected the areas of high biodiversity values to the same degree as in Western Europe.

The ongoing social and economic restructuring (mainly privatisation) has controversial impacts on land use and landscape structure. In theory, the re-establishment of small farms has a potential to increase the diversity of agricultural landscapes. In practice, large proportions of agricultural land are currently untended, and this may lead to degradation of traditional rural landscapes. Orientation towards short-term economical profits has caused increased pressure on coastal and forested ecosystems and other areas with high market value.

The existing national approaches represent multi-functional approaches to ecological networks. Based on the networks of protected areas (as core areas of the ecological networks) and interlinked by natural and semi-natural landscapes, they were both designed to support the maintenance of valuable habitats as well as the migration and dispersal of species. Although the Baltic approaches are not totally compatible with the ecological network in a pan-European sense, and the European nature conservation priorities have not been (sufficiently) considered in their designation, the theoretical and methodological experience, and planning traditions provide a strong basis for further actions.

According to provisional methodologies developed in the framework of the project, the designation of national ecological networks in the Baltic States will be based on both the existing approaches and landscape planning traditions, and the international obligations related with EU Habitat and Bird Directives, nature conservation conventions and other agreements. Therefore, the purposes of the national networks are slightly different: the Latvian and Lithuanian networks will be established for bio-ecological and eco-stabilising purposes (in Lithuania network landscape aspects are integrated). The Estonian approach tries to integrate bio-ecological, environmental and landscape aspects in designation of ecological networks.

The criteria for designation of ecological networks (and their structural elements) must take into account both the common criteria and guidelines for establishment of the PEEN and the natural characteristics of the Baltic States. For designation of core areas the qualitative criteria, naturalness and biodiversity together with the size criterion, will be used. The location and character of ecological corridors will depend on the location and habitat character of core areas. The designation of restoration areas is considered less important in the Baltic States (especially in Estonia and Latvia).

According to all three methodologies, the designation of ecological networks will be more or less based on GIS and existing digital databases. The databases that are considered to be relevant for the designation of ecological networks include similar databases for all Baltic States like CORINE Biotopes and Land-Cover maps, IBAs database, digital base maps, etc.; or specific databases on distribution of species and habitats, etc.

Baltic co-operation in the development of ecological networks between governmental and non-governmental institutions is beneficial for several reasons, but especially for exchange of ideas and experience, and for considering regional and transboundary (compatibility) aspects.

The establishment of ecological networks is practically impossible without public support or against people's will on the basis of restrictive law. Therefore public awareness and dissemination of information among all stakeholders are crucial factors for the successful implementation of ecological networks.

Note

[1] This study was supported by the Dutch Government within the framework of the project 'Development of national ecological networks in Baltic countries in the framework of a pan-European ecological network.'

References

Arts, G.H.P., Van Buuren, M., Jongman, R.H.G., Nowicki, P., Wascher, D. and Hoek, I.H.S. (1995). Editorial. *Landschap*, Special issue on ecological networks 12:3, pages 5-9.

Baldock, D., Beaufoy, G., Bennet, G. and Clark, J. (1993). *Nature conservation and new directions in the common agricultural policy*. Report for the Ministry of Agriculture, Nature Management and Fisheries of the Netherlands. Arnhem, Institute for European Environmental Policy.

Baltic Environmental Forum (BEF) (2000). *Baltic States of the environment report: Based on environmental indicators*. Riga, Baltic Environmental Forum.

Bennett, A.F. (1999). *Linkages in the landscape*. The IUCN Forest Conservation Programme. Gland, Switzerland and Cambridge, UK, IUCN.

Bennett, G. (1998). 'Guidelines for the Development of the Pan-European Ecological Network.' Draft. Council of Europe, Committee of Experts for the European Ecological Network. STRA-REP (98) 6.

Brandt, J. (1995). 'Ecological Networks in Danish Planning,' *Landschap*, Special issue on ecological networks 12:3, pages 63-76.

Bridgewater, P. (1988). 'Ecolines & Geolines: Connectivity in natural landscapes,' in Schreiber, K.-F. (ed.). *Connectivity in Landscape Ecology*. Proceedings of the 2nd international seminar of the International Association for Landscape Ecology, Münster 1987. *Münstersche Geographische Arbeiten* 29.

Burkhardt, R, Jaeger, U., Mirbach, E., Rothenburger, A. and Schwab, G. (1995). 'Planung Vernetzter Biotopsysteme,' *Landschap*, Special issue on ecological networks 12:3, pages 99-110.

Council of Europe, UNEP and European Centre for Nature Conservation (1996). *The Pan-European Biological and Landscape Diversity Strategy, a vision for Europe's natural heritage*. Council of Europe, UNEP, European Centre for Nature Conservation.

De Blust, G., Paelinckx, D. and Kuijken, E. (1995). 'The green main structure for Flanders,' *Landschap*, Special issue on ecological networks 12:3, pages 89-98.

Diamond, J.M. (1975). 'The island dilemma: Lesson of modern biogeographic studies for the design of natural reserves,' *Biological Conservation* 7, pages 129-46.

Environmental Protection Ministry of the Republic of Lithuania (EPMRL) (1998) *Republic of Lithuania. Biodiversity conservation strategy and action plan*. Vilnius, Publishing Bureau of Environmental Protection Ministry of the Republic of Lithuania.

Estonian Ministry of Environment (EME) (1997). *Estonian national environmental strategy.* Tallinn, Estonian Ministry of Environment.

Estonian Ministry of Environment (EME) (1998). *National environmental action plan: Estonia.* Tallinn, Estonian Ministry of Environment.

Estonian Ministry of the Environment (EME) and United Nations Environmental Program (UNEP) (1999). *Estonian biodiversity strategy and action plan.* Edited T. Kull. Tallinn and Tartu, Estonian Ministry of the Environment and Environmental Protection Institute of the Estonian Agricultural University.

Foppen, R.P.B., Bouwma, I.M., Kalkhoven, J.T.R., Dirksen, J. and Van Opstal, S. (2000). *Corridors of the Pan-European ecological network: Concept and examples for terrestrial and freshwater vertebrates.* Report prepared within the framework of the Committee of Experts of the pan-European ecological network under co-ordination of the European Centre for Nature Conservation.

Hanski, I. (1994). 'A practical model of metapopulation dynamics,' *Journal of Animal Ecology* 63, pages 151-62.

Hanski, I. (1998). 'Metapopulation dynamics,' *Nature* 396, pages 41-49.

Hanski, I., Poyry, J., Pakkala, T. and Kuussaari, M. (1995). 'Multiple equilibria in metapopulation dynamics,' *Nature* 377, pages 616-21.

Hobbs, R.J. (1992). 'The role of corridors in conservation: solution or bandwagon?' *Trends in Ecology and Evolution* 7, pages 389-92.

Jagomägi, J., Külvik, M., Mander, Ü. and Jacuchno, V. (1988). 'The structural-functional role of ecotones in the landscape,' *Ekologia* 7:1, pages 81-94.

Jagomägi, J. and Sepp, K. (compilers) (1999). 'Concept, principles and criteria for development of ecological networks in Estonia.' Development of national ecological networks in Baltic countries in the framework of Pan-European ecological network, Projects report. Tartu, University of Tartu and Institute of Environmental Protection. Manuscript.

Jongman, R.H.G. (1995). 'Ecological networks in Europe: congruent developments,' *Landschap,* Special issue on ecological networks 12:3, pages 123-30.

Jongman, R.H.G. and Kristiansen, I. (1998). *National and regional approaches for ecological networks in Europe.* European Centre for Nature Conservation report: STRA-REP (98) 18, submitted to the Council of Europe as a part of the implementation of the Work Programme of the Pan-European Ecological Network.

Kavaliauskas, P. (1994). 'Land Management in Lithuania: Past and Future,' *GeoJournal* 33:1, pages 97-106.

Kavaliauskas, P. (1995). 'The Nature Frame: Lithuanian experience,' *Landschap,* Special issue on ecological networks 12:3, apges 17-26.

Kavaliauskas, P. (1996). 'Lithuania: the nature frame' in Nowicki, P et al. (eds). *Perspectives on Ecological Networks.* ECNC publication series on Man and Nature, Vol. 1. Tilburg, European Centre for Nature Conservation.

Külvik, M. and Sepp, K. (1998). 'Eesti – tugev sôlm Euroopa ökovôrgustikus [Estonia – a strong knot in European ecological network],' *Eesti Loodus* 5/6, pages 198-200.

Latvian Ministry of Environmental Protection and Regional Development (LMEPRD) and United Nations Environmental Program (UNEP) (1998). *National report on biological diversity: Latvia.* Riga, Latvian Ministry of Environmental Protection and Regional Development.

Limpens, H.J.G.A. and Kapteijn, K. (1991). 'Bats, their behaviour and linear landscape elements,' *Myotis* 29, pages 63-71.

Lithuanian Fund for Nature (LFN) (1999). 'Projects No. 75666/3: Development of national ecological networks in Baltic Countries in the framework of Pan-European ecological network, I phase final report.' Vilnius, Lithuanian Fund for Nature. Manuscript.

Little, C.E. (1990). *Greenways for America.* Baltimore, John Hopkins University Press.

Mander, Ü., Jagomägi, J. and Külvik, M. (1988). 'Network of compensative areas as an ecological infrastructure of territories,' pages 35-38 in Schreiber, K.-F. (ed.). *Connectivity in Landscape Ecology.* Proceedings of the 2nd international seminar of the International Association for Landscape Ecology, Münster 1987. *Münstersche Geographische Arbeiten* 29: 35-38.

Mander, Ü., Palang, H. and Jagomägi, J. (1995). 'Ecological networks in Estonia: impact of landscape change,' *Landschap*, Special issue on ecological networks 12:3, pages 27-38.

Mierauskas, P., Sinkevicius, S., Gudzinskas, Z., Rasomavicius, V. Ivainskis, P., Kesminas, V., Kurlavicius, P., Mickevicius, E. and Baubinas, R., (2000). 'Lietuvos ekologinio tinklo koncepcija ir jo sudarymo principai [The concept of Lithuanian Ecological Network and Principles for its Creation],' *Aplinkos tyrimai, inzinerija ir vadyba* 1:11, pages 3-13.

Nikodemus O., Kreilis M., Strazdiņa B., Buša V. (2000). *Planning of ecological network in Latvia: principles and methods.* Latvian Geographers Congress, Rīga. Association of Latvian Geographers.

Opdam, P. (1990). 'Dispersal in fragmented populations: The key to survival,' in Brunce, R.H.G. and Horward, D.C. (eds). *Species dispersal in agricultural habitats.* London, New York, Belhaven Press.

Priednieks, J. and Kreilis, M. (compilers) (1999). *ECONET development in CEECs*, IUCN project No. 75598X/Latvia. Unpublished project report in University of Latvia, Riga.

Remm, K, Külvik, M., Mander, Ü. and Sepp, K. (2001). Design of the Pan-European Ecological Network: A national level attempt. In press.

Rodoman, B.B. (1974). 'Polijarzacija landsafta kak sredstvo sochraenija biosfery i rekreacionnych resursov [Polarization of landscape as a manage agent in protection of biosphere and recreational resources],' *Resursy, Sreda, Raselenije*, 150-162. Moscow, Nauka.

Sepp, K. and Mikk, M. (1998). 'Estonia' in *The development of common approach to the design and implementation of the national ecological network in Central and Eastern Europe.* Proceedings of international workshop 23-25 May 1998, Konstancin-Jeziorna, Poland, 20-26. Warsaw: IUCN Office for Central Europe.

Sepp, K., Palang, H. Mander, Ü. and Kaasik, A. (1999). 'Prospects for nature and landscape protection in Estonia,' *Landscape and Urban Planning* 46, pages 161-67.

Van Opstal, A.J.F.M. (1999). *The architecture of the PEEN: Suggestions for concept and criteria.* Wageningen and Tilburg, IKC-N and ECNC.

Van Zadelhoff, E. and Lammers, G.W. (1995). 'The Dutch Ecological Network,' *Landschap*, Special issue on ecological networks 12:3, pages 77-88.

8 Breaking Loose?
Russian Reasons to End Its
Dependence on Foreign Ports

Alf Brodin

Introduction

Background

As a consequence of the dissolution of the Former Soviet Union, foreign trade between the Russian Federal Republic and Western Europe had to adapt to an essentially new geopolitical environment. One task was to find new routes and to establish a different framework for the conduct of water-borne transport. Nevertheless, to a very large extent prevailing trade patterns, despite many discontinuities, e.g. in exchange relations, were prisoners of the legacy of the past. In the absence of immediately available better alternatives, Russian cargoes had to be carried through the now independent Baltic States to reach ports that previously were parts of the Soviet Union. These ports were originally outlined and built within the framework of a centrally planned economy and received their cargo volumes through administrative directives. To the annoyance of certain political and nationalistic circles in Russia, ports in the Baltic States competed successfully with Russian ports for Russian foreign trade cargoes.

In later years, several attempts have been made from the Russian side to address the situation by constructing new port capacity in the Gulf of Finland. The aim of this chapter is to describe and analyse the new transport geography of Russia with regard to such reassessments of needs and possibilities. Basically, the situation is characterised by two opposite tendencies: on the one hand, new and improved foreign trade routes, port competition and market economic adaptation and on the other, a neo-mercantilist evaluation of the foreign economic interests on the part of Russia: that such dependencies should be avoided and that both economic and transport efficiency support the build up of domestic capacity.

Sources, Methods and Limitations

The chapter is based on an extensive use of various sources of information, and a multitude of methods. Many secondary sources of both international and Russian origin provide the basis. Relevant data have as far a possible been collected from its sources, often the different ports, but also a number of home pages on the world-wide-web. During fieldwork, all major ports in western Russia, from Arkhangelsk on the Arctic coast and west- and southward ending in Novorossiysk on the Black Sea, have been visited at least twice during recent years. A word of caution is always appropriate, especially so when reading about agreements by different parties to the realisation of plans and investments, as the time lag from plan to final implementation is long, and more often than not, subject to delays and reversals. The reigning unpredictability can be lamented, but should not make us abstain from attempts to find up-dated information and to be cognisant about where the uncertainties reside.

What will be discussed here is limited to the parts of the fSU port sector directly affected by the geopolitical changes in areas adjacent to the Baltic Sea since the falling apart of the fSU in 1991. Although there are many interesting aspects to highlight in Russian transport patterns and in the Russian use of foreign inlets and outlets, the emphasis is put on ports and projects in Russia. For this reason, only projects on Russian soil are described in greater detail.[1]

Russian Transport Routes

The Limited Choice of Outlets

The relatively densely populated and heavily industrialised part of Russia, west of the Ural Mountains has traditionally served as the centre of industrial production, agriculture as well as the origin of most of its foreign trade. It is in this part of Russia that such major transport volumes are generated – either imported or exported – and create a demand for port capacity.

In its current shape, Russia has natural access to open sea in all four cardinal directions. A brief evaluation of the situation along these coastal fronts reveals that there are many limits to the build- up of port capacity and feeding land transportation systems. The claimed open access to major seas is in reality somewhat illusionary. In the north, Russia has only two major international ports, Murmansk and Arkhangelsk, but practically only Murmansk can handle regular all-year traffic.[2] East of these two seafront cities, along the Arctic coastline, a considerable number of mostly very small but locally important ports can be found. In the Far East, there are a number of ports located along the Pacific coastline, located thousands of kilometres away from their main markets in central Siberia, and nearly two weeks away from Moscow by normal freight train. Most of them, however, suffer from severe ice-problems and only the three most southern, Vladivostok, Vostochny and Nakhodka can be considered to be operating efficiently.

A severe problem along the whole of the Russian southeastern land border is an exceptional practical transport matter stemming from the nineteenth century. The width of the railway-gauge in the fSU area remains wider than in its neighbouring countries; 1524 mm instead of the more commonly used standard of 1435 mm. This same problem occurs along all outer land borders of the fSU, with Finland and Mongolia as the two exceptions. Along the southern coastline, in the Black Sea, only Novorossiysk, the largest of the fSU ports, and the port in Taupse have remained under Russian federal control. All other important ports in the Black Sea, like Odessa and Nikolayev, belong to the Ukraine.

To make the tour around Russia complete we must look at the Baltic Sea, where a driving force throughout Russian history has been to secure access, but once again, this has been severely curbed.[3] Within the Soviet system, the three Baltic republics controlled most of the extensive Baltic Sea coastline, and it was here that the port infrastructure was created, and the bulk of Russian exports and imports are transiting.[4]

Traditionally the likes of Mayer (1957) could clearly demarcate the hinterland of ports, but the hinterland of Russian, Baltic and many of the larger European ports, has today become increasingly hard to demarcate. Increased competition, long distance transits and the influence on the choice of transport routes from other factors than merely the price has contributed to loosen the links between the hinterland and a particular port (Hoare 1986; Klaassen 1987). When studying ports in the former Soviet system, where extreme specialisation of firms and central decisions steered the cargo flow to the port available, ports were often distant from the site of production. Average transport distances could therefore be anything from 1000 kilometres to both 2000 and 3000 kilometres (Mellor 1982; North 1996). This pattern has not changed much. Even now, in western Russia and the Baltic States, it is difficult to identify the origin of cargoes and to establish a fixed hinterland. The abundant Russian deposits of raw material and natural resources are widely scattered, but they seldom generate transport activities geared towards one particular outlet only.

The 'Containment' of Russia by the Baltic States

Looking at it in another way, since the break-up of the fSU, the three Baltic States have a number of well oversized ports, at least in relation to their own production and direct needs. If seen from a Russian perspective, several very important ports, as a result of the independence of the Baltic States, form part of an integrated infrastructure beyond direct Russian control.[5] The geopolitical importance of these ports is given by the fact 70-95 per cent of the cargoes handled are *'en route'* from or to Russia. The most important of these ports in the Baltic States, from north to south, are Tallinn, Riga, Ventspils, Liepaja and Klaipeda. (For location see Figure 8.2). It is likely that Russia wants to wield as much influence as possible over the routes and the ports as long as they belong to an interdependent transport system.

It is this Russian dependence that constitutes the basis for an analysis of Russian interests. These interests could be highlighted by two different ways of reading the situation. As mentioned in the introduction and according to a liberal view on market logic, there is plenty of room for the creation of positive interdependencies between the countries based on demand and supply of goods, available routes and transport capacity and port resources. Basically, according to this line of reasoning, there are few contradictions in relations between Baltic States and Russia. However, we would like to make a scrutiny of a second set of assumptions and the corresponding chain of argumentation: Geopolitical reasoning about the competitive nature of interests and the value of having control appear to offer a different but apt framework for understanding motives and arguments in Russian domestic politics and planning. To be forced to make use of foreign ports for both export and import operations is seen as a major annoyance by Russia, a country marked by a long tradition of autarchic thinking. The following quotation from the writings of one of the founders of the early geopolitical school, the Swedish professor Rudolf Kjellén could describe the complexity of the situation:

> 'Even state bodies have their Achilles heels and their hearts. Such vital parts are primarily the capitals and the big arteries of trade' (Kjellén 1917: 50, author's translation).

For the Baltic States, their possession of transport corridors and deep-water ports on the open coast might thus constitute an Achilles' heel of their big neighbour. It is not improbable, according to this view, that such assets will remain a source of irritation, even when other reasons for conflicts have been sorted out.[6] It is well known that relations between Russia and Baltic States have often been filled with tense since independence. There are many reasons for this state of affairs, and domestic disorder and periods of economic crises in Russia has sustained distrust. Russian transport problems are not the only problems taken into consideration when the Russian side evaluates its relationship with the Baltic States and its own needs for new port capacity. Of course, not only questions concerning transit issues are at stake from the Russian point of view. Nevertheless, transit issues have often been used as a way of executing pressure on the Baltic States for results during negotiations, or as a form of punishment, no matter what has been negotiated.

At the same time, Russia is a state with a constantly increasing dependence on world trade, and where the westbound trade routes will continue to be of great importance for foreign currency earnings. Russia may be the world's largest country, but when it comes to access to port facilities, there are certain restraints such as the control of and the handling of cargo that are nominally in foreign hands. Russian cargo owners must pay the costs for the use of these transit routes, the cargo handling and all other transport expenses, in foreign currency. It is as break-bulk points on these important routes that the ports of the Baltic States have become key-players in a large-scale geopolitical game.

Russian Western Transport Corridors[7]
Russia's transport containment has been mentioned as an often-neglected fact in the analysis of the Russian political economy. The focus will now turn to problems related to the Russian transport geography together with existing and possible

transport corridors. The problematic situation of suitable transport routes is evident when confronting Russian international trade. In almost all potential transport solutions to and from Russia, and despite an increasing share of land transport, seaports are inevitable.

An attempted illustration of all major Russian trade corridors to countries in the West is given in Figure 8.1. In principle, ten different transport corridors can be identified, but as a simplification, these have been grouped into three main categories, being numbered from 1 to 3. Each of the three main categories indicated portray one of the possible types of trade routes that are presently available.

Figure 8.1: Russian western transport corridors

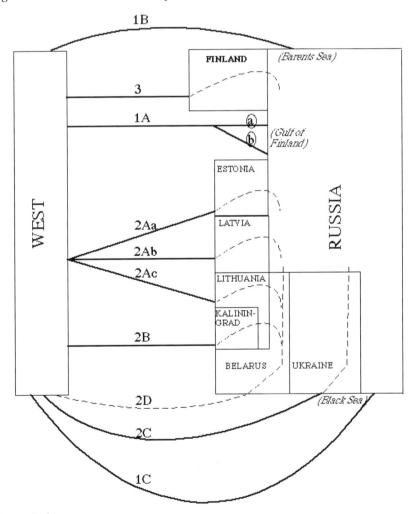

Source: Author

1   **Direct link from a Russian port to markets in the West**
   1A   *direct from a Russian port in the Gulf of Finland*
   1B   *direct from a Russian port in the Barents Sea*
   1C   *direct from a Russian port in the Black Sea*

The biggest advantage, to these three alternatives, from a domestic point of view, is that they completely avoid the involvement of a third country for transhipment.[8] The ideal corridor of the three is, of course, 1A. Not even this route is without drawbacks though, largely in the form of capacity restraints in the few existing Russian ports in the area; St Petersburg, Vyborg and Vysotsk. This route, using existing ports, has been indicated by 1Aa, while the lower leg of the arrow, 1Ab, indicates a possible future flow over projected Russian ports in the Gulf of Finland. A more detailed description of both existing ports, and those under construction, will be given later, but what is stressed here is that the *would-have-been* ideal export route, for the time being largely remains a *could-have-been* ideal export route. The 1B alternative indicates the use of ports in the Russian Barents Sea, such as Murmansk and Arkhangelsk. These two corridors, 1A and 1B, are naturally directed towards the West. The third of the corridors, 1C, suffers from longer transport distances on land and at sea , but in addition also requires the passage of the Bosporus Strait. After a number of incidents in the Turkish strait, strong resistance is mounting against the use of this corridor for larger transit volumes, of especially crude and petroleum products.[9]

2   **The six different corridors grouped under 2 all indicate a transport corridor between Russia and the markets in the West that include the crossing of one, or more, foreign borders before reaching a port**
   2A   *exported from one of the Baltic States*
   2B   *exported from Kaliningrad, in Russia, but cargoes must cross the borders Belarus/Lithuania, Latvia/Lithuania, Belarus/ before reaching a port*
   2C   *exported from a port in the Ukraine crossing one border and a long overland transport to reach a port*
   2D   *cargoes could transit practically any country bordering Russia to be transported overland, through e.g. Belarus, the Ukraine, Poland, to European destinations*

From a Russian domestic point of view, none of these four alternative corridors could be said to be ideal. All involve the crossing of one or more foreign borders, a process that presently, and for the near future, will remain a time-consuming and often insecure process. Depending on the kind of products transported and applicable customs regulations, taxes, transit fees etc. must be paid in foreign currency. Which of the different corridors that can be said to be the most suitable could probably not be determined without a deep knowledge of the type of cargoes and volumes involved. The 2A alternative remains the most widely used, 2B is in limited use, 2C is restrained by the problematic economic and administrative situation in the Ukraine, but has slightly started to regain its importance during 1999 – 2000, while 2D is used mainly by trucks carrying import cargoes, but less so for export.[10]

3   **The Finnish corridor**
    indicates a transport corridor through Finland from Russia and on to markets in the West, but still includes the crossing of a foreign border

When making use of this alternative, cargoes must cross the borders of one of the EU member states, before reaching a port destination. Having once crossed an EU border, there will be a less complicated access to other member countries to which much of the Russian export is destined. This is also the only important transit corridor through a western country and a connection that was in use even during the years of the fSU.

As shown in Figure 8.1, a number of different transport routes can be distinguished for transports between Russia and Western Europe. The choice depends on the type of cargo that is to be moved and the prices quoted. Generally, the route going through Finland, (no. 3 in Figure 8.1) has long been considered to be the safest of the three major westbound alternatives while the inland route through Poland has been considered the cheapest. All three alternatives have an estimated transit time between Rotterdam and Moscow of about one week. That is if the transport for the Baltic and Finnish alternatives are co-ordinated with a departing ship. Large-scale studies have clearly indicated that Russian companies generally regard transport costs to be the key issue in their choice of route (VTT 1997). This indicates that future links must not only be efficient but also prove cost-efficient in order to become successful among Russian users.

Of all the alternatives described above only the very first one, 1Aa (existing ports in the Gulf of Finland), and to some extent 1B (Russian North West), could be said to correspond to Russian primary needs. Other alternatives show serious drawbacks by way of dependence on other countries, money outlays or longer transport distances, or all in combination. From this respect, it can be understood that since the early 1990s Russia has argued that new port capacity should be added in the Gulf of Finland to enhance capacity where it is best needed.

The arguments brought forward so far stress the present geopolitical situation in the Baltic Sea region, and argue that relations between the countries remain tense much due to the complicated Russian transport situation The current transport and port situation causes a severe strain on the Russian economy that touches on Russian self-esteem and thereby potentially fuelling hostile attitudes towards her smaller neighbours.

The Russian Economic Situation

For Russia, as for all countries undergoing economic transition, the first years lead to deep economic recession. By the time the fall in output levelled off, output had on average fallen by more than 40 per cent. By 1999, GDP had regained growth in Russia, as in virtually all the 25 transition countries. Governance problems have in several countries, together with an endemic corruption that has proved difficult to stamp out, severely hampered a positive development.[11] Since the Russian August 1998 financial crises, economic forecasts for the future have shifted. For the first half year after the initial crisis, the tendency was very negative, and then recovery slowly started and became very positive for the last quarter of 1999 and during 2000. A turn of events that was fuelled by the resignation of President Yeltsin and the appointment of President Putin. For 1999, GDP growth landed at 3.2 per cent while estimates for 2000 indicate a growth in the range of +6.7 per cent (Bofit MIR, 1-2001). Forecasts for 2001 indicate a continued growth of +3.6 per cent (EBRD 2000). To put this in perspective though, it should still be mentioned, that if the Russian recovery could be maintained, on par with the 2000 GDP increase of 7 per cent per year, it would still take Russia some 25 years to catch up with the West.

Continued systematic subsidies given to energy and raw-material extraction industries, even during transition years, made it possible for some, through an often far from transparent process of issuing government export licenses, to re-sell locally procured primary products for export with a considerable margin (author's interviews). A process that, at the same time, generated a considerable share of the transit volume. To do business in Russia forces entrepreneurs to challenge a problematic legal system with changing rules, with a weak and problematic enforcement, corruption, high taxes and organised crime which together makes it quite an ordeal. Russian economic policy, at both national and regional levels, is strongly influenced by businesspeople that are accustomed to lobbying, corruption and paternalism.

Vested interests in the leading Russian economic circles might themselves be willing to accept certain reforms, for two reasons. First, they might decide that their long-run interests are best served by a society in which property rights are protected and the rule of law prevails rather than one ruled by lawlessness, as in much of the CIS today. Second, because it could be better to look beyond possible short term profits to create better future conditions for growth of both national economies and personal wealth. Albeit statistically very insecure, the flows of capital out of Russia indicate that Russia has remained the only capital exporter in the whole group of transition countries throughout the transition period. This could be interpreted as a sign of lacking confidence in the domestic market from capital owners.

When Vladimir Putin replaced President Boris Yeltsin, he started his period in the wake of a strong economic recovery that has followed the near fourfold devaluation of the rouble in August of 1998. Strong public support allowed Putin to win the presidential election without having to articulate a detailed economic program, but instead promised the Russian electorate the much talked about 'stronger role for the state.' The high price of money in Russia, where bank interest rates have for long been maintained in the +25 per cent/year range, has instead contributed to the wide-spread use of money surrogates (*veksels*), barter trade and in turn the generation of both tax and wage arrears (Shleifer and Treisman 2000). One result of this process, in combination with other processes described above, is that long-term financing of infrastructural projects, where the building of ports is just one example, becomes extremely difficult. This at the same time as the importance of foreign trade to the national economy is increasing. Throughout 2000 though, both macroindicators and industrial indicators have remained favourable and, perhaps most important of all, Putin has been given room for manoeuvre by a sustained +30 USD/barrel world petroleum price for most of 2000. As much as 1/3 of state incomes in 1999 were generated within the field of foreign trade, a share that is likely to have increased considerably during 2000 (Goskomstat 2000 www). Its share of state income generated through foreign trade will probably continue to grow, especially so in the wake of the new tax reform that considerably lowers personal income tax. Much of the explanation of the heavy state dependence on trade-generated incomes, and other fees, derives from the fact that 45 per cent of the economy, according to the Deputy Minister of Interior, Makarov, belongs to the shadow economy (Interfax 2001-02-09). Today when the EU accounts for a constantly increasing share, around 40 per cent, of total Russian foreign trade, and 50 - 60 per cent of foreign trade in the Baltic countries, this mounting need for trade related infrastructure is an understandable process (Bofit QIR 4-2000, Bofit MIR 1-2001 www). If transit trade is important for Russia, it is even more so for the ports, railway and trucking companies, but also for the national economies of the three Baltic States of Estonia, Latvia and Lithuania. This is shown by the fact that roughly 10-17 per cent of the 1999 GDP in these states could be derived from incomes generated directly or indirectly by Russian transit trade (Central Statistical Bureau of Latvia, Statistical Office of Estonia, Statistics Lithuania 2000 www).[12]

The Russian Transport Sector

This chapter will concentrate on the Russian port sector with the aim of discussing recent developments. As the need for port capacity can, largely, be derived from the economic well-being of a country, as described in the previous chapter, positive economic development coupled with a stable political situation is often a prerequisite for sizeable and long-term investments like ports. The main part of the chapter will discuss handling and the situation in existing ports as well as different Russian port projects in the Baltic Sea.

The Soviet Legacy for the Ports
Russian practise when it comes to the handling of cargo in ports has two typical peculiarities from Soviet times; the *first* phenomenon is the practice of loading/unloading directly into railway cars while the *second* is the imbalance in volume between loading and unloading. Two features that have proved remarkably hard to change (Ranger 1998-11-13).

Total handling in Russian ports for 2000 has been estimated to 140 mt. A total figure that could roughly be complemented by some 65 mt that were handled in the Baltic States, some 20 mt in the Ukraine and the 4-5 mt being handled in Finland to make up a much larger present total volume of no less than 230 mt.[13] A figure, if compared to the fSU high of 166 mt from 1983 and 185 mt from 1989, indicating that Russia, together with the other fSU states, over the years has become exceedingly involved in sea-borne world trade. Volumes mentioned also indicate an overall need to increase port capacity as larger volumes are being handled in the fSU area today than 10-15 years ago.[14] This could be stated, avoiding complicating the discussion by bringing in factors such as shifts over time in the patterns of trade and the relationship between the categories of the cargoes handled, processes that under market economic circumstances force transporters and ports to make changes and adapt continuously, which was never really done in fSU times.

If World Bank estimates from 1996 give a correct indication of the situation in the port sector there was only be a minor need to increase Russian port capacity. Capacity was estimated to be sufficient for most types of cargoes, but not adequate for containers and for the handling of petroleum (Hayter interview 1997-09-09). Over the few years since the results of this study were made public, it has been the ports in the neighbouring countries that have been reacting in line with the findings. Since 1997, the petroleum-handling capacity in the Baltic States has been expanded in nearly all ports. A new buoy-loading terminal has been built in Lithuania, handling in Klaipeda has been thoroughly upgraded, and the petroleum handling in Tallinn-Muuga port has been the real success story. New container terminals have been opened in both Klaipeda and Ventspils, while one is under construction in Tallinn and just inside the Finnish border capacity has been doubled in Kotka and much enhanced in Hamina. This quick decision-making and the capability to find willing investors by its foreign competitors have proved impossible to match for Russian ports. Still the rhetoric has been loud in Russia when it comes to the need to extend domestic capacity. What has been argued for during transition years is new capacity, large enough and efficient enough to make the choice of a domestic routing viable for shippers. From this respect there are few other practically possible alternatives than expansion of the 1Ab alternative in Figure 8.1 (new capacity in the Gulf or Finland).

With this development in its neighbouring countries as a background, it can be no surprise that Russian domestic calculations have tried to estimate the annual cost for Russia to make use of these foreign facilities and was in Morskie Porti (2:1997) given as USD 600-700 million per year. Other sources, such as Business in Russia (Sept. 1997) indicated USD 300 million to USD 1.5 billion per year, while the most commonly given figure during the late 1990's was USD 3 billions per year (Parfenov 1999-10-23). The figure used by Prime Minister Kasyanov in a meeting with the Leningrad oblast government in late 2000 was again USD 1.5 billion (*Moscow Times* 2000-09-13). None of these sources included any calculations, and therefore nothing can be said about the price tags that have been set to different factors and about what kind of costs have been included or not. It would be of great interest to know if such calculations include only transport costs or have been set to include e.g. 'lost' taxes and intended dues and fees only. The most interesting thing here is that transport-related advantages in the argumentation, like shorter distances, speedier handling a s o, are only superficially, if ever, mentioned. The argument used to make viable this increase in capacity has continuously been focused on the 'costs' incurred to Russia by way of 'lost' revenues. If such an analysis concentrates on short-term benefits for the port authority involved, it can always be expected as being positive. If what is at stake is the common good of Russia and its citizens in a social cost-benefit analysis, then the answer is probably far from as clear cut. What is also lacking is a presentation of the economic calculations and alternative solutions to the projects proposed. It is therefore understandable that the long-term benefit of port investment projects can easily, and often rightly, be questioned. This is especially so in an environment where an absolute minimum of the background information is made publicly available.

What Russia has at hand, which has not been, at least publicly, discussed in the Russian debate on this issue is that there are a complete set of some 15 ports in six countries, from Poland to Finland, all competing to handle its cargo. Some of these, like the ports in the Baltic States, have no other alternative than to handle Russian transit cargo. Few countries in the world have a better chance to make use of the market forces to play out one port against the others in order to secure an as cheap handling as possible with a minimum of state involvement. That state-directed investments in new capacity could possibly out-price this set of competitors is probably hard to make many western economist believe, and should perhaps, rightly, be questioned.

Ports in the Gulf of Finland
Of the list of 40 Russian seaports for which official statistics are being presented, only four can today be found in the Baltic Sea. Of these, three are in the Gulf of Finland and the fourth being Kaliningrad. During the years of the fSU, another five major Baltic ports, Tallinn, Riga, Ventspils, Liepaja and Klaipeda, could have been added to this list. The relation in turnover between these two groups of ports in 2000 indicates a 2.6 time's higher turnover in the ports of the Baltic States than what is being handled in Russian ports (see Table 8.1).[15] With such a limited Russian port sector, it is not difficult to understand the excitement showed for port projects in the main Russian outlet in the Baltic Sea. A number of factors that point in favour of establishing new Russian ports here are:

- no real competition from other Russian ports in the East, South and North;
- export and import cargoes transiting westwards most often originate from densely populated and industrialised locations in western and central parts of Russia;
- cargo owners routing cargo to/from Russian ports would prefer to avoid the reigning insecurity and costs of additional border crossings.

Apart from making new port projects attractive for investors, the argumentation is in principle also valid for the three ports in operation in the Gulf of Finland, Vyborg, Vysotsk and St Petersburg. However, they suffer from certain drawbacks. The two smaller of these three ports, Vyborg and Vysotsk, are, together with other ports in the Leningrad region, being organised under the same port administration (Kareva 2000).[16] The port in Vyborg is located in the city centre of the former Finnish town with the same name, while the port in Vysotsk is located on an island on the eastern side of the Gulf of Vyborg. Both ports are restricted by the relatively shallow waters in the gulf, in the range of 7-8 meters, and both have for several years had a turnover of approximately 0.5 and 2 mty respectively. A rapid increase for the port of Vysotsk during 2000 however, has nearly lifted its turnover to 3 mty. The turnover for both ports is dominated by different bulk cargoes and with an extreme export orientation; with 95-100 per cent being outbound. As for the port in the city of St Petersburg, the volumes are much larger, although tradition is much shorter.[17]

All port facilities in the St Petersburg region are administrated under the same Sea Port Administration and turnover figures presented are, since three years back, the combined figure for all port handling facilities in the region. In 2000, the turnover for the port area reached 32 mt, while the JSC Sea Port of St Petersburg company that runs most of the terminals in the seaport had a turnover of nearly 19 mt (PR department of the JSC 'Sea port of St Petersburg'). The three ports demonstrate different ownership forms as the port in Vyborg is state property, the port in Vysotsk has been privatised with foreign, mostly Norwegian investors, while the port in St Petersburg has largely been privatised with the help

Figure 8.2: Port geography in the Gulf of Finland

Source: Compiled by the author from various sources

of local/domestic investors. As for the two smaller of the ports, also the port in St Petersburg also has a problem with access. This is because arriving ships must enter via a near 30-km channel from the island of Kronstadt, with its limited draught of 11 meters and other limitations in navigation. As the three ports are located in the inner parts of a gulf, wintertime ice packing, due to westerly winds and low salt content in the water, is a common problem.

A geographical disadvantage that the two city ports have in common is that the ports area is completely circumvented by the city itself. This complicates plans for expansion and leads to increasing risks in handling cargo in the port area and during transport to and from the ports. On the other hand, St Petersburg has one advantage that none of the competing ports in the Baltic Sea can match, which is its direct access to the Russian canal system via the River Neva. With the European tendency towards an increased use of canals for long-distance bulk transport, this could prove to be a considerable advantage for the port in the future (Rissoan 1994).[18]

Table 8.1: Turnover in larger fSU ports, 1998-2000 (1000 tonnes)

Port	1997	1998	1999	2000	Important cargoes in the port
Russia					
St Petersburg	20.6	21.6	28.5	32.0	Oil, general cargo, containers, pulp wood
Vyborg	0.8	0.6	0.7	0.7	Pulp wood, general cargo
Vysotsk	0.9	1.8	2.0	2.9	Coal, pulp wood
Kaliningrad	3.2	4.4	3.7	2.8	Oil, coal, pulp wood, ferry cargo
Total	25.5	28.4	34.9	38.4	
Baltic states					
Tallinn	17.1	21.4	26.4	29.3	Oil, ferry cargo, pulp wood, steel, grain
Riga	10.2	13.3	11.3	13.3	General cargo, containers, pulp wood
Ventspils	36.8	36.0	34.1	34.8	Oil, oil products, chemicals, fertilisers
Liepaja	2.1	2.3	2.3	3.0	Pulp wood, steel, general cargo
Klaipeda	16.1	15.0	15.0	19.4	Oil products, fertilisers, steel, ferry cargo
Total	82.3	88.3	89.1	99.8	

Source: Statistics supplied by each of the ports listed

During the years of transition, St Petersburg has been considered an expensive port for shippers, which is a major explanation why St Petersburg has had difficulties in attracting cargo. Dues and fees have been set at levels well above competing ports in the Baltic countries (County Administrative... 2000).[19] Corruption and bureaucracy are two more factors often referred to as reasons to avoid using Russian ports, but in later years, things have clearly improved in this respect. Despite the above mentioned problems expansion plans are optimistic and the city foresees a turnover in the range of 60 mty in 2010 for the combined ports of St Petersburg.

Arguments for Port Investments

When as much as half of the Russian foreign trade volume is directed towards the Baltic Sea, our contention that the existence and control over well functioning ports in this region is of obvious vital interest to Russia is well supported. However, before describing the individual Russian port projects being planned in the Gulf of Finland, some general arguments for new port investments should first be discussed. As investments in new or extended ports often involve huge sums of money, a number of positive effects from the investment can also be identified. The crucial question is whether the effects will prove positive enough, in the long run, to give an acceptable payback on what has been invested. When new capacity appears in the market, enhanced competition will inevitably make possible profit margins shrink, if there is not a corresponding supply response. Some of the effects that are likely to lower unit costs for cargo can easily be identified as:

 − lower costs as e.g. larger ships can be accepted;
 − lower costs as a result of shorter transport distances for customers;
 − lower costs as more up-to-date equipment is introduced;
 − lower costs as traffic is not lost to other ports;
 − lower costs as the port attracts extra traffic

If the above set of statements can be fulfilled by a project it is definitely a good beginning, but there are more factors that must be evaluated. When new investments are made, it should be remembered that lowered transaction costs, which is what port developments are often hoped to result in, must be shared between the developer and users. It is rarely the case that a developer can isolate all positive effects for himself. Instead these benefits must be shared with domestic cargo owners and in an international port, such as one's being discussed here, possible welfare effects must be shared with foreign users.

To be able to calculate who will come out on top requires deep knowledge, e.g. about the price elasticity of cargoes handled, and what kind of cargoes that are expected to be handled. It would probably be more accurate to discuss a kind of 'combined elasticity.' Such calculations should also entail the competitive situation in the regional port sector, near future development for the cargoes in question as well as general economic development trends, both in the national market and in the consumer markets for the products in question. A set of questions like these could not be answered satisfactorily. It is therefore understandable that the long-term benefit of port investment projects can easily, and often rightly, be questioned. The problem is compounded in an environment where only an absolute minimum of background information is publicly available.[20]

To open up several new ports will pave the way for another risk factor; the 'hop-around' of shipping lines between the different ports. This might constitute a most severe risk for the ports in this part of the Baltic region, especially as only a minor share of the handled cargo has a local origin and with relatively similar distances to large consumer regions. The new volumes of cargo that will appear in the market just because of the availability of new port capacity are probably fairly limited, apart from eventual, not yet constructed, long distance pipelines. The effects of public transport infrastructure development on regional and national economic development in general has been a highly debated topic in economic geography for decades. Recent evidence though, has demonstrated, that 'linkages are more complex than specified heretofore in the literature and that previous estimates of these linkages are likely to be subject to specification – error and simultaneous equation bias' (Tally 1996: 1). However, some scholars emphasise the positive side and see transport investments as a 'catalyst for growth' (Garrison 1994) while others (Harvey 1990) show that such investments, despite their good intentions, run the risk of 'crowding out' other more rewarding investments.

Since President Putin was elected and the new Kasyanov government came to power, a pressure has been created in favour of the completion of proposed port projects. During his St Petersburg year Putin was indirectly involved in negotiations around these long-lived port issues, and is probably very familiar with all kinds of factors that have previously been restricting the development of these projects.

The Building of Ports in the Gulf of Finland

If one compares the flow of Russian cargoes through ports in the Baltic Sea with existing Russian port capacity, it could perhaps be placed beyond doubt that Russia needs more domestic port capacity in the Baltic Sea. In the kind of sweeping Russian economic estimations about the costs of using foreign ports, it is not stated from whose point of view the arguments for more capacity should be seen and who will benefit from it. The difficulties in finding long term financing from non-state sources for proposed ports can well be a result of this lack of transparency.

The first decision to build new ports in the Gulf of Finland was taken as early as in 1992, but President Yeltsin came to sign a second decree to build three new ports in the Gulf of Finland when he visited St Petersburg on June 6, 1997.[21] Two of the ports included in the decree, Primorsk and Bukhta Batareinaya, are primarily to handle petroleum, while the third, Ust-Luga, is to serve as a general cargo and container terminal, in its first phase, and later also for coal-transit. To organise the preconditions needed for the construction of these new ports from a juridical point of view, has proved very difficult and unpredictable.

Of the four proposed Russian port projects in the Gulf of Finland, the project in Primorsk is currently the one most likely to have the first ship dock at its quays, perhaps even before the end of 2001. As can be seen in Table 4.2 Primorsk is not only the largest, but also the most expensive of the projected ports. As in the case of the other projects, also Primorsk has an eight-year official history. Over the years, construction of the different projects has appeared to be on the point of starting, or has even been started, but work has come to a standstill again. The first of the projects to enter its construction phase was Ust-Luga, as early as 1992, but several juridical processes and financial crises have kept the project from reaching even near-completion. Land ownership, foreign direct investment legislation, JSC legislation, environmental examinations and undercover-interest infringements are just some examples of the most difficult hurdles to pass for a new project where each issue can be taken to court, resulting in months of delays. Both the ports in Primorsk and Ust-Luga are examples of exactly this problematic procedure, having passed through several court appeals, before the projects reached a stage where construction could have been fully started; if the financing had been in place. The project at Primorsk, which is intended to become the new large export terminal for crude petroleum and petroleum-products has state funding from the still state-owned pipeline operator Transneft, that got construction work going at Primorsk by early April 2000. Tank facilities and quayage for a crude petroleum terminal is under way together with the initial 300 km pipeline connection, first of all from the refinery in Kirishi, some 100 km east of St Petersburg and the bypass needed under the Neva river. This however, is a minor problem compared to the 2700 km of pipe-line, often referred to as the , needed to feed the terminal at full capacity from the petroleum fields in the Timan-Pechora fields in the northern Komi oblast.

Plans at Ust-Luga were originally to build a large container terminal, but the plans have over the years come to include nearly all possible fields of activity for a port, while the current plan includes a coal and a fertiliser terminal for export. In 1998, the project was taken over by Rosterminalogul and construction was active during 1999, but came to a standstill for parts of 2000. Now, state funding looks likely to get the port into a workable condition, perhaps during 2001, even though that was also stated during 2000.

Table 8.2: Projected ports in the Gulf of Finland

Project	Operator	Est. cost*	1:stage cap.	Full cap.	Ship size	Dist to St P	Handling
Primorsk	Transneft	3.700	12 mty	45 mty	150.000	170 km	Crude oil & products
Ust-Luga	Rosterminalugol	2.400	7 mty	35 mty	70.000	120 km	Coal, fertiliser, steel
Batareinaya	Surgutneftgas	1.000	3 mty	6 mty	40.000	60 km	Oil products
Lomonosovo	"Yantar"	200	4 mty	6 mty	30.000	45 km	Metals, container, refrig.

* = Estimation in USD million for full capacity [22]

Source: Information collected by author from various sources

The port in Bukhta Batareinaya is also to have a pipeline connection to the Surgutneftgas refinery in Kirishi, but its location, only six kilometres from the four nuclear reactor power plant in Sosnovyj Bor has proved problematic. The intended pipeline (not initiated at the time of writing) is supposed to pass near the nuclear plant, which has caused much criticism. Owing to the existence of the power plant, some 10-km in all directions is a restricted area for visitors (even for local Russians), including the intended port location, and a special permit is needed to enter.

The nearby, and the smallest of the projects, the port in Lomonosovo, has its location inside the St Petersburg city border as its biggest advantage. The port is to be built near a smaller existing port, partly by way of landfillings. In Lomonosovo, the project is promoted by local business and the regional community, but the project is currently in the hands of the Ministry of Transport, that owns the contractor Yantar, but no funds seem to be available to get construction work started in the near future.

Large-scale dredging will be needed in all the ports to form approach channels and make it possible to turn ships in the ports. For the moment, of the four port projects mentioned here, only the port in Lomonosovo, can show any cargo turnover. The four projects, of which two have been partly initiated, are all in different stages of preparation, which from one month to the next could change from a complete standstill to intensive construction work and back to a standstill the following month. If just two of these ports would come into operation within a few years' time, the result would be a considerable capacity injection into the Russian part of the Gulf of Finland.

As has probably been understood already from the short descriptions above, the necessary supporting infrastructure, from housing for workers to good road and railway connections for large scale port developments, exists in the city, but not in the surrounding Leningrad oblast, where the coastal areas needed for development can be found instead.

The Russian Exclave of Kaliningrad

Soviet port cities could often demonstrate a number of planning influences that were the result of military considerations, but few better than Kaliningrad. Here, the armed forces came to fully dominate the region. With its position, at the south-western-most corner of the country, it was a strategic location for the Soviet Union, and has become even more so for Russia. The navy in particular established itself here, with the Baltiysk base as home port for the Soviet Baltic Fleet, along with a multitude of other branches of the defence. Due to the high level of military concentration, the oblast was forbidden territory for foreigners during Soviet years, and practically continued to be so until 1993. The oblast's present position, as the last remaining Russian fortress in the west, bordering a NATO country, possibly new EU members and as en exclave, has strongly enhanced Kaliningrad's geopolitical position.

This position has during the first month of 2001 allowed the oblast to make a comeback into the highlight of European media. The first incident that appeared in US press was the allegation that Russia was moving nuclear weapons into the region (*Washington Times* 2001-01-03). This was followed within days of the news that Germany was negotiating an economic take-over as a part of a debt-for-shares-deal concentrated to the Kaliningrad region. A move that was presented as if intended to enhance German influence in the region and indirectly restore the former German region of Königsberg (*Daily Telegraph* 2001-01-21). This at the same time as one of the priorities during the Swedish presidency of the European Union, during the first half of 2001, has been the EU eastward extension. An extension that would give rise to the problem of having Kaliningrad as an enclave in-between the two future EU members of Poland and Lithuania. This is a situation that give rises to new, and still to be solved, transit and transport issues making future, but perhaps already reluctant, foreign investors even less eager to enter the region.

When it comes to commercial port activities these are concentrated in the centre of the city of Kaliningrad, where the port area is located in the mouth of the river Pregol. The port in Kaliningrad can only be reached via a 40-km long canal which permits one-way traffic for ships under 10 000 dwt. The largest of the three port basins is the Kaliningrad Sea Port, still controlled by the Ministry of Agriculture, once the former fishing port, but now nearly completely converted to normal commercial activities. The Sea Commercial Port of Kaliningrad, the now privatised remains of the former state port structure, operates the two smaller of the basins in the port. The potentially best port in the region is located at the Baltiysk Navy Base by the open sea, if the base were to open up to commercial activities.

Kaliningrad's current position as exclave has for several reasons proved to be a problem as all passenger and goods movements by train or road between the

Figure 8.3: Possible transit routes Russia-Kaliningrad

NB: lines do not indicate existing infrastructure.
Source: Compiled by the author from various sources

Kaliningrad Oblast and mainland Russia must now cross foreign territory (corridor 2B in Figure 8.1). This routing either includes the crossing of the borders of at least two neighbouring countries such as e.g. Lithuania and Belarus, or another of the combinations indicated in Figure 8.2. Russian disclosures about the contents of certain transit goods are rare, an issue that has become a bone of contention with Lithuania. A Russian proposal to create a privileged corridor from Belarus through Poland, a few years ago, stirred up bad feelings and was later withdrawn. The only possible domestic way to reach the Oblast is by sea from the St Petersburg area, but this alternative remains in limited use, although a new ferry connection is being discussed from Ust-Luga.

The problems of goods movement caused by the geographical position of the region has also lead to difficulties in the port sector. The turnover in the port of Kaliningrad has remained on more or less the same level over the last ten years and the take-off in volume that has been hoped for has so far not happened. This despite the fact that the port sector has probably lived some years in a favourable position with the former director of the fishing port, Gorbenko, being governor in the region. He has reclaimed this directorship, though strongly disputed, after losing the election in late 2000 to the commander of the Russian Baltic Fleet in the region; General Yegorov.

Since the Gulf of Finland, the only other Russian seashore in the Baltic Sea, offers few suitable locations for port establishments, the Kaliningrad region has, throughout the transition years, marketed itself as a possible alternative. There have also been a number of different port projects launched in the region, but up until the beginning of 2001, no other project than the one initiated by LUKoil for a petroleum-export terminal, has really materialised. This export terminal was opened in November of 2000 and should by late 2001 reach its full 5-mty capacity (IPR 2000 www).

From a positive point of view, the region could be looked upon as having a geographically very suitable position – acting as a possible gateway to and from mainland Russia. This has also been the idea behind major local initiatives in the region, like the long-term project to develop the 'Yantar' free trade zone, a zone that has for years been counteracted by the central administration in Moscow.[23] Since the break up of the Soviet Union, a number of different proposals have been discussed concerning the future of the oblast. Anything from business as usual, the forming of the Yantar free-zone (to become the 'Hong Kong' of Europe), forming some kind of loosely connected federative part of Lithuania, being re-integrated with Germany (at least economically), forming an independent fourth Baltic State, or some form of more or less independent unit within the Russian Federation. With an already overloaded agenda for the next few years within the EU, with internal affairs such as a common currency and external affairs such as the eastward extension, there will probably be very little chance to highlight Kaliningrad on the agenda. It can therefore be assumed that once again it is the geopolitical considerations, from a Moscow's perspective, that will get the upper hand, over what could be considered to be the best strategy from a local Kaliningrad perspective.[24]

Conclusions

Seen from a Russian geopolitical position, the ports of the Baltic States should long have lost most of their transit turnover, but the relatively quick adaptation by the ports in the Baltic states to more efficient ways of operation than their Russian competitors has not allowed this to happened. This fact is clearly demonstrated by the large transit volumes that are still today being handled in the three Baltic countries At the same time, the expected and forecasted building of new Russian port capacity has not been realised either. The complexity of the present Russian transport geographical situation, as it was demonstrated in Figure 8.1, together with years of economic recession in Russia have not made possible the realisation of the grand plans that do exist. So far, it has not been possible for Russia to break out from its port and transport containment, forming a strong link between transport geography and geopolitics.

The new Russian government that was formed in the spring of 2000 under President Putin, has probably been given an insiders view of the multidimensional problems that has made port-construction in the Gulf of Finland such an infected issue. This knowledge can probably considerably facilitates the construction of new port capacity, e.g. in the Gulf of Finland. Other factors such as the positive economic development, political stability and an inspiring, above USD 30/barrel, petroleum price, have for the first time during the transition years, paved the way to again revitalise one, two, or perhaps even all of these long talked about infrastructure projects.

This paper has not attempted to analyse these questions as an issue based on pure economic aspects, because this could well prove to be completely misleading. It might be that questions of transport economics are not the most important once. What is at stake is the securing of transport routes and domestic export outlets for the future, which is seen as a must for a country as export dependant as Russia. To revive the words of Kjellén above, what we could be witnessing is an attempt to 'heal one of Russia's wounded Archilles heels', here in the form of re-establishing a large transport artery on non-disputed Russian soil.

Post Script

In a rudimentary attempt to make me understand the logic of Russian port construction plans in the Gulf of Finland, a Russian friend in the port/shipping sector used the following example:

> 'For me as a Russian the export of our goods to earn foreign currency has the same importance as the export of Volvo's for Swedes. If you did not have a port in Gothenburg, do you sincerely think that there would not be a port project there, no matter the logics and costs, if the current alternative for Volvo and Sweden would be to use ports in Norway?'

Maybe this is the way one should look upon the Russian need for more port capacity. This instead of insisting that there should be an economic and logical idea behind a project. If this is the 'real' explanation to these port projects, then no level of efficiency, and no price level, in Baltic ports could secure a transit flow passing theses ports. From a logical way of reasoning, pure efficiency, because of the present fierce competition between the ports, could well have become the decisive factor in favour of continued large-scale transit trade. Even though the Baltic states might hope this, events during the last year has made it more likely than ever before that new Russian ports will be build in the Gulf of Finland to break previous dependence. What makes predictions insecure is the fact that the problem for Russia during transition years has not been to name its priority projects, but to achieve them.

Notes

1   In Brodin (2000) a wider approach can be found that also describes alternative Russian routes that make use of ports in the Barents Sea and transit traffic through Finland and ports in the Baltic States.

2   The detour needed to reach e.g. Hamburg from Moscow via Murmansk instead of Tallinn add some 1500 km (or some 90 per cent) to the transport distance by sea (Lloyd's Maritime Atlas 1998).

3   Losses of access to the Baltic Sea that have occurred in 1918, 1940 and in 1991.

4   Transit should here be understood as the transport of cargoes passing the port area en route to a customer in the hinterland of the port, or to a ship in the port (Vigarié 1979).

5   A perspective that sees Russia as the natural bearer of the Soviet heritage (Nove 1992).

6   What is often referred to is the large Russian ethnic minorities in Estonia (app. 30 per cent) and Latvia (app. 35 per cent) (Smith 1995). There are also unsettled border disputes between the countries.

7   In the following, the text, for simplicity, only refers to Russian export transactions. This is because export volumes are normally many times larger than import volumes, but the discussion could simultaneously be said to cover even import transactions, in the opposite direction.

8   A possible 1 D route would be shipments over ports in the Russian Far East, or overland through the Central Asian republics, but such routes include too long detours to be considered further.

9   When international passage rights in the Bosporos Strait were negotiated in 1931, on average three larger commercial ships per day passed, whereas in 1997 the average was nearly 140. 1985-97 nearly 200 accidents and groundings were registered (*Lloyd's List* 1997-11-26). In 1936, Istanbul had 900 000 inhabitants and today 10-12 millions live in the metropolitan area near the 500 meters wide Strait.

10   It should not be forgotten, though it is outside the field of study, that the overland export route is very important for the Russian export of oil and gas through several pipelines that cross e.g. Belarus, Ukrainian and Polish territory.

11   A statement by Duma anti-corruption committee chairman Nikolai Kovalev: 'a recent survey in St Petersburg found that 98 per cent of businesspeople there had suffered extortion attempts, and 96 per cent admitted bribing officials' strongly support this (Quoted in *Paralamentskaya Gazeta*, 2001-02-01). None of the transition countries has been given a very good rating in later years by the Transparency International rating of corruption levels. Russia being number 82 of 90; on par with Kenya.
(www.transparency.de/documents/cpi/2000/cpi2000.html)

[12] An extreme figure, never seen before, was given by Duma Foreign Affairs Committee Chairman Dmitrii Rogozin 'Russian transit made up an important part, according to some estimates up to 30 percent, of Estonia's GDP' (RFE 2001-02-19 WWW).

[13] Less than 5 per cent of handling in 1999 was cabotage, despite preferential handling fees that apply to cabotage cargoes and the long Russian coastline. (app. 15 per cent in Sweden the same year). Handling in Finland has often been given a disproportional importance and is only in the range of 6-8 per cent of the volume handled in ports of the Baltic States.

[14] Russian demand in 2000 was 240 mt of which 33 per cent was transhipped through neighbouring countries according to deputy minister of trp. Yakunin (Min. of Trp 2001-01-30 WWW)

[15] Calculated from the statistics as presented in Table 3.1 (98.8 / 38.4 = 2.6). For 1996, the same figure was 5.7. The large difference is, mainly, due to a below 10-mty turnover in St Petersburg in 1996 (Morskie Porti no 1 1997: 13).

[16] It should be remembered that the City of St Petersburg and Leningrad Oblast, where these ports are located are two strictly separate administrative units. St Petersburg and Moscow are the two city-states within the Russian Federation while Leningrad Oblast is one of the 87 regions.

[17] The ports in Vyborg and Vysotsk have a long tradition back into early Swedish years, while St Petersburg as a city was not first established until 1703, by Peter the Great.

[18] The latest attempt in this field has just failed though as it has proved too difficult to find return-loads from both Germany and France for a line to Moscow (*Lloyd's List* 2000-05-25).

[19] The port has announced discounts on port dues of 20-50 per cent 'with the aim of attracting new traffic' to foreign shipping lines (*Lloyd's List* 1999-01-22: 7), but the structure, special contracts, together with a general lack of transparency of the fees often makes it difficult to compare different ports.

[20] A good example of how port development projects could be handled publicly can be found in Norway 'Cost-benefit analysis for the extension of the port of Oslo and two alternative port solutions' –authors translation. Title in Norwegian: 'Nyttekostnadsanalys av utbyggning av Oslo havn og to alternative havnelösningar' (Norwegian Institute for Transport Economics 1998).

[21] The 1992 decree was named 'On Measures for the Revitalisation of the Russian Commercial Fleet.' The 1997 decree was named 'Transport and Technological Provisions for Freight Transport through Shorepoints on the Gulf of Finland.'

[22] USD 3.7 billion is the figure most frequently seen, while other sources could use completely different sums. One such example is USD 525 million given by the Rayon Administration (2000 WWW).

[23] One reason for this has been that false certificates have been issued in Kaliningrad on domestic goods qualifying it for duty-free status (Kushnirsky 1997). The name Yantar (Russian for amber) has been chosen because some 90 per cent of the world's findings of amber come from the Kaliningrad Oblast.

[24] A meeting between Governor Yakovlev and President Putin which will 'examine the future socio-economic development of Kaliningrad' has been set to March 22 2001 (Russian Regional Report 2001-02-07).

References

Avdeev, K., Deputy Head of Division of External Economic Co-Operation; City of St Petersburg; Interview in Stockholm 2000-03-23.

Brodin, A. (1999). 'Swedish Trade with the Former Soviet Union,' pages 169-215 in Alvstam, C.-G. and Lindahl, R. (eds). *Forskning om europafrågor.* Gothenburg, CERGU at Gothenburg University.

Brodin, A. (2000). 'Ports in Transition in Countries in Transition.' Dissertation, Department of Human and Economic Geography at Gothenburg University.

Dervis, K., Selowsky, M. and Wallich, C. (1996). *The Transition in Central and Eastern Europe and the Former Soviet Union.* Washington D.C., The World Bank.

EBRD Transition Report (2000). London, European Bank for Reconstruction and Development.

Hayter, D., Partner; Booz-Allen & Hamilton; London; Interview in Stockholm 1997-09-09.

Hoare, A.G. (1986). 'British ports and their export hinterlands: a rapidly changing geography,' *Geografiska Annaler* 68B:1, pages 29-41.

Holt, J. (1993). *Transport Strategies for the Russian Federation.* Washington D.C., The World Bank.

Kareva, O., Chief of Investment Department; Vyborg Rayon; Interview in Vyborg 1993-02-12 ff.

Kirkow, P. (1997). 'Transition in Russia's Principal Coastal Gateways,' *Post-Soviet Geography and Economics* 38:5, pages 296-314.

Kjellén, R. (1917). *Staten som lifsform.* Stockholm, Hugo Gebers Förlag.

Klaassen, L. (1987). *Exercises in spatial thinking.* Aldershot, Avebury.

Klink van, H.A. and Berg van den, G. (1998). 'Gateways and Intermodalism,' *Journal of Transport Geography* 6:1, pages 1-9.

Kushnirsky, F.I. (1997). 'Post Soviet attempts to establish Free Zones,' *Post-Soviet Geography and Economics* 38:3, pages 144-62.

Lloyd's List (1998-2000). Issues from the date indicated where used.

Mayer, H.M. (1957). *The port of Chicago and the St. Lawrence Seaway.* The Department of Geography, research papers no 49. Chicago, University of Chicago.

Morskie Porti (1997-2000): Issues from the month indicated where used. Moscow, Association of Sea Commercial Ports.

North, R. (1997). 'Transport in a new reality' in Bradshaw, M.J. (ed.). *Geography and Transition in the Post-Soviet Republics.* Chichester, Wiley.

Norwegian Institute for Transport Economics (1998). *Nyttekostnadsanalys av utbyggning av Oslo havn og to alternative havnelösningar.* Report no 407/1998. Oslo, Norwegian Institute of Transport Economics.

Nove, A. (1992). *An Economic History of the USSR 1917-1991.* London, Penguin.

Parfenov, A., General Director, Lenmorniiproekt; interview St Petersburg 1998-01-24 ff.

Ranger, P., TACIS-Project Manager – Novorossiysk port; Scott Wilson Kirkpatrik, London; interview in Novorossiysk 1998-11-13.

Rissoan, J.P. (1994). 'River Sea navigation in Europe,' *Journal of Transport Geography* 2:2, pages 131-41.

Russian Regional Report (2001). Weekly mail service to subscribers. New York, EastWest Institute.

Shleifer A., Treisman D., (2000). *Without a Map – Political tactics and economic reform in Russia.* Cambridge Massachusetts, MIT Press.

Smith, G. (1995). 'Ethnic Relations in the new States,' pages 34-45 in Shaw D. J. B. (ed.). *The Post Soviet Republics.* Harlow, Longman.

Tally, W. (1998). 'Linkages between transportation infrastructure investments and economic production,' *Logistics and Transportation Review* 32:1, pages 145-55.

Trolley, R. and Turton, B. (1995). *Transport systems, policy and planning – A geographical approach.* Harlow, Longman.

Vigarié, A. (1979). *Ports de Commerce et Vie Littorale.* Paris, Hachette Université.

Whitehead, D. (2000). 'Factors affecting the pattern of future demand in the ports industry,' *PIANC Bulletin* 104, pages 16-20.

World Development Report (1996). *From Plan to Market*. Washington, D.C., Oxford University Press/World Bank.

Internet Sources (WWW)

Information sources found on the World-Wide-Web – WWW (Date indicates when first visited):

Bofit – Bank of Finland Institute for Economies in Transition (2000 & 2001)
    http://www.bof.fi/bofit
    QIR = Baltic Economies – The Quarter in Review
    MIR = Russian Economy – The Month in Review
    Visited: 1997-09-05 ff. Server: Bank of Finland
Business in Russia (2000 & 2001); http://www.rg.ru/bussines/econom/
    Visited: 2000-10-23 ff. Server: Rossijskaja Gazeta
Central Statistical Bureau of Latvia (1999 & 2000) http://www.csb.lv/ajaunumi.htm
    Visited: 1999-01-05 ff. Server: Central Statistical Bureau of Latvia
Financial Times (2001) http://www.fi.com/
    Visited: 2001-01-14. Server: Financial Times
Ministry of Transportation of the Russian Federation (2001) http://www.transport.ru/
    Visited: 2001-01-30. Server: Ministry of Transport
Moscow Times (2000) http://www.moscowtimes.ru/indexes/06.html
    Visited: 2000-10-23 ff. Server: Moscow Times
Goskomstat – State Committee on Statistics (2000 and 2001) http://www.gks.ru/osnpok.htm
    Visited: 1999-01-05 ff. Server: Goskomstat
Interfax (2000 & 2001) http://www.interfax-news.com/today
    Visited 2000-01-05 ff. Server: Interfax
IPR – Strategic Business Information Database; www.siena.edu/ipri/
    Visited: 2000-11-18 ff. Server: IPR
RFE – Radio Free Europe/Radio Liberty (1999 and 2000) http://www.rferl.org/
    Visited: 1998-01-05 ff. Server: Radio Free Europe/Radio Liberty
Statistical Office of Estonia (1999&2000) http://www.stat.ee/wwwstat/eng_stat/statistics_fr.html
    Visited: 1999-01-05 ff. Server: Statistikaamet
Statistics Lithuania (1999 & 2000) http://www.std.lt/engl/default.htm
    Visited: 1999-01-05 ff. Server: Statistics Lithuania
Vyborg Rayon (2000) http://www.head.vyborg.ru/index.html
    (before 1999 at: http://www.teia.ru/vyborg/index.htm)
    Visited: 1998-01-05 ff. Server: Vyborg Rayon Administration

9 The Economics, Politics and Safety Dimensions of the Ignalina Nuclear Power Plant

Jurgis Vilemas

During the period after Lithuania regained its independence, very deep, complicated and mostly unpredictable changes in the economy, in all branches of industry without exception, took place. Very abrupt prise rises of all primary energy resources and raw materials, almost all of them being imported, together with low productivity, led to a deep decline in the output of industry and agriculture. It is evident that even now the Lithuanian economy has not yet adapted to new conditions, where competition makes it necessary to produce high-quality products and to adjust to rapid changing market. From the Soviet past the country inherited a rather modern energy sector, which has to some extent helped to smooth the transition. However, the consumer, who had become used to very cheap energy, could not change at once. The energy intensity of the Lithuanian economy is still significantly higher than in modern economies. To significantly reduce this dependency, Lithuania needs enormous investments in all sectors of the economy and that is impossible to do in short time and under the circumstances of a long-lasting general economic crisis. Only in 2001 have signs of real recovery been observed.

Big overcapacities and a good structure of the primary energy supply enabled Lithuania to avoid heavy investments in the energy sector. At the beginning of 1994 a Lithuanian energy strategy was approved for the first time [1]. It outlined a strategy for a comparatively long period – until the year 2015. It also satisfactorily predicted Lithuanian energy developments for the next five years. During the last period the whole Lithuanian economy has entered a more stable development and a considerable amount of experience and information has been gathered. Information about changes and plans in neighbouring countries and at the global scale has been analysed. The approaching membership of the EU has also had an impact on the preparation of a new updated strategy.

A series of new studies needed for comprehensive energy policy has been carried out in Lithuania in recent years (2-9). Most of work was done by joint effort of Lithuanian experts and foreign consultants using the newest and thoroughly validated modelling tools and computer programs. In October 1999 the Parliament of Lithuania approved new updated energy strategy and this paper, in some extent, incorporates main recommendations of that document, particularly related to electricity sector.

Lithuania inherited from it's Soviet past a very powerful energy sector, which was created not only for the local (Lithuanian) needs but to satisfy a much grater, regional demand. At present exports and local consumption of electricity are almost halved (Table 9.1) in comparison with 1990, but all generating plants with operating staff are completely preserved. This lies as a heavy burden on the whole economy of the country, because it increases the energy supply cost for the consumer.

Table 9.1: Changes of GDP and energy consumption, percentages

	1990	1992	1994	1996	. 1998	2000
GDP	100	74.2	56.1	60.7	68.4	65.5
Final energy	100	74.3	55.5	52.2	51.6	45.0
Final electricity	100	77.4	58.8	57.2	56.2	52.0
Export (electricity)	100	44.4	-9.2	43.1	50.8	11.2

The Lithuanian energy strategy of 1999 clearly demonstrates that for the most realistic development scenario of the Lithuanian economy the internal electricity consumption even in 2020 can be satisfied by a fraction of existing production capacities after some modernisation and refurbishment. The real dilemma for the Lithuanian government is either to find export markets or to shut down some of the generating capacity. But which parts of it? The possibility of a future open electricity market in the region will also have a significant impact. A preliminary assessment of possible electricity markets indicates that only the Ignalina Nuclear Power Plant and Combined Heat and Power Plants (CHPs) can be competitive.

The main object of the Lithuanian electricity generation structure is the Ignalina Nuclear Power Plant (INPP) with a total installed capacity of 3000 MWe. This plant is the least costly generator in Lithuania covering not only more than 80 per cent of the local demand but also offering more than 7 TWh/year for export.

The Role of Ignalina in the Lithuanian Economy

Ignalina is one of the most important enterprises in the Lithuanian power sector, performing a stabilising role during the particularly difficult period of fundamental reorganisation and restructuring of the economy. More than 80 per cent of power consumed in Lithuania is produced by the Ignalina (Figures 9.1 and 9.2) as its production cost is almost half of the production cost in existing thermal power plants. Only existing CHPs can compete.

Ignalina is not sensitive to fuel supply interruptions. This phenomenon is very common in former Soviet Union countries and power stations burning petroleum or natural gas always face this problem. The very big overcapacity of nuclear fuel production in Russia creates very favourable market conditions for nuclear fuel consumers. As a result Ignalina never had any problems with timely fuel supply.

Due to the small share of fuel costs in the total production costs of electricity in NPPs, their lack of dependency on daily fuel supplies and a big fuel inventory in the core, nuclear power plants are sometimes considered a domestic energy source independently of where the fuel supply is coming from. In Lithuania, where almost 95 per cent of organic fuel (petroleum and natural gas) is imported from one country, the nuclear power plant substantially increases the security of energy supply.

However, Ignalina NPP with the reactors similar to those in Chernobyl – the RBMK type – is considered as potentially dangerous and that is why the all neighbouring countries and especially the EU countries pay special attention to it. RBMK reactors do not have the basic design features required in Western World reactors, because the last physical barrier, preventing radioactivity from spreading in the case of a severe accident, is partially missing. That is way the Lithuanian government considers systematic safety improvements of Ignalina up to the inter-

Figure 9.1: Electricity production in Lithuania

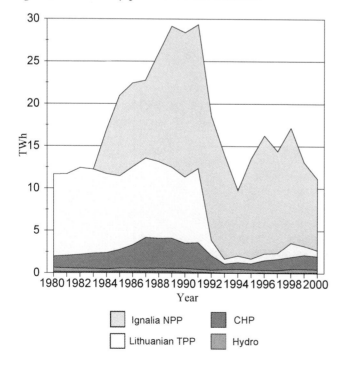

national standards as the most important priority. The achievements of recent years are really impressive and recognised by international experts.

In 1994 a Grant Agreement with the European Bank for Reconstruction and Development (EBRD) was signed for safety upgrading of the INPP. One of the conditions was that Lithuania must not to rechannel its reactors and must shut them down when the gap between channels and the graphite moderator expires. Rechannelling is a normal procedure that marks half of the lifetime of the reactor core. In 1994 information about general safety features available to the international community was extremely limited and the emotional impact from the Chernobyl accident was overwhelming. An early closure of Ignalina will have an enormous fiscal impact, especially as the Lithuanian budget is already under severe pressure. It will be a severe problem to provide large budgetary support for decommissioning and clean-up activities.

The Progress of Safety Improvement at Ignalina

Ignalina consists of two units with Soviet designed reactors of the type RBMK-1500. Unit 1 was commissioned in December 1983 and unit 2 in August 1987. The reactors used are different from the more widely used reactors RBMK-1000 that

Figure 9.2: The structure of electricity production in Lithuania

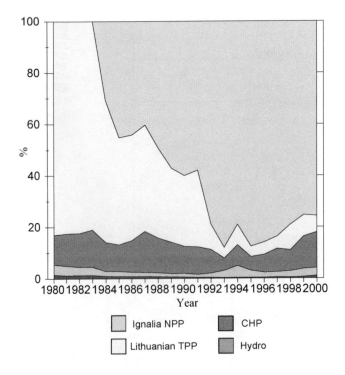

are being operated in Russia and Ukraine. The Ignalina reactors not only provide larger capacity but also have more advanced safety and operational features.

After the Chernobyl accident it became evident that RBMK reactors have specific design deficiencies which must be eliminated immediately. Some remedial safety measures at INPP were addressed and Western operational experience was introduced with the assistance of Western countries and the International Atomic Energy Agency (IAEA). But a well systematised, comprehensive safety-improvement programme did not exist at the time.

Several international studies related to the different safety aspects of Ignalina have been initiated after Lithuania had restored its independence. The first very important study was a probabilistic safety assessment (PSA) of the Ignalina. This study was initiated and financed by the Swedish Nuclear Safety Inspectorate. In this project the Swedish nuclear power plant Barsebäck, operating with BWR reactors, was used as a reference plant and the Ignalina NPP was used as the applicant plant. For this reason the study was named the 'Barselina project.' Since the study's inception in1991, four phases have been completed (10). The long-term objective was to establish common perspectives and a unified basis for assessing risks of severe accidents and establishing requirements for remedial measures.

In general, the results of the Barselina project indicate that the probability of a severe accident with core damage is of the order of 10^{-5} per reactor year – the same range as is expected for Western reactors. The analysis clearly indicates that the main contributors to the risk belong to sequences that will lead to damage or accident only in long term (1-24 hours). This demonstrates both the high redundancy of the front-line engineering safety systems and the special 'forgiving' features of the reactor type. Low power density and high heat accumulation capacity enable the reactor to survive a total loss of electrical power without core damage.

The Barselina project enabled Lithuanian authorities to start systematic planing of safety improvement at INPP in 1992. Countries of Western Europe, the USA and IAEA assisted Lithuania in carrying out a comprehensive INPP safety improvement programme. As a result the INPP Safety Improvement Programme (SIP-1) was ready in 1993. To implement the programme financial assistance was urgently needed. On 10 February 1994 a Grant Agreement was signed between Lithuania and the Nuclear Safety Account (NSA) established as an initiative by the G7 countries and administrated by the EBRD. The NSA grant was to fund a project of short-term safety upgrades in support of the SIP-1. According to the Agreement 34 million ecu were provided with some conditions. First of all Lithuania was obliged to perform an 'in depth safety assessment of the Ignalina NPP' with additional technical and financial support. It was agreed that the safety assessment was the responsibility of the INPP with the support of Western and Eastern nuclear safety experts including the reactor designer, NIKIET. The Agreement includes an effort to produce and review a Western-style safety analysis report (SAR) and to use the results as a major input for safety improvement and for licensing of the INPP Unit 1 for continued operation. The INPP and the

Lithuanian government have subsequently agreed to implement all the results of the in-depth safety assessment within new Safety Improvement programme N 2.

In addition, Lithuania has pledged to undertake a cost analysis to determine the economical features of the INPP in comparison with other existing power generators and possible new alternatives. As a part of the NSA Grant Agreement, the government of Lithuania has agreed not to extend the lifetime of either reactor beyond the time at which their fuel channels should be replaced. All Grant Agreement conditions were formulated on the basis of the very limited information available at that time about general safety features and about economic indicators of the INPP.

The Safety Analysis Report (SAR) (11) and its independent review (RSR) (12) examined three areas that are equally important to the safe operation of a any nuclear power plant: systems analyses, accident analyses and operational safety management. Various degrees of non-compliance with safety requirements were found in each area. However, none of them was severe enough to require a shutdown of the reactors while precautions were being taken.

The SAR and the RSR have made many recommendations on necessary safety improvements in design, operation and safety culture. In addition to the long list of recommendations the Ignalina Safety Panel (ISP), which was supervising all processes of the SAR and the RSR, made some special summarising recommendations.

The recommendations of the SAR, RSR and ISP were intended to aid the State Nuclear Energy Safety Inspection (VATESI) in making a licensing decision on Unit 1. VATESI was established by the newly independent Lithuanian government on 18 October 1991. An International Licensing Assistance Project was established to support VATESI during the application of the SAR, RSR and ISP results in the licensing of the Ignalina NPP.

On the basis of the recommendations just referred to, a new Safety Improvement Program (SIP-2) was developed in 1997. The SIP-2 has been continuously updated and revised annually and was fully completed in 2000.

Among the long-them safety improvement measures the most important is the development and installation of an additional, fully independent shutdown system. Because of the high safety significance of the additional shutdown system and of the considerable time necessary for the development, assessment, testing and implementation of this system, the independent review (RSR) has required that compensatory measures be implemented until the additional system is in place. In response Ignalina has developed a compensatory system, which has been installed, tested and commissioned and is now in operation in both units.

The Ignalina NPP staff has shown a very positive approach regarding the recommended implementation of changes in management and safety culture. The programme of safety culture implementation at the Ignalina NPP includes personnel notification on the plant policy in the safety and quality assurance area, workshops, personnel training and audits on safety culture and the development of new procedures. In order to improve the quality and efficiency of the training process for general operational staff, full-stop simulator was commissioned by the end of 1998. It is the most modern simulator for any nuclear power plant with RBMK reactors.

The scope and comprehensiveness of international studies conducted on the Ignalina NPP make it unique among all RBMK-type reactors. Extensive studies by international experts have determined that in terms of Probabilistic Safety Analysis indexes, the modified Ignalina NPP is comparable to Western reactors. The Ignalina NPP is the only RBMK-type plant about which this statement can be made. This does not imply that the INPP is 'identical' to Western BWR-type reactors. Ignalina is a graphite-moderated, channel-type reactor and in many constructional aspects it differs from the single-pressure vessel BWRs. The documentation of these differences is very extensive and we shall briefly summarise their conclusions.

The probability of events, such as pipe breaks and valve failures, in Ignalina is higher than for Western BWRs. The objective reasons are the higher complexity of an RBMK-type reactor, which has a considerably larger number of pipes, valves, weldings and associated equipment, and the lower level of quality control in Soviet design and construction.

On the plus side, international analyses demonstrate that the Ignalina NPP is remarkably robust and that the vast majority of initiating events will not lead to fuel overheating or the release of radioactivity from fuel. The robustness also has objective reasons. Among these reasons is the fact that channel-type construction limits the intensity of loss-of-coolant accidents. In addition, the INPP core has a considerably larger volume and a larger heat-capacity (thus a lower rate of heat-up); there are higher vertical elevations (thus higher driving force for natural circulation); and the Soviet designers compensated for lower quality control by larger volumes of water in the primary system and above the core region and by high redundancy.

When all of these factors are taken into account, the index combining event-initiation probability and consequences of events is indeed comparable to those achieved by Western plants.

However, in spite of the fact that a lot of safety improvements and analyses have been performed at the Ignalina NPP, much remains to be done. A new safety analysis report is under way and special programmes for strengthening VATESI and technical support organisations are under consideration.

The Development of Lithuania's Internal Infrastructure

During the early years of operation of Ignalina, the administrative, regulatory and scientific-technical support came from Soviet authorities outside Lithuania. Since 1991 Lithuania became fully responsible for all aspects of the operation, supervision, regulation and safety improvements of the plant. Very few believed that Lithuania would be able to developed these necessary structures in due time. This was real challenge for young Government and the response was to create the State Nuclear Energy Safety Inspection (VATESI), as already mentioned. Over the past ten years, VATESI has developed into an internationally recognised authority.

According to the Nuclear Energy Law and Nuclear Safety Convention, ratified by the Seimas (parliament), Lithuania is obliged to ensure the safety of all nuclear installations and to establish the legal framework for a nuclear safety regulatory system, namely:

- national safety rules and requirements;
- a licensing system for nuclear facilities;
- a system for analysis and assessment of nuclear installations;
- an enforcement mechanism, ensuring observance of the requirements and licensing conditions.

These huge tasks could not be performed without assistance from more experienced countries, and the assistance was offered immediately by Swedish government (1991), the EU PHARE programme and later by many countries operating nuclear power plants.

In 1994 the Lithuanian Nuclear Safety Advisory Committee was created on the initiative of the Swedish Nuclear Power Inspectorate. The Committee consists of experts from France, Finland, Germany, Japan, Sweden, the UK, Ukraine, the USA and Lithuania. The main tasks of the Committee are:

- to assist the Government and to advise VATESI on the principal safety matters related to the Ignalina NPP;
- to monitor the implementation of the safety improvements;
- to serve as the main supporter to the Government on major issues affecting safety, including design, operation, upgrading and decommissioning;
- to promote information exchange between Lithuania and other countries on current safety issues and progress with safety improvements at the INPP.

The Committee meets three to four times per year and the majority of its recommendations are implemented.

The long-term safe operation of nuclear power in any country requires competent support from local scientific and technical institutions. Notwithstanding the fact that, comparatively speaking, Lithuania is well endowed with scientific research institutions in the fields of natural and technical sciences, none of them has been heavily engaged in nuclear research, except for the ecological aspects of Ignalina's operation; nor have they participated in the design, construction or operation of Ignalina.

Thus, one of most urgent problems was to create the necessary support infrastructure able to serve the Ignalina NPP and the national regulatory agency. Some institutes of the former Lithuanian Academy of Sciences and technical universities were reoriented and their potential is now being used for this purpose.

At the present time the following organisations are performing activities in connection with the Ignalina NPP:

- The Lithuanian Energy Institute (plant safety analysis, structural analysis, radioactive waste and spent fuel management, least-cost planing, energy-demand forecasts);
- The Institute of Physics (environment monitoring around the Ignalina NPP);
- The Institute of Information Technology (computerised control systems);
- Kaunas University of Technology (material research, ageing of components, non-destructive testing);
- Vilnius Technical University (welding technology, large-components reliability).

The training and education of the Lithuanian technical support organisation's (TSO) staff has been arranged through special training courses, seminars and workshops organised by various assisting countries, the IAEA and by direct involvement in a majority of projects dedicated to safety enhancement activities. Lithuania has undertaken such projects with the strong support from majority of highly developed Western countries: Sweden, Germany, the USA, the UK, France, Finland, Italy and Denmark.

What are the TSO's main tasks in nearest future?

- scientific and technical services for the new safety-improvement programme, SIP-3;
- to assist in licensing of Unit 2;
- to create, accumulate and learn to use all needed analytical and experimental means for the assessment of ageing problems of main structural materials at Ignalina NPP;
- to be ready for the problems related to future Ignalina decommissioning and dismantling.

The Revised Lithuanian Energy Strategy and the Impact of Early Closure of Ignalina on the Economic and Political Development in Lithuania

According to Lithuania's energy law the Seimas must revise the country's energy strategy every five years. The first Lithuanian energy strategy was formulated in 1994 and the basic revision was undertaken in 1999. Among the most difficult and important issues was the fate of Ignalina NPP. Closure and decommissioning is a condition of the NSA Grant Agreement and, in addition, the current Accession Agreement for Lithuania's entry into the EU requires a decommissioning plan for nuclear and an associated energy strategy.

All previous economic analysis, based on least-cost methodology, clearly indicates that the cost of producing nuclear electricity is the lowest even taking into account necessary investments in safety improvements, decommissioning expenses and disposal of spent fuel. On the other hand, as it was demonstrated above, knowledge accumulated in recent years together with the continuous progress in safety improvement provides reason enough for a revision of basic assumptions on which the Grant Agreement was constructed. Nevertheless the opinion of the international community is important for Lithuania, which prepares for the membership in the EU and NATO.

In October 1999 the following plan for further operation of the Ignalina NPP was stated in the National Energy Strategy (NES) and approved by the Seimas (13):

'In line with the Nuclear Safety Account Grant Agreement, Unit 1 of the Ignalina NPP will be decommissioned before the year 2005, taking into consideration the terms and conditions of long-term and considerable financial assistance from the European Union, Group 7 member states and other states as well as international financial institutions.

The remaining operation period of Unit 1 must be used most efficiently and in particular during the implementation of the secondary shut down system at Unit 2.

Actions to be taken immediately are as follows:

1) to prepare a comprehensive program – in line with international requirements – for the final decommissioning, dismantling, radioactive waste and spent fuel (or transference for reprocessing) of Unit 1;
2) to initiate all necessary legal procedures for the decommissioning of Unit 1 and to harmonise appropriate Lithuanian legal acts;
3) to evaluate and clarify the costs required for decommissioning Unit 1 and identify the sources of financing, taking into consideration foreign technical and financial assistance;
4) to prepare a development programme for the Visaginas Region, taking into account the re-qualification of employees and restructuring of the sphere of industry and services;
5) to prepare a detailed programme for the restructuring of the whole power sector comprising the period before and after closure of Ignalina.'

The conditions and precise final date of the decommissioning of Unit 2 shall be fixed in the up-dated National Energy Strategy to be prepared in the year 2004, when more detailed information on the work of Unit 2 will be available.

When preparing the conditions for further operation of Unit 2 of Ignalina NPP and the final decision on its decommissioning, it will be necessary to carry out a new safety analysis; to prepare a new investment programme for further safety improvements; to issue a new license for operation, in compliance with the requirements of Western Europe; to prepare a programme for the development of infrastructure (administrative, supervision, scientific-technical support, staff training) necessary for the safe and effective operation of Ignalina NPP.

During the preparation of this strategy, the preliminary costs of the decommissioning and dismantling of Ignalina NPP, the costs of replacing Ignalina NPP with other power plants, as well as the impact on macroeconomics were calculated.

The costs of the final decommissioning of Unit 1 and management of all waste are evaluated to approximately Lt 10.4 billion. The costs of management, storage and disposal of waste and spent fuel accumulated by the year 1999 (about Lt 8 billion) are expected to be financed from international funds and the costs from the year 2000 to be covered by increasing electricity rates and improving efficiency of the whole power sector.

Investments in modernisation of the power sector due to the decommissioning of Unit 1 would amount to approximately Lt 2.8 billion by the year 2020. Financing should be in the form of international loans which are repaid from energy revenues.

The impact of restructuring of the industry and labour force of the INPP region is not yet specifically evaluated, but possible financing from EU structural funds combined with some financing from the state budget is estimated to be capable of covering the expenses of creation of new jobs, investments and economic development in the region.

The total negative consequences of the decommissioning of Unit 1 on the national economy may be up to Lt 40 billion. A further assessment of this calculation is expected to be undertaken in the near future, using more comprehensive initial information. The possible financing through credits, grants and soft loans has already been announced by the EU, international funds, international financing institutions, bilateral donors and commercial investors. Depending on the available financing from G7 countries, EU, international funds and other financing sources, the total impact of decommissioning Unit 1 on the national economy may be reduced considerably.

The future operation of Unit 2 of the Ignalina NPP would also help to gradually accumulate more funds necessary for its final decommissioning.

References

1. National Energy Strategy of the Republic of Lithuania. Executive Summary. Lithuanian Ministry of Energy, 1994.
2. National Energy Efficiency Programme. Lithuanian Ministry of Economy, 1996.
3. Least Cost Power Sector Development Programme, Republic of Lithuania. Final Report. LEI, Kaunas, 1996.
4. Lithuania Least Cost Power Sector Development Programme. November 1997.
5. Energy and Nuclear Power Planning Study for Lithuania Using IAEA Models. LEI, Kaunas, 1997.

6. Evaluation of Economic Expediency of the Replacement of Technological Channels of Ignalina NPP. LEI, Kaunas, 1996 (in Russian).
7. Baltic ring study. Final Report. January 1998.
8. Strategy for the Use of Domestic and Renewable Energy Resources. Lithuanian Energy Agency. Vilnius, 1997.
9. Least Cost Power Sector Strategy for Lithuania. Lithuanian Ministry of Economy, June 1999.
10. The Barselina Project Phase 4 Summary Report, December 1996.
11. In-depth Safety Assessment of Ignalina NPP. Final report, December 1996.
12. Review of the Ignalina Power Plant Safety Analysis Report. Final Report, June 1997.
13. National Energy Strategy. Parliament of Lithuania, Vilnius, 5 October 1999.

10 Lake Peipsi: A Transboundary Lake on the Future Border of the European Union

Per Stålnacke and Gulnara Roll[1]

Several lakes and rivers cross the boundaries between countries. Management of transboundary waters is complicated. One government cannot act on its own: co-operation between riparian countries is required to ensure good water quality and sustainable development in the shared water basins. The number of agreements on transboundary waters in Europe is today approximately 160 and shows an increasing trend (Figure 10.1). This reflects an urgent need to co-operate on management of shared water resources. However, the co-operation is not easy to achieve and there are various obstacles, such as differences in water management legislation, institutional structures and practices that stem from differences in languages, cultures as well as physical and political geography of different states. The history of developing co-operation on transboundary waters shows that 'co-operation is a striking achievement whenever ... it occurs, and there is every reason to believe that co-operation will become more elusive ... as growing human populations, enhanced capabilities, and rising expectations generate more severe conflicts of interest as well as greater demands on the earth's natural systems' (Young 1989: 4).

Figure 10.1: Existing agreements on transboundary waters in Europe, 1860-2000

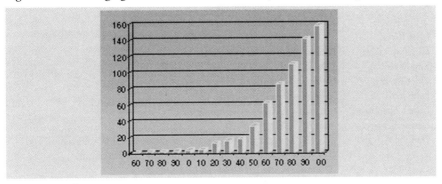

Source: UN-ECE

Because of the enlargement preparations for the European Union, management of transboundary waters has received considerable attention lately. A selected number of transboundary waters in the existing and future EU border regions are given in Table 10.1. The EC Water Framework Directive (WFD) will become a central tool for the future environmental management of transboundary river basins in Europe. The EU has recognised that the environmental problems being faced in the applicant states and beyond are far more severe than in the present member states. There is also a need for a truly integrated and functioning basin-wide co-operative scheme for the management of international waters, especially on the new border region of the European Union.

The Lake Peipsi basin is a major river basin in northern Europe and is likely to become part of the new frontier between the EU and Russia. Environmental problems such as eutrophication have been reported as being considerable in the literature.

Another important fact is that agriculture in Eastern Europe has undergone dramatic changes during the past 8-10 years. The consequences of this collapse have been immediate and have included, among other things, dramatic decreases in fertiliser use and livestock, and large areas have been taken out of production. Such abrupt and large land-use change has hardly been recorded in modern European agricultural history. Lake Peipsi is no exception from this huge and dramatic change in land use.

Prerequisites for successful environmental management of lake and river basins include the collection of basic environmental statistics and quantitative

Table 10.1: Selected transboundary watercourses and international lakes on the current and future border of the European Union

Lakes and Rivers	Countries
Lake Peipsi	Estonia – Latvia – Russia
Tisza River	Hungary – Slovakia – Ukraine – Romania
Lake Galadus	Lithuania – Poland – Russia
Daugava River	Latvia – Belarus – Russia
Nemunas River	Lithuania – Russia – Belarus
Wilija River	Lithuania – Belarus
Lyna River,	
Wegorapa River	Poland – Russia (Kaliningrad)
Bug River	Poland – Belarus – Ukraine
Oder River	Germany – Poland
Lake Inari	Finland – Russia – Norway
Lake Constance	Germany – Austria – Switzerland/ Liechtenstein
Neusiedler See	Austria – Hungary
Danube River	11 states, including 5 pre-accession states and 4 Central European and NIS states that will not be EU members in the near future (Ukraine, Romania, Moldova, Croatia)
Vjose River	Greece – Albania

estimates of the riverine loads; estimation of the pollution sources, retention and buffering capacity in the drainage basin; and knowledge of the lake water quality. Transboundary basins on the European fringe are often 'data-poor' or 'information-poor' and characterised by a highly varying quantity and quality of input data. Lake Peipsi is one such lake where the existing monitoring programmes suffer from financial limitations and a lack of harmonised monitoring strategies. As a consequence, the magnitude of the nutrient loads and sources has been uncertain for a long time.

The general objectives of this chapter are as follows:

– a physiogeographical description of Lake Peipsi and its drainage basin;
– an environmental assessment of Lake Peipsi and its drainage basin (i.e. mainly devoted to nutrients loads and sources in the drainage basin);
– an overview of the transboundary co-operation and problems in the Lake Peipsi region.

Some Basic Facts about the Lake Peipsi Region

Lake Peipsi (Figure 10.2) is particularly interesting since:

– it is the fourth largest lake in Europe (after Ladoga, Onega and Vänern), with a surface area of 3,550 km², and a volume of 25.1 km³, and a large drainage basin (47,800 km²);
– it is the largest international lake in Europe;
– it is located in the new border region of the European Union;
– it is shared by one EU state in accession (Estonia) and one non-EU state (Russia);
– the border regime is relatively newly established (i.e. 1992), and the Joint Estonian-Russian Transboundary Water Commission was established as late as 1997;
– the lake itself and its drainage basin can be considered as a combination of 'data-rich' and 'data-poor', with respect to environmental information, and the access and availability of data are scattered;
– the lake has been regarded as suffering from eutrophication problems and reduced fish stocks;
– large land-use and industrial changes have taken place and are still ongoing in the drainage basin after the collapse of the Soviet Union.

The lake, actually consists of two major subareas:

– Lake Peipsi/Chudskoe (2,610 km²)
– Lake Pihkva/Pskovskoe (710 km²)

Figure 10.2: Lake Peipsi and its drainage basin

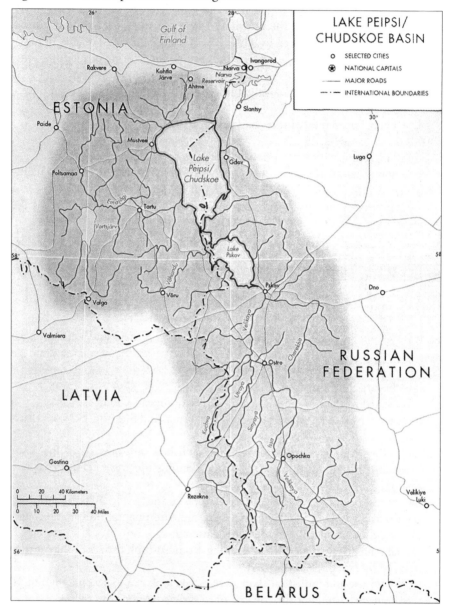

Note: Lake Peipsi covers and area of 3550 km² and it drainage basin covers 47,800 km². There are approximately 20 rivers and smaller streams that discharge into Lake Peipsi. The watersheds of the Velikaya and the Emajogi rivers (25,200 km² and 9,740 km², respectively) cover almost 80 per cent of the total drainage basin. Lake Peipsi discharges into the Narva River (length 77 km), which is the second largest river flowing into the Gulf of Finland.

Source: The World Bank

These two 'lakes' are connected by Lake Lämmijärvi/Teploe (235 km²). General morphometric data for the three subareas are given in Table 10.2.

Table 10.2: Morphometric data for the Lake Peipsi

	Lake Peipsi (Chudskoe)	Lake Lämmi (Tjoploe)	Lake Pihkva (Pskov)	The whole Lake Peipsi
Area, km²	2611	236	708	3555
% of surface area	73	7	20	100
Volume, km³	21.8	0.6	2.7	25.1
% of volume total	87	2	11	100
Depth medium, m	8.3	2.5	3.8	7.1
Depth maximum, m	12.9	15.3	5.3	15.3
Length of shoreline, km	260	83	177	520
% of total length	50	16	34	100
Distribution of the aquatory between Estonia and Russia, %	55/45	50/50	1/99	44/56

The water mass in the lake is actively stirred by wind in summer. This ensures homothermia and good aeration in spring, summer and autumn. This can also be seen in the monitoring data, where the water quality near the surface correlate well with the nutrient concentration made at the bottom of the lake at the same sampling site (Stålnacke et al. 2001). This good mixture of the water combined with high water temperature in summer leads to intensive biological activity and high trophic level. The flora and fauna of the lake are rich both in the number of species as well as in their abundance. There are about 100 macrophytes species, about 1000 algae species, 291 zooplankton species, 419 macrozoobenthos species and 33 fish species in Lake Peipsi (Pihu and Haberman 2001). Average pH is 8.1 and Secchi depth is typically around 1.6 m (Nõges et al. 1996). The water residence time is about 2 years.

Commercial fisheries are an important activity both on the Russian and Estonian sides of the lake. Fish stocks are one of the largest of any lake in Europe. Records show that average annual catches during the last 50 years have been as high as 11.6 thousand tonnes. This is 10 times the size of the catches in Lakes Ladoga or Onega (Nõges et al. 1996). The stock of the economically valuable vendace has sharply decreased in the 1990s, while the amount of pikeperch has increased (Nõges et al. 1996).

Most of the pollution load in Lake Peipsi can be attributed to activities in the river basins, which in total covers approximately 44,000 km², or 12 times the surface area of the lake itself. Over 1.1 million people (23 inh./km²) live in the drainage basin of Lake Peipsi. The population is relatively uniformly distributed within the river basin with the exception of a few large cities (e.g. city of Pskov with 206,000 inh.). Nearly 67 per cent of the drainage basin belongs to Russia; the rest belongs to Estonia (26 per cent) and Latvia (7 per cent). The Latvian part is mainly located in the Velikaya River and in this study calculated into the Russian estimates of loads and sources. There are approximately 20 rivers and smaller streams that discharge into Lake Peipsi. The watersheds of the Velikaya and the Emajogi rivers (25,200 km_ and 9,740 km_ respectively) cover almost 80 per cent of the total drainage basin. Lake Peipsi discharges into the Narva River (length 77 km), which has an annual flow of 380 m³/s and is, after the Neva River, the second largest river flowing into the Gulf of Finland.

Land Use, Natural Resources and Economic Development

Agricultural lands occupy more than 40 per cent of the total catchment territory of the Lake Peipsi. A substantial fraction of the agricultural land is today unused land or fallow land. For example, 40 per cent of the agricultural land in the Velikaya River basin is of non-arable character. Besides agricultural land, the land use in the drainage basin of Lake Peipsi is dominated by 40 per cent forested areas and approximately 8-9 per cent wetland/bogs. Forestry and processing of timber are a rapidly developing sector in Estonian industry at the moment. On the Estonian side, logging and the timber processing are becoming a noteworthy alternative for those who lost their jobs in agriculture in the regions far from cities. On the Russian side, the main impediments to the development of forestry are the absence of roads in remote forested areas and the general economic recession in the region.

Large areas of peat deposits are located in the Lake Peipsi watershed. They are not used intensively because the bigger bogs and marsh areas are under nature protection. Moreover, wetland areas of Lake Peipsi have been recognised as being of international importance. Thus Lake Peipsi and the watershed have a great potential for eco-recreation and eco-tourism.

A socio-economic survey of the Lake Peipsi region was recently published (Hinsberg et al. 2001). The study showed that the major weaknesses in the region were (i) an underdeveloped industrial and transport infrastructure, (ii) peripheral location of both Estonian and Russian sides of the transboundary region, (iii) a great number of vacant production buildings, (iv) a lot of vacant land, and (v) sparse population. In the region, in many cases of land property ownership problems remain unsolved. In addition, problems of structural unemployment due to low quality level of the existing labour resources: its shortage, low level of speaking and understanding foreign languages, 'frozen' mentalities and lack of co-operation.

Although many people in the Peipsi region see their future in tourism, the problems are also unfortunately common: low level of tourism infrastructure facilities, shortage of accommodation, few signposts, low reputation and availability of services, low maintenance order of beaches, etc. At the same time, the resources are varied and the potential, even when considering domestic tourism, is quite good. Concerning the development, the following areas are mentioned first of all: closeness to the lake, fishing activities, wind energy and cross-border co-operation (launching navigation to Russia and co-operation with the Russian border regions). Other possibilities include development of tourism (beaches, navigation (ports)), organising events based on local cultural traditions, training of guides, etc. Sectors that merit consideration as investment objects were: timber-processing industry, all forms of handicraft, processing of agricultural products, fishery and tourism (Hinsberg et al. 2001).

The Peipsi region is based on the co-operation between self-governing regions or local administrative units. From the point of view of regional development patterns, the Lake Peipsi region includes two more or less distinct subregions – the northern and central/southern Peipsi subregions.

The Northern Peipsi Subregion
Geographically, the Northern Peipsi region includes the Ida-Virumaa County in northeastern Estonia and Kingisepp and Slantsy counties in the Leningrad oblast in Russia. In contrast to the south and central region, the northern area is to a large extent dominated by the mining of oil shale. Two of the world's largest thermal power plants, consuming the oil shale, are found in Estonia. Other main branches of industry in this region are building and civil engineering, chemical industry, textile manufacture, foodstuff production and timber processing (furniture factories).

Along with the oil shale processing industry, a potential for water tourism from the Baltic Sea through Narva River to Lake Peipsi and development of recreation on the beautiful northern Peipsi coast, is under discussion among authorities and is being assessed within many regional development projects. Further development of the Northern Peipsi subregion is connected with the modernisation of the oil shale-processing industry and promoting at the same time small and medium enterprises in service, tourism and recreation.

The Central/Southern Peipsi Subregion
The central and southern part of the region covers three administrative regions of Estonia – the Counties of Jõgevamaa, Tartumaa and Põlvamaa. On the Russian side, only one major administrative region exists – the Pskov oblast region. Lakeside municipalities in the subregion are characterised by tendencies typical to peripheral areas: an unfavourable demographic situation, depopulation and underdeveloped infrastructure (Hinsberg et al. 2001). There are two major development centres in the area located in the central and southeastern part of the catchment area – Tartu in Estonia with 98,000 inhabitants and Pskov on the Russian side with 207,400 inhabitants.

In the rural and sparsely populated areas outside these two main towns, typical activities are based on milk and cattle farms, small-scale fishery, timber enterprises and food-processing factories.

Dramatic changes in land use took place in the central/southern Peipsi subregion during 1990s. When it was a part of the Soviet Union, Estonian agriculture specialised in meat and milk production, and a substantial import of mineral fertilisers and animal feedstuff was a characteristic part of the production system. The agricultural products (meat and cereals) were then exported back to Soviet Union. The years 1990 and 1991 were the start of an almost total collapse in the agricultural production due to the disintegration of the former Soviet Union. For example, in the Baltic States the mineral fertiliser use dropped by 90 per cent and livestock decreased 50 per cent from their level in late 1980s (Löfgren et al. 1999). During the early 1990s, Estonian agriculture was rapidly restructured due to the sudden decrease in demand for Estonian farm products. At the same time, large areas of arable land were taken out of production. The number of dairy cows decreased from 757,000 to 379,100 between 1990 and 1995, and the number of pigs decreased from 960,000 to 421,000 during the same time period (FAO statistics). The number of dairy cows and pigs at collective farms in the Pskov Region has also decreased substantially, from 221,400 to 113,000, and from 156,100 to 63,200, respectively (Stålnacke et al. 2001). The situation seems to have stabilised now due to a better market situation, especially in Estonia.

A similarly abrupt and massive land-use change has hardly been recorded in modern European agricultural history. Therefore, one challenging task is to study river and lake responses to the land-use changes. This question/problem is of great relevance since other Eastern European countries show similar land-use changes (e.g. Poland, Latvia,and Hungary). The exact decrease in pollution loads in rivers from agricultural sources is uncertain. However, results by Loigu and Leisk (1996) indicate that the nitrogen and phosphorus loads have decreased by 53 per cent and 44 per cent, respectively, between the late 1980s and the mid-1990s. The scattered data on the two monitored Russian rivers make such estimations highly uncertain.

Today, Estonian agricultural production is mostly for the domestic market. The amount of fertilisers applied to the agricultural fields is between 15-40 kg/ha for nitrogen and 2-10 kg/ha for phosphorus. This is 2-10 times lower than in the Nordic countries. A similar economic recession can also be seen in the Russian part of the Lake Peipsi drainage basin. Today, according to official statistical data, 21,015 tonnes of mineral fertilisers are annually used in the Russian part of the drainage (65 per cent nitrogen fertilisers; 14 per cent phosphorus; 21 per cent potassium). This corresponds to the same low unit-area applications as in Estonia. Most of it is applied to the agricultural fields in the Velikaya River catchment area. The use of organic fertilisers (manure, slurry, etc.) is also low from a Western European perspective with an estimated use of 0.8 to 2.2 t/ha (approximately 380,000 tonnes/yr).

The yield of cereals in the Velikaya River catchment area ranges from 600 to 800 kg/ha, reaching 1000 kg/ha in the Piusa and Obdekh basins and on lands near the southern coast of Lake Pskovskoe (Stålnacke et al. 2001). These values are extremely low in comparison with e.g. Sweden, where cereal yields are 5-10 times higher. Since agriculture is not profitable today, many farmers' main income is from timber from their own forests. Thirty-five per cent of the catchment area is covered by forest and the timber industry on the Estonian side is growing fast with the co-operation of Finnish companies. Good peat reserves are to be found in this subregion, but they are not exploited because of concern over the impact the activity could have on the environment. Thus, the main environmental issues in the rural areas are impacts from small-scale timber felling and diffuse agricultural pollution. Tourism and recreation are largely undeveloped because of a poor infrastructure, a sensitive coastal zone and weak public transport infrastructure. One of the major challenges in this area is to overcome the monofunctional character of the local economics that is based on fisheries and subsistence agriculture and to develop a more diverse foundation of economic development in the region based on small and medium-size entrepreneurship and focusing on fishery, organic farming and tourism.

Despite the current economic downturn and peripheral status of the region, many factors work in favour of the build-up of a transboundary regime in the Lake Peipsi area, renewing co-operation on economic issues as well as on water monitoring and management.

Environmental Monitoring

Even though the routine monitoring of Lake Peipsi in Estonia and Russia has a long and strong tradition, since the disintegration of the Soviet Union there have been no efforts to organise a joint comprehensive exchange and analysis of the available data. The collapse of the Soviet Union at the beginning of the 1990s and the economic crisis that followed have also made it difficult to maintain the monitoring programmes. In addition, the laboratory equipment in most cases is old, and chemicals and consumable supplies are too expensive or difficult to obtain.

In Estonia, the national monitoring programme for water quality in rivers and water discharge covers eight rivers, or almost 90 per cent of the total drainage area. The sampling frequency is normally monthly. In Russia, the corresponding programme includes only two rivers (the Velikaya and Gdovka Rivers). However, these two rivers cover 87 per cent of the drainage basin on the Russian side of the lake. The sampling frequency for nitrogen and phosphorus is low in the Russian rivers monitored, with only 2-6 samples per year. In addition, total-N and total-P are not standard parameters in the Russian national monitoring programme for water quality. This makes the estimation of the riverine loads from the Russian part of the drainage basin very uncertain.

Since 1996, the lake water quality programme on the Estonian side of the river has consisted of five sampling sites. On the Russian side, ten sites are regularly monitored. The lake water quality programme in Russia lacks analyses of total-N and total-P, which makes eutrophication assessment studies difficult.

Pollution Loads and Sources to Lake Peipsi

A recent assessment study showed that riverine transport is the most important pathway for the input of nutrients to Lake Peipsi (Figure 10.3). The total nutrient loads of rivers correspond to area-specific loads of approximately 5 kg/ha for nitrogen and 0.2 kg/ha for phosphorus (Stålnacke et al. 2001). The nitrogen load

Figure 10.3: Total inputs of nitrogen (upper) and phosphorus (lower) along the major pathways and estimated load at the outlet from Lake Peipsi (the Narva River at Vasknarva)

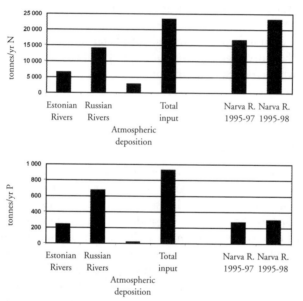

Source: Modified after Stålnacke et al. (2001)

is low from a Baltic Sea perspective and is, for example, almost two times lower than the corresponding riverine load to the Gulf of Riga. The phosphorus load is somewhat higher than the corresponding riverine load to the Gulf of Riga but almost two times lower than the average phosphorus transport in the rivers draining to the Baltic proper and the Western Baltic. The loads are also low, when comparing with two other rivers in Central Europe (the Elbe and Rhine Rivers; Figure 10.4).

The low nutrient levels in almost all the studied rivers are surprisingly low or moderate given the large share of agricultural land in the drainage basin (42 per cent). Odense River, representing a typical agricultural basin in Western Europe with approximately the same percentage of agricultural land as basins in the Peipsi region, shows area-specific loads far above the ones reported in the Peipsi basin.

Figure 10.4: Time-averaged, area-specific riverine load of nutrients (kg ha-1 yr-1) in Velikaya, Emajogi, Narva, Elbe, Rhine and Odense rivers

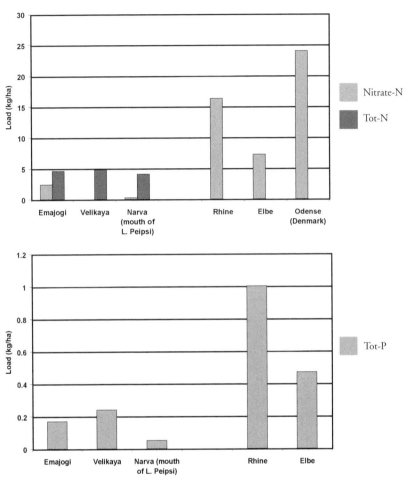

The nitrogen retention in Lake Peipsi is 1-28 per cent and the phosphorus retention 68-70 per cent. The phosphorus retention is particularly large compared to e.g. the large Swedish lakes. Nitrogen retention in Lake Peipsi seems to be lower than expected.

Less than 10 per cent of the nitrogen load from rivers originates from wastewater (Stålnacke et al. 2001; Figure 10.5). Between 55 and 80 per cent of the load originated from agriculture sources and approximately 15-30 per cent originates from forests and other diffuse sources. Of the phosphorus load, the point source discharges are responsible for approximately 20-30 per cent of the total phosphorus load to the lake (Stålnacke et al. 2001. Agricultural sources are responsible for approximately 40 per cent in Estonian rivers and 70 per cent in the Russian rivers. The two largest cities in the basin, Pskov and Tartu, are also the two largest point sources in the drainage area (Stålnacke et al. 2001). A large fraction of the effluents from point sources (i.e. wastewater from municipalities and industries) is treated in sewage treatment plants. For example, more than 90 per cent of the point source discharges to Estonian rivers is treated at sewage treatment plants (Stålnacke et al. 2001). However, 74 per cent of the wastewater in Estonia is treated using only mechanical treatment. Eighty-nine percent of the residents in Pskov are connected to sewage treatment plants. There are some uncertainties in the figures of the emissions from the point sources in Russia. This is particularly true for the people not connected to sewage treatment plants. Also noteworthy is that no sewage treatment plants in Russia have tertiary treatment, i.e. chemical precipitation.

Discharges of nutrients and organic matter have decreased substantially in the Emajogi and Velikaya Rivers during the 1990s. This is due to improved treatment efficiency at the sewage treatment plants in Pskov (Velikaya River; SWECO 1997) and Tartu (Emajogi River) (Figure 10.6). In other rivers, no significant decrease can be seen. Even though that the point source contribution to the lake is relative small in an entire lake budget perspective it may cause severe problems locally. For example, has emissions of oil products, Zn-, Ni-, Fe-, Cr- and Cu-compounds, organic and inorganic deoxidants and pesticides from industries and municipalities been identified in Velikaya river mouth and delta (Ivanov 1997; Lebedeva and Sudnitsyna 1997). The Rannapungerja, located on the northern coast carries substantially amounts of sulphate-, nitrogen- and phosphates from the mining districts in the catchment area.

The energy production from the oil-shale mining in northeastern Estonia is another source of pollution in the Peipsi region. The residual water from the ash removal systems of oil-shale-fired power stations (Narva Power Stations, former known as the Estonian and Baltic Power Stations) shows very high alkalinity (pH>12), with a large concentration of heavy metals. Despite the closed water circulation in the ash removal systems there have been leakage from the sedimentation basins in the heavy rain periods and in the snow-melting periods. The energy industry's second largest impact on environment quality is caused by sulphur and ash emission into the atmosphere. The cooling water of the power stations has a temperature of 17-18° C in the outlet river even in winter-period, and it causes thermal pollution in Narva Water Reservoir. In addition to its direct impact on the landscape, the mining of oil shale also influences the groundwater. The open cast mining method is used for up to 40 metres in depth in the oil-shale bed. However, the oil shale in the main Estonian deposit lies at a depth up to 100 metres and oil shale is extracted from underground mines. Very large amounts of water (about 190-210 million cubic metres) are annually pumped out of the mines and quarries, but to our knowledge no assessment of the environmental impact has been carried out. Another significant economic activity is the 125 MW hydropower plant located 18 km downstream from the Lake in the Narva River. The same water that drives the turbines provides cooling water for the thermal power plants mentioned above.

Figure 10.5: Source apportionment of the nitrogen and phosphorus load to Lake Peipsi, 1995-98

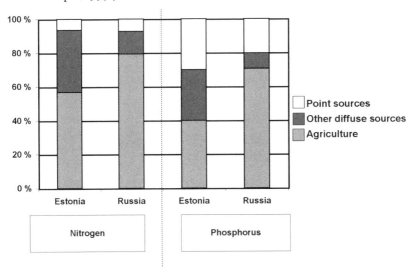

Figure 10.6: Annual emissions of nitrogen and phosphorus from point sources 1995-98 in major river basins in the Lake Peipsi drainage basin

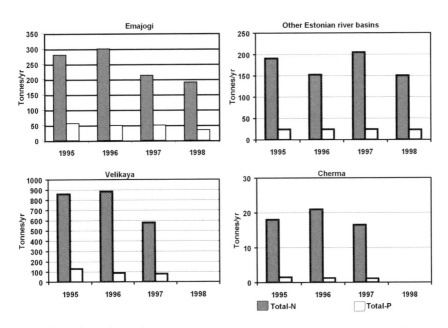

Source: Stålnacke et al. (2001)

The chemical industry produces many hazardous substances, which in wastes and in waste- water outlets can cause harm to the ecosystems. There are not enough investigations, but the first results indicate high concentrations of PCBs, phenols and phenol compounds, hydrocarbons and heavy metals.

Eutrophication Problems in Lake Peipsi

Lake Peipsi has been described as one of the most polluted lakes in the Baltic Sea region, and at the same time as one of the most biologically productive lakes, with a rich fish stock. Eutrophication is periodically indicated by blue-green water blooms, an increased abundance of macrophytes, as well as changes in species composition. The abundance of macrozoobenthos has been considered to one of the highest among lakes in Northern Europe (Nõges et al. 1996). The primary production rate has been reported to be 0.8 g C $m^{-2} d^{-1}$ (Nõges et al. 1996), which is somewhat higher than the values observed in other lakes in the Baltic Sea region. In addition, contamination with faecal micro-organisms has been prevalent due to inefficient sewage treatment or even a lack thereof. Moreover, Lake Peipsi is particularly vulnerable to pollution because it is relatively shallow (mean depth 7.1 m, maximum depth 15 m). The mean concentrations of nutrients show a clear south-north gradient with the highest concentrations in Lake Pihkva and the lowest in the northern part of the main Lake Peipsi (Nõges et al. 1996).

As pointed out earlier, Lake Peipsi is of great economic significance, first and foremost in terms of water transport and fishery. During the Soviet period, large amounts of pollutants from industrial and agricultural sources were emitted to the lake. The recent restructuring of the economy in Estonia, Latvia and the Russian Federation has most likely decreased the pollution from agricultural sources, as already mentioned. Nevertheless, the lake is under high anthropogenic influence. The different parts of the lake show different trophic states; Lake Peipsi is regarded as a eutrophic lake, Lake Lämmijärv is close to hypertrophic, and L. Pihkva is considered to be hypertophic. The eutrophication of the lake continues to rank as one of the most pervasive pollution problems. This is because the control of eutrophication is problematic due to the extremely complex cause-effect relationships involved.

Transboundary Co-operation in the Lake Peipsi Region

In 1997, Estonia and Russia agreed on the protection and sustainable development of transboundary waters, following the principles set by the UN Economic Commission for Europe's convention five years earlier, which included the Narva River basin and Lake Peipsi/Chudskoe. The collaboration was initiated in 1994, with one of the first bilateral agreements on fisheries in Lake Peipsi. In August 1997, Estonia and the Russian Federation signed an intergovernmental

'Agreement on the Protection and Sustainable Use of Transboundary Water Bodies.' Based on this agreement, Russia and Estonia established a Joint Transboundary Water Commission the same year, for co-ordination of activities on implementation of the agreement. The official representatives of the Commission consisted of (i) a Secretary General of the Estonian Ministry of the Environment (ii) a First Deputy Minister of the Russian Ministry for Natural Resources, and (iii) two Commission secretaries, representing environmental authorities in Estonia and Russia which co-ordinated activities on implementation of the transboundary water agreement. The Commission established four working groups: a working group on water protection, a working group on water management, a working group on monitoring and research, and a working group on co-operation with NGOs, local authorities and international organisations.

A fundamental task of the Commission was to act as a formal mechanism for organising co-operation across the border as well as between local interested parties and the two governments. Activities included were: management of the exchange of water monitoring data, definition of priority studies on protection and sustainable use of the resources, and agreements on common quality indicators and methods of water testing and analysis. One of the most significant achievements of the Estonian-Russian Commission for Protection and Use of Transboundary Waters so far has been to complete a comprehensive computer-based inventory of point-source pollution in the Lake Peipsi/Chudskoe and Narva River basin. Meanwhile, the Commission recently agreed to establish a joint database on water quality. The Commission is committed to developing co-operation with local authorities, stakeholders and NGOs around the lake. At its second annual meeting in 1999, the Commission adopted a decision to start preparation of a Lake Peipsi Basin Management Plan based on principles outlined in the EU Water Framework Directive. The Lake Peipsi Management Plan to be developed will build on ongoing water management activities in the lake basin by the respective governments and projects currently supported by the Danish and Swedish governments and the EU.

Effective implementation of existing monitoring programmes on Lake Peipsi is undermined by the financial limitations of the regional environmental authorities responsible and by a lack of co-ordination of monitoring activities between Estonia and Russia. Differences in institutional arrangements for monitoring and information exchange in Estonia and Russia (i.e. institutional incompatibility) as well as considerable differences in methodology and equipment used by the partners on the Estonian and Russian sides complicate the task of developing co-operation and harmonisation of the state monitoring strategies. The political and economic situation in the region is changing rapidly and this does not always allow for the development of long-term specific co-operation plans – plans are to be revised frequently. The Lake Peipsi basin is a relatively new transboundary water basin, and for this reason the procedures of international co-ordination of monitoring and management activities have yet to be elaborated. Establishing co-operation in the Lake Peipsi Basin in the situation of transition and uncertainty is challenging but at the same time it can be seen as a great opportunity to apply modern transboundary water management methodologies and tools instead of being 'track-dependent' of the methods used decades ago. In fact, the Lake Peipsi co-operation experience has attracted considerable attention from international organisations such as the World Bank, the European Commission and others as an example of a sustainable and cost-effective co-operation.

Implementation of the EU Water Framework Directive regime

Besides national and local efforts to build up co-operation to address environmental problems in the Lake Peipsi Basin, the prospects of EU membership may reinforce co-operation. According to the EU Water Framework Directive (WFD) that came into force in December 2000, rivers and lakes will need to be managed by river basin boundaries. Transboundary co-operation should be developed across member state borders or even beyond them. As Estonia is an EU accession state, the Estonian government is currently in the process of adapting national laws and the administrative system to the requirements of the EU. As a part of this work the Estonian Water Act is being revised to harmonise with the EU Water Framework Directive. River Basin Management Plans for all water basins in Estonia are to be elaborated by 2004 and Estonian international basin management plans by 2009 (Marko Tuurmann pers. comm. 2001).

Half of Lake Peipsi is located in the Russian Federation and is to be managed according to Russian legislation. Russia is not obliged to implement the EU Directive – that is a volunteer decision. The Estonian-Russian Joint Transboundary Commission has adopted a decision in 1998 that the Estonian-Russian transboundary waters will be managed in accordance with the EU Water Framework Directive. On the surface it seems that there should not be serious problems with the implementation of the Water Framework Directive in the Estonian-Russian transboundary water basin as both the EU Water Framework Directive and the Russian Water Code apply an ecosystem (basin) approach to management of waters. A closer look at the EU and Russian water legislation reveals fundamental differences in the approaches to the developing and implementing river basin management plans.

The Russian Water Code defines the basic principles of state management of the use and protection of water resources in the Russian Federation, including the distribution of responsibilities for water management among different institutions and organisations and different levels of government, ownership of water resources in Russia, rules of use and obtaining licenses for the water use. The implementation of the basin plan is left to responsible authorities – the Ministry of Natural Resources of Russia and its regional offices that have to define procedures and schedule the implementation of the Water Code.

The EU Water Framework Directive covers surface water and groundwater together as well as estuaries and marine waters and has the following main objectives: expanding the scope of water protection to all waters, surface waters and groundwater; achieving 'good status' for all waters by a certain deadline; water management based on river basins; a 'combined approach' to emission limit values and quality standards; getting the prices right; getting the citizen involved more closely and streamlining legislation (Blöch 2000). Under the Water Directive, all the EU member states are obliged to establish river basin authorities that should define water quality ecological objectives in specific water basins within stated in the directive deadlines, prepare river basin management plans and implement specific plans of actions.

The Directive establishes a deadline for achievement of ecological objectives but it leaves open to its member states to define ecological objectives depending on major water-use patterns and specific geographical conditions in water basins. One of the first difficulties in the implementation of the Directive in the Estonian-Russian transboundary water basin will be the establishment of common ecological objectives for the water basins. As there are different water quality standards used in Russia and Estonia for a number of water quality parameters, there is no common ground between experts in two countries on surface and ground water quality in the basin. To adopt common ecological objectives will require a great amount of work at expert level as well as political negotiations and decisions through the Estonian-Russian transboundary water commission, in order to achieve the common ground on the water quality in the Lake Peipsi Basin.

Another potential problem is the directive's 'full cost recovery' pricing system, which is one of the Directive's most important innovations: Member states will be required to ensure that the price charged to water consumers – e.g. for the distribution of fresh water and the collection and treatment of waste water – reflects the true costs. Full cost recovery is impossible to implement in accordance with the Russian legislation, where the use of water resources and the cost of water purification are subsidised.

Another problem is that the Directive's language is not easy to understand as it contains many new concepts from the point of view of traditional water management concepts ('Good water status,' 'full recovery cost pricing,' etc.), and text does not exist in the Russian language.

Thus, step-by-step guidelines for the development of integrated water management strategies especially for river basins on the EU external borders, based on the principles of the Water Framework Directive, should be prepared. EU technical assistance programmes, such as TACIS, should be focused on assisting non-EU member states in the implementation of joint strategies for management of the shared transboundary waters on the European borders.

Note

1   The following persons are acknowledged for their contribution:
    Ülo Sults (Tartu Environmental Research Ltd.); Anatoli Vasiliev (Tallinn Technical University); Boris Skakalsky (State Hydrological Institute); Alla Botina (Pskov Regional Committee
    for Environmental Protection); Karin Pachel (Estonian Ministry of Environment, Environment Information Centre); Tatiana Maltsman (Swedish Environmental Protection Agency);
    Tiina Nõges (Tartu University); Külli Kangur (Institute of Zoology and Botany); Madis Saluver and Olga Vassilenko (Peipsi Center for Transboundary Co-operation).
    The authors are grateful to the Estonian Ministry of Environment, the Russian Hydrometeorological Centre and Pskov Regional Committee of Environmental Protection for providing environmental data on *e.g.* water quality and water discharge. We also acknowledge all
    other participants that in one way or another have contributed to this report.
    The Swedish EPA, the Danish Ministry of Foreign Affairs and the European Union (contract
    No. EVK1-CT-2000-00076) are acknowledged for their financial contribution.

References

Hinsberg, A., Saluver, M., Vassilenko, O. (eds) (2001). 'Lake Peipsi Business Profile: Socio-Economic Survey of the Lake Peipsi Region,' *Peipsi CTC Report.*

Ivanov, S.V. (1997). 'Monitoring khimicheskogo sostava pridonnykh stred del'ty reki Velikoj' in
    *Okhrana okruzhayushchei sredy i ustojchivoe razvitie v vodosbornom bassejne Pskovo-Chudskogo
    ozera.* Tartu.

Lebedeva, O.A. and Sudnitsyna, D.N. (1997). 'Ėkologicheskij monitoring del'ty reki Velikoj' in
    *Okhrana okruzhayushchei sredy i ustojchivoe razvitie v vodosbornom bassejne Pskovo-Chudskogo
    ozera.* Tartu.

Loigu, E. and Leisk. Ü. (1996). 'Water quality of rivers in the drainage basin of Lake Peipsi,'
    Hydrobiologia 338, pages 25-35.

Löfgren, S., Gustafson, A., Steineck, S. and Stålnacke, P. (1999). 'Agricultural Development and
    Nutrient Flows in the Baltic States and Sweden after 1988,' *AMBIO* 28, pages 320-27.

Nõges, P., Nõges, T. and Jastremskij, V.V. (1996). 'Primary production of Lake Peipsi/Pihkva,'
    Hydrobiologia 338, pages 77-89.

Nõges, T., Haberman, J., Jaani, A., Laugaste, R., Lokk, S., Mäemets, A., Nõges, P., Pihu, E.,
    Starast, H., Timm, T. and Virro, T. (1996). 'General description of Lake Peipsi-Pihkva,'
    Hydrobiologia 338, pages 1-9.

Olsson, L. and Sults, Ü. (1999). *PCB, Metals and benthic fauna in some rivers draining oil-shale
    mining areas in the Lake Peipsi Catchment.* Report from a Monitoring Campaign. Västra
    Götaland, Sweden.

Pihu, E. and Haberman, J. (eds) (2001). *Lake Peipsi – Flora and Fauna. Institute of Zoology and
    Botany.* Tartu, Sulemees Publishers.

Stålnacke, P., Sults, Ü., Vasiliev, A., Skakalsky, B., Botina, A., Roll, G., Pachel, K. and Maltsman,
    T. (2001). 'Nutrient loads to Lake Peipsi,' *Jordforsk Report* 4:1.

SWECO (1997). *Development of Water Services in Pskov.* Final Report. SWECO.

Young, O. (1989). *International Co-operation: Building Regimes for Natural Resources and the Environment.* New York, Cornell University Press.

Part III

Transborder Regional Co-operation

11 Transnational Regionalism as Paradigm and Political Reality: Consequences for Comparative Research and Co-operation Praxis

James Wesley Scott[1]

This chapter touches upon the phenomenon of transboundary regionalism as a new form of political regulation and as a subject of increasing research relevance. Transboundary regionalism can be defined as a spatially integrated form of political co-operation and problem-solving that transcends the limits of nationally based administrative practice and attempts to create a sense of cohesiveness, interdependence and common interests across national boundaries. Its proliferation in recent years as a political phenomenon has been accompanied by a conspicuous increase in research on border regions and transboundary co-operation initiatives.[2]

Transboundary regionalism involves the flexible construction of international communities of interest – a process described here as 'transboundary regionalisation' – within changing global economic and political contexts. For this and other reasons it has enriched political geography by unifying a variety of issues often dealt with in isolation, including new readings of geopolitics, functional aspects of borders ('filtres,' 'gateways,' 'zones of integration,' etc.), transaction costs of transboundary co-operation as well as the cultural, historical and socio-economic contexts of specific border areas (van Houtum 2000). One of the principal tasks of research is to develop a clearer understanding of the greater political relevance of transboundary regionalism, particularly in terms of shifting scales of governance between local, national and supranational levels.[3] It should thus be sufficiently clear that the study of this phenomenon necessitates inter- and multidisciplinary approaches as well as meaningful comparative methodologies in order to go beyond mere description and typologies.

Central to our understanding of transboundary regionalism are the different economic, political and cultural/ideological variables that ultimately condition it. From both a scientific and practical standpoint, transboundary regionalism can be captured in terms of political regulation processes that seek to 'manage' globalisation; it addresses challenges to traditional, nation state-oriented, policy mechanisms by creating networked and multilevel governance structures that deal with environmental, economic, cultural, social, and other issues. At the same time, transboundary regionalism is both a result of overlying geopolitical conditions and locally embedded (or 'bottom-up') initiative. Within the scope of this article I will develop a comparative analytical framework centred around a notion of 'regime' as geopolitical context. As defined here, regimes consist of incentive structures, political imperatives, restrictions, and paradigmatic discourses of economic and political integration. They are also characterised by the actual governance structures or 'realms of co-operation' that various actor groups construct transnationally.

While regimes express the contingency of transnational political regulation, any treatment of transboundary regionalism as a political process must ultimately address its potential significance as a governance mechanism, and specifically as an effective means to deal with regional development issues in cross-border contexts. This will be done by presenting evidence from Europe and North America regarding results of transboundary regionalism, both in terms of developing multiactor networks as well as actual project-oriented results. This approach involves a high degree of generalisation but allows for a systematic comparative analysis. Indeed, experiences of the German-Polish and Arizona-Sonora borderlands, both highly asymmetric and in may ways peripheral to their respective nation states, indicate that transboundary regionalism is gradually opening up new development opportunities for disadvantaged regions. Thus, in concluding, this paper will offer several observations on the potential governance roles transboundary regionalism might assume within a future and considerably enlarged European Union.

The Analytical Framework:
Paradigms and Transboundary Regionalisation Processes

Transboundary regionalism reflects fundamental, if gradual, changes in the political geography of international relations. As Oran Young (1997) and others argue, global economic and environmental pressures have generated an increasing demand for new transnational governance mechanisms that transcend Westphalian notions of territorial sovereignty. Nation states have begun to understand that strategic and project-oriented networks joining communities, regions, and actor groups transnationally help make sense of globalisation and to anticipate its consequences. More often than not, these networks are embedded in region-building processes where, as in the case of the Baltic Sea region, Euroregions, the US-Mexican borderlands and other areas, environmental, economic and political interdependence necessitate new forums for transnational co-operation.

Organised around attempts to address specific issues of common interest, transboundary regionalism reflects the opportunities and limitations presented by the institutional frameworks within which they operate. Transboundary actors generally engage in such activities voluntarily, assuming net benefits from co-operation. In a sense, they create goal-oriented networks of 'elites' who partially transcend local contexts in defining their agendas. On the other hand, the establishment of transnational networks and communities of interest is ultimately affected by local and regional conditions. Here, we are dealing with regions constructed around specific issues of common concern. They exist as partly formalised organisations, such as the Euroregions, as well as informal alliances.

The central argument developed here is that transboundary regionalism is conditioned, among other things, by supranational integration contexts, administrative and institutional structures, policy concerns of the nation state, culture, language and history. The theoretical basis for this discussion has been gleaned from concepts of political regulation, understood as the management of change in the territorial control functions of the nation state, and the New Institutional Economics. In term of regulation, regions and cities that co-operate across national frontiers can be seen as a spatial nexus where internal and external forces interact – where the contradictions of globalisation (e.g. socio-economic polarisation, crises of political legitimacy, a weakening of the social consensus) are met with concrete strategies of social, political and economic stabilisation (Le Galés 1998; Krätke 1999). Thus, whether the actors and actor groups involved are NGOs, state or local governments, public agencies, public-private alliances, private enterprises or hybrid (interorganisational) forms thereof, realms of co-operation develop that are centred around specific regionalising projects. Such realms of co-operation are characterised by interaction structures (semi-formal and informal organisations, networks, conferences, etc.) and strategies (regional development concepts, marketing, political lobbing activities, etc.).

Figure II.I: An exemplary European transboundary co-operation 'regime'

Norms	Imperatives	Institutions	Instruments
– national (and/or senior government)-mediation	– cohesion	– ntergovernmental commissions	– structural policy incentives
– synergy: exploitation of complementarities	– 'pre-integration' of Central European states	– informal parliamentary working groups	– transboundary regional development programmes
– partnerships: multilevel policy coordination; additionality through co-financing	– decentralisation and regionalisation	– Euroregions: locally based institutions	– informational policies and transfers of co-operation know-how
	– sustainability	– European representation through voluntary organisations	
	– promotion of regional and local initiative		– publicity forums and political platforms (CEMAT, Council of Europe, AEBR)
	– development of competitive regional policies		

The theoretical approach employed in Figure 11.1 draws inspiration from Douglass North's concept of institutional change (1990) and attempts, simply stated, to identify opportunity structures, paradigmatic notions, and organisational principles that govern or guide the development of transboundary regionalism in different geographical contexts. Within this general theoretical framework, the concept of transboundary co-operation 'regimes,' as expressed by rules, policy instruments, strategic considerations and paradigmatic arguments that influence transboundary co-operation behaviours, provides a basis for comparatively analysing transboundary regionalisation as a form of political regulation (Scott 1999a). Of central importance are therefore projects of economic globalisation and interstate integration (as manifested, for example, by the European Union and the North American Free Trade Area, or NAFTA) and the institution-building process they entail (Scott 1999b). Figure 11.1 presents in generalised form a European regime for transboundary regionalism that captures the programmatic nature of the EU's interstate integration project.

Within the larger discourse of globalisation and shifting spatial scales of governance, transboundary regionalism has developed into a paradigm that links changing notions of state-society relationships to equally global ideas of change in the organisation of economic life (Loughlin 2000). Paradigms are not only ways of seeing and interpreting reality but also provide a course of action. The 'interventionist welfare state' and 'fordism' have given way to paradigms of regional empowerment, post-fordist flexible accumulation and network relationships (Rhodes 1996; Eising and Kohler-Koch 1999). These in turn have helped legitimate – and almost reify – the concept of transboundary regionalism.

As a result, the construction of transnational regions reflects processes of mediation between different spatial levels of change and the social-political regulation of that change. As Patrick Le Galès (1998) has suggested, region-building, as a form of political regulation, involves two important functions. These are: 1) the promotion of internal integration through developing the sense of regional community, including in this case the definition of transnational commonalities and 2) the process of external integration by which actors and actor groups situate their political community or region within the larger context of interstate interaction (e.g. European Union or NAFTA). Both functions involve the development of strategies that exploit available co-operation incentives and opportunities as well as the creation of new incentives by pooling resources.

The summary evidence given below offers characterisations of transboundary regionalism as it has developed in Europe and North America. While this evidence can be given here only in a highly generalised form (and thus risking a certain oversimplification of the true picture), it reveals regionalisation patterns that might help to comprehend the potential significance of transboundary regional co-operation as a governance mechanism.

Evidence from Europe: Integration Policies and Selective Political Networking
Political exigencies of integration as well as basic principles of EU policy, structural policy in particular, have decisively influenced the development of cross-border co-operation in Europe. Transboundary regionalism implies the emergence of new spatial contexts for managing societal issues and achieving a new level of intercultural integration. It is therefore perceived in many circles as a vehicle for creating a sense of 'Europeanness' and for facilitating the difficult process of EU enlargement.

Although no general consensus exists as to how it should be achieved, economic, political and spatial cohesion are viewed as essential in maintaining an effective and internationally competitive European Union (European Commission 2000, 1996). In this respect EU structural policy has acquired a decidedly strategic role. Numerous programmes and initiatives have been launched with the express goal of creating new spatial perspectives for co-operation between cities and regions in various areas of economic development and regional policy. Most prominently, the European Initiative Interreg, now in its third phase (2000-2006), has supported numerous transboundary and transnational co-operation projects since 1989. Financed out of the EU's structural funds, the present Interreg III initiative has earmarked over 4.8 billion euro to this end, making it the community's largest structural initiative. With co-financing from national and local sources, the total amount available within the Interreg framework will exceed well over 6 billion euro. In addition, programmes targeted for Central and Eastern Europe and the former Soviet Union, most prominently PHARE and TACIS, provide supplemental funds for cross-border projects on the EU's external boundaries.

Providing incentives for the creation of new communities of interest within and without nation states serves not only to instil a sense of European identity but also to diffuse innovations in, among other areas, economic promotion, job-creation schemes and revitalisation strategies.[4] As a result, transnational networks organised around specific development problems and/or perspectives have multiplied, signifying a certain degree of Europeanisation of local policies (Church and Reid 1999, 1995). In addition to networking, European goals are also being promoted by regional policy and spatial planning principles that emphasise comprehensive strategic approaches and vertical and horizontal co-ordination (EU Commission 1999). Ultimately, one of the intended effects here is to strengthen local capacities for strategic planning and local development and thereby the competitiveness of European cities and regions.

Furthermore, organisational structures of cross-border co-operation have been built up in Europe through a combination of local initiatives and supportive measures implemented by national and European Union institutions, resulting in a complex multilevel framework of formal institutions, political associations, lobbies and the incentive programmes mentioned above (von Malchus 1998). Again, formal-institutional aspects of cross-border co-operation in Europe are very much in evidence in the area of regional development and spatial planning. The Council of Europe, the European Conference of Ministers Responsible for Spatial Planning (CEMAT), the Association of European Border Regions[5], various regional authorities and local governments in border regions as well as the European Commission itself are among the institutions and agencies that have been deeply involved in promoting transnational co-operation in these areas (Blatter and Clement 2000). They have also encouraged a strategy of what might be called 'multilevel institutionalisation' in order to facilitate co-operation and the vertical and horizontal co-ordination of policy between different spatial levels. This strategy is largely based on precedents established by the Benelux countries and cross-border actors on the Dutch-German border and involves the creation of intergovernmental planning commissions representing senior governments agencies, regional working groups and voluntary associations or Euroregions made up of municipalities (and, as the case might be, counties or regions) located along national boundaries.

Cross-border regionalism manifests itself not only institutionally but also as interests and development priorities articulated in the form of strategies guiding co-operative action. Strategy development is largely informed by broader European regional development and spatial planning objectives as transmitted via various principles, documents, institutions and programmes (Scott 1998). Here again, programmatic goals of sustainable development, competitiveness, cohesion and the strengthening of local capacities – values that in fact define a specific European consensus on balancing regional development – form a basic foundation. These objectives are reflected in the Interreg initiative that, along with PHARE and TACIS in the case of Central and Eastern Europe, has provided considerable financial assistance to cross-border projects and material incentives to the development of regionalist strategies. Most importantly, Interreg mandates the elaboration of cross-border development strategies that include socio-economic and geographical analyses of regional strengths and weaknesses, the declaration of future development goals and the identification of specific projects with which to achieve them.[6]

Economic development, cross-border infrastructure and improved co-operation in environmental protection are the primary objectives outlined by the EU in assisting project-oriented co-operation. However, socio-cultural objectives are also considered. Specific emphases of development areas differs from region to region. But generally include technical infrastructure improvements, basic capital investment projects, environmental protection measures (such as the establishment of natural reserves and parks) well as cultural and youth exchange initiatives. Not surprisingly, infrastructure development features prominently in regions along the EU's border with Poland, Hungary, The Czech Republic and other Central and East European countries. In border regions such as the French-German or Dutch-German somewhat more emphasis is placed on developing informational networks between local governments and enterprises, public transportation, tourism and the co-ordination of local land-use plans (Roch, Scott and Ziegler 1998)

Having evolved out of co-operation between Germany and its western neighbours (Benelux-states, Denmark, France and Switzerland), multilevel institutionalisation appears to be gradually imposing itself as a normative organising principle of transboundary co-operation within the EU (Scott 2000). Furthermore, this concept has been applied to German-Polish, German-Czech and Austrian-Hungarian border regions in anticipation of enlargement. Interestingly enough, despite its short history of open co-operation, the German-Polish border region can boast of an impressive array of cross-border institutions. At the national and regional levels Polish-German Intergovernmental Commissions, an Environmental Council and several interagency working groups dealing with specific planning, and environmental issues have been created. At the local level, cities and towns within a distance of 40 to 80 km from the common border have established municipal associations for the specific purpose of forming four German-Polish Euroregions based on international private law (Scott and Collins 1997).

Faced with radically new geographical and geopolitical situations since 1990, political elites within the German-Polish border region have been attempting to reframe development perspectives within a broader European spatial context, an all the more urgent task due to the negative social and economic effects of de-industrialisation and massive job losses in agriculture affecting both sides of the border (Barjak 1997; Krätke 1996). The four Euroregions created since 1993 have drawn up development concepts that embrace the ambitious objective of creating *integrated economic and ecological areas* through a wide variety of measures aimed, among other things, at combating unemployment, promoting a positive sense of common border region identity, economic co-operation and good neighbourliness (Gruchman and Walk 1996). Through EU funding mechanisms provided by the Interreg and PHARE initiatives, local projects have assumed an important role in determining the prospects of German-Polish cross-border regionalism. Project examples include binational water treatment plants, joint university facilities in Frankfurt (Oder) and its Polish neighbour Slubice, joint emergency services and the development of natural areas for environmental and tourism purposes.

Evidence indicates that multilevel institutional support of cross-border co-operation in Europe appears to have contributed significantly to the development of new interregional and transnational working relationships. However, despite this sophisticated institutional framework, cross-border co-operation has fallen short of its regional development aspirations. At its most 'successful,' cross-border regionalism has mobilised public-sector co-operation in areas where public agencies have more or less direct influence over projects and project results. For example, co-operation between public agencies, universities and, to a lesser extent, non-profit organisations has been generally successful in relatively straightforward projects of clear but limited focus. As a result, uncontroversial initiatives in areas such as environmental protection (creating cross-border parklands and nature reserves), physical and transportation infrastructure, the production of basic planning materials, joint curriculum development for regional

universities, vocational training, cultural activities, local social services and public agency networking have flourished

Nevertheless, transboundary regionalism has been far less successful in stimulating private sector participation in regional development (van Houtum 1998).
Furthermore, administrative complexities associated with European programmes
appear in many instances to discourage community partnerships, promoting unilateral rather than truly binational projects (European Parliament 1997). In some
cases, such as the Spanish-Portuguese, German-Polish and German-Czech border
regions, Interreg (and PHARE) funds are often merely viewed as additional
sources of revenue rather than as genuine co-operation incentives. However, by
the same token, critical observers have emphasised that the public agencies
involved have failed to build up effective communication networks and thus to
'vertically integrate' institutions of planning co-operation.[7] Similarly, interagency
conflicts over resource allocation have often worked against the co-ordination of
regional development initiatives earmarked for the border region.

Evidence from North America:
Flexible Networks in the NAFTA Context

In contrast to the European situation, interstate integration in North America is
clearly biased towards recognising economic rather than political interdependence. A comprehensive policy-making process shared by Canada, Mexico and
the United States is not envisaged – at least not within the foreseeable future
(Doran 1996). Territorial sovereignty issues, having lost much of their salience in
Europe, remain of great importance in the North American context and only
modest moves towards the creation of supranational institutions have been made.
Still, the free-trade context sanctioned by Canada, Mexico and the United States
has provided a platform for regionalism and has prompted a rapid increase in co-
operation initiatives aimed at taking advantage of economic opportunities and/or
addressing negative side-effects of economic growth. Accordingly, transboundary
co-operation regimes in North America have evolved around economic development and environmental issues (Varady et al. 1996).

The self-styled Pacific Northwest Economic Region (PNWER), a transnational region including several US states and Canadian provinces, has framed its
strategies with regard to with basic issues affecting the economic development
perspectives of the binational region (Alper 1996; Artibise et al. 1997). These
include: infrastructure, trade, foreign investment, environmental amenities,
tourism and other areas. PNWER is unabashedly promotional and very much
driven by private-sector interests intent on exploiting the benefits of North American free trade. These activities find more concrete focus in a plethora of subregional, often single-purpose, task forces and associations, such as the Cascadia
Transportation and Trade Task Force, a multilevel coalition of governments, business associations and other groups that promote growth management and

improved mobility along the Portland-Seattle-Vancouver motorway corridor (Sparke 2001). These initiatives, while largely business oriented, have been accompanied by more critical and environmentally aware networks that seek to stave off greater exploitation of the region's natural resources (Alper 1999).

In the case of the US-Mexican borderlands, economics and the environment are even more directly tied to transboundary regionalism. Increased local/regional trade as well as large-scale foreign direct investment have helped fuel the growth of binational urban economies in San Diego (California)-Tijuana (Baja California), El Paso (Texas)-Juárez (Chihuahua), the Lower Rio Grande Valley and in the Two Nogales on the Arizona-Sonora border (Ganster, Sweedler and Clement 2000).[8] However, while economic growth in many parts of the US-Mexico Borderlands has been truly impressive, the environmental costs have been high.[9] The rapid urban development there is generally considered to be unsustainable due to scarce water resources, the inadequacy of water-treatment infrastructure and the inability of local governments to provide public services commensurate with growth, particularly on the Mexican side (Clement, Ganster and Sweedler 1999). In addition, toxic pollutants generated by the burgeoning industrial complexes on the border pose a serious threat to water quality and public health (Tiefenbacher 1998). As a result, transboundary regionalism in the US-Mexican context is both informed by business-sector concerns for the economic future of the area and promoted by NGOs and advocacy groups that address environmental and community development issues (Zabin 1997).[10]

Until recently, the formal institutional co-operation between Mexico and the United States on issues of borderlands development was notorious for a legalistic and limited approach with little consideration of local concerns (Mumme 1997). As a result of regional action new supranational institutions have been created within the NAFTA process. These include: 1) the trilateral North American Commission on Environmental Co-operation (CEC), a general advisory body, 2) the US-Mexican Border Environmental Co-operation Commission (BECC), responsible for identifying and assessing infrastructure projects to receive loans and 3) the North American Development Bank (NADBank), an agency that provides loans to certified infrastructure projects on the US-Mexican border. Furthermore, a process of developing Integrated Environmental Plans for the Border (IBEP) as well as the objective of community empowerment through involvement in project development and implementation have been incorporated into the overall policy framework (Mumme 1997; Spalding 2000).

The binational Arizona-Sonora region is an excellent example of how the process of North American economic and political integration and the burgeoning export-oriented manufacturing sector have contributed to the regional transboundary co-operation environment. Within this co-operation environment various groups, including business associations, local and state governments, NGOs and regional academic communities, interact and in certain cases have inaugurated binational regional development initiatives. The Arizona-Mexico Commission and its Sonoran counterpart, the Comisión Sonora-Arizona, are independent but symmetrically structured organisations that have provided an environment for various co-operation activities involving, state and non-state actors and emphasising economic, environmental and cultural issues.[11] While headed by the state governors, the Commissions facilitate significant private-sector and volunteer involvement and provide a central role for regional universities in project-oriented co-operation. Large international and regional firms but also non-profit foundations are among the most important sponsors of the Commissions and their activities. The work of the Commissions is decidedly project-oriented; perhaps the most ambitious and symbolically important initiative they have supported is that of marketing the image of an integrated region for investment, tourism and regional development purposes. Furthermore, the two Commissions and the working groups that have gradually emerged in the binational region pursue a general strategy of maintaining the viability of economic growth while improving environmental conditions and quality of life (Arizona-Mexico Commission 2000; 1997a). The rationale for establishing this political agenda is uncertainty over the long-term prospects for Arizona and Sonora and fears that, as peripheral states, their chances for exploiting new markets within the NAFTA context will be limited (Arizona-Mexico Commission 1997b). Competition from other regions in Canada, Mexico and the US is increasing and the border location may cease to be an advantage as international rail and road corridors are developed. This has resulted in a strategic planning exercise, the Strategic Economic Development Vision for the Arizona-Sonora Region.

The 'Vision' contemplates cohesive, mutually beneficial regional development for the transnational corridor between Phoenix and Hermosillo and is sponsored and supported by the two state governments. The actual process of developing the strategy, however, is managed by partnerships made up of universities, local governments, industrial organisations and other interested actors and groups. Financing for the strategy and its various elements has been secured from non-governmental sources and, to a lesser extent, from business contributions. Rather than focus on individual enterprises, the Arizona-Sonora Vision employs the concept of industry clusters in organising economic development initiatives. In this way, complementarities, international competitiveness quality of life indicators and the development potential of different business sectors (e.g. tourism, transportation and logistics, food-processing) within the binational region can be more effectively determined and co-operative efforts implemented.[12] Now that the study phase is completed, the main challenge facing the 'Vision' will be finding resources and the necessary political support to implement recommendations.

When weighed against the ambitious goals set by the two Commissions, the actual results achieved by these transboundary initiatives might appear meagre. Concrete results in terms of large investment projects, for example, have been few and far between because of a general lack of financial resources. Detractors insist that the Arizona-Sonora project is little more than a prestigious networking opportunity that bestows symbolic diplomatic status on those involved and pampers the political self-images of the two states.[13] Nevertheless, the Arizona-Sonora regionalist project appears to have generated a variety of mechanisms through which the binational region has been able to articulate its political interests and development concerns – both 'internally' and 'externally.' Through a routinisation of dialogue between actors on both side of the border, physical and psychological barriers to communication have been successfully diminished and more or less stable co-operation structures institutionalised.[14] This has allowed the Commissions to support project-oriented co-operation as well as lobbying activities by regional interest groups in response to national policies. However, it is also clear that the Arizona-Sonora initiative has had to establish working relationships with the national level in order to flourish. Perhaps ironically, co-operation with federal agencies remains essential, especially in matters dealing with transportation infrastructure, border-crossing formalities and the environment.

Overriding regional development issues, such as transportation, logistics, environmental concerns and the permeability of the border draw attention to the vulnerability of the US-Mexican (and particularly the Arizona-Sonoran) co-operation projects. Nevertheless, in the long run there is potentially a greater political role for US-Mexican transboundary regionalism. This appears to be taking place by focusing binational strategies in order to inform policy at various levels and in through lobbying to improve binational relations and local conditions. This carefully optimistic assessment is supported by the fact that perceptible changes in border region governance have already taken place; in exploiting the supranational agenda of NAFTA, the regional initiatives briefly discussed here have, with the specific means available to them, helped transform the political and economic policy role of the US-Mexico border. Previously considered a periphery by both federal governments – and this despite the rapid urban growth rates on the border – the national level appears to have 'rediscovered' the US-Mexico borderlands. Gradually, national agencies are attempting to work with regional and local actors in finding solutions to pressing transboundary problems. This has, in part, been signalled by the inauguration of a planning process for sustainable development in North American border regions (Spalding 2000).

Conclusions

Within the last two decades transboundary regionalist projects have emerged in both Europe and North America as important elements of political and economic integration. These alliances address a need for new forms of political negotiation and co-ordination – and in the broadest sense, regulation. They can thus be understood as pragmatic exercises in constructing the political and social foundations necessary for solving local problems that transcend national boundaries. As this paper has indicated, they are also conditioned by overlying contexts of interstate integration and are thus characteristic of the specific strategic orientations of political and economic co-operation in the two continental settings. Figure II.2 offers a synthesis of the contextual situations governing transboundary regionalism in Europe and North American and highlights prominent similarities and differences discussed above.

In the European case, the dynamics of EU integration and enlargement indicate that border region issues are beginning to enjoy a policy status in their own right. Formally, the general structural pattern of European transboundary regionalism conforms to systems of multilevel governance evolving within the EU (Hocking 1996; Marks 1997). Transboundary co-operation is regulated by institutions at national, regional and local levels, embedded in European and, to an extent, national structural policies, and is heavily dependent upon subsidies and other direct incentives. However, Europe's dense institutional and policy networks have only partially addressed the local and regional development aims of transboundary regionalism. In many cases co-operation is characterised by administrative complexity, public sector dominance and appears, furthermore, to have dampened private-sector interest. Ironically, despite their embeddedness within policy networks at other administrative levels, regional co-operation initiatives appear to be rather fragmented and 'closed' systems comprised primarily of administrative elites. As a result, action appears oriented primarily towards influencing decisions within the immediate networks but with limited external (multiplier) effects and limited citizen participation.

Figure II.2: Transboundary regionalism in comparative perspective

	EU Context	NAFTA Context (US-Mexican Borderlands)
Logics of Interstate Integration	Dominated by EU integration policies and particular interests of nations-states (integration of regions into larger EU context)	A response to NAFTA and economic integration challenges (regional self-defence)
Sectoral Bias	State-oriented and/or dominated by public sector	Interorganisational with strong non-state/NGO bias
Strategies		
formal	Integrated regional development	Integrated regional development
de facto	Subsidy-driven and focused on economic issues	Fragmented: strong business-sector/environmental protection bias
Organisational Characteristics		
formal	Multilevel governance	Interorganisational partnerships
de facto	Fragmented but 'closed' elite networks	Open-ended networks, often fragmented

In the North American context there exists, almost by definition, no broad policy platform for cross-border co-operation and much less government support for cross-border regionalism. Only in specific areas dealing with water and air quality and other environmental issues does the critical mass for forceful, multi-level action exist. However, while formal cross-border co-operation is evolving slowly, the activities of non-state actors and urban and regional strategic alliances appear to be closing some of the gaps left by formal co-operation. In contrast to the European case, transboundary regionalism in North America is decidedly entrepreneurial and at the same time 'grassroots' in focus. While state agencies provide a vital political (e.g. diplomatic) anchor, co-operation is characterised by transnational strategic alliances within which NGOs, universities and the private sector play an important role. This has been particularly the case with initiatives promoting improved economic co-operation and/or responsive cross-border environmental policies in the US-Mexican borderlands. Again however, the rather open-ended networks that characterise transboundary regionalism in North America are also fragmented in that they address a limited number of issues and only specific groups with a clear stake in regional development; no mechanism for establishing a system of multilevel governance that might integrate these initiatives within formal policy networks is as yet envisaged.

As mentioned above, the issue of transboundary governance is of major scientific and practical salience. The summary evidence presented suggests, in fact, that while the policy roles of transboundary regional co-operation appear restricted in absolute terms of political power, new 'networked' policy areas are emerging across national boundaries with considerable potential for addressing specific local interests and development issues. Although most of the empirical data presented here has been gleaned from case studies of German-Polish and US-Mexican border regions, the experiences of many other border regions in Europe also provide supporting evidence (Scott 2000; IRS 1999). In terms of governance, furthermore, the promise of transboundary regionalism appears to lie in its capacity to connect communities embedded in very different socio-economic, political and cultural contexts by creating flexible communication networks. Given the limitations of traditional, nationally-oriented policy-making mechanisms in dealing with changing political and economic environments, transboundary regionalism can justifiably be interpreted as a mechanism that lowers the transaction costs of maintaining political dialogue in complex (and often highly asymmetric) international situations.

As such, there is little doubt that as the pace of EU enlargement accelerates, transboundary regionalism will play an increasingly important role in establishing multilateral and multilevel working relationships between present EU member states and accession candidates. The German-Polish and Arizona-Sonora cases indicate that a regional development dialogue can indeed develop not only within 'peripheral' border regions but also across sharp socio-economic and cultural divides. Consequently, research focusing on the evolution of transboundary regionalism should seriously consider developing means of assessing the political relevance of transboundary regionalism based on the specific perceptions and requirements of the actors involved. From the standpoint of comparative research, these would serve as a meaningful alternative to 'benchmarking' or developing a priori criteria, a practice supported by research conducted in the name of EU policy evaluation. Additionally, more work should be devoted to analysing the manner in which socio-economic and institutional-administrative asymmetries influence network-formation, agenda-setting, priorities, strategies and, ultimately, local acceptance for transboundary co-operation initiatives.

Zincone and Agnew (2000) have convincingly argued that, as globalisation intensifies, mismatches between international economic and national political space – and the 'governance gaps' they engender – will be gradually eliminated by new transnational political arrangements. Despite its shortfalls, transboundary regionalism in Europe is addressing these governance gaps through a gradual process of internal and external integration; that is, by creating a new (if presently limited) sense of transnational regional community while projecting regional concerns onto 'higher' political arenas. Inevitably, the success of transboundary regionalism within a future EU will depend on its ability to make legible and intelligible to local communities processes of globalisation and European integration. Indeed, perhaps the central governance role of transboundary regions will be, in the sense of Zaki Laidi (1998), to create 'spaces of meaning' where complex state/society paradigms and notions of sustainability are translated into locally recognisable and acceptable agendas for action.

Notes

[1]   This article is based on research carried out with support of the German American Academic Council's TransCoop Programme. Matthew Sparke of the Department of Geography at the University of Washington was the US-American partner and contributed to the result presented here.

[2]   There is an extensive literature dealing with issues of transnational regionalism and transboundary co-operation. The special volume of *Regional Studies* (Volume 33, Number 7, 1999) edited by James Anderson and Liam O'Dowd, as well as European Research in Regional Science, Volume 10 (2000), edited by Martin van der Velde and Henk van Houtum, provide excellent overviews of the European situation with some comparisons with North America. The Spring 2000 edition of *Journal of Borderlands Studies*, edited by Joachim Blatter and Norris Clement, furthermore provides a very useful comparative overview of developments in both Europe and North America.

[3]   The term 'governance' is understood here to include the establishment and acceptance of a set of rules of conduct and norms (as embodied by social institutions) that 'define practices, assign roles and guide interaction so as to grapple with collective problems' (Stokke 1997: 28). Ernst-Otto Czempiel (1992: 250) offers a rather useful definition as well: 'Governance is the capacity to get things done without the legal competence to command that they be done.' Governance is hence more an issue of creating ideational and/or persuasive authority rather than exercising legal mandates.

4 Examples of network initiatives that have received EU funding are COAST (addressing employment and environmental problems in nine coastal cities), HYDRE (establishing a Mediterranean network of cities and regions to monitor water resources) and OUVERTURE and ECOS (complementary programmes aimed at establishing links between cities and regions with regard to various economic development policies).

5 The Association of European Border Regions (AEBR) was founded in 1971 by politicians, planners and researchers including Hans Briner, Viktor von Malchus and Alfred Mozer. This association received considerable impetus from efforts of the Dutch and German governments to sponsor local cross-border pilot projects in the area of cultural exchange and social activities. Events since 1971 have borne out the strategic role of the AEBR in influencing European debate on regional policy and, more specifically, on policies aimed at cross-border regions on the EU's internal and external borders.

6 Detailed information regarding the Interreg III initiative can be obtained through the EU Regional Policy website www.inforegio.org.

7 Reference is made to comments of German and Polish observers interviewed by the author.

8 Maquiladoras operate in similar fashion to offshore export processing centres where products are assembled at low cost for the world market Liberal fiscal regimes allow for the tax and duty free importation and re-exportation of components and other inputs. Initially restricted to a narrowly defined area along the border with the United States, Maquiladoras can now operate within the entire territory of Mexico.

9 The social costs of growth, as manifested by growing pockets of extreme poverty within the Borderlands cannot, for the sake of brevity, be touched upon here.

10 Furthermore, the internet resources available on North American environmental issues are impressive. The Interhemispheric Resource Centre, located in Silver City, New Mexico, offers an excellent compilation of websites and documents (see www.zianetcom/irc1/bordline/).

11 For information on the activities of these commissions, consult the following website: www.azmc.org.

12 See the summary description of the 'Vision' provided by the Arizona-Mexico Commission and available under

www.azcentral.com/community/azmex/amcvision.shtml.

13 Information was obtained during interviews carried out between 1997 and 1999.

14 Confirmed in interviews with persons closely associated with the two Commissions. For more detailed documentation of this research, see IRS (1999), available through the author.

References

Arizona-Mexico Commission (1997a). *AMC Agenda -Fiscal Year 1997 Draft Document.* (Document source: www.azcentral.com/community/azmex/amc97plan.shtml).

Arizona-Mexico Commission (1997b). *The Impact of the North American Free Trade Agreement on the State of Arizona: A Three Year Review, July 1997.* (Document source: www.azcentral.com/community/azmex).

Alper, D. (1996). 'The Idea of Cascadia: Emergent Transborder Regionalisms in the Pacific Northwest-Western Canada,' *Journal of Borderland Studies* XI:2, pages 1- 22.

Alper, D. (1999). 'Conflicting Transborder Visions and Agendas: Economic and Environmental Cascadians.' Paper presented at the international conference on 'Permeable Borders and Boundaries in a Globalising World' at Simon Fraser University, Vancouver, British Columbia on 25-27 August, 1999.

Artibise, A., Moudon, A. and Seltzer, E. (1997). 'Cascadia: An Emerging Regional Model,' pages 149- 74 in Geddes, R. (ed.). *Cities in Our Future.* Washington, DC, Island Press.

Barjak, F. (1997). 'Wirtschaftliche Lage und Regionalpolitik in den "Grenzräumen" der neuen Bundesländer,' *Forschungsreihe des IWH* 5, pages 29-134.

Blatter, J. and Clement, N. (2000). 'Cross-Border Cooperation in Europe: Historical Development, Institutionalization, and Contrasts with North America,' *Journal of Borderlands Studies* XV:1, pages 15-53.

Church, A. and Reid, P. (1995). 'Transfrontier Co-operation. Spatial Development Strategies and the Emergence of a New Scale of Regulation: The Anglo-French Border,' *Regional Studies* 29:3, pages 297-306.

Church, A. and Reid, P. (1999). 'Cross-Border Co-operation, Institutionalization and Political Space Across the English Channel,' *Regional Studies* 33:7, pages 643-55.

Clement, N., Ganster, P. and Sweedler, A. (1999). 'Development, Environment and Security in Asymmetrical Border Regions: European and North American Perspectives,' pages 243-81 in Eskelinen, H., Liikanen, I. and Oksa, J. (eds). *Curtains of Iron and Gold. Reconstructing Borders and Scales of Interaction.* Aldershot, Ashgate Gower.

Doran, C.F. (1996). 'When Building North America, Deepen Before Widening,' pages 69-85 in Doran, C.F. and Drischler, A.P. (eds). *A New North America, Cooperation and Enhanced Interdependence.* Westport and London, Praeger.

Eising, R. and Kohler-Koch, B. (eds) (1999). *The Transformation of Governance in the European Union.* London, Routledge.

European Commission (2000). Interview with Michel Barnier, Commissioner for Regional Policy, *Inforegio Panorama: Quarterly magazine of the actors of regional development*, October. Available at: www.inforegio.com/wbdoc/docgener/panorama/pano2_en.htm.

European Commission (1999). *European Spatial Development Perspective.* Luxemburg, ECC-EC-EAEC.

European Commission (1996). *First Report on Economic and Social Cohesion.* Luxemburg, ECC-EC-EAEC.

European Parliament (1997). Report on Cross-border and Inter-Regional Co-operation. (Prepared by the Committee on Regional Policy, Rapporteur: Riita Myller). DOC_EN\RR\325\325616.

Ganster, P., Sweedler, A. and Clement, N. (2000). 'Development, Growth and the Future of the Border Environment,' pages 73-103 in Ganster, P. (ed.). *The US-Mexican Border Environment: A Road Map to a Sustainable 2020.* San Diego, San Diego State University Press.

Gruchman, B. and Walk, F. (1996). 'Transboundary Cooperation in the Polish-German Border Region,' pages 129-38 in Scott J., Sweedler A., Ganster, P. and Eberwein W.-D. (eds). *Border Regions in Functional Transition: European and North American Perspectives.* Erkner bei Berlin, (IRS) Institute for Regional Development and Structural Policy.

Hocking, B. (1996). 'Bridging Boundaries Creating Linkages: Non-Central Governments and Multilayered Policy Environments,' *WeltTrends* 11, pages 36-51.

(IRS) Institute for Regional Development and Structural Policy (1999). *Projektbericht 1.18: Grenzübergreifende Regionalisierung: Möglichkeiten politikergänzender Kooperationsformen im deutsch-polnischen Grenzraum* (Project Report on Transboundary Regionalisation: Perspectives for Supporting Policy Networks in the German-Polish Border Region). Erkner bei Berlin, IRS.

Krätke, S. (1996). 'Where East Meets West: The German-Polish Border Region in Transformation,' *European Planning Studies* 4:5, pages 647-69.

Krätke, S. (1999). 'A Regulationist Approach to Regional Studies,' *Environment and Planning A* 31, pages 683-704.

Laidi, Z. (1998). *A World without Meaning*. London, Routledge.

Le Galés, P. (1998). 'Regulations and Governance in European Cities,' *International Journal of Urban and Regional Research* 22:3, pages 482-506.

Loughlin, J. (2000). 'The Cross-Border Challenges and Opportunities Posed by the Transformation of European Governance.' Paper presented at the international conference 'European Cross-border Co-operation: Lessons for and from Ireland,' Queens' University, Belfast 29 September-1 October, 2000.

Marks, G. (1997). 'An Actor-Centred Approach to Multi-Level Governance,' pages 20-40 in Jeffrey, C. (ed.). *The Regional Dimension of the European Union: Towards a Third Level in Europe?* London, Frank Cass.

Mumme, S. (1997). 'NAFTA and North American cross-Border Environmental Management,' pages 249-61 in Blake, G., Chai, L., Grundy-Warr, C., Pratt, M. and Schofield, C. (eds). *International Boundaries and Environmental Security: Frameworks for Regional Cooperation.* London and Amsterdam, Kluwer Law Publishers.

North, D. (1990). *Institutions, Institutional Change and Economic Performance.* Cambridge, Cambridge University Press.

Rhodes, R. (1996). 'The New Governance, Governing without Government,' *Political Studies* XLIV, pages 652-67.

Roch, I., Scott, J. and Ziegler, A. (1998). *Umweltgerechte Entwicklung von Grenzregionen durch kooperatives Handeln.* IÖR Schiftenreihe, 24, Dresden, (IÖR) Institute of Environmental and Spatial Development.

Scott, J. (1998). 'Planning Co-operation and Transboundary Regionalism – Implementing European Border Region Policies in the German-Polish Context,' *Environment and Planning C: Government and Policy* 16:5, pages 605-24.

Scott, J. (1999a). 'European and North American Contexts for Cross-Border Regionalism,' *Regional Studies* 33:7, pages 605-17.

Scott, J. (1999b). 'Evolving Regimes for Local Transboundary Co-operation: The German-Polish Experience,' pages 179-93 in Eskelinen, H., Liikanen, I. and Oksa, J. (eds). *Curtains of Iron and Gold. Reconstructing Borders and Scales of Interaction.* Aldershot, Ashgate.

Scott, J. (2000). 'Transboundary Cooperation on Germany's Borders: Strategic Regionalism through Multilevel Governance,' *Journal of Borderlands Studies* XV:1, pages 143-67.

Scott, J. and Collins, K. (1997). 'Inducing Transboundary Regionalism in Asymmetric Situations: The Case of the German-Polish Border,' *Journal of Borderlands Studies* XII:1&2, pages 97-121.

Spalding, M. (2000). 'Addressing border Environmental Problems Now and in the Future: Border XXI and Related Efforts,' pages 105-37 in Ganster, P. (ed.). *The US-Mexican Border Environment: A Road Map to a Sustainable 2020.* San Diego, San Diego State University Press.

Sparke, M. (2001). 'Not a State, But More Than a State of Mind: Cascading Cascadias and the Geo-Economics of Cross-Border Regionalism,' forthcoming in Perkmann, P. and Sum, N.-L. (eds). *Globalization, Regionalization and the Building of Cross-Border Regions.* London, Macmillan.

Tiefenbacher, J.P. (1998). 'La Frontera Química:Toxic Emissions and Spills Along the US-Mexican Border,' *Journal of Borderlands Studies* XIII:1, pages 57-77.

Van Houtum, H. (1998). *The Development of Cross-Border Economic Relations. A Theoretical and Empirical Study of the Influence of the State Border on the Development of Cross-Border Economic Relations Between Firms in Border Regions of the Netherlands and Belgium,* Tilburg, Netherlands, CentER.

Van Houtum, H. (2000). 'An Overview of European Geographical Research on Borders and Border Regions,' *Journal of Borderlands Studies* XV:1, pages 57-83.

Varady, R.G., Clonic, D., Merideth, R. and Sprouse, T. (1996). 'The U.S.-Mexican Border Environment Cooperation Commission: Collected Perspectives on the First Two Years,' *Journal of Borderlands Studies* XI :2, pages 89-119.

Von Malchus, V. (1998). 'Cross-Border Co-operation after World War II,' pages 285-95 in Hedegaard, L. and Lindström, B. (eds). *The NEBI Yearbook 1998: North European and Baltic Sea Integration*. Berlin, Heidelberg, Springer.

Young, O.D. (ed.). (1997). *Global Governance. Drawing Insights from the Environmental Experience*. Cambridge, Mass and London, MIT Press.

Zabin, C. (1997). 'Nongovernmental Institutions in Mexico's Northern Border,' *Journal of Borderlands Studies* XII:1&2, pages 41-72.

Zincone, G. and Agnew, J. (2000). 'The Second Great Transformation: The Politics of Globalisation in the Global North,' *Space and Polity* 4:1, pages 5-21.

12 Cross-border Co-operation and EU Enlargement

Birte Holst Jørgensen

Cross-border co-operation is central in the history of the European Union, community building and enlargement. Cross-border co-operation aims at bridging gaps left by former struggles, power politics and nationalist fervour. It also aims at overcoming the dividing effect of borders by putting into effect the free movement of people, goods, capital and services (European Dialogue 1997; Foucher 1998; Denters et al. 1998).

In this chapter I will elaborate on the success and shortcomings of PHARE cross-border co-operation programmes and enlargement starting with two basic assumptions on what cross-border co-operation may achieve:

1. Cross-border co-operation may lay the first foundation between neighbouring countries wanting to overcome economic, political and administrative differences, including borders between EU member states and candidate countries, between candidate countries, and between candidate countries and non-candidate countries.
2. Cross-border co-operation has the potential to fulfil the daily needs for micro integration and by doing so it also reveals the limits to micro integration by highlighting the deficiencies in national political and administrative systems. This may create a bottom-up pressure for decentralisation and deeper European integration.

The chapter analyses the background, design and implementation of the PHARE programme CREDO. It is a multi-country cross-border co-operation programme between CEC-CEC (Central and Eastern European countries) and CEC-NIC (Newly Independent States) border regions. It illustrates the delicate balance between wider and deeper European integration.

The History of European Cross-border Co-operation

Since the Second World War, co-operation across internal and external borders has increased steadily and is today a prominent feature of the European architecture. Borders are regarded as 'scars of history' (Council of Europe 1987). They protect national interests and are barriers to the mobility of people, goods, capital and services. But borders are also touchstones, which allow people to come together, to co-exist peacefully and to co-operate with one another to solve common problems. This makes co-operation across national borders an important mechanism of European integration.

Co-operation among border regions across national borders can be traced back to the years following the Second World War. It was especially concentrated to the border areas in the Benelux countries, France and Germany. Subsequently, a large number of cross-border arrangements have emerged, aiming at furthering general European integration, improving economic development, bringing people closer together and solving joint environmental problems (Dupuy 1982; Lindström 1996; Östhol 1996; Holst Jørgensen 1999).

Within the context of the Council of Europe, emphasis has been devoted to give voice to subnational authorities and other stakeholders of border regions (Holst Jørgensen 1999: 80-108). Border regions constitute an excellent framework for moulding Europe's future development because they have a vital interest in co-existence and co-operation with one another (AEBR 1995). Activities have concentrated on providing two constitutive elements:

– A legal framework for cross-border co-operation;
– Financial support for cross-border co-operation activities.

As for the first, the Council of Europe has encouraged national governments to sign the European Outline Convention on Transfrontier Co-operation between Territorial Communities or Authorities plus an additional protocol attached to it. The legal frame has progressively been ratified by member states. The enforcement depends, however, of often far-reaching internal legal adjustment and external bi- and multilateral agreements, for example the Karlsruhe Agreement from 1996 (Holst Jørgensen 1999: 91-106).

As for the second, efforts have concentrated on integrating cross-border issues into the structural policies of the European Community. In the wake of the Single European Act and the overhaul of the structural funds in 1988, the European Community reserved substantial funds to promote co-operation between neighbouring border regions. Following a series of 14 groups of pilot schemes on cross-border co-operation, the Commission launched the Interreg programme in 1990. Interreg is one of the EU initiatives. They allow the Commission to 'propose to the member states that they submit applications for assistance in respect of measures of significant interest to the Community' not covered by the member states' development plans (Official Journal of the European Communities (OJEC):

Regulation 4253/88: Article 11). The initiatives are designed to encourage co-operation across national borders, thereby supporting bottom-up integration.

Interreg received 1 billion ecu over the period 1990-94. This amount was increased to 2.6 billion ecu for the second programming period of 1995-99, which covered 59 cross-border co-operation programmes along internal and external borders of the Community. In Interreg III for the period 2000-2006, a total of 3.9 million euro has been earmarked for cross-border co-operation (OJEC 2000/ C 143/08: article 48).

Cross-border co-operation in Central and East European Countries

The fall of the Berlin Wall in 1989 not only paved the way for deeper European integration but also established political and economic relations between the European Community with the countries of Central and Eastern Europe. PHARE was created in 1989 to provide financial support for the countries' efforts to reform and rebuild their economies and thus make the transition to a market economy easier.

Recognising the importance of cross-border co-operation in the PHARE programme, the European Union has given financial support to cross-border co-operation since 1994. Approximately 20 per cent were then assigned to PHARE cross-border co-operation (CBC), Small Project Funds and multi-country CBC programmes as for example the Baltic CBC programme, the ECOS-Ouverture programme and the CREDO programme. The multi-country programme address regional rather than national issues and stresses cost-effectiveness across all partner countries.

In the period 1994-98, 820 million ecu or 18 per cent of the total PHARE funding was assigned to cross-border co-operation along the borders between EU member states and candidate countries in Central and Eastern Europe (CEC). The idea was to encourage similar cross-border co-operation at the external borders of the EU along the same lines as the co-operation already promoted by the Interreg initiative across the internal borders of the EU, and ensure EU funding on both sides of the borders. Hence, the aim of the PHARE cross-border co-operation programme was to assist PHARE regions along the external borders of the European Community in overcoming their specific development problems and to promote the creation and development of co-operation networks on either side of the border.

However, since the PHARE CBC only covered the borders adjacent to the European Community, the multi-country programme, CREDO, was adopted in 1996 to address the internal borders of the PHARE countries (CEC-CEC) as well as the external PHARE borders adjacent to the newly independent countries (CEC-NIC). In total 12 million ecu was devoted to promoting good neighbourliness, social stability and economic development in border regions. An overview of regions eligible for PHARE and CREDO is shown in Figure 12.1. This was the total PHARE set-up in the spring 1998 comprising on the one hand the PHARE CBC and on the other hand multi-country programmes, including the CREDO programme. However, this changed radically a few months later and was related to a change in the Community's enlargement policy.

During the 1990s the European Community acknowledged that the enlargement was no longer a question of if but when. Therefore, a pre-accession strategy was defined to prepare the candidate countries for EU membership. From being primarily demand-driven, PHARE in 1998 became accession-driven focusing on preparing candidate countries for full membership of the European Community. It was made a precursor to the social and regional structural funds[1].

In adopting the accession-driven approach in the new regulation in 1998 emphasis was now placed on national programmes and a reduction in the number of multi-country programmes. Cross-border co-operation was consolidated in the pre-accession strategy and the geographical scope of the PHARE CBC programme was extended from borders with the EU to include borders between candidate countries. This would allow these newly eligible border regions to also

Figure 12.1: Cross-border co-operation in Eastern and Central Europe

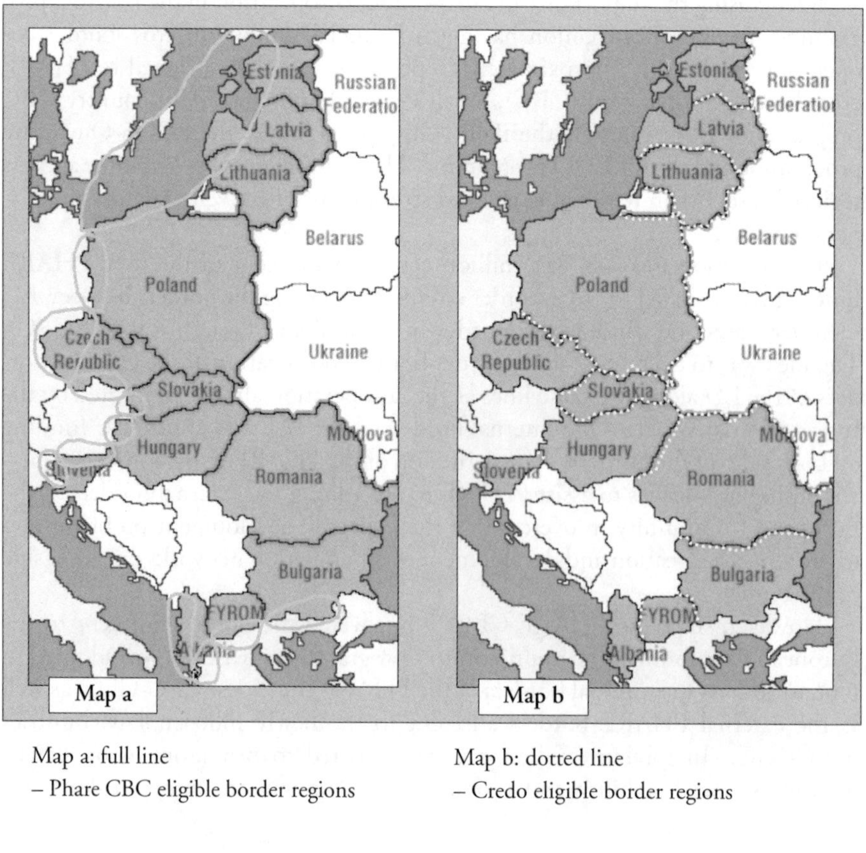

Map a: full line
– Phare CBC eligible border regions

Map b: dotted line
– Credo eligible border regions

prepare themselves for their participation in the Interreg initiative upon accession and would include them in regional development programmes in each candidate country and also be eligible for Small Projects Funds. At the same time, it was decided *not* to renew the CREDO programme. No less than 20 out of 36 border regions would be eligible under PHARE CBC. However, no immediate action was foreseen regarding the remaining 16 border regions adjacent to the newly independent countries (Russia, Belarus, Ukraine and Moldova) and the border regions between the two non-accession countries (Albania and the Former Yugoslav Republic of Macedonia).

From the point of view of preparing countries for accession, it seemed logical to concentrate on institution building and investment at the level of the national candidate country and to assure the same funding conditions for border regions regardless of their geographical location. However, let us have a look on how PHARE CBC has been implemented in the period 1994-98 and after that focus on the implementation of CREDO in order to compare the creation of favourable conditions for cross-border co-operation. This requires sensibility towards the very specific and challenging circumstances of border regions at the intersection of national borders and intra-state boundaries (Holst Jørgensen 1999: 16-25).

PHARE CBC 1994-98

The Court of Auditors carried out an audit of the PHARE CBC in 1998 in order to assess the impact of the programme in the period 1994-98 and to evaluate the effectiveness of the programme management (OJEC 2000/C 48/01). Previous to the audit an external evaluation had also been carried out (European Commission 1998)

The audit of the PHARE CBC was carried during the revision of the PHARE cross-border regulation. This timing obviously prevented any conclusions from the audit to be fuelled into the new regulation, which was prepared and implemented in an unusually speedy way for the Commission. Nevertheless, the Court of Auditors pointed out that it would have been much better to introduce a new regulation after 1999 to avoid disruption of the current programmes. Firstly, the new regulation could not address the main problems of the different implementation procedures between Interreg and PHARE funds, with member states being responsible for selection and supervision of the Interreg funds, whereas the Commission was responsible for the selection and supervision of PHARE funds. Secondly, multi-annual, and multi-country, programmes along the PHARE-PHARE borders were inappropriately disrupted (OJEC 2000/C 48/01: Article 93). Without explicitly mentioning the CREDO programme the Court of Auditors clearly emphasised that it was not a wise step to introduce radical changes in the overall cross-border co-operation set-up when the essential regulations were not changed yet and when other cross-border programmes were running. In short, the CBC did not present convincing results:

- *Lack of local priorities*: Insufficient priority was given to projects, which were primarily for the benefit of the people living in border regions (OJEC 2000/C 48/01: Article 12). Instead projects focused on national priorities (OJEC 2000/C 48/01: Article 96).
- *Centralised programme management*: Programme management procedures of both the beneficiary countries and the Commission were too centralised (OJEC 2000/C 48/01: Article 96).
- *Limited cross-border impact* (OJEC 2000/C 48/01: Article 96).
- *Delay in implementation* due to excessively large budget, relative absorption capacities for cross-border projects and limited experience of administrations in the beneficiary countries (OJEC 2000/C 48/01: Articles 10 and 96).

Furthermore, the Court of Auditors found that the new 1998 PHARE guidelines did not take into account specific details of the CBC programme. The Court was especially critical of the 2 million euro minimum size per project and suggested that a larger share of the CBC programme should focus on relatively small projects with a strong local/regional and cross-border impact (OJEC 2000/C 48/01: Article 12). Here we have a tautological problem. The reason why the Commission decided on the 2 million euro minimum size per project was the lack of capacity to manage a large number of small projects in these countries, especially at local and regional level. Therefore, the number of projects should be restricted so that existing institutions gradually could be able to manage the funds. On the other hand, the Commission favoured the set-up of small project funds and was sympathetic to transferring management of these funds to cross-border co-operation institutions similar to the Euroregions. No reflection, however, was made on how to lay the first building blocks of the emerging cross-border co-operations structures. Nor did the Commission pay any attention to the contribution of the existing programme CREDO may have made when these structures were being built.

Now let us see how the design and implementation of the CREDO programme may be the answer to some of the shortcomings apparent in the PHARE CBC. It may provide a framework for building cross-border co-operation structures in order to achieve integration across the internal PHARE borders and the external borders of PHARE in relation to non-accession countries.

The CREDO Programme

As has been mentioned, the CREDO programme was adopted in 1996 with a total of 12 million ecu.

The CREDO programme was introduced step by step. First, a Pilot Round was implemented in 20 border regions in 10 countries. In the next step, in the so-called Main Round in 1998 some 36 border regions in 12 countries were included and a support office for managing the programme was set up by the Commission. Projects included both soft projects and hard projects, i.e. both small projects, tourism development, information and experience exchange and the financially more costly infrastructure projects as bicycle paths, tourism sign posting, sewage and equipment for environmental monitoring. What mattered was that projects would raise awareness of the potential benefits of cross-border co-operation, especially at local and regional level. They should provide sustainable beneficial effects and if possible create the necessary conditions for more committed co-operation and joint actions in the future.

Local Priorities to the Benefit of People Living in Border Regions

Projects approved for funding were selected from an overwhelming pool of project applications sent by local and regional authorities, agencies and non-governmental organisations and interest groups. There were, however, difficulties along the external PHARE borders towards Belarus, Ukraine and Moldova as no funds were available to match the CREDO funds. The foreseen TACIS funds for cross-border co-operation followed another selection procedure and time of application and were not available for the many CEC-NIC projects presented in the CREDO context.

In the Pilot Round a total of 272 project application were submitted, of which 198 fulfilled the requirements for funding leading to a final selection of 46. The Main Round comprised a total of 458 applications with a total request of app. 40 million ecu although only 7.4 million ecu was available for funding. Therefore 106 projects were approved.

This local priority setting was carefully ensured in the programme design and institutional set-up. In each border region local secretariats were set up with the responsibility to raise awareness, inform about the programme and to assist a political regional border committee with representatives from sub-national authorities, labour market organisations, business councils etc. The regional border committees would assess project applications and make a final priority list together with their counterpart on the other side of the border. In the Pilot Round the Commission selected the projects for funding after some local hearing procedures. In the Main Round the priority list made by regional border committees serves as the basis for the formal approval by the Commission.

Decentralised Programme Management and Procedures

The programme management infrastructure in the Main Round was completed in all 36 border regions in 12 countries. The management support was designed in such a way that it permitted local representation, national co-ordination and a programme support office in Prague responsible towards the Commission for the daily co-ordination and administration of the programme. The overall infrastructure appears in Figure 12.2.

The infrastructure consisted of:

– National CREDO co-ordinators appointed by the Commission and often situated in a ministry or equivalent in the PHARE country.

- Regional border committees with the responsibility to assess project applications and make a priority list together with the counterpart on the other side of the border.
- Secretariats and Supervising Organisations appointed by the overall programme responsible and equipped with IT communication network making it rapid and efficient to communicate between the Central Programme Office in Prague and the local fixed points in each border region.
- Local auditors appointed by the overall programme responsible and assisting projects to set up adequate financial schemes and control the proper spending of money.
- Central Programme Office in Prague responsible for the implementation of the overall programme and the intermediate between the Commission, the national CREDO co-ordinators and the local fixed points.
- A financial structure consisting of a commercial bank managing the incoming payments by the Commission and the outgoing payments to the projects.
- A group of regional and monitor officers employed by the Central Programme office in Prague visited the projects twice during project implementation to provide a forum of dialogue about barriers and carriers for proper implementation.

It was no secret that PHARE regulations were demanding and complex (European Commission 1999: 6). Therefore, emphasis was made to solve administrative and financial matters in an efficient and flexible way minimising the inconveniences

Figure 12.2: CREDO organisational diagram

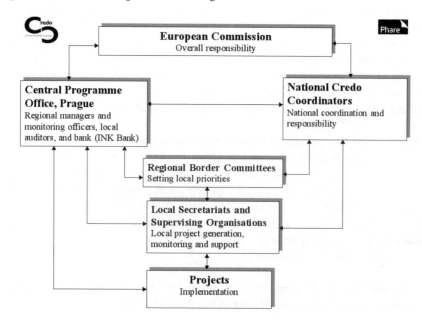

for the projects. By means of local supervising organisations and local auditors as local fixed points most problems would be solved, sometimes after consultation with the Central Programme Office and in rare cases consulting the Commission.

Cross-border Impact

It is still too early to estimate the impact of the CREDO projects as the programme activities were finalised by the end of 2000. Therefore, this assessment has the character of a preliminary evaluation regarding the following aspects:

– Co-ordination with regional policy
– Institution building
– Cross-border co-operation

Contrary to border regions receiving Interreg support, the eligible regions of the CREDO programme did not focus on developing regional programmes and strategies. However, the CREDO projects passed several informal co-ordination procedures. Firstly, the regional border committees were obliged to assess whether projects were in accordance with existing programmes and initiatives. Secondly, the projects approved were sent for comments to the EU delegations. But first and foremost, funds were scarce and not distributed over several years. First priority was to facilitate people coming together and concentrate on selected problems/issues, just like the first Article 10 pilot projects paving the way for the Interreg initiative.

One important factor in cross-border co-operation was the establishment of cross-border co-operation institutions addressing specific issues and problems of border regions. This facilitating role is often called a turntable,[2] which simultaneously allows for vertical co-ordination across the asymmetrical levels of governments of the nation state and horizontal co-ordination among often non-comparable institutions across the border. Agreements in this complex context require a turntable. Within the CREDO programme this task was a matter for the secretariats and the regional border committees, which had the potential to become a political body. Personnel in these secretariats received training and education in order to reach a common understanding of the objectives, available instruments and their fulfilment. In addition, these local officers met across the 36 border regions making their own international network of people engaged in cross-border co-operation issues and perspectives. They filled the gaps of the national administrative and political systems not necessarily suitable for addressing micro-integration issues close to the everyday problems facing people living in border regions. Not as an additional layer of government but as a contact point where actors from different levels of government, across private and public boundaries and across national borders were empowered to solve common problems.

At the level of projects, no evaluation has been concluded yet. I would like to bring forward some examples of cross-border co-operation, which – in my view – illustrate that projects do make a difference. These best-practice examples cover both soft and hard (infrastructure) projects and external and internal PHARE borders, as shown in Figure 12.3.

Figure 12.3: Best-practice examples of cross-border co-operation projects

	Soft projects	Hard projects
External PHARE borders	The Border land School in Suwalki (Poland-Belarus)	Sanitary collector – environmental protection (Poland-Ukraine)
Internal PHARE borders	COMCOFORM – chambers of commerce (Romania-Hungary)	Komarno/Komaron cultural centre (Slovakia-Hungary)

The Borderland School in Suwalki, a Polish city, was one of the few cultural projects within the CREDO programme. It was carried out by the Borderland Foundation and the Centre, a non-governmental organisation, with the aim of bringing people together in open communities in border regions. Situated in the northwestern part of Poland bordering Lithuania and Belarus, the project included a number of educational and cultural activities to which Polish, Belarussian, Lithuanian and other people attended. Workshops were held on the rich and troublesome history of the border region and study tours made in Belarus. A Belarus thematic issue of a cultural magazine *Krasnogruda* was made together with Belarussian partners. And a video was made to capture the identity, history and culture of the people living in the region. In short, the project brought academic and cultural people together, contributed to the documentation of the complex history of the border region and established a cross-border network of academia, media and other people with links to a wider European network.

In the southwestern-most part of Poland, the municipality of Ustrzyki Dolne implemented an infrastructure project to its own benefit, but indeed also to the benefit of its Ukrainian neighbours living within the boundaries of the same watershed. The municipal sewage system was improved by the construction of a sanitary collector so that sewage no longer was led to the Strwiaz River but to the sewage plant. As the history of European cross-border co-operation shows, the contacts across the border often begin in order to solve joint problems of pollution, which does not recognise borders.

Two chambers of commerce on each side of the Romanian and Hungarian border concluded a joint project, the COMCOFORM, in order to overcome some of the informational barriers when a company wanted to establish itself on the other side of the border. A joint web site was created with bilingual information on the basic legislative requirements for establishment of businesses and guidance on who to contact to get more information and assistance. The emphasis on bilingual information was quite important to stress the interests and need of the majority living in an area where also minority interests were at stake. The next step, which was not included in the CREDO project, was to translate this information to the language of the most important business partners in Europe.

The last project to be mentioned was an infrastructure project in the twin cities of Komarno-Komarom on each side of the border River Danube. Once it was one city but wars and conflicts divided it into two. For some years the two mayors of the cities had headed annual cultural events where the citizens from both sides were invited and participated. In order to improve the physical conditions and at the same time save the common heritage of an old military garrison, the restoration of the buildings were made along with the establishment of an open-air theatre in the courtyard.

Apart from the output demonstrated above, the projects produced a number of spillover effects. The project participants were introduced to the *acquis communautaire*, which should not be underestimated. Likewise, they not only got better access to the neighbour on the other side of the border but also to a network across many national boundaries.

Efficient Implementation

The CREDO programme was adopted in 1996. The Pilot Round was launched in the autumn 1997, projects were selected in December 1997, contracts signed in May 1998 and projects were to be completed by the end of 1999. The Main Round was delayed from the beginning as the Central Programme Office was first established in January 1998, five months later than expected. Although the deadline for project applications was in July 1998, the formal approval of the Commission was not made until December 1998. The project contracts were signed progressively in the autumn 1999 leaving a maximum of 12 months for project implementation. This was a particularly great challenge to the infrastructure projects as they depended on favourable weather conditions during wintertime.

Delay in implementation was first of all caused by the Commission in initiating the programme, including identifying subcontracting organisations both in the Pilot Round and in the Main Round.

When the programme management support consortium was contracted, the programme management infrastructure was set up in relatively short time. The combination of a small programme management unit in the Czech Republic and local fixed points in each border region assured together with compulsory IT communication infrastructure with Internet access to smooth and flexible communication during the programme implementation. In addition, many projects also included financial support for IT equipment and installation. Therefore the opportunity to communicate both with the local supervising organisation and with the Central Programme Office in Prague was always there. The world had apparently become much more accessible in these former remote areas of the PHARE countries.

The last important element in programme implementation was the financial management of programme funds, from programme instalment from the EU to single payments to each project. Funds were paid to a commercial bank contracted by the programme management support office to handle the overall flow of money from the Commission and to each single project account. Similar functional arrangements were implemented in some of the very advanced cross-border co-operation regions in the European community, e.g. the very prestigious Euregio along the Dutch-German border. Funds did not get stuck in national payments procedures, which as demonstrated above were not necessarily capable of managing small project funds properly. Local auditors were actively involved in consulting project managers by providing a simple financial scheme and control procedures. The constant alert of the Central Programme Office assured that the assessment of project conditions for receiving the next instalment and the transfer of money was managed on short notice.

Some Lessons Learned

Contrary to the implementation of the PHARE CBC and its shortcomings highlighted in the audit report, the CREDO programme was designed and implemented in a way that should allow for the overcoming of many difficulties associated with cross-border co-operation.

It was, however, a problem that the CREDO programme was isolated from other parts of the PHARE CBC on the one hand and the local EU delegations on the other. There was no attempt to include the programme infrastructure and the various project participants in other activities supporting cross-border co-operation. One example was the lack of co-ordination with other ongoing cross-border co-operation projects adjacent to the EU member states, where national co-ordinators could have played a more active role. Nor were the CREDO actors included in the LACE-PHARE II technical assistance scheme financed by the European Community.[3] The LACE activities were designed both for internal Community border regions and external border regions carried out and co-ordinated by the Association of European Border Regions with a secretariat in Gronau where the Euregio had its office. Most of the technical assistance was provided within the CREDO programme in a more tailor-made and focused fashion compared to activities within the framework of LACE. However, by belonging to the LACE programme better access to the interest organisations of European border regions would have been achieved. It might have created better contact with the EU Commissioners, the EU delegations and the candidate countries.

The largest frustration was, however, that the new PHARE CBC regulation did not require a link to the institutional infrastructure in place in 36 border regions supported by CREDO PHARE funds. Due to efficient communication links, a fine-meshed support and monitoring system and smooth payments of PHARE funds, the CREDO programme was finalised without serious deviations from the initial project objectives. The first elements of a cross-border co-operation structure for managing similar projects was in place. Some projects were slightly revised, the time schedule was altered, and the staff was changed. However, most of the problems were to be blamed on the delay in the overall programme implementation. It was therefore inexplicable why the Commission decided not to renew the CREDO programme or at least assure that there were linkages and transfer of experience between the CREDO programme and the new PHARE CBC.

In particular, there was an inconsistency in the EU enlargement policy towards the external borders of the PHARE countries, where 16 border regions were excluded from the new PHARE CBC regulation. After all, these areas were probably the most remote and isolated border regions of the candidate countries in Central and Eastern Europe. They are also important elements in the enlargement process, which aimed at furthering the integration of the continent by peaceful means, extending the boundaries of stability and prosperity to new members.

So what was going on? The motivations or the arguments behind cross-border co-operation were fulfilled in the CREDO programme: it brought people closer together, it was administratively cost-efficient and flexible and it built the first bricks for cross-border co-operation structures. Still nobody at national and EU level seemed to care.

This shows exactly the shortcomings of cross-border co-operation. Cross-border co-operation and micro-integration cannot be regarded isolated from the top-down EU enlargement policy towards the Central and East European countries.

Several scholars point to the inconsistency in the enlargement policy (Friis 1999). It is closely related to the internal security of the EU such as immigration and internationally organised crime. The 'border-less Europe' with the free movement of goods, services, capital and people demands a European internal security policy in order to protect the common borders towards the outside. On the one hand, the enlargement is seen as a policy instrument that can diffuse the potential security risk in the East. On the other hand the candidate countries do not demonstrate strong, efficient judicial systems and border control.

This dilemma has induced the EU to opt for a protection strategy, where the EU has refrained from gearing the applicant countries for membership (Friis 1999: 177). This is clearly shown in the incorporation of the Schengen Agreement in the EU treaties, which has made it more difficult for the applicant countries to join the EU as they have to accept 'the acquis, the whole acquis and nothing but the acquis.' The application of the Schengen rules in for example Poland has created a new division in Europe not seen since the cold war, a silver curtain (Politiken 6 December 2000). This has produced bad feelings from the neighbouring Belarus and Ukraine, who perceived the streamlining of the Polish visa-policy (since January 1998) as an unfriendly act to the business and trade relations across the border.

The future of eastward enlargement is still confused and unclear as how to bring the negotiations to a successful end: when will it take place and who will be invited? As long as this has not been clarified, the EU-policy towards cross-border co-operation remains an inconsistent affair.

Conclusion

Contrary to the shortcomings highlighted in the audit report and evaluation reports of the PHARE CBC programme, the small multi-country programme CREDO was designed and implemented in a way that overcame some of the major obstacles:

- Local priorities were ensured to the benefit of the people living in the border regions by means of a bottom-up identification and selection process sustained by regional border committees and local secretariats.
- Decentralised programme management and procedures ensured an efficient and flexible way of solving administrative and financial matters.
- The cross-border impact of the cross-border co-operation projects was shown in the informal alignment with some local and regional projects. It was clearly shown in the institution building of cross-border bodies addressing the specific issues and problems of border regions. And the many projects showed convincing examples that people were brought together to do business, to prevent pollution and to share cultural experiences and promote mutual understanding.

The former German foreign minister Mr Kinkel once said: 'Border regions are important laboratories for developing a Europe closer to the people, a democratic counterweight to globalisation and Europeanisation' (Holst Jørgensen 1999: 244). Just like the Small Project Funds, the CREDO programme has proved a successful innovation for fostering cross-border co-operation at grass-roots level. If cross-border co-operation measures are absorbed and subordinated to national schemes of accession, there is a danger that inadequate frameworks may produce a backlash for a bottom-up contribution to European integration (Holst Jørgensen 1999: 469).

On the other hand, bottom-up integration cannot be regarded as isolated from the overall EU enlargement policy. It exists and develops in an osmotic relation with the top-down integration project of the EU. As long as the enlargement policy is inconsistent, the prospects for cross-border co-operation is vulnerable to the decisions of the national and European centres and will be linked to the issue of EU enlargement. This is especially the case with the external PHARE borders, but also the case between members and non-members of the Schengen Convention. For people living in the border region it is therefore highly contradictory on the one hand to bring people together across national borders and at the same time construct a silver curtain with fierce border control measures against the outside world.

After all, borders are *the* basic political institution. They tend to protect and promote interests. They create incentives and opportunities to maintain, strengthen, blur or move the boundaries in order to meet the objectives with respect to members, applicant countries and non-applicant countries of the European Union.

Notes

1   PHARE is one of three instruments for the pre-accession. The other two are the ISPA precursor to the cohesion fund and SAPARD precursor to the agricultural funds.

2   First used by the EUREGIO co-operation along the Dutch-German border.

3   Http.//www. Lace.aebr-ageg.de/lacebr/htmp/labrp200.htm

References

AEBR (1005). Charter of Border and Cross-border Regions. Gronau.

Council of Europe (1987). The Council of Europe and Regionalism: The regional dimension in the work of the Standing conference of Local and Regional authorities of Europe (CLRAE), 1957-85. Strasbourg.

Denters, B., Schobben, R. and van der Veen, A. (1998). 'Governance of European border regions: a juridical, economic and political science approach with an application to the Dutch-German-Belgian border,' in Gerhard, B. and Schmitt-Egner, P. (eds). *Grenzüberschreitende Zusammenarbeit in Europa.* Baden-Baden, Nomos Verlagsgesellschaft.

Dupuy, P.-M. (1982). 'Legal Aspects of Transfrontier Regional Co-operation,' *West European Politics 5:4.*

European Commission (1998). *PHARE – An evaluation of PHARE Cross-border Co-operation Programme.* Final Report. Brussels.

European Commission (1999). E*nlargement: Overview of the PHARE Programme and the new Pre-accession Funds.* Proceedings of a seminar held in September 1999 at the EU Information Centre in Budapest.

European Dialogue (January-February 1997). 'Co-operation Between Regions,' in http://europa.eu.int.

Foucher, M. (1998). 'The Geopolitics of European Frontiers,' in Anderson, M. and Bort, E. (eds). *The Frontiers of Europe.* London: Pinter.

Friis, L. (1999). 'Eastern Enlargement, Schengen, JHA and All That ... Tracing the EU's Internal Security Policy towards Central and Eastern Europe,' in Friis, L. *An Ever Larger Union? EU Enlargement and European Integration.* Copenhagen, Danish Institute of International Affairs.

Holst Jørgensen, B. (1999). *Building European Cross-border Co-operation Structures.* Ph.D. series 99/2. Copenhagen, Institute of Political Science Press.

Lindström, B. (together with L. Hedegaard and N. Veggeland) (1996). *Regional Policy and Territorial Supremacy. Nordic Region Building and Institutional Change in the Wake of European Integration.* Stockholm, NordRefo.

Östhol, A. (1996). *Politisk integration och gränsöverskridande regionbildning i Europa.* Research Report 1996:1. Umeå, Umeå Universitet, Statsvetenskapliga institutionen.

Official Journal of the European Community (1998). Commission Regulation (EC) No. 2760/98 of 18 December 1998 concerning the implementation of a programme for cross-border co-operation in the framework of the PHARE programme. OJEC L 345, 19/12/1998.

Official Journal of the European Community (2000). Special report no. 5/99 concerning PHARE cross-border co-operation (1994 to 1998), accompanied by the replies of the Commission. OJEC 2000/C 48/01.

Official Journal of the European Community (2000). Communication from the Commission to the Member States of 28 April 2000 laying down guidelines for a community initiative concerning trans-european co-operation intended to encourage harmonious and balanced development of the European territory – Interreg III. OJEC 2000/C 143/08.

13 Sustainable Fragmentation: Regional Organisations in the North

By Åge Mariussen[1]

In discussing inter-national co-operation, it may be useful to make a distinction between the institutional and the organisational level (Selznick 1992).

- Organisations are rational instruments established to implement measures leading to useful and pre-determined outcomes.
- Institutions are legitimised with reference to formal decisions, which refers to values that may be directing, guiding and inspiring activities.

Nordic co-operation evolved after the end of World War II. In its early years, Nordic co-operation was pragmatic and primarily directed towards internal Nordic issues. However, the development of formalised structures can also be looked upon as a response to the security situation during the Cold War. Among the early achievements of this co-operation were the Nordic passport union, a common labour market and joint social conventions. In general, Nordic co-operation has lead to widespread institutional diffusion among Nordic countries in several policy areas. Some of the ambitions among actors in Nordic co-operation during its first 50 years may be seen as oriented towards deeper integration based on common Nordic values. However, more ambitious plans concerning economic and security integration never became a reality, as the Nordic countries joined EFTA in 1960 and Denmark became the first Nordic EC member in 1973. The dynamics of Nordic co-operation gradually became more reactive and oriented towards the European Common Market, which would evolve into the European Community *and later the European Union* As an adaptation to the EU enlargement of 1995, Nordic co-operation evolved into a more 'utilitarian' approach emphasising 'Nordic usefulness' as the rationale of co-operation in addition to the instrumental and organisational, rather than institutional, aspects of co-operation.

However, at the same time, the field grew even more complex. At the end of the Cold War several new international Councils were established to promote co-operation between Nordic countries, the new Baltic countries, Russia and – on a circumpolar basis – Canada and the USA. The common set of problems identifying these councils was the attempt to bridge the gap created by the Cold War. This was, however, done in different geographical and political directions:

- Co-operation with the Baltic countries, through the CBSS
- Co-operation with Russia, through the BEAC
- Co-operation with Russia, USA and Canada, on a circumpolar basis, through the AC

In 1995, the field was also invaded by EU Interreg programmes. They have an objective which, at least until the next round of EU enlargement from 15 to 25 is on the road, is distinctly different, to promote integration of the Europe of 15, and their neighbours.

What we see is a fragmentation at the level of institutions: co-operation is legitimised in different ways, with reference to different formal decisions, again referring to different values, pending on the differences in the networks of countries in question.

At the same time, several of the geographical areas of co-operation and activities are similar. One empirical indication of this fragmentation is a prevailing overlap between the activities of the councils and between the councils and Interreg. What is more, within the institutional framework established by the councils and programmes, thick networks between public officials and institutions, as well as civil society organisations have evolved thus increasing integration and co-operation at the operative level. Recently, the question of 'co-ordination' has been raised, in particular through the Finnish Northern Dimension initiative, but also by other actors involved.

This begs a question: How can a field with such a dense population of institutions, monitored by modern national governments with well-developed relations, where 'everybody' is talking about improved co-ordination and remain fragmented?

This chapter identifies three explanations to this case of sustainable fragmentation:

- Differences at the institutional level, in terms of values and objectives
- Lack of autonomy at the institutional level, combined with a certain inertia at the level of inter-national co-operation, preventing mutual adaptation between institutions
- Segmentation at the operational (project) level into three major project clusters, the EU programmes, the Nordic Council of Ministers (NCM) and the post-Cold War councils.

One empirical indication of this fragmentation is a prevailing overlap between the activities of the councils and between the councils and Interreg. Recently, the question of 'co-ordination' has been raised, in particular through the Finnish Northern Dimension initiative, but also by other actors involved.

From the point of view of the inter-governmental paradigm a phenomena like councils and Interreg partnerships may be seen as rational attempts to solve common problems in the North. However, in the case of the post-Cold War councils, collective decisions only managed to provide loosely organised secretariats and councils, without administrative clout. The corresponding Interreg programmes, although equipped with substantially stronger financial and administrative muscles, tend to evolve through ad hoc secretariats and partnerships firmly negotiated between national and regional-level representatives.

Once established, these arrangements all seem to be protected by changes emerging at the level of inter-national co-operation. The institutions seem to be unaffected by 'competition' from other institutions with activities in the same areas. Overlapping activities obviously does not pose any threat to existing institutions.

The networks of co-operation in Northern Europe is segmented into two main clusters, reflecting the distinction between the two different problems that invaded the field, and between the two main ministerial level contacts: to overcome the division of Northern Europe created by the Cold War and to promote European integration.

To overcome segmentation, more autonomous institutional arrangements would have been imperative, enabling the institutions of co-operation to co-ordinate more efficiently among themselves. A somewhat more pro-active attitude at the international level may also lead to certain conclusions, in terms of merging, closing down or restructuring the co-operative institutions. Apparently this does not happen.

Notably the Northern Dimension initiative attempts to bridge the gap between the two sets of problems, by focusing on converging the EU enlargement issue and the instruments of EU regional policy in order to close the east-west divide in Europe. One might speculate that a future enlargement of EU, with the Baltic countries as members, combined with an active partnership between the EU and Russia might, some day in the future, make possible a rethinking of the institutional arrangements in the north of Europe. So far, however, the Working Programme emerging from the initiative has vague objectives.

The Logic of Co-operation

Within the framework of the new intergovernmental paradigm, governments may act co-operatively as rational, collective actors, deciding to give power and resources to new, co-operative institutions, in order to solve common problems. However, these rational decisions may be offset by different forms of an institutional logic (Scharpf 1988) that 'creates frustration without disintegration.' The decision to commit power and resources to new institutions to solve common problems may be limited by well-known considerations of self-interest, restricting the field of co-operation, weakening co-operative institutions, and – in the worst-case scenario, transforming them into rhetoric with no or limited practical impact. The solution to the common problem may be found in the available arsenal of dominant institutions, thus resulting in institutional diffusion. The similarities in organisational design, both in terms of strengths and weaknesses, between the post-Cold War Councils, are obvious. As we all know, processes of diffusion and mimicking may prove to be inadequate, given the complexity of the problem at hand (DiMaggio and Powell 1983).

An alternative scenario would be the emergence of autonomous leading centres with in the co-operative institutions, capable of redefining, developing and renegotiating their own goals and mode of operation (Selznick 1992: 234-44). In the case of the EU, this has, at least partly, been achieved by the strong position of the Commission. Given a certain level of institutional autonomy, one might expect that the Councils, Interreg programmes and other arrangements would have a capacity to span the institutional landscape surrounding them and find their place in the environment. A successful mutual adaptation of new institutions into harmonious layers of 'thick institutionalisation' may solve the problem of fragmentation. These processes, however, depend upon a certain level of autonomy of the institutions enabling them to interact and thereby adapt to the environment. Autonomy may be a too scarce resource if the institution itself is a thin rhetorical shell.

Thus, institutional logic may offset rational action at all these stages. The co-operation may be deprived of adequate resources and powers of allocation. The solution to the problem may be found in some model that does not fit in well with the actual problems at hand. Fragmentation may prevail, because the institutions are too weak to be able to achieve mutual adaptation.

The Cases

The councils and programmes must be seen in the context of three historical periods, each with its own agenda.

–   *Cold War/pre-EU co-operation (1950-90).* Nordic co-operation evolved through the establishment of the Nordic Council (NC) in 1952 and the Nordic Council of Ministers (NCM) in 1971.
–   *Post-Cold War (1990-96).* Following the end of the Cold War, several regional councils were established with the purpose of developing relations between east and west, improving the environment and supporting economic development. These initiatives resulted in three new, permanent institutions: the Council of the Baltic Sea States (CBSS), established 1992, the Barents Euro-Arctic Council (BEAC), established 1993, and the Arctic Council (AC), established 1996.
–   *EU regional and enlargement policies (1995-2009).* The European Union's regional policies include instruments for international co-operation, of which

the most important is Interreg. After Finland and Sweden joined the EU in 1995, significant new resources were made available for east-west co-operation in the north of Europe. This EU-funded cross-border and Interreg co-operation was implemented through programmes with specific regulations for planning, management, funding and evaluation. New institutions and structures are now evolving through the new programming periods, from 2000-2006 and a planned period 2007-2009, where EU enlargement will be central. The Interreg programmes and secretariats are submitted to general EU regulations, determined by negotiations between DG XVI and national representatives.

The EU on its part is concerned with European integration. One of the policy instruments available is to achieve this is the Structural Funds, including the Interreg. The Interreg programmes provide new methods and devote funding of a size previously unknown for cross-border and Interreg co-operation. As the next round of EU enlargement is approaching, policies are being developed to facilitate the integration of several eastern European countries. In addition, indigenous

Figure 13.1: The geography of the four regional councils of the north

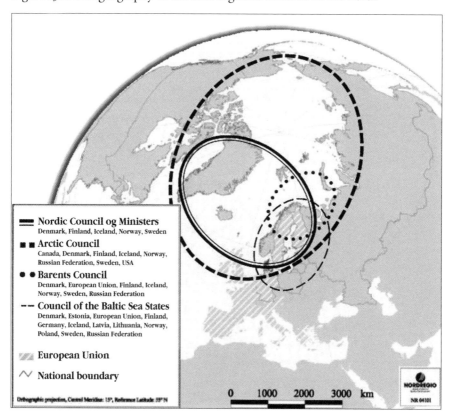

peoples' organisations (AC and BEAC), regions (BEAC and Interreg) and non-governmental organisations (AC) also participate in the co-operation processes. Given the large number of countries (22), regions and organisations active in the formal co-operation, the considerable geographical overlap, as illustrated in Figure 13.1 and in Figure 13.2 is not surprising.

The Interreg Community Initiative promotes cross-border and Interreg co-operation to encourage harmonious and balanced development of the European Territory. The Initiative covers both EU member states and non-member states. The most recent initiative, Interreg III, will run during 2000-2006 and has three strands:

- Interreg IIIA: cross-border co-operation – the promotion of integrated regional development between bordering regions.
- Interreg IIIB: transnational co-operation – contributing to an integrated and harmonious territory.
- Interreg IIIC: co-operation to improve policies and techniques of Interreg economic development.

Figure 13.2: Interreg III programmes with Nordic participation

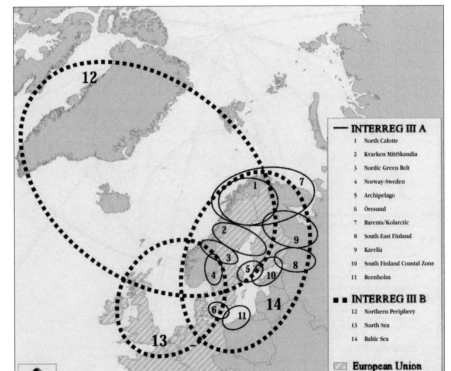

The Interreg initiative is implemented through programmes with specific geographical partners. Programme documents are of a hierarchical nature, with a regional analysis, objectives and strategies for programme interventions, definitions of priorities and measures, indicators for achievements, criteria for project selection, and monitoring and evaluation routines. There are fixed multi-annual budgets and rules for EU and national co-funding of projects.

The four regional Councils focused in this study are quite different in nature than these programmes. The NC/NCM, the CBSS, the BEAC and the AC are international organisations and platforms for implementations of projects of common interest. Only the NCM has a budget of its own which also encompasses implementation of projects.

Interreg is partly overlapping in geography as well as in content and, even more importantly, Interreg programmes probably offer the most powerful means of project implementation. While the NCM spent 16 million DKK in 2000 on cross-border Nordic co-operation, the annual Interreg III allocation for the Nordic EU member states amounted to 20 times that sum.

The three Interreg IIIB programmes, the Baltic Sea, the Northern Periphery and the North Sea, are of particular interest for the four international organisations. Interreg IIIB programmes can provide funding for projects within the following themes:

– spatial development strategies including co-operation among cities and between rural and urban areas to promote a polycentric and sustainable development;
– development of efficient and sustainable transport systems and improved access to the information society;
– promotion of the environment and good management of cultural heritage and of natural resources, in particular water resources;
– specific priorities such as promotion of integrated co-operation of maritime regions and of insular regions as well as integrated co-operation of ultra peripheral regions;
– technical assistance to establish transnational partnerships.

The geographical overlap is illustrated in Table 13.1. As we can see, the overlap is considerable. The Interreg programmes were in many cases based upon Nordic cross-border co-operation that begun some 20 years earlier. The NCM-sponsored co-operation was instrumental for these regions in obtaining EU funding. At the same time, however, the new programmes are far more important and extensive than the old ones, both in terms of funding as well as establishing partnership programmes and implementation routines.

Table 13.1: Interreg programmes 1995-99 and 2000-06 in the area covered by the
four regional councils

The Regional Councils	Interreg II 1995-99	Interreg III 2000-06
NCM Nordic Cross-border programmes: North Calotte, North Atlantic, MittNorden, Kvarken, ARKO, Østfold-Bohuslän, Øresund, Archipelago	– North Calotte – Kvarken MittSkandia – Nordic Green Belt – Borderless Co-operation – Inner Scandinavia – Archipelago – Øresund	– North Calotte – Kvarken MittSkandia – Nordic Green Belt – Norway-Sweden – Archipelago – Øresund
Arctic Council and Barents Euro-Arctic Council	– Barents – Karelia – South East Finland – North Sea	– Barents/Kolarctic – South East Finland – Karelia – Northern Periphery – North Sea

Council of Baltic Sea States	– Baltic Sea
	– South Finland
	  Costal Zone
	– Bornholm
		– Baltic Sea
		– South Finland
		  Costal Zone
		– Bornholm

Other EU Instruments: PHARE, SAPARD, ISPA, TACIS

A number of additional EU budgetary instruments are significant in relation to
the geographic and thematic areas that the four regional Councils cover. These
programmes are directed towards the external relations of the EU. We can identify two categories of relevant programmes. The first is part of the pre-accession
strategy of the EU vis-à-vis applicant countries. The strategy aims at: providing a
consistent and coherent programme to prepare the countries to join the EU; providing a single framework for various forms of EU assistance; making applicants
familiar with the procedures and policies of the Union.

The following instruments are relevant in this respect:

– PHARE under DG Enlargement: the main channel for technical co-operation with the countries of Central and Eastern Europe: institution building to
  facilitate the adoption of the Union's legislative framework, e.g. twinning projects, and investment support to bring industries and infrastructure up to EU
  standards. The budget is 1.5 billion euro.
– SAPARD (Special Accession Programme for Agriculture and Rural Development) under DG Agriculture: aid for modernisation of agriculture, agricultural and rural development. 0.5 billion euro annually.
– ISPA (Instrument for Structural Policies for Pre-Accession) under DG REGIO:
  development of transport and environmental infrastructure following the
  approach of the Cohesion Fund. Central governments are the recipients. 1 billion euro annually.

For these instruments the following countries are eligible, Bulgaria, the Czech Republic, Estonia, Hungary, Latvia, Lithuania, Poland, Romania, Slovakia and Slovenia. The PHARE programme is also directed at three non-candidate countries: Albania, the Former Yugoslav Republic of Macedonia (FYROM), Bosnia and Herzegovina. The goal is to promote the transition to democracy and market economy.

In addition, the EU has been employing TACIS since 1991 to support the transition process in the Newly Independent States, i.e. twelve former Soviet Union countries and Mongolia. TACIS provides grants to support the transfer of know-how to these countries. The intention is to foster closer economic and political links with these countries.

The North Sea Commission and the Baltic Sea Commission

In conjunction with the discussion of the Interreg programmes mention should also be made of a number of regional players operating within the same geographical area. In the North Sea area governments have been concerned about the conditions of the North Sea and government conferences have been arranged in order to address environmental concerns, e.g. leading up to the Esbjerg Declaration of 1995, with a particular focus on discharges of dangerous substances into the sea.

Also at the regional level, institutionalised co-operation has emerged with the establishment of the North Sea Commission (NSC) in 1989 under the Conference for Peripheral Maritime Regions (CPMR) in order to further partnerships between regional authorities around the North Sea. Activities entail mostly encouragement of joint development initiatives and efforts to develop common stances on various issues vis-à-vis the European Union. The activities are action-oriented and carried out by the secretariat in Viborg, Denmark, with six technical groups located regionally. Issues of common concern are business development, culture and tourism, communication and transport, environment, and fisheries. In addition to these themes, the NSC has pinpointed planning/infrastructure, education and research, regional-co-operation and EU issues as the main themes in the co-operation of the NSC and its member regions.

Under the same umbrella of the CPMR there has been an equivalent organisation for the Baltic Sea since 1996 – the Baltic Sea Commission (BSC) with its secretariat in Stockholm. With a function similar to that of the North Sea organisation, the BSC serves as a network to promote co-ordination and co-operation, to initiate and implement useful projects and provide access to European Union institutions. Its activities comprise transfer of knowledge and experience, a coastal zones inter-commission group, a youth forum, an America-Latina inter-commission group, a Mediterranean/Baltic co-operation group, and spatial planning. Both of the commissions under the CPMR have direct links to the Interreg programmes.

Attempts at Co-ordination

The question of co-ordination of the practical activities emerging in this web of institutions is on the agenda in several contexts. One of the themes has been establishing permanent secretariat functions. Establishment of a permanent secretariat has been discussed in the Arctic Council. In the Council of the Baltic Sea States, the need for co-ordination within CBSS-BEAC-NCM is stressed in the communiqué from the Ministerial Session in June 2000. A similar interest has been manifest in the NCM, where a Wise Men's Panel is discussing future strategies and has requested a special analysis of co-ordination and co-operation issues.

Possibilities of co-ordination between the four Councils, and with other co-operative bodies with the same geographical and thematic focus, are to a large extent dependent upon the way these institutions are funded and managed, the organisational muscles at disposal. One important obstacle in this respect is the difference between councils funding and not funding secretariats and activities:

– The NCM has its own budget and is supported by a permanent administration in Copenhagen. Even more structured in terms of implementation are the Interreg programmes. They have fixed budgets for several years ahead, signed agreements concerning funding and semi-permanent administrative systems, giving them at least a potential overview of all activities.
– The BEAC, the CBSS and the AC, on the other hand, do not fund activities of their own. The participating countries finance the secretariats and projects on a voluntary basis. The CBSS has a permanent secretariat in Stockholm, while the AC and BEAC secretariats rotate among the countries together with the chairmanship. These Councils therefore have weaker, often ad hoc administrations.

This distinction affects the Councils' administrative capacity, which is an important factor when it comes to co-ordinating wide-ranging and widespread activities. Secretariats without a project budget to implement have a more limited overview of project activities in the field and few instruments in order to enhance the co-ordination.

Interreg partnerships consist of representatives of the regions and the national level regional policy ministries of the countries involved. The partnership set up a secretariat. In general, the secretariat has been an ad hoc arrangement in most programmes. During the 1991-95 period the European Commission (DG REGIO) was one of the agents within the partnership. In the current (2000-2006) period, the Commission is negotiating regulations, monitoring and approving programmes, without being member of the partnership. The over all aims and objectives are laid down by negotiations between the Commission and the member countries, but the substance of the programmes, including the analysis of the region, is developed by the partnership.

Thus, a balance is struck between bottom-up analysis and programming, and top-down regulations, which may enable the programmes to move in quite different directions. However, the Interreg partnership is committed by the regulations.

One initiative with the objective to increase the co-ordination is the EU Northern Dimension and its Action Plan. Even though the practical outcome of the Action Plan remains to be seen, it has both the ambition and the potential to become an overall co-ordination instrument for activities funded by the EU. This is important also for the four regional Councils, as EU co-funding of related activities is significant. Since the Northern Dimension Action Plan clearly is a framework for EU interests, it may encourage non-EU countries to formulate their own interests.

The *EU Northern Dimension* is intended to be a mechanism for co-ordination across all Councils. The Northern Dimension aims at strengthening the position of the EU in northern Europe. The key focus is on the relationship between the countries of the EU and the Baltic Sea area and Russia.

The initiative to develop a Northern Dimension was taken by Finland as a means for focusing on the EU border with Russia. It can be seen as an attempt to construct an institutional framework for bilateral co-operation between the EU and Russia in northern Europe and as a framework for EU activities in this region in particular. If successful, the Northern Dimension could also prove to be a significant factor for co-ordination of all activities across the EU-Russian border, i.e. integrating other co-operative arrangements as well.

A first step in this direction was taken in June 2000, when the Action Plan for the Northern Dimension was approved. The Action Plan defines the geography of the Northern Dimension in rather general terms, including a flexible area from Iceland on the west to the northwestern part of Russia, from the Norwegian, Barents and Kara Seas, in the north to the southern coast of the Baltic Sea. The Plan will be carried out through EU instruments, including the Association Agreements between the EU and the member states and the applicant countries, the Partnership and Co-operation Agreement (PCA) with Russia, and the European Economic Area Agreement with Norway and Iceland. The Action Plan addresses a wide array of challenges, the most important are security, stability, democratic reforms and sustainable development, followed by the sustainable use of natural resources. In this way, the Action Plan should make it possible to incorporate most of the European activities of the Councils included in this study, in terms of measures, target groups and geography. The Action plan also refers to the actors. It places the CBSS, BEAC and AC, in one group, which 'may assume a significant role in consultation with the Council of the EU in identifying common interests of the Northern Dimension Region. Added value may be provided by coming to an agreement on common priorities.' The second group includes the NCM, together with the Baltic Council of Ministers and the Barents Regional Council, which may be 'consulted,' in accordance with EU rules, when implementing the Action Plan.

Attempts at co-ordination are taking place both at the level of the institutions themselves – i.a. through the attempts to argue for permanent secretariats and other stronger cores, at the EU level, through the Northern Dimension initiative, and within various national levels, such as the Norwegian Ministry of Foreign Affairs.

So far, these attempts have not managed to solve the shortcomings of co-ordination that are reflected in the sustained overlap of activities and spaces documented below.

Limits to Co-ordination

The question of overlap in membership is illustrated in Table 13.2, where members as well as observers are indicated both for the Councils and for Interreg programmes and accession instruments. The overall picture is one of considerable geographical overlap.

Table 13.2: Geographical overlap: members (M) and observers (O) in organisation

Arctic Council	Council of Baltic Sea States	Barents Council	Nordic Council and Nordic Council of Ministers		Interreg Baltic Sea	Interreg Northern Periphery	Interreg North Sea
M	M	M	M	Denmark	M	M	M
M	M	M	M	Finland	M	M	
M	M	M	M	Iceland		M	
M	M	M	M	Norway	M	M	M
M	M	M	M	Sweden	M	M	M
	M			Estonia	M		
	M			Latvia	M		
	M			Lithuania	M		
O	M	O		Germany	M		M
O	M	O		Poland	M		
M	M	M		Russia	M		
				Belarus	M		
O	O	O		UK		M	M
O				Netherlands			M
				Belgium			M
M		O		Canada			
M	O	O		USA			
	M	M		EU			
	O	O		France			
	O			Italy			
	O			Ukraine			
		O		Japan			

Overlapping Activities

The most wide-ranging activities are those of the Nordic Council of Ministers. As we have pointed out, this organisation has a more lengthy history than do the others and a more formalised framework. The three major areas of interest are as follows in the Nordic countries, co-operation on culture, education and research, IT, environment, resource policy, welfare, and industry. In the adjacent Areas and the Northern Dimension it is sustainable development, enlargement and economic co-operation; and in Europe/the EU to promote common Nordic viewpoints.

The three other organisations have a somewhat more specialised focus. The Council of the Baltic Sea States focuses on regional co-operation and communication, economic policy as regards investment and trade and SME industrial policy, education and research (Eurofaculty), environment and energy, nuclear safety, as well as democracy and human rights.

The Arctic Council, in turn, has a clear sustainable development profile. It includes education and research, environmental protection, emergency prevention, preparedness and response, health issues and issues relating to indigenous peoples, e.g. fisheries of the Saami people.

The Barents Council, finally, shares some themes with both the Arctic Council and the Council of the Baltic Sea States: welfare, health and culture of the indigenous peoples are high on the agenda. Education and research are also part of its activities. Another aspect of the Barents programme is activities pertaining to industrial and commercial development, infrastructure, competence enhancement and sustainable development.

However, even if their headlines and themes are the same, the actual issues in question and the geographical dimensions may be different. While the AC is interested in the Northern Sea Route between Europe and Asia, the CBSS is concerned with Via Baltica. And when the AC is working with health issues for the indigenous populations in the far north and the prospects of developing telemedicine, the BEAC and the CBSS concentrate on contagious diseases. And while the BEAC and the CBSS both work on transition of the former Soviet countries, the BEAC has Russia as the only transitional member state, while the CBSS has four additional members. Keeping the above in mind, four kinds of thematic overlap can be assessed as the most fundamental ones:

- *The overlap concerning the links to Russia.* The post-WWII Councils AC, BEAC and CBSS were all established as means to normalise relations with Russia. Economic development, environmental issues and cultural exchange are high on the agenda. Co-operation between Russia and its neighbouring countries is discussed at Council meetings, but projects themselves are carried out on a bilateral basis. There is, therefore, scope for better co-ordination.
- *The overlap between the BEAC and CBSS, on the one hand, and Interreg IIIB programmes, on the other.* There are Interreg IIIB programmes with a geography more or less identical to the Barents and Baltic Councils. Since the Councils administratively belong to the domain of the respective Ministries for Foreign Affairs and the Interreg programmes to the domain of EU regional policy, the links between them are not necessarily obvious for the Councils

themselves. But when it comes to implementation of specific projects and to co-operation with the regions in the areas, the overlap in activities is obvious.

– *Overlap between the NCM Adjacent Programme, on the one hand, and the BEAC and CBSS on the other.* The NCM Adjacent Programme provides scope to extend almost every sector of Nordic co-operation to include the Baltic Sea region. There are examples of co-funding between the Councils, e.g. when the NCM finances a significant part of the energy secretariat of the CBSS. Co-funding of projects is an efficient way to promote co-operation between the Councils, especially if operating. However, one could question the rationale behind the Nordic countries operating through several Councils at the same time to fund the same kind of activities.

– *The overlap between NCM cross-border programmes and Interreg IIIA programmes.* The NCM cross-border programmes are, in financial terms, very limited as compared with Interreg. Nordic funding is more easily accessible and may be used for activities which could otherwise be difficult due to the more complicated Interreg regulations, which is a positive result of having two sources of project funding. However, the NCM contribution is now rather marginal in financial terms, and the question is whether it will make a difference.

Table 13.3: Overlap in thematic focus

	AC	BEAC	CBSS	NCM
Democracy and human rights			x	x
Culture		x		x
Indigenous people	x	x		x
Health	x	x	x	x
Education and research		x		x
Environment	x	x	x	x
Nuclear safety		x	x	
Industrial and economic development		x	x	x
Energy		x	x	x
Transport infrastructure	x	x	x	x

Overlapping, in terms of themes and geography, is the rule and not the exception (see Table 13.3). To a certain extent, overlap in themes is moderated by different geographical orientations, as the same activity may have different orientations in different areas. To a certain extent, this also implies a different focus within each theme. Although many themes are shared, it must be borne in mind that the different councils have differing emphases.

– The NCM is a broad co-operation between governments and include practically all fields of public administration. Their Adjacent Area Framework Programme has focuses on neighbouring countries to the east, i.e. Russia and the Baltic States.

– For the BEAC, economic and democratic development in Russia, together with improving the environmental situation, is at the centre.
– For CBSS, economic development in all transition states around the Baltic Sea is in focus; this may include transport infrastructure, energy, environment, health and human rights issues.
– The AC has a broader geographical perspective. While its themes are to a large extent the same as for the other Councils, AC concern is, as a rule, focused on the most remote parts of the region.

For all four Councils attention centres on questions related to the environment. Transport and health are other issues of major importance for all. For the BEAC, the CBSS and the NCM, as well as for the Interreg programmes, economic development in a broad sense, as a means of enhancing the well being of people and encouraging stability in the region, is the main issue, together with environmental questions.

One might anticipate that the councils and the Interreg partnerships on their own initiative would sort out these things out – and establish mechanisms for co-ordination This is, however, not the case.

Conclusions

We have noticed fragmentation due to the considerable overlap both of activities and their geography. These overlaps seem to sustain in the face of numerous efforts to co-ordinate. Based on the discussion above, we may summarise factors causing fragmentation:

1. Co-operative institutions have a different history, and accordingly are legitimised with reference to somewhat different values and objectives.
2. They possess a low degree of autonomy, which prevents them from making joint decisions in favour of more co-ordination
3. Inertia at the level of international co-operation, protects institutions once they are in place against any major top-down reforms
4. In terms of geography we see fragmentation into separate clusters.

Weakness and Inertia

The EU partnerships master huge financial and administrative resources. However, a closer examination of the regulations and administration of these partnerships depicts that all programmes are determined by regulations decided after negotiations between the national governments (regional policy ministries) and the Commission. This restricts the autonomy of the programming partnership. In most programmes, the secretariats were changed during the transition from Interreg II to Interreg III, both in terms of staff and location. Indeed, in certain programmes, the location of the secretariat was turned into a battlefield between

strong national partners (the conflict between Sweden and Germany on the location of the Baltic Sea secretariat). The councils are even weaker, with no permanent secretariats, and without a budget. These weaknesses at the core are of course
also reinforced by the often loosely structured council institutions. These weaknesses tend to reduce the capacity of these institutions to evolve into what
Selznick calls institutional actors. They lack centres of their own capable of being
pro-active in relation to their founders, and develop strategies to change and
develop overall objectives and orientations.

Fragmentation is reproduced because the institutional actors at the core of the
co-operative organisations does not have sufficient autonomy and resources to act
as a firm institutional framework – and make joint decisions with the other institutions on how to divide tasks and co-ordinate areas.

At the same time, there seems to be inertia at the level of international co-
operation. It has proved relatively simple to establish new institutions. Once
established, the main outline seems to be well protected from change. There are
no joint decisions made to close down institutions, or merge them. It was quite
remarkable that although the borders of several Interreg programmes were adjusted, no programmes were merged, and no programmes were closed down. The co-
existence of quite similar Interreg programmes and councils have not resulted in
any central level decisions to merge or close down any of the councils.

Segmentation into Two Clusters

The field of co-operation is structured into two distinct sets of problems: closing
the wounds of the Cold War – and European integration. The definition of the
solutions to these problems is reflected in the history of the various institutions
and appears to be separated into two different clusters:

The Nordic countries constitute the core countries, belonging to all four
councils. The NC/NCM co-operation has the longest history (50 years), and is
most wide-ranging (covering almost every field of public administration), and
also is the most formalised and institutionalised (own budget, large number of
committees and institutions).

The three councils, the CBSS, the CEAC and the AC, were created as mechanisms of co-operation on particular geographically related issues. These organisations also became topical instruments in the aftermath of the Cold War in order
to find new means of international co-operation. Some distinguishing features
should be highlighted. The Barents Council is more oriented towards northern
European-Russian relationships, while the Arctic Council also has a North American agenda. The Council of the Baltic Sea States, for its part, is positioned
around the Baltic Sea. The Barents Council also has the particular feature that the
co-operation takes place at two levels, one intergovernmental and one regional.
There are formalised structures between regions and cities in the Baltic region as
well. In terms of institutional modelling, these councils were designed with the
same general layout: mobile secretariats, no separate project funding possibilities,
and with the main national level relation to the ministries of foreign affairs. Thus,

they constitute a network of their own and have made some attempts at mutual co-ordination between itself and the Nordic Council of Ministers.

Interreg IIIB programmes are targeted towards the Baltic Sea and the North Sea, which corresponds to the inter-regional councils, the Baltic Sea Commission and North Sea Commission, respectively. The Interreg IIIB Northern Periphery programme is directed towards parts of Finland, Iceland, Norway and Sweden. The pre-accession instruments PHARE/SAPARD/ISPA are directed towards the applicant countries to the EU, and the TACIS programme towards the Newly Independent States. Whereas the programmes have well-developed systems of mutual information, organised and streamlined within the EU framework, mechanisms of information exchange with the councils are at best random.

Now What?

A key to understand this outcome is the strategic deliberations at the international level. Here, we lack data. In the absence of relevant data, it is interesting to note that the lack of autonomous institutional actors tends to leave the national governments in charge. After all, a decision to build up a strong, autonomous organisation with a capacity to decide upon its own direction may appear to be a strategy which may lead in uncontrollable directions. At the same time, some of the 'users' of the system may also be quite happy with the state of affairs. Once they overcome the confusion, often reported by project initiators, the existence of several institutions may be seen as options for new and innovative financing strategies, enjoyed by project level actors who know their way around. Without any kind of comprehensive evaluation of what all these institutions actually achieve, we may also note that the outcome of these operative projects may or may not be affected by the fragmentation observed in the analysis. Indeed, one consequence of fragmentation is that nobody knows what a desirable outcome would be. This surely generates problems with legitimacy.

Note

[1] This chapter is based on a report to the Norwegian Ministry of Foreign Affairs, with two co-authors, Hallgeir Aalbu and Mats Brandt, with editorial assistance from Keneva Kunz. The maps were produced by Jörg Neubauer.

References

Andersen, S.S. (2000). *Hvordan er EU mulig?* TfS 4, pages 561-93.
DiMaggio, P. and Powell W.W. (1983). 'The Iron Cage revisited: Institutional Isomorphism and Collective Rationality in organisational fields,' *American Sociology Review* 48, pages 147-60.
Scharpf, F. (1988). 'The Joint decision Trap: Lessons from German federalism and European integration,' *Public Administration* 66, pages 239-78.

Selznick, F. (1992). *The Moral Commonwealth, Social Theory and the Promise of Community.* Berkeley, Los Angeles, Oxford, University of California Press.

On the Council of the Baltic Sea States
Site: http://www.baltinfo.org

Documents: Report from the Committee of Senior Officials to the 9th Ministerial Session of the Council of the Baltic Sea States 21-22 June 2000

On the Arctic Council
Sites: http://arctic-Council.usgs.gov/
                  http://www.grida.no/caff/
                  http://grida.no/amap/
                  http://www.grida.no/pame
                  http://www.ims.uaf.edu:8000/EPPR/

On the Nordic Council of Ministers
Site: http://www.norden.org

Documents: Planerna För Det Nordiska Samarbetet (C2) samt Nordiska Ministerrådets Budget för 2000. *Nordic Council of Ministers 1999-12-10*

On the European Union external and cross-border policy, Northern Dimension and the financial instruments Interreg, PHARE/ISPA/SAPARD, TACIS
Site: http://www.inforegio.cec.eu.int/wbdoc/docoffic/official/INTERREG3/
                  index_en.htm

Interreg III
Sites: http://europa.eu.int/comm/enlargement/pas/phare.htm and
                  http://www. inforegio.cec.eu.int/wbpro/pro_en.htm on Pre- Accession Strategy
                  http://europa.eu.int/comm/dgɪa/tacis/index.htm on TACIS

On the North Sea Commission and the Baltic Sea Commission
Sites: http://www.northsea.org/
                  http://www.balticseacommission.org/
                  http://www.crpm.org/ on the Conference of Peripheral Maritime Regions

14 Nordic-Baltic Ventures during the Early Post-Soviet Time: Some Company Examples

Harley Johansen [1]

Nordic companies were quick to move into the post-Soviet Baltic region during the mid-1990s, as opportunities for investment became available. The early investors represent a variety of firms, large and small, and within different sectors, yet they exhibit some similar motives and experiences. This chapter will examine the early entry of Nordic firms into the Baltic region and describe some examples of different decision factors involved. The data are derived from descriptive interviews and site visits of 34 firms at their locations within Estonia, Latvia, Lithuania and St Petersburg, Russia. Results show that significant changes in operations have occurred for some companies since their initial investment, including transfer of ownership to either the Nordic or the Baltic side, and addition of new product or service lines as markets are discovered.

The decade of the 1990s has seen major changes in the status of the Baltic Sea region. Many of the predicted forms of integration at the time of Baltic independence in 1991 at the end of the Soviet era, have not only begun, but are well under way. Integration of economic and social activities has been especially strong between Nordic and Baltic nations as means of connectivity have steadily improved. The number of daily passenger trips, e.g., between Helsinki and Tallinn has risen steadily during the decade and one can assume that other forms of interaction, such as airline passenger trips and telephone calls have paralleled this trend. In addition, the region has been discovered by the international tourist industry, which sells tours of various forms, including cruises, to tourists interested in seeing the 'Baltic capitals,' which now include both Nordic and Baltic cities. The scale of these trends was difficult to imagine at the beginning of the 1990s decade when infrastructure for nearly all forms of interaction was primitive, and the Baltic countries were struggling to meet the most basic needs. Economic progress has been especially strong in the Baltic countries as measured by both GDP and average wages (*Business Central Europe* 2000). A large share of this progress can be attributed to a steady inflow of foreign direct investment (FDI), much of which has come from the Nordic side of the region (Figure 14.1).

Rapid growth of foreign investment has been characteristic of the post-Soviet

Figure 14.1: Foreign direct investments, per capita by country

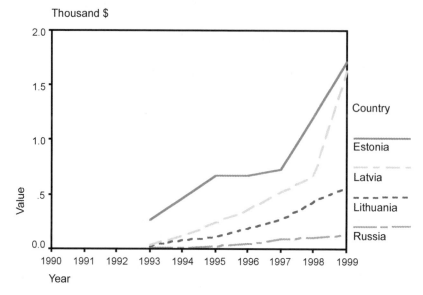

Source: *Business Central Europe*

Baltic countries since their independence in 1991. While investments from West-ern Europe and America are growing in importance today, the first wave of invest-ment came from nearby Nordic countries, motivated primarily by market oppor-tunities (Johansen 1995; Kivikari 1996). In a survey of Nordic companies with investments in Estonia, Latvia, Lithuania, and St Petersburg, Russia as of 1994, we found that most Nordic investments were in market-oriented service and retail operations located within or near the main capital cities (Johansen, Snickars and Steinbuka 2001). Manufacturing investors were motivated by both market opportunities and labour cost advantages and these were more apt to include state companies as joint-venture partners. Manufacturing companies were also most important in the large cities, but some went to non-capital city locations within each Baltic country, and these were usually acquisitions of Soviet era plants offered for privatisation.

The spread of Nordic companies into the Baltic region began in earnest after early 1991 and showed a rapid upswing during the period 1992-95 (Figure 14.2). The cumulative percentage growth curve of Nordic companies resembles a logis-tic within each Baltic country, rising sharply during the years 1991 to 1993. The continued growth trend beyond 1995 is not shown here because of the closure of data collection as of 1995, but later evidence has shown a growth from 400 listed Nordic companies in 1994 to over 2100 companies listed as active in the Baltic countries and St Petersburg as of mid-2000 (Snickars and Bourennane 2000). This high rate of FDI growth suggests a parallel to the adoption curve found in studies of innovation diffusion and a spatial process that resembles colonisation into frontier regions (Bylund 1960; Hudson 1969), although in this case, the colonisation is by western companies into the post-Soviet business frontier. In the early models of colonisation and diffusion, it was useful to look at the behavioural characteristics of actors at different stages of the growth curve. In diffusion research, this curve is called an adoption curve, with adopter categories – innovator, early adopter, early majority, late majority, and laggard, acting in order, along the logistic curve (Lionberger 1960; Johansen 1971). The earliest to join were different from each later group, as measured by information sources and quality, risk-taking ability, and general 'innovativeness,' while the last to adopt represent the least informed and most conservative in the population. If we apply this scale to companies investing in the Baltic frontier, those first investors should have some of the 'innovative' characteristics found in past adoption surveys, and they may provide some insights into the pros and cons of being earliest to the frontier.

It is for this reason that this chapter focuses on a selected group of case studies of Nordic or Nordic/Baltic joint venture companies that were already in the Baltic countries as of 1994. These companies were selected from the larger group of responding companies surveyed during 1994-95, and they represent large and small as well as a mix of companies by sector. These companies were visited during the period from November 1995 through November 1997, and therefore may reflect the changing times during those two years of transition. We are therefore looking at the early investors and will see the issues of concern to them as they adapted to the post-Soviet setting. In a few cases, we have current information on

Figure 14.2: Investment curve by year for Baltic Countries

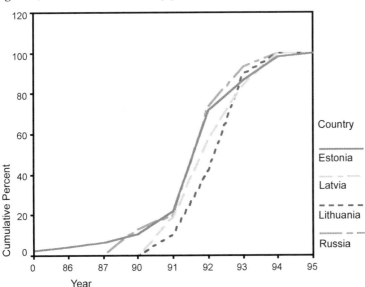

Source: Author's survey of firms

their status in 2000 and a comparison of today's situation compared to their view at the time they entered the Baltic area.

The rush of companies into the newly opened region was a response to the new market opportunities very close to the Nordic countries, including both product markets and labour markets for low cost production. These motivating factors were understandably related to the type of business of each firm. Market opportunities were strong at first because of a demand for previously unavailable western goods, and because of a temporary surge of market capacity following the sale of resources leftover from the Soviet time. Companies later learned that their long-term success would depend on the more stable, but smaller market capacity of the Baltic countries, and the gradual development of St Petersburg's market potential.

Similarly, labour market advantages were strong at first, when average wages were at or below 50 USD per month, but these advantages may be diminishing with the increase in wages by four to five times that amount during the decade. Several companies expressed a need to adjust business plans toward lower targets as they adapted to the process of transition in each Baltic setting.

Case Study Examples

The companies listed in Table 14.1 were part of a larger group of Nordic firms surveyed in 1994 that were active in the Baltic locations of Estonia, Latvia, Lithuania and St Petersburg, Russia. The companies were visited at their Baltic locations during the two years following the survey, completed in 1995 (Johansen, Snickars and Steinbuka 2001). The purpose of the visits was to observe on-site operations, sharing of site development costs or services for business operations, agglomerations of similar or unrelated firms, and the specific nature of the Baltic operation and its management. The visit at each company was arranged following the survey and based on the respondents' invitation to accept a visit. The visits involved an interview with the on-sight manager and usually a tour of the Baltic operation. It was possible in the interviews to follow up on items in the survey and to probe for reasons behind their original responses. An important dimension of the visits was the ability to learn how each company became interested in the Baltic region and what led to their investment and location decisions. Companies can thus be grouped into four decision types based on their motives and experience in the Baltic decision. These four types are:

Pioneers – companies who saw the opportunity for new market or production expansion upon the opening of the Baltic region to foreign investment in 1991, or earlier near the end of the Soviet Union.

Client-led – companies who were encouraged by their client companies to move into the Baltic region to provide them with services as they were in the west.

Network influenced – companies that found opportunities through networks involving other Nordic companies with Baltic experience. Less distinct than the other groups, network effects can and did work in conjunction with other sources of information for each of the groups and these contacts came from the feedback from pioneer companies in both Nordic and Baltic locations. In this way, the 'client-led' companies were also examples of network effects among Nordic companies.

Followers – companies who saw other companies moving to the Baltic region and the opportunity to compete for a share of the new market.

The visited companies include a variety by sector, size, origin, and decision type, as shown in Table 14.1. First we will consider the breakdown by decision type. Of the 34 cases, by far, the most common decision type among these early companies was that of 'pioneer.' This characteristic was common to 20 of the cases, where their early entry was based on the perception of market and/or production opportunities close to their home base in the Nordic countries. Good examples of this type include factory acquisitions or JVs such as Eesti Tubakas, Aseri Tellis, Tetra Pak, Gefa I Tranemo, and others in the Baltic countries, and small retail and service firms such as Ballad Sales Promotion in Russia and in Lithuania. Large firms such as Neste and Electrolux also fall into this category with their early actions to establish strong market presence in the region. In these cases entrepreneurs took the decision to invest in either production or sales and the motivation may have begun from inside the Baltic frontier (e.g., Sveja, Jetis and Vironet) or from the Nordic side (e.g., Esko Koolitus, Kunda Nordic Cement and Tetra Pak), or some combination of motives from both sides (e.g., Gefa I Tranemo and Swedish Trade Council). These early investors developed their markets and production systems as they went and brought new styles of business management and technology to the region.

Eight cases, including the four main auditing and management-consulting firms KPMG, Price Waterhouse, ICS and SIAR Bossard, were 'client-led.' These were cases where their services in western accounting standards and other business services were not available in the former Soviet setting and were needed from the beginning by their clients and other early investors. Other 'client-led' examples were construction companies Skanska and Lentek Ltd., who were encouraged to bid on contracts from other western investors within the FSU Baltic region. Skanska was first hired to renovate space in Riga for the Stockholm School of Economics, which led to other projects within the region. Lentek Ltd. was formed to take over the Finnish side of a joint venture with the Soviet Union that had been started as Finn-Stroi in the 1970s, but dissolved after the Soviet ending. Lentek has built new and renovated space for both western companies such as early entrants Neste and Philip Morris, along with government offices, banks, and other new projects in Russia. In both the Skanska and Lentek Ltd. cases, networks within the Nordic and Baltic regions were also influential in their early

Table 14.1: Companies visited at Baltic locations

Company		Visit Location	Products	Source Country
Auditing Firms/ Management Consulting				
KPMG	C	Tallinn, Estonia	Auditing firm, business consulting	Branch of KPMG Finland
Price Waterhouse	C	Riga, Latvia and Vilnius, Lithuania	Auditing and management consulting	Nordic division branch office
ICS	C	Vilnius, Lithuania	Management consulting. Serves clients with front end investment services.	Denmark
SIAR Esko Koolitus Bossard	C	Riga, Latvia	Management consulting. In Riga, Vilnius, St Petersburg and Moscow, Russia.	Nordic division
	P	Tallinn, Estonia	Business education for adults to help Estonia into market economy.	Finland
Swedish Trade Council	P	St Petersburg, Russia	Service to Swedish companies in Russia Supported by Swedish government (50%) and by consulting services (50%)	Sweden
Manufacturing Companies				
SAAB	N	Tallinn, Estonia	Auto parts supplier development.	Sweden
Eesti Tubakas	P	Tallinn, Estonia	Cigarettes	Sweden/ Estonia JV
Vironet	PN	Tallinn, Estonia	Screens for rock crushing, other mfg	Swedish/Finnish/ Estonian JV
Mistra-Autex	P	Tallinn, Estonia	Carpets for cars and trucks	Finnish/ Estonian JV
Kunda Nordic Cement	P	Kunda, Estonia	Cement	Finnish/ Estonian JV
Aseri Tellis	P	Aseri, Estonia	Bricks	Swedish/ Estonian JV
ABB	P	Tallinn, Estonia	Mfg. and service of electrical systems.	Sweden
Tetra Pak	P	Riga, Latvia and St Petersburg, Russia	Processing and packaging dairy and juice products	Sweden
Gefa I Tranemo	P	Jekabpils, Latvia	Clothing	Swedish/Latvia JV
Betomix	P	St Petersburg, Russia	Mixed, high quality concrete	Finland
Retail Firms				
Ballad Sales Promotion	P	St Petersburg, Russia	Auto parts sales via mail order. New product line after entry to Russia.	Finland
Electrolux	P	Tallinn, Estonia and Riga, Latvia	Dealership development, import, sales	Sweden

Table 14.1: Continued

Company		Visit Location	Products	Source Country
Retail Firms (cont.)				
Statoil	F	Vilnius, Lithuania	Market development, auto sales and service.	Norway
Neste	P	Vilnius, Lithuania	Auto service and fuels, retail and bulk sales	Finland, was JV with state co., now independent
Jetis	P	Kaunas, Lithuania	Import special steel and travel agency JV	Sweden/Lithuania
Sveja	P	Klaipeda, Lithuania	Import, sales and installation of bathroom fixtures	Independent, former JV with Sweden
Roxor	P	St Petersburg, Russia	Imports and sales of artificial flowers and kitchen merchandise	Sweden
Construction				
Skanska	CN	Riga, Latvia	Construction and renovation, market development.	Sweden
Lentek Ltd	CN	St Petersburg, Russia	Construction and renovation.	Finland/RussiJV
Alfa Laval	P	Riga, Latvia	Sales and installation of heating equipment, separators	Sweden
Other Business Services/import/ export				
ASG Transport Fwd	C	Tallinn, Estonia	Freight forwarding and transport services	Sweden
Latsin	P	Riga, Latvia	Logging, export and sustainable forestry.	Sweden
Artrolito	N	Klaipeda, Lithuania	Import and installation of joints (hip and knees)	Sweden/ Lithuania JV
Containership Group	P	St Petersburg, Russia and Helsinki, Finland	Container shipping facilities in St Petersburg, serving interior Russia.	Finland
Tallinna Autoveod	P	Tallinn, Estonia	Freight forwarding.	Finland/ Estonia JV
Norvista	P	St Petersburg, Russia	Travel Services. Started as branch of Finnish company, now owned by Finnair	Finland
Jetis	P	Kaunas, Lithuania	Import special steel and travel agency	Sweden JV, now independent
Marketpoint	C	St Petersburg, Russia	Advertising	Sweden/ Russia JV
Ballad Sales Promotion	N	St Petersburg, Russia	Printing and design of business logos on business gifts.	Finland

Note: C=client-led,   P=pioneer,   N=network influenced,   F=follower

development and in their decision to establish long-term presence in the new frontier.

Transportation needs led ASG to develop a facility at Tallinn when an American company, Velseco, needed their services to ship containerised oil shale to Houston, Texas. This led to other business for incoming and outgoing freight. Travel services, hotels, restaurants, and other services were important needs in the early years of Baltic FDI. Western visitors and company employees needed an/or desired a higher standard of these services than was available in the early post-Soviet setting. Norvista is an example of this type of service, providing travel connections to and from the Baltic region to western travellers at first, and later to the growing demand from within the region. The Finnish company is one of many such agencies working in the region and catering to both local and international tourists and business travellers. Originally called Area Travel, Norvista was bought by Finnair and expanded to 11 offices in the Baltic region. The company chose to locate its St Petersburg office in the main lobby of the Astoria Hotel, a prime location for this type of service. Ninety percent of Norvista's clients are now Russians travelling to Europe and Scandinavia for holidays. As in most cases of client-led investment decisions, expanded local business contacts followed the move to the Baltic region.

Network connections were evident in the cases of some companies, where they learned of business opportunities through contacts with other Nordic Baltic region companies. Examples of this include the Finnish Betomix company and its connections to other companies working in Russia such as Lentek, that needed higher quality concrete than was available locally. This led Betomix to build a plant near St Petersburg where they can serve several western clients as well as an emerging local market of construction companies. SAAB is another case of establishing an office to promote and develop supplier manufacturing capabilities in the region through its contacts with other firms such as Mistra Autex and Electrolux, already in the region. SAAB hired Peeter Tibbo as manager of the Tallinn office, a man with connections and experience working with Norma, the manufacturer of safety belts for Soviet cars. Mr. Tibbo's local connections also helped bring other western suppliers to the Baltic region to buy factories for upholstery and other fabrics for automobiles. Vironet is another case where its main customer, Finnish/Estonian JV Kunda Nordic Cement, was a market for the screen products and outside capital was needed to keep production going. Thus the Vironet JV was formed. These network connections are similar to, and often involve client-led influencing factors as mentioned earlier, so it has probably been more common than can be shown here based on the reported data. Network constructs are complex and may include connections both within and between regions among individuals, companies, and agencies involved in the early wave of investment (See Johansson and Johansson 1999 for examples of this).

Although there was evidence of some examples of 'followers' among the larger survey of companies, because the companies selected for interviews were primarily the early entries to the Baltic region, they do not fall into the 'follower' category in most cases. Statoil might be considered a follower in the auto-service station business, because it followed Neste into most markets in the region. However, in this case, the time delay was only a matter of months or a year in most locations and Statoil did seem to gain some advantage by waiting. They were able to avoid the requirement for JV partners and they also had greenfield sites in most markets. They have emerged as the leading international company in sales in the Baltic countries. As an example of networked investment forms, Statoil has combined with McDonalds in several urban locations, and they share a fuel depot with the Finnish company Neste (now Fortum) in Lithuania. Some observations about the process of investment by western companies included the immediate need to find or create office space that met western standards.

Soviet companies typically had archaic office facilities and equipment and communications systems were primitive. Just one effect of the first wave of foreign investors was increased demand for new office space, which in turn created a demand for building renovation in the region. Opportunities emerged for both local and foreign construction companies and renovation supplies throughout the Baltic capital cities. Other side-benefits of FDI occurred as western companies trained local staff in office management and procedures, including the use of modern computer and telecommunications equipment, thereby upgrading the human resources. Another immediate need was for advertising services to publicise the entry of, especially the retail and service firms in the new region. Advertising was not a big part of the Soviet economy and this service was not available in the local market. Market-point is an example of the introduction of advertising services. They developed along with some of their clients from the west, such as Gillette, and worked to sell their service to other foreign and domestic firms in the emerging market economy.

The companies listed in Table 14.1 include small and large firms engaged in both manufacturing and service or retail activities in the Baltic region. Some firms have been involved in the region for many years, even pre-dating the Soviet time, e.g. Alfa Laval, while others are new start-up companies formed to meet recent business opportunities. Probably the most common type of investment is the expansion into the Baltic region as a branch of a Nordic company, e.g., KPMG, ABB, Electrolux, and other large established firms, yet new entrepreneurial firms have emerged with Baltic/Nordic investment partnerships, such as Sveja, Pentacom, and Ballad Sales Promotion. As expected, the issues brought up by the company representatives vary somewhat by size of firm, sector, and location within the Baltic region. For example, Electrolux faced the challenge of training retail dealers throughout the region to display, sell, and service its products. Gefa I Tranemo and other manufacturers needed to transform defunct Soviet factories into profitable ventures.

Conclusions

It is clear that entry into the post-Soviet Baltic market has been motivated by perceived new opportunities in both product and labour markets compared to those of the Nordic and other European countries. The companies that took the first steps toward either joint venture, or other forms of investment saw the region as a business frontier with both challenges and potential for growth. These companies may have been the first wave of western investors into the region, but larger numbers of western firms soon followed them. Even during the early 1990s, the process of 'follow the leader' was evident as described in the case of KPMG, as was the importance of learning from each other by sharing information among western companies, as mentioned in the Alfa Laval and Electrolux cases.

These early investors have had different experiences than those arriving later, and perhaps they have had the benefit of being 'first in' in some ways. It is also likely, however, that some firms have had an easier time by waiting until the Baltic countries were more stable in terms of the rules of the game. Another finding that is revealed in the cases is the entrepreneurial nature of some of the smaller companies. Examples of this were found in Lithuania at Pentacom, and in St Petersburg at Ballad Sales Promotion. Each firm diversified to offer new and unrelated products and/or services to take advantage of market opportunities.

The Nordic business presence in the Baltic region has strengthened ties between both sides of the Baltic Sea. The rapid transfer of business technology and western products and services has led to a greatly expanded ability among the Baltic countries to participate in the larger economy of the region and the world. The common practice of Nordic firms hiring local employees in all but (and often including) the top management positions, has resulted in a rapidly upgraded workforce in the region. The experience in western business has enhanced human capital in all sectors where employees have access to computer and telecommunications technology along with new styles of doing business. The rapid rise of the three Baltic nations to EU membership consideration (with Estonia in the leading position) is evidence of the importance of early investment activities from the Nordic countries. Estonia's leading position in FDI (Figure 14.1) supports this position.

Finally, Nordic-Baltic networks that were derived from business links have also extended to include many social and cultural networks to address such issues as Baltic Sea environmental management and international agreements on other issues such as trade and tourism. The region is rapidly becoming re-connected after many years of separation and the speed of this process is a good indication of the magnitude of information-age technologies and their adoption throughout the region. Business ventures and other aspects of society all share the benefits of rapid information exchange as this infrastructure develops.

Note

[1] This research was supported by a grant INT-9401940 from the USA National Science Foundation.

References

Business Central Europe (2000). 'Monthly Statistics by Country.' December.

Bylund, E. (1960). 'Theoretical Considerations Regarding the Distribution of Settlement in Inner North Sweden,' *Geografiska Annaler*.

Hudson, J.C. (1969). 'A Location Theory for Rural Settlement,' *Annals of the Association of American Geographers* 59, pages 365-81.

Johansen, H.E. (1971). 'Diffusion of Strip Cropping in Southwestern Wisconsin,' *Annals of the Association of American Geographers* 61.

Johansen, H.E. (1995). 'Locating Western-Style Retail Outlets in the Former Soviet Baltic Rim: The Case of Neste Oy of Finland,' in Tykkylainen, M. (ed.). *Local and Regional Development During the 1990's Transition in Eastern Europe*. Aldershot, Avebury.

Johansen, H. E., Snickars, F. and Steinbuka, I. (2001). 'Nordic Investments in the Post-Soviet Baltic Frontier,' *Geografiska Annaler*, series B, 4.

Johansson, J. and Johansson, M. (1999), 'Developing Business in Eastern European Networks,' in Tornroos, J. and Nieminen, J. (eds). *Business Entry in Eastern Europe*. Helsinki, Kikimora Publications.

Kivikari, U. (1996). *The Legacy of the Hansa: The Baltic Economic Region*. Helsinki, Otava Publishing.

Lionberger, H.F. (1960). *Adoption of New Ideas and Practices*. Ames, Iowa State University.

Snickars, F. and Bourennane, M. (2000). 'Industrial Networking in the Baltic Sea Region.' Presented at Meeting on Urban Systems and Urban Networking, VASAB 2010, European Commission Regional Development Fund, Hørsholm, Denmark.

Part IV

Political Integration, Territorial Governance and Security

15 Peaceful Change but not yet Stable Peace: Military Developments in the Baltic Sea Region, 1990-2000

Frank Möller[1]

During the Cold War, the Baltic Sea region was a 'strategic backwater' (Council on Foreign Relations 1999) which received little attention in international politics. Like the European far North, the degree of tensions in the region reflected primarily the overall degree of tensions between the military blocs rather than conflicts emanating from the region itself. Unlike the far North, the issue was not primarily one of piling up and deterring one another by means of nuclear weapons. Regional security dynamics were suppressed by all-European and global dynamics reflecting the superpower antagonism. Swedish and Finnish neutrality, however, cushioned the manifestation of the superpower rivalry in the region to some extent.

The military situation in the Baltic Sea region was stable but it was a stability which left much to be desired. It had nothing to do with a 'sea of peace' as the Soviet propaganda tried hard to make one believe. Rather, it was a 'heavily armed threatening peace' (Wellmann 1999: 86). Its replacement by something else is highly welcome, the more so since – unlike in former Yugoslavia and in parts of the Russian Federation – uncovering intra-regional tensions did not unleash armed conflict in the region. It certainly did result in some kind of instability often referred to in terms of unpredictability and 'grey zones.' As compared with the rigidity of the Cold War period, however, the current instability is positive and should be addressed in terms of flexibility and openness. In particular the metaphor of 'grey zone' misses the point and still reflects Cold War thinking. It is primarily used in Estonia, Latvia, and Lithuania to describe the geographical location, perceived as uncomfortable, between NATO and Russia. It presupposes (at least) two poles between which a grey zone could be located. Yet it is a distinctive mark of the post-Cold War period that the political landscape in the Baltic Sea region is increasingly represented in its entirety, without dividing lines, spheres of influence and, thus, grey zones.

The meaning assigned to military security is deliberately being downgraded. It is transformed into a 'soft' reading of security in terms of economic and political co-operation, environmental protection, nuclear safety, people-to-people contacts, and so on. To be sure, not all actors subscribe to this point of view. In the Baltic States, for example, an emphasis on military security is still discernible, albeit less distinct than in the mid-1990s. While still focusing on NATO membership, the Baltic States are referring to membership in the European Union increasingly in terms of security (Vares 1999), thus adapting to the Finnish viewpoint (Forsberg and Ojanen 2000). In Sweden and Finland, substantial modernisation programmes in the armed forces throughout the 1990s accompany policies supporting a softer reading of security. In this case, soft security has not removed military security but both approaches are being pursued simultaneously. In Finland, for example, the civilian understanding of security displayed in the initiative on a Northern Dimension of the European Union goes hand in hand with approaching NATO to an extent inconceivable only some years ago. The Russian Federation's military restraint and co-operative policies in the Baltic Sea region are seen by the neighbouring states in part as an expression of a lack of capabilities rather than a change of intentions and (regional) great power ambitions. Yet, the overall picture which emerges ten years after the 'Charter of Paris' is one of co-operation among and within nation-states and societies in a region without insurmountable dividing lines.

Although the 1990s have been a decade of peaceful change in the Baltic Sea region, it may be premature to refer to the region in terms of a security community: Peaceful change has not yet been translated into expectations of stable peace (Deutsch et al. 1957). Yet to some extent, the Baltic Sea states – with the exception of the Russian Federation – have exhibited an even more peaceful development than some states in the ostensible Western European security community. For example, they did neither display violent secessionism nor terrorism. Conflicts over citizenship in Estonia and Latvia have been prevented from escalating by way of involving international organisations for mediation and fact-finding. Disputes on territory and borders between the Baltic States and Russia have not escalated either. The conflicts over the demarcation of the sea borders between the Baltic States have temporarily burdened bilateral relations because major economic interests were at stake. In the meantime, a search for compromise seems to have replaced intransigent positions. Non-decisions and dilatory policies appear to have been accepted as normal part of the game. The lack of border treaties with Russia in a couple of remaining cases has not prevented the European Union from starting membership negotiations with the Baltic States. This – and the EU's Northern Dimension – may prepare the ground for a less rigid approach to borders which is already discernible in many parts of the Baltic Sea region (Ahponen and Jukarainen 2000).

The Post-Cold War Setting in the Baltic Sea Region

During the 1990s, no armed conflicts occurred in the Baltic Sea region (Wallensteen and Sollenberg 2000).[2] One of the most remarkable features of the end of the Cold War in the Baltic Sea region was indeed its non-violence. While fifteen of eighteen armed conflicts in Europe between 1989 and 1993 took place in the territories of the former Soviet Union and ex-Yugoslavia (Wallensteen and Axell 1994: 333), change in the Baltic Sea region was peaceful. The process of restoring Estonian, Latvian and Lithuanian independence was basically characterised by prudent restraint and non-violence on the part of the Baltic popular movements and the Soviet central authorities. Neither the process of state formation in the Baltic States nor the political and economic turmoil in the Russian Federation brought about international violence in the Baltic Sea region.

With the termination of the validity of the 1955 'Treaty of Friendship, Co-operation and Mutual Assistance' on 1 July 1991 and the resulting dissolution of the Warsaw Treaty Organisation, the primary means of Soviet military domination over parts of Central and Eastern Europe finally disappeared. It disappeared roughly eight months after the unification of the two German states on 3 October 1990 which would not have been possible without civilian mass resistance in the German Democratic Republic in the late 1980s. The role taken by the military, in particular the Soviet forces stationed in the GDR, during the mass demonstrations was essentially one of bystanding and non-involvement based on strict instructions from Moscow (Albrecht 1995: 172). Likewise, the Baltic popular movements' non-violent resistance in the second half of the 1980s was not met with mass violence on the part of the armed forces and is to be seen as the condition of possibility for the movements' success, materialised in the independence of Estonia, Latvia and Lithuania in autumn 1991. The international accords in connection with the German unification resulted in 'the biggest reductions in armed forces on a given territory within a given brief period' (Albrecht 1995: 169). About one million troops were either disbanded or withdrawn from Germany.

The withdrawal of the Russian – former Soviet – troops from the territories of Poland, the former German Democratic Republic, Estonia, Latvia and Lithuania has aptly been called 'one of the greatest strategic retreats in human history' (Lieven 1996: 175). Altogether, thirty-seven divisions were withdrawn from Central Europe and the Baltic States (IISS 1995: 102). As long as the Soviet Union existed, the troop withdrawal caused bitter complaints among conservatives representing military interests and right-wing forces in the Soviet Congress of People's Deputies. They complained that unilateral force reductions and an overambitious foreign policy undermined Soviet security (Sharp 1991: 435). Yet, Soviet withdrawals from Eastern Europe continued. After the dissolution of the Soviet Union, the pull-out Russian troops from Estonia, Latvia and Lithuania amounted to 120,000 servicemen. The principle of withdrawal has not been called into question by the Russian authorities. Its implementation, however, caused dissatisfaction as indicated by various official and semi-official statements. These reflected, among other things, the military value attached to the Baltic republics in Soviet times, temporary political tensions between the Baltic States and the Russian Federation, and unrealistic demands on the part of the Baltic States as to scope and speed of the troop pull-out. Furthermore, the technical problems

caused delays and temporary interruptions of the troop withdrawal, thus intensi-
fying anxieties in the Baltic States for Russia's willingness to fulfil her international obligations. This disregarded, the troop pull-out progressed quite smoothly on the operational level, although a different picture emerged on the level of
rhetorics. The endeavour was completed in Lithuania on 31 August 1993 and in
Estonia and Latvia one year later.

The Russian troop pull-out from Poland – approximately 40,000 men – and
Germany – approximately 380,000 men – was completed in October 1992 and
August 1994, respectively. Altogether, 4,000 Russian servicemen were allowed to
stay in Poland until 17 September 1993 to co-ordinate the transfer of troops withdrawn from Germany (Lachowski 1994: 577). Russia was also permitted to use the
ballistic missile early warning station in Skrunda (Latvia) up to August 1998 (plus
18 months for dismantlement). In compliance with the Russian troop withdrawal agreement, dismantlement of the former Soviet nuclear submarine training
base in Paldiski (Estonia) including two small nuclear test reactors was completed in September 1995 (Raid 1996: 20). Likewise, the Skrunda radar station has
been dismantled and left by the Russian armed forces according to schedule
although it resulted in 2,500 km space between the British Islands and Greenland
being uncovered by Russian surveillance systems for the time being (Puheloinen
1999: 60).

In spite of numerous concerns as to unpredictability (e.g., Vike-Freiberga
2000; Heikka 2000: 3) – which have replaced complaints of predictable malevo-
lence – the foreign policy of the Russian Federation in the Baltic Sea region has
basically been stable (Medvedev 2000: 11-22). Even the contentious issue of Russian civilian and military transit by rail through Lithuania to supply its Kaliningrad exclave 'has not provoked conflict of any significance' (Gricius 1998: 171).
Moreover, the quantitative scope of the military transit has been rather modest
(Oldberg 1998: 7). Despite of numerous alarmed statements and threats of
counter-measures, the Russian authorities have even swallowed the Polish membership in NATO. The issue concerning the NATO membership of Estonia,
Latvia and Lithuania, however, remains contentious.

Military Developments in the Baltic Sea Region, 1989-2000

The overall military expenditure of the Baltic rim states have declined over the
period under scrutiny here. Putting Russia as a special case aside (see Table 15.1),
military expenditure in constant figures reached the low mark in 1996. Since then,
a slight increase can be observed. The overall figures for 1999 are still considerably
lower than those for 1992. However, the figures show considerable differences
across countries.

With the evaporation in 1990 of the German Democratic Republic, one
markedly militarised state disappeared from the political landscape in the Baltic
Sea region. As a percentage of the gross domestic product, the GDR with between

4.4 and 5.0 per cent had the largest share of military expenditure among the Baltic Sea states thoughout the 1980s, except for the Soviet Union. In 1989, the manpower of the regular armed forces (excluding substantial paramilitary and state security troops) was stronger than that of Sweden, Finland, Norway and Denmark combined – 173,100 as against 161,200 (IISS 1989). Moreover, the GDR hosted by far the largest contingent of Soviet forces based on foreign territory – some 380,000 men (Sharp 1990: 463).

The dissolution of the Soviet Union left a gap which the Russian Federation has neither been able nor aspired to fill. The lack of transparency of Russian military accounting – for example, the 1999 and 2000 defence budgets were 'shrouded in secrecy' (IISS 2000: 118), military related activities were hidden in the federal budget under another heading, figures are imprecise and unreliable due to, for example, practices of non-payment and barter, and so on – makes precise evaluation difficult and the figures open to rather arbitrary interpretation (IISS 1999: 108-111). As a consequence, estimations of Russian military expenditure differ significantly from one another. Yet, the estimates invariably indicate a considerable decrease in expenditure, which resulted, among other things, in limited operationability and declining technical standards. Reflecting a slight recovery of the Russian economy, total Russian military expenditure in 1999 rose in real terms and actual expenditure exceeded the budget by 24 per cent (Sköns et al. 2000: 248; IISS 2000: 115).

Table 15.1: Independent estimates of Russian military expenditure

	IMF % GDP	SIPRI 1997 $bn	SIPRI % GDP	IISS 1997 $bn	IISS % GDP	ACDA 1997 $bn	ACDA % GDP	NATO % GDP
1992	4.7	50	5.5	146	10.8	178	20	>10
1993	4.4	44	5.3	114	8.9	137	17	>10
1994	4.6	42	5.8	101	8.3	99	14	>10
1995	2.9	25	3.7	86	7.4	79	11	>7
1996	3.6	24	3.7	73	6.5	n.a.	n.a.	7
1997	3.3	25	3.8	64	5.8	n.a.	n.a.	<7
1998	2.5	n.a.	3.2	55	5.2	n.a.	n.a.	4.4

Note: n.a.: not applicable.
Source: IISS (1999: 110)

Financial scarcity cannot but have an influence on the ongoing process of military reform in the Russian Federation.[3] The reform consists of four priority areas: reductions in personnel; redirecting the armed forces to short local and regional conflicts; redirecting the armed forces to Southern and Far Eastern regions; and compensating Russia's absolute and relative conventional weakness with prioritising its nuclear forces.[4] Reacting to obvious deficiencies during the Chechen campaign, the Russian Security Council on 11 August 2000 decided to emphasise improving the conventional forces (IISS 2000: 110). Yet, lack of resources as a consequence of the weak performance of the Russian economy throughout the 1990s is inhibiting both a cost-intensive restructuring of the military and an increase in the defence budget as demanded by the military and the defence lobby in the Russian Duma. At the same time, reducing the personnel of the armed forces appears to be more expensive than maintaining them at existing levels, at least in the short run (Arbatov 1999: 201-204). Furthermore, substantial person-nel reductions have already been accompanied by a severe lack of qualified offi-cers leading to a decline in quality of education and training. On balance, the Russian military reform has mainly been one of muddling through rather than one of using the scarce resources properly and in a target-oriented manner. It has also been claimed that President Yeltsin 'clearly preferred a system with no coher-ent national security policy or institution capable of making one' (Blank 2000: 562). For example, plans of moving into the direction of professional armed forces seem to be postponed for the time being (IISS 1999: 104-111).

In the 1990s, Russian military policy was based on the 'Principal Guidance on the Military Doctrine of the Russian Federation' issued in 1993 and refined in 1998 and on 'The Basics of the State Policy of the Russian Federation on Military Development until the Year 2005' of 30 July 1998. These documents rule out for the foreseeable future the possibility of large-scale or even global warfare. Instead, they focus on local conflicts in the post-Soviet space and the individual or com-bined possession of countries adjacent to the Russian Federation of armed forces comparable or superior to Russia's (Arbatov 1999: 196-97). A new 'Concept of National Security of the Russian Federation' was approved on January 10, 2000. It emerged in the form of a presidential decree and replaced its December 1997 statist-liberal predecessor document (Wallander 2000: 9).[5] It has been followed by a new Military Doctrine and a new Foreign Policy Concept, approved by Presi-dent Putin on 20 April and 28 June 2000, respectively. Arguably, these documents should not be read as an expression of the President's personal opinion. Rather, it is to be supposed that they reflect the views of the Russian defence and security establishment more generally.

The January 2000 'Concept of National Security of the Russian Federation' re-assesses Russia's international environment by putting stronger emphasis on external threats to Russian security (Wallander 2000: 10). It also underlines the necessity to secure the country's territorial integrity and the inviolability of its borders. Taking account of Russia's dissatisfaction with both NATO's enlarge-ment process and the military intervention in Kosovo, the new elements in the document appear modest. The document stresses co-operation 'first of all' with the 'leading states of the world.' In other words, Russia still wants 'to be *with* them and *among* them' (Baranovsky 2000: 456). The document also re-evaluates the use of nuclear weapons.[6] It contemplates the use of nuclear weapons to 'repulse armed aggression, if all other means of resolving the crisis have been exhausted' (cited in Wallander 2000: 11). The threshold to the use of nuclear weapons has further been lowered in the new Military Doctrine. The document permits the use of nuclear weapons in case of a conventional attack by a non-nuclear power 'in situations critical to the national security of the Russian Federation' even if the aggressor has no formal alliance tie to a nuclear-weapon state (for the document, see *Arms Control Today*, 2000). The emphasis on nuclear weapons has however been relativised by the August 2000 decision of the National Security Council referred to above.

After the completion of the troop withdrawal, the Baltic Sea region has certainly not been in the centre of Russian military interest in the 1990s. Rather, attention was directed to the South resulting, among other things, in 'peace-keeping and war-making' in the Caucasus (Baev 1996: 115). As a corollary of this, the Russian naval forces have been reduced since 1990 by 80 per cent. Furthermore, the operationability and even floatability of parts of the remaining fleet is questionable. At the same time, the Navy's role within Russia's strategic nuclear forces is likely to be expanded in the light of START II. The situation of the conventional naval forces is characterised by the gap between Russia's maritime interests as outlined in the April 2000 Naval Doctrine on the one hand,[7] the Navy's enduring difficulties to fulfil the requirements on the other (IISS 2000: 111). Russian naval deployment and naval aviation capabilities in the Baltic Sea region reflect the general trend. The Baltic Fleet shed 56,000 sailors (Trenin 2000: 24). Alexei Arbatov (1999: 204) even speculates on the possibility of the Baltic Fleet being downgraded 'to flotilla or even squadron scale.' At present, the fleet's function is that of a coastal fleet (Puheloinen 1999: 63) comprising of not more than two destroyers and four frigates.

In the process of restructuring Russian combat units, Kaliningrad has become an 'operational strategic group' combining all land, sea and air forces under the command of The Ground and Coastal Defence Forces of the Baltic Fleet (IISS 1999: 104 and 2000: 124). Ground forces deployed in Kaliningrad oblast show a marked decline in numbers from approximately 50,000 in 1992 to 10,400 in 1999 and up again to 12,700 in 2000 (IISS 1992: 98; 1999: 116; 2000: 124). These figures call into question the aptness of the frequent complaints of excessive militarisation of Kaliningrad oblast, part and parcel of the discourse on military developments in the Baltic Sea region throughout the 1990s. The 'geo-rhetoric' usually saw the combination of Russian troop presence in Kaliningrad and the oblast's specific geographical location, i.e. separateness from Russia proper, *in itself* as a military threat to the security of the neighbouring states.

Compared with the number of military personnel on active service of the other Baltic rim states, however, 'the estimates of Russia's dominant military position [in the Baltic Sea region] will have a rather scant ground' (Moshes 1999: 62).[8] Furthermore, the November 1999 adaptation of the 'Treaty on Conventional Forces in Europe' reduces the ceilings for tanks, armoured combat vehicles and artillery systems deployed in both Kaliningrad and Pskov considerably. Under the old Treaty, approved in 1996, Russia was allowed to station 4,200 tanks, 8,760 armoured combat vehicles (ACVs) and 3,325 artillery systems in Kaliningrad as well as 1,800 tanks, 600 ACVs and 2,400 artillery systems in Pskov. These figures remained quite theoretical, in part due to lack of storage facilities. Under the new Treaty, only 855 tanks, 1,007 ACVs and 375 artillery may be stationed in Kaliningrad; 31 tanks, 139 ACVs and 91 artillery systems in Pskov (Schmidt 2000: 44-45). During the 1990s, conventional forces in Northwestern Russia have been considerably reduced. For example, massive troop cuts up to 40 percent included the disbandment in March 1999 of the Leningrad Military District's 6th Army

Table 15.2: Russian deployment and naval deployment in the Baltic Sea region, 2000

	Kaliningrad Operational Strategic Group*	Leningrad Military District (HQ St Petersburg)	Baltic Fleet (Bases Krohnstadt and Baltiysk)
Ground forces	12,700	38,100	
Main battle tanks	816	333	
Armoured combat vehicles (ACV)	850	500	
Artillery/Multiple rocket launcher/			
Mortars	345	940	
Scud/Scarab	18	18	
Attack helicopters	20	25	
Air Defence			
Fighters		185	28
Surface-to-air-missiles	50	525	
Submarines			2
Destroyers			2
Frigates/corvettes			4
Patrol/coastal combatants			26
Mine counter-measures			13
Amphibious			5
Support and misc.			130
Naval Aviation			
Combat aircraft			68
Armed helicopters			41
Naval Infantry	1,100	1,300**	
Main battle tanks	26	74	
ACV	220	230	
Artillery/Multiple rocket launcher	30	45	
Coastal Defence			
Artillery	133	134	
SS-C-1b Sepal	8		
MT-LB		360	
Air			
Combat aircraft	392		

* Commanded by The Ground and Coastal Defence Forces of the Baltic Fleet
** Subordinated to Northern Fleet

Source: IISS (2000: 123-26)

and the army corps stationed in Vyborg (Herd 1999: 202). As part of the Russian military reform launched in 1997 and resulting from a combination of political, financial and military considerations, Russia has disbanded two armies, one army corps, six divisions, eight brigades, and one squadron and has dismantled several military facilities and installations in its Northwestern areas (Lachowski 2000: 265). The remaining troops, however, are regarded as having comparatively good equipment (Puheloinen 1999: 61). Yet due to a dramatic decrease in arms production throughout the 1990s (Martelius 1999: 227), Russia's ability to maintain the current standard of equipment appears questionable.

Even if intended to mitigate concerns about an ostensible Russian superiority, singling out Russian military capabilities in the Baltic Sea region results all too easily in falling in the trap of carrying on and renewing Cold War thinking. Moreover, Russian armed forces are still often depicted in their potentially offensive function while the armed forces of the other Baltic Sea states are represented purely defensively. While Russia is called for justifying the scope of its armed forces – with some outside observers pretending to know the appropriate scope of the Russian armed forces better than Russian military planners themselves – the scope of the armed forces of the other Baltic rim states is critically assessed only seldom. While Russian armed forces are still seen as potential threat, the armed forces of the other Baltic Sea states are primarily viewed in terms of legitimate self-defence and pursuing international co-operation. Read in isolation, thus, Table 15.2 falls precisely in the trap of perpetuating Cold War threat perceptions by selecting Russian military capabilities rather than, say, Swedish or German, thus giving them a specific meaning. The table should therefore be read in the context of the arguments in the remainder of the chapter.

The advances in terms of disarmament on the part of the Russian Federation were, no doubt, to some extent involuntary. Nevertheless, they are real and at least in short- to medium-terms irreversible.[9] At the same time, they have not yet led to proportional disarmament of the other Baltic Sea states. The Nordic States, for example, still seem to suffer from the after-effects of the increase in significance of the Northern landscape and waters as theatre of strategic superpower rivalry in the mid-1980s. The 'age of the Arctic' (Young 1985-86) was characterised by the Soviet military build-up on the Kola peninsula and the US Maritime Strategy. Regardless of its name, this strategy was 'a combined navy, air force and army approach' (Tunander 1989: 51) which 'prompted a clear sense of alarm on the part of Scandinavian officialdom in particular' (Zakheim 1998: 126). Although not directly directed against the Nordic states or at any one specific Nordic State (Holst 1990; Ruhala 1988), their position was affected adversely by the transformation of the Arctic region into one of the world's most active and important areas of military operations (Young 1985-86: 160).

In the late 1980s and early 1990s, anxieties emerged in the Nordic States that the Soviet troop reduction in Central Europe might result in an increase in troop stationing in the Soviet territories adjacent to the Nordic States. These concerns were not totally unfounded (Jonson 1997: 311). They have paved the way for a careful consideration of unilateral disarmament throughout the 1990s. The historical linkage of neutrality and strong national defence in Sweden as well as the Swedish recollection of incursions of Soviet submarines in Swedish territorial waters in the 1980s have been further obstacles to disarmament on any major scale. Add to this the persistent conservatism of the foreign and security establishments (not only) in the Nordic States. Their military expenditure declined as percentage of GDP – with Sweden's figures for 1996 as a low mark in defence spending which has rapidly been corrected. In constant US dollars, however, they are exhibiting in stagnation in the Danish case and marked increase for the part of Sweden since 1996 thus reversing the trend of the early 1990s. Finland was the only country to experience a marked reduction in 1999. At the same time, Swedish manpower has been reduced considerably while Danish armed forces show an increase in personnel between 1993 and 1997. Major portions of the military budgets in the mid- and late 1990s have been consumed within Finland and Sweden by the modernisation of the air forces by way of ambitious fighter procurement programs (the Swedish air force has ordered 140 JAS-39 Gripen and the Finnish one 64 F-18C/D). In 1996 and 1997, Finland spent $610m and $660m, respectively, for F-18C/D. A supplementary budget as of February 1998 amounted to $180m. Another supplementary budget in April 1998 amounting to $1.1bn enabled the purchase of transport helicopters and the formation of a rapid-reaction force (IISS 1997: 38 and 1998: 35). In contrast, Norway has refrained from replacing its Air Force's F-5 fleet, to be phased out in near future, with Eurofighters. Plans to add five new frigates to the three frigates in service appear to be 'the last naval order for years' (IISS 2000: 39-40).

In Poland, a 'Programme for Integrating and Modernising the Polish Armed Forces for the Years 1998-2012' has been adopted by the Council of Ministers on 15 October 1998. A 'National Security Strategy' has been approved in November 1999. It was followed one month later by 'Assumptions of State Security Policy.' The substantial reduction of personnel throughout the 1990s is to be continued up to 2003. This will leave Poland with a defence establishment numbering 150,000, i.e. roughly half the level as in the early 1990s. The process of reduction in personnel is accompanied with an increasing under-qualification of the remaining personnel. This is so as the relatively healthy Polish economy attracts some of the most qualified people (Simon 2000: 2). The growth in military expenditure between 1993 and 1997 reflects mainly the inclusion of military retirement pensions and disabled personnel benefits in the military budget (Sköns et al. 1998: 211). Thus, growth in military expenditure in real terms does not always express real increase in the efforts of armament. Adaptation to NATO standards as well as modernisation and restructuring programmes, however, are likely to be reflected in future military budgets. The direct costs of joining NATO are estimated at $3bn between 1998 and 2010. Indirect costs of achieving inter-operability with NATO forces are expected to constitute some $8.3bn divided over 15 years (Sköns et al. 1999: 293). At the same time, aspiring to meet the criteria for EU membership may result in a shift of priorities once NATO membership was realised in April 1999. The rather ambitious Polish military plans may remain unfulfilled (IISS 1999: 35).

Estonia, Latvia and Lithuania are aiming at finalising their involuntary non-alignment as well. Lithuania has considerably increased its military expenditure in real terms between 1994 and 1998. The recent change of government (October 2000) may lead to delay the realisation of the envisaged aim of defence spending amounting to two percent of GDP without changing the foreign and security course in principle. In order to meet the requirements pertaining to NATO membership, the Baltic States have constantly increased their investments into the military sector and intensified both trilateral military co-operation and co-operation with the Nordic States. Although still criticised as insufficient, working together among Estonia, Latvia and Lithuania for the purpose of enhancing the military capabilities and coming closer to NATO is considerable albeit, in the case of the Baltic Battalion, still '*very* dependent upon external support' (Simon 2000: 4). Financial scarcity increasingly requires a prioritisation of either the build-up of national armed forces or participation in international military co-operation. It also necessitates a shift in emphasis from the quantitative to the qualitative aspect of co-operation. By way of participating in international military co-operation (e.g., 'Partnership for Peace') the Baltic States wish to underline their claim that they are producers, and not merely consumers, of European security and that NATO would derive benefit from including them. Therefore, the costly Baltic Battalion is considered important to national security although it does not directly enhance national defence capabilities (Bergman 2000: 19). The joint Lithuanian-Polish Battalion combines troops of a NATO member state with troops of a non-member state and is seen by Lithuania as a step on the path towards NATO membership (Lithuanian Ministry of National Defence 2000).

Table 15.3: Military expenditure as a percentage of GDP, 1985, 1989-99

	1985	1989	1990	1991	1992	1993	1994	1995	1996	1997	1998	*1999*
GER	3.2	2.8	2.8	2.3	2.1	2.0	1.8	1.7	1.6	1.6	1.5	*1.6*
DK	2.2	2.1	2.1	2.0	1.9	1.9	1.8	1.7	1.7	1.7	1.6	*1.6*
N	3.1	3.0	2.9	2.8	3.0	2.7	2.8	2.4	2.2	2.1	2.3	*2.2*
S	2.6	2.3	[2.6]	[2.5]	[2.5]	2.6	2.4	2.0	1.7	2.2	2.2	*2.3*
F	1.9	1.4	[1.6]	1.8	1.9	1.9	1.8	1.5	1.7	1.5	1.5	*1.4*
GDR	4.6	5.0	-	-	-	-	-	-	-	-	-	*-*
PL	3.0	1.8	2.7	2.3	2.3	2.6	2.3	2.2	2.2	2.1	2.1	*2.1*
EST	-	-	-	-	(0.5)	0.8	1.1	1.0	1.0	1.2	1.2	*1.5*
LAT	-	-	-	-	-	0.8	0.9	1.0	0.7	0.7	0.7	*1.0*
LIT	-	-	-	-	-	0.7	0.5	0.5	0.5	0.8	1.3	*1.0*

Note: Figures for Germany (1985, 1989, 1990) refer to the former West Germany.
[ ] SIPRI estimate; ( ) uncertain figure; for Russia, see Table 15.1.

Sources: SIPRI (1992: 264); SIPRI (1999: 320-21); SIPRI (2000: 280-81); IISS (2000: 297-98)

Table 15.4: Military expenditure in constant US dollars (US$m)

	1992	1994	1996	1997	1998	1999
Germany	49951	41906	40343	38906	39001	39543
Denmark	3224	3150	3126	3168	3205	3223
Norway	3968	3885	3554	3495	3728	3650
Sweden	[5507]	5343	4044	5399	5540	5714
Finland	2219	2120	2225	2078	2259	1913
Poland	2502	2675	2852	2983	3097	3144
Estonia	(20.1)	36.7	38.7	48.1	50.6	57.1
Latvia	—	45.0	33.8	32.8	35.2	45.7
Lithuania	—	27.7	33.9	55.7	94.2	124
Overall Sum	*[67391.1]*	*59188.4*	*56250.4*	*56284.5*	*57010*	*57413.8*

Note: Figures are at constant 1995 prices and exchange rates.

[ ] SIPRI estimate; ( ) uncertain figure; for Russia, see Table 15.1.

Source: SIPRI (2000: 274-75)

Unified Germany, while having dislocated some of its marine installations from former west to former east German bases, has been exhibiting restraint in respect to its military presence and activities in the Baltic Sea region. In particular, although currently updating its naval capabilities (IISS 2000: 40), 'Germany shows no ambitions to fill a "naval power vacuum"' (Krohn 1996: 109). Based on the 'Treaty on the Final Settlement with Respect to Germany' of 12 September 1990 and the statement made by the governments of the FRG and the GDR on 30 August 1990 in Vienna at the Negotiations on Conventional Armed Forces in Europe, the strength of the German armed forces was to be reduced to 370,000 and, as a result of budgetary constraints, has further declined since then. In 2000, for example, the German armed forces numbered some 321,000 active personnel (including 128,400 conscripts) distributed among Army (221,100 incl. 102,100 conscripts), Navy (26,600 incl. 5,500 conscripts), and Air Force (73,300 incl. 20,800 conscripts) (IISS 2000: 61-62). Germany continues its policy of renunciation of the manufacture and possession of and control over nuclear, biological, and chemical weapons. In addition, units of German armed forces assigned to NATO are permitted to be stationed in the territory of the former GDR and Berlin only without nuclear weapon carriers. Foreign armed forces and nuclear weapons or their carriers are banned from the territory of the former GDR and Berlin, too. As a result, this territory is nuclear weapons-free. With 1.5 per cent of GDP, German military expenditure reached a new nadir in 1998. In constant figures, the low mark was in 1997. Since then, a slight increase in military expenditure can be observed.

Essentially, active manpower of the armed forces of the Baltic Sea states has been more than halved from 1992 to 2000. Except for the Baltic States, there is no increase in personnel in any Baltic rim state. Estonia, Latvia and Lithuania are in the process of establishing national armed formations. The increase in personnel is thus not surprising. With the exception of the Baltic States, the Swedish air force and the Finnish Navy, the armed forces of the Baltic rim states have reduced their personnel throughout the 1990s in all three military branches. Considerable reductions in personnel have occurred in Germany, Russia and Poland. As to personnel, Russia remains the strongest military power among the Baltic rim states although only a small fraction of its overall military personnel is relevant to the Baltic region. Most recent developments show no marked changes in active manpower. Figures for Sweden and Poland remain constant in 1998 and 1999 and are further declining in 2000. Figures for Finland remain constant from 1998 to 2000. Drastic decline in personnel in Denmark's armed forces down to 24,300 in 1999 and 21,800 in 2000 results primarily from excluding civilians from the figures (while including 461 central staff). Developments in Norway display slight irregularities between 1996 and 2000. Germany continues the reductions in personnel and has 332,800 and 321,000 in 1999 and 2000, respectively. Russian armed forces in 1999 are roughly half the level of 1993. Estonia, Latvia, and Lithuania go on building their armed forces. Considerable irregularities in the figures for Lithuania and Latvia in the mid-1990s are mainly a result of including in, or excluding from, the statistics border guards and voluntary forces. Table 15.6 shows considerable mobilisable reserves in some of the Baltic Sea rim states.

Table 15.5: Active manpower of the armed forces of the Baltic Sea states, in thousands

	1991	1992	1993	1994	1995	1996	1997	1998	1999	2000
S	63.0	60.5	64.8	64.0	64.0	62.6	53.4	53.1	53.1	52.7
N	32.7	32.7	29.4	33.5	30.0	30.0	33.6	28.9	31.0	26.7
F	31.8	32.8	32.8	31.2	31.1	32.5	31.0	31.7	31.7	31.7
DK	29.4	29.2	27.7	27.0	33.1	32.9	32.9	32.1	24.3	21.8
GER	476.3	447.0	408.2	367.3	339.9	358.4	347.1	333.5	332.8	321.0
RF	-	2720.0	2030.0	1714.0	1520.0	1270.0	1240.0	1159.0	1004.1	1004.1
PL	305.0	296.5	287.5	283.6	278.6	248.5	241.8	240.7	240.7	217.3
EST	-	2.0	2.5	2.5	3.5	3.5	3.5	4.3	4.8	4.8
LAT	-	2.6	5.0	6.9	7.0	8.0	4.5	5.0	5.7	5.0
LIT	-	7.0	9.8	8.9	8.9	5.1	5.3	11.1	12.1	12.7
Sum	938.2	3630.3	2897.7	2539.1	2316.1	2051.5	1993	1899.4	1740.3	1697.8

Note: Figures include conscripts. In addition, figures for *Sweden* include active reserves (1996-2000); for *Norway* recalled reservists (1994-1997); Joint Services organisations, Home Guard permanent staff; for *Denmark* central staff while excluding civilians (1999-2000); for *Germany* active Reserve training posts, inter-service staff (1991); for *Russia* Ministry of Defence staff, centrally controlled units for electronic warfare, training, rear services (1992-2000); for *Poland* centrally controlled staffs, units/formations (1998-2000); for *Latvia* National Guard (1996-2000); centrally controlled units (1999-2000), Border Guard (1993-1996); for *Lithuania* Voluntary National Defence Force (1998-2000), Border Guard (1993-1995).

Source: IISS (1991-2000)

It should be noted, however, that military asymmetries do not *in themselves* imply instability or the existence of a threat to any one of the Baltic Sea littoral states. This is so because the functional value of military capabilities *as such* explains relatively little of the political meaning attached to them for a variety of reasons by political actors. Political meaning, in turn, is socially constructed and thus subject to possible change. Whether the meaning assigned to military capabilities changes or not is primarily a result of social practices and shared knowledge (Wendt 1995). Furthermore, the existence of military asymmetries in the Baltic Sea region remains disputed and depends on whether the overall military power of the rim states is included in the equation or if only the military power relevant to the region is takne into account (Moshes 1999). Moreover, quantitative estimations have to be complemented with qualitative assessments, albeit this is not the place to engage oneself in such an endeavour. In any case, calls for a military equilibrium in the Baltic Sea region are hardly required. NATO member states on the one side, the Russian Federation on the other, and some (voluntary or involuntary) non-aligned states in between, serving in a positive case as a bridge, in a negative case as a buffer zone – this would be a carbon-copy of the Cold War setting. Demanding a 'Baltic balance' (Zakheim 1998: 128) has connotations of the mechanical rationale underlying Cold War military planning and weapons counting to serve as a vehicle for future-oriented military planning and development in the region. And in the Baltic Sea region an automatic identification of military capabilities with at least potential threats is increasingly being replaced by an emphasis on perceiving the military in terms of co-operation and partnership.

Table 15.6: Mobilisable reserves of the armed forces of the Baltic Sea states, 2000

	Reserves (total)		Reserves (total)
Sweden	570,000	Russia	Some 20,000,000
Norway	222,000	Poland	406,000
Finland	485,000	Estonia	Some 14,000
Denmark	64,900	Latvia	14,500
Germany	364,300	Lithuania	355,650

Note: Total figures for *Sweden* include local defence and home guard and for *Norway* home guard. Figures for *Lithuania* consist of 27,000 first line (ready 72 hours, incl. 10,200 Voluntary National-al Defence Service) and 327,950 second line.
Source: IISS (2000)

Prospects and Problems

One indicator of this change consists of the diversity of internationally supported trilateral military co-operation programmes among Estonia, Latvia and Lithuania (like the Baltic Battalion, the Baltic Naval Squadron, the Baltic

Defence College, and so on). Given the anything but smooth historical relations, military co-operation between Poland and Lithuania is an even more remarkable trend (e.g., the joint Lithuanian-Polish peacekeeping battalion, LITPOLBAT). The military co-operation agreements between Poland and the Baltic States concluded on 27 September 2000 point in this direction, too: In 2001, Poland plans 66 joint projects with Lithuania, 40 with Latvia and 17 with Estonia (*Radio Free Europe/Radio Liberty* 2000b). Likewise, the Danish-German-Polish joint Multinational Corps Northwest based in Szczecin, initiated in 1994, inaugurated in 1999 and viewed suspiciously by Russia, indicates a considerable improvement in German-Polish relations since the recognition in September 1990 of the Oder-Neisse-line as a permanent border between Germany and Poland by then German Chancellor Kohl. Before then, some Polish officials had even argued for preserving some Soviet troops on Polish territory as well as Polish WTO membership as 'important guarantees of post-1945 borders with Germany' (Sharp 1991: 437). As to Lithuanian-Polish co-operation, the NATO interoperable LITPOL-BAT, based on an intergovernmental agreement of December 3, 1997, was inaugurated on April 14, 1999. It leans on the existing units. The battalion, comprised of 433 Polish and 351 Lithuanian servicemen and trained separately in their respective countries, is seen as 'an important tool of Lithuania's integration into the NATO military structures' (Lithuanian Ministry of Defence 2000). This appears to indicate the partially instrumental understanding behind Lithuanian-Polish co-operation in the military sphere as a vehicle bringing Lithuania closer to NATO. The same may be said with respect to the Baltic Battalion in particular after the recent change of its title and expansion of its functions (see below).

Although military activities in the Baltic Sea region have largely unfolded in the spirit of co-operation and partnership, some problems remain or are currently surfacing. Naval arms control regimes in the region are non-existent, and with respect to regional conventional arms control, 'the existing record of accomplishments looks modest' (Lachowski 2000: 269). Another problem is that the Russian Federation is only exceptionally included in regional military co-operation schemes. For example, Russian participation in international exercises on Lithuanian territory is limited to the preparatory phase and observer status during the actual manoeuvre (e.g. 'Baltic Challenge 98'). The Lithuanian Defence Ministry declares full Russian participation incompatible with a 1992 constitutional amendment. It prohibits Lithuania from joining 'any new political, military, economic, or any other state alliances or commonwealths formed on the basis of the former USSR' (Lithuanian Ministry of National Defence 1999). In addition, Russia at times excludes itself from co-operation by not participating in some of the frameworks in which participation has been possible, e.g. 'Partnership for Peace' (Lachowski 1999: 21; Herd 1999: 201). Whereas the Nordic Council of Ministers, the Council of the Baltic Sea States, the Northern Dimension of the European Union and parts of the United States Northern European Initiative are explicitly aiming at integrating (Northwest) Russia within a variety of mainly non-military networks, military integration policies in the Baltic Sea region –

like, arguably, in the whole of Europe – are seen by many in Russia as a dual task of 'prevent[ing] Russians from becoming disengaged, without however actually letting them in' (Baranovsky 2000: 446).

Furthermore, in some cases threat perceptions seem to remain unchanged. For example, the 'Law on the Basics of National Security' of the Republic of Lithuania unmistakably refers to the 'specific geopolitical environment, hardly predictable due to existing militarised territories and states of unstable democracy,' as 'potential external risks and dangers' to Lithuanian security. 'Military capabilities in close proximity to Lithuanian borders' are seen as an external risk. The text refers implicitly to Kaliningrad *oblast*, the demilitarisation of which is seen as one of the main tasks of Lithuanian foreign policy.[10] At the same time it has been claimed that 'on the grass-root level negative risk perceptions and assessments are being successfully overcome (people are not afraid of each other and wish to do business together)' (Moshes 1999: 61). Russian security guarantees for the Baltic States, possibly multilateralised, have been rejected point blank in 1997 although co-operation on a less pretentious level seems to be possible and realistic. For example, co-operation between Baltic and Russian border guards and law-enforcement agencies is said to be successful (Trenin 2000: 41). In September 2000, Russian Vice Admiral Vladimir Valuyev announced the Baltic Fleet's readiness to help Estonia, Latvia and Lithuania clearing their territorial waters of Soviet-era mines (*Radio Free Europe/Radio Liberty* 2000a). Russia's willingness to hand over maps of World War II minefields in the Baltic Sea has been welcomed by Baltic officials (Tiido 2000). In October 2000 Estonian inspectors visited the Russian airborne division in Pskov under the OSCE regime in order to check the accuracy of Russian military data (*Radio Free Europe/Radio Liberty* 2000c). This may serve as a confidence-building measure, in particular because Russian military forces stationed in Pskov have often been represented as 'the main concrete military threat to Estonia' (Haab 1998: 111). At the occasion of 52nd Session of the Nordic Council in November 2000, the Defence Ministers announced new military co-operation with Russia on the basis of officer exchanges between the Nordic States and the Russian Federation. Furthermore, they invited Russia to take part in 'Nordic Peace' exercises.[11]

The erasure in June 1998 of 'peacekeeping' from the title of the Baltic Battalion (BALTBAT) in order to make possible its participation in 'NATO-led peace enforcement operations' (*Estonia Today* 1999) not only considerably expands the battalion's original function of 'carry[ing] out peacekeeping operations mandated by the United Nations (UN) or by the Conference on Security and Co-operation in Europe (CSCE)' (Danish Ministry of Defence 1995). Parallel to the expansion of NATO's missions as exemplified in the Kosovo war, a clash between BaltBat's activities and Russia's perceived interests cannot be excluded. Such an eventuality has already been expected by some observers in connection with Baltic participation in KFOR and SFOR (Johnson 1999). This could be excluded as long as BaltBat was designed to perform its tasks exclusively under an UN or OSCE mandate. This is so as Russia would have influence over any such mission. Combined with the identification of 'the expansion of military blocs or alliances to the detriment of the Russian Federation's military security' as one of the main external threats to Russia's military security in the current Military Doctrine (*Arms Control Today* 2000) and the Baltic States' aspirations to enter NATO, a drastic relaxation of Baltic-Russian military relations appears unlikely. The Russian simulation in June 1999 of a Western conventional attack on Kaliningrad *oblast* is not likely to be perceived as a confidence building measure by adjacent countries, too. After having failed to stop the attack by conventional means, the Russian military 'succeeded' in defeating the virtual aggressor by using nuclear weapons (Wallander 2000: 11).

Finally, Estonia's, Latvia's and Lithuania's non-participation in the 'Treaty on Conventional Forces in Europe' (CFE) may have undesirable consequences for regional security in connection with these states' aspirations to enter NATO. The same situation would emerge if Finland and Sweden, as non-participants in the CFE regime, applied for NATO membership. Currently only the Baltic States are of concern. For as long as they remain outside the CFE-Treaty, NATO could in a crisis deploy its troops on the territory of Estonia, Latvia, and Lithuania, ie. an area uncontrolled by any conventional arms control regime. This would result in a substantial destabilisation of the regional security pattern and perceptions (Möller and Wellmann forthcoming). It would also undermine the credibility of the CFE-Treaty which, according to NATO, is 'the cornerstone of European security' (NATO 1995). Furthermore, resistance to Baltic NATO membership remains to be one of the few issues which unite Russian politicians from left to right, independent of party affiliation. The Military Doctrine, implicitly referring to the stationing of NATO troops in neighbouring countries, identifies as one of the main threats to Russian military security 'the creation (buildup) of groups of troops (forces) leading to the violation of the existing balance of forces, close to the Russian Federation's state border' (*Arms Control Today* 2000).[12]

Those NATO members which are currently exhibiting restraint in the question of Baltic membership may see their main argument supported, namely, that the disadvantages to European security emanating from Baltic NATO membership may outweigh the advantages to Baltic security. Unfortunately, even joining the CFE-Treaty prior to, or parallel with, NATO-membership would not entirely solve the problem. For Exceptional Temporary Deployment (ETD) would include the option of military reinforcement in the Baltic States amounting up to six divisions. Likewise, a Russian-Belarusian union could at least temporarily and in theory deploy under ETD four divisions against Latvia. Both options are highly destabilising and thus unwelcome. Therefore, even joining the Treaty, as Lithuania has stated to be interested in at the occasion of the OSCE Summit in Istanbul on 19 November 1999, would require 'additional arms control agreements' or at least 'mutual military restraint' in the Baltic Sea region (Schmidt 2000: 34).

Concluding Remarks: Re-imagining Baltic Security

The 1990s, the Baltic Sea region has been labelled by peaceful change. This is a tremendous achievement. The translation of peaceful change into expectations of stable peace, however, has not yet been managed. The military aspect of security, albeit declining in importance in large parts of Western Europe, is still seen as indispensable for national security. However, military developments in the region as sketched in this chapter hardly give rise to anxieties. Most importantly, the conflicts in particular between the Baltic States and Russia have been managed with political rather than military means. International organisations have made use of a variety of instruments like fact-finding and preventive diplomacy in order to ease bilateral relations and resolve conflicts (Birckenbach 1997). By and large, their recommendations have been accepted and implemented in national legislation, albeit sometimes reluctantly.

Russia, Germany and Poland have reduced their armed forces considerably throughout the 1990s. The Nordic States appear to be somewhat more hesitant as to substantial steps of disarmament. Sweden and Finland have indeed modernised their air forces considerably. Military expenditure declined in Finland and Norway and remained largely unchanged in Denmark. Sweden, on the other hand, combines reducing personnel with increasing military expenditure in constant figures from 1996 to 1999, thus reversing the decline pursued from 1990 to 1995. Estonia, Latvia and Lithuania are still developing their national armed forces. Rather ambitious plans are colliding with limited financial resources. Establishing national armed forces while at once participating in many international co-operation schemes may be difficult to sustain. On balance, 1996 and 1997 marked a low point in the Baltic Sea states' military expenditure. Since then, a slight increase can be observed. This increase can hardly be seen as a reaction to military tensions in the region since there are none. Local and regional military activities are unfolding largely in the spirit of co-operation although much remains to be done if Russia is to gain the standing of a partner of equal stature.

Membership in the European Union is increasingly represented in terms of security. This goes in particular for Finland but Estonia, Latvia and Lithuania currently seem to come closer to the Finnish viewpoint. At time of writing, the issue of Baltic NATO membership is somewhat de-dramatised and receded into the background. Yet it is likely to re-appear in 2002 when NATO will decide upon the next round of enlargement. Up to then, preparations for EU membership on the part of Estonia, Latvia, Lithuania and Poland and bringing life in the EU's Northern Dimension on the part of Finland, Denmark and Sweden are likely to dominate the political agenda in the Baltic Sea region. The Northern Dimension, explicitly aiming at integrating Northwest Russia, may serve as a remedy against isolating Russia which is excluded from both EU and NATO enlargement. In particular in conjunction with the recent re-evaluation of the Nordic co-operation with the adjacent areas (Nordic Working Group 2000) and the United States Northern European Initiative (van Ham 2000), the Northern Dimension may help in further permeating the borders between current and future EU (and perhaps NATO) members and non-members. How the EU is going to deal with the tension between making its new members implement a strict external border regime on the one hand (Schengen) and the Northern Dimension the success of which presupposes a certain openness and porosity of borders on the other hand, remains to be seen.

The argument advanced that 'Europe has no clear border' (Wæver 1998: 100) is true in particular of North Eastern Europe where the European Union reflects this borderlessness by ravelling out in the form of its Northern Dimension. To see borders as vehicles with which to tie communities together rather than separate them from one another is arguably one of the most fascinating trends in Baltic Sea co-operation. Another one is the ongoing disassociation of security from its military aspect. A third one appears to be the involvement of a growing number of non-state actors in cross-border co-operation; a fourth one the strengthening of the civil society even in former socialist parts of the region (Birckenbach, Wellmann and Karabeshkin 2000). These trends, however ambiguous and hesitant they unfold, may have the potential to influence the process of re-imagining security in a positive manner and to contribute to peaceful change in the Baltic Sea region.

Notes

1   Thanks to Arto Nokkala and Pertti Joenniemi for comments on earlier drafts of this chapter.
2   The definition of 'armed conflict' follows Wallensteen and Sollenberg (2000: 648). Thus, neither the aggression of Soviet Ministry of the Interior troops against civilians in Vilnius and Riga in January 1991 nor the violence against Lithuanian border guards at Medininkai on July 31, 1991 qualifies as 'armed conflict.'
3   In order to grasp the magnitude of the reform process it is necessary to see that military reform in Russia means much more than just reform of the armed forces. Military reform includes the reform of 'the defence industries and war mobilization assets, of the recruitment system and social security for the military, of the division of powers and authority between the branches of the government on military matters, of the system of funding defence and security, and of the organization of the executive branch and the [Ministry of Defence] itself' (Arbatov 1999: 196).
4   From this follows that 'To defend against the ubiquitous threats it perceives, Russia relies almost exclusively on nuclear weapons [...]. And since those weapons are of little relevance to today's political-economic agenda, Russia's assets are maladapted to its needs. This asymmetric defence and security posture impedes arms control and regional security agreements and helps explain the stalemate over START II and national missile defence' (Blank 2000: 562).
5   The 1997 document was 'clearly a marriage of liberal and statist views, with liberal influence defining national security in terms of domestic well-being and reform, and statist influence in articulating the kind of assertive and pro-active Russian foreign involvement that would shape and make best use of the opportunities in the international system to support Russia's primarily internal security tasks.' The August 1998 financial crisis undermined the liberal elite's economic position and the NATO-led war in Kosovo 'discredited the liberal rationale for substantial and wide-ranging security co-operation with the West' (Wallander 2000: 9-10).

6   It should be noted that the 'revival of the nuclear first-strike concept since 1993' has not yet
    been reflected in the command and control system and the operation of the armed forces
    (Arbatov 1999: 202).
7   The Naval Doctrine defines as Russia's maritime interests to guarantee access to the world's
    oceans; to prevent both discriminatory actions against Russia and domination in particular
    of adjacent seas by any states or alliances to the detriment of Russian interests; and to settle
    international conflicts over the use of the sea to the benefit of Russia (IISS 2000: 111).
8   Observers are also warning against presupposing a 100 per cent manning state of Russian
    units. Independent estimations are in part considerably lower (IISS 2000: 124).
9   The Russian disarmament advances are even clearer when we compare deployment in 1995
    with 2000. In Kaliningrad, for example, the number of ground forces decreased from 24,000
    to 12,700; main battle tanks from 870 to 816; armoured combat vehicles from 980 to 850;
    mortars from 410 to 345; attack helicopters from 52 to 20. The Baltic Fleet's submarines
    declined from 9 to 2; principal surface combatants from 23 to 6; patrol and coastal combat-
    ants from 65 to 26; mine countermeasure from 55 to 13, and so on. Naval aviation under the
    command of the Baltic Fleet decreased from 195 combat aircraft in 1995 to 68 in 2000 while
    armed helicopters increased from 35 to 41 (IISS 1995 and 2000).
10 Republic of Lithuania 'Law on the Basics of National Security,' 19 December 1996 (amend-
    ed as of 4 June 1998), Vilnius, Part Two, Chapter 9, First Section and Part One, Chapter 5
    (official translation).
11 'Nordic Peace' exercises have been held since 1997. They are joint exercises among the Nordic
    states within the framework of 'Partnership for Peace' and at once part of the collaborative
    exercises conducted under the Nordic Coordinated Arrangement for Military Peace Support,
    NORDCAPS (*FD aktuelt* 1999). The Baltic States have participated in 'Nordic Peace' exer-
    cises.
12 As Henrikki Heikka (2000: 31) points out, 'If the unipolar ambitions of the US are seen as
    the main threat to the stability of the international system, then the attempts of Russia's Baltic
    neighbours to gain formal security guarantees from Nato are not perceived by Moscow pri-
    marily as a regional security problem, but as an integral part of the most important threat to
    Russia's national security.'

References

Data used in this article are based upon the Yearbooks of the Stockholm International Peace
    Research Institute (SIPRI) 1990-2000 and the International Institute for Strategic Studies
    (IISS) 1989-2000. The IISS's *The Military Balance* is published by Brassey's, London, 1989-94
    and Oxford University Press, Oxford, 1995-2000. SIPRI's *Yearbook* is published by Oxford
    University Press, Oxford, with the following subtitles: *World Armaments and Disarmament*
    (1990-1993), *Armaments, Disarmament and International Security* (1995-2000), no subtitle in
    1994.
Ahponen, P. and Jukarainen, P. (eds). (2000). *Tearing Down the Curtain, Opening the Gates:
    Northern Boundaries in Change.* Jyväskylä, SoPhi.
Albrecht, U. (1995). 'The Peaceful Unification of Germany,' pages 168-207 in Patomäki, H. (ed.).
    Peaceful Changes in World Politics. Tampere, Tampere Peace Research Institute.
Arbatov, A.G. (1999). 'Russia: Military Reform,' pages 195-212 in Stockholm International Peace
    Research Institute. *SIPRI Yearbook 1999: Armaments, Disarmament and International Securi-
    ty.* Oxford, Oxford University Press.
Arms Control (2000). 'Russia's Military Doctrine,' May 2000, pages 29-38.
Baev, P.K. (1996). *The Russian Army in a Time of Troubles.* London, Thousand Oaks, New Delhi,
    Sage Publications.
Baranovsky, V. (2000). 'Russia: A Part of Europe or Apart from Europe?' *International Affairs*
    2000:3, pages 443-58.

Bergman, A. (2000). *Balbat – The Emergence of a Common Defence Dimension to Nordic Co-operation?* Copenhagen, Working Paper No. 22/2000, Copenhagen Peace Research Institute.

Birckenbach, H.-M. (1997). *Preventive Diplomacy through Fact-Finding: How International Organizations Review the Conflict over Citizenship in Estonia and Latvia.* Hamburg, Lit Verlag.

Birckenbach, H.-M. and Wellmann, C., assisted by Karabeshkin, L. (2000). *Zivilgesellschaft in Kaliningrad. Eine Explorationsstudie zur Förderung partnerschaftlicher Zusammenarbeit erstellt im Auftrag des Schleswig-Holsteinischen Landtags.* Kiel, Schleswig-Holstein Institute for Peace Research.

Blank, S. (2000). 'Partners in Discord Only,' *Orbis* 2000:4, pages 557-70.

Council on Foreign Relations, chairman Zbigniew Brzezinski (1999). *U.S. Policy toward North Eastern Europe,* April 1999, at http://www.cfr.org/public/pubs/baltics.html.

Danish Ministry of Defence (1995). *The Baltbat-Project. Documentation from the Danish Ministry of Defence.* Copenhagen.

Deutsch, K.W. et al. (1957). *Political Community and the North Atlantic Area: International Organization in the Light of Historical Experience.* Princeton, Princeton University Press.

Estonia Today (1999). 'The Baltic Battalion (BaltBat): Regional and International Co-operation in Action,' updated 25 October 1999.

FD aktuelt (1999). 'NORDCAPS – Nordic Co-operation in Peace Operations,' at http://www.odin.dep.no/fd, updated 13 December 1999.

Forsberg, T. and Ojanen, H. (2000). 'Finland's New Policy: Using the EU for Stability in the North,' pages 115-29 in Bonvicini, G., Vaahtoranta, T. and Wessels, W. (eds). *The Northern EU: National Views on the Emerging Security Dimension.* Helsinki and Bonn, The Finnish Institute of International Affairs and Institut für Europäische Politik.

Gricius, A. (1998). 'Russia's Exclave in the Baltic Region: A Source of Stability or Tension?', pages 149-177 in Joenniemi, P. and Prawitz, J. (eds). *Kaliningrad: The European Amber Region.* Aldershot, Ashgate.

Haab, M. (1998). 'Estonia,' pages 109-29 in Mouritzen, H. (ed.). *Bordering Russia: Theory and Prospects for Europe's Baltic Rim.* Aldershot, Ashgate.

Heikka, H. (2000). *The Evolution of Russian Grand Strategy – Implications for Europe's North.* Helsinki, The Finnish Institute of International Affairs.

Herd, G.P. (1999). 'Russia's Baltic Policy After the Meltdown,' *Security Dialogue* 1999:2, pages 197-212.

Holst, J.J. (1990). 'Northern Europe and the High North. The Strategic Setting: Parameters for Confidence Building and Arms Restraint,' pages 42-56 in Lodgaard, S. (ed.). *Naval Arms Control.* London, Newbury Park, New Delhi, Sage Publications.

Johnson, S.C. (1999). 'NATO Bombs, Russian Rhetorics and the Baltics,' *The Baltic Times* 1999:155, 22-28 April, pages 1 and 10.

Jonson, L. (1997). 'Russian Policy in Northern Europe,' pages 305-324 in Baranovsky, V. (ed.). *Russia and Europe: The Emerging Security Agenda.* Oxford, Oxford University Press.

Krohn, A. (1996). 'Germany,' pages 96-115 in Krohn, A. (ed.). *The Baltic Sea Region: National and International Security Perspectives.* Baden-Baden, Nomos Verlagsgesellschaft.

Lachowski, Z. (1994). 'Conventional Arms Control and Security Co-operation in Europe,' pages 565-95 in Stockholm International Peace Research Institute. *SIPRI Yearbook 1994.* Oxford, Oxford University Press.

Lachowski, Z. (1999). 'Prospects for Regional Arms Control in the Baltic Sea Area,' pages 9-32 in Joenniemi, P. (ed.). *Confidence-Building and Arms Control: Challenges Around the Baltic Rim.* Mariehamn, The Åland Islands Peace Institute.

Lachowski, Z. (2000). 'Building Military Stability in the Baltic Sea Region,' pages 259-73 in Hedegaard, L. and Lindström, B. (eds). *The NEBI Yearbook 2000: North European and Baltic Sea Integration.* Berlin, Heidelberg, Springer.

Lieven, A. (1996). 'Baltic Iceberg Dead Ahead: NATO Beware,' *The World Today* 1996:7, pages 175-79.

Lithuanian Ministry of National Defence (1999). *White Paper '99.* Vilnius.

Lithuanian Ministry of National Defence (2000). 'International Cooperation,' at http://www.kam.lt, updated 15 June 2000.

Martelius, J. (1999). *Neuvostoliiton/Venäjän Sotilaspolitiikka – globaalista suurvallasta alueelliseksi hegemoniksi.* Helsinki, National Defence College.

Medvedev, S. (2000). *Russia's Futures: Implications for the EU, the North and the Baltic Region.* Helsinki and Bonn, The Finnish Institute of International Affairs and Institut für Europäische Politik.

Möller, F. and Wellmann, A. (forthcoming). 'Lithuania, Latvia, Estonia,' in Giessmann, H.-J. and Gustenau, G.E. *Handbook Security 2001.* Baden-Baden, Nomos Verlagsgesellschaft.

Moshes, A. (1999). 'Russia and Security- and Confidence-Building Around the Baltic Rim,' pages 57-76 in Joenniemi, P. (ed.). *Confidence-Building and Arms Control: Challenges Around the Baltic Rim.* Mariehamn, The Åland Islands Peace Institute.

Nordic Working Group (2000). *Closer Neighbours: Proposal for a New Nordic Strategy for the Co-operation with the Adjacent Areas,* at http://www.norden.org.

North Atlantic Treaty Organization (1995). *NATO Study on Enlargement.* Brussels.

Oldberg, I. (1998). 'Kaliningrad: Problems and Prospects,' pages 1-31 in Joenniemi, P. and Prawitz, J. (eds). *Kaliningrad: The European Amber Region.* Aldershot, Ashgate.

Puheloinen, A. (1999). *Russia's Geopolitical Interests in the Baltic Area.* Helsinki, National Defence College.

Radio Free Europe/Radio Liberty (2000a). 'Baltic States Report,' 20 September.

Radio Free Europe/Radio Liberty (2000b). 'Baltic States Report,' 16 October.

Radio Free Europe/Radio Liberty (2000c). 'Baltic States Report,' 31 October.

Raid, A. (1996). 'Security Policy of the Baltic States: The Case of Estonia,' pages 8-28 in Lejins, A. and Bleiere, D. (eds). *The Baltic States: Search for Security.* Riga, Latvijas Arpolitikas Instituts.

Ruhala, K. (1988). 'Finland's Security Policy,' pages 117-29 in Möttölä, K. (ed.). *The Arctic Challenge: Nordic and Canadian Approaches to Security and Cooperation in an Emerging International Region.* Boulder and London, Westview Press.

Schmidt, H.-J. (2000). *Die Anpassung des KSE-Vertrags und die Gefährdung der globalen Rüstungskontrolle.* Frankfurt, Hessische Stiftung Friedens- und Konfliktforschung.

Sharp, J.M.O. (1990). 'Conventional Arms Control in Europe,' pages 459-507 in Stockholm International Peace Research Institute. *SIPRI Yearbook 1990: World Armaments and Disarmament.* Oxford, Oxford University Press.

Sharp, J.M.O. (1991). 'Conventional Arms Control in Europe,' pages 407-60 in Stockholm International Peace Research Institute. *SIPRI Yearbook 1991: World Armaments and Disarmament.* Oxford, Oxford University Press.

Simon, J. (2000). 'Transforming the Armed Forces of Central and East Europe,' *Strategic Forum* 2000:172.

Sköns, E. et al. (1998). 'Military Expenditure and Arms Production,' pages 185-213 in Stockholm International Peace Research Institute. *SIPRI Yearbook 1998: Armaments, Disarmament and International Security.* Oxford, Oxford University Press.

Sköns, E. et al. (1999). 'Military Expenditure,' pages 269-99 in Stockholm International Peace Research Institute. *SIPRI Yearbook 1999: Armaments, Disarmament and International Security.* Oxford, Oxford University Press.

Sköns, E. et al. (2000). 'Military Expenditure,' pages 231-59 in Stockholm International Peace Research Institute. *SIPRI Yearbook 2000: Armaments, Disarmament and International Security.* Oxford, Oxford University Press.

Tiido, H. (2000). 'The Impossibility of a "Baltic Sea Region Security",' paper presented at 'The 5th Anniversary Stockholm Conference on Baltic Sea Region Security and Cooperation,' 19 October, at http://www.usis.usemb.se/bsconf/2000/program.html.

Trenin, D. (2000). 'Security Cooperation in North-Eastern Europe: A Russian Perspective,' pages 15-54 in Trenin, D. and van Ham, P. *Russia and the United States in Northern European Security.* Helsinki and Bonn, The Finnish Institute of International Affairs and Institut für Europäische Politik.

Tunander, O. (1989). *Cold Water Politics: The Maritime Strategy and Geopolitics of the Northern Front.* London, Newbury Park, New Delhi, Sage Publications.

Van Ham, P. (2000). 'Testing Cooperative Security in Europe's New North: American Perspectives and Policies,' pages 57-95 in Trenin, D. and van Ham, P. *Russia and the United States in Northern European Security*. Helsinki and Bonn, The Finnish Institute of International Affairs and Institut für Europäische Politik.

Vares, P. (ed.) (1999). *Estonia and the European Union: In Search of Security*. Tallinn, Institute of International and Social Studies/EuroUniversity.

Vike-Freiberga, V. (2000). 'Russland ist unberechenbar,' *Der Spiegel* 2000:22, pages 198-200.

Wæver, O. (1998). 'Insecurity, Security and Asecurity in the West European Non-War Community,' pages 69-118 in Adler, E. and Barnett, M. (eds). *Security Communities*. Cambridge, Cambridge University Press.

Wallander, C. (2000). 'Wary of the West: Russian Security Policy at the Millenium,' *Arms Control Today* 2000:2, pages 7-12.

Wallensteen, P. and Axell, K. (1994). 'Conflict Resolution and the End of the Cold War,' *Journal of Peace Research* 1994:3, pages 333-49.

Wallensteen, P. and Sollenberg, M. (2000). 'Armed Conflict 1989-99,' *Journal of Peace Research* 2000:5, pages 635-49.

Wellmann, C. (1999). 'Meer des Friedens oder mehr Frieden: Perspektiven der Ostseekooperation aus friedenswissenschaftlicher Sicht,' pages 71-86 in Wellmann, C. (ed.). *Kooperation und Konflikt in der Ostseeregion*. Kiel, Landeszentrale für politische Bildung Schleswig-Holstein.

Wendt, A. (1995). 'Constructing International Politics,' *International Security* 1995:1, pages 71-81.

Young, O. (1985-86). 'The Age of the Arctic,' *Foreign Policy* 1985-86:61, pages 160-179.

Zakheim, D. (1998). 'The United States and the Nordic Countries During the Cold War,' *Cooperation and Conflict* 1998:2, pages 115-29.

16 The Development of the Armed Forces in the Baltic States

Christopher Jones[1]

A rather basic and crude analysis of the development of the armed forces of the three Baltic States since independence in 1991 would point to three crucial factors: Russia, money and will. The legacy of Russian/Soviet occupation continues to weigh heavily on the minds of the Baltic States, and though not explicitly stated in their respective national security policy documents, Russia is still regarded as a source of potential danger. The question of money is a critical one, particularly in the coming five years. Economic resources are limited and all sectors of the developing market economies have demands. The avowed goal of a defence budget of 2 per cent of national GDP is crucial to the further development of the armed forces, and the linchpin of their preparations for membership in the North Atlantic Alliance. Given the limited economic resources and the 'Russian factor,' it is not surprising that political and national consensus on the issue of developing the national armed forces is not complete. Disagreement focuses on the question of money, which derives from the question of priorities. Should the priority be membership in NATO, or good neighbourly relations (read Russia)? Further strains are evident in the way in which armed forces should be developed – what kind of defence force should they have?

This chapter presents the armament trends of the Baltic States, i.e. defence budgets and expenditure, weapons procurement, manpower, etc., and argues that since 1991, the most critical years for the development of the armed forces of Estonia, Latvia and Lithuania are the years 2000-2003. As a string of NATO applicants in Eastern Europe look forward to the next summit meeting in 2002, where it is anticipated that a second list of post-Cold War new members will be presented, the three small Baltic States have set the goal of a defence budget at 2 per cent of GDP by 2003 if not before. Whether they can achieve this matters largely on economic policy and political will. This paper does not argue the case for or against Alliance membership, though the strong link between the proposed budgets and their respective applications should be noted.

The Russian factor has influenced the development of the armed forces in these three former Soviet republics in several ways. As shown in Figure 16. 1, the geostrategic position that Estonia, Latvia and Lithuania are in has led them to seek external security guarantees in order to bolster their own national defence efforts. This in turn has meant that the development of the armed forces is done with NATO interoperability paramount in the planning, organisation, training and equipping of the Baltic armies. In the early years of re-independence the feeling of futility was evident. Why should we bother with the expense of building national defence forces, when they have served little use in our past history with Russia? To a small degree this sentiment continues, but is only a small and waning sentiment. Conditions of service in the Red Army for Baltic nationals served to argue against service in the fledgling national forces, as young men were reluctant to volunteer for duty, and less than happy to serve as conscripts. Joining the armed forces was seen as a 'waste of time' by conscription-age young men who want to get ahead in the developing economies, or dangerous due to harassment and violence within the armed forces.[2] Recent years have seen an improvement in conditions and attitudes, and the planned budget allocations for the next three to five years seek to develop this further. The image of a 'hero war' with Russia has

Figure 16.1: Approximate disposition of forces in the Baltic Sea littoral region

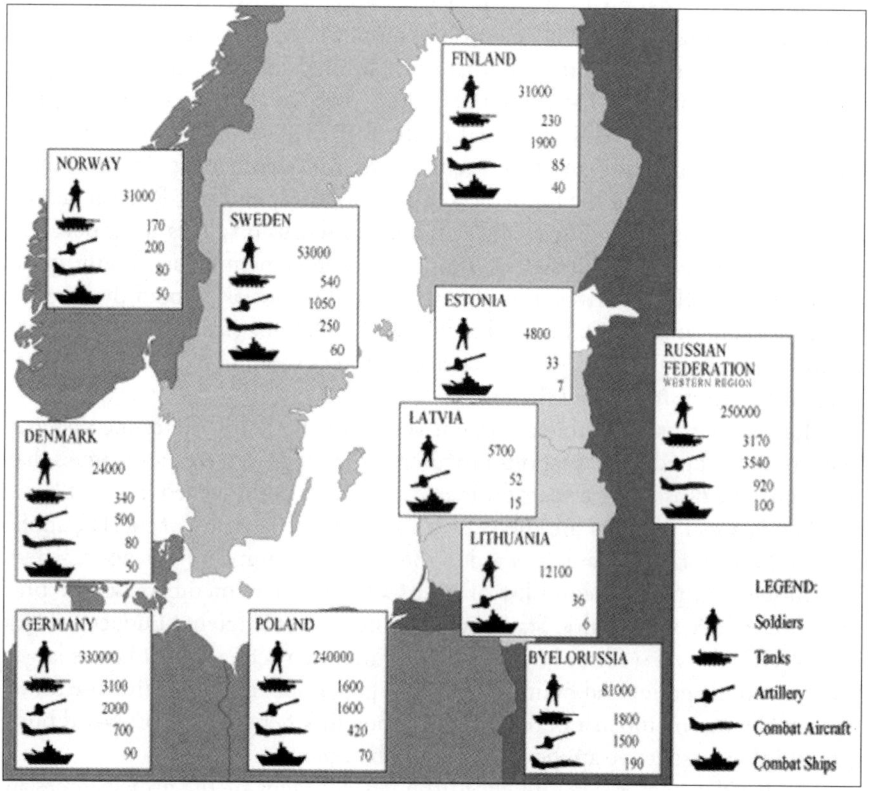

Source: Ministry of Defence 2000a

had an effect on how the armed forces are shaped. The unconscious assumption of a traditional invasion has impacted upon both the tasks that the armed forces are trained for, and the weapons that they employ to achieve them. This has led to tension between the military and political leaders in the Baltic States, as the primary political goal is membership in NATO, where peace-support and peace-keeping missions are more the norm.[3] This involves a special set of skills, force structure and weaponry, distinct from traditional counter-force warfare, as preferred by the military. This tension between the imperative of building a national defence force, and the political desire to wave the Baltic flags in Bosnia and Kosovo has been recognised by the Baltic States themselves, and by a number of their partner countries, notably Finland and Sweden who have a traditional preference for a strong national defence force.[4]

Despite the apparent strength of the Russian factor, it is not relevant for the further development of the Baltic armed forces over the next five years. The critical issues are the matter of the defence budget, and the political will necessary to ensure an increase of the defence budgets to at least 2 per cent of national GDP by 2003, as projected in Figure 16.2. Currently the GDPs of the Baltic States range from US $5bn-$10bn, and the defence budgets from US $60m-$180m. Having suffered to various degrees the effects of the Russian economic crisis of 1998, the three Baltic States are on the road to recovery. Their economic development must be seen in the context of their applications for membership in the European Union (EU), from whom they have recently received favourable economic reports, though naturally with room for improvement.[5] The key to the issue of the increase in the defence budgets is that it is linked to the growth of the economy. There is no extra money available in State funds to divert to the Defence Forces without getting further into debt, or by diverting from other sectors of the economy. The additional finances must come from economic growth. Not only that, but the allocation of budgets within the State expenditures must be made in competition with other departments, equally deserving of finance.

The goal of 2 per cent of GDP is merely that – a goal – and not written in legislature.[6] It is therefore the task of the respective governments to push the defence budget through Parliaments who may not necessarily agree with the government's priorities. This must also be done under the watchful eyes of international financial and security organisations. The International Monetary Fund recently advised the Lithuanian government to stay within its promised 1.4 per cent fiscal deficit for 2001 and to consider cutting expenditure in several sectors. However, the current coalition government of Prime Minster Paksas has proposed a budget programme that will raise the budget deficit to 3 per cent in 2001, despite an IMF agreement with the former administration to keep it to 1.7 per cent (RFE/RL 2000b; 2000c). NATO will also be paying attention to the defence budgets and spending in the Baltic States as the Alliance assesses the readiness of applicant countries prior to drawing up a list of the next round of new members.[7]

Whilst economic growth in the Baltic States should continue to increase at a sufficient rate over the next five years, barring another calamitous Russian

Figure 16.2: Projected defence budgets of the Baltic States in percentage of GDP

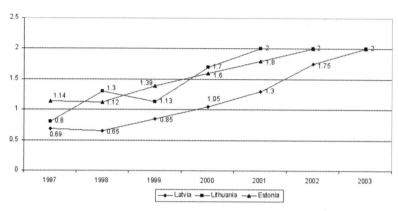

financial collapse, the more sensitive issue of the allocation of funds with State budgets is less clear. All three national administrations have faced criticism over planned budgets, with calls for cuts in the defence budget, diverting funds to the agricultural sector, local municipalities, education, etc. There is a distinct lack of broad political support for the proposed budgets, and a questioning of foreign policy priorities.[8] In his introduction to the Latvian Ministry of Defence's *White Paper 2000*, Defence Minister, Girts Valdis Kristovskis commented on the need for such support:

> 'Defence initiatives are effective only if they gain broad political and public support. That support can be generated by informing and convincing the public that the efforts of the Ministry of Defence and of the Armed Forces are effective and will guarantee the country's peace and security. Erroneous and sometimes misleading information regarding the aims and accomplishments of the defence establishment illustrates prejudices established during the past 50 years of occupation... Unfortunately, sometimes elected public officials and even the press fail to fully understand the complexity of defence issues and their effect on the entire population. As a result, analyses tend to be sceptical even to the point of questioning the need for defence of any kind' (Ministry of Defence 2000).

It is worth noting that according to the *Security Concept of the Republic of Latvia*, approved in 1997, 'delaying the improvement of its defence capabilities' is considered a real threat (Ministry of Defence 1997). Addressing the need to improve the political will behind the development of the armed forces, Estonian President Lennart Meri, speaking in October 2000, encouraged Parliamentary politicians to focus more on the development of Estonia's national defence, in order to ensure accession to NATO in 2002 or 2003 (RFE/RL 2000a).

The Defence Forces of the Baltic States [9]

No assessment of the development of the national defence forces of the three Baltic States can fail to recognise that they have made tremendous advances since regaining their independence in 1991. The fact that all three began the process of building their defence forces and the correlating bureaucratic and political structures from a very weak position speaks to the work that has been done in the intervening years. It has often been stated that they began this endeavour 'from scratch' – very little command and organisational experience, particularly at the senior and officer level; a legacy of little or no individual initiative, and poor personnel management coupled with low levels of morale; the absence of the necessary logistical and physical infrastructure, that which was not destroyed by the outgoing Russian troops or already in a severe state of disrepair or polluted by years of misuse, and a lack of even the most basic equipment. By way of example, the state of the Estonian defence forces when independence from the Soviet Union was declared was negligible. Mare Haab cites Foreign Ministry figures that report only 85 people in the defence forces in January 1992, rising to 1,100 by the end of the year (Haab 1995: 22).

Within the Soviet Red Army there was no Estonian army as such, the Estonian National Corps having been disbanded in the late 1950s. Much of the present Estonian military leadership at the colonel level dates back to this period, and these mostly from the air force, navy and signals, with few if any in the infantry or artillery, the most needed arms in the current forces. Clemmesen states that 'most Baltic former Soviet officers were trained for the technical branches, e.g. as engineers for the air surveillance, air defence or rocket forces. Relatively few were trained as infantry, field engineer or artillery officers' (1998: 239). When the task of recreating the Defence Forces began in earnest in 1992, of some 200 Estonian ex-Soviet Army officers, one-half were too old. Half of the rest were not considered to be Estonian (or 'too far gone' in terms of Soviet indoctrination to be of use in a democratically controlled and open military force), and the remainder, some 40 to 50 officers, were left to serve in the Border Guard and Land Forces. This lack of talent was largely a factor of the Soviet Army restrictions on who could become an officer. Furthermore, those with staff and leadership responsibilities were used to a small area of responsibility in an initiative-free environment. Adaptation to the defence of a small state, with wide areas of responsibility and a high degree of personal initiative, as in a Western-style army, has been slow (Clemmesen 1998: 239). Non-commissioned Estonian soldiers serving in the Red Army were often subjected to harsh treatment, particularly as conscripts, amounting to little more than 'slave labour' (Clemmesen 1998: 235). As mentioned, this has done much to damage the 'appeal' of service in the new Baltic defence forces.

Most critical in this list of deficiencies has been the personal aspect of the defence forces. It is far easier to purchase a weapon system or rebuild a military facility than it is to reorient personnel. The necessary changes are thus not only

Table 16.1: Numerical strength of the Baltic States' armed forces, 1992-99

	1993	1994	1995	1996	1997	1998	1999
Estonia							
Total Armed Forces	2,500	2,500	3,500	3,450	3,510	4,340	c. 4,800
Conscripts	-	-	-	-	-	2,490	2,870
Reserve	c. 6000 militia	c. 6,000	c. 6,000	c. 6,000	c. 14,000 [a]	c. 14,000	c. 14,000
Army	2,500	2,500	3,300	3,300	3,500	3,980	4,320
Navy	2 [b]	-	150	150	160	320	340
Air Force	-	-	-	-	-	36	140
Paramilitary [c]	2,000	2,000	2,000	2,000	2,800	2,800	2,800
Latvia							
Total Armed Forces	5,000 [d]	2,280	2,650	3,000	4,500	4,960	5,730
Conscripts	-	-	-	-	-	2,150	2,120
Reserve	16,000 Home Guard	18,000	18,000	16,500	16,600	14,600 [e]	14,500
Army	1 infantry battalion,						
1 recce. battalion	1,500	1,500	1,750	3,400	2,350	2,550	
Navy	300	900	1,000	1,000	980	880	840
Air Force	-	150	150	250	120	130	210
Paramilitary	Border Guard [f]	4,300	4,300	3,500	3,600	3,720 [g]	3,720
Lithuania							
Total Armed Forces	4,800	c. 4,900	c. 4,900	5,100	5,250	11,130 [h]	12,130
Conscripts	-	-	-	-	-	3,548	3,560
Reserve	11,000	12,000	12,000	11,000	11,000	355,650 [j]	355,650
Army	4,300	4,300	4,300	4,200	4,200	6,750	7,840
Navy	c. 250	c. 350	c. 350	350	c. 500	1,320	1, 320
Air Force	250	250	250	550	550	970	970
Paramilitary [k]	5,000	4,000	4,000	4,800	4,800	3,900	3,900

[a]   Actual size of the Defence League is some 7,500. The additional personnel are found in several auxiliary organisations, for women and children.

[b]   Formed 1 July 1993.

[c]   Border Guard, Ministry of Internal Affairs. Includes a maritime element that fulfils the task of Coast Guard.

[d]   Includes Border Guard.

[e]   National Guard.

[f]   Ministry of Internal Affairs.

[g]   Includes 220 Coast Guard.

[h]   Includes conscripts and some 2,100 Voluntary National Defence Force.

[j]   Includes 27,700 first line (including 11,100 National Defence Service); 327,950 second line (age up to 59).

[k]   Includes 400 Coast Guard.

Source: Data collated from *Military Balance* (1992-2000)

external, in the way the armed forces exercise, manoeuvre and operate, but also internal, in the way that they must now think – as Western-style, democratically controlled armed forces. Given their stated desire of membership in the Atlantic Alliance, how they speak is also a matter of concern, and their English language skills are a key test of the interoperability of the Baltic armed forces. This is not a critical factor at home, when one considers the working languages of NATO member armed forces, but it is important that the officers, unit commanders and non-commissioned officers (NCOs) can communicate with NATO partners. It is these aspects of the development of the armed forces of the Baltic States that have been the most critical, and most affected via intense co-operative pro-grammes with regional neighbours such as the Nordic states, and with NATO member armed forces, and service on international duty or in a co-operative field exercise develops these aspects further.

Given the small size of the populations in the Baltic States, between 1.5 and 3.8 million, the size of the active armed forces will always be small. The key to building a sizeable defence force with such a limitation is to develop a 'total defence' concept, with the mobilisation of age-cohorts that have received military training, and been rotated through refresher training over successive years. The total armed force available during wartime would then see the addition of the Reserve forces and the Border Guard.[10]

The National/Home Guard elements thus represent a sizeable force for these three states. One needs only to look at Table 16.1 to see how Lithuania has recent-ly formulated its Reserve force plans to include 27,700 first line troops (includ-ing 11,100 Voluntary National Defence Service), and 327,950 second line troops (age up to 59). According to Nordberg's analysis of the state of the defence forces in the Baltic States in the early 1990s, Estonia's population produces some 6,000-7,000 young men in an age cohort:

> 'If some 80-90 per cent of these were to be trained in military service the num-ber of reserves would increase by at least 5,000 men annually. The size of the Finnish Field Army is some 530,000, ten per cent of the population. With cal-culations based on the Finnish example, and training over a period of 20 years, Estonia could establish a wartime defence force of 100,000 men. A field army of that size could easily establish an efficient territorial defence covering the whole country' (Nordberg 1994: 42)

Nordberg also cites figures for Latvia and Lithuania. Latvia produces some 7,000-8,000 young men in each age cohort, which could yield an annual increase to the Reserve Forces of some 6,000-7,000. After 20 years, the wartime field army should total some 140,000 (1994: 60). The sizeably larger Lithuanian population allows an age cohort of 10,000-12,000 young men, giving a 8,000-11,000 increase in the Reserve should 80-90 per cent of these receive military training. A Lithuan-ian wartime force could thus equal 220,000 men, and allow the establishment of a comprehensive territorial defence (1994: 74, 78).

This crucial element of the defence structure is currently under review and development in all three states, as they prepare and improve their mobilisation plans. For example, Latvia is planning to expand the total number of military units according to the demands of their total defence strategy. In their long-term 12-year plan it is anticipated that the number of trained military personnel available will be approximately 50,000 troops as follows:

- Active duty forces – 6,000 soldiers
- Mobile reserve battalions (MRBs) – 27,000 soldiers
- Territorial reserve force battalions (TRFBs) – 17,000 soldiers

To achieve this level of manpower in the Latvian armed forces, together with the necessary standard of readiness and training demands, comprehensive training planning is required over the next 12-15 years to include the systematic induction of conscripts, personal training, and unit training up to the battalion level. The establishment of a Mobilisation Training Centre is scheduled for 2003, and participation is mandatory for men between 30 and 45. This is all in addition to the regular activities of the Latvian National Guard. It is anticipated that under such a mobilisation plan, Latvia will reach a ready reserve military strength of approximately 50,000 by the year 2012. Implementation of this plan has begun and is expected to accelerate as the defence budget increases, making more resources available to this effort.

Estonia

The Estonian Defence Forces consist of the regular armed forces, the Defence League (*Kaiteseliit*), the Border Guard (Piirivalve), and other units with military organisation under the Ministry of Internal Affairs, which, in time of war, will come under the command of the Commander-in-Chief of the Defence Forces (*Estonia Today* 1998: 2). The regular forces have some 4,800 personnel, in the Army, Navy and Air Force. Conscription lasts 12 months, for males aged 18-27. The Defence League is a voluntary defence force, and is modelled along similar lines to the Nordic model of 'total defence' and territorial defence strategy, although it could be argued that as this force structure was established during 1922-40, it is now a reapplication rather than adoption of this mode of national defence. Elements of this force were in existence prior to independence, and served as the main defence until the development of the regular forces was undertaken in earnest. Some 14,000 volunteers currently serve in these forces, and they have engaged in bilateral co-operation with other 'home guard' units from Sweden, Norway, Denmark, and Finland. The Border Guard was also re-established prior to independence, in September 1990, and currently has some 2,800 personnel.

The further development of the Estonian Defence Forces (EDF) is based on

Table 16.2: Current forces and equipment

Army 4,320	Navy 340
Equipment:	Equipment:[a]
RECCE 7 BRDM-2	PATROL CRAFT 3
APC 32 BTR-60/ -70/ -80 (Ex-Soviet)	2 *Grif* (RF *Zhuk*) PCI, 1 *Ahti* (Da *Maagen*) PCI
TOWED ARTY 105mm: 19 M 61-37	MINE WARFARE 4
MOR 81mm: 44; 120mm: 14	MINELAYERS 2
ATGW 10 *Mapats,* 3 RB-56 *Bill*	2 *Rymaettylae*
RL 82mm: 200 B-300	MINE COUNTERMEASURES 2
RCL 84mm: 109 *Carl Gustav*; 90mm:	2 *Kalev* (Ge *Frauenlob*) MCI
100 PV-1110;	SUPPORT AND OTHER 2
106mm: 30 M-40A1	1 *Mardus* AK, 1 *Laine* (RF *Mayak*) AK
AD GUNS 23mm: 100 ZU-23-2	
Air Force 140	Paramilitary 2,800
Equipment:	Equipment:
AC 2 AN-2, 1 PZL-140 *Wilga*	PATROL CRAFT 20
HEL 3 Mi-2	PATROL, OFFSHORE 3
	1 *Kou* (SF *Silmä*), 1 Linda (SF *Keimo*), 1 *Valvas*
	(US *Bittersweet*)
	PATROL, COASTAL 6
	3 PVL-100 (SF *Koskelo*), 1 *Pikker*,
	1 *Torm* (*Arg*), 1 *Maru* (SF *Viima*)
	PATROL, INSHORE 11
	3 PVK-001 (Type 257 KBV), 1 PVK-025
	(Type 275 KBV), 5 PVK-006 (RV)
	1 PVK-010 (RV 90), 1 PVK 017, plus 2 LCU
	SPT AND OTHER 1 *Linda* (SF *Keimo*)
	PCI (trg)
	AVN 2 L-410 UVP-1 *Turbolet*, 5 Mi-8

[a]   The Navy in November 2000 received the 74m long frigate *Beskytteren* from the Royal Danish Navy, to be renamed *Admiral Pitka*. The ship will serve as the flagship of the Estonian Navy (RFE/RL 2000b). The *Admiral Pitka* is the largest ship in any of the Baltic navies, and the transfer involved a considerable amount of final-user training.

Source: *Military Balance* 1999-2000: 87

the draft five-year plan 2000-2005, that sets out to establish a more developed and capable peacetime force structure that will provide the foundation of a planned wartime force. In addition, defence readiness is to be improved by developing rapid reaction capabilities and combat readiness. Specifically the 2000-2005 plan for the EDF includes:

–   An increase in the EDF wartime size to 25-30,000;
–   The formation of 3 light infantry reserve brigades;
–   The development of airspace surveillance capabilities;
–   The further development of mine warfare capabilities;

- The development of rapid reaction capabilities;
- The standardisation of education;
- The concentration of officer and NCO basic training in Estonia;
- The improvement of working conditions and social guarantees of military personnel;
- The development and reorganisation of the current mobilisation and readiness system;
- The development of the Logistic Concept of the EDF;
- The modernisation of the existing warehouse system, including a system for storing mobilisation supplies.

To this end, the procurement of major equipment in the period 2000-2005 will concentrate on the acquisition of communication and air surveillance, air defence, anti-tank defence and naval mine warfare (*Estonia Today* 2000). More important than the material improvements is the focus of increased spending upon the conditions of service in the EDF by improving the quality of life for personnel.

Latvia

The Latvian National Armed Forces (NAF) consists of the Territorial Defence Forces – the regular armed forces and the National Guard (*Zemessardze*), the Air Force, Navy, Military Police, Security Service and Special Tasks Unit. In addition there is the 3,500 strong Frontier Guard. The regular forces are made up of conscripts serving for 12 months, from 19-27 years old, with a current strength of some 5,500 personnel, in the Army, Navy and Air Force. The *Zemessardze* is a voluntary territorially based defence force, and is also modelled along the lines of the 'total defence' – territorial defence structure. Elements of this force were in existence prior to independence, and together with the Frontier Guard, served as the main defence until the development of the regular forces was undertaken in earnest in 1993. Some 14,500 volunteers and mandatory service soldiers currently serve in these forces, and they too have engaged in bilateral co-operation with other 'home guard' units from Sweden, Denmark, Norway and Finland.

Latvia's defence priorities explicitly state that the development of the national self-defence capabilities is paramount. NATO interoperability comes second, and will be addressed in conjunction with the primary effort where applicable (Ministry of Defence 1997). In addition to the aforementioned plans to develop the mobilisation structure and affect an increase in manpower, short- and long-term planning includes:[11]

- Consolidation of the training centres and training facilities, including the establishment of a Land Forces Training Centre to improve the professional quality of the land forces;

- Improvement of military readiness, through enhancements in the military infrastructure and training;
- The improvement to the quality of life for all service personnel, career planning, and the creation of an improved image for the Armed Forces;
- Development and acquisition of the necessary infrastructure for command, control and communications, including equipment and software to meet NATO interoperability requirements;
- Finalising the BALTPERS project, which, together with Sweden provides a unified military personnel management and information data system.

Table 16.3: Current forces and equipment

Army 2,250	Navy 840
Equipment:	Equipment:
RECCE 2 BRDM-2 APC 13 *Pskbil* m/42 TOWED ARTY 100mm: 26 K-53 MOR 82mm: 5; 120mm: 26 AD GUNS 14.5mm: 12 ZPU-4	PATROL CRAFT 12 1 *Osa* PFM (unarmed), 1 *Storm* PCC (unarmed), 2 *Ribnadzor* PC, 5 KBV 236 PC, 3 PCH MINE COUNTERMEASURES 3 2 *Kondor* II MCO, 1 *Lindou* SUPPORT AND OTHER 3 1 *Nyrat* AT, 1 *Goliat* AT, 1 diving vessel COASTAL DEFENCE 10 patrol craft: 2 *Ribnadzor* PCC, 5 KBV 236 PC, 3 PCH
Air Force 210	Paramilitary 3,720
Equipment:	Equipment:
AC 2 AN-2, 1 L-410 HEL 3 Mi-2	n/a

Source: *Military Balance* 1999-2000: 91

Figure 16.3: Number of personnel and increase in salaries, 1997-2003

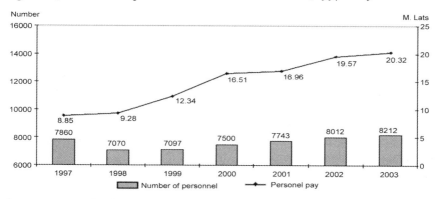

Source: Ministry of Defence 2000b

Figure 16.3 shows one of the most critical aspects of the defence budget increases
– the improvement in the quality in life for service personnel through an increase
in pay. This is a most substantial allocation, with an approximate 130 per cent
increase in salaries compared to a 4.5 per cent rise in personnel. Implemented in
July 1999, the increased salaries amounted to an average increase of over 80 per
cent across the board, enabling the Latvian NDF to keep quality personnel, and
provide them with a more amenable financial environment. It also serves to
improve the appeal of a career in the armed forces.

Specific plans for the separate arms of the NAF include the following two-
phase development goals:

1st phase	Air Force	– development of the airspace surveillance system;
		– further enhancement of transport capabilities;
		– development of search and rescue capabilities;
	Naval Forces	– completion of the maritime surveillance system;
		– development of coastal defence capabilities;
	Land Forces	– brigade and battalion structural development;
		– development of armament (anti-tank, air defence);
		– enhancement of peace support functions.
2nd phase	Air Force	– formation/deployment of air defence system;
	Naval Forces	– creation of anti submarine surveillance system;
		– improvement of coastline/anti-offshore
		operations defence system;
	Land Forces	– formation of rapid reaction forces.

Lithuania

Nordberg writes that Lithuania began the establishment of its national defence
forces a year before Latvia and Estonia, with the benefit of 1,200 ex-Soviet Army
Lithuanian officers (1994: 78). In late 1993 the Lithuanian Army was composed of
a 2,000 strong Field Brigade of eight lightly armed battalions, and a Training
Brigade, serving the basic military education of conscripts. At the same time,
some 3,000 formed the Frontier Guard. The Navy, performing the function of a
Coast guard in peacetime, was 600 strong, with 800 serving in the Air Force. The
National Defence Volunteer Force (NDVF) was created in 1991, and defended
strategic locations such as civic buildings whilst still under Soviet occupation. It
currently consists of some 12,000 men and forms a major part of the Lithuanian
National Defence and Reserve force, training several times a month in line with
their training programmes. The composition of the Reserve force has recently
undergone dramatic changes, with the addition of over 300,000 adult males up
to the age of 59. Compulsory military service is for 12 months primary service in
the regular forces, followed by subsequent service in the active reserve. Units of
the Territorial Defence and the National Guard are voluntary units.

Table 16.4: Current forces and equipment

Army 7,840	Navy 1,320
Equipment:	Equipment: [a]
RECCE 11 BRDM-2	FRIGATES 2
APC 14 BTR-60, 13 *Pskbil* m/42	2 Sov *Grisha III*, with 2 x 12 ASW RL,
MOR 120mm: 36 M-43	4 533mm TT
RL 82mm: 170 RPG-2	PATROL AND COASTAL
RCL 84mm: 119 *Carl Gustav*	COMBATANTS 4
	1 *Storm* PCI, 1 SK-21 PCI, 1 SK-23 PCI,
	1 SK-24 PCI
	SUPPORT AND OTHER 3
	1 *Valerian Uryvayev* AGOR
Air Force 970	Paramilitary 3720
Equipment:	Equipment:
AC 6 L-39, 22 AN-2, 3 AN-26, 1 AN-24, 2 L-410	n/a
HEL 3 Mi-8, 5 Mi-2	

[a]   The Navy will receive the German minesweeper *Marburg* in March 2001, after an overhaul of $800,000 of which Germany will pay the major portion (RFE/RL 2000c).

Source: *Military Balance* 1999-2000: 92

In 1998 the Ministry of Defence adopted seven long-term Security Development Programmes:

– development of the Armed Forces;
– defence infrastructure development;
– mobilisation programme;
– airspace surveillance and control programme;
– defence research and development programme;
– integral civil defence and rescue system development programme;
– interoperability and reciprocity of defence structure with NATO.

These Programmes set out to develop the current system of the control of units; improve combat readiness; prepare other structures designed to enhance the defence capability of the armed forces; the modernisation and procurement of weaponry; a review of training and education programmes; and the standardisation of the Armed Forces' command, control and communication systems (Ministry of Defence 1999). In addition, the construction of military facilities – housing and military camps – are planned, to further improve the Quality of Life issues. New training centres and facilities are planned, particularly the Conscripts Training Centre, the Peacekeeping Training Centre, the NVDF Training Centres and Battalion Training Facilities, in order to develop the combat readiness of both conscripts and the Reserve Forces.

Procurement

Procurement has naturally been a critical issue for the Baltic armed forces. The Russians left little or no equipment when they withdrew in 1994, and what infrastructure that was still intact was in very poor condition, and plagued by the overwhelming problem of pollution (Jauhiainen 1999). The initial task of equipping the armed forces was incredible, and at the very basic level – uniforms (combat and dress); personal equipment (tools, webbing, belts, packs, boots); communications (radios, computers, networks); small arms and ammunition (pistols, rifles, machine guns); unit equipment (tents, desks, canteens, medical supplies); transport (jeeps, trucks), etc. Much of this has been provided for the Baltic States, mostly in the form of donations from neighbour and partner countries, notably the four Nordic countries, Germany, the UK and the US among others. Denmark, for example, has not made any sales of military equipment to the Baltic States. When prices are listed on documents it is purely for budgetary and customs reasons. However, one should not wholly discount the ability of the Baltic States to acquire weaponry. An example is the purchase by Estonia of weaponry from Israel in 1993, concluded in January 2000, totalling $110m including interest, which enabled the equipping of the Estonian Defence Forces in the initial stages of their development.

If one were to ask whether defence equipment procurement has been a reflection of policy or the other way around, the answer would likely be that procurement policy has to operate under the severe limitation of limited funds, and the continued development of defence plans and organisation. Procurement has thus been limited to what little they can afford, and the immediate needs of the armed forces. Certainly in the last five years, procurement has been sufficient for the Baltic States to equip and deploy several national rifle platoons and companies to the SFOR, IFOR and KFOR forces in the Balkans, albeit with substantial help from partner countries. Denmark has been foremost in this respect, as it has trained and deployed rotating national companies and platoons from BALTBAT, the joint Baltic peacekeeping force, within its own deployment.

The donation of equipment has been a two-way process, as the Baltic States have made requests for equipment, or a partner country has seen a need and offered to address it. Such was the case with the significant Finnish donation of the equipment, including ammunition, for a complete field artillery battalion, consisting of 19 H105 37-61 howitzers. To a large degree this represented Finland's own priorities for defence, as such heavy equipment is not appropriate for the BALTBAT-style deployments, but clearly meant for *national* defence. Likewise, reflecting its own defence priorities, Latvia has placed a higher priority on its naval acquisitions that Lithuania, which is more land-force oriented. It should be noted that the donations are not made at random, nor are just a means of getting rid of old equipment, pawning it off on the Baltic States who will take just about anything. Certainly much of the equipment is second-hand, but has either undergone renovation or is still worthy of use, such as the German donated patrol craft.

Material donations do operate under some restrictions: obviously there are the regulations on arms transfers as stipulated in international law. Thereafter, it depends upon the availability of surplus equipment in the donor country. Finland, for example, is not cutting down its military defence as Sweden and Norway have done, so surplus material is negligible. In conjunction, it depends upon the ability to receive. The donation of the Finnish howitzers would have been of little use were the Estonians not first trained – in Finland – in how to use the equipment. Danish material support is also given in a package deal, as spare parts as well as final-user training are involved, ensuring that the recipient Baltic armed force actually benefits from the donation. Sweden too has made its donations in the context of bilateral training programmes, conducting a policy that support is dependent upon the transfer of knowledge in order to provide for long-term sustainable support. Sweden has planned to donate now-surplus equipment for an entire infantry battalion to Latvia, over the next five years, again based upon the ability to receive – that such units are in place.

Table 16.5 shows material transfer, either by purchase or by donation, to the Baltic States, from 1992 to late 2000. It refers only to major transactions of military hardware, and thus does not include details of the smaller items mentioned above.

Table 16.5: Procurement of major conventional weaponry by the Baltic States 1992-99

Year	Baltic State	Supplier	Number	Weapon designation & description	Year of order	Year of delivery	Number delivered	Comment
1993[a]	Lithuania	Russia	2	Grisha-3 Class Frigate	1992	1992	2	Lithuania will build houses in Russia in exchange [b]
			2	Stenka Class Fast Patrol Craft	1992	1992	2	Lithuania will build houses in Russia in exchange
			2	Turya Class Fast Patrol Craft	1992	1992	2	Lithuania will build houses in Russia in exchange
1994	Estonia	Germany	2	L-410UVP Turbolet Transport Aircraft	(1992)	1993	2	Former GDR equipment; gift
		..	(40)	Armoured Personnel Carrier (BTR series)	(1992)	(1993)	(40)	
	Latvia	Germany	2	L-410UVP Turbolet Transport Aircraft	(1992)	1993	2	Former GDR equipment; gift
			2	Kondor-I Class Minesweeper	1992			Former GDR equipment
			2	Osa II Class Fast Patrol Craft	1992			Former GDR equipment
	Lithuania	Germany	2	L-410UVP Turbolet Transport Aircraft	1992	1993	2	Former GDR equipment; gift
		Russia	8	L-39C Albatros Jet Trainer Aircraft	1993	1993	4	Ex-Russian Air Force; deal worth $0.08m
			2	Stenka Class Fast Patrol Craft	1992			Ex-Russian Navy
			2	Turya Class Fast Patrol Craft	1992	1993	2	Ex-Russian Navy
1995	Estonia	Denmark	1	Maagen Class Patrol Craft	(1994)	1994	1	Ex-Danish Navy
		Russia	2	Zhuk Class Patrol Craft	(1993)	(1994)		

(Table continued next page)

Table 16.5: Continued

Year	Baltic State	Supplier	Number	Weapon designation & description	Year of order	Year of delivery	Number delivered	Comment
1995 cont.		Germany	2	Kondor-I Class Minesweeper	(1993)			Former GDR equipment; armament and minesweeping gear removed before delivery
	Latvia	Germany	2	Kondor-I Class Minesweeper	(1993)	(1994)	2	
		Russia	3	Osa I Class Fast Patrol Craft	(1993)	(1994)	3	
		..	(13)	M-42 Armoured Personnel Carrier	(1993)	(1993)		
	Lithuania	Germany	3	Osa I Class Fast Patrol Craft	1993			Former GDR equipment; armament removed before delivery
		..	(4)	Antonov 2 Transport aircraft				
		..	3	Mi-8T Hip C Helicopter				
1996	Estonia	Finland	1	Silmä Class Off-shore Patrol Vessel	1994	1995	1	Ex-Finnish Frontier Guard; aid
		Germany	4	Mi-8T Hip C Helicopter	(1995)	1995	4	Former GDR equipment; for SAR; aid
			6	Osa I Class Fast Patrol Craft	(1993)	1995	6	Former GDR equipment; armament removed before delivery; aid
		Norway	1	Storm Class Fast Patrol Craft	1994	1995	1	Ex-Norwegian Navy; armament removed before delivery; gift
	Latvia	Czech Republic	20	D-30 120mm Towed Gun	(1994)	1995	20	Ex-Czech Army; aid
			25	M-53 100mm Towed Gun	1994	1995	25	Ex-Czech Army; aid
		Norway	1	Storm Class Fast Patrol Craft	1994	1995	1	Ex-Norwegian Navy; armament removed before delivery; gift
		Germany	1	Osa I Class Fast Patrol Craft	1993	1995		Ex-GDR equipment; armament removed before delivery; aid
	Lithuania	Germany	3	Osa I Class Fast Patrol Craft	1993	1995	3	Ex-GDR equipment; armament removed before delivery; aid
		Norway	1	Storm Class Fast Patrol Craft	1994	1995	1	Ex-Norwegian Navy; armament removed before delivery; gift
		Sweden	1	Victoria Class Fast Patrol Craft		1995	1	
			1	SK-21 Patrol Craft		1995	1	
		Czech Republic	18	120mm Towed Gun		1995		Ex-Czech Army; aid
1997	Estonia	France	1	Rasit-E Battlefield Radar	1995			
		Israel	(13)	Mapats Anti-tank missile	(1993)	1994-96	(13)	
		Denmark	1	Radar		1996		Aid
	Lithuania	Poland	5	Mi-2 Hoplite Helicopter	1996	1996	5	Ex-Polish Air Force; gift

Year	Baltic State	Supplier	Number	Weapon designation & description	Year of order	Year of delivery	Number delivered	Comment
			3	P-37 Barlock-A Surveillance Radar	1996	1996	3	Designation uncertain; ex-Polish Air Force
			2	P-40 Knife Rest Surveillance Radar	1996	1996	2	Ex-Polish Air Force
			2	PRV-11 Side Net Surveillance Radar	1996	1996	2	Designation uncertain; ex-Polish Air Force
1998	Estonia	Finland	19	M-61/37 105mm Towed Gun	1997		..	Ex-Finnish Army; gift
		France	..	Rasit-E Battlefield Radar	1996		..	
		Germany	2	Type 394 Frauenlob Class Minesweeper	1996	1997	2	Ex-FRG Navy; aid worth $26m; Estonian designation Kalev Class
		Sweden	8	RBS-56 Bill Anti-tank missile	1997		..	Ex-Swedish Army; loan; deal also includes 2 launchers
		USA	1	Balsam Class Depot Ship	1997	1997	1	Ex-US Coast Guard; Estonian designation Valvas Class
	Latvia	Poland	5	Mi-2 Hoplite Helicopter	(1994)	1995-97	5	Second hand
		Sweden	8	RBS-56 Bill Anti-tank missile	1997		..	Ex-Swedish Army; loan; deal also includes 2 launchers
		Finland	1	Silmä Class Off-shore Patrol Vessel	1996	1997	1	Ex-Finnish Frontier Guard; donated to Border Guard
	Lithuania	Sweden	8	RBS-56 Bill Anti-tank missile	1997		..	Ex-Swedish Army; loan; deal also includes 2 launchers
1999	Estonia	Finland	19	M-61/37 105mm Towed Gun	1997	1997-98	(19)	Ex-Finnish Army; gift
			2	Minelayer	1998	1999	2	Free transfer
		France	(1)	Rasit-E Battlefield Radar	1996	1998	(1)	
		Sweden	8	RBS-56 Bill Anti-tank missile	1997	1998	(2)	Ex-Swedish Army; loan; deal also includes 2 launchers; for use with BaltBat joint peacekeeping unit.
	Latvia	Sweden	8	RBS-56 Bill Anti-tank missile	1997	1998	(8)	Ex-Swedish Army; loan; deal also includes 2 launchers; for use with BaltBat joint peacekeeping unit.
	Lithuania	Czech Republic	2	L-39ZO Albatros Jet trainer aircraft	1998	1998	2	Deal worth $2m; to join the 4 L39C purchased in 1993
		Germany	3	Mi-8TV Hip-F Helicopter	1998	1998	3	Ex-FRG Air Force; originally former GDR equipment; aid
		Sweden	8	RBS-56 Bill Anti-tank missile	1997	1998	(8)	Ex-Swedish Army; loan; deal also includes 2 launchers; for use with BaltBat joint peacekeeping unit.
2000	Estonia	Finland	2	Minelayer	1998	1999	2	Free transfer
2001	Estonia	Denmark	1	Frigate	2000	2000	1	Renamed *Admiral Pitka*

[a] The date given refers to data recorded in the previous year.

[b] Agreement made on 8 September 1992 during negotiations for the withdrawal of Russian troops from Lithuania, under which 2,700 flats for soldiers would be built in Kaliningrad for Russian officers (Nordberg 1994: 77).

Note on conventions:

.. Data not available or applicable.

( ) Uncertain data or estimate.

Sources: Data collated from *SIPRI Yearbook* (1993-99) and *Military Balance* (1992-2000)

International Co-operation

As the Baltic States have had to develop their national armed forces from scratch, involving Western forces in the training and organisation of the national defence was a logical and very necessary step. Training standards during the Soviet era were harsh and often poor. Clemmesen notes how elements of this training regime have continued: 'the training is not aimed at developing "brain" and the ability of independent action among the soldiers. Training is anachronistic in underlining drill and learning rules by heart' (1998: 244). Thus international military co-operation has provided the essentials of basic military and officer training to the Baltic armed forces, which having been instilled in instructors, can now and in the future, be taught by Baltic servicemen. By far the greatest benefit of IMC is the training of officers and men in the standards and techniques of a Western/NATO style armed force. Noting the impact upon the Estonian Defence Forces, Lindström notes that 'the experience, educational and social aspects of international co-operation are opportunities for Estonia to improve the level of national defence capability and to overcome more rapidly the deficiencies that 50 years of having no armed forces of its own have caused' (1997: 89)

A key element of the international involvement in the development of the Baltic States' armed forces has been the Baltic Projects, a series of initiatives that have attracted international leadership, co-ordination, planning and support. Each project has a different national chair. Briefly, the series includes:

– BALTBAT, the Baltic Peacekeeping Battalion, consisting of 721 troops based upon three national light infantry rifle companies. Agreement to establish the force was made in late 1994, and elements of the force saw deployment in Bosnia in 1998, integrated into Nordic deployments. Support for BALTBAT is scheduled to terminate in 2002, by which time it is planned that the force will be self-sustaining in terms of leadership and training. The Steering Group is chaired by Denmark.

– BALTRON, the Baltic Naval Squadron, initiated in October 1996. The force should consist of three to six naval vessels, tasked with counter-mine operations. Recent reviews have estimated that BALTRON should be self-sustaining by 2003-2005. The Steering Group is chaired by Germany.

– BALTNET, the Baltic Regional Airspace Surveillance Network. Undoubtedly the most expensive to the projects, and the most reliant on international support and training. It will provide a consolidated radar picture of the region, integrated into NATO air surveillance networks. The Steering Group is chaired by Norway, with the US as the major contributor.

– BALTDEFCOL, the Baltic Defence College in Tartu, Estonia. Established in 1999, with the Dane, Colonel Michael Clemmesen as its first commanding officer. The College offers training for senior staff officers, similar to a National Defence College. Training and education places emphasis on strategic issues in the Baltic region, is conducted on NATO rules and procedures, and in English.

- BALTSEA, while not strictly a Baltic Project, is organised upon similar lines with a Steering Group. BALTSEA is the overall co-ordinating body of the listed Projects, as well as other assistance to the Baltic States. It seeks to plan and co-ordinate the many multi- and bi-lateral support programmes, to ensure that the overall support is effective and complementary, and does not produce counter-productive results, as has sometimes been the case, or doubled, with two or more countries separately providing similar support.

The Defence Budgets

Tables 16.6 and 16.7 show a growth over time in the financial resources committed to the development of the defence forces by the Baltic States. This is set to continue, in line with their aim of NATO membership. It should be noted that such targets do not necessarily entail NATO membership, as further development of the self-defence capabilities of the respective defence forces will require further increases in spending. However, the Baltic States themselves have presented these budgetary targets as being crucial to their membership applications.

The budget allocations remain dependent upon government revenue. Tax revenue has been consistently lower than planned government expenditure, and programmes are frequently under-funded, as evidenced by the fact that Latvia cut its planned and budgeted investment projects by 31 per cent in 1999, allocating only 3.8 million lats to investment. The current increases remain insufficient to provide to a wide development of the defence forces. It was concluded that the allocation for 2000 was unable to substantially alter the current situation (Ministry of Defence 2000b). In Lithuania, though 1.75 per cent of GDP was earmarked for defence, inadequate budget collection meant the actual funding was much lower (RFE/RL 2000).

Table 16.6: Military expenditure in constant US dollars, 1989-98, $m at constant 1995 prices and exchange rates

	1989	1990	1991	1992	1993	1994	1995	1996	1997	1998
Estonia	-	-	-	21.4	28.9	36.7	54.9	46.3	52.0	49.8
Latvia	-	-	-	-	38.6	45.0	43.6	33.8	43.1	32.5
Lithuania	-	-	-	-	51.3	27.7	28.8	33.9	55.8	104

Source: *SIPRI Yearbook* (1999: 313)

Table 16.7: Military expenditure as a percentage of GDP, 1989-97

		1989	1990	1991	1992	1993	1994	1995	1996	1997
Estonia		-	-	-	0.5	0.8	1.1	1.5	1.2	1.2
Latvia		-	-	-	-	0.8	0.9	1.0	0.7	0.9
Lithuania		-	-	-	-	0.7	0.5	0.5	0.5	0.8

Source: *SIPRI Yearbook* (1999: 320)

The crucial element remains the politics of the defence budget; or rather the proposed increases should be seen in the context of developing economies with limited funds and ever-increasing demands for those funds. The governments of all three Baltic States face considerable pressure in order to secure the planned spending on the Armed Forces, not least in Lithuania. In Estonia, the parliament on 20 December 2000 approved the 2001 state budget of 29.78 billion kroons ($1.71 billion), which includes an obvious increase in the allocation for defence. The Latvian parliament approved the 2001 budget on 30 November 2000. Projected State revenue is 1.436 billion lats ($2.297 billion) and expenditures 1.503 billion lats, resulting in a budget deficit of 73 million lats or 1.7 percent of GDP. The largest expenditure increases are planned for Latvia's integration into NATO and the EU (RFE/RL 2001). In Lithuania, the left-of-centre coalition government of Prime Minister Paksas has stressed the continued rise in the budget allocations to defence, in order that Lithuania can be invited to join NATO in 2002. However, the government's budget programme has not pleased everyone, and Paksas admitted that the proposed 2001 budget allocation of 1.95 per cent of GDP for defence may be cut, and the law promising an increase to 2 per cent of GDP revised. The current programme has at least put back the 2 per cent target to 2002 instead of 2001 as per the previous government (RFE/RL 2000b). A week later the Parliamentary Budget and Finance Committee recommended cutting this further, stating that given the existing financial situation, Lithuania could afford 1.83-1.85 per cent of GDP on defence. Such a cut would force the revision of Lithuania's NATO Integration Programme. Analysts have commented that the coalition government will face internal challenges over policy. The New Union/Social Liberal Party coalition members have already called for a reduction in the defence budget, and Presidential intervention was necessary to prevent a compromise of Lithuania's commitments to NATO (RFE/RL 2000c). With that battle won, the Parliament voted by 70 to 58 with nine abstentions to approve the 2001 budget.[12]

Conclusion

The impact of Russia upon the further development of the armed forces of the Baltic States is now limited chiefly to objecting to Baltic membership of NATO, though Russia does of course remain in the defence assessments of the Baltic States.[13] The dominant influence for the short- to medium-term development of the Baltic armed forces is unquestionably NATO. The current development plans, particularly the goal of increasing the national defence budgets to the NATO average of 2 per cent GDP is driven by the political policy aim of membership in the Alliance. Were membership not such an immediate political issue, it is likely that defence spending would increase at a more sustainable level over the long-term, with attention being paid to other critical areas of the economy and State budget, as suggested by recent experiences in the respective governments budget proposals for 2001. The development of the Baltic forces would remain somewhat dependent upon foreign support in the form of training, equipment donations, exercises and co-deployments. In either case, the role of the Nordic countries, both those in and outside NATO, as principal supporters of the development of the Baltic States' Armed Forces has been a key factor in the transition from the bare minimum of self-defence capabilities to the present condition, where the Baltic States act as willing and able contributors to UN and NATO peacekeeping deployments. The emphasis must now turn to strengthening the national defence forces, providing the forces with a suitable working and training environment, including salaries; weaponry commensurate to the tasks; and the establishment of a capable structure of both peacetime and wartime procedures.

The years 2000-2005 will prove crucial for the Baltic States in many respects. Each is in the process of membership application to the EU, which may be ready to invite new members by 2005. Furthermore, it is anticipated that NATO will present a list of invitees at its summit in 2002. The primary challenge in this respect will be the efforts of each applicant country first and foremost, and only then the opinions of others. It is evident that regardless of the plans for the further development of the Armed Forces of Estonia, Latvia and Lithuania, the battle to be fought is in the respective Parliaments. Budgetary commitments sufficient to the plans and programmes for the strengthening of the Armed Forces can only be met if the political will to ensure the allocation is sufficient, provided that the collected revenues allow. It could be argued that improved economic performance might alleviate some of the conflict, but political leadership will be the true test. There can be no clearer statement about the political control of the military in the Baltic States than this.

Notes

1   The author would like to thank officials at the Embassy of the Republic of Latvia in Stockholm, the Swedish Ministry of Foreign Affairs, the Finnish Ministry of Defence, and the Danish Military Attaché to Estonia for their assistance in preparing this chapter. Additional thanks for critical comments are due to Erik Männik, former head of Plans & Policy at the Estonian MoD, Pertti Joenniemi and Olav F. Knudsen.

2   (*The Baltic Times* 1997: 7). The lack of a clear career plan and low rates of pay for the armed forces has also meant the loss of trained personnel to the private sector. This is particularly true of soldiers that have received English language training and service abroad. A high-ranking Estonian defence official remarked in 1997 that BALTBAT, the Baltic peacekeeping battalion, was more harm than good as far as the Estonian Defence Forces were concerned. It was too expensive and too often the case that a young Estonian officer who spoke good English, returned from peacekeeping deployment, to be employed by a security firm in Tallinn.

3   The Commander of the Estonian Defence Forces, Major-General Johannes Kert was controversially dismissed by President Lennart Meri in June 2000, a decision later ratified by the State legislature on 28 August. It was reported that Kert was dismissed because he was 'considered too headstrong,' 'opposed reform in the armed forces,' and 'for resisting legislative control over the army leadership.' (Keesing's Record of World Events 2000a, b, c). There seems to have been some disagreement over the role and size of the armed forces. Kert later

refused to serve as the Chief of the Army, at least until the size of the army is determined (RFE/RL 2000b). Kert was known for his criticism of the emphasis on Estonian participation in PfP activities, commenting that the Estonian Defence Forces were 'living in a PfP coma,' and that such activity was draining resources from the development of the national defence forces.

4   Brigadier General Michael Clemmesen, a Danish officer who has served on an international defence advisory committee to the Baltic States and currently serves as commandant of BALTDEFCOL, the joint Baltic Defence College in Tartu, Estonia, has been quite critical of the extent to which the Baltic States have subscribed to the substantial number of PfP and Spirit of PfP exercises, in and out of the region, that are designed to practice NATO-type operations and develop interoperability. Writing in 1998, he stated that 'Eager to score as many points as possible for good PfP behaviour, the Baltic States show up, having to pay expenses that seem trivial to most outsiders, but are heavy in relation to the Baltic defence budgets... That focus on the PfP programme could be seen as proper by the other partner states applying for NATO membership... For the Baltic States, however, the situation is rather different. The exercise programme has tied up too large a part of the very limited defence budget needed for the building up of a self-defence capability from scratch' (1998: 248). Clemmesen made additional comments, in Danish, in *Nord Revy*, No. 6, 1995. Further comment has been made that the Baltic countries have not fully understood that before they are able to participate in Peace Support operations, they must have a proper national defence. In particular, Baltic State politicians see it very important to have their own flag flying in the Balkans without appreciating what it really takes.

5   Economic growth rates for the first half of 2000 showed the lingering effects of the Russian financial crisis of August 1998, particularly in Lithuania whose GDP grew by only 1.9 per cent in the first six months compared with the same period last year. Estonia's GDP grew by 6.4 per cent, and Latvia's by 5.1 per cent. In November 2000, the European Commission predicted a growth in Estonian GDP of 6.2 per cent for 2000 and 6.3 per cent for 2001. Latvia was forecast at 3.6 per cent and 4.5 per cent respectively, and for Lithuania 2.3 per cent and 3.2 per cent (RFE/RL 2000b). Should these forecasts prove correct, it would be one half of the battle won in terms of expanding the defence budgets of the three countries.

6   Estonia has a legislated minimum of 1 per cent GDP for its defence budget.

7   NATO Secretary-General, Lord Robertson, in conversation with Lithuanian Defence Minster Linas Linkevicius, recently stated that, with reference to the progress of candidate countries, 'ships swimming slowly will simply sink' (RFE/RL 2000c).

8   Leaders of two left-of-centre parties in Lithuania have criticised the government's policy of joining NATO. Vytenis Andriukaitis, chairman of the Social Democratic Party stated that 'the top priority should be good relations with Lithuania's neighbours, and efforts to join NATO should only come third,' and emphasised that NATO membership 'is certainly not the first priority.' Gediminas Dalinkevicius, vice chairman of the New Union/Social Liberal Party stated that the present government 'had worsened relations with Russia by demanding compensation for the Soviet occupation,' and that the current military spending was 'beyond the bounds of reason' and 'beyond what the country could afford' (RFE/RL 2000b).

9   Further analysis of the development of the national defence forces of the Baltic States, conducted by local practitioners, are to be found in *The Baltic Defence Review*, published by the Baltic Defence College, available at http://www.bdcol.ee/bdr/index.htm. The author particularly recommends the articles by Gundars Zalkans (Latvia), Giedre Statkeviciute (Lithuania) and Major-General Ants Laaneots (Estonia) in *Baltic Defence Review*, 1/1999.

10 To emphasise the integral role of the National Guard (NG) units in Latvia's territorial defence, and the corresponding structure of the defence forces, the Latvian Ministry of Defence stated in its *White Paper 2000*, that 'in times of national emergencies, the NG is reactivated and functions alongside the active duty forces. The Armed Forces development planning impacts the NG units the most. The NG units have now become a part of the total defence strategy, with some additional missions assigned to the NG during general mobilization and in case of armed conflict.' (Ministry of Defence 2000: 32).

11 For further information see the Latvian Ministry of Defence's *White Paper 2000*, available at http://www.mod.lv
12 'The Social Democratic coalition and the Peasant Party voted against the budget, while the Conservatives abstained, noting that they cannot support a budget that takes away 150 million litas ($37.5 million) from pensioners, school renovations and home construction, The budget anticipates revenues of 6,428 million litas and expenditures of 7,334 million litas. The planned budget deficit of 906 million litas is 13 percent larger than the planned 2000 deficit and accounts for 1.9 percent of GDP' (RFE/RL 2001).
13 Recent polls in Estonia showed that between 60 per cent to 80 per cent of the respondents believed that the Russian state was "definitely" or "possibly" a threat to "the peace and security" of Estonia.

Key to abbreviations

Equipment		Country Codes	
AC	Aircraft	Arg	Argentina
AD	Air Defence	Da	Denmark
AGOR	Oceanographic research vessel	Ge	Germany
AK	Cargo ship	RF	Russia
APC	Armoured personnel carrier	SF	Finland
ASW	Anti-submarine warfare	Sov	Soviet
AT	Tug	US	United States
ATGW	Anti-tank guided weapon		
HEL	Helicopter		
LCU	Landing craft, utility		
MCI/O	Mine countermeasures vessel inshore/offshore		
MOR	Mortar		
MSI	Minesweeper inshore		
PC/C/H/I	Patrol Craft coastal/harbour/inshore		
PFM	Fast Patrol Craft		
RECCE	Reconnaissance		
RCL	Recoilless launcher		
RL	Rocket Launcher		
TOWED ARTY	Towed Artillery		
trg	training		
TT	Torpedo Tube		

Source: *Military Balance* (1999-2000)

References

The Baltic Times (1997). 'Baltic Militaries look for answers,' 3-9 April.

Clemmesen, M. (1998). 'Foreign military assistance,' pages 227-58 in Mouritzen, H. (ed.). *Bordering Russia: Theory and Prospects for Europe's Baltic Rim*. Aldershot, England, Ashgate.

Estonia Today (1998). 'The Defence Forces,' 18 December. Tallinn, Ministry of Foreign Affairs.

Estonia Today (2000). 'Basic Facts on the Estonian Defence Forces,' 15 November. Tallinn, Ministry of Foreign Affairs.

Haab, M. (1995). 'Estonia and Europe: security and defence,' in Van Ham, Peter (ed.) *The Baltic States: Security and defence after independence, Chaillot Paper* 19, June 1995, Institute for Security Studies Western European Union.

Jauhiainen, J. (1999). 'The Conversion of Military Areas in the Baltic States,' pages 327-334, in Hedegaard, L. and Lindström, B. (eds). *The NEBI Yearbook 1999: North European and Baltic Sea Integration.* Berlin, Heidelberg, Springer.

Keesing's Record of World Events (2000a). Estonia, page 43643, Volume 46, No. 6, June. Washington DC, Keesing's Worldwide.

Keesing's Record of World Events (2000b). Estonia, page 43713, Volume 46, No. 7/8, August. Washington DC, Keesing's Worldwide.

Keesing's Record of World Events (2000c). Estonia, page 43764, Volume 46, No. 9, September. Washington DC, Keesing's Worldwide.

Lindstöm, L. (1997). 'Estonia's view of military co-operation and its prospects in the Baltic Sea Region,' pages 85-93 in *Military Co-operation and Its Prospects in the Baltic Sea Region,* Research Report, Series 2, No. 1. Helsinki, National Defence College, Department of Strategic Studies.

Military Balance (1993-2000). Royal Institute for Strategic Studies. Oxford, Oxford University Press.

Ministry of Defence (1997). *Security Concept of the Republic of Latvia.* Mimeo.

Ministry of Defence (1999*). Defence White Paper.* Ministry of Defence of the Republic of Lithuania. Available at http://www.kam.lt

Ministry of Defence (2000a). *White Paper 2000,* 'Report of the Minister of Defence of the Republic of Latvia to the Parliament on State Defence policy and Armed Forces Development for the year 2000.'

Ministry of Defence (2000b). *Trends of theDefence Budget for 1999-2003,* Ministry of Defence of the Republic of Latvia. http://www.mod.lv/english/sec_bugets/1999-2003.htm

http://www.vm.ee/eng/estoday/2000/defence-facts.htm

Nordberg, E. (1994). *The Baltic Republics: A strategic survey,* Finnish Defence Studies, No. 6. Helsinki, National Defence College.

RFE/RL (2000a). Radio Free Europe/Radio Liberty, *Baltic States Report,* Vol. 1, No. 33, 16 October.

RFE/RL (2000b). Radio Free Europe/Radio Liberty, *Baltic States Report,* Vol. 1, No. 35, 20 November.

RFE/RL (2000c). Radio Free Europe/Radio Liberty, *Baltic States Report,* Vol. 1, No. 37, 5 December.

RFE/RL (2001). Radio Free Europe/Radio Liberty, *Baltic States Report,* Vol. 1 No. 39, 10 January.

SIPRI Yearbook: Armament, Disarmaments and International Security (1993-1999). Stockholm International Peace Research Institute. Oxford, Oxford University Press.

17 Windows onto Europe or Russian Dead Ends?: The Federal Centre and the Foreign Relations of Russia's Western Regions

Jakob Hedenskog

Recent years have seen an increasing number of studies devoted to the subject of centre-periphery-relations in Russia. This contribution aims to deal with one particular aspect of the relation between the federal centre and the federal subjects of the Russian Federation, namely the regions' possibilities to develop own foreign relations.

The phenomenon of regionalism, i.e. the process of regions getting more self-government at the expense of the federal centre, dominated in the Russian Federation during the years of Boris Yeltsin's presidency. But many of Russia's 89 federal subjects or regions (i.e. republics, oblasts, krais etc.) not only expanded their powers within the Russian Federation, but also started to look for co-operation partners outside the borders of the federation. Recent years have, in fact, seen a substantial change in the international life of Russia's regions. Today, regional executives frequently go abroad both as heads of regional delegations as well as taking part in federal delegations. Russian regions open up offices of representation in other countries, as well as their foreign partners are doing in the Russian regions. Treaties are signed with foreign partners and entities of other countries on a number of issues.

Contacts with foreign partners among Russia's regions have become stronger and more substantive. This broadening of economic and cultural contacts with the outside world by Russia's regions can be seen as part of a world tendency to decentralise control of the social and economic processes and partly step down international relations that until recently was a federal monopoly to the regional level.

The foreign relations agenda for Russia's regions includes a broad spectrum of questions, with some of them not usually included in the tighter definition of traditional foreign policy. These 'new issues' are for instance ecological problems, drug trafficking, international crime and other problems that do not recognise any borders. However, for Russia's regions, foreign relations also serve other purposes. By creating transnational corporations and joint ventures with foreign firms, the regions hope to increase foreign investments and promote progress in the regional economy. Further, by developing foreign relations, many regions hope to reduce their dependence on the federal centre. By May 1999, of all the 89 subjects of the Russian Federation only 13 were self-sufficient, i.e. net-donors to the federal budget, while the others were either net recipients or depressed regions.

This process of widening international contacts has been made possible by a number of factors. Firstly, as already mentioned, by the international trends of regionalism and transborder co-operation that have also affected Russia. To a certain extent, the federal centre has been supporting transborder contacts as a tool to create a belt of good-neighbourliness along particularly the European borders of the Russian Federation. Secondly, by the growing importance of the regional executives after they started to be popularly elected in mid-1990s, which, for instance, meant that the regional leaders became true actors on the national arena.[1] For the regional leaders, developing foreign links has therefore served a political purpose as a way to show that they are effective and able to muscle their region into the competitive world arena. Thirdly, by federal legislation[2] and the bilateral power-sharing agreements[3] signed by the federal centre and half of the federal components, which specified the rights and limits of regional authority, and lifted up foreign relations as an important topic for the regions. However, the power-sharing agreements have also left room for certain ambiguities and possibilities for the regions to challenge federal directives, including those pertaining to foreign affairs.

The Russian Foreign Ministry appears to be both pleased and concerned about the increasing role that the country's far-flung regions have started to play in foreign affairs. It has generally been pleased by the role such activities have played in attracting investment and maintaining ties with ethnic Russians in the so-called 'near abroad.'

On the other hand, the Foreign Ministry has became increasingly disturbed by the ways such activities have distorted Moscow's foreign messages and by the way such activities have promoted centrifugal and even separatist tendencies across the Russian Federation. Especially the leading ethnic republics have often gone beyond the scope of the Constitution of the Russian Federation, intruding into the federal jurisdiction, as they have claimed a right to shape and carry out a 'foreign policy of the republics.'

One of the most striking examples of regional interference in the official Russian foreign policy has been the action taken by the governor of the Primorskiy Krai, Yevgeniy Nazdratenko, who has constantly refused to recognise the agreement delineating the common border reached between Russian and Chinese officials in 1991. Furthermore, in 1994-95 some republics with strong Muslim identification signed bilateral treaties with the Republic of Abkhazia, which at the time had just fought a bloody war to secede from Georgia. By doing so, the republics broke the Russian-Georgian friendship treaty signed in 1994. A final example: at a conference in Istanbul in April 1997 representatives of seven ethnic republics supported a communiqué that insisted on recognising the 'Turkish Republic of

Northern Cyprus' in complete contrast to the official line of the Russian Federation.

This contribution discusses the foreign relations of three regions in Western Russia, namely St Petersburg, the Kaliningrad Oblast and the Murmansk Oblast. It concentrates on some vital aspects of their foreign relations, their capability to attract foreign investors, their development of foreign trade and their transregional contacts across the borders. Being located on the western edge of Russia, the three regions need good relations with their western neighbours in order to further their own economic progress and to promote stability in Northwestern Europe.

All the three regions have similar positions vis-à-vis the federal centre. They are all ethnically Russian and of strategic importance to the federal centre. They have all signed bilateral power-sharing agreements with the centre.[4] However, concerning other aspects, the Murmansk and Kaliningrad Oblasts seem to be more alike, whereas the city of St Petersburg, even apart from its slightly different federal status, is somewhat different in many respects. For instance, both oblasts are border regions, while St Petersburg is located as an enclave in the Leningrad Oblast, albeit with access to the Baltic Sea and thereby to other countries.

Also, both oblasts are rather sparsely populated (approximately 1 million inhabitants each), while St Petersburg is a metropolis with almost five million inhabitants. Moreover, the oblasts are net receivers from the federal budget, while St Petersburg is one of the few net contributors to the federal budget. And finally, both oblasts are home to considerable military units, especially as hosts to important bases for the Russian Navy. St Petersburg, on the other hand, is important as the traditional centre for the country's naval shipyard industry and military-industrial complex (Hedenskog 2000b).

Let us now take a separate look at all the three regions and how they have developed their foreign relations.

St Petersburg: A City in Search of its Place

The city of St Petersburg, located as an enclave in the surrounding Leningrad Oblast, has the status of a federal subject of its own. The city was founded by Czar Peter the Great in 1703 and soon became the new capital whose task was to open up Russia to the West, to create 'a window onto Europe.' Western European artists, architects, scientists as well as experts in areas such as management, shipbuilding and engineering were personally invited by Czar Peter, and later by his successors, to create a truly European city on Russian soil. Almost from the beginning, St Petersburg residents considered their city to be the most Western, cosmopolitan and modern of all the Russian cities. Even after the Russian capital was moved back to Moscow, and Leningrad, as the former capital was named after Lenin's death in 1924, was turned into a more or less provincial industrial town, its residents preserved the idea of their city as a '*Velikii gorod*,' a great city. Today

St Petersburg has minor groups, in particular 'The Movement for Petersburg's Autonomy' (*'Dvizheniie za Avtonomiiu Peterburga*), who advocate more autonomy, or even separation, from the Russian Federation. 'The separatists' continue to propagate the idea of the uniqueness of its city, which they think belongs to the European cultural traditions, as opposed to the rest of Russia (Hedenskog 1999).

Recently, prominent Russian politicians have talked about moving the capital back to St Petersburg. The question was raised by State Duma speaker Gennadiy Seleznyov, originally a native from Leningrad, and supported by St Petersburg's governor Vladimir Yakovlev, who saw a chance for a big economic injection for his city. Seleznyov's statement advanced the idea of moving the State Duma from Moscow back to St Petersburg and giving the city on the Neva a status of capital together with Moscow. President Putin, also a native of Leningrad, called the idea 'interesting' (Titova 2000). In fact, St Petersburg has been given a prominent position within the Commonwealth of Independent States as the CIS parliament was located to the city. There have also been suggestions of moving the CIS capital from Minsk to St Petersburg. However, this might be a poor consolation for St Petersburg, since the CIS, so far, has been a rather weak organisation and the CIS parliament, in its seven years of existence, has not been able raise a single issue (Pipija 2000).

During the period of *glasnost* and *perestroika*, Leningrad established itself as the breeding ground of Russia's pro-democracy movement. It was here that reformers swept the legislature in the country's first free regional elections in 1990 and a year later won the mayor's office, bringing Anatoliy Sobchak, one of the reform-movement's front-line figures to power. On the same day the voters decided to restore the historic name of St Petersburg. During his years in office, Sobchak worked intensively to attract tourists, foreign investors and famous pop musicians to the city, with the aim of restoring St Petersburg's former glory and status as a great European city. In 1991 he appointed a former KGB officer, Vladimir Putin, who had been one of Sobchak's law students, to become chairman of the Committee on Foreign Relations. From the very beginning Putin had wide powers over foreign dealings, almost equal to the mayor's. Sobchak and his 'right hand' Putin had grandiose plans to attract large amounts of foreign investment, protect the interests of the region and implement projects with foreign partners, i.e. to turn St Petersburg into a cultural capital and international financial centre. However, as with a planned World Financial and Trade Centre, a prioritised project that was scuttled in 1995, most of the initiatives were never realised. There were many reasons for these failures. Firstly, St Petersburg lacked a well-defined programme to support investment and it took a long time to develop one (Makova 2000). Secondly, tourists did not come in the expected numbers, scared as they by stories of growing criminality and Mafia activities in Russia. Thirdly, a project to create a Free Economic Zone in the city aimed at attracting foreign investments, was never realised due to a lack of support from the federal authorities. Furthermore, the city's finances were in a critical shape. The privatisation of large industries and the conversion of the city's huge military-industrial complex proceeded slowly, and from 1991 to 1995 the industrial output in the city fell by 60 per cent (Hedenskog 1999).

In 1996, Sobchak lost the gubernatorial elections to his own deputy Vladimir Yakovlev. During Yakovlev's years in office, the city's finances have improved substantially and foreign investments increased. In 1999, after years of slow improvement, the city's investments amount jumped to $650 million, up from $309 in 1998 (Shevory 2000). The city is the second region according to total amount of foreign investments of the Russian federal subjects. however, it is by far distanced by the city of Moscow, which in 1997 attracted an astounding 68.9 per cent of all foreign investments in Russia (Sokolin 1998). The biggest investor countries in St Petersburg are the USA and Finland. St Petersburg is also second to the city of Moscow when it comes to joint ventures with foreign companies, with the Kaliningrad Oblast in the third place (Kuzmin 1999).

St Petersburg went through the financial crisis in 1998 with better results than most Russian regions, even if its residents, as everywhere in Russia, suffered heavily from the rouble crash and the empty shelves in the stores. The regional banks, however, did better than the Moscow banks, the city's finances recovered rather quickly and the entire foreign trade decreased only slightly. According to *Goskomstat*, the city's main exports are machine and metallurgic products and the main recipient countries are the USA, Finland and Germany. The main import countries are the same, but in a different order (Hedenskog 1999). After the crisis, imports of food dropped by an average of 50 per cent compared to pre-crisis levels, since the high inflation increased demand for cheaper domestic products (Shcherbakova 1999).

For many observers of St Petersburg during Yakovlev's years as governor, the improvements of the city's economy have, however, been overshadowed by the governor's struggle against the liberal opposition in the Legislative Assembly and, most of all, by the city's growing criminal record. The many high-profile killings of prominent politicians such as the city's top privatisation official Mikhail Manevich, State Duma deputy Galina Starovoitova and city legislator Viktor Novosyolov as well as several representatives of the city's business elite, have given St Petersburg the not very flattering epithet of 'criminal capital of Russia' (Hedenskog 1999).

St Petersburg is an active participator in regional cross-border co-operation and twin-town projects. It has developed a programme called 'St Petersburg – Russia's European Gateway,' providing for co-operation above all with the EU and the states around the Baltic Sea. This programme is based on proposals by many European states and organisations bearing on such areas as finance, transport, trade, culture, construction, environment conservation, the social sector and labour resources.

In 1997, joint efforts by regional authorities in Helsinki, Stockholm, Tallinn, Riga and St Petersburg produced a regional development programme, 'the Baltic Palette' ('*Baltiiskaia Palitra*'), presented in the form of an application to the European Commission (Kuzmin 1999).

To sum up, as the biggest metropolis by the Baltic Sea, St Petersburg is an attractive partner in regional transborder co-operation. With its vast consumer market, the city is a potential economic driving force for the whole Baltic area. However, it seems unlikely that the federal centre will allow the city to develop into a truly 'European city,' as aspired to by the city's intelligentsia. Also, St Petersburg has stronger ties to the centre and the historical Russian Empire, in other words is more 'Russian' than some if its residents might want to acknowledge. There seems to be little reason to the idea of bringing back the capital to St Petersburg even though the proposal enjoys some support in the higher ranks of power in Moscow among politicians with roots in St Petersburg. Judging by the economic relations and foreign investments, Moscow, rather than St Petersburg, remains Russia's 'window onto Europe.'

The Kaliningrad Oblast: A Russian Enclave in Europe

The Kaliningrad Oblast has a unique geographical location as Russia's westernmost region, situated as an exclave between Poland, Lithuania and the Baltic Sea. The area, conquered by the Soviet Army at the end of World War II, was earlier a part of the German province of East Prussia. After the war, the whole German population was either deported or fled to Germany and was replaced by Soviet, mainly ethnic Russian, Ukrainian and Belorusian, settlers. In 1946 the medieval city of Königsberg was renamed Kaliningrad in honour of the Soviet president Mikhail Kalinin, who had just died.

For the Soviet Union, the Kaliningrad Oblast became extremely important for military-strategic reasons. The Soviet Baltic Fleet's headquarters were transferred from Leningrad to Kaliningrad, and the port of Baltiysk (formerly Pillau) became a major naval base. The armed forces and the military industry became major employers in the region, to which no Western visitors were allowed and even Soviet citizens had limited access. Today, the Kaliningrad Oblast's exclave position in Russia automatically creates transit problems, since the most important railways and roads pass through Lithuania or Poland and it also makes border trade extremely important for the region.

In the early 1990s reform economists in Kaliningrad, inspired by Western experts, began to work out plans of a free economic zone, called 'Amber' ('*Yantar*') with the aim of restructuring and developing the economy and attracting foreign investments to the region. The idea was to exploit the Kaliningrad Oblast's unique geographical position close to Western Europe. Foreign investments were to be attracted by favourable taxation and customs rates, free exports, a good industrial and social infrastructure, and a cheap and well-trained work force. In September 1991 the 'Yantar' Free Economic Zone (FEZ) was officially established. The Kaliningrad Oblast was to become a centre for economic co-operation in the Baltic region and at the same time a springboard for Western firms looking for an entry into the vast Russian market. The first governor of the

Kaliningrad Oblast, Yuriy Matoczin, supported the project and expressed the high hope that the oblast in ten years would become a 'Baltic Hong Kong.'

Indeed, the 'Yantar' project had some measure of success. A tourist industry developed, especially attracting a great number of German visitors. Foreign trade increased fivefold between 1995 and 1997, and the Kaliningrad Oblast became one of the foremost places in Russia with regard to the number of enterprises with foreign investment. Germany, Poland and Lithuania of course supported the drive for economic liberalisation and political autonomy in the Kaliningrad Oblast and became its main trading partners. Lithuania and Poland opened consulates in Kaliningrad and signed agreements on visa-free travel and regional co-operation across the borders.

However, the heavy legacy of fifty years of planned economy and militarisation was still strong in the oblast and limited the development of the FEZ. The industrial products from the Kaliningrad Oblast – like from the rest of Russia – proved non-competitive on the international market. The infrastructure was more a disadvantage than an advantage, since it was lopsided and worn down, and the environmental problems were enormous and required vast investments. Moreover, the Kaliningrad Oblast's geographical location was not particularly beneficial. Instead of being a springboard to Russia, the exclave's position was a great liability. The region was isolated from the rest of Russia and was heavily dependent on energy and raw materials from other Russian regions, especially since importing electricity from the Ignalina power station in Lithuania was dismissed for politically reasons. Thus, the free zone privileges only served partly to compensate for transit and transport problems.

The overall economy of the Kaliningrad Oblast deteriorated and industrial production fell – even more than the Russian average. Even though joint ventures were numerous, the actual amount of foreign investment in the region was pitiful. Most of the joint ventures only existed on paper and mainly went into trade and services. Trade with the West was still impeded by visa, custom, transport and communication problems as well as contradictory economic legislation. In view of all these problems, the Kaliningrad Oblast was superseded by the Baltic States and Poland, which became more attractive to foreign investors and international aid programmes since they provided more stable and favourable conditions and started to show real growth. Transit trade, also Russian, with the West went over to other Baltic ports, notably Klaipeda in Lithuania. Finally, St Petersburg, rather than the Kaliningrad Oblast, seemed to be a more rational choice for foreigners wanting to reach the Russian market, being a metropolis with direct access to the Russian mainland.

The Kaliningrad Oblast's economic problems and its failure to attract Western investment were also intimately related to its status and relation with the federal powers in Moscow. The tendency toward more autonomy for the oblast was reversed by the centre for both political and economic reasons. In 1993 Moscow abolished a trade agreement which the Kaliningrad Oblast had signed with Lithuania and retained control over border and visa formalities. In 1995

Yeltsin suddenly abolished the customs exemptions of the Kaliningrad FEZ on the ground that all regions of Russia should enjoy equal terms.

Finally, in 1996 the status as FEZ was replaced by a federal law 'On Strengthening the Sovereignty of the Russian Federation on the Territory of the Kaliningrad Oblast.' According to the law, the Oblast became a 'special' economic zone (SEZ). Federal oversight was emphasised and left little room for independent foreign relations. However, the oblast also got back some favours. It became a 'free customs zone' for products imported from other states, products imported from other states and then re-exported, and products manufactured in the zone and then sent to Russia. Products were considered to have been produced in the zone if their value increased by 30 per cent (electronic products 15 per cent), which favoured processing of imported goods. However, a major obstacle for foreigners wanting to invest in the Kaliningrad Oblast was not removed – land could still not be purchased but only leased for periods yet to be settled (Oldberg 1998).

The Russian financial breakdown and political disarray in August 1998 of course affected the situation also in the Kaliningrad Oblast. Food imports, on which the city of Kaliningrad depended up to 90 per cent, stopped; shelves were emptied and prices skyrocketed; banks closed and black market exchange reappeared, bringing people to panic and despair. Governor Leonid Gorbenko threatened to suspend the payments to the federal budget since the centre did not transfer what it promised. He even declared a 'state of emergency' in the oblast, however changing it to 'situation of emergency' after the presidential administration had pointed out that the governor exceeded his powers since only the president can declare state of emergency.

The crises resulted in growing tensions between Moscow and the Kaliningrad Oblast as well as inside the region between the supporters of central control and security on the one hand and those of free market and orientation toward the west on the other (Oldberg, forthcoming).

As noticed, the Kaliningrad Oblast's geographic position makes it extremely dependent on transborder trade with the countries around the Baltic Sea. In 1997, Germany stood for 25 per cent of the Kaliningrad Oblast's total imports. Poland and Lithuania came second with 15 per cent of each. The same countries were also the main recipients of export products from the Kaliningrad Oblast with Poland accounting for more than 25 per cent and Germany and Lithuania just under 10 per cent each. The Nordic countries (Denmark, Finland, Norway and Sweden) accounted for less than 5 per cent of Kaliningrad's exports and a little over 5 per cent of the imports. Both Estonia and Latvia had hardly any trade at all (less than 2 per cent each) with the Kaliningrad Oblast, which is surprising given their geographic proximity.

The actual composition of the Kaliningrad Oblast's trade was also somewhat unusual. According to the Kaliningrad Regional State Committee on Statistics, on the import side, in 1997, 9.7 per cent of total imports were accounted for by cigarettes – over $100 million, or over $100 for every man, woman and child in the region, which leads to the likely conclusion that much of this trade, legally or illegally, went elsewhere. Most of the rest of the imports were consumer goods (food, alcohol, home appliances) and other finished products (office equipment, vehicles) or industrial inputs (building materials). On the export side, also in 1997, crude petroleum, ships/boats, fish/crustaceans and cellulose were the main export products (Dewar 2000).

Something that will probably have a great negative impact on the Kaliningrad Oblast's economy and position as a trading zone is Russia's current strategy to join the World Trade Organisation (WTO), which will mean lower customs duties to increase the sale of foreign goods on the Russian market. As the WTO requires from its members a unified legal system throughout the country, this would mean that the Kaliningrad Oblast would lose its benefits from the SEZ and attractiveness as a region where investments are profitable. The consequence of a change in the tariff regime would likely mean the cancellation of contracts for long-term cooperation, a sharp curtailment of investment and closing of many enterprises. Also, import-substituting products produced in the Kaliningrad Oblast and shipped to the rest of Russia would become more expensive than products directly imported from abroad (*EWI Russian Regional Report* 2000a).

In recent years, rather strong economic ties have been developed between the Kaliningrad Oblast and Belarus with its eccentric President Aleksandr Lukashenko. For instance, in July 1999, a document was signed that foresaw the use of the Kaliningrad Oblast ports for trans-shipping Belarus imports and exports (*EWI Russian Regional Report* 1999a). In October the same year, the co-operation was extended and a treaty that calls for setting up a system of transit through Belarus to the rest of Russia and increasing trade between Belarus and the Kaliningrad Oblast, was signed. During 1997 to 1999, the annual trade between Belarus and the Kaliningrad Oblast rose from $40 million to $150 million (*EWI Russian Regional Report* 1999b). However, due to transit problems and the critical state of the Belarus economy, with a foreign trade to some extent based on barter, prospects for further development of this trade do not seem very promising.

Co-operation with states around the Baltic Sea is of course of great importance for the Kaliningrad Oblast. In 1994, a treaty on cross-border co-operation with Poland was signed, providing for co-operation between the Kaliningrad Oblast and St Petersburg with Northeastern and coastal provinces of Poland (Kuzmin 1999). Representatives of the Kaliningrad Oblast, together with representatives of the Novgorod and Leningrad Oblasts and the city of St Petersburg also participate in the work of the Council of the Baltic Sea States, originally established in Copenhagen in 1992. The strengthening of the industrial potential of the Baltic region along with corresponding measures to protect the environment and the development of the transportation infrastructure are among the priorities of this co-operation (Matvienko 1996).

Finally, the Kaliningrad Oblast has also participated in the creation of so-called Euroregions, both in Euroregion 'Nieman' together with Polish, Lithuanian and Belarus regions, and Euroregion 'Amber' together with regions of Southern Sweden, Northern Poland, Lithuania and Latvia (Romanov 1998).

Summing up, the Kaliningrad Oblast's geographic position as separated from the rest of Russia, makes the region more anxious not only to co-operate with neighbouring states, but also to demand a greater degree of independence. However, as is the case with St Petersburg, it seems more than unlikely today that the federal centre would give the region the necessary tools to fully integrate in a Baltic Sea context.

Of great importance for the future status of the Kaliningrad Oblast is the expansion of the EU to include the neighbouring countries Poland and Lithuania. If those countries become members, the Kaliningrad Oblast will be completely surrounded by EU members. That could lead to positive economic benefits for the oblast, such as widening and strengthening business contacts and increased foreign investments, making the Kaliningrad Oblast a true 21st Century Russian 'window onto Europe.' However, one cannot exclude the opposite, that the Kaliningrad Oblast would feel exposed, squeezed between two EU countries (and possibly, two NATO countries, since Poland has already joined the alliance) and that stricter controls on Poland's and Lithuania's borders would create difficulties in trading with these countries. Instead the regional leadership would probably support further integration with the Russian economy, and the region would turn out to be a 'dead end', a bastion defending Russian superpower interests in the new united Europe.

The Murmansk Oblast:
Between Moscow and the North Pole

The Murmansk Oblast is located on the Kola Peninsula in the very northwestern part of Russia, almost halfway from Moscow to the North Pole. It borders on Norway, Finland as well as the Karelian Republic of the Russian Federation. The Kola Peninsula is a traditional border zone and meeting ground, historically characterised by intensive commercial activities for Russians, Norwegians, Saami, Finns and Swedes as well as merchants from Holland and Britain. Trade relations between Russia's North and the northern parts of Norway go back to the first written chronicles.

The first Russian settlers on the Kola Peninsula were farmers from the Republic of Novgorod, who settled along the coasts of the Barents Sea and the White Sea in the thirteenth century. Later, the Kola Peninsula was conquered by the expanding Muscovy and from the late nineteenth century the Russian Empire started to exploit the Kola Peninsula's strategic importance. In 1916 the city of Murmansk (originally named Romanov-na-Murmane) was founded.

Today, the Murmansk Oblast is still a strategically important region and home to the Russian Northern Fleet, which includes two-thirds of the Russian Navy's nuclear submarines. Within the borders of the region are six closed cities containing naval bases and important naval shipyards. The Murmansk Oblast is still one of the most militarised regions in the world. It is also one of the most environmentally vulnerable. Apart from the pollution from the region's huge mining industries, which have created ecological disaster areas around them, the Murmansk Oblast is also the region with the highest concentration of nuclear installations in the world, with around 240 reactors in use (1996), the bulk of them in nuclear submarines.

The main industries in the region are based on mining and fishing. The natural resources on the Kola Peninsula are indeed impressive. The region is home to 100 per cent of the Russian Federation's apatite production and to a substantial share of Russia's nickel and iron production as well as of other metals. More than 70 per cent of the region's exports consist of minerals and metals (Hedenskog 2000a). According to regional statistics 1994-97, exports more than doubled in dollars (*Murmanskoi oblasti 60 let: Yubileinyi statisticheskii sbornik 1998*). However, most of the export revenues do not bring wealth to the region itself since all the metallurgical companies are in the hands of oligarch structures in Moscow. Imports consist mainly of food and agricultural products as farming is underdeveloped due to harsh climatic conditions. After a rapid increase in population from the 1920s to the early 1990s, mostly due to state-financed immigration, the region today suffers from a considerable net emigration and natural population decrease (Hedenskog 2000a).

During the Cold War, the Kola Peninsula was one of the few places where NATO and the Soviet Union shared a common border, and the tense political situation in the area made it almost impossible for people to maintain contact across the borders. The end of the Cold War opened up new opportunities for regional co-operation in the Barents region. The Murmansk Oblast's foreign relations are today channelled mainly through the Barents Euro-Arctic Region (BEAR) co-operation. The BEAR was established in January 1993 when representatives from Russia, the Nordic countries and the EU Commission signed the Kirkenes Declaration, which laid down the foundation of the structure and official aims of the co-operation. A special feature of the BEAR co-operation structure is that it has two parallel bodies: the Barents Euro-Arctic Council (BEAC), where the national authorities are represented, and the Regional Council, made up of representatives from the Nordic counties and Russian units of the Barents region.[5] This form of co-operation, where the regional level is the dominating operative level, has attracted international attention, and in this sense the BEAR co-operation differs from the Baltic Sea co-operation, which is driven much more by the national governments.

On the other hand, the lack financial resources at the subnational level makes the development of multilateral arrangements difficult. Even if national interests are not in conflict with transborder arrangements and regionalisation, the processes are very much steered by government priorities. Norway is definitely the driving force in the BEAR co-operation, both as initiator of the project and because of its greater willingness to trust the actions of subgovernmental bodies. Sweden and Finland have been more hesitant and have focussed particularly on the Baltic region (Svensson 1995). The BEAR co-operation also suffers from the fact that only Sweden and Finland are EU members. The original proposal assumed Norway's membership as well but that was rejected by the Norwegian electorate in 1994. The Finnish 'Northern dimension' initiative aimed to raise EU awareness of the problems and prospects of the northern regions as the new frontier with Russia (Archer 2000).

From the Russian side, the BEAR co-operation is highly popular among the regional leaders of the participating regions. For instance, Murmansk Governor Yuriy Yevdokimov sees the BEAR co-operation as a 'model for co-operation between countries with different histories and a variety of political, economic and military backgrounds' and considers developing this model as his 'most important task.'

As the most fruitful results of the co-operation, Yevdokimov has mentioned the 'Murmansk corridor,' a project intended to improve transport and commercial development by a joint Norwegian-Russian working group, the construction of the new Russian-Finnish border crossing 'Salla,' the programme for energy efficiency and environmental protection, and the introduction of modern telecommunications systems in the participating Russian regions.

However, Yevdokimov also sees shortcomings in the BEAR project, namely the failure to inform the people of the region about the benefits from the co-operation, and the fact that the different projects have not produced the desired financial gains in Russia. In Yevdokimov's view, this is due to the large number of small projects and a lack of funding and experience in attracting private investors (*The Barents region Cooperation and visions for the future* 1999). In contrast to the regional leaders, the official Russian view of the BEAR project is, according to the Norwegian researcher Waling T. Gorter-Grønvik (1998), predominantly negative. Moscow does not financially contribute to the project at all, and much co-operation in the BEAR is seriously hampered by ministries and directorates in the centre who show no understanding of transnational regional co-operation at all. As an example, in 1998, Russia even expelled key Norwegian BEAR experts as retaliation for a diplomatic scandal.

The BEAR co-operation is a political institution, which is implemented primarily through co-operation on a wide range of projects: environmental protection, trade, infrastructure, business, culture, indigenous people, research and education. So far, the best results seem to have been achieved in the people-to-people, grass-roots area of the BEAR co-operation. In the business and investments area, as mentioned, the results have been more moderate. Perhaps expectations were too high (*The Barents region Cooperation and visions for the future* 1999).

Despite its potential advantages, foreign investments in the Murmansk Oblast are very low. From 1995 to 1998, according to Goskomstat, average foreign investments in the region from 1995 to 1998 were no more than $3 million per year, which is extremely low even by Northwest Russian standards. Despite a considerable jump in 1999 up to $14 million, the amount is lower than for comparable regions. The reason seems to be an insufficient regional investment policy, a lack of diversity of the regional industry (concentrating on two main sectors) and the strategic importance of the Murmansk Oblast, which limits foreigners' activities in the region, including the freedom of movement (Hedenskog 2000b).

As it seems, the federal centre has not been willing to give the Murmansk Oblast enough support in developing its economy in a self-sufficient way. As an example, in 1994 the Oblast Duma worked out a project of creating a Free Economic Zone called '*Murman.*' The project, which was supported by then Governor Yevgeniy Komarov, and sent to the State Duma, had the aim of creating favourable conditions for foreign investors and give the region greater control over gas and petroleum extraction, as well as over local taxes. However, the proposal was never really discussed by the State Duma (Hønneland 1995).

As an example of Russian suspicion toward foreigners, which is still a hindrance to foreign investment, one may recall the case of the Shtokman gas fields in the Barents Sea. It is one of the largest and so far practically unexploited gas finds in the world, with reserves estimated at three trillion cubic meters, situated 600 kilometres northeast of Murmansk. In the beginning of the 1990s, a consortium of international firms with Norsk Hydro in the lead nearly obtained the rights to exploit the field.

However, in December 1992, the minister for the petroleum and gas industry, Viktor Chernomyrdin, suddenly decided not to grant the rights to exploit the Shtokman field to the international consortium, but to a newly formed Russian association of military industries (Jonson 1994). After a period with no visible results at all, the State Duma, in April 2000, changed policy once again and finally decided to grant the rights to exploit the Shtokman fields to a joint venture, consisting of Rosshelf, a daughter company of Gazprom, together with French, American, Norwegian and Finnish interests. The Russian part is going to keep control over 50 per cent of the shares (plus one share), leaving 12,5 per cent each to the foreign counterparts (Reznik 2000). The example shows with what hesitation the Russian authorities let foreign investors participate in the extraction of the natural resources.

Conclusions and Thoughts about the Future

During the 1990s, the official Russian policy towards the regions' desire to develop foreign relations has been double-edged. On the one hand, the centre generally supports the regional leaders in their efforts to increase their share of foreign investments. On the other hand, it is not willing to give special rights to individual regions in order not to stimulate separatist tendencies. As a consequence, the promises of creating special free economic zones in some regions, with the main purpose of stimulating foreign investments, have been turned down by the centre. Of the regions scrutinised in this paper, the Kaliningrad Oblast went furthest with this project, whereas St Petersburg was turned down in an earlier phase and the Murmansk Oblast was never even given a fair chance.

The centre does not know whether it will fully support transborder co-operation for the regions or not. On the one hand, it has provided some legal possibilities through power-sharing agreements and federal laws. On the other hand, it does not give the necessary financial backup to the Russian participants in the Regional Council of the BEAR co-operation, which is the most far-reaching co-operation studied here.

So far the transborder co-operation has not resulted in huge foreign investments in Russia's regions, as was expected in some cases. Of the three regions studied here, only St Petersburg has attracted a considerable amount of foreign investment. The city's investment policy started to have real effect only recently, in 1999, and the sum is not particularly large neither counting per capita nor compared to Moscow's foreign investments. Generally foreign investments in the regions are still impeded by problems related to tax, credit, finance, customs, land and suspicion, making Russia a high-risk zone for investors.

At the end of the Yeltsin era, real efforts were made to subject the regional foreign relations to the guidelines of the Ministry of Foreign Affairs. As new President, Vladimir Putin has gone much further by restoring what is often called 'vertical power.' After entering office, Putin almost immediately declared war on the 'legal chaos' existing in the regions, where regional laws often conflicted with federal legislation. He particularly attacked the bilateral power-sharing agreements, which had been criticised for giving the Russian Federation an asymmetric character. No more agreements of this character will be signed, at least in the near future. On the contrary, some of the most generous existing agreements, particularly the one with Tatarstan, have already been subjected to renegotiation (*EWI Russian Regional Report* 2000b).

In May 2000 President Putin created seven new federal districts, encompassing all the 89 regions (*EWI Russian Regional Report* 2000c). In July it was decided to reform the Federation Council and exclude the regional executives from it (*RFE/RL Russian Federation Report* 2000).

The administrative reforms have quickly changed the rules of centre-periphery relations in the Russian Federation and have probably neutralised the regional leaders for a long time to come. In addition, the war in Chechnya, fought under the name of 'anti-terrorist campaign,' has effectively shown separatists in the ethnic republics that President Putin intends to keep the Russian Federation intact at any price. That these new rules also will prevent the Russian regions, including those analysed here, from developing their own foreign relations. However, this development is not exclusively dependent on the Russian federal centre's policy towards the region, but, to some extent, also on the attitude and goodwill of the neighbouring countries.

Notes

[1] Only the presidents of the ethnic republics and the mayors of Moscow and St Petersburg were popularly elected already from 1991. From the end of 1995, elections were held in a small number of ethnic Russian regions, usually loyal to Yeltsin. But from 1996-97 elections were held all over the federation.

[2] The most important new document concerning the rights and limits of the foreign relations for the subjects of the Russian Federation is a federal law 'On Co-ordination of International and Foreign Economic Relations of Components of the Russian Federation' from 4 January 1999. This allows the regions to maintain foreign relations below government level, i.e. with administrative-territorial entities of other states. With permission from the government the regions may also develop relations with institutions of other states. The regions are obliged to keep the Ministry of Foreign Affairs informed when they are going to negotiate with a foreign partner, and the treaties with foreign partners are to be published officially. The regions are also given rights to open offices of representation outside Russia, and equivalent regions of foreign states may establish missions in Russia, as long as these do not have diplomatic functions. Finally, according to federal law, the foreign relations of the regions are to be co-ordinated by the federal institutions only.

[3] The first region to sign a bilateral power-sharing agreement was the republic of Tatarstan, which together with Chechnya had refused to sign the Federation Treaty in 1992. The document from 1994 gave Tatarstan wider responsibilities, for instance concerning foreign policy, than the other republics. In practice it was confirmed as a sovereign republic united with the Russian Federation. Soon afterwards the other ethnic republics were also standing in line to sign their own power-sharing agreements. In 1996, when president Yeltsin needed support from the regional leaders for his re-election campaign, the authority to sign power-sharing agreements was extended to include other regions. A new law regarding the formal principles for future power-sharing agreements was adopted in July 1999. However, after Moscow signed its agreement in June 1998, bringing the total number to 46 , no more power-sharing agreements have been signed.

[4] The Kaliningrad Oblast was the first ethnically Russian region (together with the Sverdlovsk Oblast) to sign a bilateral power-sharing agreement with the federal powers on 12 January 1996. St Petersburg also signed its agreement in 1996 (13 June) and the Murmansk Oblast 30 October 1997. Comparing the three agreements, one finds that they are all drawn up in a similar way. However, it seems that the federal powers have become slightly more restrictive towards letting the regions develop foreign relations, since the last agreement, signed by the Murmansk Oblast, does not allow the region to sign agreements with ministries of other states, which is possible for the Kaliningrad Oblast and St Petersburg.

[5] These are: the Murmansk Oblast, the Republic of Karelia, the Arkhangelsk Oblast and the Nenets Autonomous Okrug of the Russian Federation, the provinces of Lapland and Oulu in Finland, Norrbottens län and Västerbottens län in Sweden and Finnmarks fylke, Troms fylke and Nordland fylke of Norway.

References

Archer, C. (2000). 'EU and the Common Strategy to Russia: A Bridge too Far?' in Herd, G.P. (ed.) *EU Enlargement in the North: Security Dynamics in Nordic-Baltic-EU-Russian Relations into the New Century*. Royal Military Academy Sandhurst, Conflict Studies Research Centre, F69.

The Barents region Cooperation and visions for the future (1999) (interview with Yuriy Yevdokimov). At http://www.odin.dep.no/publ/1999/barents/index-e.html. Oslo, The Norwegian State Departement. Last accessed 11 November 1999.

Dewar, S. (2000). 'Key Economic Issues,' in Baxendale, J., Dewar, S. and Gowan, D. *The EU and Kaliningrad*. London, Federal trust.

EWI Russian Regional Report (2000a). 'Change in customs duties would have big impact on Kaliningrad,' 27 September, page 8.

EWI Russian Regional Report (1999a). 'Kaliningrad's Gorbenko Meets Lukashenko,' 5 August, page 11.

EWI Russian Regional Report (1999b). 'Lukashenko in Kaliningrad,' 21 October, page 12.

EWI Russian Regional Report (2000b) 'Putin and Tatarstan,' 5 April, page 5.

EWI Russian Regional Report (2000c). 'Putin Creates Seven New Federal Districts to Better Manage the Regions,' 17 May, pages 1-2.

Gorter-Grønvik, W.T. (1998) 'History, Identities and the Barents Euro-Arctic Region: The Case of Arkhangelsk,' in Flikke, G. (ed.). *The Barents Region Revisted*. Oslo, Norwegian Institute of International Affairs.

Hedenskog, J. (1999). *Mellan självstyre och centralstyre: S:t Petersburg och dess förhållande till centralmakten under 1990-talet.* Stockholm, FOA.

Hedenskog, J. (2000a). *Mellan Nordpolen och Moskva: Murmansk oblast och relationen till centralmakten.* Stockholm, FOA.

Hedenskog, J. (2000b). 'The Foreign Relations of Russia's Western Regions,' in Oldberg, I. and Hedenskog, J. (eds). *In Dire Straits: Russia's Western Regions between Moscow and the West.* Stockholm, FOA.

Hønneland, G. (1995). 'Regionaliseringstilløp på Kola-halvøya,' *Nordisk Østforum* 2, pages 53-64.

Jonson, L. (1994). 'Russian Doctrine and the Arctic,' in Dellenbrant, J.Å. and Olsson M.-O. (eds). *The Barents Region: Security and Economic Development in the European North.* Umeå, CERUM.

Kuzmin, E. (1999). 'Russia: the Center, the Regions, and the Outside World,' *International Affairs* 45:1, pages 105-22.

Makova, M. (2000). 'In St. Petersburg, Putin's Mediocre Record in Helping Foreign Business,' *EWI Russian Regional Investor*, 20 January, pages 3-4.

Matvienko, V. (1996). 'The Center and the Regions in Foreign Policy,' *International Affairs* 42:4, pages 88-97.

Murmanskoi oblasti 60 let: Yubileinyi statisticheskii sbornik (1998). Murmansk, Murmanskii oblastnoi komitet gosudarstvennoi statistiki.

Oldberg, I. (1998). 'Kaliningrad: Problems and prospects,' in Joenniemi, P. and Prawitz J. (eds). *Kaliningrad: The European Amber Region*. London, Ashgate.

Oldberg, I. (forthcoming). 'Kaliningrad oblast – a troublesome exclave,' in *Unity or Separation: Center-Periphery Relations in the Former Soviet Union*. London, Praeger Publishers.

Pipija, B. (2000). 'Kakoi stolitsei stanet gorod na Neve?' *Nezavisimaia Gazeta – Regiony* 5, 14 March.

Reznik, I. (2000). 'Podarok Gazpromu ot Gosdumy i Rybnadzora,' *Kommersant*, 22 April.

RFE/RL Russian Federation Report (2000). 'Senators Vote to Dissolve the Upper House,' 27 July, page 1.

Romanov, S. (1998). 'Russia's Regions and Transborder Cooperation,' *International Affairs* 44:1, pages 80-90.

Shcherbakova, A. (1999). 'Local Food Producers Feed Off Crises,' *The St. Petersburg Times' Post-Crises Special '99.*

Shevory, K. (2000). 'Regional Tax Breaks Threatened by State,' *The St. Petersburg Times*, 7 March.

Sokolin, V.L. (ed.). (1998). *Rossiiskii Statisticheskii Yezhegodnik 1998.* Moscow, Goskomstat.

Svensson, B. (1995). 'National Interests and Transnational Regionalisation – Norway, Sweden and Finland Facing Russia,' in Dahlström, M., Eskelinen, H. and Wiberg, U, (eds). *The East-West Interface in the European North.* Uppsala, Nordisk samhällsgeografisk tidskrift.

Titova, I. (2000). 'Will Duma Return to St. Petersburg?' *The St. Petersburg Times*, 2 May.

18 Environmental Threats, Governmentality and Security in Northern Europe

Monica Tennberg

Making Spaces for Interventions

This chapter studies the problem of environmental security through Michel Foucault's concept of governmentality. For Foucault, the government is 'the conduct of conduct' – a form of activity aimed at shaping, guiding or affecting the conduct of some person or persons. The governed is 'a sort of complex composed of men and things.' The relations to be governed are many: men in their relations and their links to wealth, resources, the means of subsistence and climate; men in their relations with other things, customs, habits, ways of acting and thinking, and lastly, men in their relation to accidents, misfortunes, famines, epidemics, and death. Governmental rationality aims at the 'right disposition of things to be governed' leading to 'a convenient end for the governed,' not for some common good (Foucault 1991a: 93).

The state plays a central role in governmentality as the political and social guarantor of security. Foucault emphasises the security function of modern states compared with the function of maintaining territorial integrity. Security is a specific political method and practice aimed at securing the well-being of the population (Foucault 1991a: 99-100). Foucault 'turned his back to the nature' (Darier 1999: 5). The practice of governmentality, however, is the practice of problematisation, which is aimed at dealing with probable and possible events and an increasing number of potential threats. The environment has been, and is, such a field of problematisation. Foucault's method directs attention to the political practices of making environmental concerns an object of discourse and to the practices of making that discourse possible. The language of governmentality consists of different ways of making 'spaces' – that is, domains for the interventions of experts, politicians, and administrators. His approach allows the study of the political practices that define what is 'sayable' and 'doable'; these practices include the environment (Foucault 1991b: 59-61). The point in studying governmentality is not to tell the story of how it 'really' was but to study how the authorities and the rationality of governing have made the world as it is now understood (Simons 1995: 38).

Pollution as a Common Enemy

In the late 1980s, the problem of transboundary pollution was an 'acute' and 'serious' problem in the Arctic. The circumpolar countries developed a common understanding of the threats to the 'fragile' Arctic environment. Circumpolar countries set themselves a challenge to 'combat the common enemy' – the threats to the fragile environment in the North (Consultative Meeting on the Protection of the Arctic Environment 1989: 2). Two years of preparatory meetings initiated by the Finnish government led to a ministerial conference in 1991 in Rovaniemi, Finland. Here, a Declaration on the Protection of the Arctic Environment and an Action Programme, known as the Arctic Environmental Protection Strategy (AEPS), was agreed. The main aim of the strategy for Arctic co-operation was to 'identify, reduce and, as a final goal, eliminate pollution' (AEPS 1991: 4).

The states recognised their role as major actors in Arctic environmental co-operation. The responsibilities of the states was emphasised; 'It is evident and necessary to tighten up national measures: political, legal, technical, or others taken so far in nearly all environmental sectors'. Co-operation among Arctic states might further include 'accords on concrete measures' on most urgent problems such as the pollution of the sea, acidification, the accumulation of toxic chemicals, and radioactive contamination (Statement by the Finnish Delegation 1989: 2-3). No delegation suggested that the existing system of legal measures was adequate. The report of the consultative meeting concluded there were a number of areas of environmental protection that should more directly reflect the particular Arctic conditions. The existing legal instruments were seen as the basis for 'improved Arctic environmental protection through a strengthening and broader application' (Protecting the Arctic Environment 1990: 3).

Most of the participating states supported the idea of special legal measures to protect the environment in principle, but they wanted to avoid overlapping. The participants shared the view that much could be accomplished through existing conventions and agreements; a wide range of international treaties applicable to the Arctic region do exist (Statement by the Swedish Delegation 1989: 3-4). It was argued that the process of elaborating multilateral legal instruments could be 'arduous and time consuming.' The negotiation of a treaty or other legal instruments was not enough: 'The treaty must be brought into force and many well founded treaties take years to come into force because of the slow pace of the ratification process.' Moreover, it was not enough to ratify treaties. They have to be applied and implemented (Statement by the Canadian Delegation 1989: 4).

By 1991, the sense of the need for special measures in the Arctic region had largely been lost in the preparatory process. The countries aimed at a 'practical' and 'pragmatic' approach for the solutions to issues of 'common interest' (Statement by the Chair 1990: 2). The concrete measure taken by the states in 1991 was the establishment of four different working groups: the Arctic Monitoring and Assessment Program (AMAP), Conservation of Arctic Flora and Fauna (CAFF), the Protection of the Arctic Marine Environment (PAME) and Emergency

Prevention, Preparedness and Response (EPPR). These working groups have produced reports, guidelines and strategies. The ministers at the Alta meeting in 1997 concluded, after receiving the report of the AMAP on the state of the Arctic environment, that 'the Arctic, in comparison with most other areas of the world, remains a clean environment with large areas of unspoiled nature.' The ministers noted that 'in some parts of the Arctic severe pollution from local sources requires both national and international remedial action' (Alta Declaration on the Arctic Environmental Protection Strategy 1997).

The Arctic Committee of Parliamentarians has suggested that collective environmental security means to 'protect and defend the Arctic against environmental threats arising from outside the region and from unsustainable activities within the Arctic' (Second Conference of Parliamentarians of the Arctic Region Conference Statement 1996). One Arctic problem that cannot be solved by states in the region on their own is the problem of POPs (persistent organic pollutants). POPs are chemicals such as dioxin, PCBs, and DDT. These pollutants include chemicals that are used in industry and substances that are produced as the by-products of industrial processes. Some of them are designed to be toxic, such as pesticides. They remain in the environment for a long time. These chemicals can travel through air and water to regions very distant from their original sources. POPs can accumulate in organisms through the food chain and appear in food at levels of concern for human health. It is already known that POPs accumulate through long-range transport to the Arctic. According to information provided by the AMAP, all persistent organic pollutants have been found in the Arctic. Their levels are generally lower than in temperate climates. However, several substances have high levels of concentration and they are therefore expected to affect some animals (AMAP 1997: 91). No illnesses for which contaminants are known to be a direct cause have yet been reported in the Arctic but the most concerning is the situation of the Arctic indigenous peoples: 'Indigenous peoples who rely on traditional diets are likely to be more exposed to several toxic substances than the majority of people elsewhere in the world' (AMAP 1997: 172).

The concern over these pollutants is part of the Arctic Council Action Plan to Eliminate Pollution of the Arctic (ACAP). This action plan aims at strengthening and supporting national actions to reduce the problem in the Arctic region (See Report of Senior Arctic Officials to the Arctic Council 1998). Under the auspices of the Arctic Council, there is a project on POPs, food security and indigenous peoples to assess the significance of aquatic food chains as pathways to the exposure of indigenous peoples to POPs, to assess the relative importance of local and distant sources, as well as the role of the atmospheric and riverine transport of POPs in Northern Russia. Two other projects aim at identifying the major sources of PCB and the production, storage, use and waste sites within the Russian territories as well as establishing a monitoring station in Northern Russia to analyse samples of POPs (Arctic Council Activities 2000).

The AMAP report aims at developing some scientifically based criteria for the human intake of pollutants. The main criterion is human tolerance to the toxic effects of contaminants. However, analysing tolerance is not a simple task. The AMAP report talks about a 'tolerable daily intake' which includes 'safety factors' for humans. The safety factor is an attempt to account for the unknown: 'The greater the uncertainty in the toxicology, the larger the safety factor' (AMAP 1997: 173-74). Human health research is a sensitive issue for indigenous peoples. The dilemma is especially difficult in communities where traditional foods are vital to spiritual, cultural, and physical well-being. The Inuit view on the problem is: 'We are what we eat. Inuit eat Inuit foods. When I eat Inuit foods, I feel like myself again' (quoted in Huntington 1997). From the perspective of indigenous peoples, 'a new form of colonialism is created if there is no communication between scientists and indigenous peoples.' Unless there is communication between different groups, the production of knowledge on the problem of pollution is an 'affirmation of [the] existing power structure' (Petersen 1997).

The concern for AMAP is in 'balancing the information.' This means informing the population about the problem with its negative implications without causing too much panic. Giving 'balanced' information about the situation is considered a challenge. First, many factors contribute to health and illness: socio-economic conditions, health services, societal and cultural factors, individual lifestyles and behaviour, and genetics: 'Contaminants enter this already complex scene.' The variation in human exposure depends on varying environmental concentrations of contaminants, local physical and biological pathways, and the local dietary habits of people. Second, the fear of contaminants and changes in the traditional ways of life can affect both community social structure and individual well-being. The potential negative effects of contaminants on human health have to be balanced with the positive effects of consuming traditional foods. Traditional diets are high in animal foods and they are rich sources of protein and vitamins. Overall, traditional diets provide 'a strong nutritional base' for the health of the Arctic peoples. Market foods from outside the Arctic often have less protein and iron but more fat and carbohydrates. Moreover, changes in food habits follow the changes in the way of life that lead to a more sedentary life style. Therefore, a move away from traditional foods could contribute to poor health and increase the risk of diabetes and cardiovascular diseases (AMAP 1997: 172-74).

The politics of governmentality is one of bio-politics; the life of populations is an object of political and scientific concern. This type of medical discourse is part of the system of the administrative and political control of the population. From the point of view of governmentality, the administrative apparatuses of the states pose welfare in terms of people's needs and their happiness when determining the nature of 'balanced' information. Governmentality makes the population the focus of administering health and safety. Medical discourse and political practice are connected – not through the concepts, methods, and utterances of medicine but through the political practices that make a possible object for medical discourse (Foucault 1991b: 68). Indigenous peoples are also made the objects of interventions by state administrators. These practices of governmentality make the indigenous peoples objects of surveillance; tests and samples are made and medical information is collected among local populations. Individuals and groups are subjected and categorised by age, ethnic group, sex, disease and welfare regimes (Dreyfus and Rabinow 1982: 140).

Can the Climate in the North Be Securitised?

After two weeks of intensive negotiations at The Hague, the Netherlands, during November 2000, ministers and diplomats decided to suspend talks on making the Kyoto Protocol to stabilise the amount of greenhouse gases released in the atmosphere. The key political issues – including an international emissions trading system, a 'clean development mechanism,' rules for counting emissions reductions from carbon 'sinks' such as forests, and a compliance regime – could not be resolved in the time available. These talks may continue in late May 2001 in Bonn, Germany. Michael Zammit Cutajar, the Executive Secretary of the Climate Convention, emphasised that 'Global warming is one of the great challenges of the 21st century, and I trust that public reaction to our meeting here will inspire governments with the necessary sense of urgency to succeed at the next opportunity' (Press release 2000). The meeting in The Hague showed the lack of political will to make the Kyoto Protocol operational.

Despite the reminder by the representative of the Intergovernmental Panel on Climate Change at The Hague 'that the overwhelming majority of scientific experts, whilst recognising that scientific uncertainties exist, nonetheless believe that human-induced climate change is already occurring and that future change is inevitable,' negotiations were unsuccessful. According scientists, it is not a question of whether the Earth's climate will change, but rather by how much, how fast, and where. The two last decades have been the warmest this century, indeed the warmest for the last 1000 years. In addition, the sea level is rising, precipitation patterns are changing, Arctic sea ice is thinning, and the frequency and intensity of El Niño events appear to be increasing. In addition, many parts of the world have recently suffered extreme environmental events. Major heat waves, floods, droughts, and other extreme weather events have led to the significant loss of life and economic costs. The frequency and magnitude of such events are expected to increase in a warmer world. The representative concluded that 'if actions are not taken to reduce the projected increase in greenhouse gas emissions, the Earth's climate is likely to change at a rate unprecedented in the last 10,000 years with adverse consequences for society, undermining the very foundation of sustainable development. Hence, the welfare of this and future generations is in your hands' (Watson 2000).

The effort to securitise the climate at least in the Arctic is a challenge. First, in order to make the problem accountable in these states, one needs show the dynamics of interaction between global, regional and local changes. The problem is that in the scientific research of global ecology, the Earth is treated a single complex system. This approach to the global environment is made possible by the development of science and computers, which makes it possible to model the climate and through the development of the technology that allows us to monitor climate change. Planet Earth is seen as a system, 'a complex cybernetic machine' the dysfunction of which requires global management (Finger 1992: 14-17). The knowledge base of climate change and its impacts at regional and local level are incomplete and fragmented (Lange et al. 1999).

So far, the Arctic has been seen as part of the larger climatic system. Because of the feedback mechanism, the changes in the Arctic are 'globally' relevant: (1) The ocean currents dominated by the Arctic Ocean and the Nordic seas are responsible for as much as half of the Earth's heat transport to the poles and may also serve as a sink for CO_2. Alterations in this circulation may affect global climate and in particular the climate of Europe and North America, (2) The melting of the Arctic land ice sheets may cause the sea level to rise around the world, (3) Arctic soils can act as carbon sinks or sources of greenhouse gases depending on the temperature and moisture changes within the Arctic, and (4) positive feedback in higher latitudes may amplify human-induced climate change and disturbances in the circumpolar Arctic climate, which may 'substantially' influence the global climate (ACIA 2000a).

Thirdly, the natural scientists were looking for ways to make the problem relevant to society. According to the special report on the regional impacts of climate change by the Intergovernmental Panel on Climate Change (IPCC 1997), 'the projected warming in the polar regions is greater than for many other regions of the world.' Major physical and ecological changes are expected in the Arctic, especially with respect to the thawing of ice, sea ice, and the melting of snow leading to substantial changes in hydrological conditions. In the context of Barents Sea region, scientists have stressed the need to integrate the study of the natural sciences with large socio-economic studies. For example, the assessment of the changes in the water balance, in water resources, and in the ecology of freshwater and estuarine waters as a consequence of global climate change is highly relevant for the evaluation of economic and social development in the Barents Sea region. Assessing impacts is a complicated matter: (1) when considering social dynamics and processes, it is important to distinguish the dynamics of local and regional processes from the impacts of 'external' global changes and (2) natural systems and social systems have different characters and dynamics. Both traditional and modern cultures have their own kinds of sensitivity and vulnerability, although all are vulnerable in varying ways to the impacts of global changes and other adverse factors to public health (Lange et al. 1999).

Natural scientists tackle with the problem of how to frame the problem in order to promote action instead of endless political rhetoric. In order to attract attention to the changes in the North, the workshop for the Arctic Climate Impact Assessment (ACIA) concluded that 'The ministers will want to hear about direct effects on humans. So we did what was most needed' (ACIA 2000b). The problem is that the impacts of climate change are in many respects positive at least from a human-centred perspective. The impacts of climate change are related to the possible small northern extension of farming into the Arctic, the chances of increased marine ecological productivity and the increased possibilities for coastal and river navigation with new opportunities for water transport, mineral extraction, tourism and trade (see IPCC 1997). Possibly, other values might be lost as a consequence of the changes ahead. According to Claes Bernes, the ultimate question in the Arctic in relation to climate change is the threat of losing something unique in the extreme and fragile Arctic environment (Bernes 1996).

In the second case (that of the threat of climate change), the question is of how knowledge is framed and for what purpose. Foucault (1972: 185) separates 'savoir' and 'connaissance' as two different forms of knowledge. The scientific knowledge (connaissance) of environmental problems plays a role in the knowledge (savoir) of environmental management and protection (a question of decision-making authority). Concentrating on this constitutive aspect of knowledge, the subject and the object and the knowledge about them, is mutually constitutive. It is through these constitutive meanings that people talk and act. The knowledge-broker who interprets and frames knowledge for policy-makers has power in respect to 'how knowledge is framed, by whom and on behalf of what interests' (Litfin 1994: 198). Making climate change a security problem and the efforts to securitise it is a challenge not only for natural scientists but also for social scientists. The most obvious way to this is to argue the significance of the expected changes to the cultures and livelihoods of indigenous peoples. Knowledge and its framing on climate change and its impacts in the Arctic are not only regionally relevant, but possibly globally important. Among the Arctic states there are developed industrial states, including two main greenhouse gas producers – the USA and Russia. Some of the Arctic states (namely Denmark, Sweden, and Finland) belong to the European Union which has adopted a central role in the climate negotiations.

Securitised 'Hard'

The problem of radioactive contamination from Russian sources is, according to the AMAP report, 'currently only of minor importance in relation to health risks with radioactivity in the Arctic.' Local sources of radionuclides such as dumped nuclear waste, nuclear storage sites, accidents, and past explosions, have led to local radioactive contamination in the Arctic. Several radioactive sources exist in northwestern Russia: spent nuclear fuel stores, decommissioned nuclear submarines, nuclear reactors on land and onboard ships, and contained sources in the environment. They are 'a potential' for the release of considerable quantities of radionuclides (AMAP 1997: viii).

However, in the North European context politically, radioactive contamination is considered as 'a major risk along the whole eastern border of the EU,' according to the Finnish initiative for a Northern Dimension of the European Union (Lipponen 1998: 9). In the Inventory made by the European Commission on the Northern Dimension (1999: 16), the problems associated with radioactive wastes in Northwestern Russia 'are acute, and a cause for widespread concern, particularly in the neighbouring countries.' According to the Action Plan for the Northern Dimension, which was accepted by the European Council at Santa Maria da Feira in June last year, the present level of safety at nuclear plants, the absence of adequate storage facilities, and the treatment of radioactive waste and irradiate nuclear fuels are of 'major concern' to public health, the environment, and sustainable development in the region (Action Plan for the Northern Dimension 2000: 2).

The Finnish initiative for a Northern Dimension of the European Union aims to tackle this problem. The 'practical' measures proposed include enabling the decommissioning of nuclear plants through securing substitute sources of energy and finding other uses for existing nuclear power related infrastructure, and the arrangement of the safe management of radioactive wastes in the Kola peninsula. The problem of nuclear safety requires 'additional funding' from the European Union (Lipponen 1998: 3). Advancing stability in the region requires 'new decisions' to reduce environmental threats, including those from military-related nuclear waste (Lipponen 1998: 2). Such demands seem vulnerable in changing political conditions. For example, on April 6, 2000 the Council of Europe recommended suspending Russian assistance unless it called a cease-fire in Chechnya. The recommendation cast some doubt over the future of multilateral scientific projects financed by the European Union (Russian Environmental Digest 2000a). However, as such this idea of assistance to Russia is nothing new: from 1990 to 1997, the European Union distributed 355 million ecu for nuclear safety programmes. Auditors said this year it was 'not possible to quantify the scale of these programmes or how far they had been implemented' (Russian Environmental Digest 2000b).

The Action Plan (2000: 1) calls for the active involvement of the Russian Federation in the development of the idea through different existing fora of co-operation. The Soviet approach to security in the late 1980's was positive towards thinking about environmental concerns in a broader and more collective sense. This Soviet attitude towards co-operation on environmental concerns made it possible to start Arctic co-operation. In 1987, Soviet president Mikhail Gorbachev suggested co-operation in the exploitation of northern natural resources and the development of a comprehensive plan for the protection of the Arctic environment. In the late 1980's, the Russians were the first to see the new possibilities in the Arctic:

'The Arctic is a region which just a few years ago was seen mainly in the light of military and political interests, a region where many requirements for co-operation in civilian projects were put aside, left of the curb of the 'highway' of international co-operation' (Address of the Soviet Representative 1989: 1).

According to the Russian representative, 'one cannot say that military and political problems in the Arctic have been resolved, they are very palpable.' However, the situation made new political thinking possible – even in the Arctic. It is 'perestroika that gave the chance to achieve a qualitative change in politics, public attitude in the very atmosphere surrounding environmental protection problems.' According to the Russian perspective, the 'Arctic region provided and provides a lot for our country.' The Russian representative emphasised the concern for the situation in the Arctic; 'its clear tendency to deteriorate is a cause for anxiety' (Address of the Soviet Representative 1989: 1-2).

This attitude changed considerably during the 1990's. 'We worry about Putin's attitude to the environment,' says Alexei Yablokov, a biologist and a former environmental adviser to President Yeltsin. 'It's early in his term, but his actions have been "disturbing".' First, some concerns have been raised about the decision by the President Putin to abolish the state environmental committee in Russia. This has led to the criticism that he has 'turned his back on Post-Soviet Russia's bulging inventory of pollution disasters.' The argument for ending the agency is to cut costs and combat bureaucracy. Critics say that transferring the agency's jurisdiction to the Natural Resources Ministry, which helps business exploit the environment, is 'ludicrous.' 'The Ministry of Natural Resources was created to exploit nature,' says Yablokov, 'and the environment committee was created to protect it. It's an obvious conflict of interest for the ministry to be given both jobs' (Russian Environmental Digest 2000c).

Second, according to the information of the state environment committee, some 61 million out of 145 million Russians live in towns with dangerous levels of contamination. Despite this, the Atomic Energy Ministry (MINATOM) proposes to generate cash from storing and reprocessing up to 20,000 tonnes of spent nuclear fuel from reactors in as many as 14 countries in Asia and Europe. MINATOM predicted a profit of $10 billion a year from the plan. In order to fulfil the plan the government has to change the legislation that currently prevents nuclear waste imports. A MINATOM spokesperson stressed that 'We see it as an extremely valuable energy product which can be reprocessed. This is done in Japan, China, Britain, and France. I think parliament will be in favour of allowing Russia to enter the world market. It's a tremendous lever for the economy' (Russian Environmental Digest 2000c). A positive decision to change the law was made at the parliament at the end of the year.

To stop the new law permitting the import of nuclear waste, the environmentalists decided to use a 1995 law in an attempt to force the government to consult the public. They managed to collect 3 million names around the country. In the light of MINATOM's determination and the government's seeming support, spokesperson of the World Wildlife Fund doubted the prospects for a referendum. However, the petition is seen as a milestone nonetheless for the green activism: 'I would say this will not disappear. We now have a totally different Green movement than we had three or four months ago,' he says. At the very least, the call for a referendum has generated public attention. (Russian Environmental Digest 2000c.)

In the third case, the Foucaultian warning of 'nothing is an evil in itself, but everything is dangerous' (quoted in Gordon 1991: 46) should be kept in mind when discussing the efforts to securitise the environment. Russian 'irrationality' makes sense, claims Igor Leshukov from the Centre for Integration Research and Programmes in St Petersburg in his study of the relationships between the European Union and Russia. The nuclear business is a way to make money – both in terms of receiving financial assistance as well as in terms of making money in the nuclear waste business. It makes sense for Russia to behave as she does in relation to the European Union. Leshukov defines the issue of nuclear safety as 'the most tricky part' of Russian-Western co-operation in Northern Europe. Nuclear safety is 'a big and non-transparent business, both in Russia and the West,' therefore it is extremely difficult to provide for efficient public control and good management. Overall, the EU-Russia relationship is a vicious circle (Leshukov 2000.)

The Northern Dimension is a European Union project to undertake more control and responsibility for nuclear safety in Northern Europe. This is one area in which 'soft security' is mixed with the considerations of 'hard security' (Leshukov 2000). It is no wonder that the issue of nuclear safety has not been solved after so many years of attention and co-operation. The challenge is, as Timothy Luke (2000) claims, 'the poverty of practicality leads to little technicalities', that is, avoidance of meta-level discussions among political decision-makers dealing with the complexities of Russian-European Union relations. The easy way out is to put the blame on the environmentalists, who are categorised as 'spies,' 'conspirators' and 'traitors.' There is the well-known case of an environmental activist against the Federal Security Service in Russia. Nikitin was arrested by the Federal Security Service in 1996 on charges of high treason and the disclosure of state secrets while writing a report for the Norwegian environmental protection organisation Bellona about the potential risks of the radioactive contamination of the northwestern region. Finally, after three years of investigation, Nikitin was acquitted by a court (Russian Environmental Digest 2000d). The Nikitin case is not an isolated case of pressuring environmental activists and organisations. President Putin, a former director of the Russian security police, has called environmentalists foreign spies. Many Russian groups and individuals have been accused of espionage for their work against radioactive contamination and for their support of nuclear safety (Russian Environmental Digest 2000e).

Northern Environmental Threats and the Governmentality of Environmental Security

Securitising the environment justifies interventions in different spheres of the lives of peoples and groups. The study of governmentality tackles questions such as who can govern, what governing is, and what or who is governed. It means making some of activity thinkable and practicable both to its practitioners and to those upon who it is practised (Gordon 1991: 3). The three cases show different approaches to securitising environmental concerns and making spaces for governmental interventions. The first case shows the importance of the exchange of information between government officials, scientists, and indigenous peoples' groups. It has been important in forwarding the message of the impacts of the global problem of POPs locally within the Arctic. In this case, the efforts to securitise the well-being and health of indigenous peoples in the Arctic have lead to a positive outcome internationally – a global agreement to tackle the POPs has been signed. Last year, international negotiations under the auspices of the UN Environmental Programme (UNEP) produced a legally binding agreement to eliminate the twelve worst POPs. As part of the international effort, the Global Environmental Facility (GEF) will fund a two-year assessment of these pollutants in different part of the world (UNEP 2000). The second case shows that some problems cannot be securitised – or they can, but with a great difficulty. The concern over the future of the northern climate has created some interest among the northern states to solve the problem. It is difficult to securitise the future of the Arctic nature. The scientists tackle with framing the problem in a socially and politically relevant way in order to convince political decision-makers of the need for action. The impacts of climate change for human communities are 'officially' evaluated to be positive in the Arctic in terms of increasing the opportunities for travel, tourism, and exploration of natural resources, which makes it difficult to engage the interests of political decision-makers. Finally, there is no point in constructing all problems as security problems, not even as 'soft' security problems. The case of nuclear safety in the European Arctic shows (ir)rationalities on both sides. It also shows the efforts to securitise the North European environment with a mixture of hard and soft security concerns, with less hope of a quick solution. The quickest solution is to blame the environmentalists.

References

ACIA (2000a). Arctic Climate Impact Assessment Motivation. 5.5.2000.

ACIA (2000b). Report of a meeting and workshop to plan a study of the impacts of climate change on Arctic regions, 28 February – 1 March, 2000, Washington, DC, USA. pages/background.html#scoping 4.12.2000.

Action Plan for Northern Dimension with External and Cross-border Policies of the European Union 2000-2003 (2000). European Council, Santa Maria da Feira, Portugal. Press release 9401/00, 14.6.2000.

Address of the Soviet Representative (Unofficial translation) (1989), in *Consultative Meeting on the Protection of the Arctic Environment*, Annex II:1-12 and Annex III:1-25 of the Final Report, Rovaniemi, Finland, September 20-26, 989, Helsinki.

AEPS (1991). *Arctic Environmental Protection Strategy.* Rovaniemi, Finland.

Alta Declaration on the Arctic Environmental Protection Strategy (1997). Alta, Norway, June 12-13, 1997. 26.8.1999.

AMAP (1997). *Arctic Pollution Issues: A State of the Arctic Environment Report.* Oslo, AMAP.

Arctic Council Activities (2000). March 2000. http://www.arctic-council.org/ac_projects.asp

3.4.2001.

Bernes, C. (1996). *Valoa ja kaamosta. Arktinen ympäristö pohjoismaissa.* NORD 1996:24. Kööpenhamina, Pohjoismainen ministerineuvosto.

Consultative Meeting on the Protection of the Arctic Environment (1989). Report and Annex 1:1-7, Rovaniemi, Finland, September 20-26, 1989, Helsinki.

Darier, É. (1999). 'Foucault and the Environment: An Introduction,' in Darier, É (ed.). *Discourses of the Environment.* Oxford, Blackwell.

Dreyfus, H.L. and Rabinow, P. (1982). *Michel Foucault. Beyond Structuralism and Hermeneutics.* Chicago, The University of Chicago Press.

European Commission (1999). *A Northern Dimension for the Policies of the Union: An Inventory of Current Activities.*

Finger, M. (1992). 'New Horizons for Peace Research: Global Environment,' in Käkönen, J. (ed.). *Perspectives on Environmental Security.* Aldershot, Ashgate.

Foucault, M. (1972). *Archaeology of Knowledge.* London, Tavistock Publications.

Foucault, M. (1991a). 'Governmentality,' in Burchell, G., Gordon, C. and Miller, P. (eds). *The Foucault Effect. Studies in Governmentality, With two Lectures by and an interview with Michel Foucault.* Chicago, The University of Chicago Press.

Foucault, M. (1991b). 'Politics and the Study of Discourse,' in Burchell, G., Gordon, C. and Miller, P. (eds). *The Foucault Effect. Studies in Governmentality. With two Lectures by and an interview with Michel Foucault.* Chicago, The University of Chicago Press.

Gordon, C. (1991). 'Governmental Rationality: An Introduction', in Burchell, G., Gordon, C. and Miller, P. (eds). *The Foucault Effect. Studies in Governmentality. With two Lectures by and an interview with Michel Foucault.* Chicago, The University of Chicago Press.

Huntington, H. (1997). *Presentation at the Conference on Environmental Pollution in the Arctic.* Tromsø, Norway, June 4, 1997.

IPCC (1997). *The Regional Impacts of Climate Change: An Assessment of Vulnerability.* A Special Report of IPCC Working group II, Watson, R.T., Zinyowera, M.C. and Moss, R.M. (eds). Summary for Policymakers. http://www.ipcc.ch/pub/reports.htm 4.12.2000.

Lange, M.A., Bartling, B. and Grosfeld, K. (eds) (1999). *Global changes and the Barents Sea region.* Proceedings of the First International BASIS Research Conference St Petersburg, Russia, 22-25 February, 1998. Institute for Geophysics, University of Münster.

Leshukov, I. (2000). *Can the Northern Dimension Break the Vicious Circle of EU-Russia Relations?* A paper presented at a research seminar on the Northern Dimension, Finnish Institute of International Affairs, 24-26 August 2000.

Lipponen, P. (1998). *'The Northern Dimension.'* Letter to President Jacques Santer, European Commission, Brussels. Helsinki 18 February 1998.

Litfin, K. (1994). *Ozone Discourses. Science and Politics in Global Environmental Cooperation.* New York, Columbia University Press.

Luke, T. (2000*). Presentation at the Environmental Social Science Conference*, University of Tampere 23-24 November 2000.

Petersen, T. (1997). *Presentation at the Conference on Environmental Pollution in the Arctic.* Tromsø, Norway, June 4, 1997.

Press Release (2000). Climate change talks suspended. Negotiations to resume during 2001. 25.11.2000.

Protecting the Arctic Environment (1990). Report on the Yellowknife Preparatory Meeting. Yellowknife, NWT, Canada, April 18-23, 1990, Ottawa.

Report of Senior Arctic Officials to the Arctic Council (1998). Iqaluit, Canada, September 17-18, 1998. 6.7.1999.

Russian Environmental Digest (2000a). 3-9 April 2000, vol. 2 no. 14.

Russian Environmental Digest (2000b). 15-21 May 2000, vol. 2, no. 20.

Russian Environmental Digest (2000c). 20-26 November, 2000, vol. 2, no. 47.

Russian Environmental Digest (2000d). 27 March-2 April 2000, vol. 2, no. 13.

Russian Environmental Digest (2000e). 29 May-4 June, 2000, vol. 2, no. 22.

Second Conference of Parliamentarians of the Arctic Region (1996). *Conference Statement.* Yellowknife, Canada, March 14, 1996. index.htm, 26.8.1999.

Simons, J. (1995). *Foucault & the Political.* London and New York, Routledge.

Statement by the Canadian Delegation (1989). In *Consultative Meeting on the Protection of the Arctic Environment.* Annex II:1-12 and Annex III:1-25 of the Final Report, Rovaniemi, Finland, September 20-26, 1989. Helsinki.

Statement by the Chair (1990). In *Protecting the Arctic Environment. Report on the Yellowknife Preparatory Meeting.* Annex II:5, Yellowknife, NWT, Canada, April 18-23, 1990. Ottawa.

Statement by the Finnish Delegation (1989). In *Consultative Meeting on the Protection of the Arctic Environment.* Annex II:1-12 and Annex III:1-25 of the Final Report, Rovaniemi, Finland, September 20-26, 1989. Helsinki.

Statement by the Swedish Delegation (1989): In *Consultative Meeting on the Protection of the Arctic Environment.* Annex II:1-12 and Annex III:1-25 of the Final Report, Rovaniemi, Finland, September 20-26, 1989. Helsinki.

UNEP (2000). *UNEP Chemicals Undertakes US$ 5 Million project Funded by Global Environment Facility to Assess Persistent Toxic Substances Regionally.* 22 August 2000
http://irptc.unep.ch/pops/POPs_Inc/press-releases/pressrel-2k/praug22.htm 22.11.2000.

Watson, R.T. (2000). *Presentation at the Sixth Conference of Parties to the United Nations Framework Convention on Climate Change.* The Hague, Netherlands, November 13, 2000. 4.12.2000.

North European and Baltic Statistics

Compiled by Jüri Köll,
Statistics Sweden, International Consulting Office

Introduction

Jörg Neubauer

In previous issues of the NEBI Yearbook a broad picture has been traced of the substantial changes the NEBI area has undergone since the fall of the Iron Curtain. The dynamics and the general trends in population, economic integration, employment/unemployment, consumption, trade and foreign direct investment have been illustrated.

Recent events include Russia's financial crisis in August 1998 that affected numerous economies, not only those of the NEBI area. The first period of structural funding for cohesion (1995-99) is over, and a new period (2000-2006) has started. EU membership for Poland and the Baltic States is being negotiated and, not least due to participation in structural funding of the EU member states, important progress has been achieved. Privatisation in the eastern economies proceeds. The Scandinavian countries' decision to join Schengen will also affect the area.

This introduction to the Statistical Section focuses on topics of population (urbanisation, natural population decline, life expectancy), economy (concentration of economic activities) and energy (production, consumption, environment, distribution network). The spatial focus lies in the eastern NEBI area.

The data have been extracted from the statistical country/region tables in the annex. To support the findings and to place them in a wider context or to give them additional focus corresponding figures for the 15 EU member states or regional figures have been used. For more information the reader is referred to the individual country/region tables.[1]

NEBI Basics

The NEBI area covers the northern and eastern European mainland around the Baltic Sea and borders on the Barents Sea, the North Atlantic Ocean as well as the North Sea.

The region (Map 1) consists of the four Nordic countries: Denmark, Norway, Sweden and Finland; the three Baltic States: Estonia, Latvia and Lithuania; the six Russian regions of Arkhangelsk Oblast (including the Nenets autonomous area), Murmansk Oblast, the Republic of Karelia, Leningrad Oblast, the city of St Petersburg and Kaliningrad Oblast, the three coastal regions of Poland (Pomorskie, Warminsko-Mazurskie and Zachodnio-Pomorskie) as well as the three German länder of Mecklenburg-Vorpommern, Schleswig-Holstein and Hamburg. All in all this makes ten different countries or parts thereof, in which as many major languages are spoken. A majority of the population adheres to either the Catholic (Poland, Lithuania), Lutheran (northern Germany, the Nordic countries, Estonia, Latvia) or Orthodox faith (Russia) and the forms of government include three parliamentary kingdoms (Denmark, Norway, Sweden), two federal states (Germany, Russia) and five republics (Finland, Estonia, Latvia, Lithuania and Poland).

Four of the countries (Germany, Denmark, Sweden and Finland) are members of the European Union and four countries (Estonia, Latvia, Lithuania and Poland) have already commenced membership negotiations with the Commission. As a member of the EEA, Norway is also closely linked with the EU. Five countries (Denmark, Finland, Germany, Norway and Sweden) are members of the Schengen Convention. Citizens of these countries are permitted to cross borders of the Schengen member countries without passport controls.

The reorganisation of the Polish voivodships (from 49, of which ten were NEBI regions, to a 16, of which three are NEBI regions) has hardly altered the overall figures of the NEBI area. According to the new definition, the area is inhabited by 53.6 million people, slightly less than before (55 million). The decline results from 1.6 million less inhabitants from Poland and from a shrinking population in northwestern Russia, St Petersburg and Latvia. The NEBI population includes 23.9 million (44 per cent) Nordic inhabitants, 10.5 million (20 per cent) Russians, 7.6 million (14 per cent) Balts, 6.3 million (12 per cent) Germans and 5.4 million (10 per cent) Poles. The three Polish voivodships include between 1.5 million (Warminsko-Mazurskie) and 2.2 million (Pomorskie).

The NEBI population lives in an area of some 2.44 million km^2 or three-quarters of the total area of the EU15 (or roughly the size of the European Union excluding the three Nordic member states). Hence the average population density of the area is low, only 22 inhabitants/km^2, as compared with 116 inhabitants/km^2 in EU15. Higher densities can naturally be found in large city regions. However, overall the NEBI area is a region of the sparsely populated periphery.

Map 1: The North European and Baltic Sea area

Regions in Germany

1. Hamburg
2. Schleswig-Holstein
3. Mecklenburg-Vorpommern

Regions in Poland

4. Zachodnio-Pomorskie
5. Pomorskie
6. Warminsko-Mazurskie

Murmansk

Karelia   Arkhangelsk

FINLAND

NORWAY

SWEDEN   Åland

Leningrad
St Petersburg city

RUSSIAN
FEDERATI

ESTONIA

DENMARK

LATVIA

LITHUANIA

3   4   5   6

1

GERMANY   POLAND

Created by Statistics Sweden M

Population

The inhabitants of the NEBI area are unevenly distributed. The northernmost regions of Arkhangelsk, Murmansk and Karelia in Russia, Lapland in Finland, Norrbotten in Sweden and Finnmark, Troms and Nordland in Norway cover one-half of the NEBI area but contain less than 8 per cent of its population. The inhabitants tend to concentrate in the southern parts and along coastal zones. However, there are large cities, all of them situated at the coastline – Hamburg is

an exception – whereof the ten largest already host one-fourth of total NEBI population (Figure 1). Accordingly the urban systems are oriented towards the Baltic
Sea. Although differing from country to country the second biggest cities are not
even half the size of the capital. Lithuania makes an exception. St Petersburg (4.2
million) alone comprises around 50 per cent of the population of the six Russian
NEBI regions. Latvia's capital, Riga (0.8 million) comprises 41 per cent of the

Figure 1: Size distribution of NEBI cities > 10,000 inhabitants

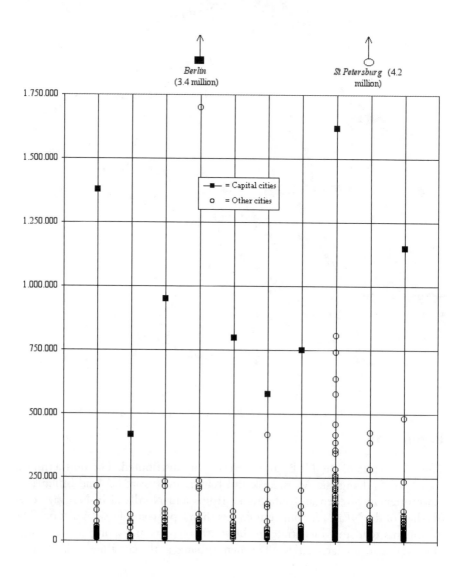

country's population. Estonia (Tallinn) and Denmark (Copenhagen) are also clearly dominated by their capital towns. Each of the NEBI countries or constituents has one or more cities with approximately half a million or more inhabitants. In the northern part of the area (e.g., Norway, Sweden and Finland) the population tends to live in smaller cities (10,000-100,000 inhabitants), which is also the case in Poland.

Urbanisation

During the second half of the 20th century, there has been a continuous urbanisation process in all NEBI countries. The intensity of urbanisation has varied from country to country. Poland reached a significant peak already in the 1950s and a smaller one in the early 1970s. Finland and Norway experienced rapid urbanisation during the 1960s and early 1970s as did Lithuania, though on a smaller scale. During the 1990s urbanisation nearly reached a standstill in Denmark and Sweden. After 1989 in most of the eastern NEBI countries, almost continuous urbanisation has been replaced by a decline in the urban population of large cities. Map 2 shows the result of the urbanisation process in 1998.

The general rate of urbanisation in the western NEBI countries is higher than in the eastern NEBI countries. The share of rural population is accordingly higher in the east than in the west. Naturally all capital regions are highly urbanised. However, also inhabitants of the most sparsely populated regions in Norway, Sweden, Finland and Russia predominately live in urban areas. Other highly urbanised areas are the Finnish triangle Helsinki-Tampere-Turku; the area between Stockholm, Gothenburg and Oslo, the Øresund region and the eastern coast of the Danish mainland. At country level the share of urban population varies from 62 per cent in Poland to 85 per cent in Denmark and the NEBI parts of Germany and Russia. Finland and Sweden are slightly less urbanised than Denmark but clearly more than the NEBI area on average and above the EU average (80 per cent).

Variations are particularly significant at the regional level. In the regions of Norrbotten (Sweden) and Murmansk (Russia) less than 20 per cent reside outside cities.[2] By contrast, rather less urbanised regions can be found in Estonia, Latvia and Poland. Lithuania is more balanced in its urbanisation. In Estonia and Latvia the disparities between adjacent regions are huge. Just south of Riga, in the Bauska region, only one fifth of the population lives in cities. In other regions, e.g. Gulbene and Cesu in Latvia and Põlvamaa and Jõgevamaa in Estonia, around one third of the population lives in urban areas. The phenomenon of highly urbanised regions neighbouring less urbanised ones is also evident in the southwestern parts of Poland.

With almost 39 million inhabitants (1999) Poland is unique regarding the distribution of urban and rural areas. Although Poland has a very high average population density, most citizens live in rural areas. This pattern is more pronounced in the southern part of the country but is also visible in the three NEBI regions along the coast. In addition nearly half of all urban Poles (in cities >10,000 inhab-

Map 2: Urbanisation rate in 1998

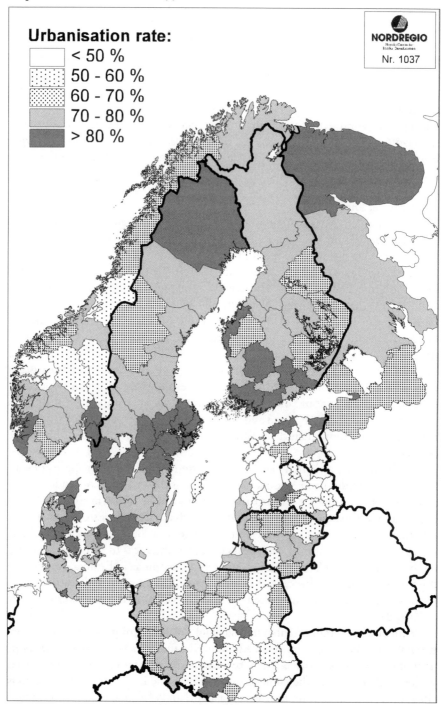

itants) live in smaller cities sized between 10,000 and 100,000 inhabitants.

Concerning the EU accession, two spatial characteristics of Poland and the Baltic States have to be taken into account. Firstly, rural areas have large populations, especially in Poland. Secondly, the urban system encompasses numerous middle-sized cities and few larger ones. These characteristics describe the situation in almost any Central and East European country. For the EU25 case the World Bank has calculated that the European Union will grow by 33 per cent in area and by 28 per cent in population. The rural population is expected to increase by 49 per cent; the urban population by only 23 per cent.

Population Dynamics

The trend towards a growing population in the Nordic countries, Germany and Poland and a decreasing population in the Baltic States and Russia continued in 1999 (Figure 2).

The year 1999 was dramatic for all six Russian NEBI regions. Without exception, total population significantly decreased. Although net migration was slightly positive in some regions (Kaliningrad, Leningrad region, Karelia, St Petersburg), it could not make up for the enormous natural population decrease. Kaliningrad is the only Russian NEBI region to experience population growth every year during the 1990s due to large immigration. However, the 1999 population decline in Kaliningrad may indicate a reversed trend. Murmansk and Arkhangelsk had again been hardest hit with a decline of more than 1 per cent (1.5 per cent and 1.2 per cent) during one year. No other NEBI region has seen so many people emigrating as has Murmansk region, which has lost the equivalent of a middle-sized town like of Tartu or Uppsala during the last decade.

The rapid population decrease in Estonia and Latvia continued in 1999 although the trend slowed down a bit. The population of Lithuania decreased only modestly as during previous years. A negative natural change is still the major factor behind population decrease in the Baltic States and is most evident in Latvia. During the spring of 2000 a census was carried out in the Baltic States. Since population registration procedures in migration and residence changes are lacking, the results of the census are expected to complete uncertain population statistics.

The population of Norway grew even faster than in 1998 due to high positive net migration and birth rates. The populations of the other Scandinavian countries also increased but less rapidly than in Norway. The Swedish population change was slightly positive. The increase was largely due to an influx of foreigners as the natural change was even more negative in 1999 than in 1998.

In Germany the population of Schleswig-Holstein increased the most. The region is among the fastest growing parts of the NEBI area. Hamburg also enjoyed a positive trend in 1999. Mecklenburg-Vorpommern continued to experience a population decline of 0.5 per cent. Here, birth rates continued to decline and net migration remained negative because of the out-migration of mainly young people to Schleswig-Holstein and Hamburg. Since 1989 Mecklenburg-Vorpommern has lost approximately 10 per cent of its population, a falling trend

Figure 2: Population change in the NEBI area 1992-99, index 1992=100

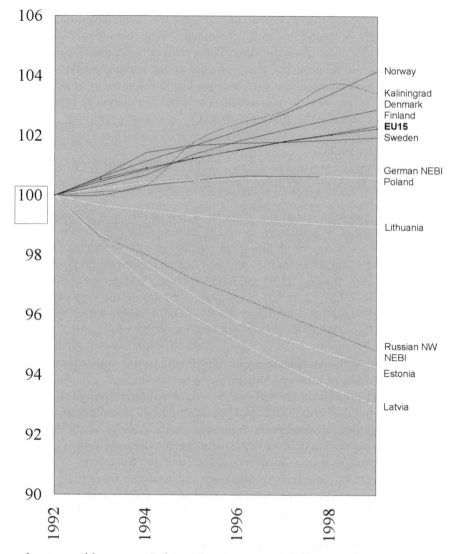

only comparable to some Baltic or Russian regions. Effects on the infrastructure are already evident in the shape of over/under-capacities in the health service system, a decreasing demand for kindergartens or a lack of pupil for schools.

In the new Polish regions there has been a positive population development as in Poland in general. Based on the population they would have had in 1995, every region experienced an increase of between ten and twenty thousand inhabitants. The trend is basically caused by positive natural change.

However, the general trend towards negative natural change in several NEBI regions, not only in those located in the eastern part, is about to cause substantial changes to the whole NEBI society. Already now the scarcity of children and great numbers of elderly people necessitate a different infrastructure to be financed by rapidly diminishing labour force. This, of course, will encourage regions to compete for population and labour. As a result regional disparities may widen.

Life Expectancy – Russian Men Expected to Die at Working Age
Life expectancy at birth indicates contemporary living standards and economic prosperity but also corresponds to the availability of social infrastructure. A big divide between East and West can be found throughout the NEBI area. In general, inhabitants of the highly developed countries (Nordic countries and Germany) are estimated to live the longest followed by Poles, who are expected to live a little bit longer than Balts. Russians live the shortest. Normally women can expect to live longer life than men. Between 1992 and 1999 life expectancy in the NEBI area varied for males from age 55 (Russia 1994/95) to 77 (Sweden 1999) and for women from age 69 (Russia 1994) to 82 (Sweden 1999).

In 1999 women from the western NEBI area were expected to reach an average age of 80, thus living six years longer than men. Women from the eastern NEBI area were supposed to live until 74 years on average, which is twelve years

Table 1: Population and migration in the NEBI area, 1993-99

	Population 1999 in million	Net migration 1999	Net migration 1993-1999[1]	Total change * 1999	Total change * 1993-1999[1]
		% of base population		% of base population	
Archangelsk	1.46	-0.6%	-2.8%	-1.2%	-6.7%
Kaliningrad	0.95	0.4%	8.7%	-0.3%	4.8%
Leningrad region	1.67	0.7%	7.2%	-0.4%	0,0%
Murmansk	1,00	-1.3%	-9.7%	-1.5%	-11.2%
Republic of Karelia	0.77	0,0%	0.5%	-0.7%	-4,0%
St Petersburg	4.66	0.2%	0.8%	-0.7%	-5.2%
Estonia	1.45	0,0%	-2.6%	-0.4%	-5.6%
Latvia	2.42	-0.1%	-2.9%	-0.6%	-7,0%
Lithuania	3.70	0,0%	-0.4%	-0.1%	-1,0%
Pomorskie	2.19	0,0%	-0.1%	0.2%	0.4%
Warminsko-Mazurskie	1.47	0,0%	-0.1%	0.2%	0.5%
Zachodnio-Pomorskie	1.73	0,0%	0,0%	0.1%	0.2%
Hamburg	1.70	0.4%	2.4%	0.3%	0.9%
Mecklenburg-Vorpommern	1.79	-0.2%	-0.8%	-0.5%	-3.7%
Schleswig-Holstein	2.78	0.5%	4.3%	0.4%	3.6%
Denmark	5.33	0.2%	1.9%	0.3%	2.8%
Finland	5.17	0.1%	0.5%	0.2%	2.2%
Norway	4.48	0.4%	1.8%	0.8%	4.2%
Sweden	8.86	0.2%	1.5%	0.1%	2.0%
Åland	0.03	0.4%	1.1%	0.3%	2.4%

* Total change is calculated as the sum of net migration and natural in-/decrease
[1] Pomorskie, Warminsko-Mazurskie and Zachodnio-Pomorskie 1998-99

longer than men. Hence there is a far bigger gap in life expectancy between East and West for men than for women. Life expectancy fluctuated during the first half of the 90s, especially for Russian men (around 8 per cent) though economic recovery in Russia and the Baltic States made it rise again in 1995. While Poles and Balts continue to increase life expectancies by systematically restructuring their society, life expectancy in Russian NEBI regions fell dramatically after the 1998 financial crisis. Note that Russia remains one of the countries reporting to the World Health Organisation with a rather low life expectancy and a huge gender gap (62 years for men and 73 for women).

The reasons are seen in the collapse of the Russian health-care system and declining living economic standards. However, a newly published study on health in Russia (March 24, 2001 issue of *The Lancet*) points to alcoholism, homelessness and unemployment as major factors. One crucial theme is the link between alcohol and mortality rate. A large number of deaths of people between 25 and 60 years of age have been related to alcoholism. Among young adults age 15-25 a leading cause of death is violence during alcohol intoxication. While men in the western NEBI countries usually die of chronic diseases, Russian men die of alcohol poisoning, accidents and infectious diseases. As a result an average Russian male of the NEBI area is expected to die at 59 years when still of working age. The

Figure 3: Development in life expectancy of men in the eastern NEBI area, 1992-99

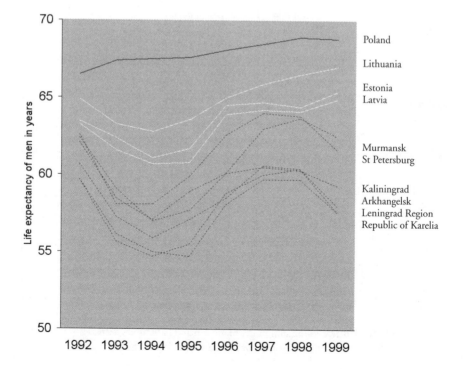

current situation is slightly better for inhabitants of the Murmansk region (men 62.5 years) and even St Petersburg (men 61.6 years) whereas inhabitants of Karelia are expected to live the shortest (men 57.6 years), which means that life expectancy for Karelian males is the same as that of Asian males from Bangladesh or India. There has been no comparable change in female life expectancy – 72 years (1999) — in Russian NEBI regions. The life expectancy of Russian men, however, started to slide long before the disintegration of the USSR.

The three Baltic States are quite similar in terms of life expectancy. Estonia, Latvia and Lithuania were doing better than Russia though following the same trend until 1998. This may be due to the strong connections to the Russian economy and system. However, since 1994 growth rates in all three Baltic economies have been among the highest in Europe supporting a longer life. Moreover, health has improved. Baltic men now live 66 years and Baltic women 77 years on average (1999), only three years less than western women. By comparison with Russia the gender gap appears smaller but is still huge. Lithuanian men and women live slightly longer than Estonians and Latvians. Obviously Lithuanians have been less affected by the post-Soviet changes as their trend lines show the smallest variation.

In contrast, life expectancy in Poland has risen continuously since 1992 supported by steadily economic growth and reforms of the health care system. This

Table 2: Life expectancy at birth in years

	1993		1994		1995		1996		1997		1998		1999	
	men	women	men	women	men	women	men	women	men	women	men	women	men	women
Archangelsk	57.3	71.1	55.9	70.0	57.1	71.0	58.5	72.1	60.6	72.0	60.4	72.7	58.0	71.1
Kaliningrad	58.5	70.9	57.1	69.8	58.9	71.4	60.1	72.1	60.5	71.6	60.3	71.4	59.3	71.2
Leningrad region	55.7	70.4	54.7	69.2	55.5	70.1	58.8	71.7	60.0	72.0	60.4	72.6	57.6	71.0
Murmansk	59.1	71.1	57.0	69.7	57.7	70.4	60.1	71.5	63.0	72.9	63.7	74.0	62.5	72.8
Republic of Karelia	56.2	70.8	55.0	69.0	54.7	69.2	58.1	71.3	59.7	71.9	59.7	72.3	57.6	70.9
St Petersburg	58.1	70.7	58.1	71.2	59.9	72.3	62.6	73.8	64.0	74.0	63.8	74.4	61.6	73.1
Estonia	62.4	73.8	61.1	73.1	61.7	74.3	64.5	75.5	64.7	76.0	64.4	75.4	65.4	76.1
Latvia	61.6	73.8	60.7	72.9	60.8	73.1	63.9	75.6	64.2	75.9	64.1	75.5	64.9	76.2
Lithuania	63.3	75.0	62.8	74.9	63.6	75.2	65.0	76.0	65.9	76.8	66.5	76.9	67.0	77.4
Pomorskie	n/a	n/a	n/a	n/a	68.5	76.3	n/a	n/a	n/a	n/a	69.2	77.4	69.9	77.9
Warminsko-Mazurskie	n/a	n/a	n/a	n/a	66.9	76.8	n/a	n/a	n/a	n/a	68.2	77.6	68.5	77.9
Zachodnio-Pomorskie	n/a	n/a	n/a	n/a	66.5	75.8	n/a	n/a	n/a	n/a	68.5	77.0	68.1	77.1
Hamburg	n/a	n/a	n/a	n/a	n/a	n/a	n/a	n/a	n/a	n/a	n/a	n/a	74.4	80.5
Mecklenburg-Vorpommern	68.6	77.3	68.6	77.6	69.6	78.1	70.2	78.5	71.0	78.9	71.5	79.4	n/a	n/a
Schleswig-Holstein	n/a	n/a	n/a	n/a	n/a	n/a	n/a	n/a	n/a	n/a	n/a	n/a	n/a	n/a
Denmark	72.5	77.8	72.5	77.8	72.6	77.8	72.9	78.0	n/a	n/a	73.7	78.6	74.0	78.8
Finland	72.1	79.5	72.8	80.2	72.8	80.2	73.0	80.5	73.4	80.5	73.5	80.8	73.7	81.0
Norway	74.2	80.3	74.9	80.6	74.8	80.8	75.4	81.1	75.5	81.0	75.5	81.3	75.6	81.1
Sweden	75.5	80.8	76.1	81.4	76.2	81.5	76.5	81.8	76.7	81.8	76.9	81.9	77.1	81.9

n/a = not available

holds true for both women (77.5 years in 1999) and men (68.8 years in 1999). Already Polish life expectancy is close the level of the highly developed Nordic countries and Germany.

The Scandinavian countries enjoy a slowly but steadily increasing life expectancy, with Sweden being ahead during the last decade. With around 80 years Nordic women live the longest in the NEBI area. Men in Denmark, Sweden and Norway usually die five years earlier. The gender gap in Finland is above seven years and, as a study has found, this is the widest national gap in the European Union. Life expectancy is 73.7 years for Finnish men and 81.0 years for Finnish women. Variations can hardly be observed since 1992.

In German NEBI regions life expectancy does not differ much from the Scandinavian figures. However there is a wider gender gap in general, topped by Mecklenburg-Vorpommern with almost eight years. The fact that Mecklenburg-Vorpommern has the shortest life expectancy among all German länder may partly be ascribed to post-wall phenomena such as those encountered in the eastern NEBI regions.

The Economy

During 1999 economic growth slowed down in most parts of the NEBI area. Despite its restructuring of the primary sector, Poland maintained its comparably high growth level (4.1 per cent) as did Finland and Sweden. Only Mecklenburg-Vorpommern, Schleswig-Holstein and Sweden experienced slightly more growth than in 1998. Russia's august 1998 financial crisis dramatically affected the economies of the Baltic States. While Latvia's growth nearly stagnated, Estonia and Lithuania GDP fell quite sharply with 1.1 per cent and 4.2 per cent, respectively, mainly due to their dependency on exports to Russia (Estonia approx. 20 per cent, Lithuania approx. 25 per cent). However, this exceptional negative performance in 1999 should not overshadow the fact that, despite population decline, growth rates in the Baltic economies are among the highest in Europe. Between 1994 and 1999 Estonia's GDP increased by well over 20 per cent and also Latvia's and Lithuania's GDP by more than 15 per cent. The Latgale area in eastern Latvia, though, is considered to be the poorest of all regions in the EU candidate countries and this affects the Latvian position in the pre-accession phase. Estonia gains from flourishing exports to predominately Nordic countries. Latvia and Lithuania generate far less GDP through exports (around 50 per cent) than does Estonia (around 80 per cent) but clearly more than the export-based economies of Sweden (45 per cent) and Finland (40 per cent). More than one-half of the Baltic trade and two-thirds of the Polish trade are with EU countries. Almost half of Russian exports are directed towards EU countries. As a result, developments in the eastern NEBI area are closely connected to developments in the EU, not least because of the Russian energy supply to the EU (see below).

Concentration of Economic Activities

Economic growth is still concentrated to capital cities and large city regions (Table 3) and the gap to rural and peripheral regions has widened. In EU and among transition countries, disparities have steadily decreased whereas regional disparities increased. In 1996 in most NEBI countries between one-fourth and one-third of GDP was generated by the capitals. Other urban areas also make significant contributions. Among the Nordic countries Denmark's economy is most dependent on its capital Copenhagen (37 per cent) whereas Stockholm contributes more modestly to Sweden's GDP (24 per cent).

Again, Poland deviates from the pattern. Warsaw contributes 12 per cent to Poland's GDP, which is far less than in other NEBI countries. However, Warsaw's contribution is generated by only 6 per cent of the national population (8 per cent of total employment). Numerous middle-sized towns and a large agrarian sector account for the major part of the GDP. According to a 1998 ILO survey, 19.2 per

Table 3: Concentration of economic activity to large NEBI city regions

	Share of nation's total*				Employment change*:	
	Population at end of 1998	Gross Domestic Product	Total employ-ment	Service employ-ment	in the country 1993-97	in the city 1993-97
		1996	1997	1997		
Copenhagen[1]	34%	37%	34%	39%	5%	5%
Tallinn[2]	37%	56%	41%	49%	-8%	-2%
Helsinki[3]	25%	33%	29%	35%	7%	11%
Riga[4]	37%	47%	44%[12]	53%[12]	-14%	-14%
Vilnius[5]	24%	28%	26%	33%	1%	2%
Oslo[6]	22%	28%[10]	26%	31%	10%	17%
Warsaw[7]	6%	12%	8%[12]	13%[12]	7%[13]	12%[13]
St Petersburg[8]	44%	54%[11]	49%	52%	-7%	-1%
Stockholm[9]	20%	24%	22%	26%	1%	5%

n/a = not available

* "National" figures (shares, change) for St Petersburg refer to the BSR parts of Russia.
[1] Københavns kommune, Frederiksberg kommune, Københavns amt, Frederiksborg amt and Roskilde amt
[2] Harjumaa
[3] Uusimaa (maakunta)
[4] Riga rajon, Riga city and Jurmala
[5] Vilnius County
[6] Oslo and Akershus fylke
[7] Warszawskie woivodship (pre-1999)
[8] St Petersburg city
[9] Stockholms län
[10] Data from 1993. The share is 31% if GDP from offshore activities is excluded.
[11] Excluding Kaliningrad oblast
[12] Data from 1998
[13] Period 1994-98

Figure 4: Production of electricity in 1998, percentage of total

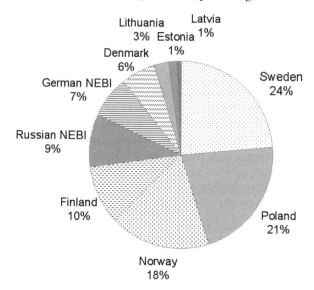

cent of the labour force declared that agriculture was their main source of income (EU15: 4.8 per cent of total employment). Agriculture is still the employer of last resort for many Poles. Almost every third person of the population is considered to depend in some way on agriculture. Because some farmers have become more efficient than others, regional differences are widening. Northern Poland in particular has not yet recovered from the collapse of the big, subsidised state farms. In Warminsko-Mazurskie, agriculture accounts for one-fourth of employment. Latvia and Lithuania employ fewer people in their agrarian sectors, though still five times more than the Scandinavian countries and Germany. Opportunities for new gainful employment would have to be developed in order to revitalise the rural areas and maintain their present population.

Energy

Northwestern Russia generates roughly one-fifth of the country's GDP. Russia accounts for 42 per cent of the EU's imported natural gas (17 per cent of total gas consumption) and 17 per cent of petroleum imports..

The production of energy in the NEBI area is based on three main sources: fossil fuel (predominately coal), water and nuclear power. In Denmark, Estonia and Poland, almost all indigenous production of electricity relies on fossil resources. Denmark and Poland depend on coal for most of their electric power. Estonia utilises domestic oil shale, whose deposits are unique within the NEBI area. The main gas producers in the NEBI area are Norway and Russia. Denmark is self-sufficient with natural gas.

In Finland, Norway and Sweden, hydro-energy plays a significant role in electricity production. Norway produces more than 90 per cent of its electricity needs from hydropower and Sweden almost half. In Latvia, too, hydropower is a significant source of indigenous electricity production. Roughly one-fifth of Russia's energy is based on hydro.

There are five NEBI countries generating energy from nuclear power. Lithuania has the highest dependency on nuclear power with the Ignalina power plant covering around 80 per cent of its electricity production. Sweden ranks second with half of its electricity volume produced by nuclear power plants. The nuclear energy produced in the three German Länder stems from four nuclear power plants in Schleswig-Holstein. There are further two nuclear power plants in NEBI Russia and two in Finland.

The use of renewable energy sources, e.g. wind power, is in general marginal in the NEBI area. Denmark is an exception, as roughly ten 10 per cent of the country's electricity is currently generated from wind and due to extensive investments, this share is expected to grow.

The exchange of electrical power shows large seasonal variations, mainly depending on accessible volumes of water and changes in demand. Finland imports significant amounts of electric energy, as do Norway and Sweden. Germany and Russia are Finland's main suppliers. Denmark is the area's greatest electricity

Table 4: Energy production and trade in the NEBI area, 1998

	Indigenous production of electricity 1996_					Electricity trade, in million kWh			Primary energy supply[2]	
	Billion	% generated from source				export	import	netto	Billion kWh	
	kWh total	fossil	hydro	nuclear	other			export	Domestic	Total
Denmark	40.9	93.1	0.1	0.0	2.4[4]	11.048	3.796	7.252	237	246
Estonia	8.5	100.0	< 0.5	0.0	0.0	528	138	390	38	59
Finland	67.3	46.0	21.9	31.2	0.0	276	9.582	-9.306	n/a	285
Germany	553.4	53.9	3.8	29.2	13.10	40.000	38.600	1.400	n/a	5.906
German NEBI	47.8[3]					2.409	6.538	-4.129[5]		
Latvia	5.8	25.7	74.3	0.0	0.0	384	914	-530	21	52
Lithuania	17.6	11.9	4.4	82.7	1.0	6.466	384	6.082	52	108
Norway	116.9	0.5	99.5	0.0	0.0	4.412	8.046	-3.634	n/a	282
Poland	142.8	96.9	3.1	0.0	0.0	8.082	4.608	3.474	1.017	1.132
Russia	826.0	68.2	19.2	12.6	0.0	106.996	29.075	77.921	n/a	24.377
Russian NEBI	62.0									
Sweden	158.6	6.2	46.8	46.6	0.4	16.799	6.102	-10.697		618.5
NEBI[6]	668.2									
EU 15	2 462.8									

1 Shares of Denmark 1996, Estonia 1996, Lithuania 1996, Norway 1996
2 Denmark, Finland, Latvia, Norway 1997
3 Estimated from 1997 balance sheets
4 Share sum <100 % due to different years (fossil share 1997)
5 Jan - Nov 1999 with Denmark, Poland, Sweden; includes Berlin and Brandenburg
6 Includes whole Polands electricity production

exporter. However, the Danish production is based on imports of coal from Poland and Russia. In 1998 the second largest exporter of electricity in the NEBI area was Lithuania. Although a significant surplus of electricity is still generated in Lithuania, the exports have steadily decreased mainly due to a lack of demand. This, of course, could be reversed when the country is fully connected to the Baltic Ring, a power line network around the Baltic Sea.

Norway and Russia are the region's main exporters of natural gas. Denmark delivers some gas to Germany and Sweden. All other NEBI countries are dependent on gas imports.

In general, the utilisation of natural gas and renewable sources is increasing whereas the use of solid fuel and nuclear power is steadily decreasing. However, the share of oil petroleum is still increasing mainly due to a growing transport sector and increasing private motorisationcar ownership.

Between 1992 and 1999 the private car ownership in the six Russian NEBI regions, Poland and the Baltic States grew fast, although car ownership in the EU15 (45 cars per 100 inhabitants) is still almost twice as high. The NEBI Germans registered more cars than the EU15 average. Here every second inhabitant owns a car. Throughout the Nordic countries car ownership is between 35 and 44 per cent, which is less than in the EU in general.

Figure 5: Car ownership in percentage of population, 1992-99

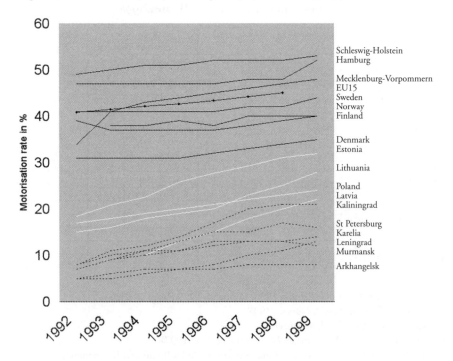

Source: European Commission (2000), National Statistics

Map 3: The energy distribution network in the NEBI area

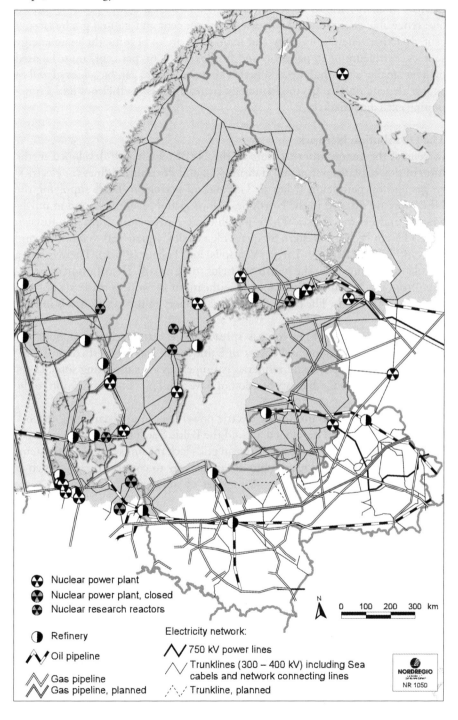

Nuclear power plant
Nuclear power plant, closed
Nuclear research reactors

Refinery

Oil pipeline

Gas pipeline
Gas pipeline, planned

Electricity network:

750 kV power lines
Trunklines (300 – 400 kV) including Sea
cabels and network connecting lines
Trunkline, planned

0   100   200   300 km

NORDREGIO
NR 1050

Agenda 21 for the Baltic Sea region, Baltic 21, sets the following goals for changes in energy use to be achieved by 2030:. Nuclear power must be phased out; renewable energy should increase by 70 per cent and natural gas by 110 per cent. Together renewable energy and natural gas are to become the main energy sources. Petroleum (- 40 per cent) and fossil solids (- 60 per cent) must be used on a far smaller scale than now. Whether these objectives can be achieved will of course, depend on changes in technology, increased energy efficiency and a functioning exchange market.

The Distribution Network
In general the energy infrastructure of the NEBI area is well developed in the form of power plants, refineries, transmission and distribution lines for electricity, gas and oil petroleum (Map 3). Gas and oil petroleum fields supplying the NEBI area are situated in the North Sea (Norway and , Denmark) and in northwestern and central Russia. Three pipeline carry petroleum from the Russian fields (Timan Pechora, western Siberia, Volga Ural, Caspian Sea) to refineries and ports in Finland (Porvoo), Latvia (Ventspils) and Poland (Plock). There is also a petroleum pipeline from the North Sea fields to Denmark. Distribution of petroleum from the North Sea fields to the southeastern network is made via ports in Rostock and Gdansk. The biggest petroleum refinery in the NEBI area is in Russia (Kirishi).

The system of pipelines for gas spreads more extensively throughout the southern Baltic Sea region and covers all Baltic States and the west coast of Sweden. In addition to ports and refineries gas pipelines are supporting some larger towns. Gas fields in the Barents Sea do not have a full pipeline connection to the NEBI area.

As a backbone for transmitting electric power over long distances, a network of trunk lines has been developed around the Baltic Sea. The network is a patchwork of national grids. The Baltic-Russian grids lack the links to adjacent systems in Finland and Poland. Preparations are under way to connect these grids so as to create a so-called Baltic Ring. A number of submarine lines connect some national grids.

Note

[1]   General note. Throughout this statistical section, the following symbols are used:

*   Data not available
-    Magnitude zero
o or o.o   Magnitude less than half of unit employed
/\ = included on the row above; \/ = included on the row below.
[2]   Statistically cities and urban population have been defined on ground of administrative units, except for the four Nordic countries, where built-up urban area is used.

References

Baltic 21 (2000).: *Baltic 21 Newsletter* 2000:1. , Stockholm. 2000

Bishop, K. and Mickiewicz, T. (2001).: 'Poland: Staying the Course?' *The Stockholm Report on Transition* 11:2. Stockholm.

European Commission (1999). 'Common strategy of the European Union on Russia,'. *Official Journal of the European Communities* 24.6.1999

European Commission (2001). *Second Report on Economic and Social Cohesion.* Luxembourg, Office for Official Publications of the European Communities.

Görmar, W., Kurnol, J. and Strade, A. (2001). 'Transnationale Kooperationen, Raumentwicklung und die Osterweiterung der Europäischen Union,' *RaumPlanung* 94. Dortmund.

Hedegaard, L. and Lindström, B. (eds) (2000).: *The NEBI Yearbook 1999: North European and Baltic Sea Integration.* Berlin, Heidelberg, Springer.

Nordregio (2000). *Regions of the Baltic States.* Nordregio Report 2000:2., Stockholm. 2000

Nordregio WP 2000:10 (2000).: *The Baltic Sea Region Yesterday, Today and Tomorrow: – Main Spatial Trends.* Nordregio WP 2000:10, Stockholm.

NORD/LB (2000).: *Nord-Ost Report* December.

SEB (2001).: 'Baltic Outlook Jan. 2001,' *Ekonomisk analys.*, Stockholm 2001-05-21.

Country/region Tables

Contents

Country/region: Estonia

Basic Data and Population
Total land and water area: 45200 square km of which agricultural land: 32%, forest and wood-land: 45%

Total population (end of the respective year or closest possible estimate):
1993 1.51 million
1994 1.49 million
1995 1.48 million
1996 1.46 million
1997 1.45 million of which 47% male, 53% female
1998 1.45 million of which 47% male, 53% female
1999 1.45 million of which 47% male, 53% female

by age groups in %	1993	1994	1995	1996	1997	1998	1999
00 - 19 years	28.1	27.8	27.4	26.9	26.4	25.9	25.5
20 - 64 years	59.1	59.2	59.2	59.3	59.4	59.7	60.0
65 - years	12.8	13.1	13.4	13.8	14.2	14.3	14.5

by nationality in % for all nationalities 0.5% or more	1993	1994	1995	1996	1997	1998	1999
1. Estonians	63.9	64.2	64.6	65.0	65.1	65.2	65.3
2. Russians	29.0	28.7	28.5	28.2	28.1	28.1	28.1
3. Ukrainians	2.7	2.6	2.6	2.6	2.5	2.5	2.5
4. Belorusians	1.6	1.5	1.5	1.5	1.5	1.5	1.5
5. Finns	1.0	1.0	0.9	0.9	0.9	0.9	0.9
6. Jews	0.2	0.2	0.2	0.2	0.2	0.2	0.2
7. Tatars	0.2	0.2	0.2	0.2	0.2	0.2	0.2

Total population has decreased from 1.53 million in 1992 to 1.45 million in 1999.

Migration in 1000 persons	1993	1994	1995	1996	1997	1998	1999
Total immigration	2.4	1.6	1.6	1.6	1.6	1.4	1.4
Total emigration	16.2	9.2	9.8	7.2	4.1	2.5	2.0
Net migration	-13.8	-7.6	-8.2	-5.7	-2.5	-1.1	-0.6
Natural in-/decrease	-6.1	-8.0	-7.3	-5.7	-5.9	-7.2	-5.9

Life expectancy at birth in years	1993	1994	1995	1996	1997	1998	1999
for men	62.4	61.1	61.7	64.5	64.7	64.4	65.4
for women	73.8	73.1	74.3	75.5	76.0	75.4	76.1

Mortality rate by homicide, assaults per 100 000 persons	1993	1994	1995	1996	1997	1998	1999
	25.8	28.2	22.2	19.9	16.3	18.3	15.7

Consumption

Food as % of total private consumption[1]	1993	1994	1995	1996	1997	1998	1999
excl self-produced	39.3	37.6	37.7	36.8	33.0	30.2	29.8
incl self-produced	*	*	*	42.6	38.1	34.9	33.8
Cars per 100 persons[2]	20.9	22.5	25.8	27.7	29.3	31.1	31.9

The number of dwellings at the end of:				
1994 was	618300	56% owned by state and local authorities,	44% by private persons
1995 was	620100	39% owned by state and local authorities,	61% by private persons
1996 was	622100	19% owned by state and local authorities,	81% by private persons
1997 was	623100	10% owned by state and local authorities,	90% by private persons
1998 was	623000	7% owned by state and local authorities,	93% by private persons
1999 was	*	*% owned by state and local authorities,	*% by private persons

Unemployment

The number of unemployed persons, (1000 persons), annual average:	1993	1994	1995	1996	1997	1998	1999
In Labour Force Surveys[3]	49.6	56.7	70.9	71.9	69.4	70.2	86.2
Registered unemployment	33.4	37.4	34.9	37.9	34.1	31.9	44.0

National Accounts

GDP in fixed prices (base year -95) in billion EEK and change in %:	1993	94/93	1994	95/94	1995	96/95	1996	97/96	1997
	39.83	-2.0%	39.03	4.3%	40.71	3.9%	42.30	10.6%	46.79
Preliminary estimates for 1998 and 1999:						98/97	1998	99/98	1999
						4.7%	49.00	-1.1%	48.47

GDP by field of activity, total in current prices in billion EEK, activity in % of total:[4]	1994	1995	1996	1997	Prel. est. 1998	Prel. est. 1999
Total at market prices	29.6	40.7	52.4	64.3	73.3	75.4
Agriculture, hunting, forestry and fishing	9.0%	7.1%	6.8%	6.0%	5.6%	5.2%
Mining, quarrying and manufacturing	18.6%	17.2%	16.2%	15.9%	15.8%	14.8%
Electricity, gas, water supply	2.9%	3.5%	3.6%	3.1%	3.3%	3.2%
Construction	5.7%	5.3%	5.2%	5.2%	5.8%	4.9%
Wholesale and retail sales	13.8%	14.8%	15.3%	15.1%	14.9%	14.5%
Transport, storage and communication	10.3%	9.4%	9.7%	10.8%	12.4%	13.2%
Public administration, education, health and social work	12.3%	13.4%	12.9%	12.2%	12.1%	13.2%
Other services	16.7%	18.9%	19.8%	20.1%	20.0%	21.7%
Unallocated banking services (-)	2.1%	1.9%	2.2%	1.8%	1.4%	1.6%
Total at basic prices	87.2%	87.7%	87.3%	86.6%	88.5%	89.1%
Taxes on products	13.8%	13.0%	13.4%	14.1%	12.6%	12.1%
Subsidies (-)	1.0%	0.7%	0.7%	0.7%	1.1%	1.2%

GDP by expenditure, total in current prices in billion EEK, expenditure as % of total:	1994	1995	1996	1997	Prel. est. 1998	Prel. est. 1999
Total	29.6	40.7	52.4	64.3	73.3	75.4
Private consumption	61.1%	58.4%	60.0%	58.4%	58.9%	57.9%
Government consumption	22.9%	25.4%	24.1%	22.1%	21.8%	23.6%
Consumption of non-profit institutions	0.5%	0.5%	0.7%	0.6%	0.6%	0.6%
Gross fixed capital formation	27.1%	26.0%	26.7%	27.9%	29.7%	25.1%
Changes in stocks	0.6%	0.7%	1.1%	3.8%	-0.3%	-0.5%
Exports (FOB)	76.0%	72.3%	67.1%	78.1%	79.9%	76.9%
Imports (FOB) (-)	87.0%	80.4%	78.6%	89.6%	90.3%	82.6%
Statistical discrepancy	-1.2%	-2.9%	-1.1%	-0.5%	-0.3%	-1.0%

GDP by income, total in current prices in billion EEK, income categories as % of total:	1994	1995	1996	1997	Prel. est. 1998	Prel. est. 1999
Total	29.6	40.7	52.4	64.3	73.3	75.4
Compensation of employees	57.3%	56.8%	53.2%	51.9%	50.7%	50.7%
wages and salaries	43.2%	43.0%	40.4%	39.5%	38.5%	38.5%
Consumption of fixed capital	11.3%	11.1%	10.8%	11.5%	13.7%	15.2%
Indirect taxes	15.4%	14.5%	14.7%	15.5%	13.6%	13.0%
Subsidies (-)	1.0%	0.7%	0.7%	0.7%	1.1%	1.2%
Operating surplus and mixed income	19.1%	20.2%	24.2%	23.6%	24.5%	23.9%
Unallocated banking services (-)	2.1%	1.9%	2.2%	1.8%	1.4%	1.6%

Foreign trade

Exports, total in million EEK, countries as % of total	1993	1994	1995	1996	1997	1998	1999
Total exports	10636	16927	21072	25037	40785	45575	43165
to Russia	22.6%	23.1%	17.7%	16.5%	18.8%	13.3%	9.2%
to Finland	20.7%	17.9%	21.5%	18.3%	15.7%	18.7%	19.4%
to Sweden	9.5%	10.9%	10.9%	11.5%	13.5%	16.7%	18.8%
to Norway	0.6%	1.5%	1.9%	1.5%	1.6%	2.1%	2.4%
to Denmark	2.4%	3.4%	3.3%	3.5%	3.2%	3.6%	3.9%
to Germany	8.0%	6.8%	7.2%	7.1%	5.6%	5.5%	7.5%
to Poland	1.1%	0.7%	1.1%	1.2%	0.9%	0.5%	0.6%
to Lithuania	3.7%	5.4%	4.7%	5.7%	6.1%	4.7%	3.9%
to Latvia	8.6%	8.2%	7.5%	8.2%	8.6%	9.4%	8.7%
to EU countries	17.8%	19.0%	54.0%	51.0%	48.5%	55.0%	62.7%
to CIS countries	30.4%	30.3%	25.1%	25.1%	26.4%	20.8%	13.4%

Imports, total in million EEK, countries as % of total	1993	1994	1995	1996	1997	1998	1999
Total imports	11830	21485	29120	38886	61662	67398	60475
from Russia	17.2%	16.7%	16.1%	13.6%	14.4%	11.1%	13.5%
from Finland	27.9%	29.9%	32.6%	29.1%	23.4%	22.6%	22.8%
from Sweden	8.9%	8.9%	8.5%	8.2%	9.1%	9.0%	9.3%
from Norway	0.5%	0.6%	0.8%	0.9%	1.1%	1.2%	1.1%
from Denmark	2.6%	2.6%	2.8%	2.8%	2.6%	2.8%	2.5%
from Germany	10.8%	10.0%	9.6%	10.0%	10.0%	10.8%	9.3%
from Poland	0.4%	0.6%	0.6%	1.1%	1.1%	1.3%	1.9%
from Lithuania	3.3%	2.6%	1.6%	1.6%	1.5%	1.6%	1.6%
from Latvia	2.3%	1.5%	2.0%	1.9%	1.8%	2.0%	2.2%
from EU countries	23.3%	23.9%	66.0%	64.6%	59.2%	60.1%	57.7%
from CIS countries	21.6%	20.4%	18.8%	17.0%	17.4%	14.2%	17.0%

Employed persons by activity

Employed by activity in 1000 persons[5]	1994	1995	1996	1997	1998	1999
All activities	693	656	646	648	640	614
Agriculture, hunting and forestry	88	63	60	54	53	48
Fishing	14	6	5	7	5	3
Mining and quarrying	11	9	9	8	8	9
Manufacturing	143	163	154	144	140	130
Electricity, gas and water supply	20	16	16	18	18	17
Construction	50	36	37	47	47	42
Wholesale and retail sales	88	83	86	90	90	87
Hotels and restaurants	19	18	18	15	14	14
Transport, storage and communication	58	66	65	60	59	63
Financial intermediation	8	7	7	8	9	9
Real estate, renting and business activities	30	32	32	35	39	39
Public administration and defence	36	36	35	34	37	37
Education	48	56	56	59	57	53
Health and social care	47	37	36	37	35	33
Other community, social and personal services	33	30	30	34	30	31
Other	7	-	-	-	-	-

Enterprises

The number of active enterprises by ownership and size	1995	1996	1997	1998	1999
all active enterprises	30527	31637	40012	35242	42768
with private domestic owners	27387	28739	36900	32782	40320
with foreign owners	1981	2019	2386	2008	2355
owned by state or local government	1159	879	726	452	93
Number of enterprises in wholesale and retail trade	14075	14586	17761	14556	16435
Enterprises with 200 or more employees	285	265	264	243	232
20 to 199 employees	3742	3588	3687	3701	3602
5 to 19 employees	8988	9424	9648	9766	9978
less than 5 employees	17512	18360	26413	21532	28956

Direct inward and outward investment

Foreign direct investment in Estonia	1994	1995	1996	1997	1998	1999
Net direct investment flow in million EEK	2819	2313	1814	3694	8074	4448
as % of the Estonian GDP for the year	9.5%	5.7%	3.5%	5.7%	11.0%	5.9%
by country: from Denmark	34	80	168	212	469	309
Finland	637	193	629	1128	1741	1713
Germany	35	56	80	188	225	60
Latvia	1	2	-3	5	-25	40
Lithuania	0	-3	-7	-37	4	105
Netherlands	198	-10	12	205	46	-21
Norway	4	57	76	747	231	191
Poland	0	0	0	0	0	0
Russia	423	-60	-5	-54	-193	74
Sweden	532	1141	180	366	4780	1435
Switzerland	11	32	37	232	25	-4
United Kingdom	89	183	42	188	387	116
United States	148	201	459	139	145	400
Stock of direct investment capital in Estonia at end of year, total	*	*	*	16456	24429	38397
of which in:						
Mining, quarrying and manufacturing	*	*	*	6096	8455	8911
Wholesale and retail trade	*	*	*	3675	5877	5432
Transport, storage and communication	*	*	*	2145	2611	10696

Estonian direct investment abroad		1994	1995	1996	1997	1998	1999
Net investment flow abroad in million EEK		30	29	484	1913	82	1240
by country: to	Denmark	0	0	-	-	0	0
	Finland	0	1	11	26	-42	-46
	Germany	0	-6	4	-1	-4	0
	Latvia	0	23	115	878	332	694
	Lithuania	0	14	26	480	35	689
	Netherlands	0	-	-	-	0	-
	Norway	0	0	-	-	-	42
	Poland	0	0	0	-	-	-
	Russia	4	-3	6	102	-31	-4
	Sweden	0	3	-1	1	23	21
	Switzerland	-	-	-	-	-	0
	United Kingdom	0	0	-	-	7	-
	United States	0	-	2	-2	0	-

Foreign loans and foreign aid

Net amount borrowed from abroad in million EEK	1994	1995	1996	1997	1998	1999
	262.1	786.8	407.6	166.9	323.3	337.2
as % of the Estonian GDP for the year	0.9%	1.9%	0.8%	0.3%	0.4%	0.4%
Foreign aid received in million EEK	1268	1032	907	1086	1331	1216
as % of the Estonian GDP for the year	4.2%	2.5%	1.7%	1.7%	1.8%	1.6%

Prices

Change in index, previous period = 100	1994	1995	1996	1997	1998	1999
Consumer price index	148	129	123	111	108	103
Producer price index for manufactured products	136	126	115	109	104	99

International sea traffic

The number of vessels in harbours	1994	1995	1996	1997	1998	1999
Arrivals from abroad	7315	8405	8683	11506	11744	13692
Departures aboard	7435	8642	8701	11401	11822	13782

International arrivals/departures[*] in harbours, 1000 persons	1994	1995	1996	1997	1998	1999
Arriving in Estonia total	1297	2142	2534	2836	3163	3454
from Finland	1105	2005	2361	2624	2879	3103
from Sweden	158	109	138	165	200	233
Departing from Estonia total	1272	2131	1978	2190	2426	2618
to Finland	1088	1999	1846	2027	2231	2394
to Sweden	148	106	131	158	185	217

[*] Cruise passengers are counted only upon arrival in the country.

International air traffic

Passengers in airports in 1000	1994	1995	1996	1997	1998	1999
Arrivals	162	177	212	247	278	270
Departures	170	184	219	255	285	275

Sources:
Questionnaires completed by the Statistical Office of Estonia.

Notes:
1) From household budget data.
2) Registration of cars. The number of passenger cars per 100 persons.
3) Figures from Labour Force Surveys or other surveys of individuals following the ILO definition of unemployed persons: Person without work, currently available for work if there should be work and actively seeking work.
4) All bank services are distributed on activities.
5) Employed persons as defined by ILO: working and paid as a wage earner, entrepreneur or a freelancer, working without direct payment in a family enterprise or farm, temporarily absent from work.
  * Data not available
  0, 0,0   Less than half of the unit employed
 - Zero

Country/region: Latvia

Basic Data and Population

Total land- and water area: 64600 square km of which agricultural land: 39%, forest and woodland: 45%

Total population (end of the respective year or closest possible estimate):
1993   2.57 million
1994   2.53 million
1995   2.50 million
1996   2.48 million
1997   2.46 million of which 46% male, 54% female
1998   2.44 million of which 46% male, 54% female
1999   2.42 million of which 46% male, 54% female

by age groups in %	1993	1994	1995	1996	1997	1998	1999
00 - 19 years	27.5	27.3	27.0	26.5	26.1	25.7	25.3
20 - 64 years	59.4	59.4	59.4	59.5	59.6	59.8	60.1
65 - years	13.1	13.3	13.6	14.0	14.3	14.5	14.6

by nationality in % for all nationalities 0.5% or more	1993	1994	1995	1996	1997	1998	1999
1. Latvians	54.2	54.8	55.1	55.3	55.5	55.7	55.8
2. Russians	33.1	32.8	32.6	32.5	32.4	32.3	32.3
3. Belarusians	4.1	4.0	4.0	4.0	3.9	3.9	3.9
4. Ukrainians	3.1	3.0	2.9	2.9	2.9	2.9	2.9
5. Poles	2.2	2.2	2.2	2.2	2.2	2.2	2.2
6. Lithuanians	1.3	1.3	1.3	1.3	1.3	1.3	1.3
7. Jews	0.5	0.5	0.5	0.4	0.4	0.4	0.3
8. Other	1.5	1.4	1.4	1.4	1.4	1.3	1.3

The total population has decreased from 2.61 million in 1992 to 2.42 million in 1999.

Migration in 1000 of persons	1993	1994	1995	1996	1997	1998	1999
Total immigration	4.1	3.0	2.8	2.7	2.9	3.1	1.8
Total emigration	32.0	21.8	13.3	10.0	9.7	6.3	3.6
Net migration	-27.9	-18.8	-10.5	-7.3	-6.8	-3.2	-1.8
Natural in/decrease	-12.4	-17.5	-17.3	-14.5	-14.7	-15.8	-13.4

Prel. data Life expectancy at birth in years	1993	1994	1995	1996	1997	1998	1999
for men	61.6	60.7	60.8	63.9	64.2	64.1	64.9
for women	73.8	72.9	73.1	75.6	75.9	75.5	76.2

Mortality rate by homocide, assaults per 100 000 persons	1993	1994	1995	1996	1997	1998	1999
	24.7	23.0	18.2	15.4	15.9	12.9	12.7

Consumption

Food as % of total private consumption[1]	1993	1994	1995	1996	1997	1998	1999
	47.7	45.9	44.2	50.9	46.8	41.0	38.2
Cars per 100 persons[2]	*	10	13	15	18	20	22

The number of dwellings at the end of:			
1993 was	960000	56% owned by state and local authorities,	44% by private persons
1994 was	953000	55% owned by state and local authorities,	45% by private persons
1995 was	952000	54% owned by state and local authorities,	46% by private persons
1996 was	953000	53% owned by state and local authorities,	47% by private persons
1997 was	954000	53% owned by state and local authorities,	47% by private persons
1998 was	955000	47% owned by state and local authorities,	53% by private persons
1999 was	956000	30% owned by state and local authorities,	70% by private persons

Unemployment

The number of unemployed persons, (1000 persons), annual average:	1993	1994	1995	1996	1997	1998	1999
In Labour Force Surveys[3]	*	*	*	245	181	167	165
Registered unemployment	60	83	81	88	91	92	116

National Accounts

GDP in fixed prices (base year -95) in million LAT and changer in %:								
1993	94/93	1994	95/94	1995	96/95	1996	97/96	1997
2353	0.6%	2368	-0.8%	2349	3.3%	2428	8.6%	2637
Preliminary estimates for 1998 and 1999:					98/97	1998	99/98	1999
					3.6%	2731	0.1%	2741

GDP by field of activity, total in current prices in million LAT, activity in % of total:[4]	1994	1995	1996	1997	Prel. est. 1998	Prel. est. 1999
Total at market prices	2043	2349	2829	3275	3589	3662
Agriculture, hunting, forestry and fishing	8.4%	9.3%	7.9%	5.1%	3.7%	3.6%
Mining, quarrying and manufacturing	17.8%	19.6%	18.4%	19.5%	15.6%	13.2%
Electricity, gas, water supply	4.6%	4.8%	4.6%	4.3%	4.6%	4.4%
Construction	5.3%	4.4%	4.1%	4.2%	5.9%	6.6%
Wholesale and retail sales	8.7%	9.8%	13.4%	14.0%	14.5%	15.7%
Transport, storage and communication	18.1%	13.8%	14.8%	14.7%	14.4%	14.4%
Public administration, education, health and social work	11.2%	12.4%	12.0%	12.3%	13.4%	12.9%
Other services	14.5%	12.4%	12.0%	13.1%	14.1%	17.2%
Total at basic prices	88.6%	86.5%	87.2%	87.2%	86.2%	88.0%
Taxes on products	11.4%	13.6%	12.8%	13.2%	14.2%	12.5%
Subsidies (-)	0.0%	0.1%	0.1%	0.4%	0.5%	0.5%

GDP by expenditure, totals in current prices in million LAT, expenditure as % of total:	1994	1995	1996	1997	Prel. est. 1998	Prel. est. 1999
Total	2043	2349	2829	3275	3589	3662
Private consumption	58.4%	62.5%	67.4%	66.4%	64.3%	*
Government consumption	20.1%	22.2%	21.6%	19.1%	21.4%	19.0%
Consumption of non-profit institutions	0.2%	0.1%	0.3%	0.3%	0.2%	*
Gross fixed capital formation	14.9%	15.1%	18.1%	18.7%	27.3%	25.0%
Changes in stocks	4.3%	2.5%	0.7%	4.0%	0.3%	1.4%
Exports (FOB)	46.5%	46.9%	50.9%	51.0%	51.3%	46.7%
Imports (FOB) (-)	44.4%	49.3%	59.0%	59.5%	64.8%	57.6%

GDP by income, total in current prices in million LAT, income categories in % of total:	1994	1995	1996	1997	1998	1999
Total	2043	2349	2829	3275	3589	3662
Compensation of employees	45.9%	48.9%	50.9%	48.9%	48.6%	*
therein wages and salaries	32.9%	35.2%	33.8%	39.7%	39.2%	*
Consumption of fixed capital	12.5%	12.2%	10.8%	10.5%	13.1%	*
Indirect taxes	13.6%	15.0%	13.7%	14.2%	15.2%	*
Subsidies (-)	0.5%	1.3%	0.9%	1.1%	1.3%	*
Operating surplus and mixed income	28.5%	25.2%	25.5%	27.5%	24.4%	*

Foreign trade

Exports, total in million LAT, countries in % of total	1993	1994	1995	1996	1997	1998	1999
Total exports	676	553	688	795	972	1069	1008
to Russia	29.6%	28.1%	25.3%	22.8%	21.0%	12.1%	6.6%
to Finland	2.0%	2.4%	3.2%	2.4%	1.5%	2.1%	1.9%
to Sweden	6.5%	6.9%	9.3%	6.6%	8.3%	10.3%	10.7%
to Norway	0.3%	0.6%	1.7%	0.7%	0.6%	0.8%	0.8%
to Denmark	0.9%	1.6%	2.0%	3.7%	3.9%	5.1%	6.1%
to Germany	6.6%	10.5%	13.6%	13.8%	13.8%	15.6%	16.9%
to Poland	3.0%	1.6%	2.5%	1.4%	1.2%	1.8%	1.8%
to Lithuania	4.3%	5.5%	5.5%	7.4%	7.5%	7.4%	7.5%
to Estonia	1.9%	2.6%	3.1%	3.7%	4.2%	4.5%	4.7%
to EU countries	33.4%	39.2%	44.0%	44.7%	48.9%	56.6%	62.5%
to CIS countries	47.6%	42.7%	38.3%	35.8%	29.5%	19.0%	12.0%

Imports, total in million LAT, countries in % of total	1993	1994	1995	1996	1997	1998	1999
Total imports	639	695	960	1278	1582	1881	1724
from Russia	28.5%	23.6%	21.7%	20.2%	15.6%	11.8%	10.5%
from Finland	4.2%	8.5%	10.4%	9.2%	9.7%	9.5%	9.1%
from Sweden	5.3%	6.4%	8.0%	7.9%	7.7%	7.2%	7.2%
from Norway	0.1%	0.5%	0.8%	1.4%	1.5%	1.6%	1.7%
from Denmark	1.8%	2.3%	2.9%	3.9%	3.5%	3.8%	3.9%
from Germany	10.0%	13.5%	15.4%	13.8%	16.0%	16.8%	15.2%
from Poland	1.0%	1.6%	1.9%	2.6%	3.2%	3.5%	4.4%
from Lithuania	9.6%	5.9%	5.5%	6.3%	6.4%	6.3%	7.3%
from Estonia	3.9%	3.5%	5.1%	5.7%	6.0%	6.6%	6.4%
from EU countries	27.4%	40.6%	49.9%	49.3%	53.2%	55.3%	54.5%
from CIS countries	38.2%	30.5%	28.2%	25.5%	19.7%	16.0%	15.0%

Employed persons by activity

Employed by activity in 1000 persons[5]	1994	1995	1996	1997	1998	1999
All activities	1083	1046	1018	1037	1043	1038
Agriculture, hunting and forestry	201	188	181	187	178	171
Fishing	8	5	5	6	6	5
Mining and quarrying	2	3	3	2	2	2
Manufacturing	209	194	180	187	171	164
Electricity, gas and water supply	16	17	19	20	19	18
Construction	60	56	58	60	63	64
Wholesale and retail sales	147	147	136	152	169	170
Hotels and restaurants	33	23	21	21	22	24
Transport, storage and communication	95	92	90	89	90	88
Financial intermediation	11	14	15	15	15	16
Real estate, renting and business activities	55	50	41	38	47	53
Public administration and defence	48	57	61	63	64	64
Education	91	91	90	91	90	89
Health and social care	66	65	62	61	62	61
Other community, social and personal services	41	44	56	45	45	49
Other	-	-	-	-	-	-

Enterprises

The number of active enterprises by ownership and size	1995	1996	1997	1998	1999
All active enterprises	31363	*	42026	43942	45823
with private domestic owners	28974	*	33161	37228	39815
with foreign owners	599	*	1635	3375	3745
owned by state or local government	1790	*	1460	1495	1598
unknown*)		*	5770	1785	781
Number of enterprises in wholesale and retail trade	14872	*	15603	17074	19490
Enterprises with 200 or more employees	387	*	391	464	375
20 to 199 employees	3480	*	3799	4323	4375
5 to 19 employees	8135	*	8903	11240	12377
less than 5 employees	19361	*	23163	23899	26266
unknown*)	-	*	5770	4016	2430

*) The number of enterprises for which classification data are not at our disposal. Neither from statistics nor from administrative sources.

Direct inward and outward investment

Foreign direct investment stock in Latvia	1994	1995	1996	1997	1998	1999
Million LAT; at the end of year	*	330.5	520.5	750.3	886.2	1057.2
as % of the Latvian GDP for the year	*	14.1%	18.4%	22.9%	24.7%	28.9%

Foreign direct investment flow in Latvia						
Million LAT	119.0	94.1	210.6	303.4	209.9	202.7
as % of the Latvian GDP for the year	5.8%	4.0%	7.4%	9.3%	5.8%	5.5%

Foreign investment stock in the company capital of enterprises registered in Latvia by investing country, 1992-97		1994	1995	1996	1997	1998	1999
Total		173.3	274.2	377.6	552.5	661.5	755.3
by country: from	Denmark	45.7	71.3	99.4	100.0	100.2	106.6
	Estonia	0.3	0.7	5.4	22.0	25.7	38.6
	Finland	3.8	7.8	10.4	16.3	30.6	39.8
	Germany	12.0	16.3	18.0	48.4	56.7	65.5
	Lithuania	0.5	0.7	0.7	0.5	1.6	2.7
	Netherlands	8.4	10.6	5.6	11.4	16.6	22.5
	Norway	0.0	0.0	1.5	1.1	26.6	28.6
	Poland	0.8	0.5	0.8	0.3	0.2	0.3
	Russia	10.3	51.3	50.8	52.7	57.0	56.4
	Sweden	5.0	7.6	18.5	26.8	44.5	63.9
	Switzerland	9.9	9.9	14.9	15.9	15.5	8.5
	United Kingdom	10.2	13.5	27.6	33.3	49.9	57.3
	United States	24.4	32.8	41.0	57.7	70.6	76.7

Foreign investment stock in the company capital of enterprises registered in Latvia by kind of activity, 1992-97	1994	1995	1996	1997	1998	1999
Total	173.3	274.2	377.6	552.5	661.5	755.3
of which in:						
Mining, quarrying, manufacture electricity, gas and water supply	39.2	49.9	65.8	136.2	130.5	157.2
Wholesale and retail trade	10.2	12.3	34.8	72.7	106.9	123.0
Transport, storage and communication	54.4	116.6	170.4	186.8	198.3	191.7
Financial intermediation	49.4	60.9	63.6	111.2	157.7	159.9

Latvian direct investment stock abroad	1994	1995	1996	1997	1998	1999
(mln LAT; at end of year)	*	124.2	116.3	131.0	159.9	142.3

Latvian direct investment flow abroad	1994	1995	1996	1997	1998	1999
(mln LAT)	35.4	35.0	-1.6	-3.5	-32.2	-9.8

Foreign loans and foreign aid

Net amount borowed from abroad	1994	1995	1996	1997	1998	1999
Million LAT.	189	217	227	218	232	359
as % of the Latvian GDP for the year	9.3%	9.2%	8.0%	6.7%	6.5%	9.8%
Foreign aid received, in million LAT	62	21	31	30	34	39
as % of the Latvian GDP for the year	3.0%	0.9%	1.1%	0.7%	1.4%	1.1%

Prices

Change in index, previous period = 100	1994	1995	1996	1997	1998	1999
Consumer price index	136	125	118	108	105	102
Producer price index for manufactured products	120	114	113	104	100	95

International sea traffic

The number of vessels in harbours	1994	1995	1996	1997	1998	1999
Arrived from abroad	*	*	*	*	*	*
Departures abroad	*	*	*	*	*	*

International arrivals/departures in harbours, in 1000 persons	1994	1995	1996	1997	1998	1999
Arriving in Latvia total	41	50	17	31	51	37
Departing from Latvia total	39	48	16	30	50	38

International air traffic

Passengers in airports in 1000	1994	1995	1996	1997	1998	1999
Arrivals	195	248	250	265	275	280
Departures	197	243	247	266	280	283

Sources

Questionnaires completed by the Central Statistical Bureau of Latvia.

Notes

1) From adjusted consumer expenditure structure data.
2) Registration of passenger cars.
3) Figures from Labour Force Surveys or other surveys of individuals, following the ILO definition of unemployed persons: Person without work, currently available for work if there
   should be work and actively seeking work.
4) All bank services are distributed on activities.
5) Employed persons as defined by ILO: working and paid as a wage earner, enterpreneur or a
   freelancer, working without direct payment in a family enterprise or farm, temporarily
   absent from work.
   * Data not available
   0, 0,0   Less than half of the unit employed
   - Zero

Country/region: Lithuania

Basic Data and Population
Total land- and water area: 65300 square km of which agricultural land: 54%, forest and wood-land: 30%

Total population (end of the respective year or closest possible estimate):
1993	3.72 million
1994	3.72 million
1995	3.71 million
1996	3.71 million
1997	3.70 million of which 47% male, 53% female
1998	3.70 million of which 47% male, 53% female
1999	3.70 million of which 47% male, 53% female

by age groups in %	1993	1994	1995	1996	1997	1998	1999
00 - 19 years	29.2	28.9	28.6	28.3	27.9	27.5	27.1
20 - 64 years	59.3	59.2	59.2	59.3	59.4	59.4	59.6
65 - years	11.5	11.8	12.1	12.4	12.7	13.1	13.3

by nationality in % for all nationalities 0.5% or more	1993	1994	1995	1996	1997	1998	1999
1. Lithuanians	80.7	81.1	81.3	81.4	81.6	81.7	81.8
2. Russians	8.7	8.5	8.4	8.3	8.2	8.2	8.1
3. Poles	7.0	7.0	7.0	7.0	6.9	6.9	6.9
4. Belorusians	1.6	1.5	1.5	1.5	1.5	1.4	1.4
5. Ukrainians	1.1	1.0	1.0	1.0	1.0	1.0	1.0

The total population has in(de-)creased from 3.74 million in 1992 to 3.70 million in 1999.

Migration in 1000 of persons	1993	1994	1995	1996	1997	1998	1999
Total immigration	2.9	1.7	2.0	3.0	2.5	2.7	2.7
Total emigration	16.0	4.2	3.8	3.9	2.5	2.1	1.4
Net migration	-13.1	-2.6	-1.8	-0.9	0.0	0.6	1.3
Natural in/decrease	0.6	-3.7	-4.1	-3.7	-3.3	-3.7	-3.6

Life expectancy at birth in years	1993	1994	1995	1996	1997	1998	1999
for men	63.3	62.8	63.6	65.0	65.9	66.5	67.0
for women	75.0	74.9	75.2	76.0	76.8	76.9	77.4

Mortality rate by homocide, assaults per 100 000 persons	1993	1994	1995	1996	1997	1998	1999
	12.5	13.4	11.7	9.3	9.1	8.2	8.0

Consumption

Food as % of total private consumption[1]	1993	1994	1995	1996	1997	1998	1999
	50.9	46.0	45.1	46.7	44.5	41.4	39.3
Cars per 100 persons[2]	16	18	19	20	23	25	28

The number of dwellings at the end of			
1994 was	1225800	13% owned by state and local authorities,	87% by private persons
1995 was	1246500	11% owned by state and local authorities,	89% by private persons
1996 was	1269600	8% owned by state and local authorities,	92% by private persons
1997 was	1277600	8% owned by state and local authorities,	92% by private persons
1998 was	1306000	3% owned by state and local authorities,	97% by private persons
1999 was	1324000	3% owned by state and local authorities,	97% by private persons

Unemployment

The number of unemployed persons, (1000 persons), annual average:	1993	1994	1995	1996	1997	1998	1999
In Labour Force Surveys[3]	*	347	347	317	257	245	263
Registered unemployment	81	66	109	125	105	114	149

National accounts

GDP in fixed prices (base year -95) in million LIT and change in %:	1993	94/93	1994	95/94	1995	96/95	1996	97/96	1997
	25861	-9.8%	23335	3.3%	24103	4.7%	25238	7.3%	27075
Preliminary estimates for 1998 and 1999:							98/97	1998	99/98	1999
							5.1%	28459	-4.2%	27256

GDP by field of activity, total in current prices in million LIT, activity in % of total:[4]	1994	1995	1996	1997	Prel. est. 1998	Prel. est. 1999
Total at market prices	16904	24103	31569	38340	42990	42535
Agriculture, hunting, forestry and fishing	10.1%	10.7%	11.2%	10.5%	9.1%	7.7%
Mining, quarrying and manufacturing	22.8%	20.7%	20.5%	18.8%	17.1%	16.8%
Electricity, gas, water supply	2.7%	3.3%	3.2%	3.7%	4.0%	4.1%
Construction	6.8%	6.5%	6.5%	6.9%	7.6%	7.0%
Wholesale and retail sales	16.6%	16.3%	15.4%	14.7%	14.4%	13.8%
Transport, storage and communication	9.5%	8.6%	8.7%	8.6%	8.5%	9.6%
Public administration, defence and compulsory social security	4.8%	5.2%	5.7%	5.3%	6.2%	6.5%
Other services*)	17.7%	18.3%	19.0%	19.6%	20.1%	22.2%
Total at basic prices	91.1%	89.5%	90.4%	88.1%	87.1%	87.6%
Taxes on products	10.1%	11.5%	10.5%	12.5%	13.9%	13.5%
Subsidies (-)	1.2%	1.0%	1.0%	0.6%	0.9%	1.1%

*) Unallocated banking services included.

GDP by expenditure, total in current prices in million LIT, expenditure as % of total:	1994	1995	1996	1997	Prel.est. 1998	Prel. est. 1999
Total	16904	24103	31569	38340	42945	42535
Private consumption	67.9%	67.3%	66.4%	65.0%	63.0%	64.8%
Government consumption	19.6%	19.7%	18.9%	19.0%	24.4%	22.5%
Consumption of non-profit institutions	0.1%	0.1%	0.1%	0.1%	0.1%	0.1%
Gross fixed capital formation	23.1%	23.0%	23.0%	24.4%	24.3%	22.5%
Changes in stocks	-4.7%	1.7%	1.5%	2.2%	0.1%	0.4%
Exports (FOB)	55.4%	53.0%	53.4%	54.5%	47.2%	39.9%
Imports (FOB) (-)	61.4%	64.8%	63.2%	65.1%	59.1%	50.2%

GDP by income, total in current prices in million LIT, income categories as % of total:	1994	1995	1996	1997	Prel.est. 1998	Prel.est. 1999
Total	16904	24103	31569	38340	42945	42535
Compensation of employees	41.2%	42.5%	40.9%	41.6%	43.4%	44.3%
therein wages and salaries	31.9%	33.8%	32.5%	32.2%	34.4%	35.2%
Consumption of fixed capital	8.9%	8.7%	9.7%	9.7%	9.8%	10.3%
Indirect taxes	11.3%	13.0%	12.1%	15.0%	14.4%	14.1%
Subsidies (-)	1.6%	1.1%	1.3%	0.9%	1.1%	1.1%
Operating surplus and mixed income	40.3%	36.9%	38.5%	34.6%	33.4%	32.4%

Foreign trade

Exports, total in million LIT, countries as % of total	1993	1994	1995	1996	1997	1998	1999
Total exports	8707	8077	10820	13420	15441	14842	12015
to Russia	33.1%	28.2%	20.4%	24.0%	24.5%	16.5%	7.0%
to Finland	0.9%	1.0%	1.1%	1.0%	0.7%	0.8%	1.0%
to Sweden	1.8%	3.1%	2.5%	1.7%	1.9%	2.6%	4.2%
to Norway	0.2%	0.6%	0.6%	0.5%	0.4%	0.5%	1.1%
to Denmark	1.5%	1.7%	2.7%	2.6%	3.4%	4.1%	6.2%
to Germany	6.8%	11.5%	14.4%	12.8%	11.4%	13.1%	16.0%
to Poland	7.0%	5.0%	3.9%	3.2%	2.3%	3.0%	4.5%
to Latvia	7.3%	8.4%	7.1%	9.2%	8.6%	11.1%	12.8%
to Estonia	2.5%	2.5%	2.2%	2.5%	2.5%	2.6%	2.4%
to EU countries	16.9%	25.8%	36.4%	32.9%	32.5%	38.0%	50.1%
to CIS countries	57.1%	46.7%	42.3%	45.4%	46.4%	35.7%	18.2%

Imports, total in million LIT, countries as % of total*)	1993	1994	1995	1996	1997	1998	1999
Total imports	9798	9355	14594	18235	22577	23174	19338
from Russia	53.7%	39.3%	31.2%	25.9%	24.3%	20.2%	19.4%
from Finland	1.3%	2.9%	3.3%	3.7%	3.4%	4.2%	4.3%
from Sweden	1.1%	2.4%	2.8%	3.1%	3.2%	3.7%	3.6%
from Norway	0.1%	0.7%	0.8%	0.9%	0.7%	0.9%	0.8%
from Denmark	2.4%	2.6%	3.5%	3.8%	4.3%	4.6%	4.9%
from Germany	9.7%	13.8%	14.3%	15.8%	18.7%	20.0%	18.0%
from Poland	2.2%	4.0%	4.2%	5.1%	5.8%	6.6%	7.0%
from Latvia	1.5%	2.7%	3.2%	3.3%	3.4%	3.9%	4.6%
from Estonia	0.8%	1.6%	1.8%	2.2%	2.4%	2.7%	2.6%
from EU countries	18.7%	26.4%	37.1%	42.4%	46.5%	50.2%	49.7%
from CIS countries	67.5%	50.3%	42.0%	32.9%	29.3%	24.7%	23.6%

*) Imported goods by country are from 1996 on broken up according to the country of consignment.

Employed persons by activity

Employed by activities in 1000 persons [5]	1994	1995	1996	1997	1998	1999
All activities	1675	1644	1659	1669	1656	1648
Agriculture, hunting and forestry	390	390	399	363	355	331
Fishing	1	2	2	2	1	1
Mining and quarrying	4	4	4	4	4	3
Manufacturing	336	302	288	289	287	283
Electricity, gas and water supply	38	42	42	41	41	40
Construction	111	115	119	119	118	109
Wholesale and retail sales	224	211	212	247	243	237
Hotels and restaurants	22	19	18	27	25	27
Transport, storage and communication	92	95	95	93	97	105
Financial intermediation	25	21	17	17	16	16
Real estate, renting and business activities	37	49	52	53	57	55
Public administration and defence	60	67	68	69	71	71
Education	140	142	147	149	153	158
Health and social care	98	103	103	107	109	111
Other community, social and personal services	97	82	94	87	80	97
Other	-	-	-	1	2	3

Enterprises

The number of active enterprises by ownership and size	1995	1996	1997	1998	1999
All active enterprises	63200	74600	86300	92324	89857
With private domestic owners					
With foreign owners					
Owned by state or local government					
Number of enterprises in wholesale and retail trade	27000	37400	41400	39406	39756
Enterprises with 200 or more employees	600	500	600	777	764
20 to 199 employees	5200	5700	6100	8700	8370
5 to 19 employees	9200	11800	13400	16391	16355
less than 5 employees	48300	56600	66100	66456	64368

Direct inward and outward investment

Foreign direct investment in Lithuania	1994	1995	1996	1997	1998	1999
Total direct investment in million LIT	125	290	610	1418	3702	1946
as % of the Lithuanian GDP for the year	0.7%	1.2%	1.9%	3.7%	8.7%	4.6%
by country: from Denmark	*	*	*	97	129	372
Estonia	*	*	*	152	81	64
Finland	*	*	*	57	1148	183
Germany	*	*	*	108	90	107
Latvia	*	*	*	2	35	13
Netherlands	*	*	*	4	-2	46
Norway	*	*	*	65	191	78
Poland	*	*	*	13	67	36
Russia	*	*	*	19	56	0
Sweden	*	*	*	170	1266	309
Switzerland	*	*	*	10	40	355
United Kingdom	*	*	*	75	130	141
United States	*	*	*	349	263	162
Stock of direct investment capital in Lithuania at the end of each year, total	*	1406	2801	4162	6501	8252
of which in:						
Mining, quarrying and manufacture	*	648	1223	1609	2173	2704
Wholesale and retail trade	*	413	910	1245	1632	2024
Transport, storage and communication	*	76	313	491	1356	1680

Lithuanian direct investment abroad		1994	1995	1996	1997	1998	1999
Total investments abroad in million LIT		*	4	0	108	17	-35
by country: in	Denmark	*	*	*	0	0	0
	Estonia	*	*	*	54	0	0
	Finland	*	*	*	-	-	-
	Germany	*	*	*	0	2	1
	Latvia	*	*	*	10	3	0
	Netherlands	*	*	*	0	-	0
	Norway	*	*	*	-	-	-
	Poland	*	*	*	0	1	1
	Russia	*	*	*	13	12	-9
	Sweden	*	*	*	-	-	-
	Switzerland	*	*	*	-	-	-
	United Kingdom	*	*	*	-	-	-
	United States	*	*	*	-	-	-

Foreign loans and foreign aid

Net amount borowed from abroad	1994	1995	1996	1997	1998	1999
Million USD (Foreign debt per year)	176.0	330.8	388.0	257.0	257.9	781.4
% of the Lithuanian GDP for the year	4.2%	5.5%	4.9%	2.7%	2.4%	7.3%
GDP, in mill. USD	4227	6026	7892	9585	10736	10649
Foreign aid received, in million USD**)	30.6	38.8	57.2	43.1	33.7	30.7
as % of the Lithuanian GDP for the year	0.7%	0.6%	0.7%	0.4%	0.3%	0.3%

**) Material value without the aid for education and technical support.

Prices

Change in index, previous year = 100	1994	1995	1996	1997	1998	1999
Consumer price index	172	140	125	109	105	101
Producer price index for manufactured products of mining, quarrying and manufacturing	145	128	117	104	93	103

International sea traffic

The number of vessels in harbours	1994	1995	1996	1997	1998	1999
Arrivals from abroad[6]	2933	3229	3411	3615	3814	3455
Departures abroad[6]	2911	3228	3440	3623	3815	3479

International arrivals/departures in harbours, 1000 persons	1994	1995	1996	1997	1998	1999
Arriving in Lithuania total	*	31.3	33.8	37.3	39.5	40.2
Departing from Lithuania total	*	26.9	28.8	32.8	36.6	38.0

International air traffic

Passengers in airports in 1000	1994	1995	1996	1997	1998	1999
Arrivals	214	204	212	238	262	269
Departures	224	214	222	241	265	272

Sources

Questionnaires completed by the Lithuanin Department of Statistics.

Notes

1) From household budget data.
2) Registration of passanger cars per 100 persons.
3) Figures from Labour Force Surveys or other surveys of individuals following the ILO definition of unemployed persons: Person without work, currently available for work if there should be work and actively seeking work.
4) All bank services are distributed on activities.
5) Employed persons as defined by ILO: working and paid as a wage earner, enterpreneur or a freelancer, working without direct payment in a family enterprise or farm, temporarily absent from work.
6) Only vessels registered in foreign countries.
 * Data not available
 0, 0,0   Less than half of the unit employed
 - Zero

Country/region: Hamburg

Basic Data and Population

Total land- and water area: 755 square km of which agricultural land: 28%, forest and woodland: 5%

Total population (end of the respective year or closest possible estimate):
1993   1.70 million
1994   1.71 million
1995   1.71 million
1996   1.71 million
1997   1.70 million of which 48% male, 52% female
1998   1.70 million of which 48% male, 52% female
1999   1.70 million of which 48% male, 52% female

by age groups in %	1993	1994	1995	1996	1997	1998	1999
00 - 19 years	17.9	17.9	17.9	17.9	17.9	17.9	18.1
20 - 64 years	65.1	65.1	65.1	65.1	65.1	65.1	65.2
65 - years	17.1	17.0	17.0	17.0	17.0	17.0	16.8

by nationality in % for all nationalities 0.5% or more	1993	1994	1995	1996	1997	1998	1999
1. Germans	84.6	84.4	84.2	84.0	84.1	84.8	84.6
2. Turks	4.2	4.2	4.2	4.2	4.2	4.1	4.0
3. Yugoslavians	1.8	1.7	1.6	1.5	1.4	1.4	1.4
4. Poles	1.1	1.1	1.1	1.1	1.1	1.1	1.1
5. Iranians	0.8	0.8	0.8	0.8	0.8	0.8	0.8
6. Afghans	0.6	0.5	0.7	0.7	0.8	0.9	0.9
7. Greeks	0.5	0.5	0.5	0.5	0.5	0.5	0.5
8. Portuguese	0.5	0.5	0.6	0.6	0.6	0.6	0.6

The total population has in(de-)creased from 1.69 million in 1992 to 1.70 million in 1999.

Migration in 1000 of persons	1993	1994	1995	1996	1997	1998	1999
Total immigration	89.2	77.5	75.1	73.9	73.6	74.9	78.7
Total emigration	70.7	70.5	68.7	70.2	74.5	76.5	71.5
Net migration	18.5	7.0	6.4	3.7	-0.9	-1.6	7.2
Natural in/decrease	-4.4	-4.0	-4.4	-3.6	-2.4	-3.0	-2.5

Life expectancy at birth in years	1986/88	1994	1995	1996	1997	1998	1999
for men	71.8	*	*	*	*	*	74.4
for women	78.6	*	*	*	*	*	80.5

Mortality rate by homicide, assaults per 100 000 persons [1]	1993	1994	1995	1996	1997	1998	1999
	3.7	2.9	2.5	2.6	2.3	2.1	2.2

Consumption

Food as % of total private consumption[2]	1993	1994	1995	1996	1997	1998	1999
	14.5	14.3	13.8	13.4	13.1	12.9	*
Cars per 100 persons[3]	47	47	47	47	48	48	52

The number of dwellings at the end of			
1993 was	808000	*% owned by state and local authorities,	*% by private persons
1994 was	816000	*% owned by state and local authorities,	*% by private persons
1995 was	824000	*% owned by state and local authorities,	*% by private persons
1996 was	832000	*% owned by state and local authorities,	*% by private persons
1997 was	839000	*% owned by state and local authorities,	*% by private persons
1998 was	847000	*% owned by state and local authorities,	*% by private persons
1999 was	853000	*% owned by state and local authorities,	*% by private persons

Unemployment

The number of unemployed persons, (1000 persons), annual average:	1993	1994	1995	1996	1997	1998	1999
In Labour Force Surveys [4]	*	*	*	*	*	*	*
Registered unemployment	62.9	71.2	77.8	83.9	92.5	90.5	84.0

National accounts

GDP in fixed prices (base year -91) in billion DEM and change in %:	1993	94/93	1994	95/94	1995	96/95	1996	97/96	1997
	121	0.9%	122	1.1%	124	1.4%	125	2.0%	128
Preliminary estimates for 1998 and 1999:						98/97	1998	99/98	1999
						2.6%	131	1.0%	132

GDP and Gross Value Added (GVA) total in current prices, activity in % of total GVA:[5]	1994	1995	1996	1997	Prel. est. 1998	Prel. est. 1999
Total GDP at market prices in billion DEM	120	124	127	131	135	138
Taxes on products less subsidies (-)	-12	-12	-12	-13	-13	-14
Unallocated banking services	5	5	5	5	5	5
Total Gross Value Added in billion DEM	113	116	119	123	127	129
Agriculture, hunting, forestry and fishing	0.3%	0.2%	0.3%	0.3%	0.3%	0.3%
Mining, quarrying and manufacturing	14.7%	14.5%	14.2%	14.2%	14.2%	13.8%
Electricity, gas, water supply	1.3%	1.3%	1.4%	1.5%	1.5%	1.3%
Construction	4.0%	3.9%	3.5%	3.3%	3.0%	2.8%
Wholesale and retail sales	14.3%	14.2%	14.1%	13.7%	*	*
Transport, storage and communication	9.8%	10.0%	9.7%	9.8%	9.9%	9.8%
Public administration, education, health and social work, social and personal services	20.8%	20.6%	20.1%	20.2%	20.0%	20.0%
Other services	33.8%	34.4%	35.8%	36.1%	36.4%	37.6%

GDP by expenditure, total in current prices in billion DEM, expenditure as % of total:						
	1994	1995	1996	1997	1998	1999
Total	*	*	*	*	*	*
Private consumption	*	*	*	*	*	*
Government consumption	*	*	*	*	*	*
Consumption of non-profit institutions	*	*	*	*	*	*
Gross fixed capital formation	*	*	*	*	*	*
Changes in stocks	*	*	*	*	*	*
Exports (FOB)	*	*	*	*	*	*
Imports (FOB) (-)	*	*	*	*	*	*
Statistical discrepancy	*	*	*	*	*	*

GDP by income, total in current prices in billion DEM, income categories as % of total:						
	1994	1995	1996	1997	1998	1999
Total	*	*	*	*	*	*
Compensation of employees	*	*	*	*	*	*
therein wages and salaries	*	*	*	*	*	*
Consumption of fixed capital	*	*	*	*	*	*
Indirect taxes	*	*	*	*	*	*
Subsidies (-)	*	*	*	*	*	*
Operating surplus and mixed income	*	*	*	*	*	*

Foreign trade

Exports, total in billion DEM, countries in % of total	1993	1994	1995	1996	1997	1998	1999
Total exports	12.8	13.3	16.1	19.8	24.6	29.7	33.0
to Russia	2.1%	2.4%	1.8%	1.8%	2.5%	1.3%	1.0%
to Finland	0.5%	0.8%	0.7%	1.3%	0.8%	0.7%	2.1%
to Sweden	2.2%	2.3%	2.0%	1.6%	1.3%	1.2%	1.0%
to Norway	1.0%	0.8%	0.7%	0.5%	0.5%	0.5%	0.4%
to Denmark	3.6%	3.6%	3.0%	2.6%	2.3%	1.9%	1.5%
to Poland	2.7%	2.5%	2.2%	2.4%	2.2%	2.2%	1.6%
to Lithuania	0.3%	0.2%	0.1%	0.2%	0.3%	0.2%	0.1%
to Latvia	0.1%	0.2%	0.2%	0.1%	0.2%	0.1%	0.1%
to Estonia	0.1%	0.1%	0.1%	0.1%	0.1%	0.1%	0.1%
to EU countries	54.5%	53.7%	54.1%	61.2%	58.2%	63.1%	64.0%
to CIS countries	2.1%	2.1%	2.0%	2.1%	2.7%	2.1%	2.0%

Imports, total in billion DEM, countries in % of total	1993	1994	1995	1996	1997	1998	1999
Total imports	47.2	48.7	44.9	46.0	54.7	58.3	64.5
from Russia	1.9%	2.0%	1.9%	2.0%	2.6%	2.0%	2.1%
from Finland	0.9%	0.9%	1.1%	0.9%	0.8%	0.5%	0.5%
from Sweden	1.8%	1.8%	1.0%	1.4%	0.9%	0.8%	0.8%
from Norway	2.2%	1.8%	1.0%	2.9%	2.5%	1.6%	1.2%
from Denmark	2.1%	1.8%	2.2%	2.8%	2.3%	1.9%	1.7%
from Poland	1.0%	0.9%	1.1%	1.0%	1.0%	1.1%	1.1%
from Lithuania	0.1%	0.1%	0.1%	0.1%	0.1%	0.2%	0.1%
from Latvia	0.2%	0.2%	0.3%	0.1%	0.1%	0.1%	0.0%
from Estonia	0.0%	0.0%	0.0%	0.1%	0.1%	0.1%	0.0%
from EU countries	42.3%	40.9%	36.7%	38.3%	37.4%	41.4%	39.1%
from CIS countries	2.6%	2.9%	2.2%	2.7%	3.0%	1.7%	1.9%

Employed persons by activity

Employed by activity in 1000 persons[6]		1994	1995	1996	1997	1998	1999
All activities		984.3	969.7	960.2	949.5	947.6	949.0
Agriculture, hunting and forestry		6.4	6.2	5.9	5.9	5.9	5.7
Fishing	/\						
Mining and quarrying	\/						
Manufacturing		147.5	139.1	136.1	131.5	121.2	115.7
Electricity, gas and water supply		10.2	9.3	8.4	8.0	7.7	7.5
Construction		53.5	52.7	51.4	49.0	48.6	48.1
Wholesale and retail sales		171.9	172.3	169.7	166.4	*	*
Hotels and restaurants (incl. in others)							
Transport, storage and communication		101.3	98.8	94.8	89.6	88.5	87.6
Financial intermediation		61.5	58.8	56.5	55.2	54.8	54.3
Real estate, renting and business activities (incl. in other)							
Public administration and defence		79.8	78.3	76.6	73.1	71.3	69.4
Education, health and social care, other community, social and personal services		193.2	195.0	198.4	201.5	206.8	210.2
Other		123.8	124.1	126.7	133.6	140.8	148.1
Not specified		*	*	*	*	*	*
		949.1	934.6	924.5	913.8	745.6	746.6

Prices

Change in index, previous period = 100	1994	1995	1996	1997	1998	1999
Consumer price index	103	102	101	102	101	101
Producer price index for manufactured products	102	101	102	101	100	99

International sea traffic

The number of vessels in harbours	1994	1995	1996	1997	1998	1999
Arrivals from abroad	12027	11679	11489	11749	11757	11626
Departures abroad	12153	11798	11635	11895	11851	11724

International arrivals/departures in harbours, 1000 persons	1994	1995	1996	1997	1998	1999
Arriving in Germany total		*	*	*	*	*	*
Departing from Germany total	*	*	*	*	*	*	

International air traffic

Passengers in airports in 1000	1994	1995	1996	1997	1998	1999
Arrivals	2196	2348	2364	2472	2581	2702
Departures	2192	2345	2357	2465	2620	2668

Sources
Questionaires completed by the Statistisches Landesamt Hamburg.

Notes
1) Death classified on codes No E960-E969, 9 Rev ICD, 1979 per 100 000 persons of population.
2) The weight is for food only without beverage and tobacco.
3) All registered vehicles on 100 persons.
4) Figures from Labour Force Surveys or other surveys of individuals following the ILO definition of unemployed persons: Person without work, currently available for work if there should be work and actively seeking work.
5) The split of GDP on activities is not available. The split of GVA on activities and the links between total GDP and total GVA are shown instead.
6) Employed persons as defined by ILO: working and paid as a wage earner, enterpreneur or a freelancer, working without direct payment in a family enterprise or farm, temporarily absent from work.
7) Price indices for Germany as a whole are used. Producer price index without food and means of enjoyment.
 * Data not available
   0, 0,0   Less than half of the unit employed
 - Zero

Country/region: Mecklenburg-Vorpommern

Basic Data and Population

Total land- and water area: 23171 square km of which agricultural land: 65%, forest and woodland: 21%

Total population (end of the respective year or closest possible estimate):	
1993	1.84 million
1994	1.83 million
1995	1.82 million
1996	1.82 million
1997	1.81 million of which 49% male, 51% female
1998	1.80 million of which 49% male, 51% female
1999	1.79 million of which 49% male, 51% female

by age groups in %	1993	1994	1995	1996	1997	1998	1999
00 - 19 years	26.3	25.8	25.2	24.7	23.9	23.1	22.3
20 - 64 years	62.1	62.3	62.3	62.5	62.7	63.1	63.2
65 - years	11.6	12.0	12.4	12.9	13.3	13.8	14.5

by nationality in % for all nationalities 0.5% or more	1993	1994	1995	1996	1997	1998	1999
1. Germans	98.9%	98.7%	98.4%	98.3%	98.4%	98.4%	98.2%
2. Romanians	0.8%	0.6%	*	*	*	*	*

The total population has decreased from 1.86 million in 1993 to 1.79 million in 1999.

Migration in 1000 of persons	1993	1994	1995	1996	1997	1998	1999
Total immigration	31.0	31.0	32.3	35.1	32.5	31.4	32.9
Total emigration	36.3	31.3	32.1	33.5	36.0	35.2	37.4
Net migration	-5.3	-0.3	0.2	1.7	-3.5	-3.7	-4.5
Natural in/decrease	-10.1	-10.9	-9.4	-7.6	-5.9	-5.4	-4.9

Life expectancy at birth in years	1993	1994	1995	1996	1997	1998	1999
for men	68.6	68.6	69.6	70.2	71.0	71.5	*
for women	77.3	77.6	78.1	78.5	78.9	79.4	*

Mortality rate by homicide	1993	1994	1995	1996	1997	1998	1999
assaults per 100 000 persons [1]	2.0	0.7	1.2	0.8	1.5	1.3	0.8

Consumption

Food as % of total private consumption[2]	1993	1994	1995	1996	1997	1998	1999
	25	24	25	24	22	19	*
Cars per 100 persons[3]	41	43	44	45	46	47	48

The number of dwellings at the end of				
1993 was	762244	*% owned by state and local authorities,	*% by private persons
1994 was	770387	*% owned by state and local authorities,	*% by private persons
1995 was	777827	*% owned by state and local authorities,	*% by private persons
1996 was	792985	*% owned by state and local authorities,	*% by private persons
1997 was	813531	*% owned by state and local authorities,	*% by private persons
1998 was	829129	*% owned by state and local authorities,	*% by private persons
1999 was	842741	*% owned by state and local authorities,	*% by private persons

Unemployment

The number of unemployed persons, (1000 persons), annual average:							
	1993	1994	1995	1996	1997	1998	1999
In Labour Force Surveys[4]	*	*	*	*	*	*	*
Registered unemployment	152.0	143.6	132.9	147.8	168.4	171.1	163.1

National accounts

GDP in fixed prices (base year -95) in billion DEM and change in %:							
	1993	94/93	1994	95/94	1995	96/95	1996	97/96	1997
	42.9	12.3%	48.2	6.4%	51.3	2.2%	52.5	0.8%	52.9
Preliminary estimates for 1997 and 1998:					98/97	1998	98/99	1999
						0.7%	53.3	1.3%	53.9

GDP and Gross Value Added (GVA) total in current prices, activity in % of total GVA:[5]	1994	1995	1996	1997	Prel. est. 1998	Prel. est. 1999
Total GDP at market prices in billion DEM	47.3	51.3	53.1	53.7	54.6	55.7
Taxes on products less subsidies (-)	-4.8	-5.1	-5.2	-5.2	-5.3	-5.7
Unallocated banking services	1.9	2.0	2.0	2.0	2.0	2.0
Total Gross Value Added in billion DEM	44.4	48.3	49.9	50.5	51.3	52.0
Agriculture, hunting, forestry and fishing	3.8%	3.8%	3.4%	3.4%	3.5%	3.3%
Mining, quarrying and manufacturing	9.5%	8.2%	8.6%	8.9%	12.1%	12.4%
Electricity, gas, water supply	2.2%	2.6%	2.9%	2.7%	/\	/\
Construction	15.1%	15.8%	14.5%	14.7%	13.4%	11.9%
Wholesale and retail sales [6]	12.4%	11.4%	11.6%	11.5%	17.5%	17.6%
Transport, storage and communication	6.3%	6.0%	5.6%	5.9%	/\	/\
Public administration, education, health and social work and personal services	32.0%	32.6%	32.4%	31.1%	30.9%	31.3%
Financial and enterprise services	18.7%	19.6%	21.0%	21.7%	22.6%	23.5%

GDP by expenditure, total in current prices in billion DEM, expenditure as % of total:	1994	1995	1996	1997	Prel. est. 1998	Prel.est. 1999
Total	47.3	51.3	53.1	53.7	54.6	55.7
Private consumption	*	*	*	*	*	*
Government consumption	*	*	*	*	*	*
Consumption of non-profit institutions	*	*	*	*	*	*
Gross fixed capital formation	*	*	*	*	*	*
Changes in stocks	*	*	*	*	*	*
Exports (FOB)	*	*	*	*	*	*
Imports (FOB) (-)	*	*	*	*	*	*
Statistical discrepancy	*	*	*	*	*	*

GDP by income, total in current prices in billion DEM, income categories as % of total:	1994	1995	1996	1997	Prel. est. 1998	Prel.est. 1999
Total	47.3	51.3	53.1	53.7	54.6	55.7
Compensation of employees	63.7%	62.9%	61.7%	60.5%	59.9%	60.3%
therein wages and salaries	52.0%	52.0%	47.6%	49.5%	46.2%	48.8%
Consumption of fixed capital	*	*	*	*	*	*
Indirect taxes	*	*	*	*	*	*
Subsidies (-)	*	*	*	*	*	*
Operating surplus and mixed income	*	*	*	*	*	*

Foreign trade

Exports, total in billion DEM, countries in % of total	1993	1994	1995	1996	1997	1998	1999
Total exports	2.89	2.59	2.72	2.12	2.60	2.57	2.54
to Russia	23.5%	6.4%	9.2%	10.5%	16.6%	9.4%	11.3%
to Finland	0.5%	0.7%	1.3%	2.1%	0.7%	2.1%	1.9%
to Sweden	1.4%	1.8%	3.7%	3.9%	2.7%	4.0%	2.8%
to Norway	8.0%	5.2%	1.2%	2.0%	1.4%	2.0%	1.5%
to Denmark	5.6%	4.7%	5.0%	4.3%	3.7%	4.8%	3.3%
to Poland	3.0%	1.9%	2.9%	7.4%	5.5%	7.3%	4.8%
to Lithuania	*	*	*	*	0.8%	1.0%	0.6%
to Latvia	*	*	*	*	0.3%	0.4%	0.5%
to Estonia	*	*	*	*	0.4%	0.6%	0.4%
to EU countries	25.1%	37.2%	42.5%	43.6%	40.1%	48.5%	38.4%
to CIS countries	*	*	*	*	*	*	*

Imports, total in billion DEM, countries in % of total	1993	1994	1995	1996	1997	1998	1999
Total imports	1.82	2.01	2.00	2.27	2.68	2.75	2.62
from Russia	3.2%	4.3%	5.6%	3.8%	5.0%	2.9%	9.4%
from Finland	5.8%	5.4%	1.2%	1.0%	1.2%	1.6%	1.5%
from Sweden	10.7%	13.5%	10.3%	15.8%	10.7%	10.6%	10.6%
from Norway	8.0%	8.0%	5.1%	5.4%	3.8%	3.2%	4.6%
from Denmark	17.9%	15.3%	16.2%	12.6%	12.2%	9.1%	8.0%
from Poland	7.8%	8.8%	11.5%	10.8%	11.6%	10.9%	9.4%
from Lithuania	*	*	*	*	1.5%	2.3%	2.0%
from Latvia	*	*	*	*	2.6%	1.9%	1.0%
from Estonia	*	*	*	*	3.4%	6.7%	1.4%
from EU countries	60.3%	60.9%	55.3%	56.2%	52.4%	48.4%	46.4%
from CIS countries	*	*	*	*	*	*	*

Employed persons by activity

Employed by activities in 1000 persons [7]	1994	1995	1996	1997	1998	1999
All activities	751.0	768.1	759.3	743.2	737.3	730.9
Agriculture, hunting and forestry	44.1	40.8	35.6	35.6	38.3	38.4
Fishing /\						
Mining and quarrying	0.6	0.6	0.5	0.4	\/	\/
Manufacturing	84.2	82.4	81.2	78.2	83.3	85.3
Electricity, gas and water supply	9.1	8.2	7.9	7.9	/\	/\
Construction	120.1	127.5	125.6	120.2	110.3	101.2
Wholesale and retail sales	125.0	126.5	126.4	129.9	178.8	178.3
Hotels and restaurants /\						
Transport, storage and communication	54.8	53.4	51.3	46.8	/\	/\
Financial intermediation \/						
Real estate, renting and business activities	64.4	67.2	69.0	69.8	72.4	72.3
Public administration and defence \/						
Education \/						
Health and social care \/						
Other community, social and personal services	248.8	261.4	261.8	254.3	254.3	255.3

Prices

Change in index, previous period = 100[8]	1994	1995	1996	1997	1998	1999
Consumer price index	104	102	102	102	101	100
Prducer price index for manufactured products	101	101	101	102	100	99

International sea traffic

The number of vessels in harbours	1994	1995	1996	1997	1998	1999
Arrivals from abroad	*	10631	13037	13102	13324	12909
Departures abroad	*	10565	13015	13084	13312	12889

International arrivals/departures in harbours, 1000 persons	1994	1995	1996	1997	1998	1999
Arriving in Germany total	*	*	*	*	*	*
Departing from Germany total	*	*	*	*	*	*

International air traffic

Passengers in airports in 1000	1994	1995	1996	1997	1998	1999
Arrivals	*	*	*	*	*	*
Departures	5	7	22	34	48	40

Sources
Questionnaires completed by the Statistisches Landesamt Mecklenburg-Vorpommern.

Notes
1) Death classified on codes No E960-E969, 9 Rev ICD, 1979 per 100 000 persons of population.
2) The weight of food and beverage in private consumption is based on the avarage value for medium income 4 persons famililies in the family budget survey.
3) The number of registered passenger cars on 100 persons.
4) Figures from Labour Force Surveys or other surveys of individuals following the ILO definition of unemployed persons: Person without work, currently available for work if there should be work and actively seeking work.
5) The split of GDP on activities is not available. The split of GVA on activities and the links between total GDP and total GVA are shown instead. Results according to ESA-95.
6) Hotels and restaurants are included here.
7) Employed persons as defined by ILO: working and paid as a wage earner, enterpreneur or a freelancer, working without direct payment in a family enterprise or farm, temporarily absent-from work. Results according to ESA-95.
8) The cost of living index in Mecklenburg-Vorpommern is used as best proxy for CPI and the producer price index for all new Bundesländern and East-Berlin is used as a proxy for PPI for Mecklenburg-Vorpommern.
   * Data not available
   0, 0,0   Less than half of the unit employed
   - Zero

Country/region: Schleswig-Holstein

Basic Data and Population
Total land- and water area: 15771 square km of which agricultural land: 73%, forest and wood-land: 9%

Total population (end of the respective year or closest possible estimate):
1993	2.69 million
1994	2.71 million
1995	2.73 million
1996	2.74 million
1997	2.76 million of which 49% male, 51% female
1998	2.77 million of which 49% male, 51% female
1999	2.78 million of which 49% male, 51% female

by age groups in %	1993	1994	1995	1996	1997	1998	1999
00 - 19 years	20.3	20.5	20.6	20.8	20.9	21.0	21.1
20 - 64 years	63.8	63.5	63.4	63.2	63.0	63.0	62.5
65 - years	15.9	16.0	16.0	16.0	16.1	16.0	16.4

by nationality in % for all nationalities 0.5% or more	1993	1994	1995	1996	1997	1998	1999
1. Germans	95.3	95.1	94.9	94.8	94.7	94.8	94.5
2. Turks	1.4	1.5	1.6	1.6	1.6	1.6	1.6
3. former Yugoslavians	0.3	0.3	0.6	0.6	0.6	0.4	0.6

The total population has increased from 2.68 million in 1992 to 2.78 million in 1999.

Migration in 1000 of persons	1993	1994	1995	1996	1997	1998	1999
Total immigration	124.7	116.2	114.8	83.0	80.4	77.9	79.8
Total emigration	106.8	99.4	93.9	63.7	65.1	66.0	65.8
Net migration	17.9	16.7	20.9	19.4	15.4	11.9	14.0
Natural in/decrease	-2.6	-3.2	-3.9	-2.5	-1.2	-2.3	-2.8

Life expectancy at birth in years	1986/88	1994	1995	1996	1997	1998	1999
for men	72.5	*	*	*	*	*	*
for women	78.7	*	*	*	*	*	*

Mortality rate by homicide, assaults per 100 000 persons[1]	1993	1994	1995	1996	1997	1998	1999
	1.2	1.2	1.6	0.8	0.8	0.8	0.8

Consumption

Food as % of total private consumption[2]	1993	1994	1995	1996	1997	1998	1999
	22.0	22.0	21.8	21.2	21.0	20.4	*
Cars per 100 persons[3]	50	51	51	52	52	52	53

The number of dwellings at the end of:			
1993 was	1185978	*% owned by state and local authorities,	*% by private persons
1994 was	1206386	*% owned by state and local authorities,	*% by private persons
1995 was	1229900	*% owned by state and local authorities,	*% by private persons
1996 was	1248831	*% owned by state and local authorities,	*% by private persons
1997 was	1269381	*% owned by state and local authorities,	*% by private persons
1998 was	1288973	*% owned by state and local authorities,	*% by private persons
1999 was	1306664	*% owned by state and local authorities,	*% by private persons

In 1993 51% was occupied by owners and 49% by tenants according to sample survey.

Unemployment

The number of unemployed persons, (1000 persons), annual average:	1993	1994	1995	1996	1997	1998	1999
In Labour Force Surveys[4]	110	124	126	116	133	124	118
Registered unemployment	94	102	102	113	127	128	122

National accounts

GDP in fixed prices (base year -95) in billion DEM and change in %:							
1993	94/93	1994	95/94	1995	96/95	1996	97/96	1997
108.8	1.1%	110.0	2.3%	112.5	0.8%	113.4	1.1%	114.7
Preliminary estimates for 1997 and 1998:					98/97	1998	99/98	1999
					1.6%	116.5	1.9%	118.7

GDP and Gross Value Added (GVA) total in current prices, activity in % of total GVA:[5]	1994	1995	1996	1997	Prel. est. 1998	Prel. est. 1999
Total at market prices in billion DEM	107.8	112.5	114.0	117.2	120.3	123.8
Taxes on products less subsidies (-)	-11.0	-11.1	-11.2	-11.3	-11.7	-12.7
Unallocated banking services	4.4	4.4	4.4	4.4	4.4	4.4
Total gross value added in billion DEM	101.2	105.8	108.1	110.3	113.0	115.5
Agriculture, hunting, forestry and fishing	2.4	2.5	2.5	2.5	2.3	2.2
Manufacturing and mining, quarrying	18.4	17.9	16.9	16.7	16.9	16.9
Electricity, gas, water supply, mining	3.0	3.0	3.5	3.0	2.7	2.9
Construction	6.3	6.1	5.5	5.1	4.9	4.6
Wholesale and retail sales[*]	12.8	12.8	13.1	13.5	13.6	13.4
Transport, storage and communication	5.8	5.7	5.5	5.7	5.8	5.7
Public administration, education, health and social work[**]	23.8	23.9	23.7	23.8	23.5	23.4
Other services	27.5	28.1	29.2	29.8	30.3	30.8

*) Includes hotels and restaurants; **) Includes personal services and households with employees

GNP by expenditure, total in current prices in billion DEM, expenditure as % of total:		1994	1995	1996	1997	Prel. est. 1998	Prel. est. 1999
Total		117.3	120.7	123.8	*	*	*
Private consumption		57.7	58.2	59.4	*	*	*
Government consumption		17.9	18.1	18.1	*	*	*
Consumption of non-profit institutions							
Gross fixed capital formation		18.3	19.1	17.7	*	*	*
Changes in stocks	\/						
Exports (FOB)		6.1	4.6	4.8	*	*	*
Imports (FOB) (-)	/\						

GDP by income, total in current prices in billion DEM, income categories as % of total:	1994	1995	1996	1997	Prel. est. 1998	Prel. est. 1999
Total	*	*	*	*	*	*
Compensation of employees	*	*	*	*	*	*
therein wages and salaries	*	*	*	*	*	*
Consumption of fixed capital	*	*	*	*	*	*
Indirect taxes	*	*	*	*	*	*
Subsidies (-)	*	*	*	*	*	*
Operating surplus and mixed income	*	*	*	*	*	*

Foreign trade

Exports, total in billion DEM, countries in % of total	1993	1994	1995	1996	1997	1998	1999
Total exports	11.6	12.9	14.0	14.7	17.1	17.8	*
to Russia	2.3%	2.2%	1.8%	2.0%	2.6%	1.9%	*
to Finland	1.0%	1.0%	1.1%	0.9%	0.7%	0.8%	*
to Sweden	3.0%	3.2%	2.6%	2.4%	2.3%	2.4%	*
to Norway	2.2%	2.6%	1.8%	2.1%	2.1%	1.7%	*
to Denmark	6.8%	6.9%	6.4%	6.7%	8.4%	8.0%	*
to Poland	2.0%	1.9%	2.1%	2.6%	2.4%	2.6%	*
to Lithuania	0.2%	0.2%	0.1%	0.2%	0.2%	0.2%	*
to Latvia	0.1%	0.2%	0.1%	0.1%	0.1%	0.1%	*
to Estonia	0.1%	0.1%	0.1%	0.2%	0.2%	0.2%	*
to EU countries	46.2%	44.2%	52.7%	55.2%	52.6%	56.8%	*
to CIS countries	*	*	*	*	*	*	*

Imports, total in billion DEM, countries in % of total	1993	1994	1995	1996	1997	1998	1999
Total imports	13.2	14.9	15.5	15.5	17.0	18.2	*
from Russia	0.7%	1.1%	0.9%	0.8%	1.1%	1.2%	*
from Finland	4.0%	4.3%	4.5%	3.7%	2.8%	3.3%	*
from Sweden	9.2%	9.1%	7.9%	9.1%	8.8%	9.9%	*
from Norway	2.7%	2.6%	2.5%	2.8%	3.1%	2.2%	*
from Denmark	16.4%	15.5%	15.8%	15.2%	14.7%	14.3%	*
from Poland	2.6%	2.1%	2.0%	2.0%	1.8%	1.7%	*
from Lithuania	0.1%	0.1%	0.2%	0.4%	0.2%	0.2%	*
from Latvia	0.1%	0.2%	0.2%	0.3%	0.3%	0.3%	*
from Estonia	0.1%	0.1%	0.2%	0.1%	0.2%	0.2%	*
from EU countries	47.3%	47.6%	64.0%	65.4%	76.3%	66.0%	*
from CIS countries	*	*	*	*	*	*	*

Employed persons by activity

Employed by activity in 1000 persons[6]		1994	1995	1996	1997	1998	1999
All activities		1245	1248	1250	1230	1231	1236
Agriculture, hunting and forestry		53	47	43	38	39	39
Fishing	/\						
Mining and quarrying	\/						
Manufacturing		*	229	218	204	188	198
Electricity, gas and water supply		*	13	17	13	12	13
Construction		111	110	106	102	98	99
Wholesale and retail sales		*	246	266	258	264	256
Hotels and restaurants	/\						
Transport, storage and communication		84	77	74	77	67	72
Financial intermediation		50	48	44	48	51	53
Real estate, renting and business activities		*	80	84	88	89	93
Public administration and defence		161	152	139	141	154	141
Education	\/						
Health and social care	\/						
Other community, social and personal services		*	246	260	261	269	273

Prices[7]

Change in index, previous period = 100	1994	1995	1996	1997	1998	1999
Consumer price index	103	102	102	102	101	100
Producer price index for manufactured products [8]	101	101	100	101	100	100

International sea traffic

The number of vessels in harbours	1994	1995	1996	1997	1998	1999
Arrivals from abroad and from Germany	57466	56994	53255	50115	50374	48970
Departures abroad and to Germany	57206	56774	53382	50164	50036	48942

International arrivals/departures in harbours, 1000 persons	1994	1995	1996	1997	1998	1999
Arriving in Germany total	*	*	*	*	*	*
Departing from Germany total	*	*	*	*	*	*

International air traffic

Passengers in airports in 1000	1994	1995	1996	1997	1998	1999
Arrivals	-	-	-	-	-	-
Departures	-	-	-	-	-	-

Sources
Questionnaires completed by the Statistisches Landesamt Schleswig-Holstein.

Notes
1) Deaths (pos. No. X85 - Y09 and Y87.1, 10.Rev. ICD, 1983) per 100 00 persons of average population the respective year.
2) The weight is based food, beverage, tobacco and consumption in restaurants in household budget data for medium income 4-person families; data for Germany as a whole.
3) Registration of passenger and combination cars July 1 the respective year .
4) Figures from Labour Force Surveys or other surveys of individuals following the ILO definition of unemployed persons: Person without work, currently available for work if there should be work and actively seeking work.
5) The split of GDP on activities is not available. The split of GVA on activities and the links between total GDP and total GVA are shown instead.
6) Employed persons as defined by ILO: working and paid as a wage earner, enterpreneur or a freelancer, working without direct payment in a family enterprise or farm, temporarily absent from work.
7) Price indices for Germany as a whole are used.
8) VAT/sales tax not included
   * Data not available
   0, 0,0   Less than half of the unit employed
 - Zero

Country/region: Denmark

Basic Data and Population

Total land- and water area: 43096 square km of which agricultural land: 62% forest and wood-land: 12%

Total population (end of the respective year or closest possible estimate):	
1993	5.20 million of which
1994	5.22 million of which
1995	5.25 million of which
1996	5.28 million of which
1997	5.29 million of which 49% male, 51% female
1998	5.31 million of which 49% male, 51% female
1999	5.33 million of which 49% male, 51% female

by age groups in %	1993	1994	1995	1996	1997	1998	1999
00 - 19 years	23.8	23.6	23.6	23.5	23.6	23.6	23.7
20 - 64 years	60.7	60.9	61.1	61.3	61.4	61.5	61.5
65 - years	15.5	15.4	15.3	15.2	15.0	14.9	14.8

by nationality in % for all nationalities 0.5% or more	1993	1994	1995	1996	1997	1998	1999
1. Danes	96.5	96.4	96.2	95.8	95.3	95.2	95.1
2. Turks	0.7	0.7	0.7	0.7	0.7	0.7	0.7
3. former Yugoslavians	-	-	-	-	0.6	0.6	0.7

The total population has increased from 5.18 millions in 1992 to 5.33 millions in 1999.

Migration in 1000 of persons	1993	1994	1995	1996	1997	1998	1999
Total immigration	43.4	45.0	63.2	54.4	50.1	51.4	50.2
Total emigration	32.3	34.7	34.6	37.3	38.4	40.3	41.3
Net migration	11.1	10.3	28.6	17.1	11.7	11.0	8.9
Natural in/decrease	4.5	8.5	6.6	6.6	7.7	7.7	7.1

Life expectancy at birth in years	1993	1994	1995	1996	1997-98	1998-99
for men	72.5	72.5	72.6	72.9	73.7	74.0
for women	77.8	77.8	77.8	78.0	78.6	78.8

Mortality rate by homicide, assaults per 100 000 persons	1993	1994	1995	1996	1997	1998	1999
assaults per 100 000 persons	4.9	5.8	4.4	4.4	5.4	*	*

Consumption

Food as % of total private consumption	1993	1994	1995	1996	1997	1998	1999
	20.0	19.0	18.9	18.5	18.2	17.9	17.9
Passenger cars per 100 persons	31	31	31	32	33	34	35

The number of dwellings at the end of:			
1991 was	2251112	*% owned by state and local authorities,	*% by private persons
1994 was	*	*% owned by state and local authorities,	*% by private persons
1995 was	2340089	*% owned by state and local authorities,	*% by private persons
1996 was	*	*% owned by state and local authorities,	*% by private persons
1997 was	*	*% owned by state and local authorities,	*% by private persons
1998 was	2357051	*% owned by state and local authorities,	*% by private persons
1999 was	2488972	21% owned by state and local authorities,	79% by private persons

Unemployment

The number of unemployed persons, (1000 persons), annual average:							
	1993	1994	1995	1996	1997	1998	1999
In Labour Force Surveys[1]	349	343	288	246	220	183	158
Registered unemployment	*	*	*	*	*	*	*

National accounts

GDP in fixed prices (base year -95) in billion DKK and change in %:									
	1993	94/93	1994	95/94	1995	96/95	1996	97/96	1997
	931.8	5.5%	982.7	2.8%	1009.8	2.5%	1035.2	3.1%	1067.7
Preliminary estimates for 1998-99:						98/97	1998	99/98	1999
						2.5%	1094.8	1.7%	1113.2

GDP by field of activity, total in current prices in billion DKK activity in % of total:	1994	1995	1996	1997	1998	Prel. est. 1999
Total at market prices	966	1010	1061	1112	1164	1216
Agriculture, hunting, forestry and fishing	2.8%	3.2%	3.1%	2.9%	2.5%	2.4%
Mining, quarrying and manufacturing	16.1%	16.0%	15.6%	15.6%	15.4%	15.1%
Electricity, gas, water supply	2.0%	2.1%	2.3%	2.2%	2.0%	1.9%
Construction	3.9%	4.1%	4.3%	4.3%	4.4%	4.2%
Wholesale and retail sales	11.9%	11.7%	11.7%	11.6%	11.4%	11.6%
Transport, storage and communication	6.8%	6.8%	6.9%	7.1%	7.2%	7.1%
Public administration, education, health and social work	20.1%	23.8%	23.6%	23.4%	23.5%	23.7%
Other services	26.1%	21.6%	21.1%	21.1%	21.3%	22.1%
Unallocated banking services (-)	3.3%	3.1%	2.9%	2.8%	2.8%	2.9%
Total at basic prices	86.4%	86.3%	85.8%	85.5%	84.9%	85.3%
Taxes on products	15.6%	15.6%	15.9%	16.1%	16.6%	16.3%
Subsidies (-)	1.9%	1.9%	1.7%	1.6%	1.5%	1.5%

GDP by expenditure, total in current prices in billion DKK, expenditure as % of total:	1994	1995	1996	1997	1998	Prel. est. 1999
Total	966	1010	1061	1112	1164	1216
Private consumption	51.1%	50.5%	50.3%	50.7%	51.1%	50.5%
Government consumption	25.9%	25.8%	25.9%	25.6%	25.8%	25.7%
Consumption of non-profit institutions	*	*	*	*	*	*
Gross fixed capital formation	17.6%	19.7%	18.9%	20.2%	21.2%	19.6%
Changes in stocks /\						
Exports (FOB)	35.5%	35.4%	35.8%	36.5%	35.3%	36.9%
Imports (FOB) (-)	30.1%	31.3%	30.8%	33.0%	33.4%	32.7%

GDP by income, total in current prices in billion DKK, income categories in % of total:	1994	1995	1996	1997	1998	Prel. est. 1999
Total	966	1010	1061	1112	1164	1216
Compensation of employees	52.2%	52.9%	52.8%	52.9%	53.3%	53.7%
therein wages and salaries	*	*	*	*	*	*
Consumption of fixed capital	14.0%	15.1%	15.0%	15.2%	14.7%	14.0%
Indirect taxes	15.6%	15.6%	15.9%	16.1%	16.6%	16.3%
Subsidies (-)	1.9%	1.9%	2.0%	1.6%	1.5%	1.5%
Operating surplus and mixed income	*	18.4%	18.2%	17.4%	16.7%	17.4%

Foreign trade

Exports, total in billion DKK, countries in % of total	1993	1994	1995	1996	1997	1998	1999
Total exports	245	270	283	296	321	323	345
to Russia	0.8%	1.0%	1.3%	1.5%	1.9%	1.5%	0.8%
to Finland	1.9%	2.3%	2.6%	2.7%	2.6%	3.0%	3.2%
to Sweden	10.0%	10.2%	10.7%	11.2%	11.3%	11.2%	11.3%
to Norway	6.7%	6.5%	6.2%	6.5%	6.2%	6.2%	6.0%
to Germany	24.6%	23.6%	23.6%	22.5%	21.2%	20.7%	20.0%
to Poland	1.3%	1.4%	1.4%	1.7%	1.8%	2.0%	1.8%
to Lithuania	0.1%	0.2%	0.3%	0.3%	0.5%	0.5%	0.5%
to Latvia	0.1%	0.1%	0.1%	0.2%	0.2%	0.3%	0.2%
to Estonia	0.1%	0.1%	0.1%	0.2%	0.2%	0.3%	0.2%
to EU countries	65.8%	64.3%	65.7%	65.6%	65.0%	65.0%	65.8%
to CIS countries	1.0%	1.3%	1.7%	1.8%	2.3%	1.9%	1.0%

Imports, total in billion DKK, countries in % of total	1993	1994	1995	1996	1997	1998	1999
Total imports	203	231	255	261	294	309	312
from Russia	1.1%	1.0%	1.0%	0.9%	0.7%	0.7%	0.7%
from Finland	2.7%	2.9%	2.9%	2.8%	2.9%	2.7%	2.7%
from Sweden	10.7%	11.1%	12.1%	12.3%	12.7%	12.7%	12.2%
from Norway	4.9%	4.8%	4.7%	5.1%	5.3%	4.7%	4.4%
from Germany	23.6%	22.9%	23.6%	22.7%	21.5%	22.0%	21.6%
from Poland	1.5%	1.7%	1.6%	1.6%	1.7%	1.7%	1.8%
from Lithuania	0.2%	0.2%	0.2%	0.3%	0.3%	0.3%	0.4%
from Latvia	0.3%	0.1%	0.1%	0.2%	0.2%	0.2%	0.3%
from Estonia	0.1%	0.1%	0.1%	0.2%	0.2%	0.2%	0.3%
from EU countries	68.7%	69.3%	71.9%	70.9%	70.4%	71.1%	71.7%
from CIS countries	1.3%	1.2%	1.1%	1.0%	0.9%	0.9%	0.8%

Employed persons by activity

Employed by activity in 1000 persons[2]		1994	1995	1996	1997	1998	1999
All activities		2812	2858	2649	2670	2699	2742
Agriculture, hunting and forestry		134	130	124	121	116	112
Fishing	/\						
Mining and quarrying	/\						
Manufacturing		500	505	486	476	478	479
Electricity, gas and water supply		21	21	18	18	18	17
Construction		163	165	154	157	161	165
Wholesale and retail sales		485	506	470	478	486	495
Hotels and restaurants	/\						
Transport, storage and communication		185	185	174	178	178	181
Financial intermediation	\/						
Real estate, renting and business activities		321	327	292	296	308	326
Public administration and defence	\/						
Education	\/						
Health and social care	\/						
Other community, social and personal services		1003	1017	916	932	943	958
Other		0	0	15	14	13	10

Enterprises

The number of active enterprises by ownership and size	1995	1996	1997	1998	1999
All active enterprises	429261	426745	421408	422078	*
With private domestic owners	*	*	*	*	*
With foreign owners	*	*	*	*	*
Owned by state or local government	*	*	*	*	*
Number of enterprises in wholesale and retail trade	*	91971	89596	87962	*
Enterprises with 200 or more employees	*	*	*	*	*
20 to 199 employees	*	*	*	*	*
5 to 19 employees	*	*	*	*	*
less than 5 employees	*	*	*	*	*

Direct inward and outward investment

Foreign direct investment in Denmark		1994	1995	1996	1997	1998	1999
Net direct investment flow in billion DKK		15.4	23.4	4.5	18.5	49.1	75.5
as % of the Danish GDP for the year		1.6%	2.3%	0.4%	1.7%	4.2%	6.2%
by country: from	Eastern European countries*)	0.0	0.0	0.0	0.0	0.0	0.0
	Finland	0.1	0.1	0.4	-0.2	*	*
	Germany	1.3	1.5	1.7	0.9	2.0	2.5
	Netherlands	3.9	2.0	-5.4	0.3	-0.5	21.8
	Norway	3.5	1.0	0.1	1.7	3.5	1.2
	Sweden	0.9	3.1	0.4	5.3	7.0	14.1
	Switzerland	0.1	0.4	-0.1	-0.5	0.5	1.7
	United Kingdom	3.5	9.7	1.0	2.4	2.6	4.2
	United States	1.4	1.4	1.8	2.0	26.7	13.8

*) Data for Estonia, Latvai, Lithuania, Poland and Russia have not been available but are included here.

The stock of direct investment capital							
in Denmark at the end of year, total	108.5	*	132.8	*	199.1	269.5
thereof in:							
Mining, quarrying and manufacture	20.0	*	26.5	*	26.7	26.6
Wholesale and retail trade	36.1	*	44.9	*	45.8	52.8
Transport, storage and communication	5.1	*	6.8	*	52.8	109.2

Danish direct investment abroad		1994	1995	1996	1997	1998	1999
Net investment flow abroad in billion DKK		7.5	17.2	14.6	27.8	30.1	84.7
by country: to	Eastern European countries*)	0.3	1.3	1.7	2.0	4.2	2.9
	Finland	0.2	0.2	0.2	0.1	*	*
	Germany	-0.1	2.5	-1.2	3.5	1.2	10.6
	Netherlands	0.1	1.2	4.8	0.7	0.9	15.1
	Norway	0.9	0.5	0.2	1.1	3.3	9.9
	Sweden	0.4	1.9	4.8	6.4	4.6	4.3
	Switzerland	0.2	2.3	0.5	1.6	-1.3	0.2
	United Kingdom	0.1	-0.2	-0.8	3.2	10.9	2.3
	United States	3.4	5.0	-1.7	1.7	-4.2	19.3

*) Data for Estonia, Latvai, Lithuania, Poland and Russia have not been available but are included here.

Foreign loans and foreign aid

Net amount borrowed from abroad	1994	1995	1996	1997	1998	1999
in billion DKK.	*	*	*	*	*	*
as % of the Danish GDP for the year	*	*	*	*	*	*

Prices

Change in index, previous period = 100	1994	1995	1996	1997	1998	1999
Consumer price index	101	102	102	102	102	102
Producer price index for manufactured products	*	105	101	102	99	100

International sea traffic

The number of vessels in harbours	1994	1995	1996	1997	1998	1999
Arrivals from abroad	*	*	*	*	*	*
Departures abroad	*	*	*	*	*	*

International arrivals/departures in harbours, 1000 persons	1994	1995	1996	1997	1998	1999
Carried by ferries to/from Denmark	*	36264	36172	36283	37534	36329

International air traffic

Passengers in airports in 1000	1994	1995	1996	1997	1998	1999
Arrivals and departures	*	*	*	*	8180	8608

Sources

Statistisk Årbog 2000 and previous years.

Notes

1) Figures from Labour Force Surveys or other surveys of individuals following the ILO definition of unemployed persons: Person without work, currently available for work if there should be work and actively seeking work.
2) Employed persons as defined by ILO: working and paid as a wage earner, entrepreneur or a freelancer, working without direct payment in a family enterprise or farm, temporarily absent from work.
 * Data not available
 0, 0,0   Less than half of the unit employed
 - Zero

Country/region: Finland

Basic Data and Population
Total land- and water area: 338145 square km of which agricultural land: 8%, forest and wood-land: 68%

Total population (end of the respective year or closest possible estimate):
1993   5.08 million of which
1994   5.10 million of which
1995   5.12 million of which
1996   5.13 million of which
1997   5.15 million of which 49% male, 51% female
1998   5.16 million of which 49% male, 51% female
1999   5.17 million of which 49% male, 51% female

by age groups in %	1993	1994	1995	1996	1997	1998	1999
00 - 19 years	25.5	25.5	25.4	25.2	25.0	24.8	24.7
20 - 64 years	60.6	60.4	60.3	60.3	60.4	60.5	60.5
65 - years	13.9	14.1	14.3	14.5	14.6	14.7	14.8

by nationality in % for all nationalities 0.5% or more	1993	1994	1995	1996	1997	1998	1999
1. Finns	*	*	98.7	*	*	98.4	98.3
2. Russians	*	*	0.2	*	*	0.3	0.4
3. Estonians	*	*	0.2	*	*	0.2	0.2
4. Swedes	*	*	0.1	*	*	0.2	0.2

The total population has increased from 5.05 mill. persons in 1992 to 5.17 mill. persons in 1999.

Migration in 1000 of persons	1993	1994	1995	1996	1997	1998	1999
Total immigration	14.8	11.6	12.2	13.3	13.6	14.2	14.7
Total emigration	6.4	8.7	9.0	10.6	9.9	10.8	12
Net migration	8.4	2.9	3.3	2.7	3.7	3.4	2.8
Natural in/decrease	13.8	17.2	13.8	11.6	10.2	7.8	8.2

Life expectancy at birth in years	1993	1994	1995	1996	1997	1998	1999
for men	72.1	72.8	72.8	73.0	73.4	73.5	73.7
for women	79.5	80.2	80.2	80.5	80.5	80.8	81.0

Mortality rate by homicide, assaults per 100 000 persons	1993	1994	1995	1996	1997	1998	1999
assaults per 100 000 persons	3.3	3.2	2.9	3.3	2.8	*	*

Consumption

Food as % of total private consumption	1993	1994	1995	1996	1997	1998	1999
	23.3	22.5	21.0	19.7	19.5	18.9	18.6
Passenger cars per 100 persons	37	37	37	38	38	39	40

The number of dwellings at the end of:

1993 was	2331406	*% owned by state and local authorities,	*% by private persons
1994 was	2352156	*% owned by state and local authorities,	*% by private persons
1995 was	2373973	*% owned by state and local authorities,	*% by private persons
1996 was	2390843	*% owned by state and local authorities,	*% by private persons
1997 was	2416378	*% owned by state and local authorities,	*% by private persons
1998 was	2449000	*% owned by state and local authorities,	*% by private persons
1999 was	*	*% owned by state and local authorities,	*% by private persons

Unemployment

The number of unemployed persons, (1000 persons), annual average:

	1993	1994	1995	1996	1997	1998	1999
In Labour Force Surveys[1]	405	408	382	363	314	285	261
Registered unemployment	482	494	466	448	408.0	372	348

National accounts

GDP in fixed prices (base year -95) in billion FIM and change in %:

1993	94/93	1994	95/94	1995	96/95	1996	97/96	1997
523.2	4.0%	543.8	3.8%	564.6	4.0%	587.2	6.3%	624.1

Preliminary estimates for 1998 and 1999:			98/97	1998	99/98	1999
			5.5%	658.3	4.0%	684.8

GDP by field of activity, total in current prices in billion FIM, activity in % of total:	1994	1995	1996	1997	Prel. est. 1998	Prel. est. 1999
Total at market prices	522.3	564.6	585.9	635.5	691.2	723.6
Agriculture, hunting, forestry and fishing	4.8%	4.1%	3.6%	3.6%	3.3%	3.2%
Mining, quarrying and manufacturing	21.6%	23.1%	21.3%	21.9%	22.4%	21.7%
Electricity, gas, water supply	2.3%	2.3%	2.3%	2.1%	2.0%	1.8%
Construction	4.1%	4.2%	4.4%	4.5%	4.9%	4.9%
Wholesale and retail sales	8.9%	8.9%	9.0%	9.5%	9.3%	9.3%
Transport, storage and communication	7.7%	7.6%	7.7%	7.8%	7.9%	8.0%
Public administration, education, health and social work	22.4%	21.9%	22.0%	21.1%	20.3%	20.1%
Other services	18.2%	18.1%	18.8%	18.5%	18.7%	19.5%
Unallocated banking services (-)	2.8%	2.5%	2.3%	2.3%	2.3%	2.1%
Total at basic prices	87.3%	87.4%	86.8%	86.6%	86.4%	86.4%
Taxes on products	12.7%	12.6%	13.2%	13.4%	13.6%	13.6%
Subsidies (-) /\						

GDP by expenditure, total in current prices in billion FIM, expenditure as % of total:[2]	1994	1995	1996	1997	Prel. est. 1998	Prel. est. 1999
Total	522.3	564.6	585.9	635.5	691.2	723.6
Private consumption	53.4%	51.7%	52.7%	50.9%	50.1%	50.3%
Government consumption	23.4%	22.8%	23.2%	22.4%	21.6%	21.5%
Consumption of non-profit institutions						
Gross fixed capital formation	15.5%	16.3%	17.0%	18.0%	18.7%	19.1%
Changes in stocks	1.4%	1.2%	-0.3%	0.4%	1.0%	0.5%
Exports (FOB)	35.1%	37.0%	37.5%	39.1%	38.7%	37.4%
Imports (FOB) (-)	29.2%	29.1%	30.0%	30.9%	29.8%	29.3%
Statistical discrepancy	0.5%	0.0%	-0.1%	0.1%	-0.2%	0.5%

GDP by income, total in current prices in billion FIM, income categories as % of total: [2]	1994	1995	1996	1997	1998	Prel.est. 1999
Total	522.3	564.6	585.9	635.5	691.2	723.6
Compensation of employees	50.7%	50.2%	50.1%	48.8%	48.5%	47.8%
therein wages and salaries	39.3%	39.2%	39.4%	38.4%	38.1%	37.6%
Consumption of fixed capital	*	*	*	*	*	*
Indirect taxes	14.5%	13.9%	14.4%	14.5%	14.6%	14.6%
Subsidies (-)	3.1%	3.3%	2.7%	2.5%	2.3%	2.2%
Operating surplus and mixed income	19.3%	21.6%	21.3%	22.9%	23.6	23.7%

Foreign trade

Exports, total in billion FIM, countries in % of total	1993	1994	1995	1996	1997	1998	1999
Total exports	134	154	176	186	213	231	233
to Russia	4.5%	5.2%	4.8%	6.1%	7.3%	6.0%	4.1%
to Sweden	11.1%	10.9%	10.1%	10.7%	9.8%	9.4%	9.9%
to Norway	3.2%	3.2%	3.0%	2.9%	2.9%	3.3%	2.8%
to Denmark	3.3%	3.4%	3.2%	3.0%	3.1%	2.8%	2.8%
to Germany	13.1%	13.4%	13.4%	12.1%	11.0%	11.8%	13.1%
to Poland	1.5%	1.7%	1.3%	1.5%	1.8%	1.8%	1.8%
to Lithuania	<0.2%	0.3%	0.3%	0.4%	0.4%	0.5%	0.4%
to Latvia	0.2%	0.5%	0.6%	0.6%	0.7%	0.7%	0.7%
to Estonia	1.4%	2.2%	2.4%	2.7%	3.2%	3.3%	3.0%
to EU countries	46.9%	46.4%	57.5%	54.5%	53.2%	56.1%	57.9%
to CIS countries	*	*	*	*	*	*	*

Imports, total in billion FIM, countries in % of total	1993	1994	1995	1996	1997	1998	1999
Total imports	103	121	129	142	161	173	177
from Russia	7.6%	8.9%	7.1%	7.2%	7.8%	6.6%	7.2%
from Sweden	10.2%	10.4%	11.7%	11.9%	12.1%	11.6%	11.2%
from Norway	4.9%	4.8%	4.1%	4.2%	3.7%	3.5%	3.6%
from Denmark	3.1%	3.0%	3.2%	3.5%	3.4%	3.6%	3.7%
from Germany	16.4%	14.7%	15.6%	15.0%	14.5%	15.2%	15.3%
from Poland	1.3%	1.3%	1.1%	0.9%	1.1%	0.9%	0.7%
from Lithuania	<0.1%	0.1%	0.1%	0.1%	0.1%	0.1%	0.1%
from Latvia	0.1%	0.1%	0.2%	0.1%	0.1%	0.2%	0.1%
from Estonia	0.7%	0.9%	1.2%	1.2%	1.4%	1.8%	1.8%
from EU countries	46.5%	43.6%	59.9%	60.3%	59.3%	59.7%	57.9%
from CIS countries	*	*	*	*	*	*	*

Employed persons by activity

Employed by activities in 1000 persons [3]		1994	1995	1996	1997	1998	1999
All activities		2054	2099	2127	2169	2222	2296
Agriculture, hunting and forestry		178	170	159	153	144	144
Fishing	/\						
Mining and quarrying	\/						
Manufacturing		428	457	461	463	475	488
Electricity, gas and water supply	/\						
Construction		109	115	118	130	139	149
Wholesale and retail sales		297	301	316	329	339	355
Hotels and restaurants	/\						
Transport, storage and communication		161	163	160	164	170	168
Financial intermediation		230	228	241	240	249	267
Real estate, renting and business activities	/\						
Public administration and defence	\/						
Education	\/						
Health and social care	\/						
Other community, social and personal services		645	659	667	684	700	719
Other		7	6	6	7	8	6

Enterprises

The number of active enterprises by ownership and size	1995	1996	1997	1998	1999
All active enterprises	189458	*	213230	219273	*
With private domestic owners	*	*	*	*	*
With foreign owners	*	*	*	*	*
Owned by state or local government	*	*	*	*	*
Number of enterprises in wholesale and retail trade	45844	*	50314	50538.0	*
Enterprises with 250 or more employees	499	*	513	533	*
20 to 249 employees	5093	*	5632	6173	*
5 to 19 employees	20955	*	24509	23071	*
less than 5 employees	162911	*	182576	189496	*

Direct inward and outward investment

Foreign direct investment in Finland.	1994	1995	1996	1997	1998	1999
Net direct investment flow in million FIM	8240	4642	5093	10975	64896	26308
as % of the Finland GDP for the year	1.6%	0.8%	0.9%	1.7%	9.5%	3.6%
by country: from Denmark	2528	-471	-57	21	2808	6690
Estonia	*	*	*	*	*	*
Germany	171	237	1269	127	472	1249
Latvia	*	*	*	*	*	*
Lithuania	*	*	*	*	*	*
Netherlands	-131	472	61	1723	-1600	10225
Norway	1405	-142	-766	134	-704	2069
Poland	*	*	*	*	*	*
Russia[**]	207	24	-24	-3	-1	*
Sweden	1506	819	339	2329	55146	5493
Switzerland	-725	439	-1427	-182	-27	1524
United Kingdom	286	799	2940	738	565	2573
United States	609	41	537	257	1222	-2840

**) Figures without reinvested earnings.

The stock of direct investment capital in Finland at the end of year, total	31846	36894	40854	51658	83855	107746
of which in:						
Mining, quarrying and manufacture	*	*	*	*	41227	49078
Wholesale and retail trade	*	*	*	*	12669	18810
Transport, storage and communication	*	*	*	*	*	*

Finland direct investments abroad. 1994	1995	1996	1997	1998	1999
Net investment flow abroad in million FIM 22447	6539	16516	27449	99645	32555
by country: to Denmark	4930	561	806	-456	-1845	150
Estonia	113	112	134	155	286	*
Germany	1086	539	2964	167	5579	-2567
Latvia	5	30	90	55	107	*
Lithuania	4	27	27	56	83	*
Netherlands	5007	-248	2166	5844	27527	9193
Norway	48	-63	1042	-84	858	1636
Poland	49	24	179	141	19	*
Russia	182	184	336	319	445	*
Sweden	591	962	4640	7467	75008	7190
Switzerland	-295	-1104	1076	857	-1130	-461
United Kingdom	5322	1594	-683	1492	797	303
United States	694	2073	-386	4575	5213	7719

Foreign loans and foreign aid

Net amount borrowed from abroad	1994	1995	1996	1997	1998	1999
in million FIM.	*	-6984	12737	*	*	*
as % of the Finland GDP for the year	*	-1.2%	2.2%	*	*	*

Prices

Change in index, previous period = 100	1994	1995	1996	1997	1998	1999
Consumer price index	101	101	101	101	101	101
Producer price index for manufactured products	102	103	99	101	99	99

International sea traffic

The number of vessels in harbours	1994	1995	1996	1997	1998	1999
Arrivals from abroad	*	23699	22891	25203	26255	27705
Departures abroard	*	*	*	*	*	*

International arrivals/departures in harbours, 1000 persons	1994	1995	1996	1997	1998	1999
Arriving in Finland total	6243	6978	7045	7617	8012	8094
Departing from Finland total	6222	6933	7007	7574	7974	8051

International air traffic

Passengers in airports in 1000	1994	1995	1996	1997	1998	1999
Arrivals and departures	4578	5113	5525	5921	6479	6715

Sources
Suomen Tilastollinen Vuosikirja 2000 and previous years.

Notes
1) Figures from Labour Force Surveys or other surveys of individuals following the ILO definition of unemployed persons: Person without work, currently available for work if there should
   be work and actively seeking work.
2) Information about the consumption of non-profit institutions and the consumption of fixed
   capital have not been available in the sources used.
3) Employed persons as defined by ILO: working and paid as a wage earner, entrepreneur or a
   freelancer, working without direct payment in a family enterprise or farm, temporarily absent
   from work.
 * Data not available
   0, 0,0   Less than half of the unit employed
 - Zero

Country/region: Åland

Basic Data and Population

Total land- and water area: 6800 square km of which land: 22%, water: 78%

Total population (end of the respective year or closest possible estimate):
1993	25.102 persons
1994	25.158 persons
1995	25.202 persons
1996	25.257 persons
1997	25.392 persons of which 49% male, 51% female
1998	25.625 persons of which 49% male, 51% female
1999	25.706 persons of which 49% male, 51% female

by age groups in %	1993	1994	1995	1996	1997	1998	1999
00 - 19 years	24.3	24.3	24.3	24.4	24.5	24.4	24.4
20 - 64 years	59.3	59.2	59.4	59.4	59.2	59.3	59.3
65 - years	16.3	16.5	16.3	16.3	16.4	16.3	16.2

by nationality in % for all nationalities 0.5% or more	1993	1994	1995	1996	1997	1998	1999
1. Finnish citizens	96.4	96.5	96.4	96.3	96.1	95.9	*
2. Swedish citizens	2.6	2.5	2.6	2.7	2.8	3.0	*

The total population has increased from 24993 persons in 1992 to 25706 persons in 1999.

Migration in persons	1993	1994	1995	1996	1997	1998	1999
Total immigration	352	389	380	446	508	595	576
Total emigration	356	377	437	425	435	446	483
Net migration	-4	12	-57	21	73	149	93
Natural in/decrease	88	42	80	9	45	74	-10

Life expectancy at birth in years	1993	1994	1995	1996	1997	1998	1999
for men	74.6	75.1	75.1	72.9	75.4	77.4	*
for women	82.6	81.8	81.1	82.7	82.3	84.8	*

Mortality rate by homicide, assaults per 100 000 persons[1]	1993	1994	1995	1996	1997	1998	1999
	4.0	0.0	0.0	0.0	*	*	*

Consumption

Food as % of total private[2] consumption	1993	1994	1995	1996	1997	1998	1999
(incl. alc. and tobacco)	*	*	22.5	*	*	*	*
(excl. alc. and tobacco)	*	*	15.8	*	*	*	*
Cars per 100 persons[3]	50	50	51	52	51	52	53

The number of dwellings at the end of:			
1993 was	11511	*% owned by state and local authorities,	*% by private persons
1994 was	11628	*% owned by state and local authorities,	*% by private persons
1995 was	11833	*% owned by state and local authorities,	*% by private persons
1996 was	11953	*% owned by state and local authorities,	*% by private persons
1997 was	11999	*% owned by state and local authorities,	*% by private persons
1998 was	10894	*% owned by state and local authorities,	*% by private persons
1999 was	*	*% owned by state and local authorities,	*% by private persons

Unemployment

The number of unemployed persons, annual average:	1993	1994	1995	1996	1997	1998	1999
In Labour Force Surveys [4]	*	*	*	*	*	*	*
Registered unemployment	836	961	810	658	527	386	314

National accounts

GDP in fixed prices (base year -90) in billion FIM and change in %:							
1993	94/93	1994	95/94	1995	96/95	1996	97/96	1997
3.07	11.5%	3.42	1.2%	3.46	5.5%	3.67	9.8%	4.03
Preliminary estimates for 1998 and 1999:					98/97	1998	99/98	1999
					*	*	*	*

GDP by field of activity, total in current prices in billion FIM, activity in % of total:[5]	1994	1995	1996	1997	1998	Prel. est. 1999
Total at market prices	3.78	3.84	4.05	4.52	*	*
Agriculture, hunting, forestry and fishing	4.5%	4.2%	3.5%	3.3%	*	*
Mining, quarrying and manufacturing	5.7%	5.8%	6.0%	5.5%	*	*
Electricity, gas, water supply	1.0%	0.8%	0.9%	0.6%	*	*
Construction	1.3%	2.0%	2.0%	2.1%	*	*
Wholesale and retail sales	6.7%	6.4%	6.2%	6.5%	*	*
Transport, storage and communication	42.2%	39.7%	40.8%	41.6%	*	*
Public administration, education, health and social work	15.3%	16.1%	16.5%	15.2%	*	*
Other services	11.9%	13.9%	15.0%	15.6%	*	*
Total at basic prices	88.6%	89.0%	90.9%	90.4%	*	*
Taxes on products	14.3%	14.3%	14.2%	14.4%	*	*
Subsidies (-)	2.9%	3.2%	3.3%	3.1%	*	*

GDP by expenditure, total in current prices in million FIM, expenditure as % of total:	1994	1995	1996	1997	1998	Prel. est. 1999
Total	3775	3842	4052	4523	*	*
Private consumption	31.8%	38.8%	36.9%	*	*	*
Government consumption	19.4%	20.4%	21.6%	*	*	*
Consumption of non-profit institutions						
Gross fixed capital formation	25.3%	28.0%	22.1%	*	*	*
Changes in stocks	-0.9%	-0.2%	0.2%	*	*	*
Exports (FOB)	102.2%	95.4%	105.0%	*	*	*
Imports (FOB) (-)	95.7%	91.5%	86.0%	*	*	*
Other external transactions net	17.8%	9.1%	0.1%	*	*	*

GDP by income, total in current prices in million FIM, income categories as % of total:	1994	1995	1996	1997	1998	Prel. est. 1999
Total	3775	3842	4052	4523	*	*
Compensation of employees	51.1%	53.5%	51.4%	*	*	*
therein wages and salaries	39.4%	41.6%	40.0%	*	*	*
Consumption of fixed capital	13.3%	12.4%	12.6%	*	*	*
Indirect taxes	14.3%	14.3%	14.2%	*	*	*
Subsidies (-)	2.9%	3.2%	-3.3%	*	*	*
Operating surplus and mixed income	24.2%	23.1%	25.0%	*	*	*

Foreign trade

Exports, total in million FIM, countries in % of total	1993	1994	1995	1996	1997	1998	1999
Total exports	3223	3856	3681	4250	*	*	*
to Russia	*	*	*	*	*	*	*
to Finland	*	*	*	*	*	*	*
to Sweden	*	*	*	*	*	*	*
to Norway	*	*	*	*	*	*	*
to Denmark	*	*	*	*	*	*	*
to Germany	*	*	*	*	*	*	*
to Poland	*	*	*	*	*	*	*
to Lithuania	*	*	*	*	*	*	*
to Latvia	*	*	*	*	*	*	*
to EU countries	*	*	*	*	*	*	*
to CIS countries	*	*	*	*	*	*	*

Imports, total in million FIM, countries in % of total	1993	1994	1995	1996	1997	1998	1999
Total imports	2350	3595	3541	3473	*	*	*
from Russia	*	*	*	*	*	*	*
from Finland	*	*	*	*	*	*	*
from Sweden	*	*	*	*	*	*	*
from Norway	*	*	*	*	*	*	*
from Denmark	*	*	*	*	*	*	*
from Germany	*	*	*	*	*	*	*
from Poland	*	*	*	*	*	*	*
from Lithuania	*	*	*	*	*	*	*
from Latvia	*	*	*	*	*	*	*
from EU countries	*	*	*	*	*	*	*
from CIS countries	*	*	*	*	*	*	*

Employed persons by activity

Employed persons by activity[6]		1994	1995	1996	1997	1998	1999
All activities		11407	11494	11652	12034	12251	*
Agriculture, hunting and forestry		1194	963	968	947	*	*
Fishing	/\						
Mining and quarrying	\/						
Manufacturing		1111	1179	1142	1160	*	*
Electricity, gas and water supply	/\						
Construction		598	605	573	630	*	*
Wholesale and retail sales		1461	1431	1436	1519	*	*
Hotels and restaurants	/\						
Transport, storage and communication		2166	2266	2260	2339	*	*
Financial intermediation	/\						
Real estate, renting and business activities		841	851	860	892	*	*
Public administration and defence		3224	3436	3924	4070	*	*
Education	/\						
Health and social care	/\						
Other community, social and personal services	\/						
Other		812	763	489	477	*	*

Enterprises

The number of active enterprises by ownership and size	1995	1996	1997	1998	1999
All active enterprises	*	*	1836	*	*
With private domestic owners	*	*	*	*	*
With foreign owners	*	*	*	*	*
Owned by state or local government	*	*	*	*	*
Number of enterprises in wholesale and retail trade	*	*	465	*	*
Enterprises with 200 or more employees	*	*	5	*	*
20 to 199 employees	*	*	45	*	*
5 to 19 employees	*	*	189	*	*
less than 5 employees	*	*	1597	*	*

Direct inward and outward investment

Foreign direct investment in Åland	1994	1995	1996	1997	1998	1999
Net direct investment flow in million FIM	*	*	*	*	*	*
as % of the Åland GDP for the year						
by country: from Denmark	*	*	*	*	*	*
Germany	*	*	*	*	*	*
Esrtonia	*	*	*	*	*	*
Latvia	*	*	*	*	*	*
Lithuania	*	*	*	*	*	*
Netherlands	*	*	*	*	*	*
Norway	*	*	*	*	*	*
Poland	*	*	*	*	*	*
Russia	*	*	*	*	*	*
Sweden	*	*	*	*	*	*
Switzerland	*	*	*	*	*	*
United Kingdom	*	*	*	*	*	*
United States	*	*	*	*	*	*
The stock of direct investment capital in Åland at the end of year, total	*	*	*	*	*	*
of which in:						
Mining, quarrying and manufacture	*	*	*	*	*	*
Wholesale and retail trade	*	*	*	*	*	*
Transport, storage and communication	*	*	*	*	*	*

Åland direct investment abroad	1994	1995	1996	1997	1998	1999
Net investment flow abroad in million FIM	*	*	*	*	*	*
by country: to Denmark	*	*	*	*	*	*
Germany	*	*	*	*	*	*
Estonia	*	*	*	*	*	*
Latvia	*	*	*	*	*	*
Lithuania	*	*	*	*	*	*
Netherlands	*	*	*	*	*	*
Norway	*	*	*	*	*	*
Poland	*	*	*	*	*	*
Russia	*	*	*	*	*	*
Sweden	*	*	*	*	*	*
Switzerland	*	*	*	*	*	*
United Kingdom	*	*	*	*	*	*
United States	*	*	*	*	*	*

Foreign loans and foreign aid

Net amount borrowed from abroad	1994	1995	1996	1997	1998	1999
in million FIM.	*	*	*	*	*	*
as % of the Åland GDP for the year	*	*	*	*	*	*

Prices

Change in index, previous period = 100	1994	1995	1996	1997	1998	1999
Consumer price index	101	101	100	102	102	*
Producer price index for manufactured products	*	*	*	*	*	*

International sea traffic

The number of vessels in harbours	1994	1995	1996	1997	1998	1999
Arrivals from abroad	4671	4444	4266	5032	4891	*
Departures abroard	*	*	*	*	*	*

International arrivals/departures in harbours, in 1000 persons	1994	1995	1996	1997	1998	1999
Arriving in Åland total	1076	1068	1156	1394	1568	*
from Finland	173	184	184	253	326	*
from Sweden	903	885	972	1141	1242	*
Departing from Åland total						
to Finland						
to Sweden						

International air traffic

Passengers in airports in 1000[*]	1994	1995	1996	1997	1998	1999
Arrivals	47	53	54	56	60	*
Departures						

*) Including passengers from Finland.

Sources
Questionnaires completed by the Department of Statistics and Economic Research in Åland.

Notes
1) Deaths per 100 000 persons classified on codes No E960-E969, 9 Rev ICD, 1979.
2) From CPI wieghts for 1990 and 1995 respectively.
3) Registration of passenger cars/ 100 persons.
4) No reliable data exist.
5) All banking services are allocatedted on activities.
6) Employed persons as defined by ILO: working and paid as a wage earner, entrepreneur or a freelancer, working without direct payment in a family enterprise or farm, temporarily absent from work.
  * Data not available
   0, 0,0   Less than half of the unit employed
 - Zero

Country/region: Norway

Basic Data and Population

Total land- and water area: 385155 square km of which agricultural land: 3 - 4%, forest and woodland: 33%

Total population (end of the respective year or closest possible estimate):
1993   4.32 million of which
1994   4.35 million of which
1995   4.37 million of which
1996   4.39 million of which
1997   4.42 million of which 49% male, 51% female
1998   4.45 million of which 49% male, 51% female
1999   4.48 million of which 50% male, 50% female

by age groups in %	1993	1994	1995	1996	1997	1998	1999
00 - 19 years	25.8	25.7	25.7	25.7	25.8	25.8	25.9
20 - 64 years	58.2	58.4	58.5	58.5	58.6	58.7	58.8
65 - years	16.1	16.0	15.9	15.8	15.7	15.5	15.3

by nationality in % for all nationalities 0.5% or more	1993	1994	1995	1996	1997	1998	1999
1. Norwegians	*	*	94.6	94.5	94.4	94.2	*
2. Swedes	*	*	0.5	0.6	0.6	0.7	*
3. Danes	*	*	0.5	0.5	0.5	0.5	*

The total population has increased from 4.3 millions in 1992 to 4.48 millions in 1999.

Migration in 1000 of persons	1993	1994	1995	1996	1997	1998	1999
Total immigration	31.7	26.9	25.7	26.4	32.0	36.7	41.7
Total emigration	18.9	19.5	19.3	20.6	21.3	22.9	22.3
Net migration	12.8	7.4	6.4	5.8	10.7	13.8	19.3
Natural in/decrease	13.1	16.0	15.1	17.1	15.2	14.2	14.1

Life expectancy at birth in years	1993	1994	1995	1996	1997	1998	1999
for men	74.2	74.9	74.8	75.4	75.5	75.5	75.6
for women	80.3	80.6	80.8	81.1	81.0	81.3	81.1

Mortality rate by homicide	1993	1994	1995	1996	1997	1998	1999
assaults per 100 000 persons	1.0	0.8	1.0	1.1	*	*	*

Consumption

Food as % of total private consumption	1993	1994	1995	1996	1997	1998	1999
	21.5	21.4	21.0	20.5	20.4	20.3	20.1
Passenger cars per 100 persons	38	38	39	38	40	40	40

The number of dwellings at the end of:				
1990 was	1751363	*% owned by state and local authorities,	*% by private persons
1994 was	*	*% owned by state and local authorities,	*% by private persons
1995 was	*	*% owned by state and local authorities,	*% by private persons
1996 was	*	*% owned by state and local authorities,	*% by private persons
1997 was	*	*% owned by state and local authorities,	*% by private persons
1998 was	*	*% owned by state and local authorities,	*% by private persons
1999 was	*	*% owned by state and local authorities,	*% by private persons

Unemployment

The number of unemployed persons (1000 persons), annual average:							
	1993	1994	1995	1996	1997	1998	1999
In Labour Force Surveys [1]	127	116	107	108	92	74	75
Registered unemployment	118	110	102	91	74	56	60

National accounts

GDP in current prices in bilion NOK and volume change in %							
	1993	94/93	1994	95/94	1995	96/95	1996	97/96	1997
	823	5.5%	868	3.8%	929	4.9%	1017	4.7%	1096
Preliminary estimates for 1998 and 1999:					98/97	1998	99/98	1999
					2.0%	1109	0.9%	1193

GDP by field of activity, total in current prices in billion NOK, activity in % of total:[2]					Prel. est.	Prel. est.
	1994	1995	1996	1997	1998	1999
Total at market prices	868	929	1017	1096	1109	1193
Agriculture, hunting, forestry and fishing	2.6%	2.4%	2.2%	2.0%	2.1%	1.9%
Mining, quarrying and manufacturing	23.4%	23.9%	26.5%	26.8%	22.7%	24.9%
Electricity, gas, water supply	2.4%	2.6%	2.1%	2.2%	2.1%	1.9%
Construction	3.3%	3.7%	3.6%	3.6%	4.0%	4.0%
Wholesale and retail sales	9.6%	9.6%	9.1%	8.8%	9.0%	8.9%
Transport, storage and communication	9.9%	9.6%	9.1%	9.1%	9.2%	8.7%
Public administration, education, health and social work	15.9%	15.6%	15.5%	15.1%	16.3%	16.2%
Other services	23.3%	22.2%	21.4%	21.5%	23.3%	22.7%
Unallocated banking services (-)	*	*	2.9%	2.7%	3.1%	3.0%
Total at basic prices	86.8%	86.5%	86.6%	86.4%	85.6%	86.5%
Taxes on products	13.2%	13.5%	13.5%	13.6%	14.1%	13.5%

GDP by expenditure, total in current prices in billion NOK, expenditure as % of total:	1994	1995	1996	1997	Prel. est. 1998	Prel. est. 1999
Total	868	929	1017	1096	1109	1193
Private consumption	47.3%	46.9%	45.8%	45.2%	47.4%	46.1%
Government consumption	21.3%	20.7%	20.3%	19.9%	21.4%	21.2%
Consumption of non-profit institutions	2.5%	2.4%	2.4%	2.3%	2.4%	2.3%
Gross fixed capital formation	21.1%	21.3%	21.3%	23.0%	25.0%	22.2%
Changes in stocks	1.6%	2.5%	1.6%	2.1%	3.4%	2.1%
Exports (FOB)	38.5%	38.4%	40.7%	40.9%	37.2%	39.0%
Imports (FOB) (-)	32.4%	32.3%	32.2%	33.4%	36.7%	33.0%

GDP by income, total in current prices in billion NOK, income categories as % of total:[3]	1994	1995	1996	1997	Prel. est. 1998	Prel. est. 1999
Total	868	929	1017	1096	1109	1193
Compensation of employees	47.8%	47.4%	46.3%	46.8%	50.4%	49.8%
therein wages and salaries	*	*	*	*	*	*
Consumption of fixed capital	*	16.2%	15.5%	15.2%	16.3%	16.1%
Indirect taxes	13.2%	13.5%	13.5%	13.6%	14.1%	13.5%
Subsidies (-)	*	*	*	*	*	*
Operating surplus and mixed income	23.5%	23.7%	25.5%	24.8%	20.0%	21.2%

Foreign trade

Exports, total in billion NOK, countries in % of total	1993	1994	1995	1996	1997	1998	1999
Total exports	227	244	266	320	342	305	355
to Russia	0.3%	0.4%	0.5%	0.6%	0.7%	0.7%	0.4%
to Finland	2.6%	3.0%	2.8%	2.2%	2.1%	2.7%	2.3%
to Sweden	8.7%	9.5%	9.8%	9.1%	8.8%	9.8%	9.4%
to Denmark	4.4%	4.7%	5.0%	4.5%	5.1%	5.7%	5.3%
to Germany	13.0%	12.1%	12.7%	11.1%	10.9%	12.3%	10.0%
to Poland	1.0%	1.0%	0.9%	0.7%	0.7%	1.1%	0.9%
to Lithuania	0.0%	0.0%	0.1%	0.1%	0.1%	0.1%	0.1%
to Latvia	0.0%	0.1%	0.1%	0.2%	0.2%	0.2%	0.1%
to Estonia	0.0%	0.0%	0.1%	0.1%	0.1%	0.1%	0.1%
to EU countries	78.3%	73.9%	77.2%	76.7%	75.9%	76.9%	74.0%
to CIS countries	0.4%	0.4%	0.5%	0.6%	0.8%	0.7%	0.5%

Imports, total in billion NOK, countries in % of total	1993	1994	1995	1996	1997	1998	1999
Total imports	171	193	208	229	252	283	267
from Russia	1.4%	2.3%	1.8%	1.6%	2.0%	1.6%	2.0%
from Finland	3.3%	3.6%	3.9%	3.5%	3.2%	3.4%	3.5%
from Sweden	14.2%	15.0%	15.4%	16.5%	15.7%	14.7%	15.1%
from Denmark	7.4%	7.4%	7.6%	7.5%	7.1%	6.7%	6.8%
from Germany	13.6%	13.9%	13.8%	13.1%	13.6%	13.5%	12.8%
from Poland	0.5%	0.5%	0.5%	0.5%	0.7%	0.7%	1.0%
from Lithuania	0.0%	0.1%	0.1%	0.1%	0.1%	0.1%	0.2%
from Latvia	0.1%	0.1%	0.2%	0.2%	0.1%	0.1%	0.2%
from Estonia	0.1%	0.1%	0.1%	0.1%	0.2%	0.2%	0.2%
from EU countries	67.2%	68.7%	71.0%	69.9%	68.0%	67.7%	67.8%
from CIS countries	1.3%	2.5%	1.9%	1.7%	2.1%	1.7%	2.1%

Employed persons by activity

Employed by activity in 1000 persons[4]		1994	1995	1996	1997	1998	1999
All activities		2035	2079	2132	2195	2248	2258
Agriculture, hunting and forestry		109	107	108	101	104	102
Fishing	/\						
Mining and quarrying		24	25	23	24	28	27
Manufacturing		304	309	318	328	325	305
Electricity, gas and water supply		22	22	21	21	18	18
Construction		114	121	126	130	141	146
Wholesale and retail sales		362	373	389	400	411	411
Hotels and restaurants	/\						
Transport, storage and communication		161	166	164	167	175	170
Financial intermediation	\/						
Real estate, renting and business activities		192	193	206	223	241	252
Public administration and defence		147	143	145	151	155	153
Education		160	165	165	169	171	179
Health and social care		344	356	372	384	383	397
Other community, social and personal services		88	93	91	92	95	96

Enterprises

The number of active enterprises by ownership and size	1995	1996	1997	1998	1999
All active enterprises	*	*	*	*	*
with private domestic owners	*	*	*	*	*
with foreign owners	*	*	*	*	*
owned by state or local government	*	*	*	*	*
Number of enterprises in wholesale and retail trade*	*	*	*	*	
Enterprises with 200 or more employees	*	*	*	*	*
20 to 199 employees	*	*	*	*	*
5 to 19 employees	*	*	*	*	*
less than 5 employees	*	*	*	*	*

Direct inward and outward investment

Foreign direct investment in Norway 1994	1995	1996	1997	1998	1999
Net direct investment flow in billion NOK	15.1	9.3	13.4	21.1	24.8	51.0
as % of the Norwegian GDP for the year	1.7%	1.0%	1.3%	1.8%	2.3%	4.3%
by country: from Denmark	1.6	0.3	-0.2	0.6	3.8	7.8
Finland	*	*	*	*	*	*
Germany	-0.1	0.3	-0.3	0.2	0.5	0.6
Estonia	*	*	*	*	*	*
Latvia	*	*	*	*	*	*
Lithuania	*	*	*	*	*	*
Netherlands	*	*	*	*	*	*
Poland	*	*	*	*	*	*
Russia	*	*	*	*	*	*
Sweden	-0.5	4.3	2.4	0.9	2.5	19.0
Switzerland	*	*	*	*	*	*
United Kingdom	6.5	-4.4	0.0	2.5	5.2	11.5
United States	3.5	0.1	10.9	0.3	-0.9	-2.0
The stock of direct investment capital in Norway at the end of year, total	110.1	118.8	135.3	164.5	194.7	231.8
of which in:						
Mining, quarrying and manufacture	67.3	71.2	86.1	103.9	124.8	138.2
Wholesale and retail trade*	16.3	17.8	19.0	20.1	22.9	25.2
Transport, storage and communication	1.3	1.6	2.7	4.5	5.4	8.4

*) incl. hotels and restaurants

Norwegian direct investment abroad	1994	1995	1996	1997	1998	1999
Net investment flow abroad in billion NOK	11.8	14.9	31.8	29.9	16	36.8
by country: to Denmark	2.9	0.2	-0.2	1.1	1.3	0.1
Estonia	*	*	*	*	*	*
Finland	*	*	*	*	*	*
Germany	0.5	0.0	0.2	0.5	-2.4	2.9
Latvia	*	*	*	*	*	*
Lithuania	*	*	*	*	*	*
Netherlands	*	*	*	*	*	*
Poland	*	*	*	*	*	*
Russia	*	*	*	*	*	*
Sweden	0.8	6.2	8.1	6.2	3.5	9.2
Switzerland	*	*	*	*	*	*
United Kingdom	-1.1	3.6	17.9	2.3	-3.2	0.7
United States	4.7	0.9	0.3	8.7	4.6	1.7

Foreign loans and foreign aid

Net amount borrowed from abroad	1994	1995	1996	1997	1998	1999
in billion NOK.	23.7	-2.2	*	*	*	*
as % of the Norwegian GDP for the year	2.7%	-0.2%	*	*	*	*

Prices

Change in index, previous period = 100	1994	1995	1996	1997	1998	1999
Consumer price index	101	102	101	103	102	102
Producer price index for manufactured products	*	104	103	*	101	102

International sea traffic

The number of vessels in harbours	1994	1995	1996	1997	1998	1999
Arrivals from abroad	*	*	*	*	*	*
Departures abroard trip abroad	*	*	*	*	*	*

International arrivals/departures in harbours, 1000 persons	1994	1995	1996	1997	1998	1999
Ferry lines Norway-abroad arrivals and departures	5147	5006	5394	5769	6032	6107

International air traffic

Passengers in airports in 1000	1994	1995	1996	1997	1998	1999
Arivals and departures	4084	4213	4737	5418	7596	7991

Sources

Statistisk Årbok 2000 and previous years.

Notes

1) Figures from Labour Force Surveys or other surveys of individuals following the ILO definition of unemployed persons: Person without work, currently available for work if there should
   be work and actively seeking work. Break in timeseries 1996 due to changes in data collection.
2) All banking services are allocated on activities for the years 1992 to 1995.
3) Information about the wages and salaries, the consumption of fixed capital, the subsidies and
   the operating surplus and mixed income have not been available in the sources used.
4) Employed persons as defined by ILO: working and paid as a wage earner, entrepreneur or a
   freelancer, working without direct payment in a family enterprise or farm, temporarily absent
   from work.
 * Data not available
   0, 0,0   Less than half of the unit employed
 - Zero

Country/region: Sweden

Basic Data and Population
Total land- and water area: 450000 square km of which agricultural land: 8%, forest and woodland: 54%

Total population (end of the respective year or closest possible estimate):
1993	8.75 million of which
1994	8.82 million of which
1995	8.84 million of which
1996	8.84 million of which
1997	8.85 million of which 49% male, 51% female
1998	8.85 million of which 49% male, 51% female
1999	8.86 million of which 49% male, 51% female

by age groups in %	1993	1994	1995	1996	1997	1998	1999
00 - 19 years	24.7	24.7	24.6	24.5	24.4	24.3	24.2
20 - 64 years	57.8	57.9	58.0	58.1	58.2	58.3	58.5
65 - years	17.6	17.5	17.5	17.5	17.4	17.4	17.3

by country of birth in % of total population, only 0.5% or more	1990	1994	1995	1996	1997	1998	1999
1. Swedes	90.8	89.5	89.4	89.3	89.2	89.1	*
2. Finns	2.5	2.4	2.3	2.3	2.3	2.2	*
3. Norwegians	0.6	0.5	0.5	0.5	0.5	0.5	*
4. Danes	0.5	0.5	0.5	0.4	0.4	0.4	*
5. Bosnia-Herzegovinians	....	0.5	0.5	0.5	0.5	0.6	*
6. former Yugoslavians	0.5	0.8	0.8	0.8	0.8	0.8	*
7. Iranians	0.5	0.6	0.6	0.6	0.6	0.6	*

The total population has increased from 8.69 millions in 1992 to 8.86 millions in 1999.

Migration in 1000 of persons	1993	1994	1995	1996	1997	1998	1999
Total immigration	61.9	83.6	45.9	39.9	44.8	49.4	49.8
Total emigration	29.9	32.7	34.0	33.9	38.5	38.5	35.7
Net migration	32.0	50.9	11.9	6.0	6.3	10.9	14.1
Natural in/decrease	21.0	20.4	9.5	1.2	-2.8	-4.2	-6.6

Life expectancy at birth in years	1993	1994	1995	1996	1997	1998	1999
for men	75.5	76.1	76.2	76.5	76.7	76.9	77.1
for women	80.8	81.4	81.5	81.8	81.8	81.9	81.9

Mortality rate by homicide, assaults per 100 000 persons	1993	1994	1995	1996	1997	1998	1999
assaults per 100 000 persons	1.3	1.2	1.0	1.3	1.1	*	*

Consumption

Food as % of total private consumption	1993	1994	1995	1996	1997	1998	1999
	18.9	18.8	18.5	17.3	16.9	16.5	16.4
Passenger cars per 100 persons	41	41	41	41	42	42	44

The number of dwellings at the end of:			
1990 was	4044768	*% owned by state and local authorities,	*% by private persons
1994 was	*	*% owned by state and local authorities,	*% by private persons
1995 was	*	*% owned by state and local authorities,	*% by private persons
1996 was	*	*% owned by state and local authorities,	*% by private persons
1997 was	*	*% owned by state and local authorities,	*% by private persons
1998 was	*	*% owned by state and local authorities,	*% by private persons
1999 was	*	*% owned by state and local authorities,	*% by private persons

Unemployment

The number of unemployed persons, (1000 persons), annual average:	1993	1994	1995	1996	1997	1998	1999
In Labour Force Surveys[1]	356	340	333	347	342	276	241
Registered unemployment	*	*	*	*	*	*	*

National accounts

GDP in fixed prices (reference year -95) in billion SEK and change in %:								
	1993	94/93	1994	95/94	1995	96/95	1996	97/96	1997
	1587	4.1%	1652	3.7%	1713	1.1%	1732	2.1%	1768
Preliminary estimates for 1998 and 1999:						98/97	1998	99/98	1999
						3.6%	1831	4.1%	1907

GDP by field of activity, total in current prices in billion SEK, activity in % of total:	1994	1995	1996	1997	1998	Prel. est. 1999
Total at market prices	1596	1713	1756	1824	1905	1995
Agriculture, hunting, forestry and fishing	2.3%	2.3%	2.2%	2.2%	2.2%	*
Mining, quarrying and manufacturing	19.6%	20.7%	20.9%	21.6%	21.9%	*
Electricity, gas, water supply	2.7%	2.7%	2.6%	2.6%	2.6%	*
Construction	4.2%	4.1%	4.0%	3.7%	3.7%	*
Wholesale and retail sales	9.5%	9.6%	9.9%	10.1%	10.2%	*
Transport, storage and communication	6.7%	6.8%	7.0%	7.1%	7.1%	*
Public administration, education, health and social work	23.4%	22.8%	22.5%	21.9%	21.6%	*
Other services	22.9%	22.8%	23.4%	23.5%	23.3%	*
Unallocated banking services (-)	3.0%	3.5%	3.7%	4.0%	3.5%	*
Total at basic prices	88.0%	88.6%	88.6%	88.8%	88.9%	*
Taxes on products	12.5%	11.9%	11.9%	11.7%	11.6%	*
Subsidies	0.5%	0.5%	0.5%	0.5%	0.5%	*

GDP by expenditure, total in current prices in billion SEK, expenditure as % of total:	1994	1995	1996	1997	1998	Prel. est. 1999
Total	1596	1713	1756	1824	1905	1995
Households and NPISH*	52.0%	50.2%	50.3%	50.6%	50.2%	50.2%
Government consumption	27.4%	26.3%	27.1%	26.5%	26.7%	26.9%
Gross fixed capital formation	15.1%	15.5%	15.7%	15.2%	16.0%	16.8%
Changes in stocks	0.8%	1.1%	0.2%	0.4%	0.8%	0.2%
Exports (FOB)	36.5%	40.5%	39.1%	42.7%	43.7%	43.7%
Imports (FOB) (-)	31.8%	33.6%	32.4%	35.4%	37.4%	37.8%

*) Non-profit institutions serving households

GDP by income, total in current prices in billion SEK, income categories as % of total:	1994	1995	1996	1997	1998	Prel. est. 1999
Total	1596	1713	1756	1824	1905	1995
Compensation of employees	56.4%	56.9%	56.8%	56.1%	56.2%	55.6%
therein wages and salaries	41.2%	41.9%	41.7%	*	*	*
Consumption of fixed capital	14.5%	12.6%	13.6%	13.6%	13.7%	13.9%
Indirect taxes	14.3%	14.4%	15.0%	15.5%	16.0%	17.5%
Subsidies (-)	4.1%	5.1%	3.6%	3.2%	2.7%	2.4%
Operating surplus and mixed income	18.9%	21.1%	18.2%	18.0%	16.8%	15.4%

Foreign trade

Exports, total in billion SEK, countries in % of total	1993	1994	1995	1996	1997	1998	1999
Total exports	388	472	568	569	633	675	702
to Russia	0.7%	0.7%	0.9%	0.9%	1.1%	0.9%	0.6%
to Finland	4.5%	4.8%	5.1%	5.2%	5.3%	5.2%	5.1%
to Norway	8.1%	8.1%	8.5%	8.4%	8.3%	8.5%	7.8%
to Denmark	6.6%	6.9%	6.1%	6.3%	6.1%	5.8%	5.6%
to Germany	14.4%	13.3%	11.7%	11.7%	11.1%	10.9%	10.6%
to Poland	0.8%	1.0%	1.3%	1.3%	1.6%	1.6%	1.8%
to Lithuania	0.1%	0.1%	0.2%	0.2%	0.2%	0.3%	0.2%
to Latvia	0.1%	0.2%	0.2%	0.2%	0.3%	0.3%	0.2%
to Estonia	0.2%	0.3%	0.3%	0.3%	0.5%	0.5%	0.5%
to EU countries	53.2%	53.2%	56.9%	57.1%	55.6%	58.0%	58.5%
to CIS countries	0.8%	0.8%	1.0%	1.0%	1.3%	1.1%	0.8%

Imports, total in billion SEK, countries in % of total	1993	1994	1995	1996	1997	1998	1999
Total imports	334	399	461	449	501	545	567
from Russia	1.0%	1.4%	1.2%	0.7%	0.6%	0.6%	0.8%
from Finland	6.2%	6.3%	5.9%	5.6%	5.3%	4.9%	5.2%
from Norway	6.4%	6.1%	7.1%	7.8%	7.7%	7.1%	7.4%
from Denmark	7.3%	6.8%	7.1%	7.5%	7.2%	6.2%	6.6%
from Germany	17.9%	18.4%	19.6%	18.8%	18.4%	17.8%	16.8%
from Poland	0.7%	0.9%	0.9%	0.9%	1.0%	1.1%	1.1%
from Lithuania	0.1%	0.2%	0.1%	0.1%	0.1%	0.2%	0.2%
from Latvia	0.2%	0.4%	0.5%	0.6%	0.6%	0.5%	0.6%
from Estonia	0.2%	0.3%	0.4%	0.6%	0.7%	0.8%	1.0%
from EU countries	55.2%	55.2%	70.6%	70.3%	69.4%	70.4%	68.9%
from CIS countries	1.0%	1.4%	1.2%	0.7%	0.7%	0.6%	0.8%

Employed persons by activity

Employed by activity in 1000 persons[2]		1994	1995	1996	1997	1998	1999
All activities		3928	3986	3963	3922	3979	4068
Agriculture, hunting and forestry		136	124	115	109	102	104
Fishing	/\						
Mining and quarrying	\/						
Manufacturing		761	802	809	800	803	797
Electricity, gas and water supply	/\						
Construction		225	230	225	218	220	225
Wholesale and retail sales		507	509	502	498	503	512
Hotels and restaurants		93	100	99	104	110	114
Transport, storage and communication		263	261	260	263	271	275
Financial intermediation		84	82	81	81	85	85
Real estate, renting and business activities		311	342	352	365	381	419
Public administration and defence		212	200	207	211	208	208
Education		315	318	315	306	323	343
Health and social care		818	819	794	763	770	776
Other community, social and personal services		200	197	201	201	200	207
Other (unknown)		3	2	2	4	4	3

Enterprises

The number of active enterprises by ownership and size	1995	1996	1997	1998	1999
All active enterprises	562765	585571	791385	810337	797338
With private domestic owners	*	*	*	*	*
With foreign owners	*	*	*	*	*
Owned by state or local government	*	*	*	*	*
Number of enterprises in wholesale and retail trade	111054	113669	119828	119735	117495
Enterprises with 200 or more employees	1626	1654	1647	1675	1712
20 to 199 employees	12202	12867	13006	13241	13717
5 to 19 employees	44205	45835	46207	47414	48360
less than 5 employees	504732	525215	730525	748007	733549

Direct inward and outward investment

Foreign direct investment in Sweden.	1994	1995	1996	1997	1998	1999
Net direct investment flow in billion SEK	49.0	103.1	34.0	83.7	155.4	503.3
as % of the Swedish GDP for the year	3.1%	6.0%	1.9%	4.6%	8.2%	25.2%
by country: from Denmark	-0.2	1.4	4.4	6.1	1.6	3.8
Estonia	*	*	*	*	*	*
Finland	-0.1	2.9	6.1	8.3	96.5	0.1
Germany	3.5	1.8	2.5	5.5	3.8	62.1
Latvia	*	*	*	*	*	*
Lithuania	*	*	*	*	*	*
Netherlands	23.1	2.2	-0.7	8.5	2.7	17.5
Norway	-0.7	9.3	7.8	6.7	1.8	3.2
Poland	*	*	*	*	*	*
Russia	-0.3	*	*	0.0	0.0	0.0
Switzerland	6.8	6.4	-0.3	-5.6	6.0	-9.7
United Kingdom	3.8	-1.2	4.4	8.8	4.3	317.3
United States	2.2	60.9	2.5	16.7	5.3	50.3
The stock of direct investment capital in Sweden at the end of year, total of which in:	*	*	*	*	*	*
Mining, quarrying and manufacture	*	*	*	*	*	*
Wholesale and retail trade	*	*	*	*	*	*
Transport, storage and communication	*	*	*	*	*	*

Swedish direct investment abroad		1994	1995	1996	1997	1998	1999
Net investment flow abroad in billion SEK		51.7	80.0	31.3	96.6	193.7	182.1
by country: to	Denmark	-0.1	2.0	-4.5	-1.4	0.7	9.3
	Estonia	0.1	0.1	0.0	0.3	2.6	1.7
	Finland	3.6	4.4	0.7	7.1	77.7	-8.1
	Germany	-3.3	-0.4	-2.9	4.9	0.1	7.1
	Latvia	0.1	0.0	0.0	0.0	0.2	0.4
	Lithuania	0.0	0.1	0.0	0.0	2.9	0.6
	Netherlands	23.7	6.6	1.5	-1.0	2.5	16.7
	Norway	-1.0	9.4	4.0	-0.2	4.4	10.7
	Poland	0.2	0.2	0.5	0.7	2.2	2.0
	Russia	-0.1	0.1	0.2	0.0	0.8	0.0
	Switzerland	-0.4	0.2	0.4	1.6	3.0	8.0
	United Kingdom	1.4	-3.0	2.4	3.2	3.4	16.0
	United States	6.2	21.2	-11.3	33.0	19.8	27.1

Foreign loans and foreign aid

Net amount borrowed from abroad	1994	1995	1996	1997	1998	1999
in billion SEK	-20.0	44.6	-27.4	-20.8	122.2	-73.0
as % of the Swedish GDP for the year	-1.3%	2.6%	-1.6%	-1.1%	6.4%	-3.7%

Prices

Change in index, previous period = 100	1994	1995	1996	1997	1998	1999
Consumer price index	102	103	100	101	101	100
Producer price index for manufactured products	105	110	98	101	100	99

International sea traffic

The number of vessels in harbours	1994	1995	1996	1997	1998	1999
Arrivals from abroad	103509	107352	113070	120434	120069	117887
Departures abroard	103620	107514	113149	120554	120073	118332

International arrivals/departures in harbours, 1000 persons	1994	1995	1996	1997	1998	1999
Arriving in Sweden total	17467	18016	18434	19154	*	*
Departing from Sweden total						

International air traffic

Passengers in airports in 1000	1994	1995	1996	1997	1998	1999
Arrivals and departures	9602	10586	11584	12819	13836	14614

Sources
Statistisk Årsbok 2001 and previous years and other statistics published.

Notes
1) Figures from Labour Force Surveys or other surveys of individuals following the ILO defini-tion of unemployed persons: Person without work, currently available for work if there should be work and actively seeking work.
2) Employed persons as defined by ILO: working and paid as a wage earner, entrepreneur or a freelancer, working without direct payment in a family enterprise or farm, temporarily absent from work.
  * Data not available
    0, 0,0   Less than half of the unit employed
  - Zero

Country/region: Poland

Basic Data and Population

Total land- and water area: 312685 square km of which agricultural land: 60%, forest and woodland: 29%

Total population (end of the respective year or closest possible estimate):
1993   38.50 million
1994   38.58 million
1995   38.61 million
1996   38.64 million
1997   38.66 million of which 49% male, 51% female
1998   38.67 million of which 49% male, 51% female
1999   38.65 million of which 49% male, 51% female

by age groups in %	1993	1994	1995	1996	1997	1998	1999
00 - 19 years	31.8	31.4	30.9	30.3	29.6	29.0	28.3
20 - 64 years	57.5	57.7	57.9	58.3	58.8	59.1	59.6
65 - years	10.7	10.9	11.2	11.4	11.6	11.9	12.1

by nationality in % for all nationalities 0.5% or more							
1.	*	*	*	*	*	*	*
2.	*	*	*	*	*	*	*

The total population has increased from 38.42 million in 1992 to 38.65 million in 1999.

Migration in 1000 of persons	1993	1994	1995	1996	1997	1998	1999
Total immigration	5.9	6.9	8.1	8.2	8.4	8.9	7.5
Total emigration	21.4	25.9	26.3	21.3	20.2	22.2	21.5
Net migration	-15.5	-19.0	-18.2	-13.1	-11.8	-13.3	-14.0
Natural in/decrease	102.0	94.9	47.0	42.7	32.5	20.3	0.6

Life expectancy at birth in years	1993	1994	1995	1996	1997	1998	1999
for men	67.4	67.5	67.6	68.1	68.5	68.9	68.8
for women	76.0	76.1	76.4	76.6	77.0	77.3	77.5

Mortality rate by homicide, assaults per 100 000 persons	1993	1994	1995	1996	1997	1998	1999
	2.7	3.0	2.8	2.6	2.4	2.1	*

Consumption

Food as % of total private consumption	1993	1994	1995	1996	1997	1998	1999
	29.9	29.5	28.7	27.3	25.2	23.3	21.4
Passengers cars per 100 persons	18	19	20	21	22	23	24

The number of dwellings in thousand at the end of:

1993 was	11366	30% owned by state and local authorities,	43% by private persons
1994 was	11434	29% owned by state and local authorities,	44% by private persons
1995 was	11491	25% owned by state and local authorities,	48% by private persons
1996 was	11547	23% owned by state and local authorities,	50% by private persons
1997 was	11613	21% owned by state and local authorities,	51% by private persons
1998 was	11688	19% owned by state and local authorities,	52% by private persons
1999 was	11763	18% owned by state and local authorities,	54% by private persons

Unemployment

The number of unemployed persons, (1000 persosns), annual average:

	1993	1994	1995	1996	1997	1998	1999
In Labour Force Surveys[1]	2427	2474	2277	2108	1923	1816	2391
Registered unemployment	2736.9	2909.6	2694.6	2507.1	2024.2	1756.5	2155.4

National accounts

GDP in current year prices in billion zlotys and change in fixed prices in %:

	1993	94/93	1994	95/94	1995	96/95	1996	97/96	1997
	156	5.2%	224	7.0%	308	6.0%	388	6.8%	472
Preliminary estimates for 1998 and 1999:						98/97	1998	99/98	1999
						4.8%	554	4.1%	617

GDP by field of activity, total in current prices in billion zlotys, activity in % of total:	1994	1995	1996	1997	1998	Prel. est. 1999
Total at market prices	225.1	308.1	387.8	472.4	553.6	617.0
Agriculture, hunting, forestry and fishing	6.0%	6.0%	5.5%	4.8%	4.1%	3.8%
Mining, quarrying and manufacturing	23.2%	24.2%	22.8%	22.7%	21.4%	20.8%
Electricity, gas, water supply	3.4%	3.4%	3.3%	3.0%	2.8%	3.2%
Construction	6.4%	6.3%	6.5%	6.9%	7.6%	7.7%
Wholesale and retail sales	17.5%	17.4%	18.2%	18.4%	18.1%	18.8%
Transport, storage and communication	6.4%	5.7%	5.6%	5.7%	5.6%	5.6%
Public administration, education, health and social work	11.2%	11.9%	12.2%	12.0%	11.9%	11.6%
Other services	12.3%	12.2%	12.8%	13.9%	16.1%	15.3%
Total at basic prices	86.4%	87.1%	86.9%	87.4%	87.6%	86.8%
Taxes on products	14.8%	13.8%	14.1%	13.3%	13.0%	13.6%
Subsidies (-)	1.2%	0.9%	1.0%	0.7%	0.6%	0.4%

GDP by expenditure, total in current prices in billion zlotys, expenditure as % of total:	1994	1995	1996	1997	1998	Prel. est. 1999
Total	225.1	308.1	387.8	472.4	549.5	617.0
Consumption of households	62.5%	60.3%	62.4%	62.8%	62.7%	63.4%
Government consumption	16.8%	16.8%	16.4%	16.1%	15.4%	15.1%
Consumption of non-profit institutions	0.9%	0.9%	0.9%	0.9%	0.9%	0.9%
Gross fixed capital formation	18.0%	18.6%	20.7%	23.5%	25.2%	26.2%
Changes in stocks	-0.3%	1.1%	1.1%	1.0%	1.0%	1.0%
Exports (FOB)	23.6%	25.3%	24.3%	25.5%	28.2%	26.2%
Imports (FOB) (-)	21.5%	23.0%	25.8%	29.8%	33.4%	32.8%

GDP by income, total in current prices in billion zlotys, income categories in % of total:	1994	1995	1996	1997	1998	Prel. est. 1999
Total	223.9	306.3	385.4	469.4	549.5	*
Compensation of employees	41.7%	41.9%	43.4%	44.2%	43.6%	*
therein wages and salaries	29.9%	29.9%	31.0%	32.0%	31.5%	*
Consumption of fixed capital	*	*	*	*	*	*
Indirect taxes	16.6%	16.0%	16.2%	15.4%	14.8%	*
Subsidies (-)	2.2%	1.6%	1.3%	1.1%	1.0%	*
Operating surplus and mixed income	43.9%	43.7%	41.7%	41.5%	42.6%	*

Foreign trade

Exports, total in billion zlotys, countries in % of total	1993	1994	1995	1996	1997	1998	1999
Total exports	25.8	39.2	55.5	65.8	84.5	98.4	108.8
to Russia	4.6%	5.4%	5.6%	6.8%	8.4%	5.6%	2.6%
to Finland	1.4%	1.7%	1.5%	1.3%	1.3%	0.9%	1.0%
to Sweden	2.2%	2.6%	2.5%	2.4%	2.4%	2.4%	2.5%
to Norway	0.5%	0.7%	0.6%	1.2%	0.8%	0.8%	1.2%
to Denmark	3.0%	3.2%	3.0%	3.0%	2.9%	2.7%	3.1%
to Germany	36.3%	35.7%	38.3%	34.4%	32.9%	36.2%	36.1%
to Lithuania	0.3%	0.7%	0.8%	0.9%	1.3%	1.5%	1.6%
to Latvia	0.2%	0.3%	0.3%	0.3%	0.5%	0.6%	0.7%
to Estonia	0.0%	0.1%	0.1%	0.2%	0.2%	0.3%	0.3%
to EU countries	63.2%	62.7%	70.0%	66.3%	64.0%	68.3%	70.5%
to CIS countries	7.4%	8.3%	10.2%	12.4%	15.3%	11.3%	6.7%

Imports, total in billion zlotys, countries in % of total	1993	1994	1995	1996	1997	1998	1999
Total imports	34.0	49.1	70.5	100.2	138.9	163.0	182.4
from Russia	6.8%	6.8%	6.7%	6.8%	6.3%	5.1%	5.9%
from Finland	2.0%	2.4%	1.9%	1.6%	1.7%	1.7%	1.8%
from Sweden	2.3%	2.8%	3.1%	2.7%	3.0%	2.9%	3.2%
from Norway	1.9%	1.7%	1.4%	1.0%	1.0%	0.8%	1.0%
from Denmark	2.4%	2.4%	2.2%	2.2%	1.9%	2.0%	1.8%
from Germany	28.0%	27.4%	26.6%	24.7%	24.1%	25.8%	25.2%
from Lithuania	0.5%	0.4%	0.2%	0.3%	0.3%	0.3%	0.4%
from Latvia	0.1%	0.0%	0.0%	0.0%	0.0%	0.1%	0.1%
from Estonia	0.0%	0.0%	0.1%	0.1%	0.1%	0.0%	0.0%
from EU countries	57.2%	57.5%	64.6%	63.9%	63.8%	65.6%	64.9%
from CIS countries	9.0%	9.4%	9.3%	9.1%	8.2%	6.5%	7.2%

Employed persons by activity

Employed by activity in 1000 persons[2]	1994	1995	1996	1997	1998	1999
All activities	15282	15486	15842	16295	16267	16009
Agriculture, hunting and forestry	4039	4194	4359	4365	4344	4322
Fishing	15	14	13	13	12	12
Mining and quarrying	377	357	339	326	297	257
Manufacturing	3071	3103	3159	3177	3100	2923
Electricity, gas and water supply	269	269	259	258	253	247
Construction	853	828	869	947	939	915
Wholesale and retail sales	1892	1903	1900	2061	2106	2094
Hotels and restaurants	176	186	188	202	222	216
Transport, storage and communication	844	838	832	865	859	838
Financial intermediation	252	268	286	305	327	389
Real estate, renting and business activities	529	554	594	688	752	776
Public administration and defence	734	738	757	786	777	757
Education	894	896	912	902	908	908
Health and social care	996	1003	1010	1029	1021	967
Other community, social and personal services	341	335	365	371	350	388

Enterprises

The number of active enterprises by ownership and size	1995	1996	1997	1998	1999
All active enterprises	1927947	2184037	2334460	2590904	2594022
With private domestic owners	1903691	2157815	2306639	2559817	2560635
With foreign owners	13654	15977	17926	20060	21237
Owned by state or local government	6856	6313	5763	6797	7931
Number of enterprises in wholesale and retail trade	855681	932999	964220	1010948	1009061
Enterprises with 200 or more employees	5078	5043	5075	5518	5788
20 to 199 employees	34937	36988	38927	41427	42138
5 to 19 employees	130724	138888	144814	154222	155113
less than 5 employees	1757208	2003118	2145644	2389737	2390983

Direct inward and outward investment

Foreign direct investment in Poland	1994	1995	1996	1997	1998	1999
Total direct investment in million zloty	4261.3	8870.9	12128.9	16098.4	22237.4	28841.9
as % of the Polish GDP for the year	1.9%	2.9%	3.1%	3.4%	4.0%	4.7%
by country: from Denmark	36.1	177.7	595.4	618.3	459.8	576.5
Baltic countries	-7.3	0.0	1.9	0.0	-2.4	0.4
Finland	16.4	38.8	63.9	103.3	157.9	155.9
Germany	640.9	1856.4	2946.7	3332.2	4773.1	4866.9
Netherlands	375.9	1578.5	3068.9	4870.2	7127.5	4783.6
Norway	21.8	92.6	26.4	143.7	86.6	61.5
Russia	0.9	14.1	15.6	-5.9	-17.5	-19.8
Sweden	92.3	225.0	230.8	282.1	893.3	821.7
Switzerland	129.5	442.2	259.4	290.9	193.9	516.2
United Kingdom	100.9	348.1	355.9	645.8	723.2	826.8
United States	594.3	1504.6	1231.5	2289.5	2611.5	1692.1
The stock of direct investment capital in Poland at the end of year, total	9234.6	19356.5	32961.9	51317.1	78766.4	108168.2
of which in:						
Mining, quarrying anf manufacture	*	*	*	*	*	*
Wholesale and retail trade	*	*	*	*	*	*
Transport, storage and communication	*	*	*	*	*	*

Polish direct investment abroad		1994	1995	1996	1997	1998	1999
Total investment abroad in million zloty		65.9	101.8	142.9	147.6	1104.0	124.2
by country: to	Denmark	0.0	0.0	0.0	0.0	0.7	0.8
	Estonia	0.0	0.0	0.0	0.0	0.0	0.4
	Finland	0.0	0.0	0.0	0.0	0.0	0.0
	Germany	1.8	7.8	67.7	105.3	-0.7	-34.5
	Latvia	0.0	0.0	0.0	0.0	0.0	0.0
	Lithuania	0.0	0.0	0.0	0.0	0.0	13.1
	Netherlands	0.5	0.7	0.2	1.3	46.5	-44.4
	Norway	0.0	0.0	0.0	0.0	0.0	-1.2
	Russia	1.8	2.9	5.9	1.6	-28.3	-4.4
	Sweden	0.0	0.5	0.5	-0.3	0.3	-2.4
	Switzerland	0.7	0.7	2.2	1.3	1.4	254.7
	United Kingdom	10.5	5.5	2.4	18.7	162.5	35.3
	United States	0.0	8.2	6.7	16.4	15.4	-47.6

Foreign loans and foreign aid

Net amount borowed from abroad	1994	1995	1996	1997	1998	1999
in million zloty.	-19474.7	1483.7	-12751.8	5241.5	9083.6	20341.0
as % of the Polish GDP for the year	-8.7%	0.5%	-3.3%	1.1%	1.6%	3.3%
Foreign aid received, in million zloty	254.5	533.4	196.8	334.6	1317.1	662.5
as % of the Polish GDP for the year	0.1%	0.2%	0.1%	0.1%	0.2%	0.1%

Prices

Change in index, previous period = 100	1994	1995	1996	1997	1998	1999
Consumer price index	132	128	120	115	112	107
Producer price index for manufactured products[3]	124	126	111	109	107	105

International sea traffic

The number of vessels in harbours	1994	1995	1996	1997	1998	1999
Arrivals from abroad	12518	14541	17365	23971	24212	27197
Departures abroad	12538	14566	17384	24015	24255	27195

International arrivals/departures in harbours, 1000 persons	1994	1995	1996	1997	1998	1999
Arriving in Poland total	450	516	713	1120	1175	1572
Departing from Poland total	432	473	640	1050	1134	1545

International air traffic

Passengers in airports in 1000	1994	1995	1996	1997	1998	1999
Arrivals	1171	1340	1432	1684	2022	2151
Departures	1174	1346	1439	1686	2014	2176

Sources
Questionnaires completed by the Central Statistical Office of Poland.

Notes
1) Figures from Labour Force Surveys or other surveys of individuals following the ILO definition of unemployed persons: Person without work, currently available for work if there should be work and actively seeking work.
2) Employed persons as defined by ILO: working and paid as a wage earner, enterpreneur or a freelancer, working without direct payment in a family enterprise or farm, temporarily absent from work.
3) 1994 and 1995 net prices – without VAT tax but including excise taxes; from 1996 on basic prices – without both VAT tax and excise taxes.
   * Data not available
   0, 0,0   Less than half of the unit employed
   - Zero

Country/region: Pomorskie

Basic Data and Population
Total land- and water area: 18293 square km of which agricultural land: 50%, forest and woodland: 36%

Total population (end of the respective year or closest possible estimate):
1995   2.17 million of which 49% male, 51% female
1998   2.19 million of which 49% male, 51% female
1999   2.19 million of which 49% male, 51% female

by age groups in %	1995	1998	1999
00 - 19 years	32.2%	30.2%	29.5%
20 - 64 years	58.2%	59.5%	60.0%
65 - years	9.6%	10.3%	10.5%

by nationality in % for all nationalities 0.5% or more			
1.	*	*	*
2.	*	*	*

The total population has increased from 2.17 million in 1995 to 2.19 million in 1999.

Migration in 1000 of persons	1995	1998	1999
Total immigration	0.8	0.9	0.7
Total emigration	2.2	1.6	1.7
Net migration	-1.4	-0.7	-1.0
Natural in/decrease	7.5	5.6	5.2

Life expectancy at birth in years	1995	1998	1999
for men	68.5	69.2	69.9
for women	76.3	77.4	77.9

Mortality rate by homicide,	1995	1998	1999
assaults per 100 000 persons	*	3.0	*

Consumption

Food as % of total private consumption	1995	1998	1999
	*	*	*

Passenger cars per 100 persons	*	*	24

The number of dwellings in thousands at the end of:		
1995 was 616	* owned by state and local authorities,	* by private persons
1998 was 630	24% owned by state and local authorities,	44% by private persons
1999 was 635	22% owned by state and local authorities,	45% by private persons

Unemployment

The number of unemployed persons, (1000 persons), annual average:	1995	1998	1999
In Labour Force Surveys[1]	141	99	115
Registered unemployment	*	*	113

Employed persons by activity

Employed by activity in 1000 persons[2]	1995	1998	1999
All activities [3]	*	776	783
Agriculture, hunting and forestry	*	115	114
Fishing	*	4	4
Mining and quarrying	*	1	1
Manufacturing	*	172	173
Electricity, gas and water supply	*	13	13
Construction	*	54	56
Wholesale and retail sales	*	123	123
Hotels and restaurants	*	17	18
Transport, storage and communication	*	61	58
Financial intermediation	*	19	23
Real estate, renting and business activities	*	44	47
Public administration and defence	*	25	25
Education	*	54	54
Health and social care	*	56	52
Other community, social and personal services	*	18	22

Enterprises

The number of active enterprises by ownership and size		1995	1998	1999
All active enterprises		104273	145899	152120
With private domestic owners		102595	144036	150120
With foreign owners		1023	1308	1339
Owned by state or local government		367	323	421
Number of enterprises in wholesale and retail trade		43144	49673	50374
Enterprises with	200 or more employees	310	297	318
	20 to 199 employees	2408	2584	2630
	5 to 19 employees	9043	9533	9722
	less than 5 employees	92512	133485	139450

Direct inward and outward investment

Foreign direct investment in Pomorskie	1995	1998	1999
Total direct investment in million zloty	*	*	*
by country: from Denmark			
Estonia			
Finland			
Germany			
Latvia			
Lithuania			
Netherlands			
Norway			
Russia			
Sweden			
Switzerland			
United Kingdom			
United States			
The stock of direct investment capital in Pomorskie at the end of year, total thereof in:	*	*	*
Mining, quarrying and manufacture			
Wholesale and retail trade			
Transport, storage and communication			

Pomorskie direct investment abroad	1995	1998	1999
Total investment abroad in million zloty	*	*	*
by country: to Denmark			
Estonia			
Finland			
Germany			
Latvia			
Lithuania			
Netherlands			
Norway			
Russia			
Sweden			
Switzerland			
United Kingdom			
United States			

Foreign loans and foreign aid to Pomorskie[4]

Net amount borowed from abroad	1995	1998	1999
Million zloty	*	*	*
Foreign aid received, in million zloty	*	*	*

International sea traffic

The number of vessels in habours	1995	1998	1999
Arrivals from abroad	4428	5417	5157
Departures aboad	4439	5430	5155

International arrivals/departures in harbours, 1000 persons	1995	1998	1999
Arriving in Poland total	113	149	185
Departing from Poland total	107	150	184

International air traffic

Passengers in airports in 1000	1995	1998	1999
Arrivals	36	54	65
Departures	36	54	65

Sources
Questionnaires completed by the Central Statistical Office of Poland.

Notes
1) Figures from Labour Force Surveys or other surveys of individuals following the ILO definition of unemployed persons: Persons without work, currently available for work if there should be work and actively seeking work.
2) Employed persons as defined by ILO: working and paid as a wage earner, enterpreneur or a freelancer, working without direct payment in a family enterprise or farm, temporarily absent from work.
3) Excluding Ministry of National Defence and Ministry of Internal Affairs.
4) Data are not available from the National Bank of Poland.
 * Data not available
   0, 0,0   Less than half of the unit employed
 - Zero

Country/region: Zachodnio-Pomorskie

Basic Data and Population

Total land- and water area: 22901 square km of which agricultural land: 49%, forest and wood-land: 35%

Total population (end of the respective year or closest possible estimate):
1995   1.72 million of which 49% male, 51% female
1998   1.73 million of which 49% male, 51% female
1999   1.73 million of which 49% male, 51% female

by age groups in %	1995	1998	1999
00 - 19 years	31.4%	29.2%	28.4%
20 - 64 years	59.1%	60.5%	61.0%
65 - years	9.5%	10.3%	10.6%

by nationality in % for all nationalities 0.5% or more			
1.	*	*	*
2.	*	*	*

The total population has increased from 1.72 million in 1995 to 1.73 million in 1999.

Migration in 1000 of persons	1995	1998	1999
Total immigration	0.4	0.4	0.3
Total emigration	1.4	0.6	0.7
Net migration	-1.0	-0.2	-0.4
Natural in/decrease	4.9	2.7	1.7

Life expectancy at birth in years	1995	1998	1999
for men	66.5	68.5	68.1
for women	75.8	77.0	77.1

Mortality rate by homicide,	1995	1998	1999
assaults per 100 000 persons	*	3	*

Consumption

Food as % of total private consumption	1995	1998	1999
	*	*	*
Passenger cars per 100 persons	*	*	21

The number of dwellings in thousands at the end of:			
1995 was	506	* owned by state and local authorities,	* by private persons
1998 was	513	29% owned by state and local authorities,	41% by private persons
1999 was	517	27% owned by state and local authorities,	42% by private persons

Unemployment

The number of unemployed persons, (1000 persons), annual average:	1995	1998	1999
In Labour Force Surveys[1]	122	119	150
Registered unemployment	*	*	119

Employed persons by activity

Employed by activity in 1000 persons[2]	1995	1998	1999
All activities[3]	*	624	599
Agriculture, hunting and forestry	*	89	88
Fishing	*	5	5
Mining and quarrying	*	1	1
Manufacturing	*	127	120
Electricity, gas and water supply	*	14	13
Construction	*	42	38
Wholesale and retail sales	*	101	97
Hotels and restaurants	*	16	15
Transport, storage and communication	*	50	50
Financial intermediation	*	15	17
Real estate, renting and business activities	*	30	33
Public administration and defence	*	23	22
Education	*	40	40
Health and social care	*	49	43
Other community, social and personal services	*	22	17

Enterprises

The number of active enterprises by ownership and size	1995	1998	1999
All active enterprises	95669	136486	140465
With private domestic owners	94148	134791	138690
With foreign owners	924	1124	1146
Owned by state or local government	391	400	462
Number of enterprises in wholesale and retail trade	41481	50317	50134
Enterprises with 200 or more employees		204	235	245
20 to 199 employees	1884	2135	2133
5 to 19 employees	7217	8156	8104
less than 5 employees	86364	125960	129983

Direct inward and outward investment[4]

Foreign direct investment in Zachodnio-Pomorskie	1995	1998	1999
Total direct investment in million zloty	*	*	*
by country: from Denmark			
Estonia			
Finland			
Germany			
Latvia			
Lithuania			
Netherlands			
Norway			
Russia			
Sweden			
Switzerland			
United Kingdom			
United States			
The stock of direct investment capital in Zachodnio-Pomorskie at the end of year, total	*	*	*
thereof in:			
Mining, quarrying and manufacture			
Wholesale and retail trade			
Transport, storage and communication			

Zachodnio-Pomorskie direct investment abroad	1995	1998	1999
Total investment abroad in million zloty	*	*	*
by country: to Denmark			
Estonia			
Finland			
Germany			
Latvia			
Lithuania			
Netherlands			
Norway			
Russia			
Sweden			
Switzerland			
United Kingdom			
United States			

Foreign loans and foreign aid to Zachodnio-Pomorskie[4]

Net amount borowed from abroad	1995	1998	1999
Million zloty.	*	*	*
Foreign aid received, in million zloty	*	*	*

International sea traffic

The number of vessels in habours	1995	1998	1999
Arrivals from abroad	9010	18395	21836
Departures aboad	9026	18425	21836

International arrivals/departures in harbours, 1000 persons	1995	1998	1999
Arriving in Poland total	382	1023	1384
Departing from Poland total	345	982	1359

International air traffic

Passengers in airports in 1000	1995	1998	1999
arrivals	0	6	7
departures	1	6	8

Sources

Questionnaires completed by the Central Statistical Office of Poland.

Notes

1) Figures from Labour Force Surveys or other surveys of individuals following the ILO definition of unemployed persons: Persons without work, currently available for work if there should be work and actively seeking work.
2) Employed persons as defined by ILO: working and paid as a wage earner, enterpreneur or a freelancer, working without direct payment in a family enterprise or farm, temporarily absent from work.
3) Excluding Ministry of National Defence and Ministry of Internal Affairs.
4) Data are not available from the National Bank of Poland.
   * Data not available
   0, 0,0   Less than half of the unit employed
   - Zero

Country/region: Warminsko-Mazurskie

Basic Data and Population
Total land- and water area: 24203 square km of which agricultural land: 54%, forest and woodland: 30%

Total population (end of the respective year or closest possible estimate):
1995   1.45 million of which 49% male, 51% female
1998   1.46 million of which 49% male, 51% female
1999   1.47 million of which 49% male, 51% female

by age groups in %	1995	1998	1999
00 - 19 years	34.0%	31.8%	31.0%
20 - 64 years	56.9%	58.3%	58.9%
65 - years	9.1%	9.9%	10.1%

by nationality in % for all nationalities 0.5% or more			
1.	*	*	*
2.	*	*	*

The total population has increased from 1.45 million in 1995 to 1.47 million in 1999.

Migration in 1000 of persons	1995	1998	1999
Total immigration	0.3	0.3	0.3
Total emigration	0.7	0.7	0.7
Net migration	-0.4	-0.4	-0.4
Natural in/decrease	6.2	4.5	4.0

Life expectancy at birth in years	1995	1998	1999
for men	66.9	68.2	68.5
for women	76.8	77.6	77.9

Mortality rate by homicide, assaults per 100 000 persons	1995	1998	1999
	*	2.3	*

Consumption

Food as % of total private consumption	1995	1998	1999
	*	*	*
Passenger cars per 100 persons	*	*	14

The number of dwellings in thousand at the end of:			
1995 was 406	* owned by state and local authorities,	* by private persons
1998 was 415.0	25% owned by state and local authorities,	48% by private persons
1999 was 418.0	23% owned by state and local authorities,	50% by private persons

Unemployment

The number of unemployed persons, (1000 persons), annual average:			
	1995	1998	1999
In Labour Force Surveys[1]	124	97	134
Registered unemployment	*	*	134

Employed persons by activity

Employed by activity in 1000 persons[2]	1995	1998	1999
All activities[3]	*	516	495
Agriculture, hunting and forestry	*	124	123
Fishing	*	1	1
Mining and quarrying	*	1	1
Manufacturing	*	107	99
Electricity, gas and water supply	*	8	8
Construction	*	29	28
Wholesale and retail sales	*	73	70
Hotels and restaurants	*	7	7
Transport, storage and communication	*	30	29
Financial intermediation	*	10	12
Real estate, renting and business activities	*	24	21
Public administration and defence	*	19	17
Education	*	34	34
Health and social care	*	37	34
Other community, social and personal services	*	12	12

Enterprises

The number of active enterprises by ownership and size	1995	1998	1999
all active enterprises	62377	78498	81740
with private domestic owners	61835	77849	80951
with foreign owners	141	242	276
owned by state or local government	321	316	424
Number of enterprises in wholesale and retail trade	27733	31423	31603
Enterprises with 200 or more employees	129	152	158
20 to 199 employees	1314	1441	1500
5 to 19 employees	3305	4218	4379
less than 5 employees	57629	72687	75703

Direct inward and outward investment[4]

Foreign direct investment in Warminsko-Mazurskie	1995	1998	1999
Total direct investment in million zloty	*	*	*
by country: from Denmark			
Estonia			
Finland			
Germany			
Latvia			
Lithuania			
Netherlands			
Norway			
Russia			
Sweden			
Switzerland			
United Kingdom			
United States			
The stock of direct investment capital in Warminsko-Mazurskie at the end of year, total thereof in:			
Mining, quarrying and manufacture			
Wholesale and retail trade			
Transport, storage and communication			

Warminsko-Mazurskie direct investment abroad	1995	1998	1999
Total investment abroad in million zloty	*	*	*
by country: to Denmark			
Estonia			
Finland			
Germany			
Latvia			
Lithuania			
Netherlands			
Norway			
Russia			
Sweden			
Switzerland			
United Kingdom			
United States			

Foreign loans and foreign aid to Warminsko-Mazurskie[4]

Net amount borowed from abroad	1995	1998	1999
Million zloty	*	*	*
Foreign aid received, in million zloty	*	*	*

International sea traffic

The number of vessels in habours	1995	1998	1999
Arrivals from abroad	1103	400	204
Departures aboad	1101	400	204

International arrivals/departures in harbours, 1000 persons	1995	1998	1999
Arriving in Poland total	21	3	3
Departing from Poland total	21	2	2

International air traffic

Passengers in airports in 1000	1995	1998	1999
Arrivals	*	1	1
Departures	*	1	1

Sources

Questionnaires completed by the Central Statistical Office of Poland.

Notes

1) Figures from Labour Force Surveys or other surveys of individuals following the ILO definition of unemployed persons: Persons without work, currently available for work if there should be work and actively seeking work.
2) Employed persons as defined by ILO: working and paid as a wage earner, enterpreneur or a freelancer, working without direct payment in a family enterprise or farm, temporarily absent from work.
3) Excluding Ministry of National Defence and Ministry of Internal Affairs.
4) Data are not available from the National Bank of Poland.
 * Data not available
   0, 0,0   Less than half of the unit employed
 - Zero

Country/region: Arkhangelsk

Basic Data and Population

Total land- and water area: 587400 square km of which agricultural land: 1%, forest and wood-
land: 42%

Total population (end of the respective year or closest possible estimate):	
1993	1.55 million
1994	1.53 million
1995	1.52 million
1996	1.51 million
1997	1.49 million of which 49% male, 51% female
1998	1.48 million of which 48% male, 52% female
1999	1.46 million of which 48% male, 52% female

by age groups in %	1993	1994	1995	1996	1997	1998	1999
00 - 19 years	30.9	30.5	29.9	29.2	28.5	27.8	27.2
20 - 64 years	59.8	59.9	60.2	60.6	61.1	61.6	62.2
65 - years	9.3	9.6	9.9	10.2	10.4	10.6	10.6

by nationality in % for all nationalities 0.5% or more	1989 census	1995	1997	1998	1999
1. Russians	92.1	95.0	*	*	*
2. Ukrainians	3.4	2.1	*	*	*
3. Belorusians	1.3	0.9	*	*	*
4. Komis	0.5	0.4	*	*	*
5. Northern ethnicities	0.5	0.2	*	*	*

The total population has decreased from 1.52 million in 1992 to 1.46 million in 1999.

Migration in 1000 of persons	1993	1994	1995	1996	1997	1998	1999
Total immigration	35.0	35.6	34.7	30.2	25.0	21.9	17.7
Total emigration	40.4	39.1	39.1	36.2	32.6	29.6	26.1
Net migration	-5.4	-3.5	-4.4	-6.0	-7.6	-7.7	-8.4
Natural in/decrease	-8.3	-9.9	-9.0	-7.8	-6.9	-6.1	-10.4

Life expectancy at birth in years	1993	1994	1995	1996	1997	1998	1999
for men	57.3	55.9	57.1	58.5	60.6	60.4	58.0
for women	71.1	70.0	71.0	72.1	72.0	72.7	71.1

Mortality rate by homicide, assaults per 100 000 persons	1993	1994	1995	1996	1997	1998	1999
	34.9	37.8	34.6	34.4	29.1	28.1	30.4

Consumption

Food as % of total private consumption[1]	1993	1994	1995	1996	1997	1998	1999
	43	45	49	51	46	52	52
Cars per 100 persons[2]	5	5	6	7	7	8	8

The number of dwellings at the end of:			
1994 was	542303	41% owned by state and local authorities,	40% by private persons
1995 was	562587	43% owned by state and local authorities,	42% by private persons
1996 was	567675	47% owned by state and local authorities,	44% by private persons
1997 was	570239	49% owned by state and local authorities,	45% by private persons
1998 was	565524	49% owned by state and local authorities,	48% by private persons
1999 was	566036	*% owned by state and local authorities,	45% by private persons

The general area, in thousand square metres, of dwellings at the end of:			
1994 was	28304	44% owned by state and local authorities,	38% by private persons
1995 was	28950	45% owned by state and local authorities,	40% by private persons
1996 was	29106	49% owned by state and local authorities,	42% by private persons
1997 was	29305	51% owned by state and local authorities,	43% by private persons
1998 was	29157	51% owned by state and local authorities,	45% by private persons
1999 was	29234	48% owned by state and local authorities,	49% by private persons

Unemployment

The number of unemployed persons, (1000 persons), annual average:	1993	1994	1995	1996	1997	1998	1999
In Labour Force Surveys [3]	48.8	74.3	84.7	92.1	91.3	108.7	113.2
Registered unemployment	22.5	38.2	58.9	55.9	56.5	45.8	24.6

Foreign trade

Exports, total in million US $, countries in % of total	1993	1994	1995	1996	1997	1998	1999
Total exports	129.6	309.9	436.5	*	*	*	*
to Finland	1.5%	9.6%	1.0%	*	*	*	*
to Sweden	10.5%	6.4%	5.5%	*	*	*	*
to Norway	11.6%	3.4%	1.0%	*	*	*	*
to Denmark	2.5%	1.1%	1.4%	*	*	*	*
to Germany	29.6%	18.6%	11.5%	*	*	*	*
to Poland	0.4%	0.3%	3.4%	*	*	*	*
to Lithuania	1.0%	1.6%	2.5%	*	*	*	*
to Latvia	0.3%	0.4%	0.2%	*	*	*	*
to Estonia	0.2%	0.7%	0.5%	*	*	*	*
to EU countries	*	*	*	*	*	*	*
to CIS countries	*	*	4.7%	*	*	*	*

Imports, total in million US $, countries in % of total	1993	1994	1995	1996	1997	1998	1999
Total imports	99.0	88.2	*	*	*	*	*
from Finland	6.9%	14.3%	*	*	*	*	*
from Sweden	0.6%	3.6%	*	*	*	*	*
from Norway	1.0%	2.3%	*	*	*	*	*
from Denmark	0.9%	1.7%	*	*	*	*	*
from Germany	18.9%	12.2%	*	*	*	*	*
from Poland	2.9%	3.9%	*	*	*	*	*
from Lithuania	0.1%	0.3%	*	*	*	*	*
from Latvia	0.1%	0.6%	*	*	*	*	*
from Estonia	0.2%	0.3%	*	*	*	*	*
from EU countries	*	*	*	*	*	*	*
from CIS countries	*	*	*	*	*	*	*

Employed persons by activity

Employed by activity in 1000 persons[4]	1994	1995	1996	1997	1998	1999
All activities	664	637	627	573	567	588
Agriculture, hunting and forestry	53	47	43	38	36	39
Fishing (included in manufacturing)						
Mining and quarrying (incl. in manufact.)						
Manufacturing	205	185	175	162	156	155
Electricity, gas and water supply (included in other community services)						
Construction	45	44	41	30	31	31
Wholesale and retail sales[5]	66	65	64	65	71	76
Hotels and restaurants (hotels incl. in other personal services, restaurants in wholesales and retail sales)						
Transport, storage and communication	83	80	79	71	67	70
Financial intermediation	7	7	7	6	6	6
Real estate, renting and business activities [8]	1	2	3	2	2	7
Public administration and defence	19	25	34	26	32	33
Education[6]	88	86	85	80	76	78
Health and social care	47	49	48	46	47	47
Other community, social and personal services [7]	36	34	37	36	35	36
Other	14	13	11	11	8	10

Enterprises

The number of active enterprises by ownership and size by ownership and size	1995	1996	1997	1998	1999
All active enterprises	14850	15821	17027	18092	19239
With private domestic owners	8049	8583	9092	9997	10571
With foreign owners	3	3	3	4	4
Owned by state or local government	2708	2785	2887	2978	3457
Number of enterprises in wholesale and retail trade	4028	4225	4566	4808	5004
Enterprises with 200 or more employees	*	*	*	*	*
20 to 199 employees	*	*	*	*	*
5 to 19 employees	*	*	*	*	*
less than 5 employees	*	*	*	*	*

Direct inward and outward investment

Foreign direct investment in Arkhangelsk	1994	1995	1996	1997	1998	1999
Total direct investment in million US $	43.5	2.5	3.5	14.6	4.3	0.2
by country: from Denmark	*	0.1	0.1	0.0	-	-
Estonia	*	-	-	-	-	-
Finland	*	-	0.0	-	-	-
Germany	*	1.7	1.1	6.8	0.9	0.0
Latvia	*	-	-	-	-	-
Lithuania	*	-	-	-	-	-
Netherlands	*	-	0.6	-	-	-
Norway	*	0.0	0.1	0.1	0.1	0.0
Poland	*	-	-	-	-	-
Sweden	*	-	-	-	-	-
Switzerland	*	-	-	-	-	-
United Kingdom	*	0.0	0.0	0.0	-	-
United States	*	0.1	0.9	6.7	2.5	0.0
The stock of direct investment capital in Arkhangelsk at the end of year, total of which in:	53.1	57.2	59.3	77.3	78.7	78.8
Mining, quarrying and manufacure	53.1	55.5	58.3	71.9	72.7	72.9
Wholesale and retail trade	0.0	1.5	0.0	0.2	0.1	0.0
Transport, storage and communication	*	0.2	0.1	0.9	0.7	0.7

Arkhangelsk direct investment abroad		1994	1995	1996	1997	1998	1999
Total investment abroad in million US $		-	-	0.1	-	-	0.0
by country: to	Denmark	-	-	-	-	-	-
	Estonia	-	-	-	-	-	-
	Finland	-	-	-	-	-	-
	Germany	-	-	-	-	-	-
	Latvia	-	-	-	-	-	-
	Lithuania	-	-	-	-	-	-
	Netherlands	-	-	-	-	-	-
	Norway	-	-	-	-	-	-
	Poland	-	-	-	-	-	-
	Sweden	-	-	-	-	-	-
	Switzerland	-	-	-	-	-	-
	United Kingdom	-	-	0.1	-	-	-
	United States	-	-	-	-	-	-

Foreign loans and foreign aid

Net amount borrowed from abroad	1994	1995	1996	1997	1998	1999
Million US $	*	196.0	*	*	*	*
Foreign aid received, in million US $	*	*	*	*	*	*

Prices

Change in index, previous period = 100	1994	1995	1996	1997	1998	1999
Consumer price index	313	245	118	107	172	132
Producer price index for manufactured products	472	285	107	113	129	166

International sea traffic

The number of vessels in harbours	1994	1995	1996	1997	1998	1999
Arrivals from abroad	462	348	265	309	272	327
Departures abroad	470	354	281	322	280	321

International arrivals/departures in harbours, 1000 persons	1994	1995	1996	1997	1998	1999
Arriving in Arkhangelsk region total	-	-	-	-	-	-
Departing from Arkhangelsk region total	-	-	-	-	-	-

International air traffic

Passengers in airports in 1000	1994	1995	1996	1997	1998	1999
Arrivals	5	10	3	1	6	1
Departures	4	8	5	4	7	1

Sources
Questionnaires completed by the Regional Committee for Statistics in Arkhangelsk region

Notes
1) From household budget data.
2) Registration of private cars per 100 persons.
3) Figures from Labour Force Surveys or other surveys of individuals following the ILO definition of unemployed persons: Person without work, currently available for work if there should
   be work and actively seeking work.
4) Employed persons as defined by ILO: working and paid as a wage earner, enterpreneur or a
   freelancer, working without direct payment in a family enterprise or farm, temporarily absent-
   from work.
5) Including public catering, logistics, sales activity and procurements.
6) Including culture, art, science and sientific service.
7) Including communal housing and public services.
8) Local government services not included
 * Data not available
   0, 0,0   Less than half of the unit employed
 - Zero

Country/region: Kaliningrad

Basic Data and Population

Total land- and water area: 15100 square km of which agricultural land: 54%, forest and wood-land: 19%

Total population (end of the respective year or closest possible estimate):
1993	0.91 million
1994	0.93 million
1995	0.93 million
1996	0.94 million
1997	0.94 million of which 48% male, 52% female
1998	0.95 million of which 48% male, 52% female
1999	0.95 million of which 48% male, 52% female

by age groups in %	1993	1994	1995	1996	1997	1998	1999
00 - 19 years	27.9	27.5	27.0	26.5	26.0	25.5	24.9
20 - 64 years	62.2	62.1	62.2	62.4	62.7	63.1	63.6
65 - years	9.9	10.4	10.8	11.1	11.3	11.4	11.5

by nationality in % for all nationalities 0.5% or more	1989 census	1996	1997	1998	1999
1. Russians	78.5	78.0	78.1	78.1	78.2
2. Belorusians	8.5	7.9	7.8	7.7	7.6
3. Ukrainians	7.2	7.4	7.4	7.4	7.4
4. Lithuanians	2.1	1.9	1.9	1.9	1.9
5. Poles	0.5	0.5	0.5	0.5	0.5

The total population has increased from 0.91 million in 1992 to 0.95 million in 1999.

Migration in 1000 of persons	1993	1994	1995	1996	1997	1998	1999
Total immigration	37.3	44.2	38.4	34.3	36.4	35.3	24.5
Total emigration	26.3	25.8	27.4	25.0	23.4	22.3	20.9
Net migration	11.0	18.4	11.0	9.3	13.0	13.0	3.6
Natural in/decrease	-4.1	-5.1	-4.7	-4.8	-5.2	-5.0	-6.4

Life expectancy at birth in years	1993	1994	1995	1996	1997	1998	1999
for men	58.5	57.1	58.9	60.1	60.5	60.3	59.3
for women	70.9	69.8	71.4	72.1	71.6	71.4	71.2

Mortality rate by homicide,	1993	1994	1995	1996	1997	1998	1999
assaults per 100 000 persons	24.6	23.7	18.9	19.2	17.5	18.2	20.9

Consumption

Food as % of	1993	1994	1995	1996	1997	1998	1999
total private consumption[1]	43	47	54	53	49	56	55
Cars per 100 persons[2]	11	12	14	17	20	21	21

The number of dwellings at the end of			
1994 was	304543	51% owned by state and local authorities,	31% by private persons
1995 was	305279	49% owned by state and local authorities,	34% by private persons
1996 was	307776	48% owned by state and local authorities,	37% by private persons
1997 was	311450	45% owned by state and local authorities,	41% by private persons
1998 was	316827	43% owned by state and local authorities,	42% by private persons
1999 was	328745	*% owned by state and local authorities,	*% by private persons

The general area, in thousand square metres, of dwellings at the end of			
1994 was	16400	51% owned by state and local authorities,	31% by private persons
1995 was	16556	50% owned by state and local authorities,	33% by private persons
1996 was	16676	48% owned by state and local authorities,	36% by private persons
1997 was	16885	46% owned by state and local authorities,	39% by private persons
1998 was	17160	42% owned by state and local authorities,	39% by private persons
1999 was	17403	41% owned by state and local authorities,	45% by private persons

Unemployment

The number of unemployed persons, (1000 persons), annual average:							
	1993	1994	1995	1996	1997	1998	1999
In Labour Force Surveys 3)	28.1	39.7	40.6	62.1	54.7	81.3	75.0
Registered unemployment	8.0	19.5	25.0	22.2	14.1	13.4	10.3

Foreign trade

Exports, total in million US $, countries in % of total	1993	1994	1995	1996	1997	1998	1999
Total exports	116.5	183.0	459.4	480.8	457.7	429.3	383.6
to Finland	6.0%	0.1%	0.4%	1.3%	1.0%	1.0%	0.8%
to Sweden	9.4%	0.5%	0.2%	0.2%	1.2%	0.5%	1.6%
to Norway	0.1%	1.1%	0.7%	0.8%	0.1%	3.1%	1.9%
to Denmark	0.2%	0.2%	0.9%	0.3%	0.2%	0.1%	0.6%
to Germany	12.9%	8.7%	5.4%	5.5%	8.0%	10.4%	10.3%
to Poland	12.0%	9.3%	2.0%	16.3%	22.3%	23.2%	24.8%
to Lithuania	-	2.2%	3.5%	4.9%	6.7%	5.6%	4.2%
to Latvia	-	1.6%	1.2%	1.3%	1.3%	2.7%	0.7%
to Estonia	-	0.2%	3.3%	1.2%	0.6%	0.7%	0.1%
to EU countries	*	*	*	*	*	*	*
to CIS countries	*	*	13.4%	12.5%	10.6%	8.2%	10.7%

Imports, total in million US $, countries in % of total	1993	1994	1995	1996	1997	1998	1999
Total imports	75.9	594.3	585.1	1030.0	1285.8	1187.9	824.1
from Finland	1.3%	2.0%	1.8%	1.1%	1.8%	0.9%	1.1%
from Sweden	-	2.0%	1.0%	0.9%	1.3%	1.3%	2.0%
from Norway	0.2%	0.9%	2.5%	2.0%	1.3%	1.6%	1.3%
from Denmark	0.4%	2.9%	1.2%	1.7%	1.4%	1.9%	1.3%
from Germany	23.7%	12.7%	8.2%	32.1%	22.8%	22.9%	37.0%
from Poland	22.4%	33.3%	15.6%	11.0%	15.9%	16.2%	13.9%
from Lithuania	2.6%	8.6%	17.6%	9.3%	15.1%	12.5%	7.5%
from Latvia	1.3%	3.2%	1.9%	1.4%	1.7%	1.9%	1.7%
from Estonia	0.3%	0.1%	0.2%	0.4%	0.6%	0.5%	0.7%
from EU countries	*	*	*	*	*	*	*
from CIS countries	*	*	16.0%	4.7%	2.9%	2.8%	2.6%

Employed persons by activity

Employed by activity in 1000 persons[4]	1994	1995	1996	1997	1998	1999
All activities	398	392	397	411	400	401
Agriculture, hunting and forestry	49	45	44	43	42	41
Fishing (included in manufacturing)	.					
Mining and quarrying (incl. in manufact.)						
Manufacturing	100	91	85	82	74	71
Electricity, gas and water supply (include in other community services)						
Construction	34	33	33	28	27	27
Wholesale and retail sales[5]	47	48	54	77	82	84
Hotels and restaurants (hotels incl. in other personal services, restaurants in wholesale and retail sales)						
Transport, storage and communication	35	33	33	32	31	31
Financial intermediation	6	6	6	6	6	5
Real estate, renting and business activities						
Public administration and defence	18	24	30	28	28	31
Education[6]	51	53	54	48	46	47
Health and social care	30	30	30	30	29	30
Other community, social and personal services[7]	20	21	21	29	26	24
Other	8	8	7	8	9	10

Enterprises

The number of active enterprises by ownership and size	1995	1996	1997	1998	1999
All active enterprises	19800	21520	23188	24587	26002
With private domestic owners	15320	15299	16869	17924	19253
With foreign owners	415	460	568	634	715
Owned by state or local government	2510	2671	2338	2434	2210
Other	1555	3090	3413	3595	3824
Number of enterprises in wholesale and retail trade	7437	7656	8176	8436	8832
Enterprises with 200 or more employees	213	213	210	233	203
20 to 199 employees	*	*	*	*	*
5 to 19 employees	*	*	*	*	*
less than 5 employees	*	*	*	*	*

Direct inward and outward investment

Foreign direct investment in Kaliningrad	1994	1995	1996	1997	1998	1999
Total direct investment in million US $	4.5	12.7	20.8	8.6	5.9	4.1
by country: from Denmark	*	0.7	0.5	-	-	-
Estonia	*	-	-	-	-	-
Finland	*	0.2	0.3	-	-	-
Germany	*	3.5	1.6	2.0	5.0	0.8
Latvia	*	0.1	-	-	-	-
Lithuania	*	0.7	-	0.5	1.0	1.3
Netherlands	*	0.1	0.1	-	-	-
Norway	*	0.1	2.5	-	-	
Poland	*	0.3	0.5	0.2	2.3	1.3
Sweden	*	3.2	2.2	2.5	0.5	-
Switzerland	*	2.5	2.1	-	-	-
United Kingdom	*	0.1	9.0	-	-	-
United States	*	0.1	-	0.1	0.1	0.1
The stock of direct investment capital in Kaliningrad at the end of year, total of which in:	*	*	*	*	*	*
Mining, quarrying and manufacture	*	*	*	*	*	*
Wholesale and retail trade	*	*	*	*	*	*
Transport, storage and communication	*	*	*	*	*	*

Kaliningrad direct investment abroad		1994	1995	1996	1997	1998	1999
Total investment abroad in million US $		*	*	0.0	*	*	*
by country: to	Denmark	*	*	0.0	*	*	*
	Estonia	*	*	–	*	*	*
	Finland	*	*	–	*	*	*
	Germany	*	*	–	*	*	*
	Latvia	*	*	–	*	*	*
	Lithuania	*	*	–	*	*	*
	Netherlands	*	*	–	*	*	*
	Norway	*	*	–	*	*	*
	Poland	*	*	–	*	*	*
	Sweden	*	*	–	*	*	*
	Switzerland	*	*	–	*	*	*
	United Kingdom	*	*	–	*	*	*
	United States	*	*	–	*	*	*

Foreign loans and foreign aid

Net amount borowed from abroad	1994	1995	1996	1997	1998	1999
Million US $	*	*	*	*	*	*
Foreign aid received, in million US $	*	*	*	*	*	*

Prices

Change in index, previous period = 100	1994	1995	1996	1997	1998	1999
Consumer price index	317	242	110	106	203	135
Producer price index for manufactured products	330	248	115	111	153	152

International sea traffic

The number of vessels in habours	1994	1995	1996	1997	1998	1999
Arrivals from abroad	*	*	*	*	*	*
Departures aboad	*	*	*	*	*	*

International arrivals/departures in harbours, 1000 persons	1994	1995	1996	1997	1998	1999
Arriving in Kalinngrad total	*	*	*	*	*	*
Departing from Kaliningrad total	*	*	*	*	*	*

International air traffic

Passengers in airports in 1000	1994	1995	1996	1997	1998	1999
Arrivals	9.8	7.7	30.1	23.1	33.1	23.9
Departures	9.8	12.6	24.3	18.8	17.1	19.5

Sources
Questionnaires completed by the Regional Committee for Statistics in Kaliningrad region.

Notes
1) From household budget data.
2) Registration of all cars.
3) Figures from Labour Force Surveys or other surveys of individuals following the ILO definition of unemployed persons: Person without work, currently available for work if there should
   be work and actively seeking work.
4) Employed persons as defined by ILO: working and paid as a wage earner, enterpreneur or a
   freelancer, working without direct payment in a family enterprise or farm, temporarily absent
   from work.
5) Including public catering, logistics, sales activity and procurements.
6) Including culture, art, science and scientific service.
7) Including communal housing and public services.
 * Data not available
   0, 0,0   Less than half of the unit employed
 - Zero

Country/region: Republic of Karelia

Basic Data and Population

Total land- and water area: 180520 square km of which agricultural land: 1%, forest and wood-land: 55%

Total population (end of the respective year or closest possible estimate):	
1993	0.79 million
1994	0.79 million
1995	0.78 million
1996	0.78 million
1997	0.78 million of which 47% male, 53% female
1998	0.77 million of which 47% male, 53% female
1999	0.77 million of which 47% male, 53% female

by age groups in %	1993	1994	1995	1996	1997	1998	1999
00 - 19 years	30.0	29.5	29.0	28.4	27.8	27.1	26.5
20 - 64 years	60.7	60.9	61.0	61.3	61.4	61.9	62.5
65 - years	9.3	9.6	10.0	10.3	10.8	11.0	11.0

by nationality in % for all nationalities 0.5% or more	1989 census	1994 microsensus	1996	1997	1998	1999
1. Karelians	10.0	10.8	*	*	*	*
2. Russians	73.6	73.7	*	*	*	*
3. Belorusians	7.0	6.7	*	*	*	*
4. Ukrainians	3.6	3.1	*	*	*	*
5. Finns	2.3	2.9	*	*	*	*
6. Veps	0.8	0.6	*	*	*	*

The total population has decreased from 0.80 million in 1992 to 0.77 million in 1999.

Migration in 1000 of persons	1993	1994	1995	1996	1997	1998	1999
Total immigration	22.1	22.4	21.9	19.3	17.1	16.1	16.1
Total emigration	21.7	20.8	19.9	19.3	16.9	16.3	16.4
Net migration	0.3	1.6	2.0	0.0	0.2	-0.2	-0.3
Natural in/decrease	-4.8	-6.5	-6.1	-4.7	-4.1	-3.9	-5.6

Life expectancy at birth in years	1993	1994	1995	1996	1997	1998	1999
for men	56.2	55.0	54.7	58.1	59.7	59.7	57.6
for women	70.8	69.0	69.2	71.3	71.9	72.3	70.9

Mortality rate by homicide, assaults per 100 000 persons	1993	1994	1995	1996	1997	1998	1999
	39.0	41.2	38.6	31.6	26.9	24.3	25.7

Consumption

Food as % of total private consumption[1]	1993	1994	1995	1996	1997	1998	1999
	49	48	50	51	50	54	56
Cars per 100 persons[2]	9	10	11	12	13	13	14

The number of dwellings at the end of:			
1994 was	61903	27.5% owned by state and local authorities,	47.4% by private persons
1995 was	62766	29.3% owned by state and local authorities,	47.5% by private persons
1996 was	63258	33.4% owned by state and local authorities,	49.2% by private persons
1997 was	62792	39.3% owned by state and local authorities,	48.9% by private persons
1998 was	62982	43.4% owned by state and local authorities,	48.8% by private persons
1999 was	63745	*% owned by state and local authorities,	*% by private persons

The general area, in thousand square metres, of dwellings at the end of:			
1994 was	14695	65% owned by state and local authorities,	14% by private persons
1995 was	14869	63% owned by state and local authorities,	18% by private persons
1996 was	14902	59% owned by state and local authorities,	27% by private persons
1997 was	15010	60% owned by state and local authorities,	30% by private persons
1998 was	15061	60% owned by state and local authorities,	32% by private persons
1999 was	15171	61% owned by state and local authorities,	33% by private persons

Unemployment

The number of unemployed persons, (1000 persons), annual average:							
	1993	1994	1995	1996	1997	1998	1999
In Labour Force Surveys [3]	40	37	40	46	47	59	65
Registered unemployment	6	10	19	25	26	22	19

Foreign trade

Exports, total in million US $, countries in % of total	1993	1994	1995	1996	1997	1998	1999
Total exports	341.0	380.8	633.0	560.3	520.3	527.5	497.7
to Finland	*	29.5%	21.8%	27.2%	31.3%	32.5%	32.5%
to Sweden	*	3.1%	1.7%	6.3%	4.7%	3.4%	6.3%
to Norway	*	1.2%	0.1%	3.2%	2.5%	2.4%	5.2%
to Denmark	*	1.1%	0.5%	0.4%	0.5%	0.1%	0.1%
to Germany	*	9.3%	6.3%	7.4%	10.7%	6.8%	3.9%
to Poland	*	2.0%	3.8%	1.0%	2.5%	0.6%	1.4%
to Lithuania	*	0.4%	0.4%	0.6%	0.6%	0.5%	0.6%
to Latvia	*	0.7%	0.4%	0.8%	0.4%	0.6%	0.7%
to Estonia	*	0.5%	0.6%	0.7%	1.0%	1.2%	3.6%
to EU countries	*	54.5%	39.3%	58.1%	64.9%	61.0%	61.5%
to CIS countries*	*	7.7%	5.5%	4.3%	1.5%	1.2%	0.9%

*) without Belorusia

Imports, total in million US $, countries in % of total	1993	1994	1995	1996	1997	1998	1999
Total imports	*	167.0	176.6	209.7	158.7	110.4	125.5
from Finland	*	24.4%	31.4%	22.1%	21.3%	23.4%	30.5%
from Sweden	*	2.9%	3.1%	2.5%	4.6%	3.3%	2.5%
from Norway	*	0.1%	0.2%	1.6%	2.8%	12.2%	11.1%
from Denmark	*	0.7%	0.3%	1.5%	1.7%	1.2%	0.2%
from Germany	*	9.0%	12.4%	15.9%	17.7%	10.7%	7.0%
from Poland	*	0.7%	0.3%	0.1%	0.6%	0.9%	0.5%
from Lithuania	*	0.3%	0.3%	0.1%	0.9%	1.4%	0.1%
from Latvia	*	0.2%	0.2%	1.0%	0.1%	0.1%	0.1%
from Estonia	*	0.2%	0.2%	0.8%	0.6%	0.7%	0.0%
from EU countries	*	60.3%	69.4%	74.2%	75.9%	55.2%	55.0%
from CIS countries	*	28.4%	17.6%	12.4%	9.4%	8.2%	5.9%

Employed persons by activity

Employed by activities in 1000 persons[4]	1994	1995	1996	1997	1998	1999
All activities	373	371	362	335	312	331
Agriculture, hunting and forestry	24	22	19	18	16	20
Fishing (included in manufacturing)						
Mining and quarrying (incl. in manufact.)						
Manufacturing	110	102	96	87	79	82
Electricity, gas and water supply (included in other community services)						
Construction	36	33	28	21	16	16
Wholesale and retail sales[5]	39	39	38	45	43	44
Hotels and restaurants (hotels incl. in other personal services, restaurants in wholesale and retail sales)						
Transport, storage and communication	45	47	50	41	37	41
Financial intermediation	4	5	4	4	4	4
Real estate, renting and business activities						
Public administration and defence	11	14	18	17	18	18
Education[6]	40	42	43	38	35	36
Health and social care	27	29	30	27	27	28
Other community, social and personal services[7] V/						
Other	37	38	36	37	37	42

Enterprises

The number of active enterprises by ownership and size	1995	1996	1997	1998	1999
All active enterprises	11323	12315	13028	13671	14666
With private domestic owners	7535	8271	8809	9216	9914
With foreign owners	92	104	124	139	155
Owned by state or local government	1803	1870	1892	1894	1973
Other ownership categories	1893	2070	2203	2422	2624
Number of enterprises in wholesale and retail trade	3886	4206	4426	4709	4982
Enterprises with 200 or more employees	*	*	*	*	*
20 to 199 employees	*	*	*	*	*
5 to 19 employees	*	*	*	*	*
less than 5 employees	*	*	*	*	*

Direct inward and outward investment

Foreign direct investment in Karelia	1994	1995	1996	1997	1998	1999
Total direct investment in million US $	13.8	16.1	2.3	3.7	5.1	4.5
by country: from Denmark	*	0.0	-	-	-	-
Estonia	*	-	-	-	-	-
Finland	*	0.6	0.5	0.4	0.1	0.1
Germany	*	2.6	0.0	-	0.0	0.0
Latvia	*	-	0.0	0.1	-	-
Lithuania	*	0.0	-	0.0	-	-
Netherlands	*	-	0.0	-	-	-
Norway	*	0.1	0.0	-	0.0	0.0
Poland	*	-	-	-	-	-
Sweden	*	0.1	0.0	0.4	0.0	0.0
Switzerland	*	0.0	-	-	-	-
United Kingdom	*	0.1	-	-	-	-
United States	*	5.4	0.4	2.4	1.7	4.0
The stock of direct investment capital in Karelia at the end of year, total of which in:	*	*	*	*	*	*
Mining, quarrying and manufacture	*	*	*	*	*	*
Wholesale and retail trade	*	*	*	*	*	*
Transport, storage and communication	*	*	*	*	*	*

Karelian direct investment abroad		1994	1995	1996	1997	1998	1999
Total investment abroad in million US $		*	*	*	*	*	*
by country: to	Denmark	*	*	*	*	*	*
	Estonia	*	*	*	*	*	*
	Finland	*	*	*	*	*	*
	Germany	*	*	*	*	*	*
	Latvia	*	*	*	*	*	*
	Lithuania	*	*	*	*	*	*
	Netherlands	*	*	*	*	*	*
	Norway	*	*	*	*	*	*
	Poland	*	*	*	*	*	*
	Sweden	*	*	*	*	*	*
	Switzerland	*	*	*	*	*	*
	United Kingdom	*	*	*	*	*	*
	United States	*	*	*	*	*	*

Foreign loans and foreign aid

Net amount borowed from abroad	1994	1995	1996	1997	1998	1999
Million US $	*	*	*	*	*	*
Foreign aid received, in million US $	*	*	*	*	*	*

Prices

Change in index, previous period = 100	1994	1995	1996	1997	1998	1999
Consumer price index	331	249	121	108	180	130
Producer price index for manufactured products	426	271	113	109	149	171

International sea traffic

The number of vessels in harbours	1994	1995	1996	1997	1998	1999
Arrivals from abroad	*	*	*	*	*	*
Departures abroad	*	*	*	*	*	*

International arrivals/departures in harbours, 1000 persons	1994	1995	1996	1997	1998	1999
Arriving in Karelia	*	*	*	*	*	*
Departing from Karelia	*	*	*	*	*	*

International air traffic

Passengers in airports in 1000	1994	1995	1996	1997	1998	1999
Arrivals	*	3.0	3.0	3.0	1.3	0.1
Departures	*	3.3	3.4	3.2	1.4	0.1

Sources
Questionnaires completed by the Regional Committee for Statistics in Republic of Karelia.

Notes
1) From household budget data.
2) Registration of all cars.
3) Figures from Labour Force Surveys or other surveys of individuals following the ILO definition of unemployed persons: Person without work, currently available for work if there should be work and actively seeking work.
4) Employed persons as defined by ILO: working and paid as a wage earner, enterpreneur or a freelancer, working without direct payment in a family enterprise or farm, temporarily absent from work.
5) Including public catering, logistics, sales activity and procurement.
6) Including culture, art, science and scientific service.
7) Including communal housing and public services.
 * Data not available
   0, 0,0   Less than half of the unit employed
 - Zero

Country/region: Leningrad Region

Basic Data and Population
Total land- and water area: 83908 square km of which agricultural land: 10%, forest and woodland: 61%

Total population (end of the respective year or closest possible estimate):	
1993	1.66 million
1994	1.67 million
1995	1.67 million
1996	1.67 million
1997	1.67 million of which 46% male, 54% female
1998	1.67 million of which 46% male, 54% female
1999	1.67 million of which 46% male, 54% female

by age groups in %	1993	1994	1995	1996	1997	1998	1999
00 - 19 years	27.5	27.2	26.7	26.1	25.5	24.9	24.2
20 - 64 years	60.3	60.3	60.5	60.8	61.1	61.6	62.3
65 - years	12.2	12.5	12.8	13.1	13.4	13.5	13.5

by nationality in % for all nationalities 0.5% or more	1989 census		1996	1997	1998	1999
1. Russians	90.9		*	*	*	*
2. Ukrainians	3,.0		*	*	*	*
3. Belorusians	2,.0		*	*	*	*
4. Finns	0.7		*	*	*	*
5. Tatars	0.5		*	*	*	*

The total population has in(de-)creased from 1.67 million in 1992 to 1.67 million in 1999.

Migration in 1000 of persons	1993	1994	1995	1996	1997	1998	1999
Total immigration	54.9	68.8	67.5	57.8	50.5	46.6	41.4
Total emigration	42.1	43.3	46.7	39.5	33.2	32.5	29.7
Net migration	12.8	25.5	20.8	18.3	17.3	14.1	11.7
Natural in/decrease	-18.0	-20.1	-18.4	-15.6	-14.1	-14.5	-19.0

Life expectancy at birth in years	1993	1994	1995	1996	1997	1998	1999
for men	55.7	54.7	55.5	58.8	60.0	60.4	57.6
for women	70.4	69.2	70.1	71.7	72.0	72.6	71.0

Mortality rate by homicide, assaults per 100 000 persons	1993	1994	1995	1996	1997	1998	1999
	36.4	34.9	34.3	26.5	27.5	24.0	30.0

Consumption

Food as % of total private consumption[1]	1993	1994	1995	1996	1997	1998	1999
	50	51	54	54	54	60	59
Cars per 100 persons[2]	6	7	7	8	10	11	13

The number of dwellings at the end of:			
1994 was	669500	64% owned by state and local authorities,	36% by private persons
1995 was	690900	54% owned by state and local authorities,	46% by private persons
1996 was	705700	54% owned by state and local authorities,	46% by private persons
1997 was	699100	53% owned by state and local authorities,	47% by private persons
1998 was	717500	51% owned by state and local authorities,	49% by private persons
1999 was	749147	48% owned by state and local authorities,	52% by private persons

The general area, in thousand square metres, of dwellings at the end of:			
1994 was	33117	67% owned by state and local authorities,	33% by private persons
1995 was	34142	49% owned by state and local authorities,	51% by private persons
1996 was	34783	48% owned by state and local authorities,	52% by private persons
1997 was	34664	47% owned by state and local authorities,	53% by private persons
1998 was	35295	45% owned by state and local authorities,	55% by private persons
1999 was	37205	44% owned by state and local authorities,	56% by private persons

Unemployment

The number of unemployed persons, (1000 persons), annual average:	1993	1994	1995	1996	1997	1998	1999
In Labour Force Surveys [3]	58.0	78.1	89.1	83.0	106.4	118.9	122.2
Registered unemployment	16.0	32.6	40.8	49.5	35.8	35.7	17.6

Foreign trade

(The export figures for 1996 and the import figures for 1995 and 1996 are included together with the figures for St Petersburg in the table for St Petersburg)

Exports, total in million US $, countries in % of total	1993	1994	1995	1996*	1997	1998	1999
Total exports	329.3	379.9	541.2		1482.6	1444.3	1520.2
to Finland	30.8%	74.9%	13.1%		13.2%	12.2%	11.8%
to Sweden	3.3%	0.6%	0.9%		42.8%	43.5%	58.6%
to Norway	0.2%	0.1%	0.6%		1.4%	0.2%	0.2%
to Denmark	*	*	55.8%		0.2%	0.2%	0.3%
to Germany	1.8%	1.8%	5.4%		2.6%	4.8%	4.1%
to Poland	0.2%	0.5%	0.2%		0.3%	0.3%	1.0%
to Lithuania	0.2%	7.9%	0.4%		3.1%	0.8%	0.5%
to Latvia	0.5%	0.5%	1.4%		6.1%	2.2%	1.7%
to Estonia	1.3%	1.4%	3.3%		5.1%	3.2%	4.3%
to EU countries	*	*	83.0%		65.9%	69.9%	82.4%
to CIS countries	*	*	3.7%		2.0%	1.4%	1.5%

Imports, total in million US $, countries in % of total	1993	1994	1995*	1996*	1997	1998	1999
Total imports	56.9	87.4			365.8	307.1	357.4
from Finland	22.0%	24.1%			16.5%	23.0%	22.5%
from Sweden	2.1%	1.1%			6.1%	6.2%	6.2%
from Norway	*	*			23.4%	2.8%	0.5%
from Denmark	*	*			2.0%	2.4%	0.7%
from Germany	30.2%	23.2%			12.2%	14.0%	19.6%
from Poland	3.2%	1.8%			1.6%	1.1%	1.0%
from Lithuania	*	*			1.0%	1.0%	0.5%
from Latvia	*	0.3%			1.2%	0.7%	0.1%
from Estonia	0.7%	0.7%			1.8%	3.1%	0.9%
from EU countries	*	*			53.4%	62.6%	73.7%
from CIS countries	*	*			6.4%	5.8%	3.6%

Employed persons by activity

Employed by activity in 1000 persons[4] [8]	1994	1995	1996	1997	1998	1999
All activities	668	678	690	674	671	696
Agriculture, hunting and forestry	95	95	81	77	69	88
Fishing (include in manufacturing)						
Mining and quarrying (incl. in manufact.)						
Manufacturing	198	191	188	168	164	171
Electricity, gas and water supply (included in other community services)						
Construction	58	59	53	72	68	64
Wholesale and retail sales[5]	63	73	89	102	113	111
Hotels and restaurants (hotels incl. in other personal services, restaurants in wholesale and retail sales)						
Transport, storage and communication	47	46	44	43	46	46
Financial intermediation	4	5	5	5	5	5
Real estate, renting and business activities	0	1	1	2	5	4
Public administration and defence	21	27	36	29	30	31
Education[6]	80	80	82	76	72	73
Health and social care	43	44	45	43	45	43
Other community, social and personal services [7]	48	42	51	49	46	49
Other	11	15	15	8	8	11

Enterprises

The number of active enterprises by ownership and size[9]	1995	1996	1997	1998	1999
All active enterprises	21627	22099	24302	26178	29061
With private domestic owners	16127	16751	16749	18027	19943
With foreign owners	108	123	147	191	221
Owned by state or local government	2093	2163	2610	2904	3105
Other ownership categories	3299	3062	3136	3065	7708
Number of enterprises in wholesale and retail trade	3690	3937	4280	4727	5592
Enterprises with 200 or more employees	*	*	*	*	*
20 to 199 employees	*	*	*	*	*
5 to 19 employees	*	*	*	*	*
less than 5 employees	*	*	*	*	*

Direct inward and outward investment

Foreign direct investment in Leningrad Reg.	1994	1995	1996	1997	1998	1999
Total direct investment in million US $ [10]	0.2	20.1	43.7	75.6	90.6	236.2
by country: from Denmark	*	-	0.0	7.0	2.1	-
Estonia	*	-	-	-	-	-
Finland	*	0.9	0.5	0.2	2.2	0.2
Germany	*	8.6	41.7	8.8	12.7	5.1
Latvia	*	-	0.0	-	-	-
Lithuania	*	-	0.0	0.0	-	-
Netherlands	*	0.1	-	-	40.0	181.3
Norway	*	-	-	0.0	22.9	2.0
Poland	*	-	-	-	-	-
Sweden	*	0.0	0.0	0.1	0.0	0.3
Switzerland	*	-	-	-	-	1.2
United Kingdom	*	0.0	0.5	0.0	0.0	10.0
United States	*	-	0.9	0.2	9.8	35.0
The stock of direct investment capital in Leningrad reg. at the end of year, total thereof in:	*	*	*	*	*	*
Mining, quarrying and manufacture	*	*	*	*	*	*
Wholesale and retail trade	*	*	*	*	*	*
Transport, storage and communication	*	*	*	*	*	*

Leningrad Reg. direct investment abroad	1994	1995	1996	1997	1998	1999
Total investment abroad in million US $	*	*	*	*	*	*
by country: to Denmark	*	*	*	*	*	*
Estonia	*	*	*	*	*	*
Finland	*	*	*	*	*	*
Germany	*	*	*	*	*	*
Latvia	*	*	*	*	*	*
Lithuania	*	*	*	*	*	*
Netherlands	*	*	*	*	*	*
Norway	*	*	*	*	*	*
Poland	*	*	*	*	*	*
Sweden	*	*	*	*	*	*
Switzerland	*	*	*	*	*	*
United Kingdom	*	*	*	*	*	*
United States	*	*	*	*	*	*

Foreign loans and foreign aid

Net amount borowed from abroad	1994	1995	1996	1997	1998	1999
Million US $	*	*	*	*	*	*
Foreign aid received, in million US $	*	*	*	*	*	*

Prices

Change in index, previous period = 100	1994	1995	1996	1997	1998	1999
Consumer price index	322	231	122	110	166	142
Producer price index for manufactured products	380	260	122	107	131	192

International sea traffic

The number of vessels in harbours	1994	1995	1996	1997	1998	1999
Arrivals from abroad	*	*	*	*	*	*
Departures abroad	*	*	*	*	*	*

International arrival/departures in harbours, 1000 persons	1994	1995	1996	1997	1998	1999
Arriving in Leningrad region	*	*	*	*	*	*
Departing from Leningrad region	*	*	*	*	*	*

International air traffic

Passengers in airports in 1000	1994	1995	1996	1997	1998	1999
Arrivals	*	*	*	*	*	*
Departures	*	*	*	*	*	*

Sources
Questionnaires completed in by the Regional Committee for Statistics in Leningrad Region.

Notes
1) From household budget data.
2) Registration of all cars.
3) Figures from Labour Force Surveys or other surveys of individuals following the ILO defi-nition of unemployed persons: Person without work, currently available for work if there should be work and actively seeking work.
4) Employed persons as defined by ILO: working and paid as a wage earner, enterpreneur or a freelancer, working without direct payment in a family enterprise or farm, temporarily absent from work.
5) Including public catering, logistics, sales activity and procurements.
6) Including culture, art, science and scientific service.
7) Including: communal housing and public service.
8) From 1999 are individuals with agricultural productions included.
9) Registered at Single State Register of Enterprises and Organisations
10) Based on information in Roubles.
 * Data not available
   0, 0,0   Less than half of the unit employed
 - Zero

Country/region: Murmansk

Basic Data and Population

Total land- and water area: 144902 square km of which agricultural land: 0.2%, wood and woodland: 37.2%

Total population (end of the respective year or closest possible estimate):
1993	1.11 million
1994	1.09 million
1995	1.07 million
1996	1.05 million of which
1997	1.03 million of which 49% male, 51% female
1998	1.02 million of which 49% male, 51% female
1999	1.00 million of which 49% male, 51% female

by age groups in %	1993	1994	1995	1996	1997	1998	1999
00 - 19 years	30.0	29.4	28.7	27.9	27.1	26.2	25.4
20 - 64 years	64.9	65.2	65.6	66.1	66.5	67.1	67.7
65 - years	5.1	5.4	5.7	6.0	6.4	6.7	6.9

by nationality in % for all nationalities 0.5% or more	1989 census	1994 microcensus	1999
1. Russians	82.9	86.2	*
2. Ukrainians	9.0	6.6	*
3. Belorusians	3.3	2.8	*
4. Tatars	1.0	0.9	*

The total population has in(de-)creased from 1.14 million in 1992 to 1.00 million in 1999.

Migration in 1000 of persons	1993	1994	1995	1996	1997	1998	1999
Total immigration	34.6	43.7	36.4	35.0	27.1	23.8	20.7
Total emigration	57.4	57.4	52.4	48.4	42.0	39.5	35.1
Net migration	-22.9	-13.7	-16.0	-13.4	-14.9	-15.7	-14.4
Natural in/decrease	-3.2	-3.5	-3.4	-1.9	-1.2	-0.6	-2.5

Life expectancy at birth in years	1993	1994	1995	1996	1997	1998	1999
for men	59.1	57.0	57.7	60.1	63.0	63.7	62.5
for women	71.1	69.7	70.4	71.5	72.9	74.0	72.8

Mortality rate by homicide, assaults per 100 000 persons	1993	1994	1995	1996	1997	1998	1999
assaults per 100 000 persons	59.7	67.5	71.3	67.4	60.1	54.4	54.3

Consumption

Food as % of total private	1993	1994	1995	1996	1997	1998	1999
consumption[1]	42	45	49	46	44	51	50
Cars per 100 persons[2]	9	11	11	13	13	13	12

The number of dwellings at the end of:			
1994 was	338920	62% owned by state and local authorities,	30% by private persons
1995 was	349895	49% owned by state and local authorities,	35% by private persons
1996 was	360706	50% owned by state and local authorities,	38% by private persons
1997 was	371073	48% owned by state and local authorities,	42% by private persons
1998 was	378268	50% owned by state and local authorities,	46% by private persons
1999 was	380108	*% owned by state and local authorities,	*% by private persons

The general area, in thousand square metres, of dwellings at the end of:			
1994 was	18475	66% owned by state and local authorities,	26% by private persons
1995 was	18913	54% owned by state and local authorities,	30% by private persons
1996 was	19228	55% owned by state and local authorities,	33% by private persons
1997 was	19761	53% owned by state and local authorities,	37% by private persons
1998 was	19666	54% owned by state and local authorities,	41% by private persons
1999 was	19653	53% owned by state and local authorities,	43% by private persons

Unemployment

The number of unemployed persons (1000 persons), annual average:							
	1993	1994	1995	1996	1997	1998	1999
In Labour Force Surveys [3]	41.4	58.9	65.5	87.0	106.0	114.6	95.4
Registered unemployment	11.5	19.5	27.5	33.5	27.8	30.2	28.6

Foreign trade

Exports, total in million US $, countries in % of total	1993	1994	1995	1996	1997	1998	1999
Total exports	426.4	615.0	851.5	1048.9	1330.5	932.9	818.8
to Finland	*	8.3%	11.9%	7.9%	7.6%	10.5%	9.4%
to Sweden	*	5.5%	8.1%	3.4%	2.9%	1.7%	2.7%
to Norway	*	16.1%	17.8%	15.8%	9.9%	15.2%	20.4%
to Denmark	*	4.9%	3.1%	3.2%	1.6%	1.8%	3.3%
to Germany	*	3.6%	3.2%	1.4%	1.3%	3.4%	3.5%
to Poland	*	*	0.0%	1.8%	2.9%	2.2%	1.5%
to Lithuania	*	0.0%	0.6%	2.8%	2.1%	3.4%	4.4%
to Latvia	*	0.0%	0.0%	0.2%	0.0%	0.0%	0.1%
to Estonia	*	0.2%	0.2%	0.3%	0.0%	*	0.1%
to EU countries	*	*	*	*	*	*	*
to CIS countries	*	*	*	*	6.3%	7.8%	5.6%

Imports, total in million US $, countries in % of total	1993	1994	1995	1996	1997	1998	1999
Total imports	147.2	176.3	299.5	264.9	254.8	202.5	253.3
from Finland	*	13.7%	13.5%	26.7%	26.9%	12.5%	8.0%
from Sweden	*	4.9%	5.0%	3.1%	2.8%	3.5%	3.8%
from Norway	*	15.5%	14.2%	20.7%	21.7%	15.7%	10.9%
from Denmark	*	2.2%	1.4%	1.0%	2.2%	4.5%	1.5%
from Germany	*	8.6%	3.8%	6.7%	4.3%	10.1%	7.5%
from Poland	*	1.0%	1.7%	2.3%	5.6%	1.9%	0.9%
from Lithuania	*	0.0%	0.1%	0.6%	0.1%	0.2%	0.0%
from Latvia	*	0.1%	0.2%	0.1%	0.1%	0.0%	0.2%
from Estonia	*	0.1%	0.2%	0.6%	0.1%	2.5%	*
from EU countries	*	*	*	*	*	*	*
from CIS countries	*	*	*	*	4.9%	6.5%	1.7%

Employed persons by activity

Employed by activity in 1000 persons [4]	1994	1995	1996	1997	1998	1999
All activities	493	472	451	431	423	423
Agriculture, hunting and forestry	13	10	9	7	6	7
Fishing[5]	27	20	15	19	2	2
Mining and quarrying (incl. in manufact.)						
Manufacturing	133	130	127	110	119	113
Electricity, gas and water supply (included in manufacturing)						
Construction	42	43	27	24	19	20
Wholesale and retail sales [6]	51	48	43	53	62	60
Hotels and restaurants	8	8	7	6	6	6
Transport, storage and communication	52	47	46	43	39	46
Financial intermediation	6	6	5	4	4	4
Real estate, renting and business activities	38	33	36	34	33	30
Public administration and defence	22	26	30	29	32	35
Education[7]	47	43	44	42	42	40
Health and social care	38	37	38	36	35	36
Other community, social and personal services[8]	16	21	24	24	24	24

Enterprises

The number of active enterprises by ownership and size		1995	1996	1997	1998	1999
All active enterprises		7373	9057	9143	10353	10437
With private domestic owners		6285	7080	5377	6505	6514
With foreign owners		167	259	91	105	106
Owned by state or local government		921	1718	1689	1811	1869
Number of enterprises in wholesale and retail trade		3418	3025	2987	3557	3512
Enterprises with	200 or more employees	*	254	*	*	*
	20 to 199 employees	*	1252	*	*	*
	5 to 19 employees	*	1075	*	*	*
	less than 5 employees	*	6476	*	*	*

Direct inward and outward investment

Foreign direct investmens in Murmansk reg.	1994	1995	1996	1997	1998	1999
Total direct investment in million US $	*	3.8	3.1	3.2	11.2	14.7
by country: from Denmark	*	-	-	-	-	-
Estonia	*	-	-	-	-	-
Finland	*	0.3	0.3	0.9	1.0	0.0
Germany	*	1.7	0.6	0.0	-	-
Latvia	*	-	-	0.0	-	-
Lithuania	*	-	-	-	-	-
Netherlands	*	0.9	-	0.4	3.9	-
Norway	*	0.1	0.5	0.5	2.9	10.4
Poland	*	-	0.0	-	-	-
Sweden	*	0.4	0.0	-	0.1	1.4
Switzerland	*	-	1.4	0.3	-	-
United Kingdom	*	0.2	0.2	0.3	1.3	2.2
United States	*	0.1	0.0	0.4	0.2	0.1
The stock of direct investment capital in Murmansk reg. at the end of year, total; in % of which in:		100%	100%	100%	100%	100%
Minining, quarrying and manufacture		10.5%	15.3%	37.4%	46.8%	50.5%
Wholesale and retail trade		9.6%	5.1%	14.5%	13.0%	42.8%
Transport, storage and communication		68.3%	67.0%	24.1%	34.5%	2.9%

Murmansk reg. direct investment abroad		1994	1995	1996	1997	1998	1999
Total investment abroad in million US $		*	-	0.0	-	0.3	0.1
by country: to	Denmark	*	-	-	-	-	-
	Estonia	*	-	-	-	-	-
	Finland	*	-	-	-	-	-
	Germany	*	-	-	-	0.3	0.1
	Latvia	*	-	-	-	-	-
	Lithuania	*	-	-	-	-	-
	Netherlands	*	-	-	-	-	-
	Norway	*	-	-	-	-	-
	Poland	*	-	0.0	-	-	-
	Sweden	*	-	-	-	-	-
	Switzerland	*	-	-	-	-	-
	United Kingdom	*	-	-	-	-	-
	United States	*	-	-	-	-	-

Foreign loans and foreign aid

Net amount borrowed from abroad	1994	1995	1996	1997	1998	1999
Million US $	*	*	*	*	*	*
Foreign aid received, in million US $	*	*	*	*	*	*

Prices

Change in index, previous period = 100	1994	1995	1996	1997	1998	1999
Consumer price index	345	231	128	115	179	136
Producer price index for manufactured products	411	196	118	112	145	199

International sea traffic

The number of vessels in harbours	1994	1995	1996	1997	1998	1999
Arrivals from abroad	*	*	*	450	417	457
Departures abroad	*	*	*	440	402	449

International arrivals/departures in harbours, 1000 persons	1994	1995	1996	1997	1998	1999
Arriving in Murmansk region total	*	*	*	*	*	*
Departing from Murmansk region total	*	*	*	*	*	*

International air traffic

Passengers in airports in 1000	1994	1995	1996	1997	1998	1999
Arrivals	*	*	*	*	*	*
Departures	*	*	*	23.9	18.4	10

Sources
Questionnaires completed in by the Regional Committee for Statistics in Murmansk region.

Notes
1) From household budget data.
2) Registration of all cars.
3) Figures from Labour Force Surveys or other surveys of individuals following the ILO definition of unemployed persons: Person without work, currently available for work if there should be work and actively seeking work.
4) Employed persons as defined by ILO: working and paid as a wage earner, enterpreneur or a freelancer, working without direct payment in a family enterprise or farm, temporarily absent from work.
5) From 1998 only the collective fishing farms, fish preparation industry moved to manufacturing
6) Including public catering, logistics, sales activity and procurements.
7) Including culture, art, science and scientific service.
8) Including communal housing and public services.
   * Data not available
   0, 0,0   Less than half of the unit employed
   - Zero

Country/region: St Petersburg

Basic Data and Population

Total land- and water area: 1399 square km of which agricultural land: 17%, forest and wood-land: 30%

Total population (enf of the respective year or closest possible estimate):
1993   4.85 million
1994   4.81 million
1995   4.77 million
1996   4.75 million
1997   4.72 million of which 45% male, 55% female
1998   4.70 million of which 45% male, 55% female
1999   4.66 million of which 45% male, 55% female

by age groups in %	1993	1994	1995	1996	1997	1998	1999
00 - 19 years	24.0	23.8	23.5	23.1	22.5	22.2	21.8
20 - 64 years	62.9	62.9	62.9	62.9	63.2	63.4	63.9
65 - years	13.1	13.3	13.6	14.0	14.3	14.4	14.3

by nationality in % for all nationalities 0.5% or more	1989 census	1996	1997	1998	1999
1. Russians	89.1	*	*	*	*
2. Ukrainians	3.0	*	*	*	*
3. Jews	2.1	*	*	*	*
4. Belorusians	1.9	*	*	*	*
5. Tatars	0.9	*	*	*	*

The total population has decreased from 4.92 million in 1992 to 4.66 million in 1999.

Migration in 1000 of persons	1993	1994	1995	1996	1997	1998	1999
Total immigration	67.0	79.2	80.4	73.2	64.2	67.7	60.7
Total emigration	83.3	74.8	72.6	59.3	60.8	53.0	51.4
Net migration	-16.3	4.4	7.8	13.9	3.4	14.7	9.3
Natural in/decrease	-53.4	-49.0	-42.9	-36.4	-32.3	-33.8	-43.0

Life expectancy at birth in years	1993	1994	1995	1996	1997	1998	1999
for men	58.1	58.1	59.9	62.6	64.0	63.8	61.6
for women	70.7	71.2	72.3	73.8	74.0	74.4	73.1

Mortality rate by homicide, assaults per 100 000 persons	1993	1994	1995	1996	1997	1998	1999
	28.1	29.0	27.0	22.5	18.6	18.9	19.8

Consumption

Food as % of total private consumption[1]	1993	1994	1995	1996	1997	1998	1999
	55	56	54	54	51	59	60
Cars per 100 persons[2]	10	11	13	15	15	17	16

The number of dwellings at the end of:			
1994 was	1515000	70% owned by state and local authorities,	30% by private persons
1995 was	1525000	57% owned by state and local authorities,	43% by private persons
1996 was	1537000	55% owned by state and local authorities,	45% by private persons
1997 was	1562000	54% owned by state and local authorities,	46% by private persons
1998 was	1566000	51% owned by state and local authorities,	49% by private persons
1999 was	1596000	50% owned by state and local authorities,	50% by private persons

The general area, in thousand square metres, of dwellings at the end of:			
1994 was	89254	67% owned by state and local authorities,	33% by private persons
1995 was	89443	63% owned by state and local authorities,	37% by private persons
1996 was	89485	61% owned by state and local authorities,	39% by private persons
1997 was	91000	59% owned by state and local authorities,	41% by private persons
1998 was	91035	56% owned by state and local authorities,	44% by private persons
1999 was	92464	54% owned by state and local authorities,	46% by private persons

Unemployment

The number of unemployed persons (1000 persons), annual average:	1993	1994	1995	1996	1997	1998	1999
In Labour Force Surveys[3]	204.6	238.4	257.5	245.8	232.3	261.8	267.8
Registered unemployment	31.3	45.2	55.3	47.4	31.9	40.6	22.8

Foreign trade[*]

*) The export figures for 1996 and the import figures for 1995 and 1996 include both St Petersburg and Leningrad Region..

Exports, total in million US $, countries in % of total	1993	1994	1995	1996	1997	1998	1999
Total exports	364.4	678.0	779.5	3065.0	1757.9	1619.2	2101.5
to Finland	22.2%	13.7%	6.9%	12.6%	6.7%	7.9%	6.7%
to Sweden	17.7%	2.8%	2.8%	20.4%	2.2%	2.1%	2.4%
to Norway	0.1%	0.3%	0.3%	0.3%	0.5%	0.5%	0.4%
to Denmark	1.8%	0.7%	0.3%	1.1%	0.4%	0.5%	0.4%
to Germany	13.3%	12.1%	13.9%	5.6%	9.7%	6.5%	7.6%
to Poland	2.3%	2.8%	1.9%	0.8%	2.9%	1.7%	0.9%
to Lithuania	0.8%	4.5%	0.8%	2.4%	2.2%	1.4%	0.5%
to Latvia	0.5%	5.1%	0.9%	3.0%	4.1%	1.6%	1.3%
to Estonia	0.5%	3.1%	0.6%	3.2%	1.7%	2.4%	2.2%
to EU countries	*	*	56.3%	*	33.8%	29.2%	42.4%
to CIS countries	*	*	10.8%	8.0%	10.0%	8.9%	6.6%

Imports, total in million US $, countries in % of total	1993	1994	1995	1996	1997	1998	1999
Total imports	249.1	363.5	4991.0	4205.0	3996.6	3545.5	2329.2
from Finland	15.0%	16.0%	8.0%	12.0%	11.8%	11.2%	8.6%
from Sweden	15.0%	5.6%	2.3%	2.3%	3.3%	3.0%	3.0%
from Norway	0.3%	1.0%	0.7%	0.8%	1.0%	0.8%	0.8%
from Denmark	5.5%	2.0%	1.3%	1.2%	2.0%	2.0%	2.0%
from Germany	19.3%	17.4%	14.1%	13.4%	13.7%	16.8%	16.6%
from Poland	1.1%	2.8%	1.9%	2.6%	3.9%	2.5%	1.8%
from Lithuania	0.4%	0.4%	0.6%	0.7%	0.4%	0.4%	0.4%
from Latvia	0.1%	0.2%	0.5%	1.0%	1.8%	0.8%	0.4%
from Estonia	0.2%	1.6%	0.8%	0.8%	0.8%	0.5%	0.2%
from EU countries	*	*	*	*	55.0%	58.7%	55.2%
from CIS countries	*	*	19.1%	12.1%	8.6%	7.4%	8.6%

Employed persons by activity

Employed by activity in 1000 persons[4] [8]	1994	1995	1996	1997	1998	1999
All activities	2353	2348	2331	2344	2330	2354
Agriculture, hunting and forestry	13	13	13	13	13	20
Fishing (included in manufacturing)						
Mining and quarrying (incl. in manufact.)						
Manufacturing	665	596	559	531	471	471
Electricity, gas and water supply (included in other community services)						
Construction	263	251	258	262	261	264
Wholesale and retail sales[5]	273	348	351	376	463	485
Hotels and restaurants (hotels incl. in other personal services, restaurants in wholesale and retail sales)						
Transport, storage and communication	227	219	211	217	212	210
Financial intermediation	27	33	30	32	32	29
Real estate, renting and business activities	10	22	26	42	41	47
Public administration and defence	53	64	79	78	89	91
Education[6]	467	454	422	414	388	382
Health and social care	161	163	157	162	159	157
Other community, social and personal services[7]	133	126	141	150	141	132
Other	61	59	84	67	60	66

Enterprises

The number of active enterprises by ownership and size[9]	1995	1996	1997	1998	1999
All active enterprises	112387	128255	148350	166485	189462
With private domestic owners	73597	87687	98322	113164	132432
With foreign owners	2136	2611	3051	3552	3847
Owned by state or local government	4662	4744	5357	6151	6832
Other ownership categories	31992	33213	41620	43618	46351
Number of enterprises in wholesale and retail trade	32910	41539	52265	61699	73562
Enterprises with 200 or more employees	*	*	*	*	*
20 to 199 employees	*	*	*	*	*
5 to 19 employees	*	*	*	*	*
less than 5 employees	*	*	*	*	*

Direct inward and outward investments

Foreign direct investment in St Petersburg	1994	1995	1996	1997	1998	1999
Total direct investment in million US $[10]	42.2	143.1	107.0	149.4	259.9	272.0
by country: from Denmark	*	0.2	-	1.1	0.1	0.1
Estonia	*	0.0	0.0	0.0	0.0	0.0
Finland	*	12.4	14.2	13.0	98.2	45.3
Germany	*	21.1	28.9	11.1	19.9	7.7
Latvia	*	-	0.0	0.0	0.0	0.0
Lithuania	*	-	0.0	0.0	0.0	-
Netherlands	*	28.6	0.2	0.1	25.6	57.8
Norway	*	0.0	0.0	0.0	0.3	2.2
Poland	*	0.0	0.2	0.0	0.0	0.0
Sweden	*	22.6	0.2	1.1	0.5	1.0
Switzerland	*	0.3	0.0	0.0	5.4	0.2
United Kingdom	*	7.8	5.1	15.0	32.4	2.4
United States	*	23.1	25.0	36.3	24	95.0
The stock of direct investment capital in St Petersburg at the end of year, total of which in:	*	*	*	*	*	*
Mining, quarrying and manufacture	*	*	*	*	*	*
Wholesale and retail trade	*	*	*	*	*	*
Transport, storage and communication	*	*	*	*	*	*

St Petersburg direct investments abroad		1994	1995	1996	1997	1998	1999
Total investments abroad in million US $		0.0	-	-	-	-	-
by country: to	Denmark						-
	Estonia						-
	Finland						0.0
	Germany						-
	Latvia						-
	Lithuania						-
	Netherlands						-
	Norway						-
	Poland						-
	Sweden						-
	Switzerland						-
	United Kingdom						-
	United States						-

Foreign loans and foreign aid

Net amount borowed from abroad	1994	1995	1996	1997	1998	1999
Million US $	*	*	*	*	*	*
Foreign aid received, in million US $	*	*	*	*	*	*

Prices

Change in index, previous period = 100	1994	1995	1996	1997	1998	1999
Consumer price index	328	225	125	113	178	141
Producer price index for manufactured products	390	240	125	107	144	142

International sea traffic

The number of vessels in harbours	1994	1995	1996	1997	1998	1999
Arrivals from abroad	4174	5014	5185	5938	5871	6319
Departures aboad	4145	4758	4940	5832	5905	6257

International arrivals/departures in harbours, 1000 persons	1994	1995	1996	1997	1998	1999
Arriving in St Petersburg total	*	118.5	89.0	85.6	104.2	115.3
Departing from St Petersburg total	*	116.4	76.5	85.0	101.5	114.9

International air traffic

Passengers in airports in 1000[11]	1994	1995	1996	1997	1998	1999
Arrivals	441.4	474.2	564.2	585.6	576.4	477.3
Departures	509.9	540.0	653.3	679.8	660.3	546.9

Sources
Questionnaires filled in by the Regional Committee for Statistics in St Petersburg.

Notes
1) From household budget data.
2) Registration of all cars.
3) Figures from Labour Force Surveys or other surveys of individuals following the ILO definition of unemployed persons: Person without work, currently available for work if there should be work and actively seeking work.
4) Employed persons as defined by ILO: working and paid as a wage earner, enterpreneur or a freelancer, working without direct payment in a family enterprise or farm, temporarily absent from work.
5) Including public catering, logistics, sales activity and procurements.
6) Including culture, art, science and scientific service.
7) Including: communal housing and public services.
8) From 1999 are individuals carrying on agricultural production included.
9) Registered at Single State Register of Enterprises and Organisations.
10) Based on information in Roubles.
11) Passengers to/from CIS countries are exluded.
  * Data not available
  0, 0,0   Less than half of the unit employed
  - Zero

List of Figures

List of Tables

Index*

---

* The index does not cover notes, figures and tables. Non-English characters are treated as follows: Danish, Norwegian and Swedish å/Å as *aa*; Danish and Norwegian æ/Æ and ø/Ø as *ae* and *oe*, respectively; Estonian, Finnish, German and Swedish ä/Ä and Estonian õ and Finnish, German and Swedish ö/Ö as *a* and *o*, respectively; Estonian, Finnish and German ü/Ü as *u*.

About the Authors and Editors

Matthew R. Auer, School of Public and Environmental Affairs, Indiana University, Bloomington, USA

Ole-Gunnar Austvik, Lillehammer University College, Norway

Alf Brodin, Economic Geography, School of Economics, Gothenburg University, Sweden

G. Gorzelak, European Institute for Regional and Local Development, University of Warsaw

Zenonas Gulbinas, Department of Landscape Geography and Cartography, Institute of Geography, Vilnius, Lithuania

Göran Hallin, Institute for Growth Policy Studies, Östersund, Sweden

Lars Hedegaard, Department of History and Social Theory, Roskilde University, Denmark

Jakob Hedenskog, Defence Research Establishment (FOA), Stockholm

Jüri Jagomägi, Regio Ltd, Tartu, Estonia

Pertti Joenniemi, Copenhagen Peace Research Institute (COPRI), Denmark

Birte Holst Jørgensen, Risø National Laboratory, Denmark

Harley Johansen, University of Idaho, Moscow, USA

Christopher Jones, Södertörns University College, Sweden and Manchester Metropolitan University, UK

Are Kaasik, Environmental Protection Institute, Estonian Agricultural University, Tartu, Estonia

Jüri Köll, Statistics Sweden, Stockholm, Sweden

Bjarne Lindström, Department of Statistics and Economic Research (ÅSUB), Mariehamn, Åland

Åge Mariussen, Nordregio, Stockholm, Sweden

Frank Möller, Schleswig-Holstein Institute for Peace Research (SHIP), Kiel, Germany

Jörg Neubauer, Nordregio, Stockholm, Sweden

Olǵerts Nikodemus, Department of Geography and Earth Sciences, University of Latvia, Riga

Eve Nilenders, School of Public and Environmental Affairs, Indiana University, Bloomington, USA

Anders Östhol, Institute of Future Studies, Stockholm, Sweden

Karin Peschel, Institute for Regional Research, Christian-Albrechts-Universität zu Kiel, Germany

Gulnara Roll, Peipsi Center for Transboundary Cooperation, Estonia

James Wesley Scott, Institut für Regionalentwicklung und Strukturplanung, Berlin

Kalev Sepp, Environmental Protection Institute, Estonian Agricultural University, Tartu, Estonia

Per Stålnacke, Jordforsk – Centre for Soil and Environmental Research, Norway

Carl-Einar Stålvant, Södertörns University College, Sweden

Bo Svensson, Institute for Growth Policy Studies, Östersund, Sweden

Monica Tennberg, Department of Social Studies, University of Lapland, Rovaniemi, Finland

Noralv Veggeland, Lillehammer University College, Norway

Jurgis Vilemas, Lithuanian Energy Institute, Kaunas

Dmitri Zimine, St Petersburg Centre for Russian Studies, Russia